Wolfram Elsner • Elyar Najmehchi

The Rise of China

Economic, Social, and Political Factors of Robust Development

palgrave
macmillan

Wolfram Elsner
University of Bremen (ret.)
Bremen, Germany

Elyar Najmehchi
Vienna, Austria

ISBN 978-3-032-20259-8 ISBN 978-3-032-20260-4 (eBook)
https://doi.org/10.1007/978-3-032-20260-4

The original submitted manuscript has been translated into English. The translation was done using artificial intelligence. A subsequent revision was performed by the author(s) to further refine the work and to ensure that the translation is appropriate concerning content and scientific correctness. It may, however, read stylistically different from a conventional translation.

This Palgrave Macmillan imprint is published by the registered company Springer Nature Switzerland AG.
The registered company address is: Gewerbestrasse 11, 6330 Cham, Switzerland

Foreword

In August 1993, returning from a honeymoon in Alaska, I found a long message on the answering machine, an archaic device that one could not, in those days, carry into the wilderness in one's pocket. The call was from an officer of the United Nations Development Program (UNDP), a long-previous housemate in Washington, DC, who was then stationed in Beijing and, as chance would have it, had also recently married a Chinese. Long story short: the UNDP needed a Chief Technical Adviser to the State Planning Commission (SPC) for "macroeconomic reform and strengthening institutions." The SPC, nestled directly under the State Council, was ostensibly a pivotal institution in the Chinese system, and there were not many Westerners who would contemplate the role in those dark days following the upheavals of 1989. But … perhaps? I asked my wife. She said that if I took the job, she could then return to visit her mother, not seen in seven years. Off I went.

There were no direct flights from the US to China, so I arrived at Beijing from Tokyo, on a cold night in January 1994. The 747 parked far out on the tarmac as no gate could accommodate it; inspectors with flashlights arrived on their bicycles before we deplaned. The mob hawking taxis into town was chaotic; the taxi itself decrepit, like all in Beijing at the time; I was overcharged. My wife arrived separately, with no problems, and joined me a day later. On the second night, deeply jetlagged, we went for a walk around 2 am, in temperatures about twenty below. Passing the gates of an old house, we heard music and peered in at the open courtyard. Perhaps a dozen middle-aged couples were moving together in the dark—practicing their ballroom dancing.

My assignment on that first visit was to give four lectures, two hours each over two days, to the section chiefs of the Planning Commission, an audience of about a dozen, middle-ranking officers. The topics covered every aspect of Western economic policy that I could think of. I wrote them out on Sunday, delivered them on Monday and Tuesday. When I finished, as a token of appreciation, my auditors pulled out their dog-eared, internal (i.e., pirated) translations of my father's books, notably the 1952 *Theory of Price Control*, which I signed on his behalf with amusement. On Wednesday, at lunch in the Great Hall of the People with two higher officials, I was offered, and accepted, the position. Remuneration was insignificant, but the work (mostly by fax from home in Texas) covered the full range of economic issues and kept me closely engaged with China for the next four years.

The State Planning Commission in those days—it has since undergone reorganizations and name changes—was, so far as I could tell, quite small. The building was perhaps twice the size of the Brookings Institution in Washington and much shabbier. On Fridays the desks would be cluttered with boxes of oranges, evidently a weekend bonus. The lunch-hour food was good but the setting drab, and like my Chinese colleagues I learned to wipe glasses and plates before using them, a precaution against hepatitis. Our meetings took place over felt-covered tables and were lubricated by tall thermos bottles full of hot tea. My wife came in with me and sat with the staff along the walls. I had the impression that to my Chinese counterparts she simply disappeared—one of their own—as soon as she sat down. My interlocutors dressed casually and were, to my eye, remarkably young.

Notwithstanding the grand title, my mission was not directly advisory. It consisted in bringing the Chinese planners into contact with people whose ideas and experience might be useful to them—and (as matters developed) in countering obviously counter-productive counsels from conventional economists, financial lobbyists, the representatives of international institutions and other self-interested actors, who began to turn up in increasing numbers at the 1990s went on.

It is impossible to know—I did not ask and no one volunteered to tell me—whether any specific visit, overseas training tour, lecture or conference that I organized over four years had any direct effect on Chinese decision-making at higher levels. Nevertheless, the parallels, in some respects, between ideas raised three decades back and institutions in today's China as described in Wolfram Elsner and Elyar Najmehchi's magnificent account are worth a moment's reflection, for they tell us something about the shock of recognition and pleasure that an institutional economist will feel as she reads this book.

Many of the activities I promulgated are hard to assess simply because I did not go along in person. I organized and sent out teams to study inflation control in Brazil, industrial policy in South Korea, municipal budgets in Texas and central banking in Washington, including the relationship of the Federal Reserve to Congress. But in other matters I was more directly involved. Teresa Ghilarducci, then at Notre Dame (and now at the New School), came to Beijing and wrote a paper on the operation of the Social Security system. I later learned that there was a pilot project in Liaoning province, and now, Elsner and Najmehchi describe the operation of a nationwide retirement security system, encompassing the still-vast rural hinterland of the People's Republic. Michael Reich of Berkeley came out and wrote a paper on the functions of independent trade unions; a few years later the National People's Assembly (National People's Congress) passed a new labor law—over the objections of the American Chamber of Commerce in China. Elsner and Najmehchi give us a chapter on the present, very advanced state of Chinese labor relations. Steve Cohen, then of the University of California and a co-founder of the Berkeley Roundtable on the International Economy, came to discuss industrial policy and to urge a balanced, European approach to transportation with an emphasis on high-speed rail. Today, China has by far the largest such network in the world.

It would be preposterous, of course, to claim credit. But as one reads Elsner and Najmehchi's catalog of China's rise—along with the vicious hostility it encounters at every turn from the West—one cannot escape the parallel to the ideological divide between mainstream and heterodox and specifically institutionalist economics—the branch of our discipline in which Elsner and I were raised. Elsner and Najmehchi have discovered in China, and bring to us here, an enormous country that has somehow found its own path, parallel in many ways to the pragmatic economics of New Deal America and early postwar Europe, focused on energy, core infrastructure, social security, negotiated labor relations, agronomy and the environment. The results, moreover, are self-evidently superior to that delivered in most of the rest of the world over the same forty or fifty years by the "Washington Consensus": privatization, deregulation, budget balance and monetary control. Hence, the vituperation, the vilification, the escalation of threat rhetoric and the effort to cut off contact—contact that might alert too many people that a different way is possible after all.

There is one area where I will go a step further on my own behalf. In 1995, a year or so into my assignment with the State Planning Commission, I began to worry, for reasons no longer entirely clear in my memory, that top policymakers in Beijing might be considering opening their financial system to Western banks and other investors. I organized a three-day meeting on "international economic issues" at Huairou, the site outside Beijing that had hosted the International Women's Conference in 1994. And I telephoned Robert Eisner, of Northwestern University. The conversation went as follows:

"Bob, have you ever been to China?" … He had not.
"I'll give you a business class ticket and the United Nations *per diem.*"
"Sounds great!"
"But there's a catch."
"What's the catch?"
"*You have to stop them from liberalizing the capital account!*"

Bob Eisner came to Huairou, along with Jane D'Arista (my colleague from days past at the House Banking Committee), my 1974 Cambridge tutor and early World Bank China hand Adrian Wood, and several others. The Chinese *apparat* turned out in force, with representatives from the People's Bank (a nest of Chicago monetarists), the Finance Ministry, the SPC and other entities. No liberalization followed. China therefore escaped the 1997 Asian crisis, and on that point, when I mentioned it at the time of my final report later that year, the response was a simple, "xie xie." I'm told that the idea came up again a decade later, just in time for the global financial crisis to again remind the Chinese leadership of the wisdom of keeping financial control.

Let me dip back into the institutionalist nexus. What does it mean to have a capitalist economy that is controlled by a national banking network and supervised by a (nominally) communist party? Elsner and Najmehchi point, accurately, to the stable medium-term outlook fostered by competent planning of transport, infrastructure, urbanization, energy security and ecological improvement, as well as a social system that fosters low rates of crime and violence, and an emphasis, recently redoubled, on defeating corruption. All this is well and good, but there is more, in my view.

In *Progress and Poverty*, Henry George long ago emphasized the dysfunctions of landlordism—of vacant real estate lots held for speculation and of the exploitation of tenants leading to decay and poverty amidst wealth and haphazard growth. These features of landlord capitalism are on ample display in (say) today's New York City, but they are muted in urban China, which largely freed itself from landlordism—to be sure, brutally, though the previous system was not less so—in the revolution. Chinese cities today have an integrity and a modernity unmatched in today's America but prefigured in the "sewer socialism" of Georgist municipal governments in Milwaukee, Toledo, Buffalo and San Francisco (among others) a century back.

Thorstein Veblen—the first and greatest of the Institutionalists—argued in *The Theory of the Business Enterprise* that the economic role of the business classes is not to encourage economic output but to obstruct it. The goal of business management, working for shareholders, is to raise the rate of profit, and for this, goods must be relatively scarce and therefore expensive. China is not free of big business, but the sheltered banking system fosters intense competition and a low rate of profit, permitting maximum advantage of new technologies and scale economies, and meanwhile flooding the world with low-cost industrial products. A recent video shows an electric-vehicle factory in Shenzhen whose floor area is larger than the city of San Francisco. Is this Veblen's fabled soviet of engineers? If it's even close, there's no wonder that the established capitalist world—the world of money-manager finance capitalism—sees an existential threat. Elsner and Najmehchi correctly identify the analytical incoherence of the China-hostile narrative, but I wonder if they are correct in describing what exists as a form of "socialism" never before seen. Perhaps indeed not seen, but imagined, and not even socialism in the utopian European sense—yet quite close to our shared intellectual home in pragmatic philosophy and evolutionary economics.

Is all well in today's China? Not entirely. China is at the forefront, along with South Korea and Japan, of a coming population crisis. It has been noted that more children were born in China in 1776 than in 2025—and a China with half today's population, not many decades from now, would find itself in a spiral of decline an decay, with a vast infrastructure that will be impossible to maintain. Something has gone quite wrong with the lived experience of women and families to make this happen. To understand what it is, and how to deal with it, will be the next great challenge for Chinese pragmatism. No country has yet recovered from a below-replacement fertility rate; a second Chinese economic and social miracle needs to be contrived, for China to become the first.

The other danger, hardly less serious but harder to spot, lies in the infiltration of mainstream "neoclassical" economics into China. The global hierarchy of academic journals, departmental ratings, appointments and prestige, headquartered in the academic West, is producing a new generation of dull economists in China, aggressive in their self-regard, whose allegiance is to the dominant doctrines that have caused, and continue to cause, so much obvious damage everywhere else. So far, these academics are merely academics and do not appear to have been very influential. But they never give up. And they are raising up a generation without the real-world knowledge, pragmatic focus and historical depth of those who brought China to where it is today. The ultimate consequence, and the risk for China, can be seen in the West, where such ideas have held sway, in quasi-totalitarian fashion—for a half-century so far.

Is there an antidote to this danger? Of course, there is. Wolfram Elsner and Elyar Najmehchi have provided it right here. May it prove equally useful those in the West who have an open mind about China as she now is and to those in China who may see the urgent need to strengthen and advance the intellectual currents that have helped to bring their homeland to her present position, both at home and in the world.

Austin, TX, USA
February 15, 2026

James K. Galbraith

Contents

About the Authors

Wolfram Elsner born 1950, is Professor of Economics (retired), University of Bremen, Germany, since 1995; studied at Universities of Cologne (MA) and Bielefeld (PhD), Germany; after Habilitation 1985 (Uni Bielefeld), he worked for ten years outside academia in regional development at city and state levels; Managing Editor, *Forum for Social Economics* (FSE), 2012–2018; President, *European Association for Evolutionary Political Economy* (EAEPE), 2012–2014 and 2014–2016; taught in many European countries, in the USA, in South Africa, Australia, Mexico, and China; Textbook *Microeconomics of Complex Economies* (Elsevier/Academic Press, 2015, 2nd ed., 2026), which received the biannual Gunnar-Myrdal Award 2017 of the EAEPE; edited a number of volumes and book series; authored books and numerous international peer-reviewed book chapters and journal articles; founding Editor-in-Chief, *Review of Evolutionary Political Economy* (REPE), 2018–2023; member of Board of Directors, *Association of Evolutionary Economics* (AFEE); member of Executive Council and Trustee, *Association of Social Economics* (ASE); member of numerous committees of AFEE and ASE; co-editor of the *International Handbook of Complexity Economics* (Routledge 2025) and the *Encyclopedia of Evolutionary and Institutional Economics* (forthcoming, Elgar 2026), served as chair, reviewer, and examiner in around 60 PhD promotions in Germany, Austria, the UK, the USA, and around 10 professorial habilitations, with 8 professors coming from his ex-PhD-students and Research/Teaching Assistants (1 the USA, 2 the UK, 2 China, 3 Germany); was awarded the ASE Service Award in 2023 for editing the FSE; Best Paper Award 2024 of the *Journal of*

Economic Issues; received the Veblen-Commons Award 2025 of AFEE for considerable contributions to evolutionary and institutional economics in his life work.

Elyar Najmehchi born 1993, Bremen, Germany, holds an MA in Economy and Society of East Asia from the University of Vienna, Austria, as well as a BA in Japanese Studies and Cultural Anthropology from the University of Tübingen, Germany. During his Bachelor studies, he learned Chinese and studied also at Peking University in Beijing and at Dôshisha University in Kyoto, Japan. He has work experience in fields such as consultancy and publishing (China), as well as the cultural field and science administration (Japan, Austria).

Abbreviations

AI	Artificial Intelligence
AIIB	Asia Infrastructure Investment Bank
APEC	Asia-Pacific Economic Co-operation
ASEAN	Association of Southeast Asian Nations
ASML	Advanced Semiconductor Materials Lithography
ASPI	Australian Strategic Policy Institute
AUKUS	Australia, the UK and the US (military alliance)
B2B	Business-to-Business
B2C	Business-to-Consumer
BDI	Bundesverband der Deutschen Industrie (Federation of German Industries)
BDN	Blue-Dot Network (Trump 1.0 initiative, alternative to the BRI)
BER	International Code of the new German capital airport "Berlin-Brandenburg"
BRI	Belt and Road Initiative ("New Silk Roads")
BRICS	Brazil, Russia, India, China, South Africa (informal international political-economic alliance of the Global South)
C2C	Consumer-to-Consumer
CAC	Cyberspace Administration of China
CAI	Comprehensive Agreement on Investment (China—EU, draft status)
CASIC	China Aerospace Science and Industry Corporation
CBDC	Central Bank Digital Currency
CCICED	China Council for International Cooperation on Environment and Development
CDU	Christian Democratic Union of Germany
CEE	Central and Eastern Europe

CELAC	Community of Latin American and Caribbean States
CFC	Central Financial Commission
CHIPS Act	Creating Helpful Incentives to Produce Semiconductors Act (US act under the Biden administration)
CIA	Central Intelligence Agency (US secret service)
CIPS	Cross-Border Inter-Bank Payments System (run by the PBoC)
CLCP	China Low-Carbon Pilot Policy
CNIPA	China National Intellectual-Property Administration
COP	Conference of the Parties (UN format of multilateral ecological conferences)
COSCO	China Ocean Shipping Company
CPC	Communist Party of China
CPTPP	Comprehensive and Progressive Agreement for Trans-Pacific Partnership
CSC	China Scholarship Council
CSCS	Corporate Social Credit System
CSRC	China Securities Regulatory Commission
DAX	Deutscher Aktienindex (German stock index)
DB	Deutsche Bahn (German Railways)
DPP	Democratic Progressive Party (Taiwan)
DSW	Deutsche Schutzvereinigung für Wertpapierbesitz (German Association for the Protection of Private Investors, part of Deutsche Bank group)
DUV	Deep Ultraviolet (advanced semiconductor production technology)
EIB	European Investment Bank (EU)
ETGE	East Turkestan Government in Exile (fundamentalist Islamic)
ETIM	East Turkestan Islamic Movement (Islamist terrorist group, focused on Uyghurs and Chinese autonomous province of Xinjiang)
ETLO	East Turkistan Liberation Organization
EV	Battery Electric Vehicles
EY	Ernst & Young (auditing company)
FAO	Food and Agriculture Organization (UN)
FDI	Foreign Direct Investment
FOCAC	Forum on China-Africa Cooperation
FRG	Federal Republic of Germany
FSDC	Financial Stability and Development Committee (Chinese Sate Council)
FYP	Five-Year Plan
G7	Group of Seven (leading Western countries)
GAFAM	Google, Apple, Facebook, Amazon and Microsoft
GDP	Gross Domestic Product

GDPC	Global Development Policy Center (University of Boston, MA, USA)
GDR	German Democratic Republic
GFC	Great Financial Crisis (2008 and following)
GIP	Green Investment Principles
GTAI	Germany Trade and Invest (investment marketing agency of German government)
HDI	Human Development Index (UN)
HRS	Household Responsibility System
HTS	Hayat Tahrir al-Sham (Islamist terror organization)
ICJ	International Court of Justice (UN)
IEA	International Energy Agency
IEEE	Institute of Electrical and Electronics Engineers
iFDI	incoming Foreign Direct Investment
ILO	International Labour Organization (UN)
IMF	International Monetary Fund
IoT	Internet of Things
IPO	Initial Public Offering
IPR	Intellectual Property Rights
ISIS	Islamic State of Iraq and Syria (Islamist terror organization)
IT	Information Technology
KMT	Kuomintang (also: GMD—Guomindang)
LAC	Latin America and the Caribbean (continental alliance of states)
LLC	Limited Liability Company
LSE	London School of Economics
LSEV	Low-Speed-E-Vehicles
MCA	Ministry of Civil Affairs (Chinese State Council)
MEE	Ministry of Ecology and Environment (Chinese State Council)
MERICS	Mercator Institute for China Studies (advisory agency of German government)
MIIT	Ministry of Industry and Information Technology (Chinese State Council)
MOST	Ministry of Science and Technology (Chinese State Council)
NASA	National Aeronautics and Space Administration (USA)
NATO	North Atlantic Treaty Organization
NDA	National Data Administration
NDRC	National Development and Reform Commission (Chinese State Council)
NED	National Endowment for Democracy (US Government)
NEP	New Economic Policy
NEV	New-Energy Vehicles (EV and hydrogen fuel-cell vehicles)
NFC	Neoliberal Financialized Capitalism

NFRA	National Financial Regulatory Administration
NGO	Non-Governmental Organization
NHC	National Health Commission
NPC	National People's Congress
OAOEV	Eastern Committee of the German Economy/Eastern Europe club (of the German trade associations)
OBOR	One Belt, One Road (see also: BRI/"New Silk Roads")
ODA	Official Development Assistance
ODI	Outbound Direct Investments (also oFDI)
OECD	Organization for Economic Co-operation and Development
oFDI	outbound Foreign Direct Investment (also: outgoing Foreign Direct Investment)
OHCHR	Office of the United Nations High Commissioner for Human Rights
PBoC	People's Bank of China (central bank)
PGII	Partnership for Global Infrastructure and Investment (Western alternative to the BRI, established by the G7)
PISA	Programme for International Student Assessment
PPP	Purchasing Power Parity
PRC	People's Republic of China
PSA	Production Sharing Agreement
QE	Quantitative Easing (Central Banks' strategies after the GFC during the 2010s)
R&D	Research and Development
RCEP	Regional Comprehensive Economic Partnership (Southeast Asian free trade zone)
RMB	Renminbi (Chinese currency)
SAMR	State Administration for Market Regulation
SCS	Shanghai Cooperation Organization
SCS	Social Credit Point System
SDGs	Sustainable Development Goals (UN)
SEATO	Southeast Asia Treaty Organization
SEZs	Special Economic Zones
SME	Socialist Market Economy
SMEE	Shanghai Micro Electronics Equipment Group
SMEs	Small and Medium-sized Enterprises
SMIC	Semiconductor Manufacturing International Corporation (China)
SOEs	State-Owned Enterprises
SPD	Social Democratic Party of Germany
SPFS	System for Transfer of Financial Messages (Sistema peredachi finansovykh soobscheniy)

SWIFT	Society for Worldwide Interbank Financial Telecommunication (Western-dominated system)
TIP	Turkistan Islamic Party (Islamist terrorist group, focused on Uyghurs and Chinese autonomous province of Xinjiang)
TPP	Trans-Pacific Partnership
TSMC	Taiwan Semiconductor Manufacturing Company
TVEs	Township and Village Enterprises (China)
ULO	Uyghur Liberation Organization
UN	United Nations
UNDP	United Nations Development Programme
UNEP	United Nations Environment Programme
UNESCO	United Nations Educational, Scientific and Cultural Organization
UNHRC	United Nations Human Rights Council
URFET	United Revolutionary Front of East Turkestan
VAC	Value-Added Chain
VETCs	Vocational Educational and Training Centers
WHO	World Health Organization (UN)
WIPO	World Intellectual Property Organization
WTO	World Trade Organization (UN)
WUC	World Uyghur Congress (focused on the Chinese autonomous province of Xinjiang)
ZTE	Zhong Xing Telecommunication Equipment Company Limited

CHAPTER 1

Introduction: Me, China, and the Chinese (by W. Elsner)

My Long-Standing Non-interest in China

About 25 years ago, I would not have bet a cent on China's future. "They want to ride the capitalist tiger? This tiger cannot be ridden! It rides you, and you will never get out of it."

The deadly illusions of the former GDR's (German Democratic Republic—former socialist East Germany) "civil rights movement" about a "soft socialism with capitalist characteristics" or a "softened capitalism with some social GDR characteristics", respectively, had to be paid for severely, despite the early promises of wealth, consumption, and a glittering world of cars and bananas, sexy entertainment and "freedom". To be paid with internal colonization and industrial degradation, joblessness, social insecurity, wage discrimination and humiliation, social setbacks, invasion of the then so-called "Besserwessies" (the know-it-alls, careerists, and gold-diggers from the West occupying the top positions), and ultimately with their self-esteem. Full German integration still has not been made, and the "winners" have even told the "losers" it was their own fault, due to their "wrong political genes", beliefs, attitudes, and behaviors, inherited from the GDR. So, at one point, politically, the "East" has even been striking back, on the far right and on the left. They had to learn: You cannot have "a bit of capitalism", just as you cannot be "a bit pregnant" … a Faustian theme …

And the Chinese want to make better? No way!

W. Elsner, E. Najmehchi, *The Rise of China*,
https://doi.org/10.1007/978-3-032-20260-4_1

But I had no idea about China's ideas, rich experience, energy, and resilience, their historically inherited great potential, their desire never to return to a "century of humiliation", then caused by European colonialism, nor to return to hunger, poverty, and underdevelopment, had no idea of the strength and mobilization capacity of this country, its people, and, yes, its "system" too. So, I still looked at this country just as skeptically, or rather, with just as much ignorance and misunderstanding, as many of my European contemporaries did—and many of them still do.

In fact, I had always kept China "at arm's length". There had been ideas to travel to China in private circles for years. Friends and family had seen pictures and heard travel reports that had made them curious about China. Seeing the Great Wall ... and the "crazy" Chinese? I brushed the idea off the table: "What am I supposed to do there!?" Their culture was too far away for me, the language apparently too complicated ...

In fact, it probably was fear of disappointment, the disappointment of not seeing a pure, clean socialism according to the ideas of a typical European intellectual do-gooder, but seeing a country that was highly unfinished, on a very long march ... and who knew where to ... Put simply, fear of losing cherished prejudices.

I certainly was not an outspoken ignoramus, definitely no longer sitting on the high Europe-centered horse, from which even today many still believe they need to preach their "values"-absolutism to the world, believing they could divide the world into good and evil, black and white, having to "save" or "punish" others as they see fit. Such arrogance and ignorance had already been driven out of me by my great antifa-social democrat history teacher in high school in the mid-1960s. And some additional ability of being (self-)critical I had learned as a "68er" student. I never wanted to give this up again, did not even want to become a "good-doing green", nor turned into other do-gooder ways. Fortunately, I also did not want to establish any new party, neither a green nor the hundredth leftist one, and chase after political posts to lecture the world from there, nor to "defend our security or interests" in foreign countries.

I knew a little bit about the history of China, also how this historical great power, with its millennia-old high culture and huge technical and scientific advantages over Europe (located at the Western edge of Eurasia), was a huge country and empire, which had never enslaved another country. I knew that China had in some way fallen behind Europe from the sixteenth century on—and finally become a victim of European colonialism and imperialism, smashed, divided, plundered, humiliated, forced into a multimillion-army of opium addicts, covered with mass murders, destroyed and left behind after that "century of humiliation" as one of the poorest developing countries in the world.[1]

Together with England, France, Germany, Italy, and Tsarist Russia, the USA also wanted to have their share of this fattest of all chunks on earth (in terms of knowledge and wisdom, products, technologies, and resources, labor, and markets). And the brutality of the English and German exploitation was then even excelled during the occupation by its East Asian competitor, the Japanese military, which let the country bleed further on and turned it into their brothel too (as armies usually do abroad).

I also knew a little about the Long March 1934–1935, about Mao Zedong, the Great Leap Forward 1958–1961, and the last great famine at that time. And I, like most "68er" intellectuals at the time, enthusiastically parroted the "Cultural Revolution" (1966–1976), knowing little about it really.

1968: The "Cultural Revolution" and the "Little Red Book"

In my generation, students at the end of the 1960s and beginning of the 1970s were reading the "Little Red Book" (*Quotations from Chairman Mao Tse-tung*, published in German in 1967) and perhaps even some of Mao's longer writings, which could be obtained everywhere during those years of the pirate-print scene as *Collected Works*—in a hope of gaining the deeper understanding promised by our student "Maoists". But Mao's small collection of aphorisms didn't tell me much. It all seemed too much out of our context. What was I, a Central European academic, supposed to learn for my profession, life practice, worldview, or politics, from something that was actually intended for poor, mostly illiterate Chinese peasants, tailored to their situation, that used images and metaphors that we in Europe could not really understand? Much of it simply seemed short and flat, while for the Chinese peasant who had experienced oppression and famine and who now perhaps (in the 1930s and 1940s) joined the People's Liberation Army (because she had no alternative to survive), it may have been extraordinarily meaningful.

Some of Mao's longer writings, however, aroused some desire in me to learn more. But unfortunately, there were the "Maoist" leaders and spokesmen at the universities who too often acted intolerantly and aggressively, so I ultimately turned away and focused on my studies and the socio-economic problems in my own country (of which there were plenty), approaching more traditional workers' parties and working in the trade unions.

In the early 1970s, I instinctively felt that China could not endure the forms and results of the "Cultural Revolution" for long. (It was only during my visits to China 40 years later that I learned about the traumas that ran deep in many Chinese families.) And the more our academic "Maoists" propagated a "permanent revolution", the more skeptical I became, and the more anxious I became about China's future. Thus, I felt better by pushing China into the farthest corner of my mind. And there it remained in a dormant state for years. There was enough to do at the "home front".

1976: Mao's Death

Mao's death reminded me of China again. Would China now sink back into chaos, now that it was just about to calm down? And how far would the Western "Empire"[2] with its claim to be the "only world power" (left) go to subjugate weakened China, that last and fattest chunk, to fragment it again and perhaps to divide it into a hundred regional, ethnic, religious-fundamentalist, and warlord areas? Just as it had subjugated or bombed less fat chunks into post-human conditions. The Empire had famously declared to "bomb Vietnam back into the Stone Age". The Vietnam War had only just ended. The victory of a small people against the Empire, David against Goliath, a victory achieved at huge cost, but with the support of the Soviet Union and China. The Empire's power was never infinite.

Development toward national sovereignty and territorial integrity had usually been made impossible under the Empire's influence, for a long time in many cases. The history of Latin America comes to mind. It was the time when the Empire directly intervened militarily everywhere.

But the USA had different plans with China and preferred a charm offensive to take advantage of the historic P.R. of China–Soviet Union schism and pull China on their side against the Soviet Union. Nixon and Mao had their historic handshake in Beijing in 1972 already. Mao, weakened domestically due to various adverse developments during his rule ("Great Leap Forward" with famine, "Cultural Revolution" with another socio-economic and political downturn), had entered some strategic alliance with Washington. Washington could therefore hope for a major "pro-Western"[3] turn of China and an opening of China for US capital, which urgently needed foreign direct investment and cheap production overseas.

At that time, I even thought I had somehow understood Mao's basic idea of a "cultural revolution", a struggle against the dangers of bureaucratization in older Eurocentric state-socialist systems, and found it worth considering. While the Mao-Nixon handshake had left me skeptical.

The Soviet Union had achieved an incredible development of productive forces, social progress, national self-defense, and international development aid and reputation, despite almost permanent invasions by the European great powers, Japan, and the USA over the decades, and despite of one of the most brutal wars of annihilation in history, with which the Nazi regime had covered the Soviet Union, and later despite a forced arms race in the Cold War 1.0, for which the Soviet Union was not made nor well prepared. The Soviet Union remained fragile throughout its history, and not only because of the constant external attacks and invasions from 1917 to 1945. For sure, mainly because of the incomparably greater availability of global resources, from natural to mental resources, and the financial capital of the "Western bloc" under the leadership of the Empire. But also, apparently, because of endogenous system-related tendencies of demobilization of human resources, as I thought.

Lenin, with his "New Economic Policy" (NEP), had the idea of catching up with a preferential development of productive forces, which should ideally have been achieved in an earlier capitalist phase, but had practically been skipped historically, with the help of more capitalist market mechanisms and small and medium-sized enterprises, under a socialist rule. But he died too early, and the rapidly emerging threat from the Nazi Reich and its terrible war of annihilation, with its relentless and highly aggressive, because racially indoctrinated, military machine, apparently no longer allowed the Soviet concept of socialism itself to be significantly further developed. The Soviet Union, in fact, never had a minute to breathe and to calmly learn and develop itself without existential pressure.

And so, this European attempt at socialism remained an economy with insufficient individual incentive mechanisms, with limited endogenous mobilization of human resources, and in principle only a real economy that was structurally not designed to generate a surplus of money capital, which would have provided power and scope for long-run strategic action, as developed capitalism typically did. This state socialism, in that early global-historical period and under that global distribution of resources in its disfavor, could not win the race to influence the world with money and capital surpluses and thus to secure relevant global resources for itself.

With the new socialist approach developed in China shortly after Mao's death, this was to become essentially different. While the Soviet Union was still somehow prospering and surging in the late 1970s, a disruptive change of basic socialist development strategy had been prepared in China, which could come to the fore only after Mao's death. While Mao's huge historic merits had lain in the 1930s through 1950s, he had even somehow prepared the coming opening and reform period through the handshake with Nixon and establishing new relations with the USA.

1976 and Following: "Gang of Four", Deng Xiaoping, Stabilization, Reform, and Opening-Up

With the end of the "Cultural Revolution", and after Mao, there was some dispute about the direction of the Communist Party of China (CPC). It was about how the Cultural Revolution could be ended, and a stable and more dynamic prospering development could finally be established. I continued to watch China with less than half an eye. And I cannot imagine today why my sympathy was diffuse at first with Mao's widow Jiang Qing and her so-called "Gang of Four". This was probably the case because the ruling forces and their media in the "West" had already pinned their hopes on the "pragmatist" Deng Xiaoping and declared him the only alternative to the continuation of the chaos of the "Cultural Revolution". Which probably was true, but their motives had certainly not been the best for the Chinese people, but rather to get access to the big chunk of China's huge resources and market. The "Cultural Revolution" had often looked like an anti-culture rampage without sense, and the "pragmatists" promised stability, opening up to Western capital, cheap Western production in China, and new markets for Western surplus production.

Stabilizing factors in the critical transition phase after Mao's passing away were long-time premier Zhou Enlai, who, however, also died in 1976, and the equally experienced Deng Xiaoping, who, in late 1978, became vice-chairman of the CPC and vice premier, and, in fact, the central person in party, government, and state. With Deng and a more pragmatic policy of the CPC, a calming down of the internal development could be established. Under this direction, China's reform and opening-up period began.

But I saw the country now quickly falling under the wings of the Empire, into a new dependency for another century, a kind of self-castration instead of a national emancipation. After thousands of years of great history again a "century of humiliation"? I quickly pushed the country back to its former place at the back of my interests. Because of the patterns of what would now become of China, I thought I knew already. How little did I know!

Just four years later, in 1982, Volkswagen, as one of the first car companies of the Western world and the first German car company in China, launched its car from Chinese production, the model "Santana", later the legendary "Golf". "Now we are producing millions of additional cars for China. A Golf (a Santana) for every Chinese!" were the messages of the German media. Imagining some hundred million combustion engines more in the world, I fantasized about a skyrocketing of global ecological collapse, for which somehow "the Chinese" then would be to blame. Another reason for me to turn away again, horrified, or uninterested at best. How could the Chinese dare to become as wealthy as the West!? Turning away again, I devoted myself to my academic work and the international academic networking with my critical, "heterodox" economic colleagues in the West. There was more rather than less to analyze then, to enlighten, to warn against the now more uninhibited, "neoliberalized", and "financialized" capitalism (NFC), which was rapidly made replacing the older "welfare state", so, more to struggle than ever. Keep working and academically fighting and enlightening everywhere at your best, about the upcoming age of economic, social, and political disintegration and the coming major financial crises. From China, the better world would not come anyway, that much seemed clear to me.

I knew nothing really. That I once again underestimated China and the Chinese, their experience in decades of national liberation, their will to development, to a significance in the world appropriate to their size, their innovation capacity, even their capacity to suffer and undergo the costs of the coming socio-economic disruptions, while they aspired and struggled further into the future, beyond just 300 million additional combustion cars, I had no idea about.

1989: Tiananmen

Tiananmen Square, the "Square at the Gate of Heavenly Peace" in Beijing opposite the old imperial "Forbidden City", then made China a center stage of world politics again a decade later.

China's reform and opening-up had, after a decade of deep socio-economic disruptions, unsurprisingly, become both a massive systemic challenge for China itself and an allurement for the West, with its already given penetration of China not only by Western capital but also Western media, public institutions, party and state foundations, non-governmental organizations (NGOs), intelligence services, etc.[4]

Apparently, numerous breaks and contradictions of the unleashed extreme growth dynamics and massive restructuring in Chinese society escalated, on the basis of which the empire now could hope to turn the rudder toward a fully socio-economic and also state and political-ideological neoliberal capitalist system in China. Which society could have withstood such radical changes in all areas of life, including an extreme redistribution of the wealth produced, with growth rates of 10–15 percent over a decade? Various disadvantages and dissatisfactions emerged among large societal sectors, including industrial workers, different and diverse motivations for changing the Reform and Opening-up strategy became virulent, even entirely conflicting goals, from more radical socialism to aspirations for a Western NFC emerged.

And this contradictory "cocktail" of unrest, having taken place in hundreds of cities and towns in China, combined, amalgamated, and culminated on Tiananmen Square. The tent city that was built on the square became suddenly, after weeks of non-violent expressions of civil unrest and discourse, the arena of increasingly violent clashes, with fully unprovoked excessive violence, perhaps sourced and staged somehow. It included the images of lynched young policemen and the burning of buses with young, unarmed soldiers around the square and in other parts of the city. Parts of the history of the Tiananmen events have been clarified since in greater detail, e.g., the nearby US embassy hosting CIA agents[5] (whatever that meant) and the discussions at the meetings of the state council and the communist party. Dramatic days….[6]

After difficult and conflictual decision-making, Tiananmen was finally cleared with police and military in June 1989. Most protesters were shocked after the burning of the policemen and soldiers and left the square deliberately, insightfully, and calmly. There were in fact only a few images that lent themselves to Western media use, except the famous "tank man" pic. And the pictures of burnt bodies of the young soldiers in their buses were of course hidden away in the West. China now could no longer be triggered into a major crisis of sovereignty, the socialist development would probably not be fully given up, how modified ever in the 1990s. And China would certainly not submit itself to the financially, technologically, and militarily superior system of the Empire, and probably would challenge sooner or later its system of unipolar "globalization", its narrated "world community" and "community of values" as coined in the West.

A historical turning point of unparalleled significance, especially since the Soviet Union was about to be handed over to the West shortly later, on a golden tray for partition and plundering, by Gorbachev and Yeltsin.

And me? I now watched with one eye, at least, with the other focused on private professional career steps I was engaged in at that time. I vaguely guessed something important had happened "outside there", but had no idea that this was a historical turning point of "reinvention" of China and the CPC on a way to where they are today, and where they could not be without that critical turn.

First, however, the "turn" was not into a straightforward socialist direction, more neoliberalism came in the 1990s rather, more privatizations, more "market", Deng's famous travel to the South ("Southern Tour") 1992 in favor of more "market" and enrichment, "market-oriented" state-owned enterprise (SOE) reforms, and the climax of China-US relations, the accession of China to the World Trade Organization (WTO) in 2001.

The political "left" in the party, a heterogeneous group in itself within party and state, including classical "planners" to non-neoliberal reformers, in opposition to the smaller groups of hardcore neoliberals, seemed to have won through the military clearing of the square, but really appeared to have strategically lost in the years after 1989. The reform debates around and after "Tiananmen" were extremely complex and "fractional", but it looked that the neoliberals, often trained in the USA, gained ground in the 1990s with strong trends of marketization, privatization, and deregulation. In the 2000s, it looked as if the emerging "Wild East", including corruption and financial shadow sectors, could seriously destabilize the party's ruling. The final turn away from an early-capitalist mode of accumulation of productive forces in the 1980s as well as from an unhampered "marketization" in the 1990s, thus, began in the 2000s, when it became clearer that corruption, spreading shadow finance, and uneven distribution effects could endanger China's entire development. The Secretary General of the party, Jiang Zemin, declared in 2002, in his last report to the National People's Congress:

> If we do not crack down on corruption, the flesh-and-blood ties between the party and the people will suffer a lot and the party will be in danger of losing its ruling position, or possibly heading for self-destruction.

In the late 2000s and early 2010s then, and namely in the era Xi Jinping, beginning 2012, a turn into the far more sophisticated, deliberately structured high-quality development that China has generated since, all considerably more based on stricter anticorruption efforts, and redistribution measures downwards, at last, seemed to take up again some essential and more leftist social(ist) reform perspectives and workers' demands around "Tiananmen". A spiral upwards in China's development seemed to have been finally manufactured from the mélange of the three previous decades of ongoing intense strategic debate. And China could avoid the infamous shock therapy, the "Soviet fate".[7]

Had I only had any idea of all that then ....

After 1989, therefore, more reinventions and turning points, on anti-corruption and a much more social(ist) development still had to follow. But these turns then were essentially under Chinese political deliberation, with less direct Western influence. Ironically, only since the 2010s, the most crucial progressive demands from "Tiananmen" became the guidelines of China's successful development.

The more the Western media outlets generated and fueled a narrative hysteria about the events on Tiananmen Sq., tabooing any socio-economic background and progressive reform content of the intentions of the great bulk of protesters, the more I felt compelled to put my own knowledge, my own experience, and my own capacity to reflect to use. Why did China do something fundamentally different than the disintegrating European state socialist countries? How can they do that? Is it from a position of strength or weakness? What kind of signal (to Washington) is this? Is a US military intervention now imminent? Or is this risk averted now? But I still was far from a comprehensive knowledge or explanation of "China's path", potentials, and next future.

What information could one get beyond the shallow narrating and permanent repetition of a "massacre" (a mantra repeated year by year up to now) of the biased media? Little in the beginning, and much less than today.[8] The monopoly of a unity-opinion press still existed in the West, and unrestricted, critical, actual and exact, investigative research, which today is more easily accessible via the internet, did not yet exist. Only a few small niche media could help.

It appeared to me that Deng's pragmatism, the deregulation and the opening to international capital, had triggered desires of the Empire for what we nowadays call a "color revolution" and related interventions below an open military intervention, as usual with the help of networks of state-sponsored NGOs. But it also seemed that behind the Chinese "pragmatism" of the time was more than that. The political compass of a national, autonomous, territorially sovereign development apparently had not been lost.

In Moscow, after the "good", but "tragic hero" Gorbachev, Boris Yeltsin was installed, who clearly enriched his clan, sold off the Soviet "silverware" and, as a "Russian dancing bear", was temporarily allowed to sit at the table with the G7 (then G8)—to be ridiculed then as a drunkard. Quickly, agreements (so-called Production Sharing Agreements—PSA) had been concluded, which allowed the USA to exploit Russian resources in separated regions. The first steps toward expropriation, fragmentation, and swallowing of the second-fattest chunk of the earth had thus already been taken.

The even fatter chunk of China could have been well integrated as the last large resource depot, largest workforce and major market in the world into the global neoliberal financialized system of hegemonic domination. It would have certainly given the declining financial capitalism for the twenty-first century one last major growth spurt and the Wall Street casino one last big party for several decades. All this seemed to fail with the clearing of Tiananmen. Western capital could come in, and even more so, after 1989 and 2001, but under the political control and increasing national sovereignty of China ...

In the ethnically culturally more distant Western autonomous provinces of China, especially Xinjiang, which had become susceptible to the then globally emerging (Islamist) fundamentalist and extremist tendencies, there emerged both in 1989 and, increasingly, in the 1990s some fertile ground for a brutalization of conflicts. This then unfolded according to patterns that had been successfully introduced with the production, organization, and military training of religious extremism à la Mujahideen (later Taliban) in Afghanistan, against the democratically elected secular and progressive-national government there, and the Soviet troops that had been called by it to come to its support.

Under the secular Sino-Soviet split, China even had collaborated with the USA against an increasing Soviet influence in Islamic Asia and Arabian countries in the 1980s, including in Afghanistan, but in the 1990s and even 2000s also against Islamist terrorism (Taliban, Al-Qaeda, Al Nusra, and Uyghur pan-Turkist Islamists, fighting with Al-Qaeda & Co. in Syria). But after the end of the Soviet Union and the increasingly prominent US-China confrontation, constellations changed and diversified, and the USA also supported Islamist groups more flexibly according to local constellations, while the Arab Gulf states and Turkey pursued their own Islamist or pan-Turkist strategies with the different Jihadists. The Uyghur "East Turkestan" terrorists against China had been a dreaded part of the Near-East Jihad among Arabs, Kurds, or the secular parts of the population, namely in Syria (more below).

The USA had also gained a dominant influence in the Central Asian former Soviet republics. Their geo-military strategy for the expansion of the "Greater Middle East" to Central Asia and then to the West of China had already been in place since Brzezinski's advisory role (until the administration of Bush Sen. in the 1990s) and since Kissinger's term and his advisory role (until the 2010s).

It was anyway an old Anglo-Saxon strategy to control the "Heartland" of the Eurasian continent, as the "key to world domination".[9] We will return to the geopolitical background of the developments in the autonomous Uyghur province of Xinjiang (see below, Part II, Chap. 13).

As an attentive and critical observer of world events, one already knew something about the role of Islamist fundamentalism, namely in Afghanistan (against the Soviet troops) and in Western Asia's conflicts, a kind of "Frankenstein's monster" of imperial strategy, with its long-run structural backlashes. These forces from the retort were designed and set to destroy all efforts of secular, progressive, or sovereign national development in "insubordinate" states, like those in Afghanistan, Iraq, Libya, and Syria. And the first Islamist-terrorist upheavals and assaults had already been reported from the Chinese autonomous province of Xinjiang since the mid-1990s. The East Turkestan Islamic Movement (ETIM) was founded in 1997, endowed and financed through a mélange of supporters from Islamic countries through the Taliban/Al-Qaeda.

At the end of the day, beyond the scandalizing and inflaming Western narratives of "Tiananmen", a surprisingly simple "message from

Tiananmen" stood in the room: "Up to here! No further! No trespassing!" And despite all internal theoretical and practical struggles about the national development strategy, about how much "market" between capitalism and socialism, and despite the economic and social upheavals through liberalization, opening, introduction of capitalist elements: The CPC apparently had learned lessons from the Afghanistan war, the decline of the Soviet Union and the state socialist countries of Central and Eastern Europe, as well as other examples in the world, "color revolutions", religious-fundamentalist terrorism and instigations of absurd violence—and in opposition to the "world opinion" they had pulled some "emergency brake", preventing a "color revolution" in China. A prerequisite as well to further develop the entire, formerly Europe-centered and Soviet-influenced socialism design, now with Chinese characteristics.[10]

Only in 2019, when the usual 30-year quarantine for US state documents for the Tiananmen case ended and US material was published, some details, as reported in this book, were confirmed, suggesting the Tiananmen outcomes were one of many conditions of a successful sovereign development of China. In some complex ways, it may be assumed, "Tiananmen" laid some groundwork for developing China into the global powerhouse that it is today.

A country, which, as a developing country with a mid-size average income, has unfolded enormous impact multipliers, or leverage effects, in all economic and life areas, a dynamic with breathtaking results—not the least in its unique ecological civilization, its renewable energies or tree-planting efforts, with measurable climate effects for all humanity. (We will deal with it in this book.)

Were it not for those fateful events around 1989, this book would not have been written in the same positive way 35 years after "Tiananmen". It might have reported then either on a kind of post-human nightmare à la Afghanistan, Libya, Syria, Palestine, or something fragmented into regional and local ethnicities, fundamentalist religions, and warlords, exploited by foreign powers, after a Soviet-type "shock therapy", or perhaps something "in between", similar to India, half successful, half limited in its development.

"Tiananmen" in retrospect from today's knowledge—The long-time GDR ambassador to China, Rolf Berthold, a contemporary witness and naturally a good connoisseur of China, looked back almost 30 years later with even a more apodictic certainty than we: "In 1989, the USA tried to convert China as the first socialist country back into capitalism. This attempt, which has gone down in the history of the country as a student coup, has failed."[11] This is apparently anything but politically correct from the perspective of today's mainstream consensus, with its annual celebration of a "massacre", including the Eurocentrist left-liberal EU intelligentsia, but probably a robust assessment from a close observer, with some reflected historical distance.

To be sure, the Empire's attempts à la Kissinger and Brzezinski to make China a neoliberal-financialized Western country and integrate it into the Western bloc could never be a one-shot "color-revolutionary" takeover as has been possible with the regime changes in many smaller and medium-sized countries. A large nuclear power certainly cannot straightforwardly be dealt with in such ways. A critical turning point could have been generated only by continuous multi-level pressures generating crises in several critical fields, dimensions, and levels. Such decades-long competing out and wearing out indeed had been successful with the Soviet Union. But such strategy explains the different phases of the US-China relations and the different mixtures between cooperation, containment, and rivalrous combat over time. In the end, the USA could never attain that critical turning point vis-à-vis China. And when all hopes for a Chinese "Soviet solution" were gone, the US strategy toward China basically changed to open hostility after the Great Financial Crisis (GFC), given the US inner and outer power positions had been considerably weakened after 2008. Shortly after 2008, Obama and H. Clinton declared their famous "Pivot to Asia" to strategically contain China.

In the meantime, however, the fog around the events of Tiananmen has largely cleared after the declassification of numerous US documents in 2019, while, in the run-up to the 30th anniversary of "Tiananmen" in the same year, media were predictably stirred up again. But also, academic interest was rekindled through the released documents.[12]

Now media language and the usual language regulations as well as photos could be examined, parallels to similar events in other countries could be drawn, compared, backgrounds analyzed, international contexts established, and surprising quotes from state and intelligence documents of the USA could be used. In contrast to the mainstream narratives of a "massacre" on Tiananmen Sq.,[13] nothing like a "massacre" by the military taking the square had occurred, according to eyewitness accounts.[14] In other parts of the city and in the country, there have been more violent fights at points. There have been serious estimations, conservative though, according to which 200–300 people were killed, which included some dozens of the killed unarmed young policemen and cadets. The *New York Times* then spoke of 400–800 dead.[15] Richard Roth, then reporting for CBS from Beijing, was another eyewitness rejecting the Western mainstream "massacre" narrative on the square.

> [W]e saw no bodies, injured people, ambulances or medical personnel — in short, nothing to even suggest, let alone prove, that a "massacre" had recently occurred in that place.[16]

He also confirmed, though, that there had been people killed by the military ***around*** Tiananmen Square, mostly in the Western part of Beijing. But the clearing of the square was mostly peaceful. Why the hardliners in that heated situation ordered the military to use violence still, as the protesters had already agreed to clear the square, can only be speculated.

Wikipedia defines a massacre as a mass murder under particularly cruel circumstances, a carnage or blood bath, which is what the collective media wordings deliberately suggest up to today. Massacre also deliberately is no category of international law, and this is exactly why the Western mainstream media are using this narrative annually up to today.

The major "success" of the media strategy around Tiananmen, thus, has been a shaping of Western popular consciousness, where the "massacre" could be indelibly anchored to this day. Thus, the most important, sophisticated, and successful part of the campaign was the methodology of the social-psychological embedding of those events for the Western populations as the actual addressees.[17]

About 35 years ago, even if only intuitively, I was not entirely wrong when I interpreted "Tiananmen" as a message from China to the Empire and the world, despite its economic and financial dependence as the "extended workbench" of the world, that it wanted to pursue its own path of national development. It certainly was highly risky, like a "ride on the razor's edge", which could easily have gone wrong. In 1989, I doubted that China would be able to realize and maintain this "message". But again, it was not the first and not the last time that China had to ride on the razor's edge ...

Meanwhile in Western Europe: "Maoists" on the Green "Long March" into the Institutions and Governments

In the subsequent decade of a crucial but apparently unspectacular development of China, my interest in China declined again. And with good reason, I thought. A number of "Maoists" from the 1970s had in the 1980s become "decent", established political careerists, and later even surprisingly warmongering, and above all vehemently anti-China, integral parts of the parliamentary and party systems, partly migrated into the mainstream parties, partly established the green parties.

Their former dream of the "permanent revolution" (no, not in Western Europe, but in China!), they had to bury. Out of this disappointment, many developed—psychologically intelligible—a deep aversion to this, now different, China, which was set to go its development path without the Western "Maoists" revolutionary romance. I already suspected: They would never make their peace with this China anymore! And they have indeed not made it to this day. Would they in some future perhaps even applaud any military intervention against China in the name of "human rights" and "Western values"? Indeed, it openly happened for the first time after WWII, ten years after "Tiananmen", 1999, with the military destruction of Yugoslavia and Serbia (the old Slavic archenemy) by Germany, the EU, the USA, and NATO, with the Greens in the German government, responsible for the ideological "antifa" narrative using "Auschwitz".

BTW, obviously, no coincidence that NATO Bombers destroyed the Chinese Embassy in Yugoslavia and killed several Chinese diplomats. The revenge of the Greens in the governments of NATO for the end of their "Maoist" dreams of a China remaining poor, inferior, vulnerable, needy of superior Western support, in a permanent cultural revolution and chaos? After all, I realized that China's history in fact moved past their traumatic China problem, and I let it rest again. After 1989 again for more than another decade …

2001: China Approved as a "Market Economy"—Admission to the World Trade Organization, and Clinton's Dream That Google, Facebook & Co. Will Take over China

The West, in the 1990s, somehow made its "tactical" peace (or truce?) with China. The basic deal from China's point of view was: We continue to organize and provide the efficient and cheap production for Western companies and consumers with well-qualified workers and infrastructure, and you allow us to self-determine our national development and support our technical-economic upgrading. This deal was sealed, for the time being, in 2001 with China's accession to the WTO, albeit with the reservation of a later review of China's qualification as a "market economy".

China had to first declare itself a "market economy" and promise to adhere to "market principles" in international trade. They did, and I (once again too superficially) noted a message for myself: "Now they are giving up any claim to an independent, even socialist development. From now on, it's all downhill for China. Now the Empire has won, after all." The USA would now, I was afraid, determine China's development via the WTO, which they controlled then, just as they have done in numerous countries via the WTO and the money from the World Bank and the International Monetary Fund (IMF). China now would also have to contribute to the global dollar dominance, through which all countries must offset US trade-balance deficits, federal debt, and military expansion, by buying and holding an overvalued dollar, in currency reserves and US Hudson (2015) treasuries.[18]

And of course, they would rely on the information dominance over Chinese society by the then only international internet monopolies, the GAFAM—Google, Apple, Facebook, Amazon, and Microsoft—which would then store every word written into a computer in China and spoken into a mobile phone, commercially evaluate it, and also, if requested, pass it on to the numerous US intelligence and military agencies. And with the help of appropriate algorithms, they would soon get a grip on Chinese public opinion.

In fact, I had, again, no idea yet that and how China, in a novel historical dimension, redefined the relation of productive forces, including having "markets" (and how effective, regulated ones!) and the relations of production, i.e., the political-economic power of a state in a long-run socialist development perspective, providing and developing the future form into which those productive forces would develop into during the twenty-first century. This book will deal with this.

In 1999, the USA had concluded a bilateral trade agreement with China, and as early as March 2000, US President Clinton confidently announced in a speech:

> We know how much the Internet has changed America, and we are already an open society. Imagine how much it could change China ... Now there's no question China has been trying to crack down on the Internet. [Chuckles.] Good luck! [Laughter.] That's sort of like trying to nail jello to the wall. [Laughter][19]

His audience laughed confidently.

Similarly, and another decade later, a Republican presidential candidate named Jon Huntsman indulged in a provincial US omnipotence-supremacy pipedream of "taking China down" via the internet during the 2011 primary campaign:

> [W]e should be reaching out to our allies and constituencies within China. They're called the young people. They're called the internet generation ... and they are bringing about change, the likes of which is going to take China down.[20]

No wonder that later, until today, frustration and aggression toward China became rampant among the ruling political elites in the USA and the EU, as everything turned out quite different than fantasized.

Since no one in the world can objectively and operationally define a "market economy", the expectations in 2001 were naturally quite different on both sides, which could typically only be glossed over with the phrase "market economy". The truth is, China *has* a market economy, it *has* markets, and effective ones, but as a system it *is not* a "market economy", let alone an NFC ("market") economy, as the Western political elites had hoped for. And even the Chinese wording of a "socialist market economy" may be flawed. More details later in this book.

The Chinese economy indeed became a market economy as a market economy could also be: with markets not being an end in themselves, not a golden calf but an instrument for increasing the prosperity of the population, not a "self-regulating", deregulated mechanism that quickly degenerates into a narrow oligopoly, not a neoliberal vehicle to primarily make the rich richer and the powerful more powerful, to serve an oversized speculative sector that only lives and acts for its own profit rates in the end, at the expense of the entire real socio-economy, but a mechanism that must prove its ability to serve national development and is accordingly controlled along, and embedded in, national development lines. This original understanding of the liberal classics, such as Adam Smith, of a "market" and an "economy" as means and not the end of human development, had already been completely lost in the West after three decades of neoliberal devastation of economy, infrastructure, society, state, and spirit. And, surprise, Chinese markets functioned again in a way that had been lost in oligopoly capitalism for a century; it reintroduced high-quality but cheap, affordable products for the average consumer ... through a true price competition.

How dynamically markets function in China, how China massively mobilizes entrepreneurship in people, how China uses its market economy without itself becoming a capitalist "market economy", and how it thus develops something completely new in the relationship between state and market, we will discuss in more detail in this book.

Around 2000/2001, I still believed more in Bill Clinton and in the Jon Huntsmans, whom history has long passed by since, than in China ... China became, for the last time, (apparently) indifferent to me.

2008: "Can Capitalism Survive China's Rise?"

But still, surprise, surprise, the world continued to change, and (more surprise), completely independent of what I thought. And information about China no longer just trickled in; it began to flow in broader currents. You could not escape it anymore. In 2008, a book about China fell into my hands that was somehow different. A title that directly addressed a "rise of China" and posed the surprising question: "Can the capitalist world economy survive China's rise?" Only later did I realize how justified this question was and how many different dimensions it had. Famous economists praised the book on the back cover. The author was a certain Li Minqi[21] from a well-known economics faculty in the USA, the University of Utah in Salt Lake City. Some 20 years earlier, I had spent some time there as a guest on a research trip to several US universities. He was also introduced (in the book) as a former political prisoner in China (1990–1992). So, another one motivated by old, unsettled grudges? The danger naturally is considerable that after political imprisonment, it becomes hard to see one's country objectively. Despite such doubts, the book seemed to me very thorough and analytical rather than flatly political.

The question of how exactly China could change the current neoliberal, financialized, and globalized world economy in its deteriorating state, with extreme inequality and growing poverty, new world records of hunger, and a climate catastrophe—nowadays termed polycrisis, remained open in the book, in my humble opinion. But alternatives were presented: China might change the hegemonic, imperial world order by displacing it as an alternative example, or, in contrast, by driving it forward, through becoming itself its most excessive manifestation, to its ecological, social, and economic limits. Exciting and frightening alternatives. It reminded me of the 300 million additional VW Golfs in China that I had fantasized about in the 1980s and 1990s. But the author, at least, clarified that China had appeared on the world stage as one, if not *the* new main actor, and this new perspective could not be avoided anymore.

Only later did I learn that some historians had long since reevaluated China's thousands of years of cultural and state history, and identified China's subjugation to the European colonial yoke and its hundred-year devastation into a poorhouse as a great historical exception, and thus had predicted a resurgence of China to a global power status as the new old historical normal.[22]

But the carefully fabricated media image of China as the cheap and dirty extended workbench of capitalism, dutifully producing every piece of Western plastic junk, was still swirling in my mind. We were "informed" on a daily basis in the Western mass media about cheap production, poverty, and environmental destruction—as if the West had nothing to do with it. So, even 20 years ago, I could not imagine, like most in the West, that China would have emerged, just a decade later, as an economic, technological, ecological, developmental, and, yes, forgive me the provocation, also as a socially progressing, leading power.[23]

After that, I started to consider China more intensively and continuously and to ask questions: Rise to a leading world power, cheap production, environmental pollution, social progress ... How does this fit together? Where does this lead to? How long can it last? I discussed, increasingly "prodded" and expectantly, among others, with my assistants—and received, even from younger people, rather dampening responses, which reflected the spectrum of political attitudes in the West:

China as "turbo capitalism", "imperialism", "dictatorship"... criticisms dependent on the political standpoints from ultraleft to conservative.

Great Financial Crisis 2008ff.: China as an Engine of the Global Economy

Then there was the Great Financial Crisis (GFC) of 2008, extending with its subsequent sovereign crises, after the Western governments had bailed out the banks, shadow banks, and billionaires, into the 2010s. It occupied everyone's minds, but critical political economists in particular ways, and still when the mainstream had already returned to neoliberal austerity business as usual. It has occupied critical economists' minds since, and triggered analyses of the particular NFC, a clearly deteriorating phase of capitalism, with the GFC being its turning point. We became occupied with its social, political, and global consequences, and the potential next crash and creeping existential crises.

It was triggered and caused by an oversized, "over-speculated" neoliberal, deregulated, and completely uninhibited financial speculation sector, which essentially only lived for itself and by inflating itself, increasingly plundered the real, producing economy, instead of serving it, and built criminal derivative pyramids (called "financial innovations") and sold them to the dumb and desperate, the greedy and those who anyway have too much left over.[24] The illusion of an eternally growing system, which logically cannot exist. In addition to the global raids on wage income, public assets, agricultural crops, or entire land areas ("land grabbing"), this system had inflated itself beyond all measure over invented cascades of fictitious capital, over derivatives of derivatives of derivatives, over debt and credit pyramids, over the servicing of loans by ever new loans (Ponzi), bubbles everywhere, and destabilized itself, the entire economy, the states, and the world—until finally even the smallest reduction of growth rates (starting in 2007 in the real estate sector) was sufficient to trigger the largest crisis worldwide in almost 80 years. Millions lost everything, those sitting at the sources lost little; they had transformed fictitious capital early enough into real assets and got bailed out and "fed" with "quantitative money easing" anyway.

For three decades, the neoliberal parties and governments had preached, practiced, and announced state withdrawal, privatization, deregulation, welfare state reduction, and a minimal state (except for police, military, judiciary, and asset management, which all was expanded instead) as the coming paradise on earth (with expanded police, courts, and military for the upcoming social conflicts in such paradise), in which there was no longer a place for "social benefaction" (supposedly no longer needed). But suddenly there were many hundreds of billions from the state budgets, and later from the central banks, to bail out private banks, investment banks, etc. from their over-speculation mess—and trillions flooded into the speculation sector in the following years ("QE"), from the central banks, for which the taxpayer is liable in the end, but that at the same time are the lobby organizations of the speculation sector. Fiscal Keynesianism virtually returned somehow, very specifically, in favor of the speculation sector. Keynesianism, politically banned for more than 30 years, suddenly appeared possible again.

And "weaponized", structurally protective "Keynes plus industrial policy" returned as well. In Germany, a demand support program was also conjured up for its own leading industry, the automotive industry. Specifically, 1.5–2.0 percent of the GDP was provided for the purchase of new cars, all of course still with old combustion technology. At that time, no one was questioning the internal combustion engine and the cheaper diesel technologies. No increased environmental standards required, no progressive structural change implied. And the big ecological fraud of the combustion engine industry, with their year-long emissions deceits and faked emission statistics, had not yet been exposed. The exhaust-gas-obscuring technology was being practiced as the usual German "auto chancellors", Schröder, Merkel, had not been fully able to block all increases of emission standards in Brussels—and it was "not recognized" yet by the German authorities. At that time, it was still the biggest luck of the automotive industry and the government to have, in a cooperative effort, prevented stricter emission limits in Brussels.[25] A "scrappage premium" for older vehicles was touted as well, safeguarding the industrial status quo with a "new" (economically well-founded, but not applied for decades) fiscal policy instrument. It helped to prevent the German economy from collapsing. A minimal fiscal success story practiced in contrast to all previous neoliberal narratives of parties, governments, media, as well as the mainstream guardians of the holy economic grail, academic chief ideologues of neoliberalism for decades. Suddenly, one could virtually be some kind of Keynesian again, which had been tabooed as the dirty child since the neoliberal upheaval in the mid-1970s.

Things somehow repeated a decade later in the Covid-19 crisis, in a global situation much more disadvantageous for the NFC, more clearly mirroring national and international deterioration of the hegemonic international NFC system. This then, through increased societal fragmentation, much more political conflict, and post-democratic state transformations in the interior policies of the West, as well as extended political overthrows and warfare in international relations, transformed things into a full-fledged "Armament Keynesianism plus industrial policy and state weaponizing", under an international win-lose system of trade, investment, policy, and people-to-people de-cooperation, decoupling, and deglobalization.

The financial sector today is structurally unchanged and larger than before, dominating more than ever the real economy, society, politics, and state in the West, in the areas of nutrition, health, and environment. We are looking back on 18 years of fragility, real disinvestment, Western deindustrialization, growth depression, intensified redistribution upwards, social and infrastructural decay, increasing state incapacity and inactivity, social fragmentation and enforced uprooting migration, the deterioration of the human right to affordable housing as well as ecological disasters, a resulting political pressure toward nationalism and extremism in the political mainstream, xenophobia, racism, warmongering, unprecedented atrocities, and genocide.

We have a term for this nowadays—polycrisis, interrelated and cumulative multiple conventional crises, which together generate a new quality of both global crisis and global change.

And then, back in 2008, China suddenly appeared on the economic and financial world stage! At that time, China still had much less weight in the world economy than it has today, but there they were making a big splash: China spent about 8 percent (!) of its then already second largest national income in the world, on a huge fiscal support program. This included, of course, investments in new technologies and in infrastructures, but above all, what has only gradually become known but is most visible today, particularly for the visitor to China: ecological investments. 2008 was, coincidentally, the year of the Olympics in Beijing, and billions of trees had already been planted up to that year, the cities with many millions of people were crisscrossed with proper and high-quality green, and huge national biodiversity parks and forest areas were established in large parts of the country, and eco-technologies were promoted everywhere, an ecological civilization in the making, "just" out of a global financial crisis—another Keynesianism, so to speak, plus deep industrial and structural changes.

It was the largest investment program in the world for years, and its investment, income, and demand effects were incomparably larger and longer lasting than Merkel's small car purchase program in Germany—and, not the least, it was the largest export promotion program for Germany for years through the 2010s. China became the economic engine of the world, and a large economic engine for Germany, of greater importance than what the German government itself achieved. All of this became increasingly effective in the 2010s, in both international trade & investment and in a structural upgrading of China.

And so it happened that after 2008, China was finally becoming "indispensable" and "unignorable"—and it suddenly stimulated my fantasies and hopes, and fears with others.

2009: "Lettels Flom Ovel Thele"

My wife got back to her older idea to satisfy my seriously awakening interest in China. But I was still not ready for a visit to China. She said: "Do you know this book, *Bliefe von dlüben*?" [Letters from over there, in a China-persiflage spelling replacing the "r"s with "l"s] I didn't know it! A German journalist and well-known satirist, Christian Y. Schmidt, had emigrated to China, married a Chinese woman, and had been writing regular satirical columns from there for several years for several German magazines. I pushed the little book from the left to the right side of the breakfast table and back for some weeks. This was not supposed to be my approach to understanding what was going on there! But then, in fact, it was. One of the then several approaches at least.

With a lot of humor about (back then, for us, apparently) "crazy" everyday behaviors of the Chinese, but also with a lot of irony and sarcasm about the prejudices about China in the Western corporate media, this little book,[26] sometimes between the lines, sometimes very directly, was also a serious and well-researched mirror of Western twisted perceptions, of the usually older, unprofessional, and wrongly researched, or outright faked stories and devastating ways our state media deal with China. There had already been a little book of this kind by the same author before, and there were more in a similar format afterwards.[27] Schmidt did not shy away from critically dealing with manufactured Western hysteria points like Tibet and Xinjiang, and daily heroes like the Dalai Lama or Ai Weiwei, and in doing so, turned the Western media language and thought regulations upside down.

In this "mirror from China", the German magazine *Der Spiegel* ["The Mirror"] stood out as the "China Basher Magazine" (Schmidt 2010, 188): Poor, incorrect information, lazy and one-sided in journalistic research, but all the more opinionated and ideologically strong, arrogant, pseudo-intellectual, Eurocentric, and absolutist in "values". "We: Good! They: Bad!"[28] Schmidt dismantled the distorted *Spiegel* reporting on China long before the scandals of more generally faked stories of the *Spiegel* became public.[29] Using the example of the usually incorrect and denunciatory "reporting" on the Summer Olympics in Beijing 2008, Schmidt was clearer with his satirical style than any direct informative report could have been. He also cleared up other Western stereotypes, such as the "Tibet liberators" among the Hollywood millionaire stars, and he did so always from the perspective of everyday life, of the man on the street, "from below", with the humor of the Chinese and the satire of the German who knows the Chinese. He took the German media to task.[30]

In this way, the author also conveyed surprising images of freedom, high levels of discussion, ease, and velocity of change in China. These images elegantly undermined the mental patterns of those who sat on their high horse of the German export world champion, as if this post-WWII national business model would not clearly drive Germany into a wall within a few years. In the 2020s, this has already become a harsh reality of the German economy and society.

The image of a rather colorful, highly discursive, sometimes obstinate and resistant, contradictions-bearing free East appeared.[31] Yes, in the evenings, people dance in the public squares of the cities, by the hundreds, quite voluntarily, relaxed, with much joy, in the Qi-Gong or Tai-Chi style, as every visitor to China has already marveled at. And in China, people laugh more than in most other countries in the world.[32] How is that? Do people in China have any reason to laugh?

At some point, Christian Schmidt had to seriously ask himself what would become of China if the Western postulates and pipe dreams for China would be implemented. The image he then painted was quite daunting. He confessed: "This China might please Angela Merkel [...] But I would have to look for a new homeland."[33]

The image of China that I got to know here was anything but a clear analytical message, but it actually made me want "more China". Now, also the gut feeling was addressed, which should complement the intellect if the quest for knowing more is to have strength and stamina. There was a breakthrough after four decades of "leaving China (relatively) aside"!

2010: "My" First Chinese Colleague

The remainder, but in fact, the beginning of my story, developed quickly. Because the groundwork had been laid. While China was becoming a prime factor in the world, I still was predominantly networked toward the West (namely in US-based academic associations). A colleague from Switzerland, whose academic networks included East Asia, told me, this famous Chinese colleague, one of the few international economics stars after 2008 who had predicted the financial crisis, was traveling in Western Europe. CHEN Ping, a complexity economist,[34] last student of Chemistry Nobel Laureate Ilya Prigogine, who, in his last academic position at the University of Texas, Austin, had analyzed certain "self-organization" capabilities and statistical "deep structures" of complex systems. This colleague commuted between Austin and his two Chinese universities in Shanghai (Fudan) and Beijing (Peking Uni). A non-neoliberal, critical economist in "our" non-orthodox networks, also prominent in China. Not one of those many neoliberal-turned returnees from the USA with the mission to take over the economic faculties at China's universities, to invite US Nobel laureates to China, to establish US-funded institutes, and to turn the universities toward the US system, as they populated Chinese academic economics from the 1980s to the 2000s. I heard he was on a lecture tour in Europe, and I should invite him to my university.

In the conversations after his lectures, I asked him questions of the usual kind, uninformed as I was. "Ok, you're not a neoliberal 'mainstreamer'. But you're also not Marxist. What options do you have in China then? How far, for example, are you allowed to criticize your government?" Perhaps this reminded him of how his former compatriots had referred to the European colonialists as barbarians. The answers were friendly and relaxed, diplomatic and disarming: "I criticize my government without problems, often in front of a large audience, for which I sometimes receive applause." "Ok, and the next morning you're in front of a government hearing committee, criticized for your criticism, right?" "Next morning I am in front of government representatives at their invitation and advise them on complex economic systems, financial sector dynamics, and economic policy measures." That hit home! I invited him several times later … and we developed some cooperation, and in 2024, we jointly edited an *International Handbook of Complexity Economics*.[35] The first Chinese person in my professional life had further broken mental dams, opened doors, not least through the calmness and self-assuredness with which he patiently answered even my crude questions. This has happened a hundred times since, with my Chinese colleagues, of whom many have become friends to me.

2010s: Chinese Students Are Coming

In the meantime, my name seemed to have somehow made its way to China. Chinese graduates were ready to go abroad anyway. And they were encouraged by their government to do so. Those trained in non-neoliberal, non-mainstream economics, and interested in postgraduate studies in non-orthodox economics, scanned the Internet for one of the few such "heterodox" professorial chairs and research groups. Some of them were explicitly interested in the upcoming fields of evolutionary and institutional economics, and some of those found me and my publications on the net. The USA and Great Britain often were still the first choice, Germany rather the second. But the Chinese graduates who suddenly inquired with me about doctoral study opportunities seemed to be informed, knew my topics and international networking. They had passed the selection process for a four-year doctoral scholarship abroad through the China Scholarship Council (CSC). A few weeks of remote testing via email, question-answer exercises, requests of writing a short paper, elaboration of the doctoral topic, an online interview—and the first Chinese doctoral student was selected to come. And we could even increase our working group without using our own budget (which would not have been available anyway). They were not just doctoral students but received contracts from my department to help me out with research and teaching. In the end, over the years, this added up to three Chinese doctoral employees and another external Chinese PhD student.

It took about a year for each to get them to the point where they didn't always jump up immediately and salute when I entered their office, and to adopt the relaxed Anglo-Saxon academic manners when communicating (in English, as we had to): addressing the professor without a title and by first name. Today, they not only have mastered this standard, but have become established professors themselves, first even in Germany (as junior professors), and finally in China (now associate and full professors).

After they had achieved PhD promotion and their professorial independence, their Chinese (professional) culture took effect: "Can we write this or that article together?" Yes, we could, and we have done until today. "When, where and how can we cooperate?" "Would you want to teach in China?" Cooperation and exchange agreements were quickly worked out. Even a Chinese dean flew in to sign an agreement with me and my department. Germany still was considered an attractive destination for a business trip anyway, not only in terms of "Industry 4.0" or "dual education". There was no shortage of Chinese funds for bringing me over to China for summer-school PhD teaching, for giving individual lectures or minor teaching sequences in regular classes, and for student exchange.

For five years, 2015–2019 (unfortunately interrupted by the Covid pandemic), we have, among other things, been running a summer school for Chinese doctoral students. A contingent of three to four additional Western professors, of different theoretical orientations, which I was asked to put together internationally, was brought in. I had suggested and could bring in colleagues from Italy, the USA, or Canada, financial and environmental economists, socio-economists, feminists, post-Keynesian, and evolutionary-institutional economists. The Western groups have been pluralistic; all major critical schools of thought should be represented over the years. They have been complemented on the Chinese side by professors who have been typically recruited from both the local (Chinese) "School of Economics" (dominated then by American "orthodoxy") and the local "School of Marxism" (usually quite worldly analysts, often with demanding formal analyses).

I wondered about something reverse happening at a German university: Inviting Chinese Marxist political economists for a pluralistic doctoral school! Impossible! We are not that pluralistic and free after all ...

One of the declared goals of a new science policy in the era of President Xi Jinping was to overcome this long-standing separation of Chinese economic faculties between Chinese Marxist political economy and Western neoliberal economic orthodoxy. This was also intended to further rejuvenate and make more attractive the Marxist faculties, in the 2010s often still considered by Chinese students as "old-fashioned", as well as to ward off the danger of a domination of Chinese economic faculties and business schools by simplistic neoliberal American mainstream "market"-model thinking and related dogmatic policy demands of the known kind. The latter had appeared ideologically strong, "modern", and to outmatch Marxist political economy since the 1980s, but practically could only advise the Government very one-dimensionally and had increasingly lost intellectual attractiveness after the GFC. By today, the Western neoliberal orthodoxy has lost traction in China also among the younger generation.

Above-mentioned Chen Ping once had explained to me how economic-policy advice has worked in China: All theoretical and ideological orientations are invited to present their proposals to the government. Practical quality and fruitfulness decide, and by no means had Marxist economists automatically have an advantage in the government. And I had thought of some of my most famous non-orthodox colleagues in the West, who after the 1970s, for decades, did not have the slightest chance of even getting close to our neoliberal governments ...

We, the Western professors in those PhD summer schools, have thus been experiencing a surprising open-mindedness and willingness to engage with a plurality of theoretical perspectives over the years. We have been fighting for such summer schools in the West for decades, and as far as they are (increasingly) taking place today, they often have to be organized outside of universities and especially outside of and without the support of the economic faculties. We have also perceived a considerable willingness to learn and cooperate in China, and a high engagement in realizing new projects—all that apparently characterizes the professional actors in China, as all the Westerners who have visited and worked in China keep telling you.

But, in the meantime, in the 2020s, in the follow-up to Trump-style anti-scientific Covid-19 "China virus" manufactured narratives, things have even worsened again in the West, reversed politically and administratively, and even in academia. In a general political climate of anxiety and the dim feelings of Western deterioration, Western politics had been in need of more enemies "out there" and clearly became more aggressive and restrictive over the 2010s in both domestic and foreign policies. China was suddenly declared as the main political enemy by the political and media castes, and any people-to-people contacts with Chinese have been put under the weirdest suspicions. Since the B. Obama–H. Clinton administration's fundamental Western strategic change after the GFC and declaration of a changing focus of the ex-hegemon from Europe toward, and against, China, a new McCarthyite Washington class of political nerds and witch-hunters is declaring that "in 2025" (postponed to 2026, then 2027 ...) the "only world power" will be "at war with China". The usual EU, UK, Japanese, Canadian, Australian, etc. satellites, dependent as they are and without any political autonomy or own conception of the world, have of course followed suit under the skirt of their big brother (or big mama).

This is exactly why they appear so upset, helpless, and panicking under Trump's second term, when big mama seems to withdraw her warm skirt and denies her former unlimited "maternalism", in fact, hegemonic paternalism. Will the EU ever learn? And does anyone in the world still care for the EU?

Those who have ever visited China, as tourists, students, academics, or other professionals, are returning with a different world view from what they had been told by Western media and politicians. And thousands of Western companies invest billions and billions, now profiting from Chinese R&D, high skills, complete and effective value-added chains and regional industry clusters, cutting-edge young start-up suppliers, and cheap bank finance, accessible and effective infrastructures, cheap and reliable energy supply, alert and helping public agencies, from a mobilizing culture with legendary "China speed" and "China experimentalism",[36] stating that they often have more freedom to venture than in the over-bureaucratic and distrustful EU and Germany.

Under such a political atmosphere in the West, universities' political bureaucracies cancel research cooperation and people-to-people contacts with China and discourage even learning the Chinese language. Universities had cooperations with Chinese Confucius Cultural Institutes for 10 or 15 years, through which informative exchange was organized and with whose help we were able to conduct teaching exchanges with Chinese professors. But cooperations have largely been cancelled under right-wing/mainstream political pressure and prosecution. Chinese delegations from industry and government representatives as well as scientists had been regular guests at our universities. Numerous companies have had a lively exchange with Chinese partners.

But the West is, in the 2020s and the foreseeable future, even perceivable locally and in our own work area, massively set back into an adverse motion toward what Trump 1.0 had issued to the USA and its satellites as "decoupling" and hybrid war.

"Five BERs and a Maglev, Please!"

Back to my Chinese visitors and PhD students in the 2010s. In the beginning, I was surprised by such cultural interchange, where I had not expected it. Nowadays, I am no longer perplexed when visitors from

China, who after a weekend trip to Berlin or Munich, ask me questions like: "Why are your trains mostly late?", "Why don't you have a seat reservation with your train ticket (but have to pay extra for it)?", "Why is there such a hustle and bustle and confusion in your stations, on your platforms, and in your (often overloaded) trains?", "Why are your railway facilities so dirty?", etc. Note, Germany once had been a dream country of engineering and good organization for the Chinese …

Such questions no longer plunge me into deep reflection and some depression. I now know that Chinese train stations work like airports: With train speeds of 350, and more recently 450 km/h, this seems appropriate. The train, track, and station concepts in Germany, on the other hand, still come from the steam engine era. In conversation with Chinese colleagues, I nowadays quickly resort to humor. I now answer: "Your trains arrive on time just because they run faster. It's just logical, no?"

In this way, I avoid thinking again about the misery of German infrastructure and German semi-privatized companies, which have been gutted through dividend, interest, and bonus payments, and expensive consulting fees, the usual neoliberal financial bleeding. I avoid thinking about the inability of the state and the incapacities and unwillingness of the political class that has learned to dance around the fiscal golden calf of austerity, the "Black Zero" or "no debt" budget, disguised and beautified as a "debt brake" (now with constitutional status). This caste now lacks even the most basic economic knowledge of a dynamic national economic circuit. I avoid despairing about the state's four-decade-long neoliberal dequalification and the resulting disinvestment, the siphoning off from the substance of former public, now privatized, companies by private "investors" with their capital-income claims.

I have always been surprised about the many times higher complexity and long-term planning of Chinese infrastructure projects. Remember the long, sad story of our capital's airport BER, which was under construction for nearly 15 years, languishing for a long time as a construction ruin. And when I, desperately, started talking ironically on all that with Chinese guests and visitors, it went like: "Should we quickly build you five BERs?" Or me: "No, please build us a Maglev (once known in Germany as Transrapid). We once invented it, but we forgot how to do it."

These are banter among colleagues who know what they are really talking about: Both sides know that the differences are not coincidental and are not differences that can be explained with simplistic stereotypes like the Chinese "authoritarian system", "dictatorship versus freedom", and other phrases for the mentally modest. Both sides know that it is about systemic differences, which at the end of complex, dynamic, and cumulative processes generate different and diverse collective and state capabilities (or cumulative incapabilities).

Those predominant simplistic Western political substitute explanations of the contemporary global change, narratives for childish minds, serving our mental laziness, emotional comfort, satiety, and deep-seated Pavlovian reflexes à la "We Good, They Bad!", leave the professional innovator, the skilled worker, technician, engineer, researcher, entrepreneur, the doer, seeker, the one willing to learn and understand, and the potentially coöperative person in us in doubt with a queasy feeling and a dissatisfaction.

And this is how all the floodgates toward wanting to understand and learn were finally opened for me, in the 2010s. Prejudices, blinders, ignorance … goodbye! Learning more about China, and about what China's development tells us about global change, was finally high on the agenda for me.

2014ff.: Conversations with German Professionals on the Plane Back from China …

So, I have been traveling to China regularly (with a three years Covid break) for 12 years now. Changchun, the city of "my" Jilin Uni, a "small town" of a population of 9 Million, in fact a second tier city in the Chinese city-levels scheme, has been the location of the first Volkswagen plant in China in the early 1980s, and is today also the location of a large Audi factory, and, in recent years, the location of a new Audi plant just for electric vehicles. Several German suppliers are thus located in the city as well, with either small production sites or service offices, and, finally, a large number of supplier and service representatives are regularly flying to Changchun.

Jilin Uni, by the way, has been ranked 57 among 732 Chinese universities, across 27 different international rankings run by different US and international institutions.[37] Globally, it appears in most research rankings between 100 and 150.[38] My German home university appears globally between the positions 300 and 350.[39]

So, I got into conversations with business travelers, in the hotel lobbies or hotel elevator, learned about their cooperations in China. On flights back home, I have learned a lot as well. You are sitting next to each other for a few hours and have some time to talk. I have asked lots of questions and people have told me about their experiences and cooperations. The experiences have been quite similar: Most have been enthusiastic about the openness, eagerness to learn, and flexibility of Chinese partners, their willingness to cooperate, and their striving for win-win situations, also about the speed of change and the ease with which new solutions can be found. Some German technicians or engineers have become reflective, sometimes even angry about their own company's hierarchy. Small business owners reflected on their home government. Nothing of that at home is keeping up with "China experimentation" and "China speed". "The German engineering plan that we had brought here did not work, and we had to make experimental changes until things worked. Even workers were involved and made a lot of suggestions. We wrote the new arrangement down, and now I have to explain the new solution to them at home", said a corporate technician, "and will have to wait for months for a 'Go' from above".

In such cases, which were new to me, I have asked myself, and the person: "What is different in the 'deep structures' here and there? What does this mean re. the attitudes, expectations, or motivations of people, what is the 'culture' of this 'other system'?"

Thus, we sometimes even touched on "systemic" questions. Fears for the future so well-known at home seem to be alien to most Chinese, some social security coupled with wide-spread optimistic expectations of advancement, income and prosperity increase, labor appreciation, and the confidence that, if their workplace will be changed, a new one will also be qualified and linked to rising income—and one will always have a number of other professional opportunities. This all contradicts our common image of China, of "dictatorship" and slavery. We will return to this with more detail.

Chinese growth will of course not be infinite, since there can be no infinite growth on a limited planet. But the growth of innovation, appreciation, prosperity, and quality of life through broad social embeddedness and security, and development through some collectivity and through national, social, and public regulatory embedding could be infinitely sustained, regardless of quantitative limits of growth.

The readers of this book will be able to better assess these aspects of a new "number one" in the global economy at the end.

… and Conversations Back Home

Landing back home in Germany, you see connecting flights canceled, gates moved several times, and people stranded in daily train chaos.[40] Welcome back to the land of the "lean" ex-public corporations, disinvesting organizations with insufficient performance but high and increasing shareholder values, the land of the emaciated public services and broken infrastructures. And the finance ministers of any coalition or neoliberal political mainstream party play the proud heroes of austerity.

Confronted with such contrast, German travelers to China, tourists, technicians, engineers and other professionals, entrepreneurs, and so on will not forget about China so quickly. Even after continuing "politically correct" instructions at home, by German political party and corporate media, about the "fact" that China can by definition be nothing else than an "autocracy" or dictatorship—the self-made experience in China should remain in the memory of many, and trigger more fundamental reflections. And they frankly speak out: All we have seen and got to know hints to China becoming No. 1 quickly.[41]

Landing in Frankfurt or Munich, you may have to transfer onto the German railway. The train may be late, you may miss a connecting train—or even get it because it also had a long delay, which, however, your railway app didn't know, the train sometimes has only one carriage in first class, wagons drive into the station in reverse order, sometimes a restaurant car missing, sometimes doors cannot be used, strange noises sometimes come from the undercarriage. Your train may also wait at some station for a new train driver, who will come with another train, which is unfortunately delayed. "We apologize for the inconvenience" is probably the most frequently heard phrase in a German Railway wagon. Functioning Wi-Fi? Not sure. Dead zones of mobile connection? Usually. Stable supply of cutting-edge technologies is still rare even in German ICEs (inter-city express trains).

For a country central in Europe, at the crossroads of North-South and East-West transport corridors, as it always was, after having opened up Middle and Eastern European countries, making cheap labor commute or relocate to Germany by the hundred thousands, after opening up African and Western Asian countries, through underdevelopment, hunger, conflicts, or wars, having refugees and other migrants flowing into Germany by hundreds of thousands as well, it was obvious for Germany that the continuation of the neoliberal austerity and divestment strategy in infrastructure and public services after 1990 would be a straightforward disaster strategy for Germany …

Using a German train, experiencing one of those hundreds of potential shortcomings of technology or service, you will get into conversation with fellow business travelers. And for some years now, experience from China seems to have increased considerably among German businesspeople. It has increasingly appeared to me that I am not alone with my "nostalgic" memories of both the days of functioning German trains and the modern Chinese railway "airports". There, you will wait at the gate and arrive at the platform relaxed, a few minutes before the train arrives and the gate is opened. You will see markers on the floor telling you where your wagon will stop. No hectic crowding, because everyone has their seat reservation with the ticket anyway. If a train there were only ten minutes late, it would be on TV in the evening and would be investigated. You will regularly get a snack in the train at the beginning, and you get food delivered to your seat anytime, but, yes, you can also get any favorite food delivered to your seat from a restaurant outside at the next station, by scanning a QR code.[42] Just one example of the highly integrated, comfortable IT-service networks in China. We might go on with highways, bridges, IT infrastructures, schools, and other services, contrasting different worlds …

When German business travelers in the train talk about such contrasts and start considering "Why can't WE actually do that?", the moods sometimes fluctuate between anger and resignation. As with many public and private services, and also, with the ex-public corporations responsible for the provision of future and infrastructure maintenance, one feels torpedoed in one's professional ethics by the system of alleged "solidity and saving", but, in fact, austerity and divesture, stock value increase, and redistribution upwards. Traveling professionals, confronted with the daily results of decades-long public de-qualification and divestment, often see quite clearly how counterproductive a flawed "market" and "business" politics is, which undermines their own professional efforts and thwarts their own professional ethics and aspirations of a reasonable economy and good society. Some start to suspect that this may have some "systemic" causes. Professionally, they are increasingly forced to think in complex systems rather than in simplistic "reductionism".

But how could we achieve a transformation toward another, more functioning, productive, innovative, inclusive, and forward-driving capitalism? In this book, we will consider further details on this, for several different economic and societal areas, and will illustrate how one area is related to the other, "systemically", both here and in China. "It's the system, stupid!"

Are Chinese Turbo Capitalists, Lovers of Dictatorship?

Are the German professionals, who have been impressed by their collaborations in China, "turbo capitalists", who appreciate some unrestrained "wild East" capitalism at work in China? Not according to my experience. Although they may enjoy finding freedom and flexibility and other good conditions for doing business. China has well-working markets. But Westerners, in fact, enjoy a working, well-regulated "market economy" there, with alert public agents and good public services.

Or are they fiery anti-democrats, who enjoy the efficiency of an alleged command economy there, and would like to have it introduced in Germany as well? Nothing of this sort could I perceive in those conversations. Many have seen from their own experience that China has chosen a quite different path. Autocracies and dictatorships have never been able to rise sustainably and comprehensively, since they always had to struggle with internal contradictions and external aggressiveness, and thus quickly wore themselves out in inner and outer wars. Autocracies and dictatorships cannot mobilize people for a peaceful ecological civilization, high-road development, societal learning and experimentation, or high-skill technological progress in the long run, as China could. China also offers peaceful coexistence, renunciation of violence, and cooperation on an equal footing to the outside world, is not threatening any other country, and is not involved in any war. Unlike the German Navy off the Chinese coasts,[43] China does not conduct military maneuvers off Helgoland…[44]

So, there must be more—let's try to find out in this book.

Among my interlocutors in airplanes and trains, there is also surprisingly little economic nationalism or anti-Chinese racism, along the lines of the long-standing European colonial thought patterns of "The Yellow Peril" or "China is the challenger that we must contain!" The ethics of professionals is fundamentally about what the famous economist Thorstein B. Veblen once called the "instinct of workmanship"[45]: The connections in our brain, namely our neocortex, and our "instincts" or behavioral dispositions are set to "coopetition", after hundreds of thousands of years of human evolution, including a massive inclination toward cooperation, designed so that we highly enjoy accomplishing things together, rejoice in a good joint result. Yes, "the journey is the destination", but both are equally important: We are proud of our result, but also of the joint path toward it, the social communication, coordination, and cooperation that we have succeeded in.

Does our revived interest in, and appreciation of that somewhat "different" Chinese system, its achievements and opportunities, also stem from our professional "instinct of workmanship", which so often is obstructed in an unorganized, deregulated, uneven, oligopolistic, oligarchic, and deteriorating Western capitalism? Some feel the systemic challenges by China more than the chances, Western politicians are focused on the challenges, Western businesses are more on the chances and opportunities side. In this book, we will learn a bit about how both aspects are working out in the world today.

In the End: Learning to Learn About China …

In this book, we will look at several central areas of China's development and policies, focused on achievements and underlying structures. Starting with micro-economic foundations, individual agents and their network structures, conditions at the workplace, innovation and entrepreneurial behavior, values and everyday behavior, labor migration and social insurance, from regions and mega-cities to the macro-economy, money and finance, to society, demography and population policies, environment, and international investments, in and out, to the embedding of agents into the national development goals, to governmental framework settings and market regulations, up to the new globalization in the Belt and Road Initiative (BRI), i.e., the "New Silk Roads". To name some of the major themes.

Only when numerous components and dimensions of a complex system do not strictly contradict each other, but are made consistent, synchronized, and convergent, can a country succeed in keeping its system sufficiently stable and successful, combining innovative change and stability, and mastering a long-run catch-up process.[46] Then such a remarkable (and so far historically unique) catch-up process also succeeds, which has made China (in a historically very short time) a global number one, not only in gross domestic product (GDP, in purchasing power, PPP), but, through an equally remarkable leverage of a still middle-income level of GDP per capita, in almost all economic, technological, ecological, and socio-economic fields.

We will take a closer look at what the success conditions of the coming general "number one" are in the twenty-first century—a return, by the way, to a thousand-year long old historical normality, at least in this limited aspect of China's sheer global significance—and particularly to take the panic away from a Western reader willing to learn. We will show that this new No. 1 exactly develops away from all traditional imperialistic or hegemonistic connotations, and what exactly this might mean for humanity and its chance to reach the end of the century under still reasonable conditions.

"China, the new number one"—can we really say that? We are talking here about more than just simple facts like the nearly 20 percent of the world's GDP (in PPP) that China now represents (USA: 15 percent). A German blogger recently summed it up nicely: Some still count aircraft carriers and thus put the USA clearly in the first place of world powers, he said, but the hegemonic world is over, although many in the West still do not understand it.[47] In this book, we will distill Bill Clinton's 1992 election slogan "It's the economy, stupid!" into another quintessence: "It's the system, stupid!". And this is far broader than traditional Eurocentrist mental dualities such as "capitalism" vs. "socialism", "democracy" vs. "autocracy", and all those simplistic and linear, but fashionable Western media coinages. We rather agree with the early insight of André Gunder Frank as expressed in his beautiful wordplay "*Re-Orient*" (Frank 1998)[48]: It is about the resurrection of the potentials of a thousand-year-long history, in a new Asian age. Along this line of dynamic thinking, the twenty-first century is the Asian and especially the Chinese one. And the blogger mentioned briefly coined it: "It's about Asia, stupid!"[49]

Among those who also had understood it early, not least as he had access to the once best data sources in the world, was former US Secretary of State Henry Kissinger. If he had known a way to prevent the rise of China, he would have taken it, and he certainly was one of those who often tried it with the well-known means and resources of the old Empire. And allegedly, he even advised both Trump 1.0 and Biden for a "Nixon reverse" strategy, i.e., that the empire should ally with Russia this time against the "more dangerous" China, in order to overpower both in the end, not simultaneously but sequentially.[50]

In his late work on China (Kissinger 2011), at least, Kissinger had presented himself from a mild and wise side: The USA will no longer be able to maintain its monopolistic world empire. They would inevitably become number two. Other studies that we will use see the USA even in third place in GDP by 2030, with India in second. We fully agree. Why this will be the case will be much clearer after having read this book.

One can no longer afford to judge China ignorantly, stubbornly, in an arrogant and presumptuous attitude, as China experts around the world argue. Trump 2.0 seems to have learned something in that respect, from his own unsuccessful hybrid wars in his first presidential term, and from the unsustainable settings and measures of the Biden era that would have led the USA into a comprehensive disaster in a short time. In some sense, therefore, Trump is acting as the decline manager of the ex-hegemon, scraping together the remaining (reduced) resources of the USA and strategically reallocating them, leaving the EU and the UK to themselves and the Ukraine war to them. The EU and the UK, on the other hand, do not appear to have comprehended the greater picture. They have only "plan A" and seem to pick any dead-end street on their way. Sitting on their "pure values-based" high war horse. The time might come when we have to ask: Does anyone in the world still care about the EU and the UK?

You may put this way as well: After the latest meeting and agreements of presidents Xi and Trump in South Korea at the end of 2025, many Western media not only said something like "China has won", but US Nobel economist Paul Krugman went a step further, clearly stating "We're Number Two!"[51]

Whatever the current global turbulences may bring forth, a more intense learning about China in the West must start again. During the last 20 years, we have even forgotten how to learn about China. The Chinese know much more about us than we know about them. Sinologists and businesspeople in the West bemoan the lack of "China competence", namely in the oligarchic media and politics. But "think twice!" In your own interest!

January 2026
Wolfram Elsner

Notes

1. The literature on Chinese history is vast today; an excellent current analysis of 2500 years of economic and technological history of China, for example, is provided by Zhao (2018). *China's Long-Term Economic Development.*

How have Economy and Governance Evolved since 500 BC? Cheltenham, UK, Northampton, Mass.: Edward Elgar.

2. The term "Empire" was made popular again in intellectual circles by the book *Empire* by Hardt and Negri (2000), which reflected the period of the new global hegemony under which the USA occupied a privileged position, especially between the defeat of the Soviet Union in 1989 and the world financial crisis 2008ff. "Empire" then meant a system with an exclusive claim to world domination (unipolarity), which the USA had been building since its entry into the Second World War and then could "harvest" by finally defeating the Soviet Union, together with their military entourage (NATO), their international financial organizations (World Bank, International Monetary Fund, etc.), its huge command over the resources of the world, and related huge financial abundance. Clearer political-economic analyses of such empire have been published later. An exemplary expression of late twentieth-century imperial-hegemonic strategy was Zbigniew Brzezinski's *The Grand Chessboard: American Primacy and Its Geostrategic Imperatives*, New York: Basic Books, 1997.
3. We will not constantly use "West" and "Western"—the everyday colloquial figure in the developed capitalist countries—in quotation marks, although it is not a clarified or useful term at all. Seen globally, cardinal directions are highly relative anyway. What, for instance, has been the "Near East" or "Middle East" for centuries from the perspective of the old colonial Europe, is in fact Western Asia. The "West" has, just like the earlier stereotypical metaphor of the "Eastern Bloc", so far been used unconsciously, if not even deliberately ideologically. No one ever in the "West" could imagine using the term "Western Bloc". So, the "West" remains a metaphor, the real content of which, as well as its effects for identity formation, generating uniform collective thinking and everyday attitudes of people, would need to be clarified. While the leading capitalist powers around the ex-hegemon, under the recent drastic global change toward multipolarity, in favor of the "Global South" and at the expense of the hegemonial capitalist system, have reorganized with a renewed subordination of the EU, UK, Japan, Australia, Canada, New Zealand etc. under US leadership and NATO, it became common to speak of the "Political West" or, more appropriate, the "Collective West". Most recently, however, "Trumpism", taking over Washington, has disrupted the "Collective West" once again.
4. The history of that, at peak times about 7000 foreign NGOs were active in China, could of course only be written in every detail much later. For a German source, see, e.g., Fitzthum (2018a, b). For a classic English-language study on earlier covert CIA operations in China, see for example Conboy and Morrison (2002). Further sources below. More generally, under the US Trump administration 2.0 (2025ff.), it became obvious how

extensively the NED has been geopolitically steering thousands of NGOs all over the world when Trump cut the NED budget in early 2025, which he considered a power center of the US-DEMs' deep imperial state.

5. See, e.g., Godfree Roberts, Snipers in the US Embassy, Beijing. The Tiananmen Enquiry, *Here Comes China*, Oct. 13, 2024, herecomeschina@substack.com
6. For detailed documentations of the events from what is known today, see, e.g., Qiao Collective, Tiananmen Protests Reading List, https://www.qiaocollective.com/education/tiananmenreadinglist, visited May 10, 2025; Godfree Roberts, Tiananmen, Parts 1–4, *Here Comes China*, Feb. 1–Feb. 21, 2024, e.g., https://herecomeschina.substack.com/p/tiananmen-part-4?back=%2Fpublish%2Fposts; id., Tiananmen Postmortem, Parts I–III, *Here Comes China*, Oct. 19–Nov. 14, 2024, e.g., https://herecomeschina.substack.com/p/tiananmen-postmortem-part-iii, all accessed May 10, 2025.
7. For details, e.g., Yuen Yuen ANG, *How China Escaped the Poverty Trap*, Ithaca (NY): Cornell University Press, 2016; Isabella Weber, *How China Escaped Shock Therapy: The Market Reform Debate*, London, New York: Routledge, 2021; Keyu Jin, *The New China Playbook: Beyond Socialism and Capitalism*, New York: Viking Press, 2023.
8. The former US Secretary of State Henry Kissinger detailed in his reflective, age-wise China book (Kissinger 2011, 419ff.) the official diplomatic history between the USA and China during the Tiananmen events, which illustrates the explosiveness of the situation. Its true intelligence knowledge would certainly have been more revealing.
9. See Halford J. Mackinder, *Der Schlüssel zur Weltherrschaft. Die Heartland-Theorie* [The Key to World Domination. The Heartland Theory], Frankfurt/M.: Westend (2019): a German translation of Mackinder's original article "The Geographical Pivot of History" (1904), which is considered the intellectual beginning of a global Western geopolitics.
10. See, for example, Wolfram Adolphi, "Chinas Planwirtschaft als dialektische Aufhebung der sowjetischen [China's Planned Economy as a Dialectical Sublation of the Soviet One]", *Das Argument* 286/2010, 1–11.
11. In a lecture in May 2018; cit. after B. Queck, "China heute [China today]", *Neue Rheinische Zeitung*, www.nrhz.de, visited April 14, 2019; see also Berthold, Rolf (2009). *Chinas Weg. 60 Jahre Volksrepublik.* [China's Path. 60 years of the People's Republic.], Berlin: Wiljo Heinen. Quotation translated by this author.
12. For example: Andrew J. Nathan "The New Tiananmen Papers: Inside the Secret Meeting That Changed China", *Foreign Affairs*, Vol. 98, No. 4 (July/August 2019), 80–91.

13. For example: Jeffrey T. Richelson and Michael L. Evans: "Tiananmen Square, 1989: The Declassified History", *The National Security Archive, George Washington University.* Online at: nsarchive2.gwu.edu, visited February 19, 2020.
14. For example: "Latin American Diplomat Eyewitness Account of June 3–4 events on Tiananmen Square", *Wikileaks*, online at: https://wikileaks.org/plusd/cables/89BEIJING18828_a.html, visited May 1, 2024.
15. Nicholas D. Kristof, "A Reassessment of How Many Died in the Military Crackdown in Beijing", *The New York Times*, June 21, 1989: https://www.nytimes.com/1989/06/21/world/a-reassessment-of-how-many-died-in-the-military-crackdown-in-beijing.html, accessed May 26, 2025.
16. Richard Roth, "There Was No "Tiananmen Square Massacre"", *CBS News*, June 4, 2009: https://www.cbsnews.com/news/there-was-no-tiananmen-square-massacre/, accessed May 25, 2025.
17. See, e.g., Austrian historian Hannes Fellner, "Zu weit oder zu zaghaft? Zu den Hintergründen des Tian'anmen-Zwischenfalls [Too far or too hesitant? On the backgrounds of the Tian'anmen incident]", *Unsere Zeit*, May 31, 2019: https://www.unsere-zeit.de/zu-weit-oder-zu-zaghaft-57499/, visited May 1, 2024.
18. The well-known economist and analyst of the financial system, Michael Hudson, one of the few who accurately predicted the global financial crisis from 2008, shows these connections in detail (e.g., Hudson 2015).
19. German translation in F. Lu, "Die Demütigung eines uralten Reichs [The Humiliation of an Ancient Empire]", *Zeit Online*, Feb. 18, 2019: https://www.zeit.de/kultur/2019-02/china-usa-weltmacht-handelskonflikt-welthandel, visited Jan. 5, 2025. This article cites the *New York Times*, which in two podcasts of Dec. 2018 revisited how the West was mistaken about China after 2000; see Michael Barbaro et al., "What the West Got Wrong About China", *The New York Times*, Dec. 4, 2018: https://www.nytimes.com/2018/12/04/podcasts/the-daily/china-rules.html, visited Jan. 5, 2025. For the full speech in English, see for example: Bill Clinton, "Full Text of Clinton's Speech on China Trade Bill", *The New York Times,* March 9, 2000: https://archive.nytimes.com/www.nytimes.com/library/world/asia/030900clinton-china-text.html, visited Jan. 5, 2025.
20. German translation in Christian Y. Schmidt, "Endlich bald Krieg [Finally soon War]", in id., *Im Jahr des Hasendrachen* [In the Year of the Hare Dragon] (Schmidt 2013), 85 f. For the original English quote, see, e.g.: P. Ford, "Huntsman's comment spurs debate in China", *The Christian Science Monitor*, Nov. 25, 2011: https://www.csmonitor.com/World/Asia-Pacific/2011/1125/Huntsman-s-comment-spurs-debate-in-China, visited Jan. 5, 2025.

21. Minqi Li, *The Rise of China and the Demise of the Capitalist World Economy* (Li 2008).
22. As a classic: André Gunder Frank, *ReORIENT. Global Economy in the Asian Age* (Frank 1998).
23. We refer again here to China's concept of ecological civilization, which we will return to in detail in this book, e.g., Xue, B., Han, B., Li, H. et al., "Understanding ecological civilization in China: From political context to science", *Ambio* 52 (2023), 1895–1909. We will of course also return to social progress in work, income, social security, downward redistribution, etc.
24. E.g., Wolfram Elsner, "Speculative financial capitalism wacking out over an 'impossible' profit rate. The infeasibility of a 'usual' real average profit rate, considering fictitious capital, and its implications", in: *Marx, Veblen, and the Foundations of Heterodox Economics: Essays in Honor of John F. Henry*, ed. by T.-H. Jo and F.S. Lee, 199–227, London, New York: Routledge, 2015; Karol Gil-Vasquez, Wolfram Elsner, "The 'Triumph of Imbecile Institutions'. Death Cults as the Enabling Myth of Late Neoliberalism. From neoliberalism to social fragmentation and identity crises, to violence, struggle for survival, and heroic death", *Journal of Economic Issues* 58(3), 2024, 1ff. (Editor's Choice Award 2024).
25. E.g., H.-J. Jakobs, *Handelsblatt Morning Briefing*, April 15, 2019.
26. C.Y. Schmidt, *Bliefe von dlüben. Der China-Crashkurs* [Lettels flom ovel thele. The China Crash-Course] (Schmidt 2010).
27. C.Y. Schmidt, *Allein unter 1,3 Milliarden, Eine Chinesische Reise von Shanghai bis Kathmandu* [Alone among 1.3 billion, A Chinese journey from Shanghai to Kathmandu] (Schmidt 2009); id., *Im Jahr des Tigerochsen* [In the Year of the Tiger Ox] (Schmidt 2011); id., *Im Jahr des Hasendrachen* [In the Year of the Hare Dragon] (Schmidt 2013).
28. As a background: Mathias Bröckers, Paul Schreyer, *Wir sind immer die Guten. Ansichten eines Putinverstehers oder wie der Kalte Krieg neu entfacht wird* [We are always the good ones. Views of a "Putin understander", or how the Cold War is reignited], Frankfurt/Main 2019.
29. For example: Kate Connolly, "Der Spiegel says top journalist faked stories for years", *The Guardian*, Dec. 19, 2018: https://www.theguardian.com/world/2018/dec/19/top-der-spiegel-journalist-resigns-over-fake-interviews, visited June 20, 2025.
30. E.g., Schmidt (2013), 177–186.
31. E.g., Schmidt (2010), 69.
32. E.g., ibid., 157.
33. Ibid.
34. Complexity economists understand the economy as a system of multiple and heterogeneous interdependent agents, recurrently interacting to solve

different common problem structures, usually located on different network topologies. Agents in such social ecologies are fundamentally uncertain, searching, learning, adapting, while countless interactions take place as they try to get coordinated to solve collective problems. Usually, with a myopic individualistic strategy, they will perform poorly together, but if they develop basic coordination and cooperation rules and informal social institutions, they may individually and collectively improve. At the same time, a short-run incentive to individualistically exploit others always looms. In the longer run, strategies, rules, and institutions are subject to an evolutionary process of diversification (searching, learning, adaptation), competition, and selection. Thus, the social ecology for each individual agent is changing all the time, and there is no chance of any absolutely and lastingly "fit" property or strategy. As a result, the system is in constant, mostly unpredictable, often surprising, often crisis-ridden dynamics and in constant development, not necessarily for the better—in stark contrast to neoliberal mainstream claims of simplistic models of "market economies" of "supply" and "demand", being "optimal", in "equilibrium", and in perfect coordination, supposedly coordinated only through "perfect" price information. In actual systems, different structures emerge, and namely under deregulated "markets", these include adverse power structures and crisis proneness, as well as social behavioral regularities (informal institutions), which are complexity reducing and may be beneficial individually and collectively but also obstructive and impeding progressive change and substantial innovation. For details, see, e.g., Wolfram Elsner, Complexity Economics as Heterodoxy. Theory and Policy, *Journal of Economic Issues* 51(4), 2017, 939–978.

35. *Routledge International Handbook of Complexity Economics*, ed. by Ping CHEN, Wolfram Elsner, and Andreas Pyka, 740 pp., Abingdon, UK, New York; Routledge/Taylor and Francis, 2025.
36. An ever-repeating theme in the industrial economics of US-oFDI to China, as, e.g., in the case of *Apple*, having become the world-class IT producer due to its lasting and increasing engagement in China; see, e.g., "Apple In China, the Industrial Commons story and Lessons for America. Factories Alone Don't Build iPhones... Commons Do", *Industrial Policy #9, Real Charts*, Substack, June 5, 2025; https://www.realchinacharts.com/p/apple-in-china-the-industrial-commons?utm_source=post-email-title&publication_id=527096&post_id=165271764&utm_campaign=email-post-title&isFreemail=true&r=ewjvb&triedRedirect=true&utm_medium=email, accessed June 6, 2025.
37. E.g., https://www.universityguru.com/de/universitaet/jilin-university-changchun, accessed May 19, 2025.

38. E.g., https://en.wikipedia.org/wiki/Jilin_University, accessed May 19, 2025.
39. https://www.uni-bremen.de/en/research/research-profile/rankings/international?sword_list%5B0%5D=Bremer&sword_list%5B1%5D=Energie&sword_list%5B2%5D=Institut&sword_list%5B3%5D=BEI&no_cache=1, accessed May 19, 2025.
40. On the technical, economic, and social disaster of the "Deutsche Bahn" [German Railways], see, for example: Luik 2019, *Schaden in der Oberleitung. Das geplante Desaster der Deutschen Bahn* [Damage in the overhead (i.e., overhead contact line). The planned disaster of Deutsche Bahn], Frankfurt/Main: Westend.
41. S. Davies, "Travelling through China, it is clear this will soon be the most powerful nation in the world", *The Telegraph*, June 15, 2025.
42. See for example: Han Peng, "You can get food delivered on China's bullet trains", *CGTN*, February 20, 2018: https://news.cgtn.com/news/7767544d34677a6333566d54/share_p.html, visited May 15, 2024.
43. See for example: Reuters, "German warship heads for South China Sea for first time in nearly two decades amid tension with Beijing", *CNN*, August 2, 2021, https://edition.cnn.com/2021/08/02/world/german-warship-south-china-sea-intl-hnk/index.html, visited January 6, 2025; Helena Legarda, "The Bundeswehr Returns to the Indo-Pacific", *Internationale Politik Quarterly*, March 20, 2024, https://ip-quarterly.com/en/bundeswehr-returns-indo-pacific, visited January 6, 2025.
44. A small German island in the North Sea, located about 70 km off the German coast.
45. Thorstein Veblen, *The instinct of workmanship and the state of the industrial arts* (Veblen 1918).
46. E.g., Wolfram Elsner, "Innovation and Information. Smooth and Ongoing Change, or Turbulence and Cognitive Over-Stress? On the Complex Deep Structure of Innovation", in: *The Elgar Companion to Information Economics*, 270–300, ed. by Daphne R. Raban and Julia Włodarczyk, Cheltenham, UK, Northampton, MA, USA: Edward Elgar, 2024; id., "Innovation depends. Between sustainable change and destructive over-turbulence: On the complex 'deep structure' of innovation", in: *China's Quest for Innovation. Institutions and Ecosystems*, ed. by Shuanping Dai and Markus Taube, Chap. 1, 10–49, London, New York: Routledge, 2020.
47. Florian Kirner, "Es geht um Asien, verdammt! [It's about Asia, stupid!]", *Free 21*, May 29, 2018: https://free21.org/es-geht-um-asien-verdammt/, visited January 6, 2025.

48. Published much later in German: A.G. Frank, *ReOrient: Globalgeschichte im Asiatischen Zeitalter* (*ReOrient: Global History in the Asean Age*), Vienna: Promedia, 2016.
49. Kirner, ibid.
50. E.g., David Ruch, "Steckt Henry Kissinger hinter Trumps Russland-Strategie? [Is Henry Kissinger behind Trump's Russia strategy?]", *T-Online*, July 26, 2018, https://www.t-online.de/nachrichten/ausland/usa/id_84177542/ex-aussenminister-steckt-henry-kissinger-hinter-trumps-russland-strategie-.html, visited May 5, 2024.
51. Paul Krugmann, "We're Number Two!", Nov. 3, 2025; https://paulkrugmann.substanck.com/p/were-number-two; visited Nov. 5, 2025.

Selected and Recommended Literature

Conboy, Kenneth, and James Morrison. 2002. *The CIA's Secret War in Tibet.* Lawrence, KS: University Press of Kansas.

Frank, Andre Gunder. 1998. *ReOrient. Global Economy in the Asian Age*. Oakland, CA: University of California Press.

Hudson, Michael. 2015. *Finance as Warfare*. Bristol: World Economics Association.

Kissinger, Henry A. 2011. *On China*. New York: Penguin.

Li, Minqi. 2008. *The Rise of China and the Demise of the Capitalist World Economy.* London: Pluto Press.

Zhao, Hongjun. 2018. *China's Long-Term Economic Development. How Have Economy and Governance Evolved Since 500 BC?* Cheltenham and Northampton, MA: Edward Elgar.

Further Cited Literature

Fitzthum, Robert, 2018a. *China verstehen. Vom Aufstieg zur Wirtschaftsmacht und der Eindämmungspolitik der USA* [Understanding China. On the rise to economic power and the containment policy of the USA], Vienna: Promedia.

Fitzthum, Robert, 2018b. Der nächste Feind [The next enemy]. *Rubikon*, October 31, 2018, https://www.rubikon.news/artikel/der-nachste-feind. Accessed October 13, 2024.

Hardt, Michael, and Antonio Negri. 2000. *Empire*. Cambridge, MA: Harvard University Press.

Luik, Arno, 2019, *Schaden in der Oberleitung. Das geplante Desaster der Deutschen Bahn* [Damage in the overhead line. The planned disaster of Deutsche Bahn]. Frankfurt: Westend.

Schmidt, Christian Y., 2009. *Allein unter 1,3 Milliarden. Eine chinesische Reise von Shanghai bis Kathmandu* [Alone among 1.3 billion, A Chinese journey from Shanghai to Kathmandu]. Reinbek: Rowohlt.
Schmidt, Christian Y., 2010. *Bliefe von dlüben. Der China-Crashkurs* [Letters flom ovel thele. The China Crash-Course]. Reinbek: Rowohlt.
Schmidt, Christian Y., 2011. *Im Jahr des Tigerochsen* [In the Year of the Tigerox]. Berlin: Verbrecher.
Schmidt, Christian Y., 2013. *Im Jahr des Hasendrachen* [In the Year of the Hare Dragon]. Berlin: Verbrecher Verlag.
Veblen, Thorstein Bunde. 1918. *The Instinct of Workmanship and the State of the Industrial Arts.* New York: B.W. Huebsch.

PART I

Learning to Comprehend China ... or a Hybrid Warfare

CHAPTER 2

What Strikes a China Traveler ...

The Air Has Become Excellent in Beijing ...

Let's start with one of the older, more tame and harmless China stereotypes: "China, that's early industrial pollution, you see it in the annual winter smog in Beijing."

In fact, the times of severe air pollution in China's capital are over! Long gone. We will have astonishing things to report below about the rise to a leading ecological nation of the former crude industrial polluter China, which produced the cheap goods for the developed capitalist world so that its wages could be kept low by deindustrialization, and its environment somewhat cleaner, at least from industrial production. The ecological mobilization and participation of the Chinese in environmental policy in fact is breathtaking. Their ecological civilization is far ahead of Western capitalism today, and the air in the big multi-million cities has become of leading quality worldwide. On your very first day there, you will recognize the high and quickly increasing share of new-energy vehicles (NEV) (electric battery vehicles -EV- and hydrogen fuel-cell vehicles) in the traffic.

When I [W.E.] landed in Beijing in 2014 and met one of my ex-PhD students who had picked me up for a quick coffee, I could hardly go on speaking after half an hour. When I stayed in Beijing for a week in 2023, I enjoyed the good air, not the slightest idea of a scratchy throat.

The "bad air" in the northeastern multimillion cities on the eastern coastal areas has always been mixed up in the West anyway with the

W. Elsner, E. Najmehchi, *The Rise of China*,
https://doi.org/10.1007/978-3-032-20260-4_2

million-year-old natural phenomenon of sand and dust storms coming in from the huge deserts in the West. While it has often been suggested in the Western media that related earlier spectacular pictures had been indicative of China's "ecological problems", this obviously was not only *not* the case, but also, as a part of pushing China to the front of global ecology protecting nations, this has been brought to an end as well through the unprecedented size order in which China has built the *Great Green Walls* of forestation, with large parts of the country's surface covered now by thousands of new planted forests, national parks, national protection zones, and biodiversity zones. We will provide details below in Part II, Chap. 11.

So, in the early 2010s, it had quickly become clear that there would no longer be too many of the yearly winter smog images from Beijing anymore. Chinese citizens nowadays no longer have to put up with smog. The party, National People's Congress, and government announced the end of the old industrial development model in the early 2010s, stabilizing growth on a downward path of GDP growth toward around 5 percent p.a. This included giving up the rather unsophisticated development model of "world export champion" of export orientation at any cost (leaving this to the Germans). They also abandoned the model of "extended workbench" for the developed capitalist countries in 2012. All-winter smog was no longer compatible with this and a "war against air pollution" was declared in 2014.[1]

And for this they did not need 30 years. Within a few years, air quality in Beijing drastically improved, resulting also in a measurable rise in life expectancy since.[2] Only ten years ago, you would get a sore throat shortly after landing in Beijing, but today, you won't notice anything like that even after staying in the city for longer. I first cautiously asked some British colleagues, who had been working and living in Beijing for years, about it... The answer came quickly and clearly: "Yes, it's quite extraordinary what has been achieved here in this field." The same question then to Chinese colleagues, and the answers here: "Yes, we did it." And the numbers speak for themselves: China's continuous complex and multi-dimensional efforts in reducing air pollution in general now account for over "three-quarters of the global decline in pollution since 2013".[3] Many have spoken of "the miracle of Beijing (of Tianjin, Shanghai, Guangzhou etc.)".

But let's add to personal travel experience some energy and emission figures on China's new and dynamic programmatic "ecological civilization".

Coal Exit, China Style: In 5 Rather Than 30 Years

Some other statistical data already provide a bigger picture:[4] Since 2015, China has been particularly pushing for structural change away from old-energy technologies. In 2017 alone, coal production capacities of 150 million tons were shut down in China, and 1000 coal mines were closed nationwide. Since then, coal has been massively cracked down on in mining, as direct energy source, and for power generation. Only the most efficient sorts of coal have been left in use at all, and older coal-based power plants have, in huge investment efforts, been quickly replaced by the newest-generation ultra-efficient plants with only half of the emissions of those still working in the West. But the dominating trend has been gross coal substitution by renewable energy. Here, China is globally leading in national energy shares and low-emission outcomes. Let's look at some details.

There has been some short-run rebound in permits for (newest-generation) coal power plants in the post-Covid era,[5] as the shutdowns in 2017 to 2019 had proved to be too radical and shutdown speed needed to be somewhat reduced, when there was the first large post-Covid economic and export upswing in 2020 and 2021 (when China had left the first Covid phase behind and opened again, while the West then was under lockdown and needed lots of commodities).

But emissions now have already peaked and are falling again since mid-2024, while officially this was only aimed for by 2030, according to analyses such as those by the *International Energy Agency* (IEA) and *Carbon Brief*.[6] This is due to the fact that a record number of low-carbon energy sources have been installed—in huge mega-watt numbers absolutely and considerably increasing in their shares of the national energy mix—and that coal plants themselves are now running less often and burning less coal overall.[7] Moreover, China's state president Xi had announced at the UN General Assembly in Fall 2020 to "achieve carbon neutrality before 2060".[8] Western China and energy expert institutions commented on this by pointing to the experience that China's ecological speed has typically become faster and more radical in reality compared to their written or verbal announcements. And in September 2025, a day after Trump—again—called climate change a "scam" at the UN General Assembly, Xi reiterated his pledge to further drastically reduce China's emissions and increase NEV production, wind, and solar power over the next decade. In an indirect response to Trump, Xi noted: "while some country is acting against it, the international community should stay focused on the right direction." Trump wrongly claimed that China has "very few wind farms" domestically and only builds them abroad. In fact, China's wind power dwarves that of the USA, as *Politico* reports:

> In just the first five months of this year [2025] it [China] added 46 gigawatts of new wind energy, enough to power more than 30 million homes. During the same period, Trump's government has frozen permits for several wind farms proposed or under construction in the Atlantic, where the U.S. has a small fraction of offshore turbines compared with China.[9]

In addition, in 2016 alone, steel capacities of 65 million tons were also shut down in China. Since then, China has aggressively forced numerous steel mills to shut down, cut production, and electrify its furnaces in recent years, in a push to reduce harmful small particles in the air considerably by 2025.[10] In the coal and steel industries, we are talking about 2–4 million jobs that have already been finished and switched to other sectors. Such dynamics of structural change would be unimaginable in the leading Western countries, where emission goals for 2030/2035 are increasingly getting out of reach, and political and industrial change has become sticky rather.

New and Renewable Energies

While in China's "war against air pollution", dozens of coal-fired power plants were shut down in Beijing alone, and hundreds across the country, coal was replaced namely by solar energy (photovoltaics), of which Beijing alone, with its roughly 22 million population, produces more than Germany as a whole (83 million inhabitants). And while hundreds of old, emission-intensive industrial plants and environmentally harmful iron and steel productions were closed, the number of cars in the big cities had been limited, and new registrations were possible for NEVs only. The share of NEVs in new registrations has surpassed 50 percent in 2024. 400,000 buses were already on the road as electric, hybrid, or hydrogen buses in 2019, accounting for 90 percent of all new energy buses worldwide.[11] End of 2024: 554,000 NEV buses (84 percent of them pure electric), 81 percent of all buses in China.[12] And there are NEV dredgers, ships, and all kinds of vehicles and machines in the field as well.

We will consider more below about solar, wind, and water energies, hydrogen and induction-current based traffic, Thorium and fusion-energy technologies, on planned reduction of energy consumption per GDP unit, and planned reduction of emission intensity per energy-input unit. "Chinese Experimentalism", Western experts say: Always trying several pathways simultaneously. And we will always be behind with our data from last or this year, when you will read them. "China Speed", again, as the literature is saying.

Traffic Avoidance on a Large Scale: The Example of the New Capital Province "Jing-Jin-Ji"

The shutdowns of old power plants, the avoidance of coal (and increasingly also oil and gas), in populous Beijing are also part of large urban planning projects to generally modernize and decentralize the entire capital region and thus avoid traffic. The capital is to be relieved and decentralized, an effort, in which the province surrounding Beijing, *Hebei* (which is abbreviated in Chinese with "Ji"), with its 75 million population, plays a crucial role: It is to become the new *capital province*, which, in addition to Bei*jing*, includes the port city of Tian*jin* (approximately 17 million inhabitants). A project grabbing the attention of urban and regional planners internationally: Jing-Jin-Ji,[13] which occupies an area about twice the size of South Korea.[14] Ministries and authorities and corresponding residential areas have already been outsourced from Beijing. Car trips are being shifted to new, high-performance rail lines to reduce traffic jams in and around Beijing.

And the Western traveler enjoys the results: Beijing has become relieved, traffic-wise. Traffic is quickly and flexibly steered by lights and lanes, AI, and (yes) cameras, traffic jams largely reduced, broad secured bicycle lanes, a livable, green bicycling city, livable and walkable residential areas ... and comfortable 350/450 kmh-bullet trains going out to everywhere, with train stations like little airports. We will get back to it.

Faster Growth in Rural Areas

In place of the shutdown of old industries, infrastructure is being built for economic integration, especially in the rural provinces in the west of the country, which have been developed with force since the 2010s. For years, they have already been growing faster than the urban eastern cities and provinces, who often have taken on partnerships for rural areas.

The last remnants of extreme poverty in more remote rural areas were completely eradicated in 2020.[15] (More on this later.) The villages and towns there, with their entrepreneurial individual farmers, and their cooperatives and village communities, have rapidly caught up in per-capita income. This has been supported by fiber optic networks and fast Wi-Fi, EVs of all kinds, motorcycles, three-wheel or four-wheel, one-seat or two-seat E-pickups, and the establishment of new industrial plants. Also, SOEs have taken over sponsorships for rural areas.

Many village communities have drawn on their marketing experience, e.g., with their historical township and village enterprises (TVEs), as once so-called Taobao online traders and "Taobao villages", which may market their specialized agricultural products independently. Taobao has been one of the first Chinese online platforms for retail, introduced by parent company Alibaba in 2003.[16]

With the favorable development of rural regions, more than 100 million of the former nearly 300 million migrant workers have already returned to their villages because they find income there in the newly emerged industries, such as in agricultural online trade.

But while the intended national urbanization ratio is still to increase, according to the last (14th) Five-Year-Plan (FYP), from now 67 percent to around 70 percent, still more migrant workers and their families are receiving Hukou (registration) in their target areas in the east to settle there permanently. But many still have their Hukou in the regions of their origin, and their property too, and thus may keep a lifelong right to return to their land there. More later.

Traffic and Ecological Management of Mega-Cities

There is practically no experience, and therefore little comprehension of the Western traveler, on what it means to manage multi-million cities well and at the same time transform them into green and sustainable systems.

There are numerous examples of large metropolises that, under the conditions of NFC development, are languishing in both social and ecological terms and have often degenerated into nightmares. Global representative polls have repeatedly shown that poverty reduction and affordable housing, especially in urban areas, are among the main issues faced by billions of people under Western-dominated NFC globalization and private urban land grabbing, and that these are what they expect from any democratic government.[17] We know of the mega-cities, where little really works, basic human cultural needs are no longer met, and basic social and ecological problems can no longer be solved. Even the peripheries of the mega-cities in the global centers, like Paris, London, or larger and smaller US cities, often seem like abandoned urban wasteland.

Many of the largest cities in the world are in China, and for the Western visitor, who typically expects barely governable typical "First-" or "Third-World" mega-cities, they appear not only "new" in the sense of only having been built in the last few decades, but also surprisingly well organized, obviously socially integrated, clean and well maintained, relaxed, often beautiful in the sense of a high-quality and varied architecture and a decentralized city-structure, and, above all, surprisingly green.[18] On top of that, nowadays they are also surprisingly quiet, due to the high share of NEV traffic, which even approaches 80 percent in some cities.

These first examples illustrate how fast structural change has been driven in an ecological direction. It could be something akin to the much-cited and long-promised "green capitalism" in Western countries. In fact, it is a novel, green kind of socialism to come, a socialism as we do not yet know it. We will return to the issue in more detail.

However, one thing appears for sure already: What applied in China yesterday no longer applies today, and what applies in China today will no longer apply tomorrow. China is changing faster than we can look, analyze, and write down. China Speed, once more.

Back to the energy mix: while in the late 2010s millions of households were quickly connected to a gas supply instead of coal-fired power plants, those days are now over again. Western media, however, remain unimpressed: A German TV report on Beijing's energy transition at the end of the 2010s focused solely on the fact that not everything went smoothly. It bemoaned how "unaesthetic" it was to lay gas lines on the surface in some residential areas, merely to provide main pipes quickly for certain older, now converted neighborhoods. The interviewed Chinese residents, however, apparently had no problem expressing their criticism in front of a

Western television camera—for example, that the gas initially arrived with too little pressure.

And yes, Chinese, so the general and mostly surprising experience of the Western China traveler nowadays, obviously do not let themselves be deprived of anything. They are active and mobilized, enjoy arguing, and—with public support—even express their interests and take part in local planning and decision-making. And in the mid-2020s, they are not only heavily involved in discussions on social media—where public agencies participate on an equal footing—but also have access to tens of thousands of local citizens' service and parliamentary outreach offices. There, they can walk in to comment or petition on planning projects, leave their ideas on draft laws displayed for public review, request public services, and receive advice from staff and even legal personnel available to them at any time. A new quality of public discourse has been achieved on all ongoing public changes, from local residential issues to national ones. Reports on this are abundant.[19] But more on that later, too.

So, fortunately, people have other ways to express criticism in their residential areas, districts, cities, and provinces—sharing their interests, ideas, and proposals—without having to wait until the next election to express them vaguely through a mark on the ballot, or until a Western TV team comes to interview them. We will return to social mobilization and participation of people in China later.

Why and How "China No. 1"? The New Old Historical Normal

China's rise to the new "number one" status is a systemic challenge for the West in manifold respects, historically the second serious and systemic challenge after the Soviet Union.[20] Thus, Western reactions to the new facts and dynamics in China—once characterized by curiosity, a desire to understand, and an interest in cooperation—are now a mixture of reflexive panic over perceived decline and growing hostility.

How can we dare to speak of China being the new No. 1? Well, first, it has had the largest GDP of the countries in the world, in PPP, since 2016, as mentioned, and as we will explain in more detail. The Chinese population in total can thus afford more goods and services for their GDP than the US population. There are complex causal factors to explain that, relating to low inflation rates, high available income through cheap services, public and private, or accessible, efficient, and cheap infrastructure use. And this will soon also apply to nominal GDP in terms of currency exchange rates over the next few years, according to all analyzable factors and all serious published forecasts.

Second, what really makes China "No. 1" appears to be the comprehensive and huge leverages that China can apply, based on a still relatively small GDP per capita, into all areas and factors of growth and advancement, be it education, labor skills, sciences and engineering, R&D, social security and social services, social mobilization and participation, millions of business start-ups, infrastructures, industry clusters and value-added chains (VAC), cities and rural development, alert public agencies and proactive policies, the "developmental" and "entrepreneurial state". This leverage has propelled China into the top areas of the world, the top ranks of international comparisons, in education, science, technology, ecology, industrial and market structures and efficiency, and many other economic, societal, and even military fields. We will examine many seminal critical factors in this book and find that, in nearly every field, China is set to become "number one".

Upon closer consideration, we must admit that it would be a miracle if this were *not* the case. Why should a country of such size, capable of mobilizing enormous economies of scale in any compressible aspect, remain one of the poorest developing countries in the world, plagued by mass disease and famine, as it was when it freed itself from European, Japanese, and US colonialism, exploitation, and plundering? And not only does mere size play a role here, but some considerably superior systemic efficacy, as we will illustrate for many areas.

And what we see, therefore, is nothing other than a return to a thousand-year-long historical normal, in which both the century of Chinese humiliation and the 300–400 years of European and Anglo-Saxon colonial and imperial dominance, in the longue durée and in long historical retrospect, were the exception rather than the rule. Thus, there is "nothing surprising in China's innovative rise".[21] The world is returning, in its socio-economic and political-economic structures, to a new-old historical normal. So, West, please relax, and enjoy the journey! And find your active but peaceful role in the new world emerging. Adapt!

More on this in the next chapters.

Notes

1. For example: Sara Flounders, "Planning Can Save the Planet: China Chooses Renewable Energy", *Workers World*, April 23, 2019: https://www.workers.org/2019/04/42006/, visited May 9, 2024.
2. For example, Jessie Yeung, "Chinese people are living two years longer thanks to 'war on pollution,' report says", *CNN*, August 30, 2023: https://edition.cnn.com/2023/08/30/asia/air-pollution-report-china-south-asia-intl-hnk-scn/index.html, visited May 9, 2024. That report stated that China's pollution levels in 2021 were down 42% from 2013, while rising in other Southeast-Asian countries.
3. For example, Zhong Wenxing, "China's War Against Pollution Extraordinarily Successful: University of Chicago Researcher", *Air Quality Life Index (AQLI)*, March 25, 2022: https://aqli.epic.uchicago.edu/news/chinas-war-against-pollution-extraordinarily-successful-university-of-chicago-researcher/, visited May 9, 2024.
4. For example, F. Schmid, "China im globalen Kapitalismus [China in global capitalism]" (Schmid 2017), p. 43; also Flounders, ibid.
5. For example, Lauri Myllyvirta & Byford Tsang, "China Pledged to 'Strictly Control' Coal. The Opposite Happened." *Foreign Policy*, November 12, 2023: https://foreignpolicy.com/2023/11/12/china-coal-climate-change-carbon-emissions-pledge-plants-apec/, visited May 9, 2024.
6. E.g., Lauri Myllyvirta, "Analysis: China's emissions set to fall in 2024 after record growth in clean energy", *Carbon Brief*, November 13, 2023: https://www.carbonbrief.org/analysis-chinas-emissions-set-to-fall-in-2024-after-record-growth-in-clean-energy/, visited May 9, 2024.
7. For example, Hannah Ritchie, "China is building more coal plants but might burn less coal", *Sustainability by numbers*, February 14, 2024: https://www.sustainabilitybynumbers.com/p/china-coal-plants, visited May 9, 2024. Ritchie shows that according to the National Energy Administration (NEA) of China, plants are now only running at around 50% of the time, compared to around 70% in the first decade of the 2000s.
8. For example, Lie et al., "The Carbon Brief Profile: China", *Carbon Brief*, November 30, 2023: https://interactive.carbonbrief.org/the-carbon-brief-profile-china/, visited May 9, 2024.
9. Sara Schonhardt, "China doubles down on climate—a day after Trump called it a 'scam', *Politico*, September 25, 2025: https://www.politico.com/news/2025/09/24/china-doubles-down-on-climate-wind-and-solar-pledges-a-day-after-trump-called-them-a-scam-00579411, visited September 26, 2025.
10. For example, Victoria Bela, "China bans new steel plants in drive to 'defend the blue sky' and cut atmospheric pollution", *South China Morning Post*,

December 8, 2023: https://www.scmp.com/news/china/science/article/3244421/china-bans-new-steel-plants-drive-defend-blue-sky-and-cut-atmospheric-pollution, visited May 9, 2024. Bela notes, for example: "In Hebei, China's top steel producing province, the number of iron and steel companies has been cut by nearly 70 percent in a bid to meet local targets ..."

11. For example, Flounders, ibid.
12. For example, Xiaoying You, "How China's buses shaped the world's EV revolution", *BBC*, December 6, 2023: https://www.bbc.com/future/article/20231206-climate-change-how-chinas-electric-vehicle-revolution-began-with-buses, visited May 9, 2024.
13. For example, Mark Preen, "The Beijing-Tianjin-Hebei Integration Plan", *China Briefing*, April 26, 2018: https://www.china-briefing.com/news/the-beijing-tianjin-hebei-integration-plan/, visited May 10, 2024.
14. For example, Reuters, "China approves $36-billion railway plan for Jing-Jin-Ji megacity", *Reuters*, November 28, 2016: https://www.reuters.com/article/us-china-infrastructure/china-approves-36-billion-railway-plan-for-jing-jin-ji-megacity-idUSKBN13N050/, visited May 10, 2024.
15. For example, Robert Walker & Yang Lichao, "China's move to measuring relative poverty: implications for social protection", *International Labour Organization*: https://webapps.ilo.org/static/english/intserv/working-papers/wp023/index.html, visited May 10, 2024.
16. Taobao.com is among the top 10 most visited websites globally. The economic activities of farmers in China have a millennia-old tradition. While in the People's Republic of China the distribution of agricultural mass products is regulated by the state, farmers, cooperatives, and villages are allowed to market specialty products independently, which has economically activated the rural provinces for a long time and has already brought considerable prosperity to many villages and communities. In fact, the TVEs had been the national experimental predecessors since the 1960s of the national "reform and opening-up" period that began in 1978.
17. Most recently, e.g., Nira Data, *Democracy Perception Index 2025*, Berlin 2025, covering representative interviews of 111,000 respondents in 100 countries.
18. See for example the report in the German *Focus-online*, an economic magazine unsuspected of any China sympathies: Melchior Poppe, "Trip der Superlative: In Shanghai erlebe ich, wie die Stadt der Zukunft aussieht [Trip of superlatives: In Shanghai I experience what the city of the future looks like]", September 2, 2019: https://www.focus.de/perspektiven/14-laender-14-reporter/24-stunden-superlative-trip-der-superlative-in-shanghai-erlebe-ich-wie-die-stadt-der-zukunft-aussieht_id_10066047.html, visited May 10, 2024.

19. E.g., Robert Fitzthum, "Das reale China. In Shanghai-Hongqiao hat sich ein System kommunaler Basisdemokratie etabliert, das westlichen China-Klischees widerspricht [The real China. A system of communal basic democracy]", Part 1, April 23, 2025; https://www.manova.news/artikel/das-reale-china; officially termed "Whole-process people's democracy" or "democracy that works" e.g., http://www.scio.gov.cn/zfbps/ndhf/2021n_2242/202207/t20220704_130720.html, all visited June 6, 2025.
20. For example: Jörg Kronauer, *Der Rivale: Chinas Aufstieg zur Weltmacht und die Gegenwehr des Westens* [The Rival: China's Rise to World Power and the West's Resistance], Hamburg, 2019.
21. Richard Ghiasy, "Nothing surprising in China's innovative rise. China's innovation is not an anomalous awakening but rather the reassertion of tradition interrupted by gunboats, opium and colonialism", *Asia Times*, Nov. 4, 2025.

Further Cited Literature

Schmid, Fred, 2017. China im globalen Kapitalismus [China in global capitalism]. In *Krise des Globalen Kapitalismus. Und jetzt Wohin?* [Crisis of global capitalism. And now where to?]. Munich: Institut für sozial-ökologische Wirtschaftsforschung (ISW), Report Nr. 109.

CHAPTER 3

Turning Tides in the West: From Willingness to Learn Toward Fear, Envy, and Bashing—and Back Again?

Divided Western Countries: Peaceful Coexistence or "At War with China 2027"?

But we seem to be further away from a relaxed stance than we were just 20 years ago. Much, however, has happened since. The GFC and its aftermath—years-long Western sovereign crises, both fiscal and monetary—suddenly changed the world and marked a major Western strategic turning point at the end of the 2000s. Another turning point seems to have been the Covid years. Public atmospheres have stiffened and narrowed since then; aggressive "pacification" appears to have made cancel culture and censorship common, and political policing has become widespread. It reflects a pervasive culture and politics of fear over systemic decline, coupled with an aggressive effort to combat it.

Management textbooks say otherwise: If we lose market share while our competitors gain it—as the West is currently losing "market share" in virtually every field to the benefit of China and the Global South—what do these textbooks recommend that corporate leadership do? Calling the Mafia, getting the Kalashnikovs out of the strongroom, walking over to the HQ of the competitor, and shooting it down? Not in a civilized "market economy" of the West! We would rather have to get our best people together in a conclave and consider why we are losing. What does the competitor do better? Elaborate on a new, better strategy! Reinvent yourself! Qualify yourself! And then start talking and bargaining,

W. Elsner, E. Najmehchi, *The Rise of China*,
https://doi.org/10.1007/978-3-032-20260-4_3

self-confidently. Since neoliberal politicians usually want to think and act like "entrepreneurs", why don't they do so at the first serious strategic opportunity?

The corporate economy is different. Our countries are obviously split in this respect. The corporate economy goes East, following the chances, and is led by their profit prospects. And the countries are split person-wise. Those in the West who have traveled to China as professionals, entrepreneurs, students, or simply tourists return with—and retain—a view of the country very different from the one they started with. Our many conversations with Chinese travelers and entrepreneurs (see, e.g., above in the introduction) have always been extremely enlightening in this respect.

In this book, we will show more about how the Western corporate economy actually operates in terms of new trade and VAC structures with and in China—a most exciting story that the West needs to understand.

But Western politics and media appear to be ever more combative, as it appears. They struggle in a fight against their own systemic decline, and the atmosphere is ever more one of narrowness, protectionism, inhibiting human-to-human contacts, and anxiousness. And anxiousness is a bad advisor, obviously. China has repeatedly invited the West to talk and bargain on anything. No one in the world is claiming that the current global economic structures are unchangeable and could not be improved and made more sustainable, least of all China.

Thus, on the one hand, there still seems to be a certain willingness for peaceful coexistence, peaceful competition, and cooperation in the populations and among internationally active professionals, entrepreneurs, managers, students, or tourists, i.e., for an open, relaxed, self-confident, productive, and non-envious recognition and hands-on engagement. This is associated with a desire for a critical understanding of, and learning from useful Chinese experience, knowledge, and solutions for major future problems.

On the other hand, there is an increasingly aggressive, hostile, and emotionalized fight in politics and the media against the newly declared "challenger" and new "public enemy no. 1", often with tacit envious emulation of Chinese knowledge, mostly motivated by fear of one's own systemic decline, with threats of a "big war with China" in the next few years. China allegedly then breaks the given "rule-based international order", spies on us with 5G, controls Hollywood scripts, and is about to subjugate the entire world. In the end, every Chinese exchange student, project partner, or tourist is suspected of being a spy, and any international people-to-people contact needs to be prohibited. Decoupling, de-risking, de-linking, which would be set to end global exchange and humankind as we knew them. Wrong-way drivers.

It then even appears audacious how China confronts the USA (and the German Navy) off the Chinese coast![1] And quickly then, it becomes obvious for many in media and politics that there is no peaceful coexistence feasible with China.[2] Dictatorship, police state, concentration camps for minorities, such have become leading themes in Western media when it comes to China, usually based on self-citation merry-go-rounds. Escalating Western sanctions have been implemented, and the hot war seems inevitable not only to the majority of weird hardliners in Washington but even to the strange political castes in Brussels, Paris, London, and Berlin, sooner or later.[3] We are seriously approaching a situation that the great evolutionary and institutional economist Thorstein Veblen had already described in 1914 as "the triumph of imbecile institutions over life and culture".[4]

In between, of course, and fortunately, there is still a spectrum of options, depending on the publication medium and the targeted public. Often an amount of factual information and assessments is conveyed to professional circles. Although the focus in the so-called tabloid media and in public and private radio and TV is increasingly tending toward aggressive reaction, there is always some chance left in our minds for the survival of humankind.

The Number of Publications on China Has Exploded, with Little Intellectual Development: Narratives of Threat, Fear, and Bashing Still Dominate

There is hardly a day that goes by without some major report on and from China in the newspapers, magazines, and websites, often full-print-page articles or long blog posts, and hardly a month without a new book on China. Especially starting from about 2017, dozens of books about China have been published each year, general-information books in the first years, more specialized ones more recently.

It relates to the fact that China has also increasingly appeared in the news and headlines on a daily basis, due to its striking levels of new policies set out in many policy fields, but also to its prominent involvement in the Trump and Biden administrations' trade and technology wars, a self-declared hybrid war in the long run.[5]

The entirety of all print and online publications, popular and academic, has virtually become unmanageable in recent years. Therefore, only a few examples shall be considered in the following, which is not intended to be a full-fledged "literature review".

A whole field of (anti-)China books has emerged, often simply regurgitating similar themes ad infinitum, not rarely applying fearmongering and sensationalism for profit. German-language publications on China hardly differ in their perspectives from those of the Anglosphere. So, we may include some German books in our literature overview, which are representative and should basically allow us to capture the main perspectives on China that are "out there":

- First, there is a narrative of a global *existential systemic struggle against China*. An ex-editor-in-chief of the leading German mainstream newspaper *Die Zeit*, for example, published a book entitled *China First. Die Welt auf dem Weg ins chinesische Jahrhundert* [China First. The World on the Way to the Chinese Century] in 2019. Although it flatly turns the Western way of thinking—namely that of the USA—upside down and projects it onto "the enemy", China, the author, T. Sommer, still falls on the somewhat reflective side of the literature spectrum.

  In the subtitle, he shares the forecast that the twenty-first century will be the Asian and especially the Chinese one (see already A.G. Frank 1998, as mentioned). It is recognized that China will be the new number one, and Sommer coins a reversal of a German saying about a "sack of rice falling in China", used to indicate something that does not matter at all: "When a sack of rice falls in China today, the earth trembles." Whether this really helps understanding China or rather subtly mobilizes old fears of the Yellow Peril (alternatively, red menace) remains open.

  But at the same time, the book serves the prevailing "we-good—they-bad" reflex. It projects a twisted worldview and the real policy of a counterproductive, nationalistic, egoistic political hustle and bustle onto China. It suggests that China is just as egomaniacal, aggressive, unpredictable, and destructive as that real estate tycoon in Washington in his historical attempt to counter US decline and rebalance its reduced resources.

  With this, the book in fact opens the door to a "Germany-EU First" strategy. From this point on, practically all means in international disputes are justified by Western "liberal intellectuals". Such literature opens up a dangerous game, underpinned by well-established stereotypes such as "Orwellian surveillance state", "red magnates", "Xi Jinping: Make China Great Again", "China is buying us up", and "How much China is too much?". Of course, it prevents a productive understanding of, and a cooperative attitude toward, China.

This, apparently, is not the aim in the prevailing market of opinions and sentiments. The focus is no longer on informing about China or even trying to understand it, but rather on rallying the "us" and bringing one's own society into formation. For Germany in particular, it is, rather banally, about preserving the privileges of this export world champion—imagined as fighting a final battle for its future place in the sun.

Self-defined "liberal" intellectuals like that author are too prudent to directly spread verbal-military hostilities against China. But when it comes to advocating and developing peaceful coexistence and win-win cooperation with China, he seems to lack the courage.

- Particularly, there is the narrative of a threat posed by China's "world domination". Everything can always be framed in a more hostile and more frightening way. A "world power China" is immediately seen in most of the literature as a threat to "us". If we look at the last 300–400 years of European colonial world dominance, these ongoing hostile and defensive attitudes—still tacitly racism-based—are comprehensible. In the era of Western colonialism and imperialism, the world has always been treated as an object of plundering and destruction: a carrier of "our" resources, its (inferior) populations working for us, later also buying our products, and in recent decades, even serving as our outsourced garbage dump. Colonialism and imperialism have cost tens of millions of lives, ruined countries, made the world more unequal, and brought it to the brink of ecological collapse. Knowing European/Anglo-Saxon history and ways of thinking, the West may fear China's revenge—and may project onto China the expectation that it will become similar to the European-Anglo-Saxon empires. Europe as the historical rule and benchmark.[6]

  In this part of the literature spectrum is, for example, a Chinese German journalist named F. Lee, a multi-newspaper and book author. For such people, China always only "lurks" and "threatens"—through products, technologies, in space, and so on.[7]

Also, in F. Sieren's, *Future? China!*,[8] for example, the "We-are-existentially-threatened!" narrative dominates. It is somewhat moderated at the end by a plea for cooperation on an equal footing. But before that, the wave of looming threats is extensively surfed: "Beijing is slowly hollowing out Europe", "President Xi is harassing" the Chinese "civil society", and "incorporating his neighbors". This fearmongering aims to rally "us" in a "survival" fight against the new enemy.

Caught in Western-manufactured fantasies of "Chinese world domination" and in the self-fabricated trap of "downgrading before comprehending" is also S. Scheuer's *The Masterplan: China's Path to World Domination*.[9] Here too, the Chinese state is little more than Big Brother and, in the end, "Europe's missing response".

Without the projection of a new enemy, many popular books about China would simply be boring and clueless. Western media and publishers rarely consider presenting China in its original tone, not believing that China means what it says.

The "Technology-Theft" Narrative: Turning Historical and Current Realities Upside Down

On another "eternal" theme, cross-cutting the literature: the great old cock-and-bull story, "*China is stealing our technology*", nowadays hugely at odds with the experience and statements of Western companies, still lingers in some literature up to now. Particularly in the US Congress and the US political caste, you have those majorities living in their fantasy worlds of the last century. In Germany, the variation of our cherished old worldview—of "Made in Germany", of German engineering, of the world-market leader and export world champion, still fantasized against all facts—has always been particularly popular. Against all the facts of the recently decaying German post-WWII model, now that the old Anglo-Saxon Heartland geostrategy has finally been successfully implemented, and the US's greatest post-WWII capitalist industrial competitor has been isolated from Russian energy supply and thus dethroned.

All Western industrialized countries are well known to have grown big through massive protectionist state intervention and by learning from others and imitating them ("theft").[10] Even medieval Europe (e.g., Marco Polo, the Hanseatic League's trade on the Northern Old Silk Road via

Novgorod, and European trade through the Southern Old Silk Roads via Northern Italy) brought significant inventions, technologies, and products from China, and later colonial Europe explicitly and more systematically plundered China's knowledge base.[11]

As mentioned, German technicians, engineers, managers, and entrepreneurs who have been doing business in China nowadays are closer to reality. Recent survey results about the declining international value of "Made in Germany", for instance, should have somewhat shaken the German politicians' ideal self-image by now.[12] Ongoing international technology screenings and rankings have placed China at the top in the great bulk of technology fields for years, and China's general reputation now ranks higher among the world's population than that of the USA. Those technology rankings, in fact, rarely mention the EU at all. After all, the German model of the export world champion has proved unsustainable in today's decomposing world, and rather risky and destabilizing.

Long-term continental and national cycles of ascent have never occurred in world history without imitation and learning from the more advanced—neither in England, the USA, Prussia and Germany nor in Japan or South Korea. And they have never occurred without the overarching, organizing, and coordinating long-term commitment of a developmental and entrepreneurial state with high state competence.[13] But the NFC state has unlearned such historical experience.

The history of Chinese scientific and technical inventions and developments, which usually took place more than a millennium on average before similar developments in Europe[14] and were largely not independently invented in Europe but rather "imported" from China, could fill volumes.[15] According to some estimates, up to 60 percent of the knowledge of today's world originates from China.[16]

China's inventions and innovations in all fields of science and technology, many of which preceded those of Europe by 1000 years or more, include the printing press and papermaking, the steam engine, knowledge of (equivalents to) Newton's laws of motion, advanced mathematics and numerics, knowledge of sunspots, comets, and astronomy in general, the armillary sphere, coal mining, gas drilling, and coal and gas usage, the mechanical clock, the seismograph, hot-air balloons, the parachute, manned kite flights, chain drives for machines, paddle steamers, the use of propellers and rotors, water pumps, spinning wheels and textile manufacturing, magnetism and the compass, gunpowder, cannons, fireworks, multi-stage rockets, earthquake-proof dam and bridge construction, shipping, irrigation canals, and ship lifts. In medicine, they already knew about sterile laboratories, immunology, vaccinations, blood circulation, biorhythms, and endocrinology and hormones. China's engineers built gigantic ships and knew the principle of internal bulkheads in shipbuilding, high-precision cartography, the Mercator projection, navigation, sailing against the wind and corresponding sailcloth technology, as well as iron and steel production, blast furnaces, seed drills and grain winnowing, plows, and more...

For some in China, Marco Polo[17] came to symbolize the great European theft of Chinese knowledge and technologies, which facilitated Europe's rise. Chinese sailing and navigation technologies allowed Europe to expand its maritime reach.[18] After the subjugation of China in the 1840s, the remaining technological and scientific knowledge was finally plundered and transferred to Europe.

Who "steals" from whom nowadays has become contentious again. Western companies have invested tens of billions not only in production but increasingly in research and development in China.[19] They consider China a "fitness center" for Western corporations. Chinese regional clusters, start-up scenes, and VACs are unique, and thus Western firms do resist slamming the door on cooperation, which has repeatedly been offered by China, but is bedeviled by Western media and wild political circuses—apparently out of arrogance, but truly out of fear of decline.

The Permanent "Collapse of China": Debt Crises, Currency Devaluations, Bank, Real Estate, Political and Other Collapses ... That Did Not Occur

Western psychological projections onto "the Other" extend to the idea of "China as the center of a new world financial crisis". The "danger from China" is often presented as a seemingly analytical prediction: that China is the center of the next world financial crisis, as it is highly indebted, has a real estate bubble and other investment bubbles, overextends its lending to other countries as part of its New Silk Road Initiative, and so on.[20]

It will be shown in this book that China is a country that has all the critical instruments at its disposal to protect itself against an upcoming next global financial crisis. The central government, while its debt has somewhat increased in recent years—to about 80 percent of GDP as of 2023—is still less indebted than most Western industrialized countries.[21]

China's companies are largely indebted in Renminbi and mainly to public banks in China, and the indebtedness of Chinese private households is offset by considerable assets in the form of widespread home ownership and investments. The savings rate on earned income in China is still very high, and all debt, unlike in the USA, is primarily taken on for investment purposes, rather than for non-durable consumption.[22] Therefore, China's economic development overall is "resilient and sustainable",[23] despite Washington's trade, economic, technological, and hybrid war. Macroeconomic investment ratios are comparably very high, and domestic consumption now is being pushed higher, as the entire "business model" is transformed toward reliance on the domestic economy and increasing trade with the more than 150 partner countries of the Belt and Road Initiative (BRI) in the Global South—the famous *dual circulation* with reliance on the domestic economy and on external exchange with reliable partners. In all, little risk of economic or financial collapse is visible …

The next financial and real crisis is much more likely to be caused by the gigantic public and private debt in the USA, approaching 40 trillion dollars for the federal government alone. The speculative bubbles present in all investment areas on Wall Street—be it stocks, bonds, derivatives, gold, real estate, or other real assets—amount to pyramids of derivatives of derivatives on the order of hundreds of trillions of dollars; some speak of 1.5 quadrillion dollars printed on financial papers in total.[24] This entails the impossibility of achieving even halfway reasonable returns on these amounts of mainly fictitious capital. This is especially true when the Wall Street financial industry can no longer maintain the inflow of global stray capital to support the demand for dollars, maintain the dollar's value, and guarantee sufficient profit rates to attract global free investment money, and thus be able to finance the huge amounts of US Treasuries caused by the overly corrupt and expensive US military and military-industrial complex. One of the weakest points of the dollar system is indeed federal state bonds, with considerable amounts of debt restructuring expected in 2025 and beyond. In 2025, the federal government will have to pay already over 5 percent on Treasuries. On a global scale, the dollar is declining both as a transaction unit for trade and as a reserve unit for central banks. The latter have swapped huge amounts of Treasuries for gold and local currencies in recent years.

We will look at some of the facts that, taken together, do not provide a basis for invoking China as the next cause of a global financial crisis.

Among other things, we will examine China's abundant currency reserves, the increasing use of the Yuan and E-Yuan both in international trade and as a reserve currency in the *Cross-Border Inter-Bank Payments System* (CIPS) run by China's central bank, the *People's Bank of China* (PBoC), and its highly effective international system of development banks and development finance, as embedded in the Global South in general and the BRICS in particular.

We will also have a look at the Chinese real-estate sector and its organized shrinking from 2021 onward to a new sustainable equilibrium—another predicted collapse that did not occur.

The "Globe Under China's Scepter" and Other Fairy Tales for Childlike Media Victims ... While Even Corporate Leaders Have Been Silenced ... and the Corporate Economy Just Votes with Their Feet

Variants of verbal warfare—such as "China's scepter", "Europe's kowtow", "espionage", "submission", and "police state"—go along with increasing media and political pressure on Western corporations to decouple from and leave China.[25]

Which, however, decouples in a different sense: by bringing their Western first-tier suppliers to China and having them invest in production and R&D themselves, and by building complete VACs in China independent of supply parts from the West, which could be subject to further sanctioning campaigns. Decoupling, the corporate way—the opposite of what Western media oligarchs and the political caste intended. In China nowadays, there exists a largely autarkic German economy, autarkic vis-à-vis the West.

Nevertheless, they forced even Germany's No. 1, Volkswagen, to withdraw from its factory in Urumqi, although over the years Volkswagen had deployed several independent international advisors to investigate its Xinjiang factory's VACs, which repeatedly proved that there was no sign of "forced labor"; on the contrary, Uyghurs' wages were above average. But facts no longer matter to fearmongers in their political and media profiling race.[26] The neoliberal greens and new neoliberal social democrats, with their political majority in the state-owned corporation

Volkswagen, pushed through, and the company had to withdraw from Xinjiang.

Even big-business bosses in Germany are silenced with respect to China and no longer speak up in the German media. CEO interviews on corporate China strategy have become rare. Instead, they vote with their feet—through investments, which have hugely increased in recent years—guided by their profit expectations and their requirements to learn cutting-edge technologies in their "China fitness center". They now evade the new media's dominance over politics and the political dominance over private capital.[27]

You have to ride at the top of the new anti-China wave of presumptions, half-truths, and misinformation to profit your media oligopoly and win elections for your political party with maximally stark verbalizations. A blogger sees the "globe under China's scepter",[28] while others paint an imperial China and Europe's kowtow to the new "emperor" of China.[29] Not only will Putin knock at your door tomorrow morning, but Xi will as well.

The necessary and omnipresent new enemy, on the one hand, is on the brink of collapse, as we have nearly sanctioned him to death, but, on the other hand, is still strong enough to devour us all tomorrow.

At its core, this all reflects the fact that "the Europeans", the EU, have largely lost any forward-looking strategic capacity in the face of a new world moving toward multipolarity. But instead of addressing four decades of neoliberalism, financialization, and the degeneration of capitalism into a redistribution machine favoring the top—instead of being the innovation, production, and investment system it once was—it seems easier to play the "Us–Them" game and blame China for the fact that the NFC has driven itself into systemic decline.

As mentioned, there is also criticism of the managers of Daimler, Siemens, and Volkswagen, who are accused of opportunism toward China. In the media bureaucracies, they can afford such a moralizing mentality that has become fashionable, because there, German export surpluses do not have to be earned. So what should top managers do when the late NFC in its declining period at home can no longer generate the dynamics to earn the wages for their German employees to large portions in China? Volkswagen, for instance, has always earned around 40 percent of its corporate profits in China.

Value-Added Chains, Trade, and Investment: De-coupling, Friend-Shoring, Hybrid War, and Other Conceptions That Have Failed

But things are changing further, and investments here or there have increasingly turned into direct rivalry. With the EU's, Eurozone's, and, in particular, Germany's lasting quasi-zero growth and relative economic decline, it has become more obvious that the capacities Western corporations have built up in China (and, to a smaller extent, also in the USA) are now being reduced in the EU and in Germany.

Moreover, the production capacities in China are not only "made in China for China", but have also become exports from China, and thus direct competition for domestic production in the German and EU markets, and even more so in third markets. No wonder the EU is now complaining that it does not export much to China anymore. The largely autarkic EU corporate economy in China no longer needs to import supply parts from the EU.

They seem to have no idea into what they have forced their own Western corporations, as they do not seem to understand the economy at all…

Desperately installing protective measures—from Chinese M&A bans to protective and often prohibitive customs tariffs against Chinese exports (which, in large part, are in fact commodities of Western corporations)—and forcing Western capital to move out of China and pursue "friendshoring" to India, Vietnam, etc., as well as exerting political arbitrariness over capital, cannot change much in the basic structures of international VACs, as has turned out. Some third "friendly" countries simply relabel Chinese products as, say, Indonesian ones, while most other products "made in, say, Vietnam" still have 90 percent of their value added from Chinese supply parts. We have seen how, with some politically enforced "friendshoring", these imports (of supplies) from China have hugely increased.

No Western politician seems to grasp what they have done to their own corporate economy in their helpless, desperate, defensive, and protective struggle against systemic decline. They have no idea of potential longer-term progressive strategies that address the root causes and critical factors of what an international economy is in the current global shift toward multipolarity and the Global South.

This book will deal more extensively in relevant chapters with the real economy, industrial policies, and forward-looking strategies.

Who Will Care for Germany, the EU, or the UK, and Who Is Getting Isolated?

For several years, German Green Party politicians—particularly when in government—acted in media-conform manners regarding the corporate economy, also not needing to earn their wages, of course. After some years in office, they turned out to be extremely overbearing in politics, issuing the most bureaucratic orders and "musts" of green transformations, neglecting what the economy can and cannot achieve in the short run, and cutting traditional energy too quickly, merely to import expensive fracking gas, etc. In Germany, not even after a full political term were the Greens and the Social Democrats able to cope, and both had to step down. Both parties lost considerably in the recent elections (beginning of 2025) and have long passed their peak.

Just as the famous saying goes: "All people are wise – some before, others after." And if the media-political trends in the EU continue, it will probably be far "afterwards" again before the EU becomes wise, when another child has fallen into the well. In the meantime, all over the world, people are reconsidering: "What do we really need the EU (Germany, France) and the UK, respectively, for?"

But still, the next escalation step is always in view—from ideological warfare to domestic censorship—toward the next hot war, be it Ukraine, the Baltic Sea, or sanctions escalations: "We are at war with Russia!" and "Ceterum censeo, Russia esse delendam!" There is virtually no Plan B beyond Plan A—total victory in war—left among EU and UK political elites. Eurasia will be split for at least three or four generations by Western politicians, who feel and behave like war heroes. Diplomacy is yesterday's scrap; it is weakness and cowardice. But you will never see any of them—or their children—in the war trenches.

One cannot imagine how the internal political climate of thought and speech has changed, and how criminal laws have been transformed, with basic legal principles dramatically altered—for example, the burden of proof reversed. Nowadays, you may go to jail for expressing a well-founded opinion or even merely hinting at historical facts. While the world struggles successfully to free itself, through however difficult processes, the EU is returning to a dark age...

Does anyone still care about such an EU? Given the speeches in recent years or the answers in TV interviews of African prime ministers, heads of state, or foreign ministers, Africa no longer pays much attention to its old colonial suppressor. The world is set to move forward.

Cultural decoupling, too: While, for example, 160 Goethe Institutes (German cultural institutes) in almost 100 countries—including China—have, since the early 1950s, been considered "good" cultural foreign policy, Chinese Confucius Institutes, which have been promoting Chinese culture, language, and educational cooperation since around 2013, are simply labeled "propaganda", or even "espionage".[30] They have to be, if not outright closed, then again detached from German universities. Chinese language courses are now offered by institutions from Taiwan. Many sinologists must make a 180-degree political turnaround or face being silenced. Few sinologists still dare to express themselves publicly, and those who do are constrained by the new oppressive climate of ubiquitous enemies, spies, and looming wars.

International isolation (China? Or rather ourselves?) and decoupling[31] are likely to create the conditions for a hot war.

As a simple final example of hysteria: "IT dictatorship" and China's "reinvention of dictatorship". The book *We Have Been Harmonized: Life in China's Surveillance State* (the German title changed to *The Reinvention of Dictatorship: How China Is Building the Digital Surveillance State and Challenging Us*)[32] is a perfect instance. The realm of evil is clearly identified, and the "we" emotions are appealingly sharpened. A place at the top of the wave has been guaranteed for books like these ever since.

Undefined, dark, only vaguely perceived enemies and dangers: Wilhelm II, the German Kaiser, knew, in the face of the "malice of the world" against "us", no political parties anymore—only "Germans"—before going into WWI with cheers against "the evil ones". The ideological mechanisms were further perfected to justify WWII and have been refined with ever more sophisticated social psychology since. In these books, Cold War 2.0 was fully developed and anticipated. The infamous election poster of the CDU (German Christian Democrats) from 1953, showing the Russian "subhuman" waiting viciously for us as victims with the fearmongering slogan "All roads of Marxism lead to Moscow!"[33] is referenced (un-)cheerfully in this book, in its last chapter: "The Future: When All Roads Lead to Beijing."

Such books lead to an open refusal to understand anyone else, the total "we" formation, and the preemptive justification of any aggression, violence, or war as "self-defense". While virtually everything in this book is wrong regarding the assessment of Chinese developments and policies on cybersecurity, AI, big data, 5G/6G, as well as social and ecological behavioral nudges.

We will explain these matters with facts, details, experiences, and cases, even in such usually sensitive fields. Much more is to come.

Notes

1. For example, Franka Lu, "Die Demütigung eines uralten Reichs [The Humiliation of an Ancient Empire]", *Zeit Online*, February 18, 2019: https://www.zeit.de/kultur/2019-02/china-usa-weltmacht-handelskonflikt-welthandel, visited May 12, 2024.
2. "Keine friedliche Koexistenz [No Peaceful Coexistence]", *German Foreign Policy*, November 28, 2019: https://www.german-foreign-policy.com/news/detail/8119, visited May 12, 2024.
3. "No Peaceful Coexistence", ibid.
4. Thorstein Veblen, *The Instinct of Workmanship and the State of the Industrial Arts*, New York, NY: Macmillan, 1914, p. 25.
5. It is not by coincidence that the publication trends follow Washington's intensified anti-China policies, beginning in the Obama period (after 2008). Trump then started an explicit trade war in 2018, and Biden continued and did not revoke any of Trump 1.0's measures. So, apparently, it is a common, joint, bipartisan "Washington strategy", independent of a DEM or REP president, and independent of the president's personal character. Unsurprisingly, Trump 2.0 continues and intensifies this strategy in his second term, and under his terms, we have experienced unprecedented kinds of measures that, if realized, would cut trade between the two countries down to zero in a short spell. Virtually all Chinese goods have come under some trade prohibition or prohibitive protective custom tariff. We have basically seen a tool set that, in the twenty-first century, can indeed set the two largest economies of the world to zero exchange and 100% decoupling. Of course, the USA would not be able to stand that for long, and therefore, some more pragmatic live-and-let-live arrangement will probably be bargained. But the world has already looked into a global abyss of splitting the world into two separated blocs, which had been unthinkable since the aftermath of the Great Depression 1929ff. We can and will of course not follow any of the erratic details changing on a daily basis, but more on all that later in this book.
6. See for example: A. Vltchek, "Who gives US the right to lecture China about rights?", *Information Clearing House*, December 11, 2019: https://www.informationclearinghouse.info/52688.htm, visited May 14, 2024.

7. For example: F. Lee, "Der Größenwahn der chinesischen Führungsriege. Im Weltall, auf der Straße, im virtuellen Raum: High-Tech-Produkte aus China lauern überall [The Megalomania of the Chinese Leadership. In space, on the street, in virtual space: High-tech products from China are lurking everywhere]", *taz*, January 14, 2019: https://taz.de/Der-Groessenwahn-der-chinesischen-Fuehrungsriege/!5561479/, visited May 14, 2024.
8. F. Sieren (2023). *Future? China! How The New Superpower Is Changing The West.* Singapore: WSPC.
9. S. Scheuer, *Der Masterplan: Chinas Weg zur Weltherrschaft* [The Masterplan: China's Path to World Domination], Freiburg, 2018 (Scheuer 2018).
10. For example: H.-J. Chang, *Kicking Away the Ladder. Development Strategy in Historical Perspective*, London, New York: Anthem Press, 2002.
11. For example, what are known as the "four great inventions", namely papermaking, printing, gunpowder, and the compass, originated in China. On this, see for example Joseph Needham's classic book series *Science and Civilization in China*, Cambridge: Cambridge University Press, 1954–present. More on this later.
12. For example, *Steingarts Morning Briefing*, October 9, 2019; *Handelsblatt Morning Briefing*, October 24, 2019; more recently, W. Muenchau, "Germany is on the brink of economic decline", *New Statesman*, March 20, 2024: https://www.newstatesman.com/comment/2024/03/germany-is-on-the-brink-of-economic-decline, visited May 17, 2024.
13. For example: Vincent J. Geloso, Alexander W. Salter, "State capacity and economic development: Causal mechanism or correlative filter?", *Journal of Economic Behavior and Organization* 170 (2020), 372–385.
14. E.g., the technology listings in Hongjun ZHAO, *China's Long-Term Economic Development. How have Economy and Governance Evolved since 500 BC?*, Cheltenham, UK, Northampton, MA, USA: Edward Elgar, 2018.
15. A short version of the above-mentioned now 26-volume series by British scientist and Cambridge professor Joseph Needham, which his students are still working on, is provided for example by: Robert K.G. Temple, *The Genius of China: 3000 Years of Science, Discovery, and Invention*, New York: Simon & Schuster, 1986.
16. Larry Romanoff, "History of Chinese Inventions. The Present and the Future", *Transcend Media Service*, December 23, 2019: https://www.transcend.org/tms/2019/12/history-of-chinese-inventions-the-present-and-the-future-recent-chinese-state-of-the-art-innovations/, visited May 17, 2024.

17. For a well-researched account that Marco Polo did in fact visit China, see for example: Hans Ulrich Vogel (2012). *Marco Polo "Was" in China: New Evidence from Currencies, Salts and Revenues*, Leiden: Brill.
18. "In 1782 [Samuel] Bentham travelled along the Siberian route to China, visiting Kyakhta and its Chinese pendant Naimatchin, and then spending over a month at the border fluvial city of Nerchinsk, where he was able to study Chinese ship designs, particularly those of junks. Back in Europe, he campaigned for the introduction of watertight compartments, an idea which he acknowledged he had got from seeing large Chinese vessels in Siberia." As for example the *Wikipedia* entry to Samuel Bentham, philosopher Jeremy Bentham's brother, notes: https://en.wikipedia.org/wiki/Samuel_Bentham, accessed June 19, 2025.
19. Note the example of the company *Bosch China*, which is a central research hub from which the German company Bosch learns overall; for example: Melchior Poppe, "Warum in spätestens 20 Jahren kein Chinese mehr ein Auto kaufen wird [Why in at most 20 years no Chinese will buy a car anymore]", *Focus*, September 2, 2019: https://www.focus.de/perspektiven/14-laender-14-reporter/14-laender-14-reporter-china-warum-in-spaetestens-20-jahren-kein-chinese-mehr-ein-auto-kaufen-wird_id_10077546.html, visited May 17, 2024. In January 2023, Bosch announced it would invest another one billion Euros into its Chinese R&D facilities. See: Gustav Theile, "Bosch investiert eine Milliarde in China [Bosch invests one billion in China]", *FAZ*, January 13, 2023: https://www.faz.net/aktuell/wirtschaft/unternehmen/bosch-investiert-eine-milliarde-in-china-18598508.html, visited May 17, 2024.
20. "As has been the case since 1951, all economists, professors, authors and politicians must ignore the data and must predict and explain China's inevitable doom." Godfree Roberts, *Here Comes China. Open Source Intelligence*, herecomeschina@substack.com, June 16, 2025, accessed June 16, 2025.
21. For example: "China Government Debt to GDP", *Trading Economics* (based on IMF data): https://tradingeconomics.com/china/government-debt-to-gdp, visited May 17, 2024.
22. See for example: *Solvecon Forex Report*, December 16, 2019, p. 12.
23. Ibid.
24. E.g., W. Elsner, "Speculative financial capitalism wacking out over an 'impossible' profit rate. The infeasibility of a 'usual' real average profit rate, considering fictitious capital, and its implications", in: *Marx, Veblen, and the Foundations of Heterodox Economics: Essays in Honor of John F. Henry*, ed. by T.-H. Jo and F.S. Lee, 199–227, London, New York: Routledge, 2015.

25. As an example for medial de-coupling and preparation for the next war: "Was zum Teufel hat Volkswagen in diesem Polizeistaat verloren? [What the hell is Volkswagen doing in this police state?]", *Sueddeutsche Zeitung*, November 26, 2019; https://www.sueddeutsche.de/politik/china-cables-wolkswagen-xinjiang-1.4696629, visited January 7, 2025.
26. "Menschenrechte: Grüne fordern Aufklärung im VW-Werk Urumqi [Human rights: Greens demand clarification at VW plant in Urumqi]", *Welt*, November 29, 2019: https://www.welt.de/regionales/niedersachsen/article203934614/Menschenrechte-Gruene-fordern-Aufklaerung-im-VW-Werk-Urumqi.html, visited May 18, 2024.
27. The last theoretical discussion among historians on capital versus political dominance took place in the 1960s regarding the German Nazi Reich: How far was the German pursuit of the resources of the Soviet Union determined by capital fractions versus capital being subordinated to and exploited by the Nazi racist strategy? Apparently, the relatively relaxed post-WWII division of labor and the relative dominance structures of media and politics vis-à-vis corporate capital have to be reevaluated for the newly formed Western political bloc since the late 2010s, presumably in favor of a new political—and now media—dominance over the corporate economy.
28. "Globus unter dem Zepter Chinas? [Globe under China's scepter?]", January 29, 2019; online at: www.gerojenner.com, visited April 17, 2019.
29. F. Böge, "Europas Kotau vor China [Europe's kowtow to China]", *FAZ*, March 12, 2018: https://www.faz.net/aktuell/politik/ausland/china-politik-europa-hat-keinen-plan-faz-kommentar-15488644.html, visited May 18, 2024; K. Müller, "Kotau des Kanzlers vor China [The chancellor's kowtow to China]", *Frankfurter Rundschau*, June 23, 2023: https://www.fr.de/meinung/kotau-des-kanzlers-vor-china-92360698.html, visited May 18, 2024.
30. See for example also: Hans-Georg Moeller, "US targeting of Confucius Institutes is just the latest push to gain free and open access to China", *SCMP*, August 21, 2020: https://www.scmp.com/comment/opinion/article/3098006/us-targeting-confucius-institutes-just-latest-push-gain-free-and, visited May 18, 2024. Moeller sees as another cause especially of US hostilities toward Confucius Institutes the fact that state-funded public educational institutes on private US college campuses represent a systemic contradiction of its "free-market" ideology and thus a hurdle in the mission to "open-up" (meaning privatize and control) the Chinese education sector and China in general for US capital.
31. The decoupling policy of the USA and its dependent followers now shows all characteristics of a hybrid war: destruction of the existing supply and

value chains, exclusion of non-compliant countries (China, Russia, etc.) from the US-dominated international financial system, including the World Bank and IMF, SWIFT etc., restriction of travel freedom for Chinese in the West, choking off scientific exchange with China and others, pressure on other countries not to import Chinese technologies, a new US agency to exert pressure on companies from third countries not to use Chinese technologies, etc.; for example Wolfgang Müller, "US-Wirtschaftskrieg, EU-Ambivalenz – Wie der Westen den Aufstieg Chinas stoppen will [US Economic War, EU Ambivalence – How the West Wants to Stop China's Rise]", *isw-Report* 119, Munich, December 2019, p. 18 ff. This does not remain without reactions: China builds new, more effective international VACs with the independent world, Huawei presents a new phone without any US components within a year, etc. And unprecedented escalations are going on, with trade, investment and technology wars, top scientists, Chinese and others, moving out of the USA and of the West to China, foreign students in the USA being incarcerated and deported. And on all fronts, from trade to chips and to people-to-people traveling, China seems to be winning. We will give further details and cases in this book.

32. K. Strittmatter, *We Have Been Harmonized: Life in China's Surveillance State*, New York: Mariner Books, 2020.
33. For an image of this poster, visit: https://upload.wikimedia.org/wikipedia/commons/a/a1/CDU_Wahlkampfplakat_-_kaspl010.JPG, visited May 18, 2024.

Selected and Recommended Literature

Frank, Andre Gunder. 1998. *ReOrient. Global Economy in the Asian Age.* Oakland, CA: University of California Press.

Sieren, Frank. 2023. *Future? China! How The New Superpower Is Changing The West.* Singapore: WSPC.

Vogel, Hans Ulrich. 2012. *Marco Polo "Was" in China: New Evidence from Currencies, Salts and Revenues.* Leiden: Brill.

Further Cited Literature

Scheuer, Stephan, 2018. *Der Masterplan: Chinas Weg zur Weltherrschaft* [The Masterplan: China's Path to World Domination]. Freiburg: Herder.

CHAPTER 4

Learning to Comprehend China Means Comprehending Ourselves

The Fears of Decline or: It Hurts to Recognize the Changing World

China's development is, in countless aspects, novel, pathbreaking, and breathtaking, but it is perceived by many in the West as a threat to their very existence. And rightly so: China will, in many complex ways and through its sheer overwhelming dynamics, disrupt global structures. Thus, the days of the good old and comfortable neocolonial global structures—namely the one-sided North–South exploitation systems, so comfortable, cozy, and enriching for the West—are over. The lazy, wealthy, privileged existence of the West will soon be completely past, and we have already learned in the West that continuing improvement of well-being is no longer the prime goal of the economy, at least not in an NFC economy.

The West is already in crisis mode, critically adapting to fewer cheap resources flowing from the South to the North. The economy can no longer be considered an instrument for improving people's well-being. On the contrary, people must get used to living with less wealth and more work and must serve the economic and financial sectors instead. If you see it as a threat to the old collective West, you are probably right. But whether you also see it as a chance—at least for yourself—depends on you.

The confrontation between the media industry and large parts of party politics in the West contributes to the fears and uncertainty with which

W. Elsner, E. Najmehchi, *The Rise of China*,
https://doi.org/10.1007/978-3-032-20260-4_4

many in the "West" view China. But could we one day (re)turn to an attitude of curiosity, learning, and understanding of "the other"?

In science and in the philosophy of knowledge and insight (epistemology), it is known that alternative, competing theories and explanatory approaches can, in the first instance, only be understood "immanently"—that is, by "going into" the approach: getting to know its ontology, axioms, assumptions, tacit prerequisites, contexts, basic reference cases, its "paradigmatic" worldview, and the history of its development path up to the present. This applies not only to complex scientific paradigms but also to national cultures, which are complex systems as well and can only be understood in their, as it is called today, "path-dependent" history. Thus, "history matters" and context matters, as complexity economists say. This approach would prevent us from making a premature judgment and condemnation of what has not even been understood yet.[1]

In Bremen, our hometown, there is a "Peace Tunnel" under one of the railway bridges near the main station, at both ends of which it says:

> Recognizing is the gate to comprehension. Comprehension is the gate to recognizing.

This circularity in the process of approaching new realities shows how easily two scaredy-cats can block each other and are more likely to go to war than to recognize, understand, or comprehend—a so-called prisoners' dilemma if the perspectives and mental horizons of the agents involved are too myopic, that is, narrow and short-term.

No need to mention that comprehension is not "approval". Achieving the capacity for critical approval would require another complex dynamic: we tend to endorse "the other" the more we know of it, understand its history, and comprehend it, as we tend to realize that they are just as good or bad as we are—sometimes whiter, sometimes blacker, but mostly lighter or darker shades of grey. Above all, when we realize that they struggle with the same basic problems as we do, seeking and testing solutions just as we do ourselves, we might become capable of understanding how they got to where they are now, and how we got to where we are now. While the result of better recognition is by no means determined, our judgment would, by all means, become a more qualified one.

How can we ensure that understanding has a chance, and that the world is not maliciously pushed to the brink of ruin again—this time, probably beyond it? How can we prevent ourselves from being pushed into the ideological trenches of Cold War 2.0, which is currently in full swing? How do we manage to understand the real, common, and collective problems of humanity—our problems as well as theirs—and tackle them cooperatively, in order simply to reach the end of this century as humankind?

"Governing Differences" and a polycentric, pragmatist modus vivendi have often been advocated in Western literature for the pacification of our own societies and apply, by analogy, to the systemic diversity and multipolarity of the twenty-first-century world structure. In this book, we will learn how, in China, they have been used to think about humankind and about their manifold global initiatives of "building a community with a shared future for mankind".

The voices of active understanding have always existed, of course, simply because such thinking is naturally human and in our joint long-term interest. Nowadays, our striving for long-term ways of thinking and for some minimal collective rationality has come under pressure in the West and is increasingly being "cancelled" by an oligarchic media industry and a cartelized mainstream-party politics.

One of the few prominent politicians to have advocated a priority of "understanding" toward China was, surprisingly and out of a wisdom of age, Henry Kissinger, in his book on China:

> Any attempt to understand China's [...] world role in the 21st century must begin [...] with a basic appreciation of the traditional context.[2]

Before him, on the scientific and historiographic side, the already mentioned André G. Frank[3] provided a historically informed approach to understanding why China in the twenty-first century will be "number one" again, and that this is, at least in terms of purely quantitative world shares, nothing other than the restoration of a thousand-year-old historical normality.

For example, it has sometimes been recognized and analyzed how China managed to escape the "trap" of economic dependence on the USA, and thus also political blackmail.[4] It has also been recognized how China, early on, abandoned the always short-term and not very wise export world-champion model as its development model and initiated a more independent, domestic-oriented path of development.

Thus, the country has considerably reduced its export surpluses since 2008, while the last remaining old "export world champion", Germany, with its formerly successful but now highly fragile and vulnerable model, is suffering in the new world. Decades-long export champion industries, such as the German machine tool industry, although highly engaged in China itself, have recently changed their strategy by 180 degrees and called for protective trade measures. Without a concept, strategy, or any better-adapted Plan B, Germany is now forced to oscillate between the USA—admiring and largely copying Trump's policies—and other global agents like China.

Similarly, the economic chief commentator of the British *Financial Times*, Martin Wolf, in a reflection on the global situation under this new systemic competition, entitled *The Challenge of One World, Two Systems*, comes to the wise conclusion that, in the end, one has to "embrace the complexity" of the situation and take a "path of maturity": "Unbridled strategic competition between China and the West would be a disaster."[5]

In the highly arrogant ruling German media industry, a former editor-in-chief of a corporate-economy newspaper, who was dismissed for too much independent thinking and then ran his own *Morning Briefing* for professionals, occasionally stands out. He has regularly commented on China's development with the intention to comprehend, and he often dismisses the countless crisis prophecies of the German media. China has been growing slower, yes, but it has not been a crisis phenomenon; it was planned. China *is* already "number one", he has kept arguing, and the gap to the rest is growing year by year. China's per capita GDP growth was over 360 percent from 2000 to 2020; the growth rates in Germany and the USA were 27 and 24 percent, respectively. The difference can no longer be explained by China's lower starting level, he argues, and he points to an explanation by sustained effectiveness: "The USA snubs the world, China connects it."[6]

Xi's so-called "Chinese dream of a moderately prosperous society" (more on this below) is, according to this important voice, superior to the neoliberal "the-winner-takes-it-all" society. China's "crises", "bubbles", or "extreme debt" are "Western alarmism", a courageous statement in a media world nowadays headed toward war:

> The West's warnings of a Chinese aging society, a bursting of the local real estate bubble and the consequences of too high debt are in truth Western hopes disguised as fear. The new world power has been going its way despite all these challenges for decades (...) The officials of the Communist Party also debate at [the] People's Congress with a seriousness and openness that one could only wish for in the Bundestag and on Capitol Hill.[7]

This is what openness and the mental capacity to comprehend could look like, and what true "quality journalism" could be as well—explaining, realistic, and thus action-relevant for people and professionals who want to change the world for the better, vilified (or honored, really?) by the mainstream as "do-gooders".

Comprehending China ...?

The title of the present book could also have been *Comprehending China*. But this title was already taken—by a book that comes close to this one in its attempt not to fall into the "We-They" trap and to end up in the trenches, where our options then become limited to zero and our future may become very short. R. Fitzthum's book *Comprehending China*,[8,9] by an Austrian author who has been living in China for decades, shows that China is not a threat to Europe but an opportunity: Why should China have an interest in aggression and war when it is fully occupied with itself and self-sufficient in its development?

China has carried the great bulk of the global elimination of poverty and is now successfully and measurably redistributing downward, toward greater equality, with sensational real-wage increases, tax relief for lower- and middle-income earners, collective social-insurance funds, expanding social programs, and affordable, accessible public services and infrastructure. The Chinese Gini coefficient has been radically reduced over the last 15 years, as we will show and explain in this book.

There should actually be a stir in liberal and leftist hearts in Europe—if they truly wanted to comprehend.

Those three topics alone—poverty eradication, reduction of inequality, and the massive development of all kinds of common goods and services for the people (which we will discuss later)—already indicate a system(at)ic difference from the NFC. None of these issues seems to be actionable in the West any longer. Instead, redistribution becomes ever more extreme, with the top 0.1 percent "as if by a miracle" always becoming richer, through all upswings and, even more so, through crises—overall plutocratic systems, as Aristotle characterized them.

… OR DO EUROPEAN "LIBERAL" INTELLECTUALS DETERMINE THE FUTURE OF CHINA?

The Austrian Fitzthum does not even shy away from the S-question, the "system-" or "socialism-" question—something that traditionally only the European/Anglo-Saxon political left was concerned with. Against the infamous "we-know-it-all-and-better" attitude, usually prevalent in the Eurocentric and West-centric left, he sets a pleasant, refreshingly clear, simple, and pragmatic attitude:

The CPC matured through a hundred years of national emancipation, existential threats, numerous setbacks, civil-war battles, countless discussions, several course adjustments, multiple "self-reinventions", and endless learning. It overcame European, US, and Japanese colonialisms as well as the Guomindang military/Chiang Kai-shek dictatorship; it survived famines, hostile interventions, isolation, and Western sanctions since 1949; it repeatedly realigned China's development in difficult phases and generated a country that has taken new paths—paths humanity had not taken before. According to Fitzthum, such a political force can be expected to define for itself what the "right path to socialism" is, "with Chinese characteristics".

There is no need for European intellectuals who are trapped in the Eurocentric tradition of top-down state socialism and who believe they know better what the "true", "real", "genuine", or "ideal" socialism for China should be.

China, by the way, is eager to learn at all levels, as those familiar with the country have always observed. Chinese scholars have also initiated global scientific associations to engage in dialogue with Western intellectuals—for example, the *World Association of Political Economy* (WAPE), where non-neoliberal economists have gathered for nearly 20 years (since 2006), or the *World Association of China Studies* (WACS), where Western scholars from many fields have convened for almost a decade (founded in 2016).

Unlike the Eurocentric intellectual hubris, pharisaism, bigotry, and global value-driven crusades of many leftist parties, China has been strikingly humble. Since the early 1950s—through its first articulation of the principle of peaceful coexistence—it has made clear that the Chinese path is not an export commodity: it is defined by Chinese characteristics and therefore not transferable or imposable on other countries.

Others, such as the Italian Marxist philosopher Domenico Losurdo or the aforementioned critical financial economist Michael Hudson, speak of "neoliberal leftists" or "leftists infiltrated by neoliberalism". These are, for example, the leftist currents in Western Europe that no longer show interest in overcoming the NFC, nor in economic justice, or even in workers' issues.[10] We will return to both Hudson and Losurdo later in this book.

The CPC, by the way, appears far more modest—despite its considerable achievements—than many of the judgmental European Greens, liberals, and leftist intellectuals, the educated "do-gooders". For decades, they have been debating "green transitions" without ever managing to make any impact on the NFC. Instead, they have grown accustomed to defeats, resigned themselves to cemented minority positions in parliaments, adapted to them, and patiently draped themselves for the next opportunity to join a government coalition.

For decades, Western professionals, visitors, and observers have witnessed in China economic, technological, social, and ecological dynamics unfolding at a pace unique in the world—dynamics that progressives in Europe who dream of a better future can only imagine. What is happening there today should, in fact, make European Green and leftist hearts beat faster, instead of hardening them.

Modesty "with Chinese Characteristics": The Chinese Way Will Not Be Exported

As mentioned, China—its people, the CPC, and its state leadership—is hardly "imperialistic" in these matters. Many features of the Chinese development path have become part of everyday life, shaping how people think, speak, and act regarding national development, ecological civilization, individual and organizational credibility, company managers, bureaucrats, politicians, party members, inequality aversion, or international solidarity. Yet it is always emphasized: what China develops applies only to China; it is not exported as a revolution or a universal development model. Advice is welcome at any time—they like to learn—but please, no ignorant prescriptions!

Such refreshing modesty would, of course, also be welcome from the so-called "defenders of our freedom" and the crusaders of the "imperial mode of living"[11]—typically "defended" in and by foreign countries—in Washington, Berlin, Paris, London, Brussels, or Tokyo. Even most green, orange, or pink parties struggle with modesty. Today, imperialism finds its breeding ground among those who impose their moral universalism on the world. It is no coincidence that A.G. Frank concluded his world-historical analysis with the ironic remark: "The Eurocentric Emperor Has No Clothes".

We will, of course, resolve the provocations that we have voiced here so far into a better comprehension of what is going on in China and the world, using facts from many areas.

… Even Learning from China? Transfer Streams Turned Around …

Assuming we manage to recognize and comprehend China, what could we learn? And if we learn something, do we still have the collective/public capacity to act in favor of necessary changes?

The *Centre for European Economic Research* attests in its innovation reports that Germany and leading Western countries, in terms of their "innovation capabilities", have been losing ranks in international rankings since 2005. A report concludes for Germany: "Long-known deficits are not addressed or are addressed too slowly; opportunities are not sufficiently exploited." Among the top positions in the global rankings are East Asian countries like Singapore and South Korea. China has consistently been gaining ranks over the last decade, even overtaking Japan.[12] Germany is nowadays widely considered to be rather locked into a path where it could crash with its model of heavy upward redistribution, austerity, restrictions, "black-zero" debt brakes,[13] demonization of the state and "market" idolization, and an overall particularly dogmatic neoliberalism. This has even entailed an end to the "export world champion" and "technology world champion" status. *Made in Germany* and trust in German companies are internationally on a downward trajectory.[14]

On the other hand, the usual international rankings show China's strengthened position. As even the *Australian Strategic Policy Institute*

(ASPI), an entity financed by the international Western armaments industries and governments, has put it:

> China's global lead extends to 37 out of 44 technologies that ASPI is now tracking, covering a range of crucial technology fields spanning defence, space, robotics, energy, the environment, biotechnology, artificial intelligence (AI), advanced materials and key quantum technology areas. The Critical Technology Tracker shows that, for some technologies, all of the world's top 10 leading research institutions are based in China and are collectively generating nine times more high-impact research papers than the second-ranked country (most often the US). Notably, the Chinese Academy of Sciences ranks highly (and often first or second) across many of the 44 technologies included ...[15]

Research-intensive German companies, such as Bosch, have increasingly sourced innovations from their Chinese subsidiaries. A German report suggested some years ago that it is "only a matter of time before innovations come from China in droves"[16] and illustrated, for example, the completely different approach to mobility innovations there: intelligent roads instead of intelligent cars, public infrastructure investments instead of isolated corporate solutions. It asked: "What can (or must) we Germans learn from the Chinese?"[17] It is a willingness to learn and openness to experimentation, supported by pro-innovation policies and regulated markets, that gives China an edge over the United States as a location for innovation in all cutting-edge scientific and technological areas, such as artificial intelligence and quantum computing.[18]

As mentioned, all major German corporations have been heavily investing in China over the last decade, in both production and assembly and R&D centers, and all first-tier system supplier firms and most second-tier suppliers are present in China, no longer with production alone, but with R&D centers themselves, all heavily aligned in joint ventures with the leading Chinese assemblers as well as connected in their VACs with usually dozens of Chinese suppliers and service firms, most of them young, cutting-edge startups, often not older than five years. They have often publicly stated that without being part of the Chinese production system and the Chinese sales market, they would have no chance in their international markets.

We are speaking of technological fields ranging from all kinds of materials, biomaterials, energy forms, renewables, thorium nuclear, fusion, through new chip technologies such as photonics, through AI and quantum computing, new dimensions of laser, stealth technologies, speed technologies ... of whatever you may think of, and of whatever you may never have heard of, you will find China at the top of breakthroughs, inventions, innovations, applications, and new combinations ... on a weekly, even daily, basis.

And we are speaking of an integrated economic ecology spanning from a huge potential of skilled and motivated workers and engineers, through complete and flexible VACs and abundant supplier scenes in efficient regional industry clusters, stable and sufficient energy, data, and computing-capacity supplies, cutting-edge intelligent hard infrastructures that are cheap and accessible, an efficient service ecology, alert, well-informed, and helpful public agents partaking in industrial discussions, clearly communicated national development targets, an open, high-speed, and experimental business climate, international openness, and markets that are well regulated but mostly in free competition, including price competition. This systemic integration is highly effective and competitive.

We will get back to these themes.

"Comprehending China", however, as we will argue, also implies understanding that private, collective, and state action to further national development is systemic and cannot simply be transferred or copied to other national systems. Appropriate "absorption capacities" would always have to be built up first before one can learn from another national system. Conversely, this also applied to China's long catch-up and rise process and its learning from Western industrial nations. At the end of our journey through the numerous economic, social, and ecological areas and policy fields of China, we will show in more detail what it means to say: "It's the system, stupid!" But even with this in mind, recognizing, understanding, learning, and cooperating, as everyday experience shows, are by no means impossible. And, in fact, there is only one survival strategy for national systems: understanding, peaceful coexistence, learning, and cooperation, as a well-known German banker-blogger put it:

> The alternative is meaningful cooperation. For Europe [...] the policy approach of the Hanseatic League should apply. Economic exchange (not sanctions!) promotes cultural exchange and understanding. This is active

peace policy. From trade comes prosperity. [...] Tolerance meant understanding this connection.[19]

On International Polls: Emerging Comprehension and Trust, Country Reputations: "Trusting China More Than the USA" ...New Tourism Waves to China, People-to-People Exchanges, and YouTube Posts

Let's briefly turn to a topic that appears to be somewhat at the sideline, and surprising too, but nonetheless is an important part of the overall picture. How do people in nations worldwide feel about leading countries, and China in particular? This is of interest, especially when the result surprisingly deviates from the media average.

Many average citizens in the Collective West (and even more so in non-Western countries) seem to have developed a surprisingly different view from the Western Bloc's media coverage.

Sometimes people's views surface in polls that seem to be based on certain pragmatic rather than ideological "value-war" considerations and their own practical life experiences. Even direct knowledge about China from tourism, professional relations, or travel reports on the internet contributes, which nowadays is full of Western young people's accounts of travels in China. A surprising number of young people even report that they live in China. By all means, these young people are surprisingly well informed about China. One of them, out of dozens if not hundreds of YouTube vloggers, has been the travel reporter and live streamer "Speed" (or: "IShowSpeed") with his millions of followers.[20]

Another surprising "media" phenomenon appeared in the context of the US prosecution of TikTok, a company originally established by the Chinese, but spun off from the Chinese parent company long ago, headquartered in Singapore and majority-owned by US financial investors—facts all unknown to much of the US public, so that the US bipartisan and media campaign against the "Chinese spy TikTok" could be pushed through the media and the political caste. But US youngsters already had their own year-long experience with TikTok, and a movement of resistance emerged among the multimillion users. The US version of TikTok has, however, not been banned, in spite of a deadline set by the bipartisan Congress, according to a new law passed under the Biden administration. The Trump administration no longer prosecuted TikTok and used it for social media posts instead, later announcing a deal that would allow US investors to fully acquire and control it (including its algorithms).[21] But before Trump came to office in early 2025, there had already emerged an ironic youth movement in the US: the alleged "TikTok refugees," by millions, declared leaving TikTok in the face of its total ban, but in fact added another platform as a fallback, and surprisingly, this was a genuinely Chinese one. In hundreds of thousands, they suddenly appeared within the domestic Chinese IT ecology, on the platform Little Red Book, "Red Note", or just "Red", in Chinese: Xiaohongshu.[22] They not only realized the huge creative options they had on that platform, but the Chinese were obviously surprised by many US youth coming onto it and into the Chinese IT ecology. A Chinese official speaker of the foreign ministry would later say upon media questions, "No, we do not do anything against that. We welcome the people-to-people exchange that has emerged here." What happened then was more exciting than anything before on TikTok: tens of thousands of direct contacts between US and Chinese youth emerged—direct communications. In the USA, the "TikTok refugees" ironically called it "Getting me my new Chinese spy". Thousands of direct people-to-people exchanges occurred, where young people exchanged posts, facts, and videos about their relative opinions and living conditions, about prices of this and that, health insurance costs, hospital services, guns and no guns in the residential neighborhoods, the possibilities of (women) walking outside after dark, etc. What has happened here has been nothing less than a new global youth phenomenon and movement.

Another example of how the world is changing, based on people's experiences and evolving opinions of each other's countries.

It has been well known for decades that the priorities and views of populations in the Political West can be contrary to what their governments, state parties, official NGOs, and media industry declare politically correct, opportune, trendy, or TINA ("there is no alternative", M. Thatcher). This especially applies to fundamental human issues such as war and military interventions, environmental issues, or social justice and equality. This could even apply to China at times.

A representative survey by the poll research group *Civey* on behalf of the US-allied German "Atlantic-Bridge",[23] which is not suspected of being "pro-China", surprisingly surfaced in the media some years ago. It stated, among other things, that 80 percent of Germans rated the relationship with the USA, still in the Trump 1.0 period, as "negative" or "very negative", and 60 percent advocated a "greater distancing" from the USA.[24] And 90 percent spoke out against the interventions of the German military in foreign countries. Most spectacularly, however, over 42 percent considered China at that time to be a better partner than the USA (only 23 percent held the opposite opinion). Notably, this applied to over 56 percent of the voters of the Left Party, whose professional politicians would rather not be identified with any proximity to China.

In 2019, a survey by the Forsa Institute among 2000 executives of medium-sized companies yielded a similar result, according to which China was considered a more reliable trading partner than the USA or Great Britain.[25] During the Biden term, the USA partly regained credibility among Western countries and, correspondingly, trust in China decreased, but direct investments (FDI) in China by German companies nevertheless reached record levels, cementing China's status as Germany's most important trading partner.[26]

While the *net* flow of FDI into China has decreased over the last years (as of 2024), this is connected to a large outflow of FDI from Chinese companies into third countries such as Vietnam, Mexico, or Hungary in order to sidestep tariffs and trade quotas of the USA and the EU.[27]

Some foreign businesses in China have followed strategies of diversification and derisking their VACs after the Covid-shock. Some have pulled out profits as their projects reached maturity. Michael Hart, the president of the *American Chamber of Commerce in China*, has stated:

> The withdrawal of profits does not necessarily indicate that companies are unhappy with China, but rather that their investments here have matured.[28]

And the balance of trust has shifted again with Trump's second term, indicating inconsistency, erratic volatility, and a lack of reliability on the part of the USA, while Western companies again prefer China for long-term investments.

But do positive views by Western people toward China really gain practical significance? Or are they always just snapshots? Even if this were to continue in the coming years, it could not, according to all experience, influence the politics of the mainstream parties or governments in the West. Given their increasing hostility and verbal warfare against China, it may always be subject to a rapid change for the worse.

We are already seeing the latter in the USA, where Washington's aggressive policy to contain rising China started under Trump and continued under Biden, and has apparently succeeded in redirecting frustrations and depressions toward an external "enemy", poisoning the public climate and generating distrust and aggression against everything "Chinese" (or Asian). A poll by the *Pew Research Center* showed a continuous deterioration in public opinion toward China since 2017, with 81 percent "unfavorable" and 43 percent "very unfavorable" in 2024.[29] European countries exhibit a more mixed picture. Although a negative trend is observable, according to a poll in 11 EU countries[30] by the *European Council on Foreign Relations* in April 2023, 43 percent declared that China remains a necessary partner for Europe with which it must strategically cooperate. Only 24 percent saw China as a rival and 11 percent as an adversary.[31]

In Eastern Europe, Serbia and Hungary have become outliers with a positive opinion of China in recent years. According to a recent poll by the *International Republican Institute*, 14 percent of Serbians saw China as their most important ally (second place after Russia) and 88 percent viewed China as "highly favorable" in general, while 36 percent saw the US as the "most important threat" to Serbia. Also, in North Macedonia, Bosnia and Herzegovina, and Albania, 56, 53, and 43 percent of respondents, respectively, viewed China as "highly" or "somewhat" favorable.[32] A 2022 poll by the *Central and Eastern European Center for Asian Studies* found that around 51 percent of Hungarians had favorable views of China, indicating a positive trend linked to increasing economic ties.[33]

In African, Latin American, and Asian countries, as well as in Russia, the positive correlation between direct contacts of the population with Chinese companies and workers, Chinese infrastructure investments, and positive public opinion is even more pronounced. In Kenya, 72 percent; in Nigeria, 80 percent; and in Mexico, 57 percent viewed China "favorably" in a 2023 *Pew Research poll.*[34] Especially since the war in Ukraine and the subsequent fallout with Western countries, public opinion of China in Russia has soared, with a record 71 percent approving of China's leadership, while views of Western countries have plummeted, according to a 2023 *Gallup* poll.[35]

A recent international poll[36] of 4900 adults in 41 countries, showing 7-day moving averages of daily surveys between Jan. 1, 2024, and May 30, 2025, conducted by *Morning Consult* for *Axios*, has exhibited a continuously increasing international reputation of China and a rapid deterioration of the US reputation since January 2025, in the Trump 2.0 term, as noted above. China's international reputation surpassed that of the USA in early 2025.

Finally, in a "Democracy Perception Index 2025",[37] sponsored by a Western "Alliance of Democracies" and regularly polled from over 110,000 respondents in 100 countries, 52 percent of the countries reported that the goal of democracy is to improve living standards and well-being. This oddly contrasts with the study's ongoing characterization of China as "non-democratic", while exactly this—improving people's well-being—has been the very quintessence and *raison d'être* of the PR China, developed over decades in its development conception of *Whole-Process People's Democracy*,[38] and which has continuously, for centuries and millennia, characterized the entire South-East Asian understanding of the state, government, culture, and democracy. Yet people in the world apparently are more consistent in their evaluations than the Collective West's self-declared exclusive democracies. Thus, for the first time in the series of these polls,

> more countries around the world have a positive view of China than of the USA.[39]

This all matters as it is embedded in a larger relational context. The context spans from a weakening dollar, through a fall in foreign visitors and students to the USA, to a huge brain drain of top scientists in all disciplines who have left the USA in a considerable emigration wave since Trump 1.0. Hundreds and thousands of high-ranked scientists, notably Chinese and non-Chinese, have left the USA in the last decade, most of them for top positions at Chinese universities and research institutes, and notably, even non-Chinese scientists have been hired at Chinese institutions.

And the bigger picture will be painted in this book.

In a complex and volatile landscape of subjective global sentiments, let us make and continue our modest contribution here to ensuring and stabilizing a well-founded and qualified recognition, comprehension, and development toward increased mutual trust in the future. China and the potentials of Western cooperation with it deserve it. Humankind would win.

Understanding China? Understanding Ourselves? What's Next?

What remains for this book? How do we develop a productive, truly and sustainably problem-solving approach to global relations in the possible spectrum between peaceful coexistence and cooperation on the one hand, and hostilities, ideological trenches, sanction regimes, expansionism and interventionism, and hot war on the other? To this end, we will evaluate facts and insights about China in many areas and from the international literature.

We know from practical life experience that sometimes we "can't see the forest for the trees". We see the details but do not recognize that these form a system with its own quality. We will have to learn to recognize both the many and manifold Chinese "trees" and the dynamic Chinese "forest". We know that it requires a delicate cognitive performance to generate a "gestalt switch", so that we recognize things in context or see them differently than usual.

Economists, for example, have been struggling for 200 years to explain the interrelationships of the economic system and have tried to bring their theoretical paradigms into handy characteristic formulas: "It's about labor costs." "No, it's about overall economic demand." "It's about the money supply." "No, it's about income distribution." "It's about public saving." "No, it's about public investing." "It's about the prevailing social institutions." "No, it's about the natural environment and future provision", and so on. One can try to "switch" back and forth between competing, and often also complementary, theoretical paradigms, but they will not dissolve and merge into a cheap compromise or "average". The "truth" may reveal itself in the long term through the interaction of paradigms with each other and with reality. It might then contain certain elements of several, but with a specific, own, new quality and systemic character.

Everyone also knows the example of the sudden cognitive gestalt switch in the drawing, in which some see the head of an old woman, others the contours of a young woman. Once I have fixed my perception on the head of the old woman, it will be difficult for me to recognize the young woman, even if another person helps me and explains the young woman's contours to me. Often it takes me a long time to make the switch. Again and again, I have to look and detach myself from "my view" of the picture and gain distance. Suddenly, "the other" is there; I see it as a whole, as a "picture", as a system. And I suddenly wonder why I couldn't see the now "obvious" for so long. And it may also slip away from me again; I have to rework the realization, the understanding of "the other", again and again.

It is nothing other than normal, real daily life that this book is about. For many, China is far away, but by now it has also become so close. We may open up a new world and better understand our own. We wish to arouse interest with information and backgrounds, to get to know China better in its unprecedented change. So, let us now approach the "inside" of this "new number one": "What's going on in China?" Why and in what way is this country different? Could a "paradigm shift" toward new, better forms of globalization, global environmental development, and also for cooperation for us—and, we are setting the bar high—for the future of humankind, become possible with China? Let's go and see.

Notes

1. In this context, "intercultural" books such as the German book by S. Baron, G. Yin-Baron, 2018. *Die Chinesen. Psychogramm einer Weltmacht* [The Chinese. Psychogram of a World Power], Berlin: Econ., which strive

for an explanation and understanding of Chinese culture and social psychology, are to be recommended.
2. Kissinger (2011), 20 f. (The numbers are in year-2000 prices and in PPP.)
3. Frank (1998).
4. E.g., Isabella M. Weber, *How China Escaped Shock Therapy: The Market Reform Debate*, London, New York: Routledge, 2021.
5. Martin Wolf, "The challenge of one world, two systems", *Financial Times*, January 29, 2019: https://www.ft.com/content/b20a0d62-23b1-11e9-b329-c7e6ceb5ffdf, visited May 20, 2024.
6. *Steingarts Morning Briefing*, April 18, 2019.
7. Ibid. Translated by the authors.
8. R. Fitzthum, *China verstehen: Vom Aufstieg zur Wirtschaftsmacht und der Eindämmungspolitik der USA* [Understanding China. On the rise to economic power and the containment policy of the USA], Vienna, 2018 (Fitzthum 2018a).
9. For recent English books outside the ideological trenches, on top of books mentioned earlier, we just name another one at this point: Roland Boer, *Socialism with Chinese Characteristics: A Guide for Foreigners* (Boer 2021).
10. For example: Michael Hudson, "America's Neoliberal Financialization Policy vs. China's Industrial Socialism", *michael-hudson.com*, April 14, 2021: https://michael-hudson.com/2021/04/americas-neoliberal-financialization-policy-vs-chinas-industrial-socialism/, visited May 21, 2024; and Domenico Losurdo, "Has China Turned to Capitalism?—Reflections on the Transition from Capitalism to Socialism", *International Critical Thought* 7/2017, 15–31.
11. See Ulrich Brand, Markus Wissen, *The Imperial Mode of Living. Everyday Life and the Ecological Crisis of Capitalism*. London, 2021.
12. ZEW – Leibniz Centre for European Economic Research, "Innovationsindikator 2023 [Innovation Indicator 2023]", *ZEW*, 2023: https://www.innovationsindikator.de/fileadmin/innovationsindikator/downloads/Innovationsindikator-2023.pdf, visited May 21, 2024. Quote translated by the author.
13. For example: Guy Chazan, "How Germany's 'debt brake' broke the budget", *Financial Times*, November 23, 2023: https://www.ft.com/content/60674329-5be3-4802-a05a-851ee2990efd, visited May 21, 2024.
14. For example: Euronews & AP, "Experts slash economic growth forecast for 'ailing' Germany", *Euronews*, March 27, 2024: https://www.euronews.com/business/2024/03/27/experts-slash-economic-growth-for-germany; Jessica Parker & Damien McGuinness, "German economy is in 'troubled waters' – ministry", *BBC News*, February 21, 2024: https://

www.bbc.com/news/world-europe-68361717, both visited June 16, 2025.
15. https://www.aspi.org.au/report/critical-technology-tracker/, accessed June 14, 2025.
16. M. Poppe, "Warum in spätestens 20 Jahren kein Chinese mehr ein Auto kaufen wird [Why in at most 20 years no Chinese will buy a car anymore]", *Focus*, September 2, 2019: https://www.focus.de/perspektiven/14-laender-14-reporter/14-laender-14-reporter-china-warum-in-spaetestens-20-jahren-kein-chinese-mehr-ein-auto-kaufen-wird_id_10077546.html, visited May 17, 2024.
17. Ibid. (Quotes translated by the authors.)
18. For example: Matt Sheehan, "How China Became an Innovation Powerhouse", *Carnegie Endowment*, January 10, 2023: https://carnegieendowment.org/posts/2023/01/how-china-became-an-innovation-powerhouse?lang=en, visited May 23, 2024.
19. Folker Hellmeyer, *Solvecon Forex Report* 23.4.2019, p. 4. (Translated by the authors.)
20. "IShowSpeed" on *YouTube*: https://www.youtube.com/c/ISHOWSPEED, accessed June 16, 2025.
21. See for example: George Wright, "White House outlines TikTok deal that would give US control of algorithm", *BBC*, September 21, 2025: https://www.bbc.com/news/articles/c89dd747yz7o, visited October 3, 2025.
22. Yitian Zhang, "How to Install the English Version of Xiaohongshu (Little Red Book) in 2025?", *DFC Studio*, September 19, 2024: https://dfc-studio.com/blog/how-to-install-the-english-version-of-xiaohongshu-little-red-book-in-2024/, accessed June 15, 2025.
23. "Atlantik-Brücke" [Atlantic-Bridge] is a German non-profit association that aims to promote European-American and especially German-American relations, i.e., "Transatlanticism", for example: https://www.atlantik-bruecke.org/en/atlantik-bruckes-beginnings/, visited May 23, 2024.
24. E.g., P. Carstens, "Deutsche haben mehr Vertrauen in China als in Amerika [Germans trust China more than the USA]", *Frankfurter Allgemeine Zeitung*: February 8, 2019, https://www.faz.net/aktuell/politik/inland/umfrage-deutsche-haben-mehr-vertrauen-in-china-als-in-amerika-16031359.html, visited May 23, 2024.
25. For example: *Weser-Kurier*, May 28, 2019, p. 17.
26. For example: H. Meyer, "Vertrauen in China sinkt – Investitionen aber nicht [Trust in China is falling – but not investment]", *Bundesverband deutscher Banken* [Association of German Banks], March 21, 2024: https://bankenverband.de/finanzbildung/vertrauen-china-sinkt-investitionen-aber-nicht, visited May 23, 2024; also: S. Marsh, "Exclusive:

German investment in China rises to record high", *Reuters*, February 14, 2024: https://www.reuters.com/markets/german-investment-china-rises-new-record-high-2024-02-14/, visited May 23, 2024.

27. See D. Lubin, "Collapsing foreign direct investment might not be all bad for China's economy", *Chatham House*, December 15, 2023, https://www.chathamhouse.org/2023/12/collapsing-foreign-direct-investment-might-not-be-all-bad-chinas-economy, visited May 23, 2024.
28. A. Liang, "Why businesses are pulling billions in profits from China", *BBC*, November 14, 2023, https://www.bbc.com/news/business-67353177, visited May 23, 2024.
29. C. Huang, L. Silver, L. Clancy, "Americans Remain Critical of China", *Pew Research Center*, May 1, 2024: https://www.pewresearch.org/global/2024/05/01/americans-remain-critical-of-china/#:~:text=Today%2C%2081%25%20of%20U.S.%20adults,in%20recent%20years%20(71%25), visited May 23, 2024.
30. These being Austria, Bulgaria, Denmark, France, Germany, Hungary, Italy, the Netherlands, Poland, Spain, and Sweden.
31. A. Bachulska, "Recent Polling Uncovers the Blind Spots in the European China Debate", *China Observers in Central and Eastern Europe (CHOICE),* July 4, 2023, https://chinaobservers.eu/recent-polling-uncovers-the-blind-spots-in-the-european-china-debate/, visited May 23, 2024.
32. S. Turčalo, "Xi's Visit and a New Poll: The Geopolitical Contest for the Western Balkans", *Just Security*, May 20, 2024, https://www.justsecurity.org/95830/china-serbia-western-balkans-poll/, visited May 23, 2024.
33. B. Szalai, R. Standish, "New Polls Show Increased Support In Hungary For Ties With China", *Radio Free Europe*, July 24, 2022, https://www.rferl.org/a/hungary-china-ties-warming-standish/31957393.html, visited May 23, 2024.
34. L. Silver, C. Huang, L. Clancy, "China's Approach to Foreign Policy Gets Largely Negative Reviews in 24-Country Survey: Still, views of China – and its soft power – are more positive in middle-income countries", *Pew Research Center*, July 27, 2023, https://www.pewresearch.org/global/2023/07/27/chinas-approach-to-foreign-policy-gets-largely-negative-reviews-in-24-country-survey/, visited May 23, 2024.
35. G. Zapryanova, B. Vigers, "Russians Continue to Warm to China", *Gallup*, December 7, 2023, https://news.gallup.com/poll/545267/russians-continue-warm-china.aspx, visited May 23, 2024.
36. Emily Peck, "Exclusive: China's global favorability rising, views of the U.S. turn negative", *Axios*, June 2, 2025: https://www.axios.com/2025/06/02/china-us-global-opinions, accessed June 15, 2025.

37. Democracy Perception Index 2025, https://146165116.fs1.hubspotuser-content-eu1.net/hubfs/146165116/DPI%202025.pdf, accessed June 15, 2025.
38. E.g., "Whole Process People's Democracy", *China Insight*: https://www.idcpc.gov.cn/english2023/dzwk/zgkx/202307/P020230717028654090872.pdf, accessed June 15, 2025.
39. Democracy Perception Index 2025, ibid., p. 5.

Selected and Recommended Literature

Boer, Roland. 2021. *Socialism with Chinese Characteristics: A Guide for Foreigners.* Singapore: Springer.

Frank, Andre Gunder. 1998. *ReOrient. Global Economy in the Asian Age.* Oakland, CA: University of California Press.

Kissinger, Henry A. 2011. *On China.* New York: Penguin.

Further Cited Literature

Fitzthum, Robert, 2018a. *China verstehen. Vom Aufstieg zur Wirtschaftsmacht und der Eindämmungspolitik der USA* [Understanding China. On the rise to economic power and the containment policy of the USA], Vienna: Promedia.

PART II

From a Poor Developing Country to a Leading Nation: Structures and Processes of Social and Economic Success and Robustness

CHAPTER 5

"A Planned Economy? Oh Gosh!"

Yes, But Different Where Plans Are Not Just Election-Campaign Fakes—The 14th Five-Year Plan (2021–2025), Grand Development Objectives and Mobilizations, the 15th FYP and Long-Range Planning Toward 2035, Governance Reforms, and "China Experimentation"

With its FYPs, China has developed and provides an information tool that gives insight into its ongoing reform, restructuring, and development. If we want to know about the various development fields, policy areas, programs, and measures, the FYPs contain most of what one needs to understand China's development—a comprehensive national program that is more than just a regular government plan.

As we refer to the (now expiring) 14th FYP, we will find many cross-connections among the complex, integrated, and largely overlapping policy areas, issues, and chapters. We will briefly list issues from the 14th FYP document as well as further policy aspects of this five-year period. As an overview, we will present keywords for major areas,[1] many of which will be outlined in more detail throughout this book:

1. ***Economic performance, growth, and income***: The shift from traditional overall growth toward qualitative growth and building a "moderately prosperous society" ("Vision 2035"); increasing

W. Elsner, E. Najmehchi, *The Rise of China*,
https://doi.org/10.1007/978-3-032-20260-4_5

per-capita GDP while keeping average annual GDP growth "within an appropriate (i.e., moderate) range"; given current turbulent conditions, no explicit GDP growth target has been set for the first time.

2. ***Industrial modernization***: Strengthening the industrial economy, manufacturing, and the service sector; maintaining and upgrading even "old" industries through automation and increasingly high-quality productive forces.
3. ***Innovation and R&D capacities, science and technology***: Increasing R&D spending above GDP growth, targeting clusters of leading technology areas.
4. "***Dual circulation***": Reorienting the economy toward the domestic market and demand, while promoting international trade and investment with reliable partner countries for sustainable development ("domestic–international dual circulation").
5. ***Rural revitalization*** through better infrastructure and (public) services, equalizing income distribution, promoting a two-way flow of resources between rural and urban areas to boost rural dynamics, and boosting agricultural production capacity, diversification, and structural adjustment.
6. ***Urbanization strategies***: Further reforming the household registration system (*Hukou*) by lifting registration restrictions and granting urban residency status for rural migrants and students; determining a national target urbanization rate; promoting people-centered, qualitative urban development toward more livable, green, and eco-friendly cities and metropolises; improving affordable housing, accessible social services, infrastructure, urban local participatory governance and management, and new city centers.
7. ***Regional dynamics***: Improving regional economic structures and development, equalizing division of labor, through planning and quality-oriented, ecological development.
8. ***International opening up and BRI cooperation***: Further advancement of the "reform and opening-up" process, encouraging incoming foreign direct investment (iFDI), furthering the "Belt and Road Initiative (BRI)", and promoting multi-dimensional, multi-level win-win cooperation—from trade, inward/outward FDI, technology, and innovation, through education, to people-to-people contacts.

9. ***Ecological civilization***: Green development and accelerating climate policy, promoting renewable energy—including fusion energy or nuclear thorium technology—long-distance transport, and storage technologies; reaching maximum CO_2 emissions by 2030 and complete carbon neutrality before 2060; continuing forestation programs and the green-cities program; emission-free companies, industrial zones, or data centers; chemical-free agriculture; sustainable marine economy and fishing; new-energy vehicles (NEVs); high-speed trains and Maglevs; ecological lifestyles ("Ant Forest" app) and consumer products.
10. ***Education, employment, and entrepreneurship***: Increasing employment opportunities through the development of employability skills and entrepreneurship; strengthening and protecting young start-up firms; public education for all, as well as enrollment numbers in higher education, fostering job creation.
11. ***Social security***: Expanding, integrating, and collectivizing universal social security; adapting to demographic issues—maternity leave and insurance, infrastructure for children, school support, young-family support and financial assistance, local spaces for children in cities; old-age policies—gray-hair economy, consumption, local infrastructure, recreation and tai chi, pension funds, care systems, networking among the elderly.
12. ***Public healthcare***: Strengthening "Healthy China"—improving universal medical insurance, affordability, and quality; improving hospitals, healthcare personnel and their remuneration, local residential accessibility of healthcare services; promoting sports and health campaigns.
13. ***Culture: general trust and happiness***: Maintaining world-leading levels of general trust and happiness in international polls; developing social trustworthiness; promoting education and cultural industries (books, movies, music, theatre, travel, public sports, and mass dancing).
14. ***Public security***: Ensuring economic security in the areas of food, energy, services, and resources; political participation in the local residential area; local People's Mediation Committees.
15. ***Public infrastructure***: Expanding public infrastructure—from the high-speed rail network, substituting inland flights, through accessible and cost-free IT infrastructure, recreational facilities

within walking distance in residential areas, to local civil information and advice centers providing all public services.

16. ***Digitization***: Building a "Digital China" —strengthening capacities in big data and cyberspace; building a "digital economy", highly integrated digital services, "digital society", and "digital government"; data protection and individual information sovereignty: new Data Security Law (DSL), Personal Information Protection Law (PIPL), and Civil Code—individual rights and protection against private data collection, reviewing one's data in civic centers; local social credit-point systems; cracking down on previously predatory IT oligopolies.
17. ***State and markets: industrial, fiscal, and monetary policies***: Promoting synergies between government market regulation and resource allocation through markets, within the framework of proactive industrial policies; reforming fiscal and monetary policy, regulating the central-bank and general-bank system, and the financial sector to better serve the real economy and national development, protect firms and start-ups, and provide accessible housing and infrastructure; cracking down on over-speculated real-estate oligopolies.
18. ***Poverty elimination***: Continuing earlier poverty eradication (2021) through multidimensional policy integration; developing rural low-income groups and areas; further preventing vulnerable groups from slipping back into poverty; integrating forestation, agricultural, peasant, and village-development policies.
19. ***Population policy and population aging, ethnic minorities***: From One- to Two- and Three-Child Policies; expanding local family counseling and support, maternal and child health care, and school relief; elderly care; minority policy: major minorities live in self-governed autonomous provinces, prefectures, and counties; multilingual and multicultural education; an overall multireligious culture.
20. ***Developing democracy—"Whole-Process People's Democracy"***: Expanding community-level participatory governance in residential civic centers and communities (shequ); integrating lower levels of the state into civil society and self-governance (e.g., People's Mediation Committees); improving women's rights and empowerment—women now form the majority of start-up owners; National People's Congresses (NPC) and parallel Chinese People's Political Consultative Conferences (CPPCC) at all administrative

levels: local, municipal/autonomous regions/provincial, and national.

21. ***"One Country, Two Systems" policy***: Taiwan—socio-economic integration in Cross-Strait relations; Fujian integration and settlement model; fostering people-to-people contacts; Hong Kong and Macau.
22. ***International relations***: Foreign policy principles of peaceful coexistence; primacy of diplomacy; integration of global initiatives, development programs, and funding programs for the Global South into UN South-South Cooperation; BRI cooperative forums with Africa, Latin America and the Caribbean, Central Asia, and the Arab world; strategic cooperation through BRICS and the SCO.

The surprising and dizzying breadth of policy fields and measures indicates a swift and ongoing process of qualification, restructuring, and adaptation to current circumstances, embedded in a long-term perspective. This stands in remarkable contrast to the frequent petrification of long-term developmental decision-making under the late neoliberal austerity regimes of Western NFC, where socially progressive reforms mostly appear unattainable because they are allegedly unaffordable, while public and private bureaucracies entrench restrictive existing power structures.

As an ironic saying goes: In the West, governments may change, but politics and policies remain the same; in China, the government doesn't change, but policies are changing all the time.

In the West, facing dwindling prospects for social advancement (notorious PISA results send their regards,[2] as do declining public health, increasing inequality, and the growth of poverty sectors), many simply cling to what they have achieved. Optimism for the future and social dynamism lag behind amid widespread defensive attitudes, while conflicts and struggles dominate in the face of deepening social divisions. Burnout, fatigue, demotivation, and dropout are widespread. In the end, understandably, a hedgehog mentality, narrow-mindedness, resentment, and xenophobia displace open social conditions, perspectives, and attitudes. Fears of decline and threat generate their own social psychology and political culture. Things are developing differently in large parts of the Global South, particularly in Southeast Asia.

The Chinese 14th Five-Year Plan followed a major restructuring of the central government (known as the State Council) and its ministries by the 13th National People's Congress (NPC, 2018–2023) in 2018. The 14th

NPC (2023–2028[3]) subsequently implemented another minor reform of the State Council in 2023. This demonstrates that the central government and its agencies are subject to continuous adaptation and reform.

Some of the main restructuring measures, as documented by observers such as *NPC Observer*[4] and *China Briefing*,[5] are as follows:

- The ***Ministry of Science and Technology*** (MOST) has received increased importance and authority ("macro-management functions") in supporting scientific and technological developments (in areas such as AI, quantum science, green technologies, etc.). This follows China's "new type of whole-nation system" (新型举国体制, *xinxing juguo tizhi*), a vivid figurative expression, which has been in place since 2019. The system had originally been introduced during the classic planned-economy period. After fading during the reform and opening-up era following 1978, it was reintroduced at a more sophisticated level to increase the government's role in mobilizing resources in key areas, now integrating market mechanisms.[6] This has allowed quicker, more qualified, and better-calibrated responses to US technological and decoupling pressures[7] and was designed to strengthen China's technological self-reliance. Furthermore, a new ***Central Science and Technology Commission*** was established as a "body for coordinating decision-making and deliberation", administered by MOST.[8] Additionally, the ***Ministry of Industry and Information Technology*** (MIIT), responsible for planning and implementing industrial policies and technical standards, was reorganized, taking over certain responsibilities related to high-tech development and industrialization, including specialized international cooperative high-tech industrial development zones.[9]
- A new National ***Financial Regulatory Administration*** (NFRA) was established to oversee, regulate, and develop the financial industry. In addition, a ***Central Financial Commission*** (CFC), described as a "body for coordinating decision-making and deliberation" of the CPC Central Committee, was created.[10] This indicates a major focus of China on developing and opening up the financial sector during the 14th FYP period and beyond.
- In that context, the ***People's Bank of China*** (PBoC), China's central bank, was reorganized. For example, regular supervision of the private financial sector (banks, investment funds, P2P credit associations, etc.) was transferred to the NFRA (above). The NFRA now super-

vises the entire financial industry in coordination with the PBoC, while securities fall under the supervision of the ***China Securities Regulatory Commission*** (CSRC).[11] The PBoC has increased responsibilities for regulating public banks, overseeing top bankers' salary and bonus caps, and supporting broader national development goals and programs, such as the affordable housing program for low-wage migrant workers, who are not to spend more than 10 percent of their income on housing. Together with the ***State Administration for Market Regulation*** (China's competition authority, below), the PBoC has taken the lead in cracking down on predatory financial and informational practices established by IT oligopolies and conglomerates (such as Alibaba/Ant Financial Group) against farmers, SMEs, and private households, culminating in the breakup of Alibaba and its earlier financial branch (2021–2023). The PBoC has also taken responsibility for the deliberate downscaling of over-speculated real-estate sector oligopolies (Evergrande, Country Garden, and similar firms), advising banks to cover the costs of non-performing loans (2022–2024). Overall, the PBoC now oversees national development goals and far exceeds the narrow austerity obsession characteristic of neoliberal central banks in NFC.

- A ***National Data Administration*** (NDA) was created under the State Council's ***National Development and Reform Commission*** (NDRC). It is tasked with coordinating and promoting "the development of basic data systems" and overseeing "the integrated sharing, development, and use of data resources".[12] This includes regulating the digital economy and implementing a national big-data and AI strategy, while also safeguarding new individual data-protection rights under the Data Security Law, Personal Information Protection Law, and Civil Code.[13]
- The ***China National Intellectual Property Administration*** (CNIPA), China's patent and trademark office, was elevated to a top-level agency under the State Council, putting it on par with the powerful ***State Administration for Market Regulation*** (SAMR). The latter has intervened massively in recent years against oligopolies, mainly in network industries such as IT, due to their cumulative concentration tendencies.[14] Despite having dismantled Alibaba and converted Ant Financial Group into a regularly controlled bank, SAMR has also required the top 40 IT companies to open up their platforms, making them interoperable and non-exclusive, and rewrit-

ing their customer contracts. Chinese citizens now have a one-click option to prevent any private data collection from their internet activity. Even public agencies are prohibited from using, for example, health data for any local social credit-point experiments.[15]

- The ***Ministry of Ecology and Environment*** (MEE), responsible for environmental protection, green development, and implementing *ecological civilization* (above), was assigned environment-related science and technology policies previously overseen by MOST.[16]
- The ***National Health Commission*** (NHC), founded in 2018, took over responsibility for health technology from MOST. It ceded some responsibilities to the ***Ministry of Civil Affairs*** (MCA), particularly regarding population aging, including transferring oversight of the ***China Association on Aging***.[17]

These are just some exemplary government restructurings as of 2025, with more detail provided in later chapters of this book. However, they already indicate that government restructuring goes hand in hand with new FYP priorities and major development objectives. The restructurings of 2019–2023 reflect new goals and challenges, including technology and R&D, financial modernization, nationwide ecological restructuring, the shrinking and aging population, and the West's decoupling and hybrid wars in trade, investment, technology, science, education, and people-to-people exchanges.

The Berlin-based *Mercator Institute for China Studies* (MERICS) analyzed the 14th FYP in detail[18] and identified its most important features as follows:

- The shift from quantitative to qualitative growth. This is linked to the "inward cycle" of the broader *dual-circulation strategy*, aimed at strengthening domestic economic and social development, boosting private consumption, and reducing dependence on Western imports and technology. Instead of conventional growth targets, "systemic resilience" and "self-sufficiency" were emphasized.
- For the objective of "new quality growth", technological innovation, digitalization, and scientific progress through basic research were identified as key areas. Highlighted were fields such as "blockchain, semiconductors, and next-generation AI", where, for example, blockchain and distributed-ledger technology already permeates the entire Chinese financial and monetary sectors (e.g., E-Yuan, money

transfers, interbank balancing). In addition, China has effectively won the "chip war" through new technologies, designs, and "outside-the-box" solutions.

- Another key area was *national security*, understood broadly to include food, economic, social, energy, technology, and military security.
- It was clarified that the plan did not imply "decoupling" from the global economy. Rather, the "dual circulation strategy" indicates that the international cycle remains essential.
- A number of national "key projects" (27) were identified in the areas of "urbanization, infrastructure, and regional coordination", including airports, roads, and railways. Other areas were noted as remaining unchanged from the 13th FYP, such as culture, agriculture and rural development, sustainability and ecology, healthcare, and the extension or improvement of public services.
- A new emphasis was placed on "systemic resilience", against the background of the Chinese government's unexpectedly negative experience with the US Trump 1.0 administration (2017–2020). Systemic resilience is to be achieved by strengthening the domestic economy against external risks and international challenges, which connects back to the overarching theme of dual circulation (above).[19]

This rough overview may appear, to Western readers who have been largely unaware of China or who have relied solely on Western mainstream media, to be too benevolent toward China. Therefore, we will provide more detailed information, citing sources from around the world, covering the full breadth of views, data, and analyses from East and West, North and South.

In fact, these FYPs indicate a surprising—and for many, overwhelming—broad and deep reform and opening dynamic, which appears unparalleled in large parts of sclerotized state and oligopoly bureaucracies in the West. As this book will show, such highly integrated FYPs, embedded in long-term development perspectives, are more than just colorful words or verbal fireworks that lose their value after an election campaign.

These policy dynamics are actively implemented so that everyone—the average Chinese citizen, young families, students, start-up entrepreneurs, scientists, professionals of all kinds, large corporations, and even Western companies and financial investors—can orient themselves through them. FYPs, rather than being rigid top-down quantitative prescriptions as they once were under Eurocentric approaches to socialism, serve as national orientations that support and facilitate professional, social, and private life through multiple channels. They coordinate, guide, and mobilize many activities and forces. We will discuss this in detail in several areas.

The plan was published after China celebrated its 70th anniversary in October 2019 and reflected on an impressive development success: the country had solved a number of humanity's challenges within a few decades. For example, it had more than doubled the life expectancy of its population, eradicated absolute poverty and illiteracy, and largely achieved gender equality in most basic socio-economic areas—a historically unique catch-up process for a large nation (figures later).[20] Without long-term perspectives and national goal-setting, understood and embraced by the people so as to mobilize them, such achievements would not have been possible.

Even the US-dominated World Bank elaborated on that "secret" of China in a study using the example of the "explosive" development of the Chinese railway system: the coordination of state, companies, banks, and science created long-term planning security for all agents involved, enabling long-term loans for investments at low interest rates, since the nation stands behind the projects. This coordination also facilitated standardization and minimized risks. The World Bank, which normally imposes counter-programs of "free" and deregulated markets on its debtors, attributes a key role to such opposing systemic mechanisms. China was able to build and maintain two-thirds of the global high-speed rail network in just ten years—and today boasts one of the best railway systems in the world in terms of punctuality, comfort, service, and moderate fares. As a result of many interrelated efficiency and cost factors—definitely not "state subsidies", nor "low wages", and not even mainly economies of large scale[21]—a kilometer of high-speed rail track in China can be produced at about a third lower cost than in comparable Western countries. Here too, the World Bank highlights the speed at which complex infrastructure can be built when actors receive "clear leadership and responsibilities".[22] The World Bank also calculates the CO_2 savings achieved because the Chinese high-speed rail system can now effectively replace numerous domestic flights.[23] This is expected to increase in the near future with new generations of faster bullet trains and a new maglev generation (magnetic levitation, ex-German Transrapid) coming into operation. Bullet trains will connect all major cities, running mostly on an hourly schedule, with much shorter waiting times compared to flying. More details are provided later in this book.

All this becomes feasible through high policy and agency integration, holistic and long-term socio-economic thinking, and comprehensive planning and framework provision.

Planning for the sake of planning? Planning to serve state bureaucracies? As we may have known it from the late, outcompeted, and exhausted Soviet Union? No longer in China. Instead, vibrant planning verifiably improves people's well-being. The lists above are meant to illustrate elements of a nation's and socio-economic system's success. Here, our goal is simply to arouse interest, not to anticipate everything.

Outlook: The 15th FYP (2026–2030)

The Fourth Plenary Session of the 20th Central Committee in October 2025 marked a critical juncture in China's policy trajectory, laying the groundwork for the 15th FYP. Preliminary reporting already pointed out some central priorities: These include bolstering technological, organizational, and macro-steering innovations. They are set to advance, among others, an "AI Plus" strategy to accelerate a comprehensive digital transformation. They are designed, further, to strengthen economic resilience through structural balancing (e.g., continuing downgrading of the real-estate sector), industrial upgrading (even of "old" industries), through supply-chain security, balancing market competition (stepping down overly fierce and counterproductive rivalry, e.g., in the EV sector). And they are heading toward expanding domestic consumptive demand. This all-embracing framework plan also reaffirms China's commitment to green development and the ecological civilization, shifting from controlling energy consumption to targeting carbon emissions, while maintaining the long-term goal of carbon neutrality by 2060.[24] This planning frame is also a decisive stepping stone to what is considered a socialist modernization to be further operationalized and realized by 2035.

The prioritization of manufacturing embraces a "modern industrial system", combining new, emerging sectors, such as aerospace, biomanufacturing, hydrogen, new materials, and quantum technology, and upgrades to traditional industries like mining, chemicals, and machinery. High and sustained investment, along with accelerated adoption of digital, smart, and green technologies, aims to consolidate China's industrial leadership across a growing range of sectors, from electric vehicles to wind turbines.[25]

Early information about the plan (which has been decided in the "Two Sessions" in March 2026 and been published in its entirety thereafter), thus, has already indicated that industrial, technological, and macroeconomic *autonomy* has become a core factor of China's planning of the coming years, a further development of the "grand idea" of the 14th FYP of "dual circulation", i.e., a complete domestic circuit combined with an intensifying global exchange with reliable countries: This aims to reduce dependence on foreign technology, particularly amid US (and EU) export restrictions on semiconductors and other advanced equipment, and the closing of their domestic economies against Chinese products, technologies, and firms, while securing critical resources and imports such as rare earth elements.

So, next to domestic priorities, the 15th FYP of course emphasizes China's global role. For example, through "high-level opening-up", "two-way investment cooperation" (i/oFDI), and the Belt and Road Initiative, China seeks to integrate its industrial capacity, capital, and technology with the markets, labor, and resources of other economies.[26] The FYP envisions deeper multilateral engagement to stabilize supply chains, promote international cooperation, and advance a governance model that balances efficiency, equity, and long-term strategic planning[27]—something that can be seen as a counter-proposal to the US-EU "decoupling" strategy. In fact, the 15th FYP will further rebuild and reshape the global VACs.

The 15th FYP thus articulates a vision of economic resilience through technological sovereignty, industrial strength, and trade and FDI networks, which all have emerged in direct reaction to geopolitical realities. It consolidates state control over critical sectors, extends China's influence in global economic governance, and positions the country as both a stabilizer and an ongoing engine of global growth. The plan aims to project continuity and opportunity for the world economy over the next five years amid geopolitical frictions and rising protectionism by the US-led West, while simultaneously reshaping the competitive landscape across key industries.

In a more domestic perspective, a major new "grand idea" of the 15th FYP is the overarching conception of "*New-Quality Productive Forces*" (NQPF), which can be seen as wrapping up the technological-industrial strategy. However, it is too often falsely reduced to just technological-industrial modernization. It will be much broader, encompassing a comprehensive *social modernization*. This will include a further upgrading of skills, schooling, vocational training, higher education, and R&D, while upgrading social security and insurance, developing child-, motherhood-, family-, and old-age infrastructures and networks, expanding self-governed local People's Mediation Committees (of which there are 690,000 in the country), and the more than 10,000 Community Service Centers that provide social services, legal consultation services, etc. In this way, it appears obvious that the idea of comprehensive modernization has an eye on the "socialist modernization" 2035 and, further, on the second centenary goal of 2049 (100th PRC anniversary), a "great, modern socialist country that is prosperous, strong, democratic, culturally advanced, harmonious and beautiful, and reasonably pollution free", to use repeated wording of Xi Jinping. The 15th FYP thus should be comprehended as a door opener to such an integrated technological, industrial, economic, social, and "popular" development, which deliberately includes democratic development toward what is called in China the "whole-process people's democracy". And in 2030, it should be judged by such integrative performance.

Notes

1. A summary of the plan can be accessed at: https://english.www.gov.cn/w/14thfiveyearplan/, visited May 25, 2024. For a full outline in English, see for example: https://www.fujian.gov.cn/english/news/202108/t20210809_5665713.htm#C3, visited May 25, 2024.
2. "Programme for International Student Assessment", a worldwide comparative study of student performance in different educational systems carried out by the OECD.
3. Note that NPC and FYP periods are not synchronic.
4. Changhao Wei, "A Guide to China's 2023 State Council Restructuring", *NPC Observer*, March 7, 2023: https://npcobserver.com/2023/03/china-npc-2023-state-council-reorganization/, visited May 25, 2024.
5. Arendse Huld, "Chinese Government Restructuring Explained – Changes to State Council Agencies", *China Briefing*, October 19, 2023: https://www.china-briefing.com/news/chinese-government-restructuring-explained-changes-to-state-council-agencies/, visited May 26, 2024.
6. E.g., Xiao Tan, Yao Song, "China's 'Whole Nation' Effort to Advance the Tech Industry", *The Diplomat*, April 21, 2022: https://thediplomat.com/2022/04/chinas-whole-nation-effort-to-advance-the-tech-industry/, visited May 26, 2024.
7. E.g., "The tech wars are about to enter a fiery new phase", *The Economist*, April 25, 2024: https://www.economist.com/international/2024/04/25/the-tech-wars-are-about-to-enter-a-fiery-new-phase, visited May 26, 2024.

8. Wei, ibid.
9. Huld, ibid.
10. Wei, ibid.
11. Huld, ibid.
12. Wei, ibid.
13. E.g., Tracy Qu, Xinmei Shen, Ben Jiang, "China's proposed National Data Bureau to become a powerful tool for Beijing to ratchet up development of digital economy, analysts say", *SCMP*, March 8, 2023: https://www.scmp.com/tech/policy/article/3212823/chinas-proposed-national-data-bureau-become-powerful-tool-beijing-ratchet-development-digital, visited May 26, 2024.
14. Wei, ibid.
15. One would wonder whether the West, namely the EU, struggling on those issues for decades, would ever be able to exert such restrictions on Western *Big Tech*. The EU, rather, is using Big Tech to execute its internet cancellation and data-collection policies.
16. Huld, ibid.
17. Ibid.
18. E.g., Nis Grünberg, "China's 14th Five-Year Plan – strengthening the domestic base to become a superpower", *MERICS*, April 9, 2021: https://merics.org/de/kommentar/chinas-14th-five-year-plan-strengthening-domestic-base-become-superpower, visited May 30, 2024.
19. Ibid.
20. For example: David Li, "70 Jahre Volksrepublik China: Spektakuläres Laboratorium für Entwicklungspolitik [70 years People's Republic of China: Spectacular laboratory for development policy]", *Weltwirtschaft und Entwicklung* 9/2019, 2–3.
21. We will discuss the true factors behind Chinese production efficiency, speed, and cost in this book. They are partly surprising, but by no means miraculous—rather, they reflect solid economics—and have little to do with the narratives that Western politicians and media like to believe, and encourage us to believe as well.
22. Cited and translated from: Georg Fahrion, "Die Bahn kommt – in China wirklich [The train arrives – in China for real]", *Spiegel*, December 14, 2019: https://www.spiegel.de/politik/ausland/eisenbahn-in-china-co2-ersparnis-ist-gering-noch-a-1300727.html, visited May 30, 2024.
23. Ibid.
24. Arendse Huld, "China's 15th Five-Year Plan: What We Know So Far", *China Briefing*, June 2, 2025: https://www.china-briefing.com/news/chinas-15th-five-year-plan-what-we-know-so-far/, visited November 11, 2025.

25. Alexander Brown, "China bets on manufacturing to carry growth in the next 5 years", In: *MERICS China Essentials special issue: China's next Five-Year Plan*, *MERICS*, October 30, 2025: https://merics.org/en/merics-briefs/merics-china-essentials-special-issue-chinas-next-five-year-plan, visited November 11, 2025.
26. "What China's 15th Five-Year Plan will bring to the world: Global Times editorial", *Global Times*, October 25, 2025: https://www.globaltimes.cn/page/202510/1346494.shtml, visited November 11, 2025.
27. Ibid.

CHAPTER 6

"Economy, Finance, and Money? A State-Subsidized Economy!"

Also Different: Economy and Finance, Technology and Skills, the Deep Structure of Robust Development—Agile Industrial Policy, Banking, Regulation and Deregulation, State and "Market", Cracking Down on Big-Tech, Real-Estate, and Finance Oligopolies

Bottom Up: Corporations, Small Businesses, Industries, and Government—"Agile Structural Policies", the Example of E-Mobility

Embeddedness, social trust, information flows: We already mentioned the widespread impression of Western professional travelers of the surprising ease and speed with which the Chinese deal with organizational, technological, and structural change. As we will show in the chapter on the social welfare system, this is partly due to the high degree of security of employability (not straightforward job stability) and the high certainty of expectations that the Chinese economic and social system can convey to people with their widely known national development goals. At the same time, people are given sufficient flexibility to adapt to rapid change, while

W. Elsner, E. Najmehchi, *The Rise of China*,
https://doi.org/10.1007/978-3-032-20260-4_6

maintaining a surprising range of options and keeping a feeling of social embeddedness.

Corresponding mechanisms for the labor market had also been developed in earlier decades by some Scandinavian countries under the keyword "flexicurity", a combination of then sufficient labor market flexibility and income security as well as social security. It had resulted in a culture where temporary unemployment, given a good replacement income, further education in unemployment phases, and good follow-up perspectives, were much more accepted than elsewhere in the West. That principle, no longer existent in more neoliberal Scandinavia nowadays, was further developed in the Chinese system: Existential insecurity is low in China today, thanks to the social insurance system, the safety and embeddedness functions of societal network structures (Guanxi, Danwei, below), the generally positive expectations of most Chinese regarding their income increase, housing and infrastructure accessibilities, the increasing purchasing power of their available income, and subjective perception of their integration into the publicly communicated national development goals.

Guanxi (literally meaning "relationships") in China refers to the network of personal relationships, which hardly leaves any decision unaffected. Formal contracts and agreements are often seen only as a guideline, from which one may deviate in favor of maintaining "guanxi".
Danwei (literally meaning "unit") was, after the family, the smallest social unit in the early People's Republic of China (PRC), based on the work sphere, with comprehensive social provision functions re. jobs, housing, social security, medical care, school supply, conflict mediation, and other social and supply issues.

This allows most Chinese to deal surprisingly easily, quickly, and flexibly with change and innovation—in contrast to many areas in the West, where people, under the impression of relatively rigid structures and the risk of potential loss of achieved social positions, by all means cling to what they achieved. This is connected to the fact that the Western NFC can no longer realize its earlier promise of a broad social and professional upward mobility nor nowadays even a general increase of well-being.

Staged and overlapping local and regional relationship systems, in combination with formal national regulation and system-wide integration, provide overall network structures that are favorable for a high level of general trust[1] and thus for the willingness to innovate and the openness to rapid information flow between people, organizations, industrial actors, and localities, which in the literature has been referred to as "Open Innovation".[2] It results in a general attitude of experimentation and learning, which has constituted a "philosophy" of the Chinese economy and industrial policy in particular.

China Experimentalism and China Speed: The entire political philosophy, from the setting of standards in industries (below) to the systemic question of the "path to socialism with Chinese characteristics", has been characterized as *Chinese Experimentalism*.[3] This is said to have emerged from the Chinese historical experience of nonlinear and discontinuous developments, and from the development goals, early experiments, failures, and corrections of a novel system, for which there had been and still are no models or master plans to refer to.

In addition, in the international business world, a related concept has emerged: *China Speed*, which refers to the high speed of Chinese developments. This also ties back to the observation that even successful Western high-tech companies—such as the German corporation Bosch—are increasingly seeing innovations emerge from their Chinese branches. Today, it is often Western corporations that learn from China, rather than vice versa[4] (more below).

National goals, market taming, and corporate regulation: There is a saying that particularly applies to China's developmental philosophy: Those who act may make mistakes. Those who don't act make a mistake. Applied to China's socio-economy: Those who experiment may make mistakes. And those who make mistakes, but are not discouraged and learn, may be successful in the end. But those who only secure the prevailing industry, distribution, property, and power structures—like neoliberal governments of any coalition of the different fractions of the one big neoliberal party—are making a mistake, which in the end does not even benefit their own clientele, as recent decades have increasingly shown.

The structures and structural changes required for experimentalism are evident in China's integrated structural policy, technology policy, product innovation policy, startup policy, anti-oligopoly policy, bank and credit policy, as well as policy toward the large SOEs.

Industrial policy principles: Chinese *structural policies* display certain characteristics:

- A systematic interplay of *regulation, deregulation, and re-regulation*, marked by phased and alternating cycles of standard-setting/regulation and "letting go".
- Ensuring the *flow of information* against an overly excessive and potentially counterproductive protection of intellectual property rights (IPR, patent protection).
- Political independence and *dominance of politics* over large corporations.
- Direct company subsidies are generally avoided: Instead, indirect support is provided to groups of companies, industries, technologies, products, networks, or regional clusters through more sophisticated and targeted strategies aligned with national priorities. These include investments in education and skills, basic and applied research, information flows in general, and the provision of both general and specialized infrastructure—whether hard or soft, easily accessible, and cost-free. Additional support is offered through targeted bank (credit) support, fostering supplier support through encouraging start-ups, network support, cluster and VAC strengthening, and, in the case of final (consumer) products, by strengthening product demand.[5] This stands in stark contrast to the current approach of massive company-based multibillion subsidies in the West (namely the EU) for attracted singular "lighthouse" projects that serve the ecological transformation.

The Chinese government, for example, allows innovations—namely by startups and SMEs in new, emerging industries—to run for longer time periods in order to determine which technological standards prove to be most appropriate. Only thereafter will regulation and standardization be decreed. And then a selection process will take place in the then "embedded" and regulated market.

In this way, China's government apparently uses regulations and deregulations not per se, but pragmatically. Even deregulations, such as the removal of maximum ticket prices in the airline industry some years ago, apparently do not occur in blind "market" faith, but mostly only for certain situations and periods, guided by the criterion of broader public benefit and intended outcomes.[6]

Intellectual Property Rights, Credible China, Rule of Law: Naturally, balancing open innovation (open information, open source…) with a guarantee of *IPR* and patented knowledge, which is usually owned by large corporations, is challenging. As we will explore in more detail, the *Credible China* and rule-of-law policies represent a clear political and cultural priority orientation for China's public actors, companies, and citizens. This means, for example, that Western international corporations, often operating through joint ventures in China, get their patents and proprietary IPR confirmed according to the law and secured before Chinese courts. They would get compensated in case of a misuse by a Chinese company (while those who have violated patents or copyrights of foreign companies are punished).[7]

Among Chinese market agents, namely large versus small firms, however, the public philosophy and practice seem to be slightly different.[8]

Generally, it is well-known that an overly restrictive IPR regime tends to weaken positive effects of other factors[9] such as education, credit supply, or infrastructures (and all those factors mentioned in the last bullet point above). Moreover, in Western economic literature and practice, it has long been acknowledged that open innovation, i.e., a far-from-total protection of patents, is more economically effective than perfect patent protection.[10] However, large corporations in deregulated neoliberal "markets" in NFC often use patents merely as assets in their portfolios to further drive up their "shareholder value", rather than as tools for genuine innovation, investment, or technological development. Frequently, they neither develop these patents themselves nor make productive use of them. Patent and IPR protection, according to extensive scientific and practical experience of the last three decades, was driven far beyond an economically productive level since the 1990s, under the pressure of large corporations, their cartels, and associations, especially Big-Tech, the large IT oligopolies of NFC.

Chinese central and provincial governments, therefore, ensure that IPR are regulated in such a way that they do not restrict the flow of information too much, especially to startups and young SMEs. In addition, they can rely on strategically important SOEs in key sectors to facilitate both intra- and inter-industry information flows, especially in support of SMEs and startups.

In fact, China apparently avoids excessive protection of knowledge (patents, software, designs, and the like) at critical points even among its large IT corporations, which would only too gladly shield their knowledge advantages against others. Here, the political priority rather seems to be that "information must flow"—so that it reaches where it is most effectively used, which is often in the newer, younger, and smaller companies (more on a case below).

Effective regulated markets, price competition, low prices, and purchasing power: In this respect, the political system generates an effective market that would no longer exist under the deregulated, oligopolistic conditions of NFC "markets". And in the end, several markets in China have recently demonstrated their ability to effectively maintain low costs and low prices. Low costs will result from the economies of scale in production, driven by the vast Chinese interior aggregate demand potential. But this alone does not sufficiently explain, for instance, the developments in the global car and, namely, electric-vehicles (EV) or new-energy vehicles (NEV) sector of recent years, where Chinese manufacturers have attained an international dominance by unique combinations of low costs/low prices and cutting-edge technical qualities and design.

And the fact that efficient economic production conditions leading to low-cost advantages will also translate into low prices—resulting in an average 50–60 percent price advantage of Chinese EV/NEV over Western cars—indicates that the Chinese socio-economic system and its regulated competitive markets have revived a mechanism that in the West has not been working anymore for over a century: industry-wide price competition. In China, young people, young professionals, and young families can afford a small state-of-the-art family-EV for under 10,000 USD, while Western policymakers apparently find their only "solution" in high protective custom tariffs against Chinese products, as practiced by the EU and USA, and which they simplistically claim are "subsidized", unable to look behind the veils of their simple world models to uncover the true sophisticated socio-economic mechanisms at work.

At times, some very strong forms of price competition may have to be somewhat moderated in order to prevent negative secondary effects on production and firm structures. The Chinese government is pursuing such moderation nowadays, particularly within the EV/NEV manufacturing sector.

Macroeconomically, low costs and price competition contribute to consistently lower inflation rates and an increasing difference in the purchasing power parities (PPP) between China and the West, which has made the Chinese GDP the largest in the world in PPP since 2016. Despite having a lower nominal GDP overall than the USA, China's population can often afford a higher level of real well-being.

The example of patent use: Returning to efficient socio-economic production conditions and to efficient information flows throughout the economy: Specifically, questions such as the appropriate level of patent protection for the patent holders, the duration of a patent's exclusivity, and whether patent holders should always have a licensing obligation, and if so, under what conditions (for example, at what prices), need to be addressed. In China, government and state agencies seem to pursue the philosophy that patent protection for the big ones should be limited to favor information access for the small ones, that licensing should always be done early, but that everything also is a question of appropriate licensing fees.

The example of SOEs: As a crucial element of its structural policies, the government scaled back the previous close relationships and formal privileges granted to the SOEs,[11] while simultaneously demanding meaningful contributions to national development from them and empowering them for that task. While they were subjected to market mechanisms and had to compete with private corporations, they were also empowered to lead technological development and investment directions within their respective industries and sectors—a role they embraced and fulfilled, particularly throughout the 2010s.

Limiting the power of Big Tech and other oligopolies: Capitalists of all kinds, no matter how rich and powerful they may be, must respect the dominance of politics and national development goals. The central government's dominance over large private corporations in China is certainly greater than the current level of political dominance over big capital in the West, although it has been increasing considerably in recent years, as this feature of neoliberal market capitalism is fading. Even the flagship automotive industry, traditionally almost untouchable in the West, was clearly subjected in China to the anti-corruption policy that finally was most seriously implemented under Xi Jinping beginning in 2012. Since then, the Chinese government has been determined to eliminate the political influence of large private corporations, particularly network oligopolies in the IT sector.[12] In this book, we will examine the cases of the EV industry, the crackdown on the IT sector, on the real estate sector, and on the banking and financial sector.

Agile industrial policy: The example of NEVs and the mini-E-vehicles industry: China is known to be the country that, pulling further ahead of leading capitalist countries, has moved beyond the era of combustion engines and pioneered E-mobility along with other alternative energy technologies (hydrogen, induction solar power). China has by far the largest stock of electric cars, including 99 percent of all electric buses worldwide, as well as electric trucks, electric forklifts, electric two-wheelers, power shovels, E-ships, future airplanes, etc. As early as 2017, more than half of all electric cars worldwide were registered in China.[13] The numbers continue to develop exponentially upwards and clearly diverge with the numbers in capitalist countries: As of 2023, China was responsible for more than 58 percent of all EVs sold globally, five times the US market and seven times the German market. By December 2023, 20.4 million EVs were registered in China (compared to Europe's 11.8 million and US' 4.7 million).[14]

The numbers are developing dynamically, whether in terms of absolute numbers of EVs on the road (e.g., 32 million in China by mid-2025), the share of newly registered cars (with over 50 percent being NEVs), the percentage of EVs among all vehicles, or the volume of EV exports, and whatever other indicators usually are reported. China is advancing and leading everywhere, and with increasing margins.

In China's major cities, blue license plates, required for the registration of vehicles with combustion engines, are virtually no longer available. Practically, only green license plates for EVs/NEVs, hybrids, or other alternative drives are issued.

And new production facilities for cars with combustion engines have no longer been permitted in China since the early 2020s. Production facilities for NEVs are preferably awarded to those cities that have made a particular contribution to clean mobility.[15] By 2035, only NEVs will be sold in China.[16]

And most Western experts admit that China's ecological policies are faster, more radical, and tend to deliver practical results well ahead of their original timelines. In fact, there are numerous examples of this already, where China has advanced ecologically beyond its international commitments, namely with respect to climate policy, which we will present later in the book.

A wealth of parallel technological lines: With *full electrification of all vehicles* on China's streets targeted within the next 10–15 years, for the transition time, fuel-saving "bridging" technologies have also been developed, such as a new diesel engine by Weichai Power, with a thermal efficiency of over 53 percent. This could translate into annual fuel savings of about 31 million tons and a reduction of carbon emissions by 97 million tons.[17]

Combined with experiments of hundreds of kilometers of solar-plated highway driving surfaces, where vehicles are propelled by induction power, as well as new-generation high-speed trains and maglev systems, this illustrates another aspect of China's technological and structural dynamism: a permanent rich parallelism of experiments. China recognizes that EVs do not represent the "end of history" of ecological mobility and has a range of parallel technological developments running in competition.

A post-individual traffic system, and a sharing economy: Already in 2018, the Chinese branch of the German corporation *Bosch* had stated that "in no more than 20 years, no Chinese will buy a car anymore".[18] This observation came in the context of Chinese developments toward a post-personal vehicle future, where instead of NEVs being equipped with numerous high-cost sensors and other intelligent technical equipment, the infrastructure around them will be upgraded via a single cloud, allowing for even more efficient traffic management through interconnected vehicles ("Internet of Things" in traffic) and autonomous driving. According to the Bosch China chief engineer:

> In 10 to 20 years from now, Chinese consumers won't buy cars anymore, because when everything from your power bank to bicycles and vehicles is connected through the network, any and all resources can simply be shared. The system at the core of it will make everything available to everyone at anytime and anywhere.[19]

This leads to another characteristic of the deep structure of a strong, resilient, and dynamic structural change in China, a widespread *sharing economy*, an idea discussed in Western green, alternative, and leftist circles for long, but remaining at the fringes there like many a green-leftist pipedream. More on this in China below.

How the low-speed electric mini-vehicles industry emerged: As of 2024, China had over 350 million electric bicycles[20] and over 6 million so-called low-speed electric vehicles (Low-Speed-E-Vehicles, LSEV) as of 2021,[21] i.e., three- or four-wheeled, single or two-seaters, passenger cars or transporters/pick-ups, on the roads. However, still in the mid-2010s, most of these LSEVs initially did not meet the generally applicable standards and were therefore not entitled to participate in public traffic. The vehicles were restricted to private spaces, company premises, yards, sports fields, and so on. Several dozens of SMEs stemming from E-bike production increasingly produced LSEVs for this "gray market". Legally, they were in a "gray" area, but at the same time, they acquired considerable know-how on such mini cars.

Comprehensive joint learning: Interestingly, these companies and "gray" productions were not prohibited or hindered by the government; rather, their production numbers were statistically recorded and analyzed, and their products were researched.[22] Typically for Chinese "agile" structural policy, the process obviously was one of a broad joint learning among SMEs and start-ups, researchers, and public agencies taking part on equal footing in specialized forums and chat groups in social media.

"Stealing patents" among Chinese: "Information must flow": Against this backdrop, the large car corporations, which are also the large EV manufacturers, approached the central government in 2017 with demands to restrict the LSEV industry, arguing that it not only produced "illegal" vehicles but also infringed on numerous patents held by the larger industry players. In a decision that drew significant attention across China, the central government rejected the request.[23] According to the central government, the "stealing" of patented knowledge for electric motors inside of China was mainly a matter of negotiations between patent holders and patent users over licensing fees. Beyond that, the prevailing principle was that "information must flow". Total patent protection and knowledge monopolization by large corporations was not an option. A stance that drew significant attention in China in 2018.

However, the government had already begun evaluating the LSEV industry and was in the process of establishing formal industry standards for these types of vehicles. It resulted in the legalization of many of those SMEs and their products that met the new standards. Others, which did not meet the standards, were phased out. Thus, since 2019, LSEVs have increasingly appeared on China's streets and will make local traffic more

Meanwhile: German/EU Automotive Industrial Policy: Covering Up the Emissions Scandal, Dilution of Fleet-Emission Targets, Missing the Climate-Goals

A review of the automotive policy of the German federal government and the German-led EU-Commission over the last two decades reveals a contrasting paradigm of preserving structures of power, oligopolization, cartelization, and ossification. In parallel with the

"Trump 2.0" US protective tariffs on Chinese EVs in 2024, the EU swiftly followed suit, increasing sales prices of Chinese vehicles on average by around 50 percent. These tariffs aimed to:

1. Shield the Western automotive industry from competition,
2. Keep their sales prices high,
3. Protect their slow ecological innovation speed,
4. Keep their high-emission combustion fleet still saleable,
5. Safeguard their profits and stakeholders' dividends.

For the sake of competition, ecological innovation, and future viability, EU and German car corporations nevertheless move over to their China "fitness center", as leading industry representatives had put it.

While US car manufacturers such as Ford or GM, and even a few EU corporations, have begun a *general retreat* from the global and particularly the Chinese market (e.g., retreating from or altogether leaving countries such as Indonesia, Thailand, New Zealand, Australia, China itself, and the EU), China has moved in the opposite direction. Thus, in 2023, especially with brands such as BYD, China became the world's largest auto exporter, beating Germany and Japan.[24]

Not only does the EU—particularly Germany—undermine its already endangered international climate commitments through its protectionist policies favoring large automotive corporations, but it is recently also further weakening its own agreed-upon rules and standards for EU automotive fleet emissions. As a result, its climate goals for 2030/2035 are steadily fading away.

flexible and less energy-intensive, serving little businesses, as they replace sedans.

Agile structural policy in China in a nutshell: In sum, China's agile, ecological, forward pushing, and structurally transformative industrial policy, now prevailing both in terms of worldwide sales and ecological performance over the West's structures-preserving, alleged "market" approaches, relies, as illustrated in the example, on the following key elements[25]:

- Flexible product development, including by SMEs and startups, sometimes even with technologies "borrowed" from big corporations.
- Early envisioning of new target applications (new target markets), including by new SMEs and startups, in which local and provincial governments as well as banks help support "their" SMEs/startups.
- Openness of information, fast information flow, and parallel, open innovation even between large companies and SMEs/startups.
- A temporary flexible, phased regulation (deregulation and regulation phases) by the central government, based on data analyses from early product applications and market developments, embedded in a national process of joint learning and discussion in social media, with equal participation from public agencies.

These are just some of the policy principles as seen in the case of the NEV mini vehicles. The industrial policy approach applied to more important new national focus technologies and markets, such as, currently, AI, is much broader in scope. It includes parallel efforts in developing human skills (from school children up to university study programs), basic and applied research, market development, making use of economies of scale, targeted financing and bank crediting, infrastructure development, applications and final consumption support for new groups of products, local cluster and VACs support, market structure, competition and price policies, etc. We will touch on further applications of this industrial policy "with Chinese characteristics", or more precisely, with the characteristics of a flexibly and openly planned economic system, on several occasions in this book.

Industrial, innovation, and ecological policy: Chinese industrial/structural policy in the vehicle industry also demonstrates that structural policies are not only essentially linked with innovation and technological development, but nowadays are also inseparably integrated with environmental policy. By 2050, right after China's big symbolic year (2049: 100 years of the People's Republic of China), internal combustion engines are no longer to be used throughout the country. Until then, increasing production and import quotas for NEVs are mandatory. By 2025 already, no combustion vehicles could be imported any more.

Given actual figures and dynamic developments in recent years, the 2050 target will be met much earlier, as is usual in all fields of the Chinese ecological civilization. The quotas for blue license plates are being reduced in China at a high pace.

And the environmental development requires that further mobility research does not fixate on the current technological state of electric mobility. Battery-free e-mobility concepts are being developed, such as a

Challenges for EU Car Manufacturers, and Their Building of an Autarkic Western Economy Within China

This is a particular challenge for the formerly leading German automotive industry. No wonder, thus, that German car manufacturers have built new factories and R&D centers for EVs directly in China, as this seems to be more cost-effective than converting existing production facilities in Germany to accommodate NEV production.[28] And their main, first-tier system suppliers have done the same. They have stated publicly that they cannot afford to stay out of China, and no longer just because of the large market (and related economies of scale), but also due to the efficiency of the Chinese suppliers, local clusters and VACs, the high skill level of the Chinese labor force—workers, technicians, and engineers—and the strength of Chinese R&D in complementary supply-part areas such as AI and autonomous driving, sensors, and new battery technologies.

Western car manufacturers then no longer only serve the Chinese market from within China ("In China for China"); they also source their supply chains locally, becoming independent from Western sanctions. As a result, they also import fewer components from the EU and finally have even begun to export out of China, not only to third countries but also into their home countries, where they compete with their own home factories.

No wonder, thus, that the EU car industry has been running into declining exports and a considerable crisis. As part of their very own de-risking strategy, they have built a full-fledged autarkic Western economy *within China*. A de-risking result that EU-bureaucracy boss von der Leyen would not have imagined when pushing her EU sanctioning crusade, including making prescriptions for China, bashing, and offending China (while being 90 percent dependent on China for rare earths). The EU, in their notorious hubris and neocolonial "values" attitude, has not only unlearned cooperation and diplomacy but also lost sight of a realist perspective on their own declining resources, diminishing potentials, and true vulnerabilities.

solar highway, as indicated, where solar panels are embedded in the roadway,[26] as well as hydrogen technology (fuel cells)[27] and other technological-organizational mobility concepts, including increasingly intelligent roads.

Systemic differences of mobility—the example of the Bosch corporation: This all reveals a systemic difference, for example in the two different paradigms of e-mobility, as experienced by the company *Bosch* in Germany and in China: While German car manufacturers have to plan "state-free", as the state infrastructure remains simple and "dumb", and therefore have to develop the electric car into a mobile supercomputer capable of intelligent and autonomous driving on a still non-responsive road infrastructure (further complicated by competing systems among manufacturers), China is embedding intelligence also into the infrastructure itself. This allows electric cars to remain relatively sleek machines, rather than being turned into expensive, mobile computer fortresses.[29]

Thus, for instance, Bosch, with its 60,000 Chinese employees (having invested another 1 billion USD in China in 2023), has learned that it can achieve technological advances in China that would not have been possible in the West.[30] Against this background, the fantastic-sounding prediction that no Chinese citizen will buy a car anymore in 20 years becomes understandable. By then, comprehensive technical and organizational mobility concepts in China will have advanced so far that individual mobility will primarily be accessed through rental services rather than car ownership.

Indications that the Chinese might slowly say goodbye to their own sedan are nowadays already being given in conversations with Chinese people. Again, different forms of car sharing and multiple car ownership are spreading.

Old Western green and leftist dreams … realizing in China: Green and left-leaning hearts in the EU should, in fact, beat faster when faced with such rates of progress. Yet, entrenched political positions—rooted in a long-standing fear of systemic decline and the loss of Western hegemony—may offer a certain comfort through their very familiarity.

The environmentally oriented industrial policy in China differs from the decades-long talks and quarreling about "green" or "red" ecological policies, which mostly remained on the surface of the problems and their dynamics.

To stay with the example of the auto industry: China was the first country to seriously address the environmental disaster of diesel trucks, which, in endless bumper-to-bumper convoys stretching for hundreds of kilometers, occupy and block the right lanes of German (and other Western) highways, while, sometimes right next to the highway, few freight trains run on old tracks. This logistics problem has been politically ignored for decades in the West due to the influence of powerful car corporations. In China, on the other hand, the Ministry of Environment did not hesitate to decommission trucks with conventional diesel technology which no longer met increasingly strict emissions targets, and it had the power to do so.[31] In 2018–2019, China moved decisively to remove more than 1 million outdated diesel trucks from the roads.[32]

In addition, stricter ecological controls were introduced. And when environmental controls are announced in China, the announcement is followed by action: Then *it will be* controlled, shut down, and punished. Saving the environment in reality—instead of greenish-leftist perpetual discourse. We will illustrate this for several areas in Chap. 11. "Ecology? Biggest Polluter!" below. We will also address the replacement of intolerable diesel ship traffic on the seas (including tourist cruise shipping) by electric freight trains and ships.

There is no question that a country, and system, like China is capable of handling the complex task associated with this, e.g., the reorganizing of truck traffic onto electric rail—another ecological task that has been discussed in Germany and other Western countries for decades, while the opposite is happening ("but nice that we talked about it again"). And what causes short-term operational costs, pays off in the medium and long term through macroeconomic development boosts and increased prosperity, and thereby also through a more motivated and innovative population.

On the other hand, in NFC, the pressure to realize the highest possible returns in the shortest possible time is too great. Complex industrial and ecological reform and restructuring projects are thus becoming increasingly less feasible. The German capital airport BER, Deutsche Bahn, IT infrastructure, schools, hospitals, and more—all send their regards when it comes to achieving self-declared CO_2 reduction goals. Over four decades of neoliberal ideological dominance, governments of the various party coalitions have "sustainably" dismantled the state and rendered it incapable of action, especially when faced with the major complex future problems.

In China's *Entrepreneurial and Developmental State*, with its large companies embedded in the long-term national development strategy, even the business rationality and model may change.

Example Volvo: Again, with the example of the automotive industry: In early 2019, the European car manufacturer Volvo, whose majority shareholder is the Chinese company Geely, became the first and only automaker to unilaterally announce the bold and ecologically revolutionary decision to limit the top speed of all its cars to 180 km/h. On the company's website, Volvo announced that by 2025, half of the cars sold will have an electric or hybrid drive, by 2030, all cars sold will be electric, and by 2040, the entire value chain is expected to be climate neutral. An observation was brought to the point by the corporate newspaper *Handelsblatt*: "Since the Swedish car manufacturer Volvo has a Chinese owner, nothing seems impossible anymore."[33] In 2023, Volvo, with its new 65,000 sqm R&D center in Shanghai and its refocusing on "new drives, design and sustainability", has in fact seen "the most successful year in Volvo's history" in terms of sales figures.[34]

Macro Proper, and Its Deep Structure: GDP, Consumption, and Purchasing Power

GDP: nominal versus PPP, country rankings: As is well-known, in terms of *nominal GDP* (i.e. in simple currency parities, measured and compared in any currency, usually USD), China still is the no. 2 economy after the USA.

However, it is less known that it has been no. 1 in *GDP in purchasing power parities* (PPP) since 2016 already. Purchasing power parities (PPP) measure the quantity of goods and services a population can buy with its nominal GDP, based on an idealized common basket of commodities. This gives hints toward several properties in the "deep structure" of an economy: The purchasing power of a population mirrors the "domestic value" of a GDP in terms of purchasable goods and services. High purchasing power is associated with more equal domestic income and wealth distributions, as well as the high quality, accessibility, and low price of the population's endowment with infrastructures, and sustained low inflation rates.

In terms of GDP in PPP, long-term time series show a growing gap between China's values and those of the USA, with graphs displaying an increasingly pronounced scissor-shaped divergence. This tells us that the quantitative amount of goods and services the Chinese population can afford with its nominal GDP (which itself is approaching that of the USA) is increasingly larger than that of the USA, showing that real economic provision is continuously rising.

This also relates to other factors, such as China having over 30 percent of the world's industrial capacity, efficient industry clusters and complete

VACs, cheap and safe energy supplies, and effective public-transport and IT networks.

It may also be attributed to the fact that China is the largest trading nation in history, with its government however carefully managing foreign trade to maintain a balanced position. Trade surplus in China, thus, contrary to widespread presumptions in the West, does not contribute much to China’s GDP—significantly less than in the USA, Japan, or namely, Germany. Note that the ratio of global export share to global population share is disproportionately low for China, at 0.8, while it is 7(!) for Germany, still the country most attached to its old business model of “world export champion”.

It is unsurprising, of course, that the world’s (now second) largest population (recently surpassed by India) generates the largest GDP, ceteris paribus. But the structural divergence between the USA and China in nominal versus PPP-adjusted GDP hints at a different systemic aspect of the socio-economies as indicated.

In terms of PPP, still, a recent ranking of the IMF/WB (2024) lists China, USA, India, Japan, Russia, and Germany as the top six economies. Notably, Germany has fallen from third to fourth and now to fifth place, while Russia has steadily risen to occupy fifth place.

It should also be noted that aggregate figures alone say little about per-capita GDP, disposable income, or the consumption of goods and services, all of which remain significantly lower than in long-established capitalist economies. More on this later.

The mid-term forecasts tell us that China will very soon hold the no. 1 spot also in terms of nominal GDP. Bloomberg says this will be the case by 2028.[35] Recent growth forecasts by the IMF and WB (2024) indicate that China alone accounts for nearly one-third of global GDP growth each year. Long-term projections by Standard Chartered Bank for 2030 and beyond foresee a global ranking led by China, followed by India and the USA.[36]

GDP per capita, nominal and in PPP—a different picture in terms of per-capita GDP: In nominal GDPpc, China is approaching 14,000 USD according to current IMF/WB statistics, which places it in the 60 s among all countries and still slightly below the global average. By this measure, China may still consider itself a developing country. One of China’s “centenary goals” set for the year 2021, i.e., the 100th anniversary of the CPC, was to become a *moderately prosperous society*. Given the figures and considering that in 1949 the country began as one of the world's poorest developing nations, one might agree that they have accomplished this goal.

In terms of GDPpc in PPP, the numbers are considerably higher, exceeding 23,000 USD in 2024 (IMF), which places China at around 70th in the global ranking and already slightly above the world's average GDPpc in PPP. Bloomberg has forecasted that, in GDPpc in PPP, China will have jumped up 56 ranks in the period 2000–2025.[37] However you look at it, this is not only one of the few successful catch-up cases in the hegemonic era of the USA as the "sole world power", but also a historically unique rise of a country within such a short period.

Quality over Quantity, a "Chinese Dream", ecological civilization: However, China is turning away from quantities as a measure in the mid-term. While it still cares about a target of 5 percent annual GDP growth, does China really want to become the no. 1 in terms of GDPpc (be it nominal or in PPP)? We cannot imagine what it would mean to the world if China's nominal GDP per capita were to reach the current average level of the USA. Some Western economists have tried to calculate and even argue that it would only be fair to grant China the same level of "wealth" that Americans currently enjoy. China is far beyond that. Currently, China accounts for approximately 19 percent of the world's population and also about 19 percent of global GDP, placing it, as said, close to the world average. In this book, however, we will show how China is able to leverage its "medium-sized" GDPpc to achieve substantial progress in all kinds of areas, such as technology, social policies, and world development.

But the Western-culture-based "number one" mentality is largely absent from China's ambitions. Its second centenary goal for its rejuvenation set for the year 2049, the 100th anniversary of the People's Republic of China (PRC), is not becoming a "number one" but a "modern socialist country that is prosperous, strong, democratic, culturally advanced, harmonious and beautiful", according to official declarations. Evidently, constructing a form of socialism, one that is unprecedented and quite different from the Eurocentric, top-down models that we knew, appears to be more important for China than achieving "Western-style" nominal wealth by all means.

In recent years, the Party Congresses, the National People's Congresses (NPC), and the State Council have increasingly emphasized the importance of quality over quantity. They thus promote the so-called *Chinese Dream* and the "pursuit of happiness", while prioritizing ecology, expanding substantive people's democracy, fostering a socialist civilization, and advancing China's *ecological civilization*. This approach includes goals such as inclusive growth, the development of high-quality productive forces (skilled labor and advanced technology), and high-quality consumption of goods and services. Considering future consumption, President Xi repeatedly spoke out against a model of excessive consumption.

The city of Shenzhen, for example, has been designated as an experimental and pioneering city tasked with establishing a socio-economic-ecological system that could eventually replace GDP as a measure of development. In this context, the city is developing a regional *Human Development Index* (HDI) aligned with UN standards for this vast metropolitan and rapidly growing region. This may also be one reason (alongside the uncertainties inherent in forecasting under such unpredictable international conditions) that the 14th FYP no longer included specific quantitative growth targets (although the "5 percent growth" have always been imminent in Chinese policies so far).

Real consumption and protein intake—USA and China compared: Given the lower Chinese GDPpc (compared to the USA) and the high savings rate of Chinese households, resulting in a low consumption ratio, there have been widespread allegations in the West that China's household consumption would be significantly lower than in the developed West. However, this view solely considers simple aggregate monetary values and overlooks the implications that arise from the mentioned divergence between nominal and purchasing power-based GDP and their related aggregates, such as household consumption in this case, both domestically (divergence of nominal GDP vs. GDP in PPP) and internationally (divergence of GDP in PPP between China and the USA).

The conclusion is that the purchasing power of Chinese households is increasing disproportionately, and that nominal aggregates (money values, household consumption expenditures) are becoming less reliable for evaluating consumption. If purchasing powers diverge between China (and similarly many other countries in the Global South with increasing purchasing power and disproportionately increasing GDP in PPP) and the USA (and other Western developed countries), household consumption should be measured and compared in actual *consumption volumes*.

Researchers have done exactly that, confirming that China's consumption levels are not nearly as low as monetary expenditures might suggest. The gap between China and developed capitalist countries in household consumption is significantly narrower when measured in actual consumption volumes. In terms of food consumption, China has even surpassed the levels of developed countries. Regarding housing, both the number of residential units per capita and the per-capita floor area are comparable to those in the West. Considering service consumption, China's consumption volume is also on par with the developed countries of the Collective West. In-depth statistical analysis shows that the physical volume of consumption is, in fact, nearly twice as high as what expenditure data indicate.[38] Obviously, most of this effect stems from the considerable price advantages (and lower inflation rates) in China over the price levels in the political West, which all is mirrored in the PPPs.

As an example, the overall indicator of socio-economic well-being of a population, life expectancy, in China (78.6 yrs.) surpassed that of the USA (77.4 yrs.) in 2020 (acc. to the WB). They have come on par again in 2025 (79 yrs.).

As a more specific indicator, the average Chinese now eats more protein than an American, according to the UN food agency. The milestone was reached in 2021, according to United Nations data.[39]

We will now turn to more areas, factors, and processes in the deep structure of the economy and its "superficial" aggregates, such as the GDP, explaining more on the resilience of a socio-economy.

Financial Sector: Between State Banks and Crowdfunding, SOEs and Startups, Regulation and Openness, Incoming FDI, and Financial Inclusion

Apart from Wall Street, Chinese currency reserves, and managed indebtedness: The Chinese financial system has widely proved to be fundamentally resistant to international financial crises. Today this seems even more the case than during the GFC. China has no relevant external debt, and particularly none with the US-dominated international financial organizations (IMF, WB) or with the Wall Street banks. There are no foreign holdings of Chinese state bonds or equivalent debt papers. It is exclusively indebted to its own central bank, the PBoC, or other state banks, and exclusively in its own currency, Renminbi (RMB). With foreign-currency reserves of well over three trillion US dollars (3.2–3.3 Trill., constantly since 2015), China is also not susceptible to any external speculation.[40] Both international financial economists (Michael Hudson, Jack Rasmus, and others) and central bankers, including IMF leaders, have confirmed

China's capacities to widely safeguard itself against international financial turbulences.[41]

While the national government's debt ratio remains moderate (89 percent of GDP), even after absorbing some provincial debt, certain provinces and cities have at times faced considerable debt levels. This has been due partly to excessive investment projects driven by competition with other provinces, and partly to the crisis in an oversized real-estate sector, where over-speculation necessitated bankruptcies of certain corporations and a downsizing of the industry to a more sustainable level (more on that later). Therefore, in 2024, the central government undertook a major refinancing effort for provinces and cities.

Companies' and private households' debt ratios usually have adequate assets on the other side of their balances. As far as households had strongly speculated in multiple condominiums in the last two decades, their assets may have suffered in recent years with the deliberate real-estate downsizing by the central government. The PBoC, however, has been running a nationwide accessible-housing program that involves purchasing condominiums that were put for sale again by private households; in order to provide them to low-wage migrant workers to ensure they have access to affordable housing (more later).

The banking sector and the role of state banks: China's banking sector consists essentially of the Chinese central bank (PBoC), four traditional major state-owned banks ("Big Four") and a number of newer public specialty banks, mostly for international trade, international development, and the new global investment project of the "New Silk Road" (BRI, more below). They are committed to the national development strategy and act primarily as public investment and development banks, both domestically and internationally. The former exclusive relationship of the four major banks with the SOEs has long been dissolved in favor of more openness, flexibility, and the obligation to promote SMEs and young startups.[42]

For the large SOEs, the banks have played the role of "trimming" them into modern, competitive, and strategically advancing companies, which has largely been successful.[43] Chinese SOEs are no longer industrial dinosaurs, like the Deutsche Bahn for example, which, instead of providing services, has been beautifying itself for the stock market for decades, shoveling millions to its former executives and expensive consultants, disinvesting over decades in order to generate and distribute profits, bonuses, interest, and dividends. Chinese SOEs, rather, are now a stable backbone in all strategically important industries, providing technological, infrastructural, and general strategic impulses and driving them forward.[44]

Bank credit versus stock invest—less capital costs of Chinese firms: Private companies in China are considerably less dependent on private stock and bond markets. They are much more bound to their banks and financed to a greater extent by conventional bank loan. They thus have much less pumped-up speculative and fictitious stock market values. *BYD*, for instance, usually had a formal stock market value of only a tenth of *Tesla's* on Wall Street, thereby bearing much lower capital costs in terms of profits and dividends to be paid, as well as avoiding excessive ceremonial top managers' remunerations and bonuses, profit costs redistributed upward to the top 1 percent of the wealth and income oligarchy.

This is another major reason why Chinese companies can produce and sell cheaper than their Western counterparts and are more price-competitive. The usual Western media and politicians' narrative of "unfair" competition and "Chinese subsidies" ignores these basic economic deep-system facts of a much less financialized economy and serves merely as a lullaby for the average little-informed Western media consumer. Lacking an elementary socio-economic and circuit-oriented understanding themselves (beyond simplistic neoliberal doctrines), they inculcate their readers and entire populations as children.

Bank credit and bank protection for start-ups: The dominant enterprise-bank relation in China ensures an investment-oriented credit supply for companies, including SMEs and young start-up entrepreneurs. The public financing system is legally committed to the national development goals and therefore must ensure credit supply, even without "free financial markets".

In the West, these have come to mostly revolve around themselves, live for themselves, and enrich themselves at the expense of the real, manufacturing economy, which they own and command, fuse or fillet as they see fit, using their stocks and bonds for building derivative fictitious-capital pyramids, as fits best to their asset strategy, balance, and profit.[45]

The "old-fashioned" Chinese bank system has thus deliberately generated young mass entrepreneurship with hundreds of thousands of new startups,[46] which are critical for the improvement of industrial structures, the promotion and diffusion of innovation and technology, and for effective VACs and spatial industry clusters. The Western corporate industry in China heavily relies on them for both production and R&D, as second-tier supplies and services providers, and Western corporate representatives have repeatedly explained that these are indispensable for their own global economic success (more on this later).[47]

In this respect, China is able to practice a better "market economy", with less petrified oligopolistic power structures, as we have already argued. China, in fact, is home to almost one-third of all startups worldwide that have a financial-sector capitalization of more than 1 billion US dollars,[48] whereas start-up activity in Western countries such as Germany is relatively low and rather declining in the longer run. As of 2024, China boasted a total of 369 so-called *unicorns* (i.e., startups valued at more than 1 bill. USD), with China's *ByteDance* being the most valuable unicorn worldwide (valued alone well over 200 bill. USD).[49]

Mass entrepreneurship, thus, appears only possible with a nationally committed, coordinated, and integrated credit and capital sector that is politically obliged to serve the real economy, provides sufficient social and financial security for founders, and protects them against takeover bids from big corp.

And notably, high profitability of companies is ensured indeed with such expansive, investment-oriented credit security.[50]

Financial-sector reform and regulation of the P2P-credit sector: During the phase of "reform and opening-up 1.0", from 1978 onwards, with its enormous growth rates, structural disruptions, and unprecedented increases of many private incomes, the state banking system was still focused on SOEs. Therefore, in view of the growing crediting needs of private firms and businesses, and against the background of the Chinese culture of family, clan, cooperative, and village community networks (Guanxi culture, see above), a large informal ("P2P") credit sector emerged. Given the rapid and substantial accumulation of wealth and assets, it quickly took on an extraordinary scale as a bank-independent area. With relatively high interest rates in China at the time (1980s through early 2000s), it offered excellent investment opportunities for the *nouveau riche*, not least as a means of hiding income and wealth from taxation. Following fundamental financial sector reforms and the regulation of the informal private credit sector in the mid-2010s, this former gray area of crediting, speculation, and tax evasion was significantly curtailed.

These regulations had become necessary especially in light of the transformation of the financial sector toward online services and platforms, the number of which had exploded from 2012 onwards.[51] All kinds of offers—from comprehensive capital collection (crowdfunding) to credit granting, financial investment, and various forms of speculation—were widely available on the internet. It was also associated with opaque, uncontrolled, and potentially destabilizing money-creation processes, on top of notorious tax evasion and adverse distribution effects. Although the extensive informal P2P financial sector in some sense contributed to greater social inclusion and financial "literacy" of many households, it ultimately undermined its own original motivations of small-scale crowdfunding and local lending to households and founders based on family, clan, and Guanxi structures. In the initial period of Chinese socio-economic stabilization, characterized by lower inflation rates, and lower interest rates, mainly during the next major reform period under Xi Jinping (after 2012), there was also a decline in the perceived risk among private households and a corresponding decrease in precautionary savings for potential life risks.[52] Finally, this informal financial sector, with rampant transfers, credit, securitization, and derivative pyramids on its own and widespread speculation euphoria, increasingly became a risk for overall economic stability. In 2015, the P2P networks finally generated a major crisis in the small-loan sector, with losses for many small investors.[53]

As a result, regular rules and standards were set for this part of the financial sector, and out of the originally 6000 P2P platforms, 1800 were officially legalized and licensed.[54] This took place in the context of a major governance reform for all segments of the financial sector, where the banking, insurance, and P2P segments were subjected to unified financial rules and administrative control executed by the PBoC and assigned directly to the state president.

Shadow banks, which had emerged in the informal financial sector with a total volume of about 10 trillion USD, were also partly banned and partly legalized and regulated.[55] Overall, this preserved the formerly informal Chinese financial sector as a whole, but regulated it transparently and connected it with the formal sector, which increased stability and made the sector more effective.[56]

Apparently, the Chinese government's approach to stabilization and regulation did not pursue any prohibition of the P2P segment, but rather an approval of new smaller sized private structures, resembling the industrial-policy approach for the e-mobility sector as mentioned. The "agile" regulatory philosophy also applied to the small-scale financial sector.

Cryptocurrency ban: Bans were issued in some extreme cases, where platforms and networks had proved a proximity to criminality (tax evasion, predatory interests and credit contracts, and other financial fraud) and then were executed quickly. For example, the extremely speculative and volatile cryptocurrency system was banned early on. China was one of the first countries to ban "Bitcoin&Co.", which had been "mined" under opaque conditions and at opaque places.

This affected the emerging "Wild West" ("Wild East") of Bitcoin mining, for which global focal points had emerged early on in some peripheral regions of China,[57] most notably the city of *Ordos* (Erduosi), located on the border of the *Kubuqi* and *Mu-Us* deserts (both part of the Gobi Desert). Factors contributing to this included the computing know-how available in China, the easily available and cheap computing capacity, and favorable electricity prices.[58] The mining activities in old factory halls of large abandoned old-industrial areas of Ordos had been noticed because of unexplainable electricity consumption. Centers with hundreds of connected computers were eventually excavated.

Not least because of that enormous power consumption, which develops exponentially in the decentralized use of cryptocurrencies through their ever-expanding so-called blockchains (Distributed Ledger Technology), the production and use of cryptocurrency was banned in China in 2019.

The E-Yuan: Today, China, with its PBoC and state banks, is at the forefront of a state-backed e-currency, or "Central Bank Digital Currency". Utilizing a more sustainable, centrally guaranteed blockchain technology for safer and faster transactions, the *Digital Renminbi*, or *E-Yuan*, has become the most widely used e-currency internationally, essentially underpinning the entire international economic and financial transactions within the BRICS+ framework.[59]

Alipay&Co.: However, the private internet-based financial sector, including purchasing and payment transfers as well as crediting, has increasingly come to be dominated by large private universal IT companies such as Alibaba (Alipay), Tencent (WeChat Pay), Baidu (Baidu Wallet), and others. These companies now provide the most comprehensive, integrated service platforms and apps for nationwide payment and lending systems to households and businesses. They effectively combine communication with payment systems and other online tools into user-friendly apps. They have built a comprehensive online payment infrastructure, supported by the most advanced hardware and software for mobile telephony.

In China, hardly anyone pays with cash anymore, nor uses physical credit cards. People usually pay using their phone wallet apps with QR codes. And for foreigners, it is easy nowadays to have their home bank accounts and credit cards approved either by physical credit card or with their Western payment system (Apple Pay) or through easy approval of Western credit cards in Alipay, WeChat Pay, etc.

Mobile payment with a mobile phone has been the dominant form of payment for many years. China has in its history made several technological leaps by skipping certain stages that the West had gone through; e.g., they largely skipped landline phoning and jumped to mobile technology or skipped physical credit cards and jumped to mobile payment.

As cash is very uncommon in cities and credit cards have become obsolete, Alipay and WeChat Pay process far more sales with mobile payments than all credit card companies worldwide combined. With *Ant Group's* (an *Alibaba* affiliate) financial app, SMEs and private households can effectively manage their entire finances, also integrating advertising tools, sales platforms, and more. It is used by hundreds of millions of households.

State control of Big-Tech finance, safeguarding and regulating competition—The Alibaba/Ant Group case: Obviously, the analysis of related big data helps prevent financial bubbles and crises. Since the introduction of mobile payment systems in China, the mass data have been carefully monitored and scrutinized by PBoC financial regulators and the *State Administration for Market Regulation*, the national competition watchdog agency operating under the *Anti-Monopoly Commission*, which is part of the State Council.

The most famous case of big-tech financial regulation was the intervention involving *Alibaba*'s financial branch, *Ant Group*, when the state legislators suddenly and spectacularly halted its initial public offering (IPO), one of the largest IPOs ever planned, just days before it was scheduled to take place at the end of 2020. Under the uncertain atmosphere caused by the Covid pandemic during 2020, Ant Group had concluded millions of dubious credit contracts with private households at a volume of hundreds of millions of dollars. It turned out that households found it virtually impossible to exit these contracts (adhesion contracts). Ultimately, Alibaba was broken up, its Ant Group was forced to become a regular registered and regulated bank, household credit contracts had to be rewritten, and the IPO was cancelled in 2021. Ultimately, it was fined in 2023 for violating regulations.[60]

Subsequently, in 2021 and 2022, the entire IT sector, nearly 40 of the largest tech companies, were scrutinized for their platform policies, re. exclusivity and insufficient interoperability for households, as well as their advertising and sales practices targeting farmers and SMEs. They were forced to rewrite exclusive contracts and guarantee easy interoperability. The cases indicated strong government control of the tech and finance sector. We will return to some details of the case later.

Crediting and venture capital, opening-up 2.0: In all, the uniformly regulated financial sector achieves high levels of performance in many respects, in terms of credit supply, payment transactions, and IT infrastructures, but also in terms of providing venture capital by banks, specialist banks, big-tech corporations, and P2P networks. During the 2010s, the volume of venture capital in China had caught up with that of the US venture capital sector within just a few years[61] and is expected to soon surpass it.[62]

The surprisingly generous opening of the Chinese financial sector to foreign banks, investment companies, financial funds, insurance companies, etc. in recent years has considerably altered the previously low level of foreign financial capital investment in China, which was formerly less than two percent of the finance-sector's volume. It has shown that certain deregulations, within the larger framework of increasing the openness to iFDI in a number of industries in China, even in service sectors like health and education, have become affordable and successful.[63]

Financial governance and supervision: In the past, the supervision of the Chinese financial system was fragmented among the PBoC and three separate regulatory authorities for banks, insurance, and securities trading. In 2017, supervision was comprehensively reformed, centralized, placed directly within the government, and, as mentioned, operationally handed over to the PBoC.[64] For this new coordinated supervision, a *Financial Stability and Development Committee* (FSDC) was formed, which was later absorbed into the *Central Financial Commission* (CFC), established in 2023. (On government restructurings during the 13th and 14th FYPs, see above, Chap. 5.) Observers have noted that the central government and the PBoC do act relatively autonomously, "without being neutralized by bankers and other lobbyists".[65]

The international significance of Chinese currency: Against this background, the international relevance and external value of the Chinese currency tend to grow. Obviously, the larger the share of the Chinese economy in the world economy, the greater the weight of the RMB in the global currency concert (the currency basket, with which global economic indicators are calculated). While the USA has always sought to prevent any increase in the share of other currencies in international trade and bank reserves, and while the US dollar still maintains a relative dominance in international business and financial transactions, a new international currency regime will eventually be required, one based on a "basket" of currencies reflecting the actual, contemporary shares in world GDP. This would not only change global statistics but also apply to the weights of countries' votes and their special drawing rights in IMF/WB. For instance, although the Chinese share of the world economy (trade, GDP) has now approached 20 percent, the RMB has been included in the IMF's "currency basket" with a weight of only 5 percent. The disproportionately growing trade within the BRICS+, ASEAN, and the highly dynamic South-East Asian *Regional Comprehensive Economic Partnership* (RCEP) economic integration areas, for instance, will exert a strong force in favor of a changing global currency system with more adequate weights for national currencies.

Considering the RMB's international relevance, the "New Silk Roads" (BRI) are of great importance: More than a trillion USD of actual infrastructure investments and up to five trillion of already mobilized credit capital for BRI projects are billed in RMB, which further increases their significance and value. The RMB will foreseeably become one of the most important currencies for transactions and for holding reserves.

In fact, as mentioned, there is an ongoing ***de-dollarization*** of transaction currencies in world trade and a shift toward the use of RMB and other local currencies for international invoicing.[66] Regarding reserve currencies, the "flight" of many central banks into currencies other than the dollar, as well as into gold, and the widespread repatriation of their gold reserves from the USA, also speak a clear language.

As another example, the City of London has been trading RMB since 2014. In 2019, the daily trading volume in RMB was around 80 billion GBP, an increase of 30 percent over 2018. By 2023, the figure had risen to over 100 billion GBP.[67] This correlates with the fact that Chinese companies had heavily invested in the UK.[68]

The USA and EU have regularly accused China of "strategically undervaluing" the external value of the RMB, given China's international competitiveness and increasing export volumes. However, the PBoC has repeatedly conducted support purchases to maintain a moderately high RMB exchange rate.[69] Only in the current economic, financial, currency, and technology war initiated by Washington has China reacted more decisively with a lower exchange rate to support its trade position and counteract US import tariffs.

Antitrust, Anti-monopoly, and Competition Policies Continued: The Case of the Crackdown on Real Estate Oligopolies

The real estate sector in China had evolved over decades into an oversized and systemically important economic pillar. Contributing approximately 23 percent to the country's GDP, it had become a crucial component of China's economy.

This was driven and supported not only by the general long-run economic development and growth dynamic, but in particular by the increasing household incomes, which are said to have elevated half a billion people into middle-income ranges. The private savings ratio in China has been extraordinary for long and still is today (nearly 32 percent of disposable income). Families and family clans tended to pool their savings and invest them jointly in condominiums, given that homeownership in China was the norm, accounting for over 90 percent of all housing. Given long-lasting construction booms, it seemed obvious to invest in a second, third, or fourth condominium, usually beyond one's own or one's family needs and usage. These could be rented out or, often enough, simply left empty. The central government, and mainly provincial governments, allowed that spiral to continue (perhaps for too long), a self-enforcing upward feedback mechanism that operated smoothly for a long time.

Which, however, is particularly risky in real estate, given the long capital turnover periods and high indebtedness of construction and real estate companies at times. Thus, province governments were repeatedly instructed by the central government not to endlessly sell tenures to urban developers merely to generate budget revenues. And eventually, the long-running real-estate boom somehow came to an end. Significant misalignments and escalating risks in the sector, driven by the large, accumulated debts of real estate groups, prompted the central government to initiate a fundamental policy shift and overdue macroeconomic correction.[70]

The Rise of the Real Estate Sector: From Basic Housing to a Speculative Bubble

Historically, the real estate sector played a key role in providing affordable housing for the population. During this phase (up to the 2010s), structural issues and potential maldevelopments were largely overlooked. Later, as Chinese households grew wealthier and the country maintained a high savings rate, real estate became a favored investment vehicle, as indicated above. The promise of secure value appreciation and consistent price growth turned real estate into an apparently risk-free investment for private households. Today's number of over 90 percent property ownership is an exceptionally high figure by global standards.[71]

This trend, however, led to severe overheating of the market. China's *price-to-income ratio* of 12.4 (as of 2022, already down from 2021) far exceeded the international average of 3 to 6.[72] Concurrently, mortgage burdens on households rose dramatically.

A striking example of the sector's imbalance was the company *Country Garden*, a real estate giant that reported a 6.7 billion USD loss in the first half of 2023 and struggled with over 150 billion USD in total debt,[73] having been declared in default in October 2023.[74]

Evergrande, another prominent company, underscored the sector's crisis: millions of apartments in hundreds of cities remained unfinished, making the crisis tangible for many affected individuals. Becoming the world's most valuable real estate company in 2018, it filed for bankruptcy in 2023 and was finally ordered to liquidate by a Hong Kong court in January 2024, due to failing to come up with viable debt restructuring plans.[75] In March 2024, it was fined almost 580 million USD by the CSRC for financial misconduct such as overstating and falsifying its revenue.[76] Additionally, one of the "Big Four" accounting firms, *PricewaterhouseCoopers* (PwC), was fined another 62 million US dollars by the state regulator, along with a six-month business suspension for its role as an auditor in "covering up" and "even condoning" Evergrande's conduct.[77]

The State-Led Restructuring of the Real Estate Sector

To address the challenges in a sustainable manner, the Chinese government thus implemented a complex, multidimensional policy response to correct the structural imbalance of the real estate sector. While president Xi Jinping emphasized, "Houses are for living, not for speculation",[78] the primary aim was to deflate the real estate bubble in an orderly manner without triggering sectoral or macroeconomic risks.

Key measures included that

- There would be *no public bail-out* for Evergrande, Country Garden, and some few others in trouble; they would be left to go bankrupt.

- There would be *no public financial assistance from the government budget for the banks*, which were held responsible for dubiously financing these corporations; the banks would have to bear the losses.[79]
- A *white list* was established, identifying those private real-estate companies deemed worthy of survival and support for a future, downsized real-estate sector.[80]
- These companies, together with public real estate and construction firms, were tasked with *completing the housing and residential development areas left unfinished* by the bankrupt companies.
- The PBoC was assigned responsibility for purchasing condominiums from private households wanting to sell their devaluated, overshot properties, as part of the *national accessible housing program* for low-wage migrant worker families (see above for details on this program).[81] Initiatives like these, already underway in cities such as Shenzhen,[82] have aimed to provide a social safety net amid the real estate sector's restructuring.

New Investment Opportunities for Household Savings, a Broader Economic Orientation

Beyond downsizing and reforming the real estate sector, China is also promoting diversified investment options for private households. Industrial bonds and investments in start-up funds are being positioned as alternatives to real estate.[83] With this, China's industrial capital market, now already twice the size of Wall Street, may be further expanded.

Such measures are part of a broader economic reorientation. The real estate sector has only been the second major industry for this crackdown on petrified oligopolistic structures. The big-tech IT sector had been the first case (see above on Alibaba&Co.). Moving away from oligopolistic structures, namely in so-called *network industries* with their cumulative effects toward size growth, and from a "winner-takes-all" model, the government is now fostering more controlled competition. Start-ups and innovative enterprises are being actively supported, particularly in emerging industries such as alternative energy, NEVs, AI, and robotics. China aims to establish a global leadership role in these strategic sectors by however adopting a more efficient industrial organization than the often sclerotic, oligopolistic, and cartelized structures that deregulated neoliberal "markets" tend to rapidly produce.[84]

Paving the Way for the 15th FYP, a "New Era" of "New-Quality Productive Forces"

Reforming the IT and real estate sectors has been a cornerstone of China's transition to a "New Era". The government is addressing the dangers of an overheated and speculation-driven oligopolistic economy to create more sustainable structures in the long run. Through *state-managed bankruptcies*, accompanying *social cushioning* measures for households and workers, and the development of *alternative investment channels*, the real estate sector is being downsized without triggering a full-scale economic crisis. At the same time, China is positioning itself for the future by laying the groundwork for more diversified and innovation-driven economic growth.

The new "grand idea" that is central here, which is to be found in the new *15th FYP* (2026–2030), is *new-quality productive forces*. This applies to

- The completion of the *Made in China 2025* program in the 14th FYP, i.e., cutting-edge technological developments,
- The continuation of the *Dual Circulation* strategy (as already emphasized in the 14th FYP), strengthening the domestic circuit by maintaining, modernizing, and automating even the "old" industries to enhance national independence amid the Western hybrid war,
- Strengthening the domestic circuit also through a *new-quality service economy* and high-quality commodity and services consumption.

Technology and Innovation

What We Have Touched on So Far

We have already touched on some remarkable aspects of Chinese technological innovation dynamics, such as quantum technology and quantum computers, the lead in flight speeds or stealth technologies in military systems, in e-mobility, alternative energy vehicles and intelligent infrastructure, in payment systems, and other fields. Spectacular inventions and developments are coming out every week in all fields, and there are whole websites, blogs, journals, and newspapers, from both West and East, that just pursue and record Chinese technological inventions, including fusion energy, Thorium salt-based energy, solar landscapes, new power storage technologies, high-voltage intelligent grids, the 600 km/h maglev, a solar-powered plane/drone that flies at an altitude of 20 km and can stay there for months,[85] the bullet-train network substituting airplanes and ocean ships, bio and health research, material research, laser, optronic and biological semiconductors, or space and submarine technologies.

China's Technological Lead

The "National Innovation System" of China in the field of photovoltaics (solar energy), for example, has been intensively researched.[86] These studies have confirmed the typical features of the innovation system, such as the combined "drivers" of government orientations and market dynamics, of regional clustering and networking, safe energy supplies, public R&D, and local economic promotion.[87] And only through public orientation, promotion, and coordination of private innovative activities could China succeed in its long-lasting catching-up process, which is unique in recent history.[88]

China's innovation dynamics have for instance been mirrored in terms of patent statistics. As early as 2014, China became the leading innovation nation with a growing lead in terms of the number of patents: The country now records more than half of all patent applications worldwide. Long-term data series from the *World Intellectual Property Organization* (WIPO) show that China has left the USA behind in terms of patent applications, and for 2022, the WIPO recorded 4.2 million patents in force for China, followed by the USA (3.3 million) and Japan (2 million). In 2023, the heavily sanctioned (by the West) Chinese telecommunications company *Huawei* was the top filer of patents worldwide (6494 WIPO applications), with *Samsung* being second (3924 applications).[89]

China is nowadays not only leading safely in high-quality patents but also ranks high in the famous *Nature* scientific-publication rankings,[90] various international university and top researcher rankings, and in attracting international leading researchers, both Chinese and from around the world, to its universities. Additionally, in several innovation-field analyses, such as in the above mentioned Australian Strategic Policy Institute's (ASPI) regular five-years *Technology Tracker*, China has led in 57 out of 64 defined technology fields in 2023. The 64 fields span defense, space, energy, environment, artificial intelligence, biotechnology, robotics, cyber, computing, advanced materials, and key quantum technology.[91]

This upswing appears to be historically linked to what some claim was a clarification of property rights for inventions (IPR) since the mid-2000s,[92] although, as we have discussed, individualist PR-protection per se is no sustainable solution. It may not exclude a collective further use of the information, even if against licensing fees. China's patent and IP law seems to be far less restrictive than that of the USA and the West, even if recent reforms have made it more protective and reliable, not least in order to attract foreign investors.[93]

"Headlong Pace"
Former US military engineer and technology blogger Fred Reed wrote a remarkable systemic evaluation as early as 2017:

> To one watching the advance of Chinese science and technology, or to me anyway, several things stand out. First, the headlong pace. Second, the amount of it that appears aimed at making China independent of the West technologically and getting the United States off Beijing's back. Third, the apparent calculated focus. It looks like intelligent design, as distinct from America's competitive scrabbling for profit by special interests, the hope being that this might inadvertently benefit the country as a whole. [...] While Beijing works to benefit China, rapidly increasing its techno-industrial clout, Washington spends insanely on weaponry. It is trying to apply a military solution to a commercial problem.[94]

The Example of AI: Big Data, Big Analysis, Big Governance—and the "DeepSeek Shock"

AI: AI is commonly regarded today as *the* key technology for the foreseeable future. It is a "cross-cutting technology" that is equally central to scientific research, industrial production, or remote control, diagnosis, and steering (the so-called Internet of Things—IoT). AI is based on the processing of previously unknown amounts of data ("big data") and their automated analysis, simulation, and prediction ("machine learning") with novel non-deterministic (non-analytical) mathematical-statistical methods. These methods are supposed to approximate complex processes and previously exclusive abilities of the human brain (such as relevance selection of perceptions and memories, pattern recognition, interactive adaptations), but at the same time compensate for specific weaknesses of the human brain in the area of both logical-analytical and statistical analysis of large numbers.[95]

Structural policy for comprehensive application of AI: Among the entire set of structural-policy success factors that we mentioned, public education expenditures and startups, with appropriate knowledge, capital, and credit endowment, are central factors of a nation's innovative capacity. As early as 2017, China had already provided 7.3 billion USD for startups in the field of AI alone, almost as much as the rest of the world combined (USA 5.8 billion, the "rest" 2.0 billion).[96] By 2027, Chinese investment in AI is forecast to reach 38.1 billion USD.[97] And it probably will be more.

AI, declared one of the prime focus technologies of the future, is of course subject to the usual set of China's structural-change policy that we have discussed, far beyond just expenditures for startups. "AI" is embedded in the usual comprehensive approach, beginning with a conception of generating computational and *AI literacy* already among school beginners, systematically expanded through to final high school classes; extended to hundreds of specialized university AI education programs; multifaceted basic and applied public research capacities and institutes; AI-based startups; AI-based big-tech and manufacturing-company developments; AI related spatial clusters, networks, and VACs; further, supporting data centers, AI-related specialized semiconductors and specialized supercomputers; further, providing sufficient, safe, and cheap green power as needed for AI, brought everywhere in the country from the huge solar parks in the sun-abundant West through efficient high-voltage grids, leading, at high speed, to AI applications in processes and products everywhere.

For instance, early on, IT company Alibaba set up a budget of 16 billion euros for AI; the city of Tianjin provided 13 billion euros for AI. There are more than 70 AI degree programs on offer.[98]

An application of lessons learned from "simpler" industrial-policy cases like solar, wind, or NEVs, in the last few decades. "China speed", now more routinized: less driven by search, experimentation, and detours, and more by the systematic application of an already developed comprehensive and dynamic structural approach.

New old historical normality again: Note again that much of this is simply a return to a thousand-year-long historical "normal", in which China has consistently been technologically ahead. It would also be an obvious "anomaly" if the world's (second) largest country (now second behind India in population, but still by far the largest in terms of GDP at PPP) were not also a leading techno-economy.

But as China is still a developing country, with its per-capita GDP only recently reaching the world average and having entered the group of middle-income countries, according to the WB, we may not meaningfully compare per-capita figures. A conversion of R&D expenditures per capita for AI would not be appropriate since China still has to "carry along" an above-average proportion of people who still are distant from higher education and science. Basic structures simply are incommensurable compared with those of developed capitalist economies.

On the other hand, China's astonishingly high leverage into innovation and technology from just a "medium" per-capita GDP appears ultimately explainable only through its specific systemic capacity. Another "structural" factor entering "the game". More on that later.

EU, Germany, and China: Note that the EU once declared in its *Treaty of Lisbon* (2000) that it wanted to become the "most dynamic knowledge-based economic area in the world". But the EU has been in constant relative decline in innovation and technology on a global scale. In the ASPI technology trackers mentioned, the EU mostly did not even appear at rank 3, but often 4 or 5, displaying a steady decline over the institute's five-year reports.

Recently, a leading entrepreneur and owner of a technology company has described Germany in the context of AI as "a living museum".[99] No wonder, then, that German entrepreneurs mention AI first when discussing industrial relations between Germany and China. A chairman of the *East Committee of the German Corporate Economy*, for example, said early in the AI wave that China would become an industrial and technology partner in AI on an equal footing, and that a multi-billion-dollar state research program on AI, along with the "exceptional (private) financial resources" available to Chinese companies, had contributed to that.[100] For AI development, there would be a "treasure trove of data" and "a huge number of excellent scientists and researchers" available.[101]

AI-facilitating governance: Speaking of *big data*: There is hardly a conference in China where dozens of scientists from large research institutes do not openly, relaxedly, and transparently discuss their nationally and internationally networked big-data analyses for everyday processes, such as traffic planning and fluid management of megacities, determining the best parking spaces for hundreds of thousands of rental e-bikes, the routes of Uber taxis, and the paths or purchase decisions of millions of consumers in a city per day. More on data, personal data protection, and individual data sovereignty within that framework will follow in dedicated chapters below (See Chap. 10: "Places and Housing? Poor Villages and Monster Cities!", as well as Chap. 12: "Democracy? Dictatorship!").

China's production activities are also already being predicted using big data and big analysis, for example, on a geospatial basis with real-time satellite imagery, quantum communication, radar screening, and many more application fields.[102]

The fact that, in Western media, the keywords "big data", "AI", etc. in the context of China immediately trigger narratives of "surveillance" and "dictatorship" appears simplistic and one-sided against the background of the much more complex Chinese socio-economic and political realities. Just the framework steering ("governance") of the daily streams of millions of people in China's many mega-cities, based on big data and AI, is indispensable for effective "Mega-City Management".[103] Without it, the many Chinese megacities would collapse just like most of the other "Third World" nightmares of multi-million cities. Again, more on big data, governance, and democratic rights later.

"Governance" here does not mean detailed control of individuals, which is technically feasible for sure, but the establishment of systems that set framework conditions, to which agents can adapt flexibly and with certain degrees of freedom. In entities such as the state, municipalities, as well as private or public organizations, such framework conditions for enabling efficient dynamics are to be set. *Smart cities*, also in the USA and EU, are using vast amounts of control and steering measures for city flows nowadays. Chinese citizens and Western tourists alike enjoy walkable, cyclable, and easily drivable cities with relatively little traffic congestion and convenient access to streets, public spaces, service offices, and store facilities. The overall atmosphere in Chinese public spaces is safe, relaxed, and welcoming. Police presence, especially compared to the often-heavy deployment seen in the West and namely most US cities, is drastically lower in Chinese cities.

Certainly, this cannot be taken as an ultimate "proof" of the non-existence of surveillance and control. However, the degree to which people feel and act freely, relaxed, and keen to debate (also with foreigners) in public spaces (including social media) may serve as another indication of the increasingly open character of the Chinese society and its public life. As said, more details will follow later.

The ChatGPT versus DeepSeek case: More recent developments in AI, such as chatbots based on so-called "Large Language Models" (LLMs), whose potentials are currently increasing by the day, have apparently revealed what some characterized as a qualitative divergence between China and the USA. The two seem to be "travelling on entirely different tracks", as China expert Manya Koetse wrote. Namely, ChatGPT, developed by the US company *OpenAI*, was perceived as rather indicative of a Western approach to AI applications, which would emphasize "individualism, personal autonomy, decentralization, and globalization", while the Chinese approach would rather consider AI as a national and state-regulated tool for economic growth and development, for national cyber sovereignty, collective support, and national security. Koetse wrote:

> The way AI is applied in the west is not necessarily suitable for the Chinese market and vice versa. The arrival of ChatGPT shows the unique paths of the eagle and the dragon, each engaged in their own race on different tracks. This doesn't mean there's nothing to learn from one another—we just have to go beyond competitive thinking and beyond geopolitical implications.[104]

The success of ChatGPT and the initially less successful Chinese counterparts led analysts such as Koetse to conclude that this might be due to a more complex language-model training in Chinese, a focus on fast applications, particular political sensitivities, or a different systemic approach. This view, however, was upended by the "DeepSeek Shock" in early 2025.

DeepSeek, a Chinese AI company founded only in mid-2023, developed its DeepSeek-R1 model with a budget of reportedly only around 5.6 million USD.[105] In contrast, OpenAI's GPT-4, released in 2023 as well, was estimated to have cost around 100 million USD to develop. Despite its much smaller budget, benchmark tests indicated that DeepSeek-R1 could answer questions, solve logic problems, and write computer programs at performance levels comparable to and even outpacing ChatGPT.[106] DeepSeek achieved this milestone swiftly, releasing its chatbot in January 2025. Three weeks later, it had already become the most-downloaded free app on the iOS App Store in the USA, surpassing ChatGPT.[107]

The success of DeepSeek led to significant repercussions in the stock market. During January 2025, Nvidia's stock price, for example, temporarily dropped by 18 percent, resulting in a nominal loss of ca. 600 billion USD in stock value—the largest single-day loss in US stock market history.[108] The decline was attributed to concerns that DeepSeek's efficient AI models could reduce the demand for Nvidia's high-end GPUs, which are essential for training advanced AI systems.

DeepSeek's rapid advancement can be seen as just another outcome of China's comprehensive and complex innovation policy, which neither uses nor needs corporate subsidies. It has particularly aimed at reducing reliance on foreign technology and bolstering domestic innovation, especially in response to the intensifying US hybrid war, e.g., the increasing sanctions on key technologies (namely semiconductors), which in turn have massively incentivized China to accelerate its domestic capacities in semiconductors, photonics, quantum computing, AI applications, and many more future critical fields.

This very condition and environment enabled startups like DeepSeek to thrive and make a quick breakthrough in AI development. China's success has also prompted a general reevaluation of AI strategies globally. It demonstrated that significant advancements could be achieved with strategic government sector support, including also high-level primary, secondary, and tertiary education (most of DeepSeek's top researchers were fresh graduates from top Chinese universities), challenging the notion that only heavily funded big-tech oligopolies can lead to innovation. This, therefore, has even been called "AI's Sputnik moment" by some experts.[109]

It has also intensified discussions about the balance between open-source collaboration and proprietary development in the AI community, as DeepSeek's success was in part also tied to its open-source (OS) nature, originally stemming from the Linux idea of the early 1990s. Unlike OpenAI's GPT-4, which remained closed-source, DeepSeek released several "open-weight" models, including *DeepSeek-Coder* and *DeepSeek-LLM*, allowing researchers and developers worldwide to access the program kernel and improve upon their work, which has been widely praised in the scientific community.[110]

The OS approach gave DeepSeek an edge in rapid innovation, as open-source communities could refine and optimize its models. China's strategy thus appears to *favor open innovation*, leveraging global talent while also pushing state-backed AI projects and investment. The "DeepSeek Shock" illustrates how strategic company innovation embedded in a complex supportive-policy system can enable rapid advancements with comparatively limited resources.

One can again observe a certain Western naivety combined with hubris in dealing with China. As an observer noted: "The DeepSeek panic […] tells us less about China than it does about western neuroses."[111] One predictable Western response was indeed to again raise the unsubstantiated claim: "The technology must have been stolen!" (OpenAI) This not only despite the fact that DeepSeek *outperformed* the Western models, but also the irony that "OpenAI itself built its whole business by scraping the entirety of the internet to train its model", which led to many mocking responses to OpenAI's accusation.[112]

A 2024 report on China's AI innovation policy by the Washington-based *Information Technology and Innovation Foundation* (ITIF), one of the world's leading think tanks for science and technology policy, had already concluded that

> The narrative that China is merely a copier is false and outdated

as it had already become the global leader in AI research publications, the unsurprising prediction being:

> Now, it [China] has developed an AI innovation ecosystem that rivals that of the United States, producing cutting-edge models that exceed those of its global peers. If this trend continues, the U.S. may soon find itself in the position of copying China.[113]

Western Hubris Still Alive: "China Is Not Innovative", the Immortal "Chinese Spy", Decoupling, the Trump "China Initiative" … and the Intellectual Brain Drain from USA to China

In light of the *Cyberspace Administration of China*'s (CAC) introduction of new regulations for AI in April 2023, China expert John Naughton observed in the recent divergence of AI approaches a general pattern in Western naivety, misjudgment, and ideology on China, which repeats itself over and over again, namely that China would not be able to sufficiently adapt to new circumstances and "would crumble" instead. "We may be proved wrong again", he writes:

> It is often said that insanity is doing the same thing over and over and expecting different results. Something similar applies to western thinking about the People's Republic of China.[114]

China has developed indeed into a technologically leading country with a unique leverage effect between average middle-income level and technological-organizational innovation performance. It has emerged as a leader in research, development, and application, despite having faced comprehensive technology embargoes from the West throughout its entire history. Several of China's leading areas, as partly mentioned above, have been identified as follows: Electromobility and other alternative-energy vehicles, solar, quantum technology, high-speed trains and magnetic levitation technology, brain–machine interfaces, supersonic rocket technology, IT-telecommunication (6G), biological batteries, AI chips, medical and gene research, nuclear research and particle accelerator technology, space research and radio telescope technology, material research in natural materials, 3D-printed house construction, etc.[115]

However, official media narratives in the Collective West are supposed to generate a different, hostile image of "the Chinese". According to those, China allegedly has an education system that only educates for adaptation, imitation, good test results, but little creativity. So, they need to steal. From the Political West. For instance, Carly Fiorina, former CEO of Hewlett-Packard, had claimed in 2015 that Chinese people could not be creative: "They are not terribly imaginative. They're not entrepreneurial, they don't innovate, that is why they are stealing our intellectual property."[116] *McKinsey* echoed this sentiment then: China could only make the "light" innovations, only make products cheaper, and only gradually improve them; they were only limitedly successful in scientific or engineering breakthroughs.[117] A commentator wrote about it: "The claim is complete rubbish for more reasons than I have room to account here."[118] US senator Marsha Blackburn wrote on Twitter (X) in December 2020: "China has a 5,000 year history of cheating and stealing."

Feeding Western populations with such (racial?) stereotypes can of course not go well for long and has already had measurable consequences, including a drastic rise in hate crimes against people of Asian descent in most Western countries. According to Cai Jinliang, chairman of *United Chinese Americans* (UCA), racial hatred against Asians in the USA has reached "a state of crisis", fueled by such anti-Chinese rhetoric, as well as Washington's anti-Chinese policies, such as the Trump-1.0-era *China Initiative*, which had continued under the Biden administration.[119] It put any Chinese in the USA, particularly scientists, under suspicion of espionage. According to a *Pew Research* survey of 2023, almost one-third (32 percent) of Asian adults in the USA report personally knowing "an Asian person in the U.S. who has been threatened or attacked because of their race or ethnicity since the COVID-19 pandemic began in 2020".[120]

In the meantime, hundreds of top, highly awarded Chinese scientists have left the USA to assume professorships, lead institutes, head work groups and research facilities, and receive project funding at top Chinese universities and institutes. And white American scientists are following them under Trump 2.0. The *brain drain out of the USA into China* is considerable, and even top US universities have declared the brain drain of Chinese scholars, researchers, and PhD students will leave gaps in the research landscape that will not be easily filled again.

The Nexperia case: Even greater radicalism has spread across the right-wing, fear- and warmongering governments of an EU, which is stuck in a steep and rapid decline toward global insignificance. The self-proclaimed champions of neoliberal "values", "rules"-abiding conduct, and "market enthusiasm" have revealed themselves to be, in practice, the most zealous state bureaucrats, regulationists, and interventionists—when it comes to foreign, namely Chinese (and, where applicable, Russian) assets. In their desperate struggle for some identity in the world changing around them, and against their deterioration, they have turned out to be, in fact, disregarders of property rights, in effect, quite conventional Eurocentrist "old" top-down state-socialist ("Stalinist") compulsory expropriators and nationalizers, when it comes to foreigners and their assets.[121]

In September 2025, to seize the Chinese semiconductor firm *Nexperia*[122] and appropriate its valuable technological assets and know-how to the advantage of the Dutch state, the (then) far-right nationalist and racist government of the Netherlands even revived a law of 1952, meant for wartime and never applied before, using it as a legal basis for what basically amounted to a "state-socialist" type expropriation (although "state-capitalist" expropriation might be the more accurate term here). The law applied here nicely demonstrates the state of mind of nowadays' EU governments: They consider themselves being in a war (against their own descent).

The firm has since been placed under direct state control. This marks a new, escalatory variant of "decoupling", a *Trump-squared* approach, whose likely (and well-considered) tumbling consequences for the EU automotive industry (dependent as it is on Nexperia's chips, and then quickly at risk of supply shortages) appear to be designed to further strain EU–China relations and disrupt international law and rules.

While Trump and Xi met in person in South Korea in October 2025 to negotiate a comprehensive de-escalation package for US–China relations, certain actors within several member governments of the, otherwise increasingly isolated, EU seem intent on manufacturing chaos, pursuing further economic fragmentation and conflict escalation. This is hardly a prudent strategy for halting the EU's decline. That particular Dutch government in question, notably, was voted out of office only weeks after its breach of fundamental principles of the international order. But "liberal" governments mostly are not different, when it comes to China, Russia, and other "enemies".

According to available information as of the end of 2025, the expropriation of Nexperia was carried out under US pressure. American officials reportedly insisted that changes in the company's ownership structure were necessary to avoid US export restrictions, and Washington's influence proved decisive, as *CNN* reported.[123] In line with this pressure, the Dutch government justified its disruptive move by hiding behind the Trump administration's so-called 50-percent ownership rule for inclusion in the US Entity List—a provision that, if applied broadly, would have affected further tens of thousands of Chinese firms, including Nexperia itself.

The UK government had already forced Nexperia in 2022 to sell its microchip factory, the UK's biggest one then, of course, and, deliberately from the side of the UK government, at less than original price and market value.

The Chinese parent company *Wingtech* had purchased the suffering Dutch company Nexperia at the end of 2019, hugely invested in it, and brought the suffering company up again to profitability, significantly increasing its assets and value. Under the Wingtech ownership, Nexperia contributed 130 million euro in corporate tax to the Dutch government. In all, a convenient victim of the Dutch government to enrich itself.[124]

Following the expropriation, China of course announced retaliatory export bans on Nexperia chips to the EU, later partially retracting them after diplomatic signals suggested that the Netherlands might consider relinquishing control of the company if exports resumed.[125] In early November 2025, Beijing eased these export restrictions, while calling for reciprocal gestures of goodwill from The Hague. But the ultimate status of Nexperia's Dutch operations thus remained unclear by late 2025.[126]

The central issue, however, lies not in these tactical maneuvers or justificatory details, but in the *original transgression*. How much the EU ever may be Washington's vassal, the *original sin* against international law has in fact been made in the EU, and no excuse can undo the very fact. The expropriation of foreign property *as such*—particularly by an EU member state that collectively presents itself as the global guardian of "values" and "rules". Its behavior mirrored precisely those authoritarian economic practices it always so readily has condemned.

Moreover, since the initial rationale for the expropriation effectively lapsed with the *Trump–Xi agreement* reached shortly after, which included the drop of the "50%-share rule" for the US entity list by the White House, the Dutch government should immediately have reversed its measures. That it has not done so is, to say the least, revealing; one may reasonably infer that it has "acquired a taste" for such practices and intends to retain them as leverage in future dealings with China.

Regardless of shifting circumstances or evolving justifications, what truly matters is the *precedent itself*—a symptom of a broader trend of politically motivated property seizures and *politization of the international economy*. It applies also to the roughly 300 billion USD in Russian Central Bank assets or to the 9 billion USD in Afghan, and the around 3 billion USD of Venezuelan Central Bank reserves. Within NATO and EU circles, open discussions have already taken place about the potential *confiscation of Chinese property in the USA and Europe* in the event of a future crisis. Some 145 billion USD assets in the USA and some 83 billion USD in the EU were already considered candidates for future confiscations.[127] The temptations for breaking up the international order appear substantial—and growing.

This initial act, the fall from grace, is fundamental rather than contingent. Whatever political compromises or pragmatic reversals may follow, the expropriation, the original sin, has occurred, and its implications will remain ...

Learning to Understand China ... and Ourselves?

Some system and policy elements: We addressed some industrial, scientific, and financial policy backgrounds of China's success, and we may generalize from several components of a policy for high socio-economic dynamics and resilience:

- Large-scale state investments in education, science, and research in cross-sectional industries and technologies,
- Analysis and definition of long-term target application fields ("target markets"),
- Coordination, organization, and promotion of cooperation and networking among actors along the value chains,
- Inclusion of local SMEs in international value chains,

- Promotion and embedding of innovative entrepreneurs (startups and young SMEs),
- Securing financial conditions (equity capital and loans) for startups and SMEs, providing sufficient venture capital,
- Use of state banks to empower large state-owned companies in key sectors for modernization and strategic investment,
- Inclusion of large private companies in national development goals,
- Ensuring high physical and social ("hard" and "soft") infrastructure facilities both through direct public investments and by obliging large companies to infrastructure investments,
- Dominance of political development priorities over the narrow and short-term self-interests of corporations, independence of the government from lobbying ("rent seeking") of large companies,
- Establishment of an anti-corruption control system,
- Big data collections and analyses for observing, forecasting, and framework control of sectoral developments,
- Temporal flexibility and interaction between deregulation and regulation, standard setting only after analysis of sector dynamics, then letting go, using the flexibility and selection capacity of a market mechanism for adaptation to regulations and standards.

Contrasting perspectives: One could encapsulate this in the words of a Western commentator: "[T]he private sector is there to serve the nation, not vice versa."[128] The contrasting program of a helpless and inefficient staggering into the future under flawed narratives of a free "market economy" is offered in Germany. Referring again to the example of AI, conservative entrepreneurs and some leftist critics agree on insufficient framework setting by the different governments of all usual color combinations. For the key technology of the twenty-first century, the earlier "grand" coalition in Berlin (of right-wing Christian Conservatives and neoliberal Social Democrats) only managed to provide 3 billion euros in 2019, for the period 2019–2025. The finance minister, however, made it clear shortly after that he only wanted to provide 500 million from the federal budget, and the 50 million promised for 2019 was initially "blocked".[129]

It thus began already with a false start, compounded by the lack of developmental vision among the new generations of neoliberal politicians, political ideologues, and party bureaucrats, who only know the party rituals. Over decades of neoliberal decline, they have lost any understanding of the economy as a dynamic, circular system, favoring instead a conception of austerity modeled on the private household of the Swabian housewife.[130] The basic economic knowledge of John Maynard Keynes, of an economy as a *cumulative circuit*, which was able to help the world out of the depression of the 1930s, no longer exists in this political class. The urgently needed public investments are sacrificed in favor of the fetish of a static *black zero* in the state budget. But suddenly, they become very "dynamic", even enshrining the most extreme restrictions in the constitution. Only to throw everything overboard, mobilizing several hundred billion up to a trillion euros for war preparation.

Against the backdrop of domestic political misery, and of the fact that their CEOs no longer have a voice in their media and get bashed and pressured for their rational decisions, German corporations have long voted with their feet and entered cooperations with American and Chinese corporations in the field of AI. For example, they are now developing autonomous driving together with Chinese internet corporations and their subsidiaries. This is not about the ever-ready knockout narratives: "They are not a market economy!", "They are not free!", "Dictatorship!", "Police state!", "Hong Kong!", "Corona!", etc., this is about substance, i.e., the future of the national economy. We would agree with corporate representatives that those who aspire to be the political personnel of the corporations, who claim to be thinking "like entrepreneurs", are really doing disservice to their own clientele.[131]

Returning to AI and IT, these obviously also have the potential for political use and misuse, including behavior analysis, control, and manipulation. In the case of China, we will return to various current experiments in social-behavior control and nudging, in a chapter on the diverse local social credit point approaches. Here, we will briefly consider also the IT sector from an industrial-policy perspective.

Understanding China and Ourselves: The Example of IT

Characteristics of the industry and the intensified rivalry between US and Chinese giants: The IT industry is closely connected with AI technology and industry, as it has become the main generator of big data and, due to its "first-mover" position, also a co-developer and main user of "big analysis". Every internet user has an individual personal profile at Google, Facebook, or Amazon, due to the electronic "traces" she inevitably leaves behind, which are stored, evaluated, and used for more business.

The same technology, of course, applies in the first instance to the Chinese IT giants Alibaba, Baidu, and Tencent. And as in the USA and the West, the "big five sisters", Google, Apple, Facebook (Meta), Amazon, and Microsoft (GAFAM),[132] are networked with the US state, secret services, and the Pentagon, and provide them with data and analyses; in China, some data flow between Tencent, Alibaba, and Co. and state agencies is ensured as well.

A potential future-oriented, socially useful applicability of big data and AI is, for example, Google's ability to accurately predict unemployment in the USA on a regional basis, based on internet research and search criteria of its users—and in real time.[133] If the US state were capable and willing to act in terms of social policy, it could prepare for upcoming regional centers of unemployment and act preventively. We mentioned another positive example: the traffic steering of multimillion mega-cities.

Network Technologies, Network Industries, and the "Market"

Network technologies: A necessary consideration regarding the peculiarity of the IT sector: The material and immaterial products (hardware and software) of the IT industry are organized around digital microelectronic processes, which are called network technologies. In the individualistic worldview of the mainstream, the so-called "neoclassical" and neoliberal "market equilibrium" economics, "competitive" *private goods* prevail, which entitle the owner to exclude all others from the enjoyment of the good. The benefit for the owner-consumer is all the greater the fewer others possess the good; the use and consumption of the good thus is "rivalrous".

In contrast, the world today is full of "cooperative" goods, below the level of the collective community goods proper (commons). They are based on today's dominant network technologies. Here, the benefit of the good for the individual user is the greater the more of it is available, and the more other users belong to the same network as myself and are capable of communicating with me—altogether, the "installed base" of the network.

Network effects, competing standards, and (non-)interoperability: Since these technologies, "goods", and related services are thus "cumulative", they exhibit so-called *network effects*. The greater the network, the more attractive it is for new entrants, and the larger the network will get. The growth of a technological communication standard of a certain network, therefore, leads in principle to global standardization and may render the producer and owner of this standard a monopolist if, for example, they were a first mover and were able to assert their standard early against potential competing standards. Eventually, they may become so powerful as to refuse interoperability with other competing networks, technologies, and standards, as, for instance, has almost always been the business policy of *Microsoft*. This explains, in a technical way, why we live in a world dominated by a group of international oligopolies, each of which may gain a power greater than that of most states in the world.[134]

Zero marginal costs and oligopolistic prices: Note that the cumulative network effects lead to huge economies of scale, so that the marginal costs of service provision for another marginal individual user mostly tend toward zero. With zero marginal costs, *conventional price theory no longer applies*, and you can no longer determine a "perfect" "competitive" price. Real prices stem from dynamic strategic rivalry (including investment, innovation expenses, non-interoperability, and technical internet proprietary and exclusion strategies) among the oligopolists and from their power positions alike.

Narrow oligopolies, "competition", and anti-trust policy: In the old-industrial, analog, mechanical-manufacturing world, today's global monopolies of (at peak times) almost 90 percent world market share, such as Microsoft's operating system, would have been unthinkable. In that world, competition authorities became active when a steel conglomerate perhaps had 20 percent of the national market share.

In the world of network technologies, however, with their massive cumulative growth (i.e., network) effects, the entire idea of "competition" and the "free market" is undermined. That's why the West and its mainstream economics can no longer present any convincing concept of "workable markets" or of what really is a "market economy", as it still loves to present itself in contrast to China.

"Markets" have been deliberately deregulated under new neoliberal mainstream-economic "market" conceptions since the 1970s, claiming "free markets" to be more "dynamic" and innovative, thus "competitive", even under narrow oligopolistic structures. They quickly abandoned their former competition theory and competition, anti-trust, and anti-cartelization policies during the 1980s, as they no longer had the criteria to analyze or regulate their new power structures. Critics have analyzed this as a backslide to medieval times and consider the new structures of network industries that have emerged since the 1980s *techno-feudalism*.[135]

Right-skewed centrality/size/power distributions: By all means, "free", deregulated markets, particularly when driven by Big Finance, tend to degenerate even more quickly into *power structures*. Statistically, they take the form of networks with highly right-skewed distributions of centrality, size, and power, where a few dominant nodes emerge as the "too big to fails". When these critical nodes encounter distress, the instability cascades through the network, threatening entire value-added chains (VACs) and entire industries.

In addition, network industries, through their inherent power structures, have become an even larger and faster engine of income redistribution from bottom to top under NFC than ever before under conventional capitalism.

Open-source competition and the platform economy: To be sure, pure monopolies are rare, and even Microsoft was never a truly global monopoly at its peak. Creative minds continually challenge monopolists through open-source approaches, such as the early *Linux* or *Android* movements, allowing users to remain interoperable with oligopoly products. Competing large corporations can also establish sufficiently large "installed bases" with alternative standards to achieve economies of scale. Today, dynamic rivalry manifests in new ways through the platform economy, which generates scale, network, and profit effects; connects different user groups, producers, and sellers; collects big data on unprecedented scales; and integrates AI, machine learning, and cloud computing in transformative ways.

Re-regulation and integration in national strategies: The world of network technologies, network industries, and "platform economies" is a dynamic, often aggressive rivalry around innovations and standards within oligopolistic structures, which repeatedly produce considerable volatilities and turbulences in the deregulated neoliberal "market economy". The big-tech oligopolies in the West, dominating the platform economy, are nevertheless considered national assets of the hegemon and fully integrated into its imperial and hybrid-war strategy, while other Western nations and power blocs, such as the EU, are desperately struggling with (usually weak) attempts to regulate, sometimes tax, and sometimes punish them.

We indicated already, and will illustrate more below, how China cracked down on its IT oligopoly and regulated this crucial oligopolistic sector to better serve households and the national development goals.

Against this background, it becomes clear why the systemic rivalry between rising and declining powers manifests primarily as a technology war, centered on the major companies on both sides. On the Western side are GAFAM—Google, Apple, Facebook, Amazon, Microsoft—extended by OpenAI and others; on the Chinese side are BATX—Baidu, Alibaba, Tencent, Xiaomi—along with Huawei, ZTE, ByteDance, and others. The dynamics of these industries are increasingly politicized and have become central to the geostrategic rivalry of our time, encompassing struggles over hegemony, containment, technological catching-up, and the emergence of a multipolar world.

Cross-Sector Industrial Policies: Some "Commonalization" of Profits and Anti-monopoly Policy

Regulation here and there: Chinese decision-makers appear fully aware of the conditions inherent to network industries—particularly their tendencies toward oligopolization, concentration of power, and politicization—and have no intention of buying into the West's simplistic narrative of an ideal, deregulated "market" when shaping IT industries and technologies. The development of the world under Western hegemony has long exposed the flaws in these old fairy tales. Even within the West, the established forces now moving toward the politicization and re-regulation of major industries no longer believe in them. Judged by Western experience, a "free market economy" in networked, platform-driven sectors inevitably tends to produce a few industrial-financial giants.

With their capital, these actors can dominate the economy, society, and politics, yet they often exhibit a narrow horizon and a limited, individualistic "rationality". Even within exclusive power circles, they are unable to develop a collective rationality capable of considering the common good or advancing the nation as a whole. As a result, long-term social and ecological initiatives from governments in such economies are largely absent, which helps explain why the West is struggling to meet its declared climate targets for 2030, 2035, and 2050.

Internet-infrastructural supply: China's IT-oriented industrial and structural-change policies have taken a different path, producing some remarkable outcomes. Anyone arriving at a hotel in China and asking for the Wi-Fi password will likely be met with a friendly smile, as proprietary codes are often unnecessary. In cities, seamless Wi-Fi coverage connects users across public, commercial, and private spaces without interruption. This contrasts sharply with Western telecommunications and postal services, which often suffer from coverage gaps and uneven service quality.

In Chinese cities, mobile phone users benefit from a dense, virtually costless service infrastructure, including readily available charging stations and cables. Similarly, there is a high density of electric vehicle charging stations—massive infrastructure investments that cost billions and which IT and automotive companies are effectively required to fund because of state mandates. More broadly, across wide areas, the government obliges private corporations to dedicate a portion of their profits to provide essential infrastructure and services nationwide.

Corporate contributions to national development: The "political-economic deal" behind this is that, for example, entrepreneurs may become very rich (more on the recent tendency to cap the incomes of top managers and the super-rich below), but they must contribute from their profits to the provision of certain community goods (infrastructures). This means, for example, that even the most remote village in China now gets fast internet. The state prescribes some "socialization" of profits.

Jack Ma, former schoolteacher and founder of *Alibaba*, has for a long time been not only one of the richest Chinese but also one of the most original, creative, and productive IT entrepreneurs, often termed an IT "rockstar". He has been a representative of exactly this socio-political "deal", which recognizes the dominance of politics and integrates corporate investments into the national development strategy. Ma has defended it and even did not shy away from harshly criticizing a US president once at the *World Economic Forum* in Davos (CH).[136]

Entrepreneurs-CPC relationship, Xi's meetings with entrepreneurs: Ma, for example, is a member of the CPC. Chinese often laugh at his famous phrase, once told to every foreigner: "I love the party like my mother, but I don't go to bed with my mother." It humorously captures a serious point: even the wealthiest capitalists in China respect the primacy of politics. They do not attempt to form a party of capitalists, but instead develop their businesses in critical cooperation with the state and the CPC.

Jack Ma, like many other wealthy and influential entrepreneurs, serves on a strategic advisory board established by the CPC. This board coordinates corporate strategies with the national development strategy, drawing on the international experience of private companies. Chinese capitalists generally earn well, enjoy regular liberties, and benefit from both financial (banking) and political support in domestic and international business. Forming a party of capital or capitalism would, of course, be infeasible. In a dynamic, experimental, and successful economy like China's, however, any desire to do so is largely unnecessary and practically insignificant.

In recent years, such as in spring 2025, President Xi has demonstratively and repeatedly met with entrepreneurs, sometimes from both large corporations and SMEs, sometimes from Chinese and international corporations, and sometimes from certain industries or cross-technologies. The results have been impressive over the years: thorough initiatives to open up the financial and other service sectors for iFDI.

More details on the crackdown on, and re-regulation of the IT and platform oligopolies: Indicative of the primacy of politics over corporations have been the developments in recent years, namely the crackdowns on IT and platform companies in general, and on *Alibaba* in particular. After a public confrontation by Ma with the PBoC and competition-agency regulators and their regulations, starting in Fall 2020, after the first Covid-19 lockdown period in Spring that year, Ma was apparently forced to keep a low profile.

But further investigation had already started into the financial practices of Alibaba's financial branch, *Ant Group*, which was set to pursue what was said to be one of the largest *Initial Public Offerings* (IPO) ever, to be carried out at the Wall Street and Shanghai stock markets, expected to raise some 37 billion USD. The investigation culminated in the Shanghai Stock Exchange halting the IPO in late 2020, a few days before the scheduled date, due to concerns over financial practices. This resulted in a statement by the PBoC that Ant Group had, in fact, been evolving into a financial company with immoral practices vis-à-vis households, deriving the majority of its revenues from potentially nonlegal financial activities. It should therefore be regulated as a regular bank.

There had been government warnings against certain practices of the IT-industry for years. But by the end of 2020, however, it was found, with the help of household protests, that Alibaba had (mis)used its dominant position in the payment system, with *Alipay* having 1 billion users and more than 50 percent market share in the payments sector, to push its Ant Group into household *micro credits* during the first wave of uncertainty under Corona in spring 2020. By June 2020, Ant Group was estimated to have issued more than 330 billion USD in microcredits to around 100 million households.

Ant Group also worked to the detriment of regular banks, to which it shifted the credits, using the banks' usual capital deposit of 20 percent of a credit sum, while itself providing only 2 percent of its own capital as security.

On top of that, it turned out that households had little chance to exit the contracts (adhesion contracts), and Alibaba had already exclusively cross-linked credit platforms (Huabei and Jiebei[137]) with Alipay and other platforms and services, such as the *Taobao* platform for private online purchases or sales by households, farmers, or SMEs.

In the end, Ant Group had to pay a fine of 2.8 billion USD. Alibaba and Ant Group were split up, with Ant Group becoming a regular financial holding with an online-banking business under standard banking-sector regulation. Payment services, credit services, and e-commerce platforms had to be opened and disentangled.

Subsequently, the government cracked down on the exclusive contracts of the IT-corporations' platforms and summoned 35 of the largest IT-platform companies (incl. taxi services like Didi, delivery services like Meituan, etc.), *ordering their platforms to be interoperable "with one click" and non-exclusive.*

The government declared:

> The IT corporations must "open their walled gardens", "break more digital barriers!"[138]

For Alibaba, this led to a more thorough restructuring in 2023, turning it into a holding company with its subsidiaries separated into six independent firms. The ownership structure and corporate governance of Ant Group also underwent further changes, with Ma's shareholder voting rights drastically reduced and no other single shareholder holding a controlling stake. These changes were lauded by the government as steps toward transparency and accountability.[139]

This did not hurt the corporations' stock values too much. For instance, in October 2020, Alibaba had a stock value of 320 billion USD; by February 2021, this had declined to 235 billion, but the decline stabilized, and stock value began rising again. Ant Group's stock value just before the IPO had been 280 billion. The IPO, now within China (Shanghai, Shenzhen, Hong Kong), has made Alibaba and Ant Group together more valuable today.

Nowadays, there are strict guidelines in place for the ethical behavior of Chinese (IT) companies to be "lawful, reasonable, empathic", both domestically and internationally.[140]

Trust in the state and government: One of the "remote" side effects of that entire process was that the usual international trust polls (all conducted by US institutions, universities and companies, such as universities in *Stanford*, *San Diego*, and *Boston*, the *MIT*, or the *Edelman Trust Barometer*[141]), which, among general-trust surveys, also measure specific trust in governments across more than 120 countries, have consistently placed China in the top three in both general social trust among people and trust in the Chinese government.

The same applies to several regularly surveyed international comparative happiness rankings (such as the *Ipsos Happiness Index*[142]), in which China has consistently appeared among the top three countries in recent years.

Structural Policies and Economic Resilience

Trade- and tech-war resilience: Trump 1.0 era: This entire constellation of factors has so far prevented China, despite short-term disadvantages, from becoming the loser in the US' strategies of trade, technology, and hybrid warfare, economic disintegration, fragmentation, decoupling, disruption, and chaos strategy.

One of the few constructive and cooperative aspects was the *Phase One Deal* under Trump 1.0, concluded in January 2020 with the US election year in view. It aimed to restore the *status quo ante* for US farmers and prevent mass bankruptcies among them, while leaving China's domestic technological capacities and international value-chain optimization intact. The deal served as a mock victory for the dealmaker, intended to market to his electorate as a proof of strength in Fall 2020. In hindsight, while

Biden maintained and even expanded Trump's tariff approach, analysts widely concluded that the trade war was a failure on the side of the USA[143] and did not significantly affect China's structural capabilities.[144] In 2019 alone, in response to Washington's technology war, China implemented monetary and fiscal measures exceeding 600 billion USD, while further opening its economy to foreign trade and investment, later visa-free mass tourism as well, continuing its ongoing "Opening and Reform Era 2.0".

According to the quintessence of studies in economics, banking and finance, as well as IT technology, Trump achieved the opposite of what he intended in his simplistic, static "dealer" worldview: In fact, he initiated a process, which Biden subsequently continued and intensified, that increasingly triggered China to become more independent from the USA, with new geographic and company-based structures for Chinese trade, VACs, and i/oFDI. This process is likely to be completed sooner rather than later.

The trade conflict and bargaining in 2025 already saw a very different power structure between the USA and China in many respects, be it general trade, semiconductor technologies, or China's rare earths. And the Trump administration not only was forced to bargain but also to make major concessions, compared to its original intentions.

The example of Huawei's spectacular turnaround: A company-related illustration had been that, for example, Huawei was able to present its first mobile phone completely free of US components as early as December 2019, just one year after Trump's technology war specifically targeted the company.[145]

Only recently, in mid-2025, Huawei's founder, REN Zhengfei, gave a crucial and enlightening interview to the *Financial Times*, explaining the specific strategies that enabled the company to turn around from the brink of collapse in 2020, after Trump 1.0's sudden expulsion of Huawei from the USA, to becoming a globally leading IT company at the cutting edge in most growth sectors. Western media, however, referring to the interview, largely focused on a single aspect of the story: Huawei's chip capacities. "Huawei plays down its chipmaking capabilities", as the *FT* itself mistakenly wrote.[146] Those who listened more closely, however, better understood the spectacular content. China's *People's Daily* framed it differently: "The more open the country, the more progress we make". REN himself had explained:

> We are using math to compensate for physical limitations. We add Moore's laws by non-Moore solutions; we use cluster computing to support weaker

> single silicon chips. In the end, we achieve equivalent practical results [...] Software cannot be sanctioned, it is based on math, code, and algorithms, software cannot be blocked.[147]

What REN illustrates here is a clear example of China's *experimentalism* at *China speed*. Under Trump 2.0, US companies such as *Nvidia* were blocked by the White House from trading advanced semiconductors with China. And with the compliance of the Dutch government, the leading Dutch supplier of EUV lithography (extreme ultraviolet-lithography) for sub-7 nm semiconductors, *ASML*, was also prohibited from exporting its advanced machines to China. In the end, there were even attempts to block the sharing of semiconductor design software with China, aiming to prevent Chinese access to 4-, 3-, or 2-nm chips.

More recently, the Dutch government went so far as to fully intervene in the operations of a private Chinese semiconductor company in the EU, Nexperia, halting its business entirely and placing it under state bureaucratic control and Dutch appropriation. This represents a far-right Dutch deviation from the market economy—a quasi-socialization. Measures like these from the West, the USA, and the EU are increasingly authoritarian, autocratic, and seemingly desperate.[148]

Increased Chinese resilience under Trump 2.0: However, all of this reflects a static, linear, and mechanistic—and often frightened and desperate—Western mindset, leaving little room for forward-looking bargaining, strategically shaped division of labor, or constructive cooperation. Meanwhile, China has already become far more resilient, advanced, and prepared to face Trump 2.0 and his EU allies than it was under Trump 1.0.

In terms of semiconductors, REN indicated that China has leveraged intelligence to combine non-cutting-edge chips in ways that achieve the same speed and functionality as the most advanced 4- or 2-nm-chips from, say, *Nvidia* or the *Taiwan Semiconductor Manufacturing Company* (TSMC). Beyond the microelectronics, China now controls alternative technologies for improving chip performance, e.g., optical constructions that allow optronic or photonic chips to reach computational speeds surpassing even most advanced Western microelectronic chips, using light rather than electrons. Mass production and application of this new kind of "chip" (no longer "semiconductors") is expected within one to two years.

And again, China is simultaneously developing alternative chip materials and computation-construction principles, including the use of new biological or biochemical materials for specialized applications.

Thus, the USA has effectively lost the "chip war", having inadvertently compelled China to rely even more heavily on its own capacities, which in turn has greatly accelerated research and innovation in the country.

More generally, China had prepared for a Trump 2.0 era and its disruptive hybrid war.

In terms of trade, China is now far less dependent on the USA than it was in the years following 2017. In 2023, only 15 percent of China's exports went to the USA, representing less than 3 percent of its GDP—a significant decline from the Trump 1.0 era. Chinese trade has become far more geographically diversified, spanning over 150 partner countries within the Belt and Road Initiative across Asia, Africa, and Latin America, as well as deepening ties with the ASEAN region and the South-East Asian RCEP.

While China has already strengthened and now leads across most technology areas, there has also been an empowerment of Western capital in terms of inward FDI (iFDI), traditionally in manufacturing but increasingly in services and finance. This has been facilitated by an extended and intensified strategy of *reform and opening*, alongside the strengthening of the domestic economic macrocircuit. By 2025, more foreign-invested enterprises are active in China than in 2017. These companies not only generate substantial profits from their Chinese operations but have also repatriated significant portions of their earnings, at times even reducing the net stock of invested capital.[149]

Last but not least, after years of escalating provocations from Washington—encouraged by both political factions in Congress, which pursue essentially identical strategies toward China—and following years of limited diplomacy punctuated by increasingly sharp warnings to both the Trump and Biden administrations, China finally played two new cards during the early-2025 trade frenzy under Trump 2.0.

First, Beijing stopped responding to Trump's increasingly absurd tariff-rate announcements. Once tariffs exceeded roughly 60 percent—the approximate average cost-price advantage of Chinese goods—trade was effectively blocked anyway. So when Trump announced tariffs of 125 percent or even 245 percent, Chinese officials simply dismissed the figures as meaningless. One might as well have spoken of 1000 or 10,000 percent tariffs, since anything above 60 percent had no practical effect. China's Ministry of Foreign Affairs publicly characterized Trump's "numbers game" as irrelevant, stating that no further reaction would follow. Up until then, China had responded with counter-tariffs but consistently emphasized that it would not be intimidated by the Trump administration's trade war.

US ports and retail shelves began to run empty, inflation rose further, and the dollar gradually depreciated. American soy and other farmers once again suffered, as they had under China's initial import restrictions starting in 2017.

On top of this, China revealed its true leverage for the first time: control over rare-earth exports. A complete halt would have paralyzed Western high-tech and climate-relevant industries, as well as Western military operations, within a few months. The West quickly and painfully realized this vulnerability.

Suddenly, Washington initiated trade talks with China, culminating in a major deal by June 2025. Trump's critics in the United States have since labeled him "TACO"—*Trump Always Chickens Out*—whenever China retaliates decisively.

China's stance, behavior, and the outcomes of the deals were widely regarded as a "victory", both internationally and within Washington's political arena. It also served as an encouragement for third countries, where China was increasingly seen as a leading coordinator of the Global South. As many Western experts remarked: "Trump Will Make China Great Again."[150] And, as a side effect, an *entire Chinese export-control regime* seems to be emerging.[151]

A NYT comment: Thomas L. Friedman of the *New York Times* had visited Huawei's research campus in Shanghai and commented in an Op-Ed:

> I Just Saw the Future. It Was Not in America. [...] at least do your homework. There is too little of that in both parties today and too much consensus that the politically safe space is to hammer Beijing, chant a few rounds of 'U.S.A., U.S.A.', issue some platitudes that democracies will always out-innovate autocracies and call it a day. [...] I prefer to express my patriotism by being brutally honest [...] I believe the best future for both of China and US, on the eve of the AI revolution, is a strategy called: Made in America by American workers in partnership with Chinese capital and technology.[152]

More to Come on Fakes, Emotions, and Fearmongering on China's Rise and Path to Sovereignty

Fake statements, hubris, and emotional arousal: That Op-Ed was one of a few exceptions in the Western media and mental landscape. Fake news, mass psychology, opinion-making, and the manipulation of media-driven voter moods have become pervasive. Today, the global oligarchic media and entertainment industries largely pursue the purpose of whipping up emotions in the population, often appealing to the lowest instincts that lie dormant within people, and to the simplest childish ways of thinking. Media, governments, and official political parties have driven Western populations into a war-like state of mind to better maintain their own political command through ever less representative formal parliamentary majorities.

As another case of manipulation, Trump, for example, apparently owed his first election victory in 2016 to the massive misuse of purchased Facebook personal data and the targeted dissemination of a worldview built on an unprecedented culture of erratic fake statements.[153]

Why this could later be blamed on *the Russian* will remain the secret of the Washington DEMs,[154] those who, as repeatedly documented online, have orchestrated election interventions, overthrows of elected governments, and color revolutions in dozens of countries over the past decades.

China seems to have largely escaped the Western media-intellectual-political patterns of "values" hubris, emotional arousals, and war- and fearmongering. It largely continues to maintain diplomatic language and behavior. Unsurprisingly, it is a prime target for media sensationalism and political bashing, with its own media and IT sectors particularly in the crosshairs.

Versus Chinese everyday culture: We will explore this in greater detail later in the book. Today, many travelers to China are surprised to find that the average Chinese are open, relaxed, friendly, and helpful, showing neither hubris, supremacy, nor xenophobia. The internet is full of related travel reports of Western (mainly young) people. Chinese are often better informed about the world, and particularly about Western countries, than the average Westerner is about China. They usually know more about us than we do about them and show greater interest in our societies than Westerners do in theirs, as Chinese students consistently outperform

Western peers also in geography on the international *PISA* rankings. Oppressed, anxious, dumbed-down slaves or "human bots" certainly look different than today's Chinese.

More people-to-people exchanges: We usually then ask ourselves how this can be, given that they don't have Google, Facebook, Wikipedia, "free press", "free politics", etc. In fact, the "free West" today is becoming more restrictive in people-to-people exchanges between Chinese and Western citizens than China. The "pro-Western" Taiwanese government, for instance, limits young people's exchanges with the mainland,[155] and Washington has rejected China's late-2023 initiative for 50,000 young Americans to visit China.[156]

Returning to "freedom and the internet" below: The Chinese Google is called *Baidu*, which, alongside Google, is the most visited search engine in the world, used in many countries. The average Chinese user has developed her own "cyber sovereignty", often operating at a higher level of sophistication than the typical Western user. We will return in a specialized chapter to the related complex conceptions of "information", "freedom", and "democracy", as well as the emergence of socially and ecologically responsible mass behavior, and examine the role and practice of the internet in China across the various contexts.

Notes

1. E.g., Graebner et al. (2021), Dai and Elsner (2021), Elsner and Schwardt (2014, 2015).
2. For China, e.g., Guo Wenbo et al., "Inter-Organizational Governance and Trilateral Trust Building: A Case Study of Crowdsourcing-Based Open Innovation in China" (Guo et al. 2017).
3. E.g., Carsten Herrmann-Pillath (2017), 309–340, 520ff.; "Chinese Experiments in Socialist Modernisation", special issue of *Wenhua Zongsheng* 3(1), 2025.
4. E.g., Poppe (2019).
5. E.g., Godfree Roberts, "How China Outplayed the West and the WTO", *Here Comes China*, June 21, 2025, herecomeschina@substack.com
6. E.g., Li Kai et al., "Public interest or regulatory capture: Theory and evidence from China's airfare deregulation" (Li et al. 2019).
7. E.g., Cao Yin, "Courts' IP decisions win respect", *China Daily*, July 13, 2018, p. 1; this case was about the US brand "Michael Jordan"—the Chinese company had to change the Chinese syllable spelling of their product to avoid linguistic similarities to the US brand. This was ordered

by the Vice President of China's highest court and publicly associated by her with the goal of "Credible China". "Michael Jordan" had to be compensated.

8. In the following, e.g., Dai and Yang (2017).
9. Li Chenhui, Lian Xubei, Zhang Zhi, "Public education expenditure, institution development, and regional innovations: an empirical evidence from China", *Economics e-journal* 3/2018: https://www.econstor.eu/bitstream/10419/176565/1/1016508158.pdf, visited May 30, 2024.
10. E.g., Bernhard Ganglmair, "Geschäftsgeheimnisse besser zu schützen, kann dem Gemeinwohl entgegenstehen [Better protection of trade secrets can be contrary to the common good]", *ZEW—Leibniz Centre for European Economic Research*, March 13, 2019: https://www.zew.de/das-zew/aktuelles/geschaeftsgeheimnisse-besser-zu-schuetzen-kann-dem-gemeinwohl-entgegenstehen, visited May 30, 2024.
11. E.g., Yan Shuo, "Corporate Political Connections and the Finance-Growth Nexus: Evidence from China", *SSRN*, June 4, 2018: https://papers.ssrn.com/sol3/papers.cfm?abstract_id=3190274, visited May 30, 2024.
12. E.g., Zhang Lanying et al., "Controlling Corporate Power in China: Case Studies of Seed Companies and Water Distribution" (Zhang et al. 2018).
13. E.g., Falk Hartig, "China: Das Reich der E-Autos [China: The Realm of Electric Cars]", *Blätter für deutsche und internationale Politik* 6/2018, 25–28.
14. See "Charts: China's global electric car dominance", *Adamas Intelligence*, April 19, 2024: https://www.adamasintel.com/charts-china-global-electric-car-dominance/, visited May 31, 2024; and "China has 20.41 million new energy vehicles running on roads by end of 2023", *Gasgoo*, January 15, 2024: https://autonews.gasgoo.com/m/70030708.html, visited May 31, 2024.
15. E.g., *China Daily*, July 11, 2018, p. 6.
16. E.g., Sean Fleming, "China joins list of nations banning the sale of old-style fossil-fueled vehicles", *World Economic Forum*, November 11, 2020: https://www.weforum.org/agenda/2020/11/china-bans-fossil-fuel-vehicles-electric/, visited May 31, 2024.
17. E.g., Dannie Peng, "China leads improvements in fossil fuel engine efficiency to fill electric gap", *South China Morning Post*, April 23, 2024: https://www.scmp.com/news/china/science/article/3259991/china-leads-improvements-fossil-fuel-engine-efficiency-fill-electric-gap, visited May 31, 2024.
18. Poppe (2019).
19. Frank Schuengel, "The Chinese will probably no longer buy cars 20 years from now", *Visor*, December 26, 2018: https://visor.ph/industry/the-

chinese-will-probably-no-longer-buy-cars-20-years-from-now/, visited May 31, 2024.
20. E.g., "China has over 350 mln electric bicycles", *Xinhua*, May 7, 2024: https://english.news.cn/20240507/ee7db5383a69442ebe0fcdb9da478cb0/c.html, visited May 31, 2024.
21. E.g., "Hyperdrive Daily: The Jon Snow of China's Electric Car Market", *Bloomberg News*, July 26, 2021: https://www.bloomberg.com/news/newsletters/2021-07-26/hyperdrive-daily-the-jon-snow-of-china-s-electric-car-market, visited May 31, 2024.
22. More detail: Dai and Liu (2017).
23. Ibid.
24. E.g., David J. Lynch, Jeanne Whalen, "U.S. and Chinese automakers are headed in completely different directions", *Washington Post*, May 18, 2024: https://www.washingtonpost.com/business/2024/05/18/china-us-ev-cars/, visited May 31, 2024.
25. Dai and Liu (2017).
26. See for example: R. Burdett-Gardiner, "China Moves to Solar Powered Roads", *The Renewable Energy Hub*, July 27, 2023: https://www.renewableenergyhub.co.uk/blog/china-moves-to-solar-powered-roads, visited June 1, 2024.
27. E.g., C. Kühl, "Hydrogen set to be the next booming sector for Chinese cleantech", *Science Business*, April 18, 2024: https://sciencebusiness.net/news/hydrogen/hydrogen-set-be-next-booming-sector-chinese-cleantech, visited June 1, 2024.
28. In certain areas, such as the battery cell, the car industry largely relies on Chinese technology, as the discussion about a planned European battery cell factory in Germany has shown. The Chinese knowledge advantage relates to the fact that in East Asia 80 percent of all e-mobility batteries are manufactured. According to the German *FAZ*, that first European battery cell factory of the Chinese firm CATL can be described as "a case of Chinese development aid for Germany". See T. Piller, "Chinas Entwicklungshilfe für Batterien aus Deutschland [China's development aid for batteries from Germany]", *FAZ*, October 2, 2023: https://www.faz.net/aktuell/wirtschaft/unternehmen/catl-in-thueringen-chinas-entwicklungshilfe-fuer-batterien-aus-deutschland-19214239.html, visited June 1, 2024. For another case of Chinese "development aid" for Europe, see for example: T. Kiefer, "Smart Driving Technology Center in Berlin: So entwickelt Nio Technologien für den europäischen Markt [Smart Driving Technology Center in Berlin: how Nio develops technologies for the European market]", *automotiveIT*, April 17, 2024.
29. Poppe (2019) (similarly also: AHK Greater China, "Kurzanalyse und Strategiepapier 'Smart and Connected Mobility im Sichuan Becken'

[Short analysis and strategy paper 'Smart and Connected Mobility in the Sichuan Basin']", published by BMUB, Berlin, 2018).

30. Ibid.
31. "Strengere Regeln: China geht den Lastwagen an den Kragen [Stricter rules: China is cracking down on trucks]", *FAZ*, January 6, 2019: https://www.faz.net/aktuell/wirtschaft/china-erhebt-strengere-regeln-fuer-diesel-lkw-15974829.html, visited June 1, 2024.
32. Ibid.
33. D. Fockenbrock, "Volvos Tempolimit regt zum Nachdenken an—Doch Nachahmer wird es kaum finden [Volvo's speed limit provokes thought—But it will hardly find imitators]", *Handelsblatt*, March 6, 2019.
34. J. Oliveira, "Neue globale Strategie: Wie Volvo unter der Geely-Flagge Erfolge erzielt [New global strategy: How Volvo achieves success under the Geely flag]", *Automobil Produktion*, December 14, 2023: https://www.automobil-produktion.de/management/wie-volvo-unter-geely-flagge-erfolge-erzielt-617.html, visited June 1, 2024.
35. For example: Tom Hancock, Enda Curran, "China Set to Topple U.S. as Biggest Economy Sooner After Virus", *Bloomberg*, January 14, 2021: https://www.bloomberg.com/news/articles/2021-01-14/a-year-after-covid-began-china-s-economy-is-beating-the-world, visited October 28, 2025.
36. For example: Enda Curran, "These Could Be the World's Biggest Economies by 2030", *Bloomberg*, January 8, 2019: https://www.bloomberg.com/news/articles/2019-01-08/world-s-biggest-economies-seen-dominated-by-asian-ems-by-2030, visited October 28, 2025.
37. Alexandre Tanzi, Wei Lu, "China to Leapfrog 56 Nations During Quarter-Century Income Surge", *Bloomberg*, November 17, 2020: https://www.bloomberg.com/news/articles/2020-11-17/china-to-leapfrog-56-nations-during-quarter-century-income-surge, visited October 28, 2025.
38. Zichen Wang, "China's Consumption Is Not Nearly as Low as It Appears: CF40 Policy Brief", *Pekingnology* and *The East is Red—CCG* July 17, 2025, eastisred@substack.com, visited July 18, 2025.
39. E.g., Victoria Bela, "Average Chinese national now eats more protein than an American: UN food agency", *South China Morning Post* July 18, 2024, https://www.scmp.com/news/china/science/article/3270808/average-chinese-national-now-eats-more-protein-american-united-nations, visited July 18, 2025.
40. E.g., "China's forex reserves rise to 3.2457 trillion USD", *Xinhua*, April 7, 2024: https://english.www.gov.cn/archive/statistics/202404/07/content_WS661289c1c6d0868f4e8e5d3f.html, visited June 2, 2024.

41. For example: G. Braunberger, "Bei einer Finanzkrise: Warum China besser vorbereitet ist als der Westen [In a financial crisis: Why China is better prepared than the West]", *FAZ*, January 26, 2019: https://www.faz.net/aktuell/finanzen/finanzmarkt/warum-china-auf-eine-finanzkrise-besser-vorbereitet-ist-als-der-westen-16008190.html, visited June 2, 2024. See also: Kadri (2017).
42. For one of the most informative studies on the development of the Chinese financial sector, from the formal banking sector to earlier informal and "gray" financing forms, on the new, internet-based and since 2016 formally approved and regulated crowdfunding sector, on the connections of the finance sector with the large IT companies, and on the role of the financial sector as promotor of technological development, infrastructures and start-ups, see: Andrea S. Funk, *Crowdfunding in China*, Cham (CH), 2019.
43. Since 1990, smaller, strategically unimportant state-owned companies began to be sold (privatized), while the strategically important larger state-owned companies were modernized, made more efficient, and put into strategic positions, pushing their respective industries; e.g., Zhang (2018), 106ff.
44. E.g., Kunzmann (2018), 67ff.
45. E.g., Wolfram Elsner, "Speculative financial capitalism wacking out over an 'impossible' profit rate. The infeasibility of a 'usual' real average profit rate, considering fictitious capital, and its implications," in: *Marx, Veblen, and the Foundations of Heterodox Economics: Essays in Honor of John F. Henry*, ed. by Tae-Hee Jo and Frederic S. Lee, 199–227, London, New York: Routledge, 2015.
46. E.g., Canfei He, Jiangyong Lu, Haifeng Qian, "Entrepreneurship in China", *Small Business Economics* 52 (2019), 563–572.
47. E.g., D. Fischer, "Neuartige Innovationsmuster in der chinesischen Industrie—Entrepreneurship in China [Novel Innovation Patterns in the Chinese Industry—Entrepreneurship in China]", in: J. Freimuth, M. Schädler (eds.), *Chinas Innovationsstrategie in der globalen Wissensökonomie* [China's Innovation Strategy in the Global Knowledge Economy], Wiesbaden: Springer-Gabler, 2017, 179–204; Y. Lai, N.S. Vonortas, "Regional entrepreneurial ecosystems in China", *Industrial and Corporate Change* 28(4), 2019, 875–897.
48. E.g., *Solvecon Forex-Report*, April 8, 2019, p. 3.
49. E.g., Xinhua, "China home to 369 unicorn enterprises: report", *China Daily*, April 29, 2024: https://global.chinadaily.com.cn/a/202404/29/WS662efd44a31082fc043c4962.html, visited June 2, 2024.
50. E.g., Fu Tong, "What determines firms' access to credit in the absence of effective economic institutions: evidence from China" (Fu 2017).

51. E.g., Xu Jianguo, "China's Internet Finance: A Critical Review", *China & World Economy* 25(4), 2017, 78–92.
52. E.g., Chai Shijun et al., "Social Networks and Informal Financial Inclusion in the People's Republic of China", *ADBI Working Paper*, No. 802, January 2018: https://www.adb.org/sites/default/files/publication/399046/adbi-wp802.pdf, visited January 8, 2025.
53. E.g., Xu (2017) (see above).
54. E.g., *China Daily*, July 11, 2018, p. 14.
55. E.g., Stephen Engle, "China $10 Trillion Shadow Bank Crackdown Has Long Way to Go", *Bloomberg News*, May 28, 2018: https://www.bloomberg.com/news/articles/2018-05-28/china-s-10-trillion-shadow-bank-crackdown-has-a-long-way-to-go, visited June 2, 2024.
56. E.g., Chai et al. (2018).
57. E.g., "China kontrolliert zwei Drittel des globalen Bitcoin-Netzwerks [China controls two-thirds of the global Bitcoin network]", *Deutsche Wirtschaftsnachrichten*, December 15, 2019: https://deutsche-wirtschafts-nachrichten.de/501362/china-kontrolliert-zwei-drittel-des-globalen-bitcoin-netzwerks, visited June 2, 2024.
58. E.g., Garrick Hileman, Michael Rauchs, *Global Cryptocurrency Benchmarking Study*, Cambridge Centre for Alternative Finance, Cambridge, UK, 2017.
59. E.g., Laura He, "China makes major push in its ambitious digital yuan project", *CNN*, April 24, 2023: https://edition.cnn.com/2023/04/24/economy/china-digital-yuan-government-salary-intl-hnk/index.html, visited June 2, 2024.
60. E.g., Arjun Kharpal, "China hits Alibaba affiliate Ant Group with $985 million fine for violating various regulations", *CNBC*, July 7, 2023: https://www.cnbc.com/2023/07/07/china-hits-alibaba-affiliate-ant-group-hit-with-985-million-fine.html, visited June 2, 2024.
61. For the years 2012–2017, e.g., *Steingarts Morning Briefing*, May 16, 2019, 6ff.
62. As of 2023, the USA and China (rank 1 and 2 resp.) dominate global high value VC funding with a 70 percent share. For example: "US and China dominate global high value VC funding deals volume with 70% share in 2023, reveals GlobalData", *GlobalData*, February 7, 2024: https://www.globaldata.com/media/business-fundamentals/us-and-china-dominate-global-high-value-vc-funding-deals-volume-with-70-share-in-2023-reveals-globaldata/, visited June 2, 2024.
63. More detail: Zhang Fan, *The Institutional Evolution of China, Government vs Market* (Zhang 2018), 227ff.
64. Zhang (2018), 217ff.
65. Rasmus (2017), p. 256.

66. Two examples of the trend of "de-dollarization": Summer Said, Stephen Kalin, "Saudi Arabia Considers Accepting Yuan Instead of Dollars for Chinese Oil Sales", *Wall Street Journal*, March 15, 2022: https://www.wsj.com/articles/saudi-arabia-considers-accepting-yuan-instead-of-dollars-for-chinese-oil-sales-11647351541, visited June 2, 2024. And: "De-dollarization: Is the US dollar losing its dominance?", *J.P. Morgan*, August 31, 2023: https://www.jpmorgan.com/insights/global-research/currencies/de-dollarization, visited June 2, 2024. The J.P. Morgan report mentions that "In July 2023, Bolivia became the latest South American country—after Brazil and Argentina—to pay for imports and exports using the Chinese renminbi."
67. E.g., City of London Corporation and The People's Bank of China Representative Office for Europe, *London RMB Business Bi-annual Report* 16(2), 2023, p. 4: https://www.cityoflondon.gov.uk/assets/Business/london-rmb-biannual-report-dec2023.pdf, visited June 2, 2024.
68. E.g., Arendse Huld, "China-Germany Bilateral Direct Investment: Trends and Outlook", *China Briefing*, February 5, 2024: https://www.china-briefing.com/news/germany-china-investment-trends-and-outlook/, visited June 2, 2024.
69. For example Rasmus (2017), 252ff.
70. E.g., Eric Li, "Chinese New Economy and Globalisation—The Sequel", presentation at the *Khazanah Megatrends Forum 2023*, October 2, 2023: https://www.youtube.com/watch?v=Vb835NzfzFw, visited January 18, 2025.
71. "Real estate conundrum, Retail sales still well below trend & Don't lose your makers (skilled producers)", *Real China Charts.*
72. E.g., Hsiao-Yi Chan, "Relationship Between Housing Price and Income in China", *Highlights in Business, Economics and Management* (24) 2024, 1888–1895: https://drpress.org/ojs/index.php/HBEM/article/view/16612/16130, visited January 19, 2025.
73. "Chinese developer Country Garden reports $6.7bn loss amid fears of another Evergrande", *The Guardian*, August 31, 2023: https://www.theguardian.com/world/2023/aug/31/country-garden-chinese-property-developer-reports-half-year-finanical-loss-fears-default-risk, visited January 19, 2025.
74. Laura He, "Country Garden has defaulted on its debt. What's next?", *CNN*, October 27, 2023: https://edition.cnn.com/country-garden-default-debt-what-next/index.html, visited January 19, 2025.
75. Mariko Oi, "Evergrande: Crisis-hit Chinese property giant ordered to liquidate", *BBC*, January 29, 2024: https://www.bbc.com/news/business-67562522, visited January 19, 2025.

76. Jiahui Huang, "China Securities Regulator Fines Evergrande Unit $580 Million", *The Wall Street Journal*, May 31, 2024: https://www.wsj.com/finance/regulation/china-securities-regulator-fines-evergrande-and-founder-586-million-b2d9fe60, visited January 19, 2025.
77. "China fines PwC $62 million for its role in the Evergrande collapse", *CNN Business*, September 13, 2024: https://edition.cnn.com/2024/09/13/business/china-fines-pwc-evergrande-collapse/index.html, visited January 19, 2025.
78. "Chinese officials begin crackdown on real-estate speculation", *Asia Financial*, Jan. 29, 2021: https://www.asiafinancial.com/chinese-officials-begin-crackdown-on-real-estate-speculation, visited January 18, 2025.
79. "China's property lifeline exposes banks to big losses, job cuts", *South China Morning Post*, November 28, 2023: https://www.scmp.com/business/banking-finance/article/3243045/chinas-property-lifeline-exposes-banks-big-losses-job-cuts, visited January 18, 2025.
80. E.g., W. Hirn, "Immobilien: Weiße Liste, rote Zahlen [Real estate: white list, red figures]", *ChinaHirn*, February 13, 2024: https://www.china-hirn.de/2024/02/13/wirtschaft-i-immobilien-weisse-liste-rote-zahlen/, visited January 18, 2025.
81. E.g., Yulu Ao, Ji Siqi, "China property: Beijing launches US$41 billion of funds to buy unsold homes, repurchase of 'idle' land in drive to rescue housing market", *South China Morning Post*, May 17, 2024: https://www.scmp.com/business/china-business/article/3263127/china-property-beijing-launches-us41-billion-fund-buy-unsold-homes-major-drive-rescue-housing-market, visited January 19, 2025.
82. E.g., Chen Bo, Han Wei, "Shenzhen Starts to Buy up and Transform Unsold Homes to Bolster Market", *Caixin Global*, August 9, 2024: https://www.caixinglobal.com/2024-08-09/shenzhen-starts-to-buy-up-and-transform-unsold-homes-to-bolster-market-102224713.html, visited January 19, 2025.
83. E.g., *Real China Charts*, October 18, 2023: https://www.realchinacharts.com/p/real-estate-conundrum-retail-sales, visited January 18, 2025.
84. E.g., "China's New Growth Strategy Backed by Robots", *International Federation of Robotics*, August 29, 2024: https://ifr.org/ifr-press-releases/news/chinas-new-growth-strategy-backed-by-robots, visited January 19, 2025.
85. Just picking one example, Ling Xin, "China's biggest solar-powered drone completes first test flight", *SCMP*, September 5, 2022: https://www.scmp.com/news/china/science/article/3191396/chinas-biggest-solar-powered-drone-completes-first-test-flight, visited June 6, 2024.

86. E.g., Mahmood Shubbak, "The technological system of production and innovation: The case of photovoltaic technology in China", *Research Policy* 48(4), 2019, 993–1015.
87. Ibid.
88. E.g., Juan R. Perilla Jimenez, "Mainstream and evolutionary views of technology, economic growth and catching up", *Journal of Evolutionary Economics* 29(3), 2019, 823–852; Yandong Zhao, Miao Liao, "Chinese perspectives on responsible innovation", in: *International Handbook on Responsible Innovation*, ed. by R. von Schomberg, J. Hankins, 426–440, Cheltenham, Northampton: E. Elgar, 2019.
89. E.g., Anton Shilov, "China filed 25% more patents than the U.S. in 2023—heavily sanctioned Huawei led all companies worldwide despite bans", *Tom's Hardware*, March 17, 2024: https://www.tomshardware.com/tech-industry/china-filed-25-more-patents-than-the-us-in-2023-banned-huawei-led-all-companies-worldwide-despite-heavy-us-sanctions, visited June 4, 2024.
90. The latest (2025) *Nature Index* again sees China with upward numbers in research output over 2024 (+17 percent), while the five Western countries following in the ranks 2–6 (USA, Germany, UK, Japan, France) are losing around 10 percent (except Germany (−2 percent) and behind them Canada, Switzerland, Australia, and Italy are losing ranks as well). See: https://www.nature.com/nature-index/research-leaders/2025/country/all/global, visited July 22, 2025.
91. Jennifer Wong Leung, Stephan Robin, Danielle Cave, "ASPI's two-decade Critical Technology Tracker: The rewards of long-term research investment", *Australian Strategic Policy Institute*, August 28, 2024: https://www.aspi.org.au/report/aspis-two-decade-critical-technology-tracker/, visited August 12, 2025.
92. E.g., Hu Albert G., Gary H. Jefferson, "A great wall of patents: What is behind China's recent patent explosion?", *Journal of Development Economics* 90 (2009), 57–68.
93. E.g., Can Huang, Cong Cao, Wim Coreynen, "Stronger and more just? Recent reforms of China's intellectual property rights system and their implications", *Asia Pacific Journal of Innovation and Entrepreneurship*, December 18, 2023: https://www.emerald.com/insight/content/doi/10.1108/APJIE-04-2023-0081/full/html#sec013, visited June 4, 2024.
94. Fred Reed, "China Tech: Interesting Bits and Pieces", *Information Clearing House*, June 30, 2017: https://www.informationclearinghouse.info/47364.htm, visited June 4, 2024.

95. E.g., Baban Hasnat, "Big Data: An Institutional Perspective on Opportunities and Challenges", *Journal of Economic Issues* 52(2), 2018, 580–588.
96. Ibid.
97. Sun Chi, "China's investment in AI expected to reach $38.1b in 2027", *China Daily*, October 23, 2023: https://global.chinadaily.com.cn/a/202308/23/WS64e5b34fa31035260b81dc9f.html, visited June 4, 2024.
98. E.g., Jörg Kronauer, "Planlos in die Zukunft [Planless into the future]", *junge Welt*, March 19, 2019.
99. Hasnat, ibid.
100. Wolfgang Buechele, "No reason to be afraid of China", *LinkedIn*, May 21, 2019: https://www.linkedin.com/pulse/reason-afraid-china-dr-wolfgang-buechele, visited June 4, 2024.
101. Ibid.
102. Ibid.
103. More detail in: Hasnat, "Big Data: An Institutional Perspective on Opportunities ..." (Hasnat 2018).
104. Manya Koetse, "In the race for AI supremacy, China and the US are travelling on entirely different tracks", *The Guardian*, January 9, 2024: https://www.theguardian.com/world/2024/jan/09/in-the-race-for-ai-supremacy-china-and-the-us-are-travelling-on-entirely-different-tracks, visited June 4, 2024.
105. E.g., Mary Whitfill Roeloffs, "What Is DeepSeek? New Chinese AI Startup Rivals OpenAI—And Claims It's Far Cheaper", *Forbes*, January 27, 2025: https://www.forbes.com/sites/maryroeloffs/2025/01/27/what-is-deepseek-new-chinese-ai-startup-rivals-openai-and-claims-its-far-cheaper/, visited February 14, 2025.
106. Ibid.
107. E.g., James Vincent, "The DeepSeek panic reveals an AI world ready to blow", *The Guardian*, January 28, 2025: https://www.theguardian.com/commentisfree/2025/jan/28/deepseek-r1-ai-world-chinese-chatbot-tech-world-western, visited February 14, 2025.
108. See for example: Shirin Ghaffary, Rachel Metz, "DeepSeek Challenges Everyone's Assumptions About AI Costs", *Bloomberg*, January 28, 2025: https://www.bloomberg.com/news/articles/2025-01-28/deepseek-ai-platform-brings-a-1-trillion-market-reckoning-on-cost, visited February 14, 2025.
109. Ibid.
110. See for example: Elizabeth Gibney, "China's cheap, open AI model DeepSeek thrills scientists", *Nature*, January 23, 2025: https://www.nature.com/articles/d41586-025-00229-6, visited February 14, 2025.

111. Vincent (2025), ibid.
112. Tim Marcin, "OpenAI accuses Chinese competitor DeepSeek of stealing data, internet digs into the 'irony'", *Mashable*, January 29, 2025: https://mashable.com/article/internet-reactions-jokes-openai-deepseek, visited February 14, 2025.
113. Nicole Hinojosa, "China May Soon Be the Top AI Innovator in the World, New Report Finds", *Information Technology and Innovation Foundation*, August 26, 2024: https://itif.org/publications/2024/08/26/china-may-soon-be-the-top-ai-innovator-in-the-world-new-report-finds/, visited February 14, 2025.
114. John Naughton, "Can China keep generative AI under its control? Well, it contained the internet", *The Guardian*, April 22, 2023: https://www.theguardian.com/commentisfree/2023/apr/22/can-china-keep-generative-ai-under-its-control-well-it-contained-the-internet, visited June 4, 2024.
115. E.g., Larry Romanoff, "History of Chinese Inventions. The Present and the Future", *Transcend Media Service*, December 23, 2019: https://www.transcend.org/tms/2019/12/history-of-chinese-inventions-the-present-and-the-future-recent-chinese-state-of-the-art-innovations/, visited May 17, 2024.
116. Tom Huddleston, "Carly Fiorina Says the Chinese 'Don't Innovate'", *Time Magazine*, May 26, 2015: https://time.com/3897081/carly-fiorina-china-innovation/, visited June 7, 2024.
117. Eva Dou, "Chinese Innovation: Now Comes the Hard Part, Says Study", *The Wall Street Journal*, October 21, 2015: https://www.wsj.com/articles/BL-CJB-27938, visited June 7, 2024.
118. Romanoff, ibid.
119. See: Mark Magnier, "Chinese-Americans protest US Senator Marsha Blackburn's tweet over China's 'cheating and stealing'", *South China Morning Post*, December 10, 2020: https://www.scmp.com/news/china/article/3113280/chinese-americans-protest-us-senator-marsha-blackburns-tweets-over, visited June 16, 2024; Stuart Anderson, "Chinese Students Still Denied Visas Under Trump Immigration Order", *Forbes*, April 11, 2023: https://www.forbes.com/sites/stuartanderson/2023/04/11/chinese-students-still-denied-visas-under-trump-immigration-order/, visited June 16, 2024.
120. Pew Research also found that the Covid-19 pandemic has added fuel to the fire, especially with stigmatizing designations such as "Chinese Virus" made by then-president Trump, among others. E.g., Neil G. Ruiz, Carolyne Im, Ziyao Tian, "Discrimination Experiences Shape Most Asian Americans' Lives", *Pew Research Center*, November 30, 2023: https://www.pewresearch.org/race-and-ethnicity/2023/11/30/

discrimination-experiences-shape-most-asian-americans-lives/, visited June 16, 2024.
121. E.g., Drago Bosnic, "Western 'Normalization': Stealing Russian, Chinese and Others' Foreign Assets", *Global Research*, October 25, 2025.
122. See for example: Finbarr Bermingham, "Dutch seized Nexperia over fears Chinese owners planned to move chip production to China", *South China Morning Post*, October 18, 2025: https://www.scmp.com/news/china/diplomacy/article/3329476/dutch-seized-nexperia-over-fears-chinese-owners-planned-move-chip-production-china, visited November 9, 2025.
123. John Liu, "How a Dutch chipmaker got caught up in the US-China tech war", *CNN*, October 15, 2025: https://edition.cnn.com/2025/10/15/tech/netherlands-nexperia-us-china-tech-war-intl-hnk, visited November 11, 2025.
124. E.g., Zichen Wang, "Dutch govt accused of freezing operations of Chinese semiconductor giant's chipmaker Nexperia", *Pekingnology*, October 12, 2025.
125. For example: Jowi Morales, "Dutch government allegedly folds to supply chain pressure, will relinquish control of Nexperia in China spat—reports say deal contingent upon China allowing firm to resume chip exports", *Tom's Hardware*, November 7, 2025: https://www.tomshardware.com/tech-industry/dutch-government-allegedly-folds-to-supply-chain-pressure-will-relinquish-control-of-nexperia-in-china-spat-reports-say-deal-contingent-upon-china-allowing-firm-to-resume-chip-exports, visited November 11, 2025.
126. For example: dpa, "China lockert Ausfuhrregeln für Nexperia-Chips nach Europa [China relaxes export rules for Nexperia chips to Europe]", *Handelsblatt*, November 9, 2025: https://www.handelsblatt.com/dpa/halbleiterkrise-china-lockert-ausfuhrregeln-fuer-nexperia-chips-nach-europa/100172806.html, visited November 11, 2025.
127. E.g., *CNN* reported July 11, 2024; see also, e.g., G. Roberts, *Here Comes China*, *Substack*, July 20, 2024; *Global Research*, October 25, 2025.
128. Andre Vltchek, "Why the West is Determined to Ignore China's Success", *Dissident Voice*, July 18, 2019: https://dissidentvoice.org/2019/07/why-the-west-is-determined-to-ignore-chinas-success/, visited June 7, 2024.
129. For example: Jörg Kronauer, "Planlos in die Zukunft [Planless into the future]", *junge Welt*, March 19, 2019.
130. "Swabia is a prosperous region in the south-west of Germany and its people, especially its supposedly thrifty housewives, became an emblem of German economic-policy orientation during the Europe crisis. According to the myth of the Swabian housewife, governments should follow the

same principles as individual households when making economic decisions." (Lukas Haffert, "Swabian Housewife Economics is Good for Everyone?", *Brave New Europe*, March 26, 2019: https://braveneweurope.com/lukas-haffert-swabian-housewife-economics-is-good-for-everyone, visited June 7, 2024.)

131. A former CEO of the German stock exchange, *Deutsche Börse Group*, T. Weimer, criticized the German government in a speech 2024, calling it a "sheer catastrophe", and stating that interest in investing in Germany has collapsed, because "[o]ur reputation in the world has never been as bad as it is now—never before". He criticized the ideologization of politics and missing investments into digitalization; "Schiere Katastrophe [Sheer catastrophe]", *Welt*, June 7, 2024: https://www.welt.de/wirtschaft/article251910022/Deutsche-Boerse-CEO-Weimer-ueber-Treffen-mit-Habeck-Eine-schiere-Katastrophe.html, visited June 7, 2024.
132. From the financial-capital perspective, the group extends to the "magnificent 7": Alphabet (Google), Amazon, Apple, Meta Platforms (Facebook etc.), Microsoft, Nvidia, and Tesla. As of 2025, Broadcom entered the group, while Tesla had to leave it.
133. Hasnat (2018), 584f.
134. In the year 2020, among the 100 largest economic entities in the world, there are only 22 states, but 78 corporations. Thus, 78 corporations are essentially comparable in size economically to the 22 largest countries in the world.
135. E.g., Yanis Varoufakis (2024). *Technofeudalism: What Killed Capitalism*, London: Penguin.
136. More detail in, e.g., Rügemer (2018), 278f.
137. See for example: "Ant Group starts to differentiate consumer loan business Jiebei from bank loans", *Reuters*, November 8, 2021: https://www.reuters.com/business/ant-group-starts-differentiate-consumer-loan-business-jiebei-bank-loans-2021-11-08/, visited August 16, 2025.
138. Coco Feng, "China's internet giants must step up opening their 'walled gardens', state media says, ahead of Tencent flagship game's return to Douyin", *South China Morning Post*, January 17, 2024: https://www.scmp.com/tech/big-tech/article/3248762/chinas-internet-giants-must-step-opening-their-walled-gardens-state-media-says-ahead-tencent, visited August 16, 2025.
139. On more detail, e.g., Zhang (2024). *High Wire: How China Regulates Big Tech and Governs Its Economy*, New York, NY, USA: Oxford Univ. Press, 261ff. Zhang notes: "China's approach to regulating its tech giants provides a salient lesson for other countries aiming to control Big Tech." (p. 276).

140. E.g., Jin (2023), *New China Playbook.*
141. E.g., Edelman Trust Institute, "2025 Edelman Trust Barometer": https://www.edelman.de/sites/g/files/aatuss401/files/2025-01/2025%20Edelman%20Trust%20Barometer_Germany%20Report.pdf, visited July 21, 2025.
142. E.g., *Ipsos Happiness Index 2025, A 30-Country Global Advisor Survey*, 3-2025, https://www.ipsos.com/sites/default/files/ct/news/documents/2025-03/Ipsos-Global-Happiness-Index-2025_1.pdf, visited July 21, 2025.
143. There have been multiple studies on the negative impacts of the trade war on the US economy in the Trump 1.0 era. E.g., Pablo D. Fajgelbaum, Amit K. Khandelwal, "The Economic Impacts of the US–China Trade War", *Annual Review of Economics*, 14, 2022; Inu Manak, "The Cost of Trump's Trade War with China Is Still Adding Up", *Council on Foreign Relations*, April 18, 2023: https://www.cfr.org/blog/cost-trumps-trade-war-china-still-adding, visited June 8, 2024; Phil Gramm, Donald J. Boudreaux, "Trump's Trade War Was a Loser", *The Wall Street Journal*, September 11, 2023: https://www.wsj.com/articles/trumps-trade-war-was-a-loser-employment-manufacturing-international-economy-tariffs-unemployment-9d8a7c7c, visited June 8, 2024; Gramm and Boudreaux concluded that the tariffs "destroyed jobs in Michigan, Pennsylvania and Wisconsin and made all Americans worse off."
144. E.g., former WB president Robert Zoellick, see S. Zeise, "Trumps Parallelwelt [Trump's Parallel World]", *junge Welt*, January 15, 2020; also, well-known US-economist Dean Baker in an interview, see "Die chinesische Wirtschaft wurde kaum getroffen [The Chinese economy was hardly hit]", *junge Welt*, February 15, 2020.
145. E.g., Asa Fitch, Dan Strumpf, "Huawei Manages to Make Smartphones Without American Chips", *The Wall Street Journal*, December 1, 2019, https://www.wsj.com/articles/huawei-manages-to-make-smartphones-without-american-chips-11575196201, visited June 9, 2024.
146. James Kynge, Kiran Stacey, "China's Huawei plays down its chipmaking capabilities", *Financial Times*, July 2, 2019: https://www.ft.com/content/3c0f59c2-9c43-11e9-b8ce-8b459ed04726, visited July 19, 2025.
147. Translated by the authors at *ChinaHirn*: Wolfgang Hirn, "Wan Hua Zheng 万花阵 I Was Huawei-Gründer Ren Zhengfei wirklich sagte—und warum es wichtig ist/Von Liu Zhengrong* Wan Hua Zheng 万花阵 [What Huawei founder Ren Zhengfei really said—and why it matters/By Liu Zhengrong*]", *China Hirn*, June 20, 2025, https://www.chinahirn.de/2025/06/20/wan-hua-zheng-%e4%b8%87%e8%8a%b1%e9%98%b5-

i-was-huawei-gruender-ren-zhengfei-wirklich-sagte-und-warum-es-wichtig-ist-von-liu-zhengrong/, visited July 21, 2025.

148. E.g., Sarah Shamim and News Agencies, "Why has Dutch government taken control of China-owned chipmaker Nexperia?", *Al Jazeera*, October 14, 2025: https://www.aljazeera.com/news/2025/10/14/why-has-dutch-government-taken-control-of-china-owned-chipmaker-nexperia, visited October 29, 2025.
149. E.g., Kevin Yao, "China moves to encourage foreign reinvestment as FDI slumps", *Reuters*, July 18, 2025: https://www.reuters.com/world/china/china-moves-encourage-foreign-reinvestment-fdi-slumps-2025-07-18/, visited October 29, 2025.
150. E.g., Andy Rothman, "Trump Will Make China Great Again", *Sinica*, June 18, 2025: https://www.sinicapodcast.com/p/trump-will-make-china-great-again, visited July 22, 2025.
151. E.g., Kyle Chan, "China's emerging export control regime", *High Capacity*, substack.com, Oct. 18, 2025.
152. Thomas L. Friedman, "I Just Saw the Future. It Was Not in America", *New York Times*, April 2, 2025, https://www.nytimes.com/2025/04/02/opinion/trump-tariffs-china.html, visited July 7, 2025.
153. E.g., Ingo Dachwitz, Tomas Rudl, Simon Rebiger, "Was wir über den Skandal um Facebook und Cambridge Analytica wissen [What we know about the scandal around Facebook and Cambridge Analytica]", *Netzpolitik.org*, March 21, 2018, https://netzpolitik.org/2018/cambridge-analytica-was-wir-ueber-das-groesste-datenleck-in-der-geschichte-von-facebook-wissen/, visited June 9, 2024.
154. Hardly necessary to mention that, in the *Second Cold War* of the West, "the Russian" once again serves as the epitome of evil. Yet reducing Trump's fake culture to nothing but a result of Russian interference, as the "liberal" media do, amounts to a near-total mental self-obliteration on the part of the Western "left-liberals".
155. E.g., Lawrence Chung, "Taiwan bans academic exchanges with 3 mainland Chinese universities", *South China Morning Post*, February 20, 2025: https://www.scmp.com/news/china/politics/article/3299492/taiwan-bans-academic-exchanges-3-mainland-chinese-universities, visited July 21, 2025.
156. While US companies remain supportive, e.g., American Chamber of Commerce in China, "Bridging Borders: One Year into the "50,000 Students" Initiative", *AmCham China*, November 15, 2024: https://www.amchamchina.org/wp-content/uploads/2024/11/AmCham-China-Report-on-US-Students-2024.pdf, visited July 21, 2025.

Selected and Recommended Literature

Dai, Shuanping, and G. Liu. 2017. Emergence of new products and agile innovation in a catching-up economy: Evidence from the low-speed electric vehicle industry in the Shandong Province, China. In *EAEPE Annual Conference, Budapest, mimeo.*

Dai, Shuanping and Wolfram Elsner. 2021. Shrinking trust in growing China: A trade-off between fast growth, change and institutionalized cooperation? Forum for social economics. *Taylor & Francis Journals* 50 (3): 297–315, July.

Elsner, Wolfram, and Henning Schwardt. 2014. Trust and arena size. Expectations, institutions, general trust, and critical population and group sizes. *Journal of Institutional Economics* 10 (1): 107–134.

Elsner, Wolfram, and Henning Schwardt. 2015. From emergent cooperation to contextual trust, and to general trust: overlapping meso-sized interaction arenas and cooperation platforms as a foundation of pro-social behavior. *Forum for Social Economics* 44 (1): 69–86.

Guo, Wenbo, Jing Feng, Brad McKenna, and Pengzhu Zhang. 2017. Inter-Organizational Governance and trilateral trust building: A case study of crowdsourcing-based open innovation in China. *Asian Business & Management* 16 (3): 187–207.

Hasnat, Baban. 2018. Big Data: An institutional perspective on opportunities and challenges. *Journal of Economic Issues* 52 (2): 580–588.

Herrmann-Pillath, Carsten. 2017. *China's Economic Culture. The Ritual Order of State and Markets.* London, New York: Routledge.

Jin, Keyu. 2023. *The New China Playbook: Beyond Socialism and Capitalism.* New York: Viking Press.

Kadri, Ali. 2017. The Saudi palace coup, the oil market, China and the US. *Real-World Economics Review* 82. http://www.paecon.net/PAEReview/issue82/Kadri82.pdf.

Poppe, Melchior. 2019. Trip der Superlative: In Shanghai erlebe ich, wie die Stadt der Zukunft aussieht [Trip of superlatives: In Shanghai I experience what the city of the future looks like]. September 2, 2019. https://www.focus.de/perspektiven/14-laender-14-reporter/24-stunden-superlative-trip-der-superlative-in-shanghai-erlebe-ich-wie-die-stadt-der-zukunftaussieht_id_10066047.html visited May 10, 2024.

Vincent, James. 2025. The DeepSeek panic reveals an AI world ready to blow. *The Guardian, January* 28, 2025. https://www.theguardian.com/commentisfree/2025/jan/28/deepseek-r1-ai-world-chinese-chatbot-tech-worldwestern, visited February 14, 2025.

Xu Jianguo. 2017. China's internet finance: A critical review. *China & World Economy* 25 (4): 78–92.

Varoufakis, Yanis. 2024. *Technofeudalism: What Killed Capitalism.* London: Penguin.

Zhang, Angela Huyue. 2024. *High Wire: How China Regulates Big Tech and Governs Its Economy.* New York, NY: Oxford University Press.

Zhang, Fan. 2018. *The Institutional Evolution of China, Government vs Market.* Cheltenham and Northampton, MA, USA: Edward Elgar.

Zhang, Lanying, Guanqi Li, and Huili He. 2018. Controlling corporate power in China: Case studies of seed companies and water distribution. *American Journal of Economics and Sociology* 77 (2): 511–540.

Further Cited Literature

Chai, Shijun, et al. 2018. Social networks and informal financial inclusion in the People's Republic of China. In *ADBI Working Paper 802.*

Dai, Shuanping, and Guanzhong Yang. 2017. Does social inducement lead to higher open innovation investment? An experimental study. In *Working Papers on East Asian Studies 112.* University of Duisburg-Essen. https://www.uni-due.de/imperia/md/cont ent/in-east/about/publications_green_series/paper112-2017.pdf. Accessed May 30, 2024.

Fu, Tong. 2017. What determines firms' access to credit in the absence of effective economic institutions: evidence from China. *Economics. The Open-Access, Open-Assessment E-Journal* 11 (31): 1–27.

Graebner, Claudius, Wolfram Elsner, and Alex Lascaux. 2021. Trust and social control: Sources of cooperation, performance, and stability in informal value transfer systems. *Computational Economics* 58 (4): 1077–1102.

Kunzmann, Marcel, 2018. *Theorie, System und Praxis des Sozialismus in China* [Theory, System and Practice of Socialism in China]. 2nd ed. Berlin: Verlag Mirco Kolarczik

Li, Kai, Cheryl Long, and Wei Wan. 2019. Public interest or regulatory capture: Theory and evidence from China's airfare deregulation. *Journal of Economic Behavior & Organization* 161:343–365.

Rasmus, Jack. 2017. *Central Bankers at the End of Their Rope? Monetary Policy and the Coming Depression.* Atlanta, GA: Clarity Press.

Rügemer, Werner, 2018. *Die Kapitalisten des 21. Jahrhunderts. Gemeinverständlicher Abriss zum Aufstieg der neuen Finanzakteure* [The capitalists of the 21st century. A general outline of the rise of the new financial players]. Cologne: PapyRossa.

CHAPTER 7

"State Ownership? Help!"

But Different from What You Expected

Agile State Firms, Diverse Ownership Forms and Business Models, Entrepreneurship and Start-Ups, and a Sharing Economy

A "Commonality" Orientation? China's Big "Sharing Economy"

Justin Yifu Lin, former Chief Economist and Senior Vice President of the World Bank (2008–2012) and now Dean of the Institute of New Structural Economics at Peking University, refers to China's strategy of strengthening the deep structures of its economy as a "new structural economic approach".[1]

This includes, among other things, the principle of regulated, organized, and transparent giving and taking at the macroeconomic level. The large IT corporations, for example, have grown because they have provided platforms and services based on an initially publicly provided network infrastructure, which is used by hundreds of thousands of companies and sometimes hundreds of millions of people. On such platforms, "open innovation" can be pursued between large industrial corporations in the automotive, aircraft, or shipbuilding sectors, as well as in other "B2B", "B2C", and even "C2C" sales or exchanges. Specialized industries and platforms have been able to establish themselves on the basis of network infrastructure and the widespread availability of computers with their software systems. Two well-known examples are the accommodation platform

W. Elsner, E. Najmehchi, *The Rise of China*,
https://doi.org/10.1007/978-3-032-20260-4_7

Airbnb and the passenger transport service *Uber*. Here, private households "share" their apartments or cars with other private households: a "platform economy" as a "sharing economy".

Under the specific systemic and cultural conditions of China, the platform and sharing economy seems to have developed in an even more comprehensive manner than in the West. The boundaries between "providers" and "consumers" of goods and services appear to be becoming more fluid: providers are also consumers, and consumers, as users, are also producers who at least co-design the product ("prosumers"). Thus, supply structures become more differentiated—for example, in passenger transport, where, in addition to traditional taxis, a widespread Uber-style system (the Chinese variant is called DiDi, which acquired Uber China in 2016) and an individual, private car-sharing system have emerged.

While "sharing" forms of production have long been a success factor of regional industrial agglomerations—as was already the case in the classic Silicon Valley with regard to qualified labor, knowledge, machinery, and production capacities in general—today in China almost everything possible is being "shared". Individuals buy cars in order to share them, regardless of whether they drive them themselves or not. A simple registration makes this possible; in operation, the rest is often handled by specialized local internet platforms and their mobile apps. The same applies to the use of plots of land, houses, and apartments, IT hardware, or even in educational matters (sharing of teaching materials and knowledge).[2]

Thus, the Chinese sharing economy has continued to grow in recent years, with transactions reaching around 555 billion US dollars in 2022—an increase of 3.9 percent from the previous year.[3] An analysis of the main reasons for this steady growth identifies five distinctive features in particular as its basis:

- Vast smartphone proliferation,
- The proliferation of QR-codes,
- Convenient payment systems (such as Alipay and WeChat Pay),
- Real name registration (minimizing chances of abuse),
- And the backing of internet giants (the so-called BATs: "Baidu-Alibaba-Tencent triumvirate").[4]

To some extent, the apparent difference in sharing between Europe and China can also be explained by China's aforementioned economic policy experimentalism. The Chinese tend to "act first, then set the rules and standards", whereas the Europeans first define the rules (and employ lawyers to secure property rights) and only then begin implementation.[5] Experimentalism and a different culture in dealing with property issues seem to make a difference. The Chinese culture of networking and sharing is also cited as a reason why, according to a high-ranking Chinese Bosch manager, it might be that in 20 years no Chinese person will buy their own car anymore.[6]

So, is socialism "with Chinese characteristics" (Xi Jinping) also emerging through a sharing economy? A world of sharing—this was previously known only from esoteric circles. However, the sharing economy prevalent in China today could serve as a systemic, individual-entrepreneurial "substructure" for innovation and for new structures of provision and use, similar to technological start-ups in agile industrial policy (see above). If these should one day become more standardized, they could bring an innovation boost to the service sector. Here too, it can be assumed that after a few years of "Wild East", standardization, regulation, and broader social embedding will take place, so that the experiment of comprehensive sharing—fully integrated into the national development process—is likely to unfold.

Those who wish can see in this the signs of a socialization "from below", which could contribute building blocks to a later socialism "with Chinese characteristics", based on the culture of social networks (Guanxi, Danwei, and so on). We will return to this in the third part. "Chinese characteristics" seem to manifest themselves in various forms of property and rights of disposal over land and goods, as well as in the organizational and legal forms of companies.

Land Use in China: Effectivity Despite Weak and Informal Property Rights

In China, land is fundamentally collective property and is therefore formally subject to the state and its various levels of government (central, provincial, and municipal). Private ownership of land, nature, and resources is thus not possible. Only agriculturally used land can also be formally owned by villages and cooperatives.

Private individuals and companies can therefore only lease land—that is, obtain "land use rights"—with the duration depending on the type of land use and the investments made on it. For urban residential or industrial uses, leases usually last between 40 and 70 years. Farming families generally receive land use rights for 30 years.

The prediction made by the ruling "neoclassical"–neoliberal economics for an economy and society without strong, preferably unrestricted private ownership of land is clear: such an economy cannot function. It must either shift toward unconditional private ownership of land, nature, and resources, or remain highly "inefficient" and ultimately perish.[7]

However, China has apparently provided counterevidence. Since the bourgeois revolution of 1911, and especially since the founding of the People's Republic in 1949, China has practiced various forms of property side by side: land distribution to landless peasants (i.e., individual land ownership), then collectivization and collective ownership of various kinds as people's communes, cooperatives, and village communities, as well as urban and state land ownership. This has resulted in a historically grown "patchwork" of different, often purely informal, possession and use rights for a multitude of state and private actors, which in recent years has indeed been recognized in the literature as a "puzzle",[8] if not a mystery, and has attracted considerable research interest.[9]

Even the so-called Household Responsibility System (HRS), which was introduced locally and experimentally during the reform and opening phase beginning in 1978, gave farmers the possibility to market independently, cooperatively, or communally, and then officially became the basis of all land use rights for agricultural enterprises—and finally also for private companies in rural regions from 1981—has by no means completely eliminated the "vaguely" defined property rights. Ownership remained collective, but land use was embedded in an incentive system with private marketing opportunities, as well as clear responsibilities for the soil.[10]

In any case, China's various land reforms have led to a relatively equal land distribution—more precisely, a distribution of land use rights.[11] Income distribution (more on this below), and thus ultimately political power distribution, could be balanced, and economic productivity could be improved in the long term.[12] Therefore, the focus is more on the distribution of use rights and, of course, on responsibilities when resources are mobilized, and economic effectiveness is to be increased (an old economic insight[13]), rather than on clearly assigned, unrestricted, and "eternal" property rights.

Since China's recent reforms, especially after 2017, further international opening, the strategy of "Credible China", reliable rule of law (more on this below), greater individual security, and simpler circulation (saleability) of land use rights are increasingly being considered.[14] Individual use rights are therefore being strengthened. However, public, state, and other forms of collective property (village, cooperative) remain undisputed.

State-Owned, Private, Cooperative, "For-Profit" or "Non-Profit": The Plurality of Entrepreneurial Forms

Corporate forms in China are also exceptionally diverse, which is historically conditioned. This diversity has been consciously maintained, and it typically proves to be an economic, socio-economic, innovation-driven, and overall systemic strength.[15] Systems with heterogeneous forms and actors, as is generally known from complex systems research, are usually more shock-resistant ("resilient") than homogenized and uniform systems—such as the deregulated, highly concentrated, and oligopolistic markets of financial capitalism—in which innovative SMEs and start-ups sooner or later fall under the financial dependence and direction of large financial industry complexes, even if their "company" or "brand" is sometimes maintained externally.

In China, in addition to the classic large state-owned enterprises (SOEs), large private corporations also exist, some of which are former state-owned enterprises that have been privatized. In addition, there are countless private SMEs, many of which were also formerly state-owned, as well as numerous private start-ups, a significant stock of cooperative production units (and not only in agriculture), and local collective or municipal Township and Village Enterprises (TVEs). Lastly, there is a multitude of explicit non-profit or social enterprises (social entrepreneurship). Through this system, corporate structures in China can apparently generate a special regional resilience.[16]

The prediction of the prevailing "neoclassical"–neoliberal economic theory would be that only the "most efficient", i.e., purely private, profit-oriented companies would prevail and survive in the market; otherwise, the system would collapse due to "inefficiencies". Here too, China's reality and pragmatic approach refute these hypothetical constructs of an abstract ideology, which still attempts to legitimize itself with a pseudo-precise, yet overly simplistic, mathematical model, mimicking the physical mechanics of the early nineteenth century.

As already explained, private companies in China are also diversely embedded in value chains, networks, (production and financing) relationships within the banking industry, informal institutional arrangements (local and regional cultures), and, finally, formal public regulations.[17] A maximum profit rate is therefore not the exclusive—and sometimes not even the dominant—criterion in the entrepreneurial "deep structure" of China (that is, in business relationships and interactions). Often, a company's role in value chains, cooperative innovation performance, or local service provision is more decisive, for example in securing the necessary capital and credit resources.

Exemplary of the real-world and historically effective (rather than formally exact "efficient") nature of various non-standard business forms was the importance of municipal or cooperative TVEs (see above)[18] for China's economic rise. TVEs emerged at the end of the 1950s as an extension of rural community production, services, and marketing of specialty products beyond the state-prescribed production quotas for agricultural mass products. After the start of the reform and opening period in 1978, most state-owned enterprises remained rigid and not very innovative, and the large SOEs were downright dinosaurs, which could only be mobilized for strategic innovations through privatizations, threats of privatizations, and, above all, the officially created possibility of corporate bankruptcy. During this time, it was the TVEs that seized opportunities in product diversification, product and process innovations, networking, and internationalization, thereby transforming China's corporate landscape.

From the corporate perspective, "reform and opening" as well as innovation emerged at the end of the 1970s and the beginning of the 1980s (and had been prepared since the late 1950s) "from the countryside"—rather than from the large state-owned enterprises in the major cities. The TVE sector expanded rapidly in terms of the number of firms, employment, and value creation, demonstrating to all other (state-owned) companies "how it was done".

TVEs were by no means uniform in terms of company or ownership structure. Cooperative, public, private capital, stock corporations, or even purely private individual companies were formed. Their only common starting point was their origin in rural regions and former village communities. Many later became large corporations. They helped the Chinese economy to comprehensively "get off the ground" in the 1980s and were increasingly supported by the state. Ultimately, it was in part their achievement that the large state-owned companies, maintained in strategically important areas, became modern, innovative, strategically forward-looking international companies.

Notes

1. For example: Lin (2017).
2. For example: Li Qiangzhi, "Institutional Innovation and Sharing Economy Development", lecture at the Tianjin Forum "Innovation and Cooperation", July 8, 2017, mimeo.
3. See for example: Xinhua, "China's sharing economy sustains growth momentum", *State Council Information Office*, February 27, 2023: http://english.scio.gov.cn/chinavoices/2023-02/27/content_85130740.htm#:~:text=China's%20sharing%20economy%20maintained%20steady,on%20year%2C%20said%20the%20report, visited June 15, 2024.
4. "5 Reasons Why Chinese Sharing Economy Future Is Looking Promising", *SAMPi*, December 27, 2023: https://sampi.co/reasons-chinese-sharing-economy-future/, visited June 15, 2024.
5. For example: Zhang Xinhong, "Status and Trends of Chinese Sharing Economy", lecture at the Tianjin Forum "Innovation and Cooperation", July 8, 2017, mimeo.
6. Melchior Poppe, "Trip der Superlative: In Shanghai erlebe ich, wie die Stadt der Zukunft aussieht [Trip of superlatives: In Shanghai I experience what the city of the future looks like]", September 2, 2019: https://www.focus.de/perspektiven/14-laender-14-reporter/24-stunden-superlative-trip-der-superlative-in-shanghai-erlebe-ich-wie-die-stadt-der-zukunftaussieht_ id_10066047.html visited May 10, 2024.
7. For a detailed critical discussion: Peter Ho, "In defense of endogenous, spontaneously ordered development: institutional functionalism and Chinese property rights", *Journal of Peasant Studies* 40(6), 2013, pp. 1087–1118.
8. For example: Ho (2013), ibid.; Paddy Ireland, Gaofeng Meng, "Post-capitalist property", *Economy and Society* 46(3–4), 2017, pp. 369–397.
9. The recent literature on the use of commons confirms that the economic effectiveness of their use actually depends on the specific characteristics of the usage arrangements, and individualistic property rights in "markets" are by no means a solution in general.
10. Ireland and Meng (2017), ibid.
11. "Post-capitalist property", as argued by Ireland and Meng (2017), must indeed not only be characterized by clearly defined collective forms of ownership, but is very much compatible with a wide range of institutional possibilities.

12. Qunyi Liu, “Rethinking Land Reform in East Asia: Egalitarian or Inegalitarian?”, *Journal of Economic Issues* 52(3), 2018, pp. 694–716.
13. John R. Commons, *Institutional economics. Its place in political economy.* New York: Macmillan. 2 Vols., First published 1934. Reprint: New Brunswick, N.J.: Transaction Publishers, 1990.
14. For example: Yanlong Zhang, “Rise of Contract: On the Institutional Account of Rural Land Titling in China”, mimeo., *Chinese Academy of Social Sciences*, Beijing, 2018.
15. For example: Zhang (2018), p. 110ff.
16. For example: Jane Hardy, Yassamin Imani, Beini Zhuang, “Regional resilience and global production networks in China: An open political economy perspective”, *Competition and Change* 22(1), 2018, pp. 63–80.
17. See also ibid.
18. See also, for example: “Township and Village Enterprises” on *Wikipedia*: https://en.wikipedia.org/wiki/Township_and_Village_Enterprises, visited July 3, 2024.

Selected and Recommended Literature

Ireland, Paddy, and Gaofeng Meng. 2017. Post-capitalist property. *Economy and Society* 46 (3–4): 369–397.

Lin, Justin Yifu. 2017. Lessons from China and East Asia's catch up: the new structural economics perspective. In *Mapping a New World Order*, ed. V. Popov and P. Dutkiewicz, 53–70. Cheltenham and Northampton, MA: Edward Elgar.

Zhang, Fan. 2018. *The Institutional Evolution of China, Government vs Market.* Cheltenham and Northampton, MA, USA: Edward Elgar.

CHAPTER 8

"Distribution? Only Poor Wretches and Billionaires!"

Income Growth and Downward Redistribution: Poverty Elimination, Wage Increases, Tax Cuts, Purchasing Power, and Inclusion—A Middle-Income Nation Emerging, and Pressure on Oligopolies and Billionaires

China Has Eradicated the World's Largest Mass Poverty

China is the first, and so far probably the only, country in the world that has not only achieved but even "over-fulfilled" the United Nations Millennium Development Goal number one—the fight against poverty—by halving the proportion of people living on less than one US dollar a day between 1990 and 2015. Between 1981 and 2013 alone, in just 32 years, China lifted more than 850 million people out of poverty, reducing their number from 878 million to 25 million.[1] By 2020, absolute poverty in China had been completely eradicated.[2]

The poverty line, as defined by the World Bank, was set at 1.90 US dollars per day at that time (as of 2022, it has been raised to 2.15 USD). The Chinese statistical poverty line is even more stringent, at 2.30 US dollars per day. China follows the strict "Lower Middle-Income Class Poverty

W. Elsner, E. Najmehchi, *The Rise of China*,
https://doi.org/10.1007/978-3-032-20260-4_8

Line".[3] Even by this stricter criterion, poverty had been eliminated in China by 2020.

Between 1990 and 2013, a total of 1.074 billion people worldwide were lifted out of poverty—70 percent of this achievement is attributable to China's contribution. While China's poverty rate fell from 88.3 percent of the population in 1981 to 1.9 percent in 2013 (and to 0.0 percent in 2020), the global poverty rate fell from 42.3 percent to 10.9 percent over the same period.

However, absolute poverty is currently rising again on some continents, such as Africa and Latin America. Even Europe and the USA are increasingly affected by problems of rising relative poverty, dependence on food aid, and, in the case of the USA, a clear decline in average life expectancy. This occurs alongside neoliberal austerity policies, economic stagnation, and intensified upward redistribution.

China has thus made income distribution more equal "from the bottom up". This success, in addition to technological achievements, remains the most well-known and somewhat recognized accomplishment of the People's Republic of China in the West. However, the fact that 850 million people can be lifted out of absolute poverty in just over three decades is likely beyond the imagination of most Europeans and North Americans. Sustainable, stable poverty eradication for hundreds of millions of people cannot be achieved through philanthropic distribution of alms from the rich to the poor, through state "welfare", or through pure work pressure and control-and-sanction regimes à la "Hartz IV"[4]; it can only be accomplished through the creation of hundreds of millions of jobs.

13 Million New Jobs Per Year, Development of Rural Areas, and Greater Income Equality

Dynamics of Job Creation

In the West, there exists generally only a limited awareness of the key fundamentals for comprehensive poverty eradication. These include:

- A massive development of rural areas,
- The creation of a vast number of jobs and their necessary infrastructures,
- Massive organized structural change,

- Extraordinary wage increases to multiplicatively stimulate the domestic economy,
- The establishment of wage replacement systems to prevent human and social capital from deteriorating again.

Since China is driving an extraordinarily rapid industrial structural change, in which a large number of old, ecologically unsustainable, and low-skilled jobs (in coal, steel, low-cost manufacturing, or waste recycling for the West) are being eliminated, it must create at least 11 million new jobs each year just to prevent unemployment from rising. In fact, between 2013 and 2016 alone, 13 million more sustainable and higher-skilled jobs were created annually.[5] Even in 2023, after more uncertain economic conditions in the "post-Covid" period, including an increase in youth unemployment, China was able to create 12.44 million new urban jobs, exceeding its set target of 12 million, while still acknowledging that "more efforts will be needed to stabilize employment" in 2024 and beyond, according to China's Ministry of Human Resources and Social Security.[6]

The current focus of infrastructure investments is on rural areas,[7] which are catching up with urban regions due to their now higher growth rates. Regional development will be discussed in more detail later.

Fiscal Effectiveness of Infrastructure Investments

The fact that public infrastructure can finance itself not only economically and socially, but even fiscally in the narrower sense—through medium-term higher tax and fee revenues—is an old economic insight from the 1940s, already confirmed in reality since the New Deal in the USA in the 1930s. This simple macroeconomic and circular economic principle is also demonstrated today by China, whose central state budget, despite investments in the trillions, is far less indebted than the state budgets of the neoliberal "savings" and austerity proponents in financial capitalist countries, whose structures effectively redistribute wealth from bottom to top.

What SPD (Social Democratic Party of Germany) finance minister Karl Schiller understood at the end of the 1960s, and with which he brilliantly managed the first cyclical post-war crisis of the Federal Republic of Germany in 1967 for years to come, would probably be regarded as nothing more than noise from another galaxy by today's federal or state finance ministers, regardless of party affiliation. The banker, academic, and government advisor John Maynard Keynes—whose experiences, insights, theories, and practical programs saved England, parts of Europe, and the world from the worst effects of the Great Depression and the world wars, and who justified state investments against typical "market" blockades—was knowledge that Karl Schiller still knew and heeded. Just until recently, Keynes was probably regarded as the devil incarnate by most German neoliberal finance ministers, even if they owned an SPD party membership card. For such a minister, Friedrich von Hayek, the forefather of extreme "market" ideology and the ultimately authoritarian redistribution system called neoliberalism, is likely regarded as a representative of God on earth.

Land Reforms

To eradicate poverty, improve the incomes of the poorest, and structurally enhance China's income distribution, the land reforms mentioned above have contributed significantly. A relatively equal distribution of land, combined with the Household Responsibility System (HRS), which gave farmers the opportunity to market their produce independently, cooperatively, or communally, enabled hundreds of millions of people to earn their own income and historically improved income distribution in China over the long term. The typically more unequal distribution associated with sustained, rapid growth (the famous Kuznets effect, discussed further below[8]) has thus been demonstrably mitigated in rural China.[9]

Significant Wage and Salary Increases

However, due to China's sustainable poverty reduction and, in particular, its development model of the "New Normal", which has a stronger domestic orientation, not only have the incomes of self-employed people in cities and rural areas inevitably grown, but the wages and salaries of workers and employees, as well as their social security systems and benefits, have also increased.

Otherwise, a longer-lasting catch-up and ascent process would not be conceivable. The era of low wages as an international "competitive factor", beyond China's organizational and scale-related productivity advantages, has effectively ended since the late 2000s.

For some time now, China has been pursuing the *high road* of development, and wage and salary growth has since been at least in line with productivity progress—something that workers in financial capitalism, with its ever-widening gap between wage growth and productivity growth, have only dreamed of for decades.

The average hourly wages of Chinese workers, for example, tripled in real terms between 2006 and 2016, from 1.20 USD to 3.60 USD (Mexico: 2.10 USD; Thailand: 2.20 USD; Brazil: 2.70 USD; India: 0.70 USD). During the same period, real wage incomes stagnated or fell in Western capitalist countries. Real wage increases alone between 2013 and 2016 amounted to between 6.3 and 8.8 percent per year in China.[10] Within the ten years of the 12th and 13th Five-Year Plans, i.e., between 2011 and 2020, real incomes doubled, which mathematically corresponds to an average annual wage increase of just over six percent. Even after the globally challenging Covid-19 shock, Chinese real wage growth was still expected to reach 4.1 percent in 2024, exceeding Europe (0.9 percent), North America (2 percent), and the global average (1 percent).[11]

As a result, Chinese minimum wages have also been steadily increased and are now, in some cases, higher than those in individual peripheral EU member states. Unlike in neoliberal capitalist systems, however, minimum wages—set by local governments according to local conditions—are effectively enforced. Compliance is strictly monitored by public commissions, and non-compliance is severely punished. This represents a public taboo in many Western countries, but it is routinely reported in Chinese media. The employee's right to lodge complaints will be discussed below.

Thus, after the eradication of absolute poverty, China is also improving income distribution among the next lower- and middle-income levels of workers and employees, elevating many into the middle-income range.

Thus, Western Low-Cost Production Moves Away ...

Companies that previously took advantage of China's low wages to carry out labor-intensive, mostly simple production with minimal skill requirements are now relocating to other countries, particularly in Southeast Asia, with lower wage levels. Among these are Thailand, Vietnam,[12] Pakistan, Bangladesh, Myanmar, Laos, and Cambodia. German entrepreneurs express similar views, and China has even factored this into its national revaluation strategy. In the future, most low-cost plastic goods for Western mass-market consumers will no longer bear the label "Made in China".

Tax Simplification and Relief for Lower and Middle Incomes

Finally, alongside land reforms, poverty eradication, minimum wage increases, and political support for wage and salary growth (discussed further below), China is also improving the net income situation for the majority of workers. Most recently, this occurred in 2019 through a comprehensive tax reform. The latest income tax reform was passed by the National People's Congress in 2018 and has been in effect since January 1, 2019.

The income tax law for labor income has been further simplified.[13] For lower and middle incomes, there are now seven flat tax rates, all of which have been reduced. In lower-wage brackets, rates have in some cases been cut to less than 50 percent of their previous levels—for example, from 7 percent to 3 percent for monthly wage income up to approximately €1300, and from 16 percent to 8 percent for monthly wage income up to approximately €2800. The top tax rate, applied to monthly incomes up to €14,000, is 28 percent.[14]

Even middle- and high-income earners are currently experiencing tax relief of between 8 and 35 percent. As a result, more people have been paying significantly lower taxes since 2019, and wage and income taxes now serve even more clearly as a secondary source of revenue for the state. These are simple and immediate effects, in contrast to decades of "tax relief" rhetoric in neoliberal systems, which in reality must compensate for tax reductions on capital income at the expense of mass income (wages and value-added tax). Unlike neoliberal capitalist states, which have constantly increased the tax burden on lower incomes through the "unnoticeable" but burdensome value-added tax, China has reduced its value-added tax in several steps (2018, 2019).[15]

In capitalist wage-tax states, wage and income taxes are typically by far the main source of revenue for the state, while capital taxes are treated as secondary. In China, by contrast, corporate taxes from companies constitute a far larger share of state revenue than wage and income taxes—a typical feature of socialist tax systems and an important systemic difference from neoliberal capitalism (discussed further in Part III).

In this way, net income distribution is further improved toward greater equality. China also redistributes downward, in contrast to Western countries, an effect already reflected in income distribution measures (discussed further below).

Additional tax cuts—both direct taxes and value-added tax—were also, as previously mentioned, implemented as cyclical and anticipated structural measures against the economic pressure from Washington, as was decided at the 2nd plenary session of the 13th National People's Congress in March 2019.

China's Rich, and How Income Distribution Is Made More Equal Also from the Top

Yes, China has rich, very rich, and super-rich individuals, and many of them: the population of millionaires and billionaires is relatively high by international standards. According to the 2024 *Hurun Global Rich List*,[16] China has over 800 billionaires—the highest number worldwide—and over six million millionaires in 2022, placing it second after the USA; this figure is projected to rise to 12 million by 2026, according to Credit Suisse.[17] Interestingly, seven of the ten richest self-made women in the world are Chinese.[18]

This issue has many aspects, which are most intensively researched and discussed within China itself, but are often morally condemned in the West, where, so far, little has been done—or has been possible—to redistribute wealth from the richest. Below are some recent aspects of Chinese analyses and measures, including a look at the general statistical measure of income equality in a society: the so-called Gini coefficient.[19]

The neoclassical-neoliberal economic model consistently presents a worldview in which high income inequality (and, consequently, high wealth inequality) creates positive incentives for the "most productive", who, through their special efforts and innovative ideas, are assumed to raise GDP. According to this ideology, a "trickle-down" mechanism then benefits everyone through additional jobs and income effects, and no distribution of income or wealth is considered too unequal.

In contrast, empirical evidence and more realistic economic theories indicate that significant inequality of income and wealth tends to generate serious negative economic consequences. This is due to:

- Innovative resources of many people remaining unused,
- The overall productivity demonstrably decreasing,
- The marginal performance of the rich (and consumption relative to income) decreasing,

- Excess money due to lack of demand being increasingly unproductively and speculatively invested or often even hoarded,
- Capital thus flowing into wrong uses and luxury consumption,
- And many unproductive ceremonial structures being built,

which leads to:

- Corruption and plutocracies spreading,
- Societal frustration arising,
- General trust in society degenerating,
- And the economic society as a whole becoming ossified.[20]

We also observe a temporal dynamic of income inequality in a rapidly growing economy like China's: the well-known Kuznets effect. This describes a process in which an initially relatively equal society, experiencing strong economic growth, first develops an increasingly unequal income distribution. Such inequality can only be gradually reduced—with a significant time lag—through redistribution efforts, typically when the society enters phases of slower growth and lower turbulence, accompanied by the development of social policies and the construction of a welfare state.[21]

In fact, China has traditionally, and in line with socialist principles, maintained an income distribution—measured by the Gini coefficient—that has been more equal than that of comparable developing countries since the 1960s. Its Gini coefficient was about 0.3 points, or roughly 30 percentage points, lower than in countries such as Brazil or Mexico.[22] Only during the reform and opening period, and with sustained strong growth statistically recorded from the late 1980s, did China's Gini coefficient increase noticeably, even surpassing that of Japan and other established, developed industrial countries. Around 2010, it stood just under 0.5, which is relatively high in international comparison. For context, very unequal countries—such as South American oligarchic "banana republics" and other middle-income countries (Brazil, Mexico, and others)—typically have Gini coefficients between 0.5 and 0.7, signaling extreme social inequality. In contrast, the former social-democratic, more equal Scandinavian countries recorded coefficients of 0.3 or below during their peak periods (1950s to 1970s), and to some extent, still today.

The peak of income inequality in China occurred between 2008 and 2010, when the Gini coefficient reached 0.49.[23] Since then, it has been declining toward 0.43.[24] Such seemingly "small" statistical movements actually reflect changes in the distribution effects of billions of individual exchange relationships and countless interactions, which must have been systematically re-regulated and institutionally re-embedded to produce greater equality at the aggregate (macroeconomic) level. This implies that when such seemingly minor numerical changes in a highly aggregated statistical measure persist over several years, they are not coincidental but rather result from structural changes in the national economic distribution mechanisms. This interpretation becomes plausible when one considers the totality of Chinese economic and social policy.

We have already seen some of the mechanisms that have been developed in China and are being applied in the process of evolving into a society "in the early stage of socialism" (see Part III below):

- Elimination of colonially inherited mass poverty, which was exacerbated by errors in early development (see above),
- Promotion of long-lasting, strong wage and salary increases, especially in lower and middle wage and salary ranges,
- Strong economic development, particularly in regions where absolute poverty was concentrated in the past—namely, the western and peripheral rural areas—partly achieved through land reforms that promoted increasingly equal distribution,
- Reforms of the income tax with significantly reduced tax rates, especially in lower and middle wage and salary levels.

New Downward Redistribution Policy

For some years now, the consequences of a direct redistribution policy have been becoming apparent, intended to promote a more equal income distribution "from the top".[25] According to a decision by the CPC in 2013, when the Gini coefficient was about 0.45, top incomes were to be reduced by 30 percent. As we have already seen, profits from large corporations are partly used, through industrial policy regulation, to fund general infrastructure investments and thereby contribute to the commons. In addition, the wealth and income of the richest Chinese are now subject to significantly higher taxation.

The top incomes of billionaires are in the social policy spotlight and are regularly published in a list of the richest, the so-called *Hurun List* (as cited above), the Chinese counterpart to the American *Forbes List*. While the societal function of the Forbes List in Anglo-Saxon neoliberal financial capitalism is to maintain admiration for "the rich and powerful", the ideological fixation on the "upper class", and the aspirations of the many millions left behind, the Hurun List tends to reinforce general suspicion of active corruption among the more inequality-averse Chinese. This has tangible consequences: "About half of the 1,000 richest Chinese have seen their wealth shrink in recent years—mainly due to higher taxation and the fight against corruption [...] Not a few on the list were arrested for corruption as a result of their listing."[26]

One of China's leading economic government advisors, Chen Zongsheng, who has conducted extensive research on the Kuznets effect and the "inverted U-function" of China's temporal income distribution, declared at an international conference in Tianjin in 2017 the ambitious goal of a politically initiated reduction of the Gini coefficient by 30 percent. As mentioned, this is a highly complex endeavor, aiming to indirectly influence myriads of interactions and their aggregated distribution effects through regulations. The medium-term target coefficient is thus expected to be around 0.32, which would indicate above-average equality in international comparison. This would place China roughly at the level of Germany.[27]

China is thus likely to be one of the very few growing economies in the world—if not the only one—in which the Gini coefficient is being reduced over the long term. Equality has historically been a core social value in China. As demonstrated in other examples, China replaces the singular goal of economic growth with a multi-objective system that emphasizes equality and participation.[28] Moreover, it is, with considerable certainty, the only country capable of exerting political influence over such complex targets.

Notes

1. For example: Le Tian, "What you should know about China's poverty alleviation campaign", *CGTN*, October 17, 2018: https://news.cgtn.com/news/3d3d774d796b444f7a457a6333566d54/share_p.html visited July 6, 2024.
2. See for example the 2022 World Bank report: The World Bank, Development Research Center of the State Council, the People's Republic of China, 2022. *Four Decades of Poverty Reduction in China*. Washington DC: World Bank, p. 46: https://thedocs.worldbank.org/en/doc/bdadc16a4f5c1c88a839c0f905cde802-0070012022/original/Poverty-Synthesis-Report-final.pdf visited on July 6, 2024.
3. For example: Kunzmann 2018, pp. 76 ff.; Schmid 2017, p. 49.

4. The former colloquial name of the German unemployment benefit system, "Arbeitslosengeld II", was overhauled and renamed "Bürgergeld" in 2023. The "Hartz reforms" were initially introduced in 2002 as part of the German neoliberal "Agenda 2010" reforms, which had a devastating impact on the welfare system and labor market.
5. For example: Schmid 2017, pp. 44–45.
6. Liangping Gao, Ellen Zhang, Ryan Woo, "China adds 12.44 mln urban jobs in 2023, says more effort needed this year", *Reuters*, January 24, 2024: https://www.reuters.com/world/china/china-adds-1244-mln-urban-jobs-2023says-more-effort-needed-this-year-2024-01-24/ visited July 6, 2024.
7. See for example the "Rural Vitalization Strategy Plan 2018-2022"; *China Daily*, July 6, 2018, p. 3.
8. Kuznets, Simon, "Economic Growth and Income Inequality", *American Economic Review* 45(1), 1955, pp. 1–28.
9. Liu 2018, pp. 703–715.
10. Ibid., pp. 45–47.
11. Charmaine Jacob, "Asia-Pacific will see the biggest jump in real salary next year. Here are the top performers", *CNBC*, November 8, 2023: https://www.cnbc.com/2023/11/09/india-indonesia-china-to-see-biggest-jump-in-real-salary-in-2024.html visited July 7, 2024.
12. On the historical phenomenon of Vietnam's development from a victim of the US war and economic sanctions to a US-friendly neoliberal model with rampant inequality and corruption, see for example: Nick Davies, "Vietnam 40 years on: how a communist victory gave way to capitalist corruption", *The Guardian*, April 22, 2015: https://www.theguardian.com/news/2015/apr/22/vietnam-40-years-on-how-communist-victory-gave-way-to-capitalist-corruption visited July 13, 2024.
13. Michelle Zhou, Jason Jiang, Murray Sarelius, Sheila Zhang, "One giant step forward in Chinese IIT reform", *International Tax Review*, December 10, 2018: https://www.internationaltaxreview.com/article/2a68raha94goaj1osa4fk/one-giant-step-forward-in-chinese-iit-reform visited July 13, 2024.
14. Ibid for the new comprehensive income tax rates, the amounts in EUR were calculated by the author based on the 2019 currency value and exchange rates.
15. For example: "Chinese Government announces significant reduction to VAT rates as China enters new VAT legislative phase", *KPMG*, March 8, 2019: https://kpmg.com/cn/en/home/insights/2019/03/china-tax-alert-08.html visited July 13, 2024.
16. See: Hurun Report, "Hurun Global Rich List 2024", *Hurun.net*, March 26, 2024: https://www.hurun.net/en-US/Info/

Detail?num=K851WM942LBU visited July 14, 2024. The *Forbes* list presents quite different numbers, with China at 473, coming in second place after the USA. See: Rob LaFranco, Grace Chung, Chase Peterson-Withorn, "Forbes' 38th Annual World's Billionaires List: Facts And Figures 2024", *Forbes*, Apr 2, 2024: https://www.forbes.com/sites/chasewithorn/2024/04/02/forbes-38th-annual-worlds-billionaires-list-facts-and-figures-2024/ visited July 14, 2024.

17. See: "The Global Wealth Report. Raw data material.", *Credit Suisse*: https://www.credit-suisse.com/about-us/en/reports-research/global-wealth-report/tables.html visited July 14, 2024.
18. See for example: Julie Cooper, "Meet the seven women in China dominating the business world", *CEO Magazine*, October 17, 2023: https://www.theceomagazine.com/business/management-leadership/richest-self-made-women-china/ visited July 14, 2024.
19. The *Gini coefficient* is calculated as follows: On the horizontal axis, the population is divided into equal groups, usually by deciles—from the poorest 10 percent, then the second poorest 10 percent, the third poorest, and so on, up to the richest 10 percent. On the vertical axis, the cumulative share of income of these population groups in the total GDP (national income) is plotted. In the case of perfect income distribution—where 10, 20, 30, … percent of the population own exactly 10, 20, 30, … percent of total income—a diagonal line is formed through the square. In reality, with imperfect income distribution, a curve forms below the diagonal, typically rising slowly at first (e.g., the bottom 10 percent may hold only 1 percent of total income) and ending steeply (e.g., the top 10 percent may hold 30 percent of total income). The Gini coefficient is the ratio of the area between the diagonal and the curve to the area of the entire triangle. It equals 0 in the case of perfect equality and 1 in the case of perfect inequality, where a single individual receives the entire income.
20. Chris Dillow, "Eight Reasons Why Inequality Ruins the Economy", *Evonomics*, May 25, 2018: https://evonomics.com/eight-reasons-why-inequality-kills-prosperity-chris-dillow/ visited July 14, 2024. In detail for example also: Richard Wilkinson, Kate Pickett, 2010. *The Spirit Level: Why Equality is Better for Everyone*, London: Penguin Books Limited.
21. Over a horizontal axis of per capita income (on which a long-term growing economy then moves to the right over time), an inverted U-curve of the Gini coefficient would then show.
22. Liu 2018, p. 712 ff.
23. For example: Kunzmann 2018, pp. 82–83. Zhang 2018, pp. 167–171.
24. Some sources differ from the official numbers, being either higher or lower due to different methodologies of calculation. The World Bank figures are significantly lower for example, in part also due to factoring in cheaper

prices in rural areas, recording a peak of 0.43 in 2010, which has decreased to 0.37 in 2020. Nevertheless, most sources record a significant decline in inequality since the 2010s. See: World Bank, "Gini index – China": https://data.worldbank.org/indicator/SI.POV.GINI?locations=CN visited July 14, 2024.

25. Chen Zongsheng, *Keynote*, Tianjin Forum, July 2017, mimeo.
26. Kunzmann 2018, p. 83f. (Quote translated by the author). This also remains true for the post-Covid era, which has otherwise seen drastic wealth increases of the top 1% worldwide. See for example: Minh Hieu, "China's 5 most affluent billionaires lose $3.1B in collective net worth", *VnExpress*, April 7, 2024: https://e.vnexpress.net/news/business/companies/china-s-5-most-affluent-billionaires-lose-3-1b-in-collective-net-worth-4730640.html visited July 20, 2024.
27. International comparisons and ranking lists vary depending on the specific data bases and variables (for example, current income or wealth, gross domestic product or gross national income, gross income, income after taxes or disposable income, etc.) used for calculation. This is why in some statistical calculations, the Chinese Gini coefficient has even been rising again since 2016: https://www.ceicdata.com/en/china/resident-income-distribution/gini-coefficient visited July 20, 2024.
28. For example: Keqing HAN, "China's Social Transition and Social Welfare Reform", in: *Social Welfare in Transitional China*, Heidelberg et al.: Springer, 2019, pp. 17–47.

Selected and Recommended Literature

Liu, Qunyi. 2018. Rethinking Land Reform in East Asia: Egalitarian or Inegalitarian? *Journal of Economic Issues* 52 (3): 694–716.

Zhang, Fan. 2018. *The Institutional Evolution of China, Government vs Market.* Cheltenham and Northampton, MA, USA: Edward Elgar.

Further Cited Literature

Kunzmann, Marcel, 2018. *Theorie, System und Praxis des Sozialismus in China* [Theory, System and Practice of Socialism in China]. 2nd ed. Berlin: Verlag Mirco Kolarczik

Schmid, Fred, 2017. China im globalen Kapitalismus [China in global capitalism]. In *Krise des Globalen Kapitalismus. Und jetzt Wohin?* [Crisis of global capitalism. And now where to?]. Munich: Institut für sozial-ökologische Wirtschaftsforschung (ISW), Report Nr. 109.

CHAPTER 9

"Labor? Slave Work!"

Labor and Social Dynamics: Labor Rights and Worker Activity, Social Security and Health Care, Migrant Workers and "Hukou", Social Mobilization, Women's Emancipation, and Population Policy

UN: "High Human Development" of China and a Holistic Social Policy

The various areas of Chinese social and economic policy form a mosaic whose social dimension—despite the novelty of many measures and the flexible, experimental character of almost all policy areas—is increasingly emerging as a coherent whole. Two overarching tendencies can be identified:

Since the 12th Five-Year Plan (2011–2015) and the beginning of the Xi/Li era—marked by the 18th Party Congress of the CPC in 2012 and the 12th National People's Congress in 2013—and again since their second term (from 2017/2018) and the 13th Five-Year Plan (2016–2020), China has been shifting its entire socio-economic performance assessment away from the "market" gross domestic product (GDP) as a purely quantitative measure toward more qualitative indicators of success, particularly those emphasizing quality of life.

The GDP aggregates both beneficial and harmful—or even contradictory—activities that do not necessarily enhance the actual quality of life

W. Elsner, E. Najmehchi, *The Rise of China*,
https://doi.org/10.1007/978-3-032-20260-4_9

and may, in fact, reduce it. It simply sums them up insofar as they generate monetary income "in the market". Consequently, since the 1970s, criticism of GDP and growth as sole measures of progress (one is reminded here of the Club of Rome's 1972 report *The Limits to Growth*), researchers, international development organizations, and the United Nations have developed alternative indicators of socio-economic success. These rely largely on a broad spectrum of so-called social indicators.

The UN, for example, analyzes national development through the *Human Development Index* (HDI), which China now also references. Moreover, China increasingly adopts qualitative success indicators derived from recent happiness research and places greater emphasis on qualitative themes such as the rule of law and democratic mobilization and participation in its developmental framework.

According to the United Nations, China has been classified as a country of "high human development" since 2010, based on the criteria of the HDI.[1] Its overall quality of life has been improving faster than that of most countries worldwide: child mortality has fallen below the levels of some developed capitalist industrial nations, while life expectancy, literacy rates, and access to employment, education, and culture have continued to rise. Absolute poverty, as previously mentioned, has been eradicated. From a social and ecological perspective, these achievements would, in fact, resonate strongly with the ideals of many leftist and green-liberal observers in the West.

A massive job-creation program (see above) ensures fundamentally adequate employment opportunities and genuine occupational choices for the population. At the same time, extensive support and social embedding of both high-tech start-ups and agricultural enterprises—facilitated, for instance, through the *Household Responsibility System* (HRS) and platforms such as Taobao—provide broad-based alternatives for self-employed income generation.

Significant wage and salary increases, along with tax relief measures targeted especially at lower- and middle-income groups, have further enhanced social equality and justice. Minimum wages are now in some cases even higher than those in certain EU member states. Their enforcement is strictly monitored, employees have an individual right of legal action in cases of non-compliance, and violations are subject to sanctions. These mechanisms embody the *social human rights* promoted by the United Nations—serving as a sharp contrast to the widespread wage dumping observed in neoliberal capitalist economies.

In addition, we will now address the following areas of Chinese social development and labor policy:

- ***Nationwide introduction of social insurance***, which has laid the institutional foundation for a comprehensive welfare system;
- ***New Labor Law***, in force since 2008, which implements international ILO standards and establishes working conditions that in some respects even exceed those regulated in countries such as Germany. It has created a consistent labor practice and a labor law jurisprudence in which legal provisions and everyday reality do not systematically diverge—as is often characteristic of developed capitalist states. Unlike German employees, Chinese workers can directly and individually assert their labor rights in court without having to endure lengthy and costly legal proceedings that frequently end in compensation settlements after years of delay. In dismissal cases, however, as in many countries, the disruption of the employment relationship is typically assumed, meaning reinstatement is generally difficult to achieve through legal action;
- ***Equal rights of women***, particularly regarding pay equity and representation across professions and leadership positions;
- ***Migrant workers***, the residential registration system (Hukou), and the related question of local social rights and entitlements;
- ***Social mobilization, inclusion, and local political participation***, which represent key elements of China's ongoing efforts to strengthen social cohesion and participatory governance.

From Zero to 1.4 Billion in 10 Years: Comprehensive Social Insurance

Access to Healthcare

China succeeded in eradicating most major epidemic diseases at an early stage. However, its healthcare system—essentially clinic-based—still lags significantly behind the equipment standards of some developed capitalist countries. Among the remaining (though steadily declining) challenges are hospital overcrowding and relatively high out-of-pocket expenses for certain services. Nevertheless, broad access to medical care is generally ensured, evidenced, for example, by a doubling of the number of hospital beds within ten years to more than five million (as of 2015). This system has since been supplemented by a network of rural doctors.[2]

Since 2009, the population has also been integrated into the universal health insurance system established in the early 2000s. With around 1.4 billion insured persons, the entire population is now covered. This means that, on average, about 100 million people were included in the health insurance system each year. Officially, universal health coverage was planned to be achieved by 2020, but the goal was already reached ahead of schedule in 2018.

Non-commercial health apps help Chinese citizens in their daily lives to adopt health-conscious behaviors, and the renewed promotion of traditional medical knowledge among the population also contributes to this.[3] This has been part of China's "Healthy China 2030" strategy, announced in 2016.[4] In particular, by placing greater emphasis on disease prevention and promoting health technologies, medical AI, and telemedicine (internet-based services), issues such as hospital overcrowding and the general lack of access to and affordability of healthcare services have been addressed.

Due to an aging population combined with rising per capita income, the demand for healthcare services has increased dramatically in China in recent years. This has led the government to introduce market-liberalizing measures to attract foreign investment into the growing healthcare sector, such as allowing Chinese-foreign joint venture hospitals[5] and expanding investment opportunities in various subsectors of the pharmaceutical and healthcare industries in 2019.[6]

Nevertheless, due to the volatile nature of the healthcare sector—particularly the risks associated with over-privatization and deregulation—the industry remains heavily regulated and closely monitored by the Central Supervision Commission (CSC), with an increased emphasis on combating corruption, especially since 2020.[7]

Healthcare: Some Statistics

A brief look at the statistics highlights the quantitative growth and successes of China's healthcare sector, as well as the corresponding improvements in overall population health over recent decades:

- While the average annual healthcare spending per capita has increased significantly since the beginning of the century, having risen from 42

USD in 2000 to 398 USD in 2016,[8] it managed to stay comparably low in relation to GDP per capita, being at 5.38 percent compared to the US' 17.36 percent in 2021, for example (the world average being at 10.35 percent).[9]

- China has almost doubled its number of hospital beds per 1000 people since the 1990s (2.5 in 1999), surpassing the USA in 2012, with the USA standing at 2.9 (similar to world average) and China at 4.3 (similar to European average) in 2017, according to the World Health Organization.[10] Similar numbers are recorded for physicians per 1000 people, having increased from 1.1 in 2002 to 2.4 in 2020, according to OECD health data, putting it above the East Asia and Pacific average,[11] as well as the number of nurses and midwives per 1000 inhabitants, with 1 in 2004 rising to 3.3 in 2020.[12]
- The maternal mortality rate has decreased from 97 per 100,000 births in 1990 to 58 in 2000 and 23 in 2020 (with the world average at 223), according to the World Bank.[13]
- Lastly, life expectancy has also continuously risen in China, being at almost 79 years in 2023 (increased from 73 in 2001, which is still the 2023 world average), having surpassed the USA in 2020, which in 2022 stood at 77 (both world average and the USA have seen an in part temporary decrease in life expectancy since Covid-19 started at the end of 2019).[14]

China's Covid Response

Contrary to the portrayal by many Western media outlets, China acted swiftly, effectively, and transparently in response to the outbreak of Covid-19. This assessment is also supported by statements from the World Health Organization (WHO), which praised China's initial handling of the crisis,[15] and numerous health professionals, as for example reported in the world's foremost medical journal, *The Lancet*.[16]

By quickly implementing stringent lockdown measures, widespread testing, and aggressive contact tracing when Covid started spreading in early 2020, China was able to almost fully contain the virus within its borders. China's previous experiences with viral disease outbreaks such as that of SARS in 2002 (and errors in its handling, resulting in public criticism) have led it to set up preventive structures such as improved reporting mechanisms for future pandemic outbreaks and de-privatization efforts of rural healthcare on the advice of its major virologists.[17]

The quick and coordinated response, which significantly mitigated the potential impact of the pandemic within China, saved potentially thousands of lives and set a benchmark for other nations to follow. Furthermore, Chinese virologists identified the virus as early as late December 2019, warned the WHO on December 31, and transparently and swiftly shared all available data on the virus with the WHO and the global community on January 8, 2020.[18] All these measures had "bought the world time", according to the WHO director-general, Tedros Adhanom Ghebreyesus.[19]

Had other countries, particularly in the West, adopted similar measures, the global spread of the virus might have been largely preventable. However, the response in many neoliberal and deregulated Western economies was slow, uncoordinated, and under-resourced. Many governments, particularly in the USA and parts of Europe, underestimated the severity of the pandemic and failed to implement effective public health measures in time. This lack of preparedness and the inadequate response resulted in thousands if not millions of preventable deaths and a devastating toll on healthcare systems and economies.[20]

In an effort to deflect blame for their own failures, some media outlets and Western leaders, especially US president Donald Trump, began to propagate conspiracy theories, such as the "lab leak" hypothesis, suggesting that the virus had escaped from a laboratory in Wuhan. These theories, however, as of late 2024, still lack any credible scientific support, and most recent studies and statements from the global scientific community, including publications in respected journals such as *Nature*,[21] rather reinforce the hypothesis that the virus likely originated from a wet market in Wuhan. Most recently, at the time of writing, another study supporting this hypothesis was published on September 19, 2024, in the major scientific journal *Cell*.[22] In fact, the Chinese government already shut down the wet market in Wuhan on January 1, 2020, less than a month after the first patients were identified,[23] and announced on February 24, 2020, to ban all wild animal trade in China.[24]

Prominent scientists have repeatedly attacked the "lab leak" and other similar hypotheses, emphasizing that there is no credible evidence to support them, warning of the dangers of scientific misinformation and conspiracy theories.[25] While the origins of Covid-19 have certainly not yet been fully clarified in all their details as of 2025, the focus on such scientifically *unsubstantiated* claims not only undermines scientific discourse but also distracts from the real issue of global health preparedness and response. This reckless rhetoric around Covid and its origins (including racist phrases used by Trump such as "Kung-Flu" and "China Virus") has furthermore had an impact on increasing racism against East and Southeast Asians, especially Asian Americans in the USA, as we have already reported above.

Western countries, especially the USA, have also attempted to delegitimize China's efforts in vaccine development and distribution. Despite the successful rollout of Chinese vaccines like Sinopharm and Sinovac, which have been approved by the WHO[26] and used in numerous countries, there has been a concerted effort to undermine their credibility. The most striking example is an investigative report published by *Reuters* in June 2024, which uncovered a wide-scale Pentagon-led misinformation campaign aimed to discredit Chinese-made vaccines in the Philippines, endangering and potentially costing many lives.[27] These allegations of ineffectiveness and attempts to ban Chinese vaccines, without any solid evidence, reflect a geopolitical game merging profit-driven motives with a projection of Western failures in managing the pandemic by aiming to delegitimize China.

The ongoing mutations of the virus, such as the Alpha, Delta, and Omicron variants, have largely emerged from, and initially spread in, regions where public health measures were poorly implemented or difficult to implement, rather than from China.[28]

Faced with these variants such as Omicron, which is much more aggressive in its transmission but less severe in terms of illness for many cases, the Chinese government first reacted by implementing stringent lockdowns and other drastic measures to prevent further spread, based on the maxim of putting people's lives over anything else. These "zero-Covid" measures, while effective in curbing transmission, led to understandable frustration and protest among the population (often via social media), especially with this new Omicron wave. The Chinese government, recognizing the concerns of its citizens, responded to these protests by easing lockdown restrictions and adjusting its Covid-19 policies in December 2022.[29] This flexibility in policymaking, aimed at balancing public health with social stability, demonstrates a responsiveness of the Chinese government to the public mood that is often overlooked in Western narratives.

Overall, China's response to Covid-19 has been judged highly successful according to evaluations by the WHO and international experts. The country not only managed to contain the virus effectively within its borders but also provided critical medical supplies and expertise to countries around the world. Despite facing significant challenges and international scrutiny, China's approach has been characterized by a high degree of coordination and adaptability, in stark contrast to the chaotic and often ineffective responses seen in many other countries. This had the result of China having had one of the lowest per capita infection and mortality rates globally (7.16 deaths per 100,000 population), while countries such as the USA (341.11 deaths per 100,000 population) and the UK (325.13 deaths per 100,000 population, as of March 2023) have had among the highest.[30]

The global pandemic has laid bare the strengths and weaknesses of different political and healthcare systems. While no country has been perfect in its response, China's approach stands out as a case study in effective crisis management. The lessons learned from China's experience could provide valuable insights for building more resilient and equitable public health systems and pandemic response infrastructure worldwide. As the world continues to grapple with the ongoing effects and aftermath of the Covid-19 pandemic, and future pandemics are sure to happen,[31] it is crucial to move beyond politicized narratives and focus on collaborative efforts to enhance global health security.

Pension Insurance

A personal social insurance system—including pension, health, accident, unemployment, and maternity insurance—was first decided upon in 1993 and prepared from that time onward. It was necessary as a supplement to company reforms, privatizations, and labor law reforms, since the old, exclusively company-based social networks and social security systems (Danwei, see above) were too narrow and inflexible.[32] However, a comprehensive social insurance law was only passed in 2011. Following this overhaul, China has seen unprecedented improvements in pension coverage, especially over the last two decades. Between 2009 and 2012 alone, the proportion of people enrolled in pension insurance nearly doubled, from 30 to 55 percent.[33] By 2023, over one billion people (more than 70 percent) had already been included in the system, making it the largest pension system in the world.[34] Here too, full coverage is now foreseeable.

Remaining challenges include relatively low pension benefit rates and rural–urban disparities, with urban workers often receiving better coverage and higher benefits. A particularly pressing issue is the insufficient funds and long-term sustainability of the pension system; a 2019 report by the Chinese Academy of Social Sciences estimated that basic urban pensions could be depleted by 2035.[35] This has prompted the government to draw up plans in 2024 to gradually raise the retirement age over the following five years. As of 2024, China's retirement age remained one of the lowest in the world—"60 for men, 55 for women in white-collar jobs, and 50 for working-class women"[36]—despite a life expectancy higher than or on par with that of the USA and a rapidly aging population placing strain on the pension system. According to a pension development report released in late 2023, a retirement age of 65 "may be the final result after adjustment".[37]

"Working-Class Security"

For the social dimension of all this, a central sentiment in China's national security strategy can be summarized as follows: "For China, development and working-class security are key to national security."[38] Such a sociopolitical commitment—echoed, for example, in Xi Jinping's party congress speech from October 2017[39]—may seem quite foreign to most people in the West, where the focus is often on "saving", "austerity", "tightening the belt", "market-compliant democracy", the primacy of "the economy", and redistribution upwards.

Working Conditions Compared: Examples

We have thus learned quite a bit about the specific working conditions in China beyond mere wage issues. Working conditions in China have been broadly evolving since the 2000s. For example, in 2017, members of German trade unions compiled an extensive collection of materials and a detailed comparison of working conditions in both countries following an informational trip to China.[40] But how can one even consider comparing a country that was until recently a very poor developing nation with one of the richest countries in the world?

Well, because China has also developed an enormous "multiplier" in terms of work and social affairs, progressing from modest average incomes to broad socio-economic and ecological achievements. It has emancipated itself under its own management from being merely a site of low-wage production for the West and has developed into a social leadership power. The familiar "knockout" arguments of neoliberal financial capitalism—"no money", "too expensive", or "competitive disadvantage"—simply do not apply and are therefore not accepted. Freed from the austerity regime and the upward redistribution imperative, China can pursue what it deems right.

Thus, with active state promotion, high-tech companies in China are now experimenting with a four-day workweek at full wage compensation.[41] Chinese labor law strictly limits the working day to eight hours.[42] In this context, the so-called "996 working hour system"—meaning working (often unpaid) overtime from 9:00 a.m. to 9:00 p.m., six days a week—which emerged primarily over the last decade, especially among IT companies, has faced growing criticism and backlash from both the Chinese population (for example, through online protests[43]) and the government. On August 27, 2021, the Supreme People's Court declared the practice illegal.[44] Since then, the government has increasingly cracked down on companies implementing the 996 system, positioning itself on the side of the workers. This has already prompted tech giants such as Douyin, Tencent, and Kuaishou to revise their work policies, although, as of 2024, the practice has not yet been fully eradicated.[45]

Temporary employment contracts in China are also subject to stricter restrictions than in countries such as Germany, where a former chancellor once prided himself on having created the "best" low-wage sector in Europe.[46] Temporary workers in China receive absolute "equal pay", meaning the same compensation for the same work, and benefit from lower retirement ages, even *after* the planned reforms (Germany's retirement age will reach 67 by 2029). Arguments like "We can't afford it!" or "No money available…" are not accepted in this context.

Another Reason Why Western Cheap Production Has Left China

In the past, large Western companies in China profited greatly from low wages and lax environmental regulations. It is therefore unsurprising that they strongly oppose social progress and the new Chinese labor law—which was intended simply to bring the labor market in line with ILO standards, which their own governments have also ratified.[47] This opposition has not hindered China, and complaints about the country's supposed loss of international competitiveness have had no effect. On the contrary, China's "socialist high road" of development—unconstrained by the argument of "no money!"—is proving far more sustainable and effective than the "neoliberal low road".

Alongside the caravan of low-cost production moving along the neoliberal low road toward countries such as Vietnam and India, the Taiwanese IT giant Foxconn announced in 2017 plans to construct a 10-billion USD technology park in Wisconsin, USA, in a deal with then-President Donald Trump, who hailed it as "the eighth wonder of the world".[48] In Wisconsin, at the heart of Trump's America, the wages of disenfranchised and impoverished workers, as well as environmental standards, were already lower than in China.[49] For Trump's "America First" agenda, the project represented a potential revival of US tech manufacturing, as the campus was planned to produce flat-panel displays and other devices. For Foxconn, the deal was especially important in the context of Trump's trade war against China, which threatened its largest customer, Apple. Yet only a few years later, in 2021, Foxconn announced it would "drastically scale back" its planned investment to just 673 million USD, reducing the number of new jobs from 13,000 to 1454. Among the reasons cited were the lack of crucial suppliers for flat-panel display production near Wisconsin, as well as local opposition—especially concerning high costs for taxpayers, extensive water rights, and the acquisition and demolition of houses for the project.[50] Rise and fall …

Equal Work and Payment, and Equal Start-Up Conditions for Women

China's long journey from feudalism, colonial devastation, and economic backwardness to an exemplary, ILO-compliant, and forward-looking labor law—together with a corresponding workplace reality—also represents a path toward genuine gender equality in employment. A few illustrative highlights:

- China's female labor force participation rate stood at 60.5 percent in 2023 (male: 72.1 percent), which is more than ten percentage points above the global average of 48.7 percent and higher than in countries such as Germany (56.4 percent) and the USA (56.5 percent). Particularly noteworthy is its relatively narrow gender gap of 11.6 percentage points—far below the global average of 24.4 percent in 2023—where a lower gap indicates greater equality.[51] As of 2022, women accounted for over 43 percent of China's total labor force.[52] According to the Global Gender Gap Index, China ranked 45th out of 146 countries in the category of "Economic Participation and Opportunity" for women, placing it ahead of several Western European countries such as Denmark (46), Spain (48), France (51), and Germany (88).[53]
- By 2020, the majority of the then over 30 million university students in China were female (over 52 percent).[54]
- A quarter of all entrepreneurs in China are female; 43 of the world's approximately 100 self-made female billionaires come from China; no other country has so many women who have accumulated such wealth (the USA standing at 30).[55] (On wealth redistribution, see above.)
- Fifty-five percent of all internet companies are founded and led by women. In the leadership levels of the IT sector, more than half are women.[56]
- As early as 2013, women held approximately 44 percent of middle and upper management positions in Chinese companies—a remarkable figure achieved without the need for protracted debates or

state-imposed regulations concerning "women in leadership" or gender quotas.

"[D]iscrimination against women" and "the exclusion or restriction of women from lawfully enjoying and exercising their various rights and interests" (Art. 2, *Law of the People's Republic of China on the Protection of Women's Rights and Interests*) are rigorously investigated and punished. Following China's economic rise in the early twenty-first century—and in response to increasing foreign cultural influences—a new official self-conception emerged, defined in deliberate contrast to that of the (capitalist and liberal) West, which is often criticized for its high levels of social degradation and the sexual exploitation of women. In contrast, China promotes a fundamentally different understanding of gender equality, grounded in its own "Core Socialist Values" rather than in the liberal feminism prevalent in many Western societies.[57]

Fighting Over- and Under-Population: From "One-Child Policy" (and Its Adverse Side Effects) to "Two-Child Policy" and the Current "Three-Child Policy"

As we have seen in several other key policy areas (and will continue to see), China has been the only country in the world to systematically attempt to address the collective challenge of "global overpopulation"—or, put in more differentiated terms, to pursue a policy of *sustainable population development*.[58] While comparable countries such as India have often experienced their largely uncontrolled population growth translating directly into poverty, hunger, and increasing dependence on foreign aid, China at least dared to undertake another large-scale social experiment.

China's One-Child Policy was introduced in 1979–1980 and officially ended in 2015, after having been gradually relaxed for several years. The generation born during the era of the One-Child Policy now ranges in age from roughly 10 to 45 years (as of 2025), encompassing much of China's younger and middle-aged population.

From the outset, there were numerous exceptions to the policy. Ethnic minority couples and those living in rural areas were often permitted to have two (or more) children. By 2004, the policy had been further relaxed; for instance, in Shanghai, divorced and remarried partners were allowed to have an additional child even if they each already had one from previous marriages. Further adjustments followed in 2013, allowing couples in which at least one partner was an only child to have two children.

By 2016, the One-Child Policy was officially replaced by a Two-Child Policy, permitting every couple to have two children. As birth rates continued to decline—largely due to modernization and rising prosperity—considerations emerged by 2018 to introduce a Three-Child Policy as an upper limit. On May 31, 2021, the nationwide Three-Child Policy was formally announced. Finally, in response to China's first population decline in six decades, the Sichuan provincial government lifted all restrictions on the number of children that residents could have in early 2023.[59]

Due to longer education periods, expanded career opportunities for women, and increased income and consumption possibilities, China's population growth rate has naturally declined for socio-economic reasons—a development also observed in other economically advanced countries with typically higher per capita income levels, such as Germany. To counteract this trend, China has begun introducing incentives to encourage higher birth rates.

A comparable situation can be found in Germany, where persistently low fertility rates have led to a declining population. In response, the government has implemented measures such as flexible parental leave and financial incentives to promote family formation. However, since the 1960s, Germany's economic model has also relied heavily on immigration and the active recruitment of young, already qualified workers from abroad—first from Italy, Greece, and Spain, and more recently from countries such as Syria—to stabilize its labor market and sustain economic growth.

In terms of population development, China's One-Child Policy was largely successful. In 2012, the average birth rate was 1.55 children per woman, placing China 181st out of 224 countries in population growth.[60] According to the Chinese government, the policy reduced the number of births by about 300 million between 1994 and 2004 alone. However, the target population of 1.2 billion was still exceeded by roughly 150 million by 2014.

Nevertheless, China's population curve shows a clear stabilization and a steady population size beginning in 2022, especially in comparison to India, whose population explosion continues largely unabated and with far less public problem-solving capacity. India surpassed China as the most populous country in the world in 2023.[61]

However, important reasons for the relaxation and eventual end of the One-Child Policy were the unforeseen side effects, which quickly prompted the first reactions and adjustments in Chinese population policy. In China, rational and self-determined family planning is not hindered by religious beliefs or superstitions, so every couple always knew the gender of their expected child early on. An old tradition in Confucian ethics, which emphasized male succession, apparently still exerted a strong influence, leading to the abortion of many female fetuses (reportedly up to 50 abortions per 100 births at the peak). China's free, unbiased, secular, and purely scientific approach to birth policy initially allowed this. However, the early determination of a fetus's gender was later banned by the government for a time.[62]

The preference for male offspring also meant that boys were excessively protected and pampered by their parents and grandparents.[63] This created generations often referred to as "little emperors", who received the best possible education, career opportunities, income, and consumption possibilities. The negative long-term effects of this development have been widely criticized, particularly the rise in individualistic and egocentric behaviors. Critics argue that the "little emperors" often exhibit relatively low social competence. It was clear that China could not afford such developments in the long run.

As a result, the quantitative ratio of boys to girls (the sex ratio at birth) shifted, reaching 1.2 boys for every newborn girl in 2009. This has created a situation in which girls in the younger and middle generations are now at an advantage and highly sought after. This secondary effect has also given rise to so-called "little empresses".

The roughly 30-year population policy experiment cannot simply be dismissed as a pure failure. It remains both a contribution and a lesson in addressing one of humanity's most pressing problems. Extrapolated to the world population, the quantitative effect in China—300 million fewer people—would correspond to approximately 1.5 billion fewer people globally.

In 2022, the average birth rate in China—driven more by socio-economic factors (and since 2020 partly by the Covid pandemic and related policies) than by active population control—was only 1.2 children per woman, resulting in a slow population decline (1.7 before Covid, now slowly rebounding).[64] However, the One-Child Policy also incurred social costs, which are becoming increasingly apparent. Put bluntly, the pampered "little emperors" and "little empresses" of the One-Child Policy era now need to be guided away from narcissism, egoism, individualism, and consumerism toward more socially responsible and ecologically sustainable behavior. This topic will be revisited in the third part when discussing the country's future prospects.

However, further secondary effects of the One-Child Policy, combined with socio-economically influenced reproductive behavior, could also impact the pension system. China's previously low retirement ages (60 for men and 55 for women) have become increasingly unsustainable, prompting the decision to gradually raise the retirement age starting in 2024, following an extended period of planning and academic discussion.[65]

Social Mobilization: Inclusion, Participation, and a "Whole-Process" Democracy

In discussions on Chinese labor law and working conditions, as well as on wage and income increases, tax reliefs, social insurance, and redistribution measures, we have already seen how much social movements of workers and employees have driven the country's social development. This has generally been supported by the respective local organizational structures of the CPC, as well as by the CPC as a whole, with its nearly 100 million members. It is common in social movements for workers and employees to view the CPC and the central government as being on their side, while corporate leaders often align with local and provincial governments, whose "champions" they are.[66]

China is the most strike-prone country in the world.[67] Strikes are not only less regulated than, for example, in Germany, but their range of topics is also more broadly related to the working and living conditions of working people. Strikes occur for all sorts of goals: higher incomes, better working conditions, greater social insurance benefits from companies, and even more corporate investment activities and innovations—typically supported by the CPC.

The described social mobilization is not only an element of China's innovative development dynamic. Many Chinese commentators see it as a tool to increase state capacity.[68] This highlights a close connection between society and the state, which is certainly not a one-way street.

The mosaic we are piecing together here should not suggest comprehensive harmony; it remains one of social conflict between workers and capitalist elites, in which local and provincial authorities are often eager to support a "trouble-free" management process.[69] For those who want to see it this way, China will remain a class society for the foreseeable future, with several hundred million workers and employees, dozens of millions of self-employed entrepreneurs, and a few million large and small capitalists—necessarily marked by class struggle. But, as the Italian philosopher Domenico Losurdo, already quoted, says: The capitalist class does not hold state power and foreseeably will not do.

This may already explain why the Chinese state does not have a one-sided, socially narrow, structurally inhibiting, short-term orientation that prevents social and ecological progress. It is possibly for this reason that workers and employees in China have already "achieved more than 'independent' and 'free' trade unions in the West".[70]

This highly mobilized workforce and society as a whole, which is quite palpable to foreigners in China, is both conflict- and cooperation-ready and seems no longer willing to "let the wool be pulled over their eyes", as we will continue to illustrate. A public that discusses issues intensively on social media and through other channels has become a core social actor in China, interacting closely with politics and showing high sensitivity regarding ethics, quality of life, environmental protection, and forward-looking life planning.[71]

This sharply contrasts with the image often painted by Western media of China as an "autocracy", "dictatorship", "police state", or "prison". Another Western China observer provocatively comments on this contrast: "[The Chinese] citizens have much more say about how their country is governed, than those in the West."[72] We will still see what the Chinese way of social mobilization and participation concretely means at the local participation level.

However, what we can recognize—or even merely suspect—here must ultimately reflect back on our own understanding of "democracy", which remains trapped in the formal, ossified rituals of a largely neoliberal party oligopoly and a detached representative parliament. This is an understanding in which we have already resigned ourselves en masse to feeling betrayed by parties, coalitions, and governments after every election, and have given up expecting any progressive changes from politics. We have learned to be modest and settled into our niches. Our imaginations must open up to new, substantive forms of democracy for the future—forms that will not be possible without direct social mobilization and participation.

If we continue to wait for the G7 or the UN to solve humanity's problems, humanity will hardly survive the end of this century. If we continue to submit to our self-imposed taboos born of resignation and refuse to open our minds, the energies and hopeful ideas of our children and grandchildren—the "Fridays-for-Future" generation—will be in vain. The "Fridays-for-Future" students seem to be starting to understand this. Our last hope?

Notes

1. Kunzmann 2018, p. 77 ff.
2. For example: Kunzmann 2018, p. 79f.
3. For example: Andrea Bernardi, Francesco Grillo, Donni Wang, *The Innovation Paradox Versus Innovation with Chinese Characteristics: Through the Lens of Healthcare and Economic Policy*, Presentation at the annual meeting of the *European Association for Evolutionary Political Economy*, Warsaw 2019.
4. For example: Xiaodong Tan, Xiangxiang Liu, Haiyan Shao, "Healthy China 2030: A Vision for Health Care", *Value in Health Regional Issues*, Vol. 12, May 2017, pp. 112–114.
5. Qian Zhou, "Key Considerations for Entering China's Healthcare Market", *China Briefing*, April 29, 2024: https://www.china-briefing.com/news/key-considerations-for-entering-chinas-healthcare-market/ visited July 21, 2024.
6. For example: Elyar Najmehchi, "China's healthcare sector promising for 2020 and beyond", *China Daily*, December 25, 2019: https://www.chinadaily.com.cn/a/201912/25/WS5e02bfeaa310cf3e35580799.html visited July 21, 2024.
7. Zhou, ibid.
8. Najmehchi, ibid.
9. World Bank, "Current health expenditure (% of GDP)", April 15, 2024: https://data.worldbank.org/indicator/SH.XPD.CHEX.GD.ZS visited July 21, 2024.
10. World Bank, "Hospital beds (per 1,000 people)—China, United States": https://data.worldbank.org/indicator/SH.MED.BEDS.ZS?locations=CN-US visited July 21, 2024, based on World Health Organization Data.
11. World Bank, "Physicians (per 1,000 people)—China": https://data.worldbank.org/indicator/SH.MED.PHYS.ZS?locations=CN visited July 21, 2024.

12. World Bank, "Nurses and midwives (per 1,000 people) - China": https://data.worldbank.org/indicator/SH.MED.NUMW.P3?locations=CN visited July 21, 2024.
13. World Bank, "Maternal mortality ratio (modeled estimate, per 100,000 live births) – China": https://data.worldbank.org/indicator/SH.STA.MMRT?locations=CN visited July 21, 2024.
14. World Bank, "Life expectancy at birth, total (years) - , China, World, United States": https://data.worldbank.org/indicator/SP.DYN.LE00.IN?end=2023&locations=CO.-CN-1W-US&skipRedirection=true&start=2000&view=chart visited July 21, 2024.
15. "WHO chief praises China's virus fight, urges more from world", *Associated Press*, February 15, 2020: https://apnews.com/article/d305b8c6fc-c5ac1f1a6e24382e6769fb visited September 28, 2024.
16. Talha Burki, "China's successful control of COVID-19", *The Lancet,* Volume 20, Issue 11, pp. 1240–1241, November 2020, October 22, 2020: https://www.thelancet.com/journals/laninf/article/PIIS1473-3099(20)30800-8/fulltext visited September 28, 2024.
17. John Nkengasong, "China's response to a novel coronavirus stands in stark contrast to the 2002 SARS outbreak response", *Nature Medicine,* Volume 26, pp. 310–311, 2020, January 27, 2020: https://www.nature.com/articles/s41591-020-0771-1 visited September 28, 2024.
18. Natasha Khan, "New Virus Discovered by Chinese Scientists Investigating Pneumonia Outbreak", *The Wall Street Journal*, January 8, 2020: https://www.wsj.com/articles/new-virus-discovered-by-chinese-scientists-investigating-pneumonia-outbreak-11578485668 visited September 28, 2024.
19. Associated Press, ibid. (see above).
20. Amanda Holpuch, "US could have averted 40% of Covid deaths, says panel examining Trump's policies", *The Guardian*, February 11, 2021: https://www.theguardian.com/us-news/2021/feb/10/us-coronavirus-response-donald-trump-health-policy visited September 28, 2024.
21. Amy Maxmen, "Wuhan market was epicentre of pandemic's start, studies suggest", *Nature*, February 27, 2022: https://www.nature.com/articles/d41586-022-00584-8 visited September 28, 2024.
22. Alexander Crits-Christoph et al., "Genetic tracing of market wildlife and viruses at the epicenter of the COVID-19 pandemic", *Cell*, Volume 187, Issue 19, pp. 5468–5482, September 19, 2024: https://www.cell.com/cell/fulltext/S0092-8674(24)00901-2 visited September 28, 2024.
23. John Nkengasong, ibid. (see above).
24. "China bans trade, consumption of wild animals due to coronavirus", *Reuters*, February 25, 2020: https://www.reuters.com/article/us-china-

health-wildlife/china-bans-trade-consumption-of-wild-animals-due-to-coronavirus-idUSKCN20J069/ visited September 28, 2024.

25. James Alwine et al., "The harms of promoting the lab leak hypothesis for SARS-CoV-2 origins without evidence", *Journal of Virology*, Volume 98, No. 9, August 1, 2024: https://journals.asm.org/doi/10.1128/jvi.01240-24 visited September 28, 2024.
26. "The Sinopharm COVID-19 vaccine: What you need to know", *World Health Organization*, June 10, 2022: https://www.who.int/news-room/feature-stories/detail/the-sinopharm-covid-19-vaccine-what-you-need-to-know visited September 29, 2024.
27. Chris Bing, Joel Schectman, "Pentagon ran secret anti-vax campaign to undermine China during pandemic", *Reuters*, June 14, 2024: https://www.reuters.com/investigates/special-report/usa-covid-propaganda/ visited September 28, 2024.
28. Kathy Katella, "Omicron and its Subvariants: A Guide to What We Know", *Yale Medicine*, September 1, 2023: https://www.yalemedicine.org/news/5-things-to-know-omicron visited September 28, 2024.
29. Frances Mao, "China abandons key parts of zero-Covid strategy after protests", *BBC*, December 7, 2023: https://www.bbc.com/news/world-asia-china-63855508 visited September 28, 2024.
30. "Mortality Analyses", *Johns Hopkins University & Medicine Coronavirus Resource Center*, March 16, 2023: https://coronavirus.jhu.edu/data/mortality visited September 28, 2024.
31. Karen Feldscher, "The next pandemic: not if, but when", *Harvard T.H. Chan School of Public Health*, September 12, 2024: https://www.hsph.harvard.edu/news/features/next-pandemic-not-if-but-when/ visited September 28, 2024.
32. For example: ZHANG Fan 2018, p. 109 ff.
33. Andrea Vilela, "Pension coverage in China and the expansion of the New Rural Social Pension", *HelpAge International*, 2013: https://www.helpage.org/silo/files/pension-watch-briefing-11-pension-coverage-in-china.pdf visited July 27, 2024.
34. See for example: Li Yang, "Towards equity and sustainability? China's pension system reform moves center stage", *World Inequality Lab – Working Paper N° 2021/13*, April 2021: https://wid.world/wp-content/uploads/2021/04/WorldInequalityLab_WP2021_13_China_PensionSystem.pdf visited July 27, 2024. And: "Number of people covered by public pension insurance in China from 2013 to 2023", *Statista*, June 28, 2024: https://www.statista.com/statistics/234072/number-of-pension-insurance-contributors-in-china/ visited July 27, 2024.
35. See for example: Zhou Xinda, Tang Hanyu, Denise Jia, "China's pension plan faces prospect of change or going bust", *Caixin Global*, May 27,

2024: https://www.caixinglobal.com/2024-05-27/cover-story-chinas-pension-plan-faces-prospect-for-change-or-going-bust-102200228.html visited July 27, 2024.

36. Kelly Ng, "China to raise retirement age as population gets older", *BBC*, July 23, 2024: https://www.bbc.com/news/articles/cpd9v48yn8ro visited July 27, 2024.
37. Ibid.
38. Cited after Kadri 2017, p. 41.
39. For example: "Full text of Xi Jinping's report at 19th CPC National Congress", *Xinhua*, November 3, 2017: http://www.xinhuanet.com/english/special/2017-11/03/c_136725942.htm visited July 27, 2024.
40. Stiftung Asienhaus in cooperation with the Forum Arbeitswelten e.V. and express (ed.), "Chinesische Arbeitswelten - in China und in der Welt [Chinese working environments - in China and in the world]", Pdf online at: http://forumarbeitswelten.de:8080/faw/themenbereiche/arbeiterbewegung-arbeitskaempfe-und-arbeitsbedingungen/2016-01_arbeitswelten-in-china__web.pdf/view visited July 28, 2024; see also Küsters 2018, p. 18f.; more also under: Internationaler Gewerkschaftlicher Arbeitskreis Köln IGAKK [International Trade Union Working Group Cologne IGAKK], visited July 28, 2024.
41. For example: Rügemer 2018, pp. 277–280.
42. See the full text: *Labour Law of the People's Republic of China*: http://www.npc.gov.cn/zgrdw/englishnpc/ Law/2007-12/12/content_1383754.htm visited July 28, 2024. See Chapter IV Working Hours, Rest and Vacations.
43. This has also spawned a youth counterculture movement named *Fo Xi*, meaning "Buddha-like" or "Buddha-like mindset", which is highly critical of what can be called the "Burnout Society", as coined by philosopher Byung-Chul Han (2015), whose book was highly popular also in China. Rather than the workaholic mindset of "996", it emphasizes the value of a tranquil life, promoting a more humane work-life balance. See for example: Xinhua, "Chinese youth adopt "Buddha-like" mindset in face of modern pressures", *China Daily*, March 14, 2018: https://www.chinadaily.com.cn/a/201803/14/WS5aa9420ca3106e7dcc141abd.html visited July 28, 2024.
44. Zheping Huang, "China Spells Out How Excessive '996' Work Culture is Illegal", *Bloomberg*, August 27, 2021: https://www.bloomberg.com/news/articles/2021-08-27/china-s-top-court-says-excessive-996-work-culture-is-illegal visited July 28, 2024.
45. See for example: Juliette Pitt, "What does China's ban on the '996' work culture mean for companies?", *The China-Britain Business Council (CBBC)*, October 22, 2021: https://focus.cbbc.org/what-does-the-

recent-ban-on-996-mean-for-chinas-future-work-culture/ visited July 28, 2024.

46. See for example: Sarah Marsh, Holger Hansen, "The dark side of Germany's jobs miracle", *Reuters*, February 8, 2012: https://www.reuters.com/article/world/the-dark-side-of-germany-s-jobs-miracle-idUSTRE8170P7/ visited July 28, 2024.
47. Werner Rügemer, "Die Volksrepublik China und ihre globale Bedeutung. Teil 2 [The People's Republic of China and its global significance. Part 2]", *World Economy*, May 20, 2019: https://www.world-economy.eu/nachrichten/detail/die-volksrepublik-china-und-ihre-globale-bedeutung-teil-2/ visited August 3, 2024.
48. Reuters, "Foxconn mostly abandons $10 billion Wisconsin project touted by Trump", *CNBC*, April 21, 2021: https://www.cnbc.com/2021/04/21/foxconn-mostly-abandons-10-billion-wisconsin-project-touted-by-trump.html visited August 3, 2024.
49. Rügemer, ibid.
50. Reuters, Ibid.
51. World Bank, "Labor force participation rate (% of population)", *World Bank Group: Gender Data Portal*: https://liveprod.worldbank.org/en/indicator/sl-tlf-acti-zs?view=trend&geos=CHN_USA_DEU_WLD visited August 3, 2024.
52. Lucia Brancaccio, "Navigating Women's Employment in China: Recent Advancements and Ongoing Challenges", *China Briefing*, March 8, 2024: https://www.china-briefing.com/news/navigating-womens-employment-in-china-recent-advancements-and-ongoing-challenges/ visited August 3, 2024.
53. World Economic Forum, "Global Gender Gap Report 2023", *weforum.org*, p. 17: https://www3.weforum.org/docs/WEF_GGGR_2023.pdf visited August 3, 2024. There are also no Western European countries in the top ten.
54. For example: Yujing Lu, Du, Wei, 2023, "Women's Education in China: Past and Present", *SHS Web of Conferences 152, 02001,* p. 3: https://www.shs-conferences.org/articles/shsconf/pdf/2023/01/shsconf_sschd2023_02001.pdf visited August 3, 2024.
55. Natalie Wu, "The World's Richest Self-Made Women In 2024", *Forbes*, April 3, 2024: https://www.forbes.com/sites/nataliewu/2024/04/03/the-worlds-richest-self-made-women-in-2024-taylor-swift-kim-kardashian-rihanna/ visited August 3, 2024.
56. See: Kathrin Gerlof, "Frauen in China. Die Rolle der Erde [Women in China: The Role of the Earth]", *Neues Deutschland*, October 2, 2019. And: Shree Lahiri, "Entrepreneurial Behaviour is Big in China", *SheAtWork*,

January 30, 2023: https://sheatwork.com/entrepreneurial-behaviour-is-big-in-china/ visited August 3, 2024.

57. On "Core Socialist Values", see for example: Gow, Michael, 2017, "The Core Socialist Values of the Chinese Dream: Towards a Chinese Integral State." *Critical Asian Studies* 49 (1): 92–116.
58. In more recent discussions, the focus has shifted toward the more differentiated concept of *sustainable population growth* rather than the simplistic notion of "overpopulation". The core issue identified today is not so much the absolute number of people in a country, but rather the *rate* of population growth in relation to ecological limits, economic requirements, and social equity. Historically—and still today—non-Western countries and their populations, including China, have often been blamed for "having too many people" or "reproducing too quickly", while the socio-economic causes of such demographic trends have largely been ignored. In reality, the wealthiest 10 percent of the global population account for over half of all carbon emissions, meaning that excessive consumption—primarily in Western countries—constitutes the main ecological threat. This overconsumption is itself causally linked to the economic exploitation of developing countries, which in turn contributes to the very population growth for which they are then blamed.
59. Megan Fisher, "Sichuan: Couples in Chinese province allowed to have unlimited children", *BBC*, January 30, 2023: https://www.bbc.com/news/world-asia-china-64457367 visited August 4, 2024.
60. See for example "One-child policy" on Wikipedia: https://en.wikipedia.org/wiki/One-child_policy visited August 4, 2024.
61. Hannah Ellis-Petersen, "India overtakes China to become world's most populous country", *The Guardian*, April 24, 2023: https://www.theguardian.com/world/2023/apr/24/india-overtakes-china-to-become-worlds-most-populous-country visited August 4, 2024.
62. For example: *Steingarts Morning Briefing*, February 25, 2020.
63. However, it has also been found, among other things, that only children have higher educational success than children with siblings: Lao Yehui, Dong Zhiqiang, "The only child, birth order and educational outcomes", *Economics e-journal*, 2019–7.
64. World Bank, "Fertility rate, total (births per woman) – China", *World Bank Group Data*: https://data.worldbank.org/indicator/SP.DYN.TFRT.IN?locations=CN visited August 4, 2024. A constant population requires a birth rate of approx. 2.1 children per couple.
65. See for example: CAI Yong, CHENG Yuan, "Pension Reform in China: Challenges and Opportunities", *Journal of Economic Surveys* 28(4), 2014, pp. 636–651.

66. Teresa Wright, "Labour protest in China's private sector: responses to Chinese communism with capitalist characteristics", *Economy and Society* 47(3), 2018, pp. 382–402.
67. For example: Rügemer 2018, p. 275 ff.
68. For example: GAO Jia, SU Yuanyuan, *Social Mobilisation in Post-Industrial China. The Case of Rural Urbanisation*, Cheltenham, UK, Northampton, MA, USA: E. Elgar, 2019, esp. p. 184 ff.
69. For example: YANG Xuehui, CHEN Feng, "Seeking solutions: how local governments handle collective labour disputes", in: Ray Yep u.a. (Ed.), *Handbook on Urban Development in China*, Cheltenham, UK, Northampton, MA, USA: E. Elgar, 2019, p. 313 ff.
70. Werner Rügemer, "Die Volksrepublik China und ihre globale Bedeutung. Teil 2 [The People's Republic of China and its global significance. Part 2]", *World Economy*, May 20, 2019: https://www.world-economy.eu/nachrichten/detail/die-volksrepublik-china-und-ihre-globale-bedeutung-teil-2/ visited August 3, 2024. Quote translated by the authors.
71. For example: Y. Zhao, M. Liao, "Chinese perspectives on responsible innovation", in: *International Handbook on Responsible Innovation*, 2019, especially and with examples: pp. 429–431, 436–438.
72. Andre Vltchek, "Why the West is Determined to Ignore China's Success", *Dissident Voice*, July 18, 2019: https://dissidentvoice.org/2019/07/why-the-west-is-determined-to-ignore-chinas-success/ visited June 7, 2024.

Selected and Recommended Literature

Kadri, Ali. 2017. The Saudi palace coup, the oil market, China and the US. *Real-World Economics Review* 82. http://www.paecon.net/PAEReview/issue82/Kadri82.pdf.

Further Cited Literature

Han, Byung-Chul. 2015. *The Burnout Society*. Redwood City, CA: Stanford University Press.

Kunzmann, Marcel, 2018. *Theorie, System und Praxis des Sozialismus in China* [Theory, System and Practice of Socialism in China]. 2nd ed. Berlin: Verlag Mirco Kolarczik

Küsters, Günter, 2018. *Das Verhältnis von EU und China im Kontext globaler Machtverschiebungen und der aktuellen Kontroverse um Chinas Großprojekt der 'Neuen Seidenstraße'* [The relationship between the EU and China in the context of global power shifts and the current controversy surrounding China's major 'New Silk Road' project], presentation, *Attac*: https://www.attac.de/

fileadmin/user_upload/Kampagnen/Europa/workshops/Guenter_Kuesters_Verhaeltnis_von_EU_und_China.pdf. Accessed January 14, 2025.
Rügemer, Werner, 2018. *Die Kapitalisten des 21. Jahrhunderts. Gemeinverständlicher Abriss zum Aufstieg der neuen Finanzakteure* [The capitalists of the 21st century. A general outline of the rise of the new financial players]. Cologne: PapyRossa.

CHAPTER 10

"Places and Housing? Poor Villages and Monster Cities!"

Rural Catch-Up and Regional Convergence, New Cooperation Regions, Green and Livable Mega-Cities, New Forests Around New Skyscrapers, the Network of Green Cities, Accessible Public Services, Local Participation, and Self-Governance

Infrastructures, Industry Policy, and Urbanization Policy as Regional Strategies

One of the "great divergences"[1] in the world—the gradient between city and countryside and the structural underdevelopment of rural areas compared to urban ones—is being eliminated in China today. Even German politicians, who apparently also occasionally travel to China themselves and do not always judge the country from afar, report "remarkable progress" being made in China's rural regions.[2]

Of central importance in this context are China's public banks, which, here too, do not simply act as short-term profit maximizers but (must) provide so-called "patient capital", which does not demand short-term maximum returns for national development projects.

The spatial distribution of the population between city and countryside is indeed a direct subject of the central government's policy. As of late 2023, China's urbanization rate stands at around 66 percent.[3] Behind this

W. Elsner, E. Najmehchi, *The Rise of China*,
https://doi.org/10.1007/978-3-032-20260-4_10

are considerations for creating an efficient and sustainable spatial structure and aligning per capita incomes across the different rural and urban provinces.[4]

But the distribution of the population among the cities—and thus the entire urban system—is now also being put to the test. Between large cities of around 27 million inhabitants and smaller ones, considered "underdeveloped", with an average of less than one million residents, a total of five defined city tiers have emerged from a development policy perspective.

This has long been the approach to spatial planning in China. However, this system is now regarded as overly differentiated and as promoting excessively large concentrations of population.[5] Many cities are now simply considered too big, with an overconcentration of large, especially state-owned, enterprises.

Novel Cooperation Regions

We have reported above on the new decentralized government region, the cooperative region "Jing-Jin-Ji", with its 130 million inhabitants in the province of Hebei. A highly complex, integrated planning of traffic flows, public services, and infrastructure decentralizes settlement structures and reduces traffic congestion by relocating millions of jobs from the overloaded capital, Beijing. Beijing is being developed as a center of culture and technology, Tianjin as a center of production and trade, and the entire province of Hebei as an area for housing, business, and regional food production. High-speed trains connect these centers within a maximum of one hour's travel time, and endless traffic jams and smog alerts are expected to become a thing of the past in Beijing—even during winter. Regional and urban policy is also an integrated environmental policy. Announced in 2015, the relocation of government offices, ministries, universities, hospitals, and up to 1200 industrial enterprises from Beijing to new areas began in 2017.

Experiments with so-called polycentric and functionally differentiated regional structures have been underway for a long time—beginning with the Special Economic Zones (SEZs) of the early 1980s, the "city clusters" along the Pearl River and the Yangtze River Delta, and other regional pilot projects in the 1990s. Since the early 2000s, about a dozen new regional cooperations between cities and their surrounding areas have been established in connection with the reform of the Hukou system. These were based on agreed concepts, plans, and sometimes even national legislation. One such example is the "ecological plan of the Poyang Lake region" for the "Middle Yangtze" cooperation area, which includes the major cities of Wuhan and Changsha, as well as the smaller city of Nanchang.[6]

Thus, through new forms of cooperative regions, the negative aspects of isolated and competitive localism, regionalism, and federalism—also well known in the West—are being overcome. Public administrative structures are being flexibly adapted to the scale of the respective challenges and to the spatial reach of the collective goods that must be managed. Mutual public blockades between territorial entities can therefore be addressed and made more sustainable. Such issues also arise prominently in German federalism—for example, in matters of fiscal equalization among the states, in the desirable "reorganization of the federal territory" under Article 29 of the Constitution,[7] or in municipal territorial reforms (such as the city-state problem).

Mega-City Management: Innovative Urban Planning and Urban Ecology—From "Smart Cities" to "Wise Cities"

During my [W.E.'s] first stay in China, I happened to meet a British colleague again at a conference in Beijing.

Me: "What are you doing here?"

He: "I work at the Chinese Academy of Sciences and live in Beijing."

Me: "Can you live here, in this monster city?"

He: "Very well, in fact. You see Chinese cities the wrong way. I live in a pleasant residential area in the center of the city, have good neighbors, and have made new friends."

Me: "Yes, but this traffic! Constant traffic jams!"

He: "I don't have a car—just my sports bike. And I'm getting to know this city more and more comfortably by bike—without any traffic jams."

He clearly enjoyed my surprise. Oh, I had to digest that first … and steered the conversation onto safe ground—onto the two lectures we still had to give that afternoon.

Since then, I have certainly noticed the many wide bicycle lanes in Beijing, generously and safely separated from car traffic. Rental bikes are available on every street corner in the city center.

Good, sustainable management of cooperative regions with more than 100 million inhabitants—and of individual megacities with 15, 20, or even 25 million people—requires, as already mentioned several times, a new and distinctive quality of knowledge and analysis. Above all, it requires insights into the average behavior of people in public transport, their shopping and leisure habits, and their average time management over daily, weekly, monthly, and annual cycles—commonly referred to as "big data".

The nightmares of capitalist megacities, for example in South and Southeast Asia, with their exploding slums, their ungovernability, and their sometimes entirely lacking quality of life,[8] can be prevented through Chinese urban policy.[9]

Therefore, Chinese cities are being developed into intelligent, electronically traffic-controlled "Smart Cities", where average human movements are recorded and analyzed. The corresponding cyber infrastructure is integrated into numerous interdisciplinary research projects to study the space-time perceptions and related behaviors of people. The stated goals are to improve quality of life, social cohesion, and urban governance.[10]

All these issues are widely and critically discussed in China through public debates, scientific conferences, publicly accessible literature, and concrete measures. Nevertheless, Western media apparently believe they know the Chinese truth better, assuming that only a new surveillance dictatorship is intended in China. Anyone who has freed themselves from the psychologically and emotionally suggestive "good-versus-evil" agitation of Western opinion journalism ("Our Smart Cities: good! Chinese Smart Cities: Dictatorship!") can observe Chinese development: Even the largest Chinese megacities are well organized and well managed—not the stereotypical "third-world behemoths", but surprisingly clean and diverse cities with good preservation services and a relatively relaxed atmosphere. We will return to facial recognition and the notion of a "cyber dictatorship" further below.

The internal settlement structure is characterized by groups of high-rise buildings, each with its own architecture and color scheme, fully equipped with infrastructure and interspersed with abundant green spaces. The high-rises typically contain a residential-commercial mix, even in central city districts. New parks and trees are being planted systematically across the city. All technical possibilities are applied to implement experiences in afforestation and greening. Since 2017, a Green Cities Network of 285 cities has been emerging in China, now boasting the largest eco-city development program in the world.[11] Or, as the late journalist André Vltchek described it:

> [China's] cities became clean, green, ecological, full of public parks, exercise machines for adults and children. Urban centres are now overflowing with a first class public transportation (all ecological), with impressive museums, concert halls, excellent universities and medical centers. [...] No beggars, no slums, no misery. [...] Foreigners who come to China for the first time are shocked: China looks much wealthier than the US or UK. [...] China does not need to have average incomes of some $50,000+ per capita to prosper, to give its people an increasingly great life, to protect the environment, and to promote great culture.[12]

The financial capitalist principle of the Western banking and real estate industry—short-term profit maximization for every square meter of land and soil—does not seem to apply, or at least does not dominate, considering the openness and diversity of urban uses.

The former chief architect of the Barcelona City Council and international star architect Vicente Guallart, who today primarily acts as an idea generator for the ecologization, humanization, and downsizing of large cities, stated in a speech at the Tianjin Forum in 2017 on possible ways from AI-based "Smart Cities" to ecologically sustainable "Wise Cities":

> The country where I can realize most of my ideas is China.[13]

Urban Mobilization and Participation, and Local Subsidiarity: Urban Neighborhood Communities (*Shequ*)

Neighborhood exchange and relationships are fundamentally easier to organize in rural regions than in the rather anonymous city. Villages have smaller, more manageable networks, traditionally higher general levels of trust, and consequently greater social obligation. (The flip side of strong institutional cooperation can, of course, always be social control and the hardening of social relationships.) The city, however, is by no means a large, unstructured, anonymous mass. Even urban space is physically and socially organized in many ways—into districts, sub-centers, quarters, neighborhoods, and street or house communities.

In China, in addition to family and clan networks, as well as the former traditional work and life units of the Danwei and the more extensive Guanxi networks in residential areas, there exists another level of societal self-organization, mobilization, participation, and capacity to act: the urban neighborhood living environment.

Modern forms of residential communities, which have existed in various forms since the beginning of the People's Republic, are the so-called *Shequ*. Since the 1990s, they have also replaced the Danwei, which shaped all aspects of life—including consumption, leisure, and social security—through the work collective. The *Shequ*, on the other hand, are residence-based. Just as with the Danwei, it is their task—and their right—to take over state functions through societal self-organization.

Thus, the lowest levels of the state dissolve into society—a feature shared with former European state socialist states. Civil societal forms of organization, for example, assumed the lower levels of state jurisdiction in the GDR in the form of company committees. For minor and medium offenses, the state was reduced and potentially replaced by societal self-organization. Offenses and criminal actions in the company context were judged by committees of colleagues. The judgments typically did not result in prison sentences, in contrast to the USA, the country with the highest percentage of its population behind bars. Instead, they enabled the continuation of work, social relationships, and social integration. Those punished could be rehabilitated faster and were less likely to face lifelong stigmatization and subsequent criminal behavior during or after prison.

Similarly, the *Shequ*'s residential committees, whose members are drawn from the local community, are today responsible in Chinese cities for advising and assisting with birth planning and childcare, gender equality, elder care, support for the disabled and the poor, social security, environment, culture and education, public safety, and conflict mediation.[14] They also create income opportunities for the poor and assist with problems faced by homeowners and apartment dwellers—which is almost everyone. More recently, they have played a substantial role in establishing mutual-help structures among neighbors through local volunteers during Covid lockdowns.[15] State authorities are supportive of the *Shequ*, and the CPC establishes its own *Shequ* party committees in parallel.

In the wake of rapid urbanization, the *Shequ* emerged in part as an urban counterpart to various Chinese experiments with village grassroots democracy and self-governance that were initiated in the 1980s.[16] These unique urban institutions of semi-state-integrated self-governance are constantly evolving and have developed into entities closer to social service providers and highly integrated local community institutions with elected representatives, rather than the forms of representative local councils that also exist in Western cities, which often suffer from low participation rates and general disinterest among constituents.

Thus, it is possible that a development path is being pursued here that could lead to further social mobilization, learned participation, the dissolution of lower levels of state bureaucracy, and ultimately, in a changed—perhaps more peaceful and relaxed— world situation, to new forms of comprehensive, substantial (direct) local democracy and governance, which nonetheless differ significantly from common Western models.

Notes

1. Losurdo (2017, 2017b).
2. Rosa Luxemburg Foundation, „Impressionen aus China – Aktuelle Entwicklungen nach dem 18. Parteitag der KPCh [Impressions from China – Current developments after the 18th Party Congress of the CPC]".
3. See for example: "Degree of urbanization in China in selected years from 1980 to 2023", *Statista*, January 17, 2024: https://www.statista.com/statistics/270162/urbanization-in-china/ visited August 11, 2024.
4. Chen Zongsheng, Keynote, Tianjin Forum 2017, mimeo.
5. Zheng Yongnian, National University of Singapore, Keynote, Tianjin Forum 2017, mimeo.
6. For example: Yao, Changcheng, "Research on the Formation of Functionally Polycentric Structures from the Perspective of Knowledge Collaboration: A Case Study of Eight City Clusters in China", Jilin University, School of Economics, 2018, mimeo.
7. Known as the "Basic Law for the Federal Republic of Germany" ("Grundgesetz").
8. For the description of Southeast Asian megacities, for example: A. Vltchek, "China's BRI Could Save Destroyed Southeast Asia", *Countercurrents.org*, August 11, 2019: https://countercurrents.org/2019/08/ chinas-bri-could-save-destroyed-south-east-asia/ visited August 12, 2024.
9. 83 of the 100 worst-polluted cities worldwide are located in capitalist and neoliberal India, according to the 2023 IQAir World Air Quality Report. See: Helen Regan, "The world's 100 worst polluted cities are in Asia — and 83 of them are in just one country", *CNN*, April 26, 2024: https://edition.cnn.com/2024/03/18/ climate/air-pollution-report-2023-asia-climate-intl-hnk/index.html visited August 12, 2024.

10. For example: Shen Z., "Overview: Big Data Support for Urban Planning and Management in China", in: Shen Z., Li, M. (Eds.), *Big Data Support of Urban Planning and Management, Advances in Geographic Information Science*, Cham, CH: Springer, 2018.
11. See for example also: "Eco-cities in China" on *Wikipedia*: https://en.wikipedia.org/wiki/Eco-cities_in_China visited August 12, 2024.
12. André Vltchek, "Why the west is determined to ignore China's success", *New Age*, July 20, 2019: https://www.newagebd.net/article/78988/article/35972 visited August 12, 2024.
13. Vincente Guallart, Keynote, Tianjin Forum 2017, mimeo.
14. For example: Thomas Heberer, "Urban neighborhood communities (*shequ*) as new institutions of urban governance", in: *Handbook on Urban Development in China*, 2019, pp. 360–391.
15. See for example: Toby Lincoln, "The urban history that makes China's coronavirus lockdown possible", *SBS News: Dateline*, March 5, 2024: https://www.sbs.com.au/news/dateline/article/the-urban-history-that-makes-chinas-coronavirus-lockdown-possible/cg1t6fm9c visited July 10, 2025.
16. See for example: Yong Xu, "Villagers' Self-Governance in Rural China", in: *The Palgrave Handbook of Local Governance in Contemporary China*, 2019, pp. 285–298.

Selected and Recommended Literature

Losurdo, Domenico. 2017. Has China turned to capitalism?—Reflections on the transition from capitalism to socialism. *International Critical Thought* 7 (2017): 15–31.

Shen, Zhenjiang, and Miaoyi Li, eds. 2018. *Big Data Support of Urban Planning and Management, Advances in Geographic Information Science*. Cham: Springer.

Further Cited Literature

Losurdo, Domenico. 2017b. China und das Ende der 'kolumbianischen Epoche' [China and the end of the 'Columbian Epoch']. *Marxistische Blätter* 3 (2017): 52–62.

CHAPTER 11

"Ecology? Biggest Polluter!"

From the Dependent "Work Bench" of the West to Ecological World Champion: Renewable-Energy Networks, Intelligent Grids and Batteries, New-Energy Mobility, New Forests, Reversing Desertification, and the "Ant Forest" App, Ahead of 2035 Goals, Improving Air and Climate for the World, Toward an Eco-Civilization

From Dependency Back to Sovereignty: From the Extended Work Bench of the West's (Dirtiest) Industries to Ecological Emancipation

"China, the number one polluter", "Largest CO_2 emitter", and similar reports from a bygone era still dominate most official Western media. In fact, at some point during its recent rise, China did become the absolute largest CO_2 emitter, accounting for 28 percent of all global emissions—ahead of the USA, which accounts for 16 percent.

But half the truth can also be a complete lie. China's CO_2 emissions curve already began to plateau in 2011, and year-on-year emissions have not increased since then—unlike in comparable capitalist India, a firm part of the imperial system of rule, and relative to the global average. Absolute emissions have already been falling since 2024.[1]

W. Elsner, E. Najmehchi, *The Rise of China*,
https://doi.org/10.1007/978-3-032-20260-4_11

Emission numbers can indeed decrease for various reasons in a country. This might result from comprehensive deindustrialization and extensive "offshore production" abroad, as in the case of the USA and other developed Western capitalist states, which have outsourced many of their emitting industries to low-wage, low-standard countries. It can also result from drastic losses in growth and an absolute reduction of GDP, as in the case of Russia after its pro-capitalist turn in the 1990s. In China, however, the exact opposite is true: tremendous GDP growth, and therefore logically, already an increase in ecological productivity, meaning a reduction of CO_2 per unit of product. While considerable technological improvements are still possible and are being realized in large steps, we will return to China's internationally low per capita emissions.

Some authors even claim that China is *the* driver of climate catastrophe and an impending ecological collapse per se, because it wants to rise and therefore "necessarily" grow—because it, "due to its rule", must seduce people into mass consumption, because it follows an "investment mania", and finally must "export" its "overcapacities" and apply its capital in other countries.[2] The switch from coal to gas in China achieves nothing; the system is, in any case, a nightmare and requires a "real" revolution.[3] Statements like these seem to come from another galaxy, or at least a bygone world. They are indeed based on the author's dissertation at the University of California, Los Angeles, from 1989. Apparently, they are still used to generate an endless loop and various new editions of the thesis that the Chinese system will not work. They are also good enough to supply local journals and mass media with variants of the narrative that everything in China is much worse than feared. One inevitably wonders when the author will finally question the findings of a 35-year-old work and adapt to the realities of the twenty-first century.

The projection of one's own perception horizon and development perspectives of one's own system onto "the other" always plays a role as well. For example, Trump's Washington pursues a destructive "America First" approach for all sides, yet many Western media outlets take pleasure in accusing China of pursuing a "China-First Policy".[4] Sigmund Freud would have been delighted. Therefore, we must examine the ecological reality of today's China based on facts rather than fakes.

To understand the correlations, explanatory factors, and future prospects of a country's environmental activity, we must first consider meaningful "structural" indicators. For example, as of 2022, China ranks only *36th in the world for CO_2 emissions per capita*, with just over half the per capita emissions of the USA. It ranks behind Japan, Australia, and Canada, and despite its above-average industrial share of GDP, it is only slightly above the world average and below the average of all high-income countries.[5] A country with a low industrial share and a large service sector, such as Switzerland, naturally performs well in this regard, regardless of population size.

China does, in fact, have a nearly thirty-year history of a crude, dependent economy with ecologically harmful mass production, closely tied to Western cheap production and a correspondingly high industrial share. This history of serving as an extended workbench for the West is now, however, being left behind by the country, which is showing a steep rise in the ecological efficiency levels of the most developed industrial countries. This trend is stable and allows a clear forecast that China will achieve lower emissions per unit of product than the richest capitalist countries in the future.

Increases in energy efficiency in China are also evident in the fact that the growth of energy consumption has been limited to only a third of GDP growth. Thus, China will be noticeably more efficient than the Western industrial nations in terms of energy consumption in the coming years.[6]

The business model of these Western industrial nations will likely continue to shift their own labor-intensive and ecologically harmful production of mass goods to the underdeveloped world, in order to appear ecologically responsible "on the home front" and provide healthier living conditions. For example, it is estimated that about 30 percent of Germany's emission reductions since 1990 are due to production relocations to China and other countries.[7] So much for Germany as an "eco-pioneer".

Germany is also the third-largest waste exporter in the world, after the USA and Japan. Others were expected to burn our production and consumption residues, so that the resulting CO_2 emissions would not count toward our balance. China, however, put a stop to this a few years ago.

The leading capitalist industrial countries, such as initially Great Britain and then the USA, have almost completely deindustrialized as part of their outsourcing strategy. In Trump's world, even simple industrial production was to be brought back, coupled with a revaluation of environmental protection. Increases in CO_2 emissions were probably counted as proof of success by the Trump administration.

Is this balance sheet unfair to capitalism? No. The Western capitalism that dominates the world, under the direction of the US empire, has never seriously considered advancing ecological development globally in its approach to globalization. Instead of providing new, environmentally friendly technologies and production methods that could have benefited everyone, it preferred to care only for its own "front yard" (it is better not to look into American backyards anyway). As a result, the world has become the ecological disaster we are experiencing today, not least because of the outsourced production of the rich countries.

China was one of the few exceptions among developing countries. As one of the poorest developing countries, it was initially more or less at the mercy of the logic of capitalist systems. It was able to play the role of an "outsourced" extended workbench relatively long and effectively, as its population was socially integrated, organized, and orderly—despite poverty—and could act uniformly. But China also played the role of the production backyard "dialectically", with the clear national development goal of resurgence and improving living conditions for its people. This was to be achieved with a commitment to technical, organizational, and management learning, constant product development, process innovations, and the overall "high road" of development, albeit also with the help of trade surpluses.

Thus, China had to increasingly force the West not to simply leave it with the worst dirt production. Rather, in a balancing act between low costs on the one hand and high qualification and organizational effectiveness on the other, between a "take what you can get" approach and a "demand better" stance, China increasingly carried out technologically higher-value, cutting-edge production—not only within China but also increasingly in collaboration with Western partners. This became increasingly attractive for Western technology corporations, as they were dealing with a qualified, motivated, well-organized, and learning workforce that, due to systemic reasons, was flexible and came with corresponding management. Western corporations also appreciated this. In fact, the emerging socialist-style development and high production efficiency in China did not exclude each other; on a long-term and national level, they even conditioned and reinforced each other, as China demonstrates.

Much of this process, in which China assumed an increasingly assertive role, has been, and still is, blamed on China as "technology theft". This is despite the fact that particularly ecological production technologies were rarely exported to China or applied there by Western companies. Other sensitive technologies exported to China were often deliberately outdated, as the case of the Chinese aircraft industry shows, which lagged about two decades behind due to the delivery of outdated technology until the 2010s.

In fact, the USA has imposed a technology embargo on China since the beginning of the People's Republic, which effectively excluded it from important technological developments throughout its entire development, except perhaps in consumer goods technologies.[8] Therefore, China did not acquire any patents during its period of national construction and the Cultural Revolution, when it temporarily missed the advent of basic computer technology. If at all, it had to purchase all patents and licenses from the West at a high price.[9] This is why China remains one of the largest payers of license fees in the world today. No Western company has ever voluntarily transferred top knowledge in sensitive areas to China, nor was it ever permitted to do so.[10]

Only since the 2000s has China been able to reconnect with its millennia-long technological and scientific leadership and, in the field of cutting-edge technology, catch up again—soon to lead in all technology fields. It is already becoming apparent that the country has taken the lead in many areas, bypassing or even overtaking Western technologies.[11] The renewed technology war by the USA is now attempting to stop China's rise to "number one", for example by excluding Chinese scientists and companies from the International Astronautics Congress in Washington in October 2019[12] or through a new 2024 Florida law restricting the hiring of Chinese researchers at state universities[13] and putting the renewal of the US–China science pact on hold.[14] However, an economic and technology war offers no perspective for a solution, and the USA may feel this most painfully.

A scientific decoupling from China—which overtook the USA and EU in the number of scientific publications in 2021 and ranked first in the natural sciences and second overall in the global *Nature Index*—is detrimental "for both sides", even according to *The Economist*. The publication states that collaboration benefits "American institutions slightly more than Chinese ones", citing a 2020 study that found "when papers co-written with Chinese scientists were excluded, the number of American publications in science and engineering fell slightly between 2014 and 2018". This occurs in the context of a sharp decrease in student visas issued to Chinese nationals and the number of jointly authored papers by American and Chinese researchers falling for the first time since 2020.[15]

Capitalism, for its part, has never helped any developing country achieve a targeted national ecological emancipation, even though countries like Germany naturally like to sell good eco-technologies. For the design and implementation of a national "eco-development strategy" in developing and emerging countries, however, it probably lacked the will, the financial motive, and in recent decades certainly the necessary collective capacity to act.

China had to achieve ecological emancipation on its own, and it began to do so when it was still a developing country with a very low per capita income. Today, it has just risen to the level of countries with medium per capita incomes, still only around number 70 in the country ranking. Ecologically, it therefore had to get deep onto its knees before accumulating enough income, knowledge, savings, investments, and capacities to make a real "leap forward" and become the "primary ecological world power", as we will see.

A War on CO_2-Emissions: Ecological Industrial Policies, Regulation, and Social Mobilization … and a Market Economy As It Could Be

Let us return to the (alleged) "CO_2-emissions world champion" of the past. We have already reported on ecologically oriented urban and regional development. Today, the entire urban and regional development in China is subject to a "Low-Carbon Pilot Policy" (CLCP—China Low-Carbon Pilot Policy). Regions and city sizes, urban and rural areas, are being redefined with the goal of minimizing traffic-related CO_2 emissions across various policy fields and actor areas. Mobility (cars, rail, airplanes), industrial policy, spatial planning, building architecture, and consumer behavior are networked under the premise of low CO_2 emissions.[16]

China also demonstrates, for example, that companies forced to invest in greater efficiency and more innovation due to stricter CO_2 regulations become more competitive in the medium term.[17] Furthermore, provinces and cities that have implemented the CLCP intensively—as always, regions have degrees of freedom here—experience higher regional growth.[18]

This is how a market economy could and should indeed work: as a flexible adjustment mechanism responding to what humanity needs, wants, and dictates in decisions. Seen in this light, China has understood the market economy better than the German government, which for decades has regularly defended the short-term profit interests of the German automotive industry in Brussels while trying to prevent stricter ecological emission standards.

The times when we hold cheap plastic from China in our hands are soon over. The capitalist caravan of ecologically disadvantageous, cheap production for hundreds of millions of Western low-wage earners must move on—due to higher wages and now also ever-higher ecological standards. There is no longer room for it in China.

China is successfully betting on environmental technologies as drivers of growth and productivity, and its provinces and cities are being "pushed" into a "race to the top". In this way, it proves that "market competition" does not necessarily have to lead to a "race to the bottom".[19] China is even planning to become a country with a *Net Zero Carbon Economy* by 2060[20] while fully maintaining its development goals.[21] In 2020, it pledged to reach peak emissions by 2030—a target that was achieved prematurely in 2024, as mentioned above.[22] Even today, the country is recognized as the world's largest producer of renewable energies.[23]

No More Imports of Western Household Waste

As already mentioned, the time when China was willing to be the garbage dump of the Western world is over. Our production, packaging, consumption, and waste orgies have been aptly described as an "imperial mode of living"[24] or even "waste colonialism".[25] The illusion of having an "ecological consciousness" is possible only because most of the waste "to be recycled" has been exported to less developed countries. Thus, countries such as the USA, which used to export nearly 4000 shipping containers of waste to China every day,[26] must now find other buyers, because since 2018 China no longer imports plastic waste. Other East Asian countries have already followed suit. This waste is now being shipped to poorer countries that cannot yet afford to resist contamination from the West and its "clean" production and lifestyle.

All of this is now being ensured by the promoted and significantly increased ecological awareness in China, the ecological attention of citizens toward companies, and considerable ecological activism—and ecological protest where necessary.[27]

Goodbye to Old Coal Mines and Coal-Fired Plants, Toward the World Champion of Renewables, Intelligent Grids and Novel Batteries ... and New-Energy Forms of Mobility

We have reported that coal mining has already been scaled down and many coal-fired power plants in China have been shut down. Yes, the air is cleaner in Beijing—no more scratchy throats. We also wrote about the world market leader in photovoltaics, which generates more solar power on Beijing's roofs alone than the Federal Republic of Germany. The share of renewable and carbon-free energies continues to grow dynamically in China.[28] Having already produced 57 percent of the world's patents in renewable energy by 2018[29] and over 80 percent of the world's solar manufacturing capacity as of 2024,[30] according to estimates from the IEA (International Energy Agency), China's share of global renewable energy capacity is expected to reach nearly 40 percent by 2030[31] and already accounts for 43 percent of global renewable capacity growth.[32] By May 2024, clean energy had already generated a record-high 44 percent of China's electricity, with coal reaching its record-low share.[33]

China is the leading producer in the field of e-mobility, ranging from e-vehicles of all kinds to e-trucks and e-forklifts. Leaded gasoline was phased out in China in the 1990s within just one year—from decision to completion. Today, the prescribed minimum standards for gasoline efficiency ensure that the fleet consumption of German car manufacturers in China is lower than in Germany itself![34]

No wonder there are 1.8 million public charging stations for e-vehicles in China—14 times as many as in the USA[35]—with more than half of the world's EVs on Chinese roads.[36] By 2019, car manufacturers were already required to sell ten percent of their vehicles as electric cars. With numerous Chinese EV brands emerging in recent years, such as BYD and Nio, as major competitors to Tesla in technology, battery power, and affordability, car buyers had 71 new electric car models to choose from in 2024 alone.[37] License plates, which are raffled off in the big cities (in Beijing, for example, only 100,000 new plates were issued in 2018), are in the vast majority green plates for cars with alternative drives—blue plates for combustion vehicles are no longer issued in the largest cities.

Thus, about 20 million cars with combustion engines are taken off the road each year. In this context, the Chinese government also banned the manufacture of 553 car models in 2018, developed by Chinese car corporations—mostly in joint ventures with Western car companies and intended for series production—due to excessively high fuel consumption. The list of such facts, which would be a medium-sized sensation in countries such as Germany and indeed evokes thoughts of a creeping "suicide of the German car manufacturers"[38] due to their slow progress, could be continued.

Research and development are being carried out on all fronts. We have reported on the first highway test tracks for battery-independent e-mobility using solar panels and induction current. We have also mentioned hydrogen-based drives as an alternative. Within a few years, the export of vehicles with combustion engines to China will end, and by 2050, combustion engines should only be seen in museums in China.

In December 2019, a new strategic decision by the Chinese government regarding future mobility technologies caused considerable stress in the German automotive industry. In view of the increasingly apparent downsides of mass battery production—worldwide difficulties in lithium sourcing and high permanent power consumption—for established e-mobility, China now intends to proceed in a technology-open manner.[39] Hydrogen, solar panel induction, and other technologies are officially on par with battery-based e-mobility, and hydrogen fuel cells even seem better suited for long distances,[40] while battery-dependent e-vehicles will probably only be effective for short distances. While the German automotive industry had just begun to switch to e-cars, not least with a view to sales in China and Chinese technological progress requirements, German mobility experts described this next major step by China as "absolutely correct".[41]

However, the extent to which the German automotive industry can muster the planning, investment, and reorganization capacities to keep up with the next major strategic step in mobility technology is the big question that Germany's automotive industry and top politicians have yet to answer. China is already converting its electric car production to reduce the number of cheap vehicles with shorter lifespans and shift production toward higher-quality models with longer lifespans, putting international car production under increasing pressure.[42]

Therefore, calls are now being made across industry, the business press, and by the Minister of Economic Affairs—including toward the EU—to finally develop a German and EU-wide industrial policy (as we have already mentioned above). Only then could Germany and the EU develop a genuine public capacity for action that would put them on an equal footing with China and enable cooperative development for the future, instead of wavering indecisively between vulnerability and mutual dependencies. However, the ideological and mental barriers in the neoliberal model country of

Schmidt-Kohl-Schröder-Merkel-Scholz-Merz, along with the German historical proclivity to always look for and find the "enemy" in the "East", should not be underestimated. Indicative of this counterproductive mentality is the ultimately self-defeating strategy of preferring to impose tariffs on Chinese-made EVs—which actually hurts consumers and Western manufacturers in China alike—over developing its own effective industrial policy.[43]

We also pointed out the largest and most efficient high-speed rail network in the world, which, with 45,000 kilometers of tracks as of 2024,[44] comprises more than double the combined length of the rest of the world's high-speed networks.[45] The system of "bullet trains", whose standard speed is currently 350 kilometers per hour and may soon reach 450 kilometers per hour with newly introduced generations of trains (peak speeds already around 430 km/h), is being expanded rapidly, aiming to reach 70,000 kilometers by 2035,[46] instead of being reduced as is the case in Germany. Train travel is so attractive, comfortable, stress-free, cheap, reliable (punctuality of nearly 99 percent[47]), and fast that it can replace numerous individual car journeys and already many flights.[48]

Shifting Freight Onto the Rails: One Million Diesel Trucks Taken Off the Roads Within Three Years

For its ecological turnaround, China is primarily relying on electrified rail transport. Electric trains are now the main means of transporting goods and will inevitably replace a portion of the massive shipping traffic in freight transport between Asia and Europe. In recent years, the number of China–Europe freight trains has set continuous year-on-year records, partly influenced by new geopolitical uncertainties along traditional freight lines, such as the Red Sea since late 2023, shipping problems in the Black Sea, and a general increase in maritime transport costs.[49]

The environmentally harmful truck convoys that slowly crawl bumper to bumper on the right lanes of the German Autobahns are an increasingly rare sight in China. This aligns with the almost daily reports from China's ecological front. To further reduce CO_2 and soot emissions, about one million diesel trucks that failed to comply with the new fuel and engine standards were decommissioned in the northern regions around Beijing by the end of 2020 alone,[50] as even the German public-service media—which otherwise rarely has a good word to say about China—reported.[51] Railways now handle large-scale distribution as a matter of course, while local small-scale distribution is managed by electric trucks of various sizes.[52]

"Recycle to Ride": A Subway Ticket or a Mobile Recharge for 20 Empty Plastic Bottles

China is brimming with ecological ideas and experiments. For example, in Beijing's subway stations, there are hundreds of special recycling machines that accept empty plastic bottles as payment for a ticket.[53] Depending on how many empty PET bottles one deposits, one also receives credits for subway tickets or even for mobile recharge and mobile network usage. The machines are also installed in schools, residential areas, and shopping centers, with a total of 5000 machines expected throughout Beijing.

In this way, the working population is motivated to collect and recycle, in sharp contrast to many Western countries, where this task is often delegated to homeless people or poor pensioners who have otherwise been failed by the system. It's about promoting ecological behaviors among the masses. Collection and recycling of empty containers can even be enjoyable for many, such as students, when it allows them to earn credits for their smartphones.

Goodbye, Domestic Flights: The Maglev Train Soon with 600, Even 1000 Kilometers Per Hour

One of the biggest emitters of CO_2 is the aviation industry. Today, short- and medium-haul flights in China offer only marginal advantages compared to the bullet trains, which on routes such as between Beijing and Shanghai show almost no time disadvantage. The new trains, reaching speeds of up to 450 kilometers per hour, will further reduce the appeal of domestic air travel.

In China, the technology of the maglev (magnetic levitation) train is among the most advanced in the world, alongside Japan. In 2019, a new maglev train capable of reaching 600 kilometers per hour was introduced, with the first model produced and unveiled in 2021—then the fastest ground transportation system on the planet.[54] So far, there are only a few operational maglev routes, such as the legendary Shanghai line connecting the airport with the city center, which has been in service since 2003.

As of 2024, China has also successfully tested a new hyperloop maglev system (operating inside a low-vacuum tube), developed by the state-owned *China Aerospace Science and Industry Corporation* (CASIC) under the name "T-Flight". In its initial tests in early 2024, it reached speeds of up to 623 km/h, with the second test phase aiming for 1000 km/h—already surpassing passenger jet speeds—and a third phase envisioning speeds of up to 4000 km/h.[55] New routes using this hyperloop maglev technology could make air travel between major destinations virtually obsolete: the projected travel time for a future ultra-high-speed line between Shanghai and Beijing is just one and a half hours, far faster than today's high-speed rail (4.5–6.5 hours) and even flights (over 2 hours, not counting airport procedures).[56]

These developments demonstrate that, in the long run, short- and medium-haul flights—especially domestic ones—will become relics of the carbon age. And the electricity powering the trains will increasingly come from sources other than coal. If any country is capable of realizing this transition, it is, as things stand, China.

Trees, Trees, Trees … Reforestation on Mega Scales

If you arrive in one of China's megacities expecting the usual sprawling metropolises common in many developing countries of Southeast Asia, Latin America, or Africa, you will be astonished by the cleanliness and orderliness of the cities and their surroundings. We have already reported much about this. There are no large homeless camps in parks or under bridges throughout the city, as can be seen, for example, in San Francisco or Los Angeles.

When I [W.E.] first arrived more than ten years ago, my initial impression—actually the second, after the throat irritation at the airport—was formed during the roughly 150-kilometer drive from Beijing to Tianjin: countless trees lined both sides of the highway. Relatively young trees, each supported by bamboo frames, stretched in green belts 50–100 meters deep, with caretakers tending to them everywhere. I later learned that this massive tree-planting effort had begun in 2008, launched both in preparation for the Beijing Olympics and as part of an ecological investment program following the financial crisis. My research revealed that a six-billion-dollar tree-planting program was implemented in the Beijing region in 2008–2009. At that time, China invested a remarkable eight percent of its GDP—about 550 billion US dollars—making it the world's economic locomotive until around 2015, a development that notably helped Germany, which achieved export records to China during that period (see also above, introduction).

In fact, a national reforestation program has existed in China since 1978. Since 1998, a nationwide ban on deforestation has been in place, and since 2000, an additional re-naturalization initiative—the "Grain for Green" program—has been implemented to convert agricultural land back into forest.[57]

The same impression is confirmed during a train ride through the countryside: villages and fields appear in good and well-kept condition. The concept of a "moderately prosperous society"[58] is indeed tangible, and its meaning becomes clear—not primarily material affluence but rather prosperity in terms of time and quality of life. People in the villages and fields do not toil under hardship nor do they sit in massive agricultural machines; they work calmly, with enough time to converse and connect with one another.

A Road Sweeper, and a Ranger of the Green City

Cleaning staff with their rickshaws or electric sweeping vehicles are present everywhere on streets and highways—both men and women alike. They are often seen during their breaks, each responsible for a stretch of several hundred meters to a few kilometers. Sometimes they rest at the roadside, even on the right lane, and every driver instinctively swerves widely around them. They are the quiet authorities of the public road space, and no one would think of polluting their workplace with litter.

Manual street cleaning, which is a demanding and often low-paid job worldwide, has been made easier in China through modern, environmentally friendly electric sweepers. Since 2023, autonomous electric sweeping vehicles have also been introduced in parks and public spaces—machines that can guide themselves, detect, sweep, and sort trash, and even recharge autonomously in cities such as Shenzhen and Guangzhou.[59]

These visible agents of clean and green cities help shape individual behavior and ecological awareness—even among drivers. And it works: overall, China's cities appear remarkably clean and well maintained. The many parks, green spaces, and trees contribute to this impression, and the decentralized city structures allow light and air to circulate more freely.

When we ask Chinese people what penalty they would face for throwing plastic waste on the street, they look at us in disbelief. The answer is always the same: *I would never even think of doing that.*

What is valued here can also be seen in a television report from 2015 by a Chinese journalist. The report showed how wind carried piles of waste from countless construction sites into the streets. The footage caused an outcry on social media, prompting the Minister for Environmental Protection to appear before the cameras two weeks later and announce an immediate clean-up plan: company yards and construction sites were to be cleared and all waste piles covered with green nets, under threat of heavy penalties. No sooner said than done—since then, green nets have become a defining feature of construction sites and company premises across China.

Meanwhile at Home: "Red-Green" Madness At the Local Nature

Today, that same Chinese journalist could come to our German hometown of Bremen and film the misery of our green spaces and roadsides: plastic waste everywhere, especially in the so-called "city green" or "roadside green", even along highway entrances and exits. After nights of compulsive, uninhibited partying, binge drinking, and barbecuing, the meadows are littered with debris. On the inner-city dykes, there are more bottle caps than blades of grass—many bottles, of course, smashed. Much of the leftover plastic and packaging is blown by the night wind toward the riverbank, and from there into the river—and ultimately into the North Sea.

Thus, the city, which was governed for almost thirty years by a "Red-Green" coalition (social democrats and greens), contributes disproportionately to the death of the world's oceans. The plastic cargo drifting downstream from its "free" party zones on the river beaches is unmistakable. The general environmental awareness and everyday behavior here are, frankly, subterranean.

Local politics, however, has other priorities: it must posture on world affairs and condemn China "in the strongest possible terms", as all parties jointly did in December 2019. Twenty-five years of green environmental senators have passed by the city's ecology—and by the behavior of its growing scene of obsessive partygoers—without leaving a trace. The second local state religion, football, adds its own weekend contribution to the ecological disaster.

In neoliberal capitalism, the environment has become the last major unregulated societal field. Environmental law exists, to be sure, but no one knows or enforces it; there are no signs, no visible rules, no equivalent of the "security" apparatus that governs other areas of life. Nature serves as capitalism's safety valve: a space where all social frustrations can be vented "freely". Because nature cannot defend itself immediately, there is no direct feedback on one's actions. Once a year, a symbolic spring "cleanup day" by school classes is meant to suggest that the problem has been solved.

Unsurprisingly, the green spaces are in a state of neglect. Urban ecology hardly exists anymore—fiscal austerity and the so-called "debt brake" have long since taken their toll. And where no one maintains or cares for the city's greenery, civic awareness, and responsibility decay as well, until irresponsibility becomes the moral norm.

The satirical climax of this unprofessionalism, incompetence, and degradation of both nature and human work comes with the outsourced and privatized "green care" services. These roll over nature with heavy, environmentally harmful machinery: leaf blowers spewing exhaust, lawn trimmers tearing through grass with plastic cords, and large mowers shredding plastic waste into micro-fragments that can never again be removed from nature.

The "Fridays for Future" generation will soon realize that, in a neoliberal, financialized, and austerity-bound country, they have little chance of changing these structures—even if, one day, a green chancellor manages to juggle environmental protection as a temporary political performance.

On Ecological Civilization: China's Network of "Forest Cities"

In China, the green, interwoven cities are not only being ecologically restructured at the regional and provincial level. In 2017, construction began on the country's first true "Forest City", in Liuzhou, Guangxi Province.[60] Powered entirely by renewable energy, the city's trees are expected to absorb 10,000 tons of CO_2 and 57 tons of water-polluting substances each year. Designed by Italian architect Stefano Boeri, Liuzhou Forest City is envisioned as a "village" of about 30,000 inhabitants. Its buildings are covered with one million plants from around 100 different species and 40,000 trees—together producing roughly 900 tons of oxygen annually.

The process of greening cities and buildings is steadily progressing. As of 2021, 192 cities had already been certified as "Forest Cities" under the "National Forest City Action" program, initiated in 2004.[61] Between 2013 and 2018, participating cities created, on average, over 13,000 hectares of forest area per year.[62] By 2025, around 300 cities have been recognized as "Forest Cities" and networked to support one another in this effort. By 2035, this network is expected to become an integral part of the "National Plan for a More Beautiful China".[63]

Since 2004, numerous scientific studies have examined the ecological benefits of China's "forest cities". For example, a 2021 study found that the construction of forest cities reduced CO_2 emissions by 1.71 percent, equivalent to approximately 1.79 million tons. Additional benefits include improvements in quality of life through expanded green spaces, which reduce the carbon content of urban air and lower $PM_{2.5}$ concentrations (air pollution).[64] A "forest city" does not merely entail increased vegetation. It also integrates green transportation, low-carbon industries, and sustainable infrastructure. One example is the "green–blue integrated infrastructure" plan in Weifang (Shandong province), which seeks to "reduce water pollution, mitigate urban flood and provide recreational opportunities simultaneously".[65]

Forestation: 24 Percent of the Country as National Parks, Special Biological Protection and Development Zones, Wetlands—Saving Species, Boosting Biodiversity, Cleaning Up Air, Water, and Soil, Reintroducing Traditional Agricultural Methods

By the early 2000s, China had already established 1757 nature reserves.[66] In addition, there are thousands of special protection areas, a scientifically classified system of zones dedicated to biological protection and sustainable development. These range from simple hunting, fishing, and tree-felling prohibition zones, as well as water protection zones, to highly specialized areas such as "Tree Protoplasm Resource Protection Zones".

Today, these areas together amount to more than 11,000 nature reserves.[67] By 2023, approximately 18 percent of China's land area (compared to about 13 percent in the USA) was designated as protection and development zones, a proportion that continues to grow.[68] As a result, China's forest coverage has expanded from just under 17 percent in 1990 to over 23 percent in 2022,[69] with a net annual increase of 1.94 million hectares between 2010 and 2020. This makes China the global leader in net forest area gain by a wide margin, while Brazil, by contrast, ranks first in net loss due to the world's highest deforestation rate.[70]

Traditional agricultural methods have been reintroduced on a large scale to further improve ecological conditions. For example, traditional fish farming has been revived in irrigated rice fields across southern China, enhancing local flora and fauna while reducing the use of herbicides, pesticides, and chemical fertilizers.[71]

UNO: China the Only Country Pushing Back Global Desertification, Compensating for Global Forest Loss, Improving Air and Climate for the World

Until recently, China lost approximately 2000 square kilometers of fertile land each year to desertification, resulting in considerable costs, from sandstorms to the relocation of about one million people whose habitats had become uninhabitable. The problems were also partly self-inflicted, due to previous industrial and agricultural overuse of soil and water resources.[72]

Today, China is the only country in the world that has managed to reverse the general spread of deserts. Since the "Great Wall" has a historically positive meaning in China, it is also a matter of national identity, which has inspired the naming of the *Great Green Wall.* Since 1978, 70 billion trees have been planted around the Gobi Desert alone, which stretches across northwest China. By 2050, the Great Green Wall is expected to encompass almost 100 billion trees, planted over a length of 4500 kilometers and a width of up to 100 kilometers or more.[73] Overall, the project is expected to create more than 35 million hectares of new forest, roughly the size of Germany.[74] It is already the world's largest artificial forest and will, by 2050, become "the world's largest ecological engineering project".[75] This is nothing less than "by far the most comprehensive nature conservation program in human history",[76] and according to the UN, it serves as a model for land reclamation projects around the world.[77]

According to a decision by the CPC, China officially pledges to green *25 percent of its territory* (that is, almost 2.5 million km^2) by 2050 and has in fact already achieved 23 percent of the land area being covered with forest.[78] Of this, over 70 million hectares of forest have been regrown in the last decade alone, making China account "for more than 25% of the world's new green areas".[79] Even the American space agency NASA confirmed in early 2019 that China "dominates the greening of the earth", followed by India.[80] This has been achieved through the world's largest increase in forests, a mobilization of the population for tree planting, restoration of wetlands, renaturation of agricultural land ("Grain to Green" program), and its total of over 11,000 nature reserves. The number of new trees is approaching 100 billion, CO_2 sequestration is enormous; climate and precipitation are already improving on a large scale; and apples, nuts, dates, and chestnuts can be harvested.[81] In 2022, China's Special Envoy for Climate Change announced at Davos that it will plant another

70 billion trees by 2030 as part of the World Economic Forum's 1t.org initiative for ecosystem restoration.[82]

Seen in this light, it is hardly surprising that China consistently meets the environmental goals of its five-year plans, as well as its UN climate programs, in terms of air, soil, and water quality, solid waste management, and the restoration of the Yangtze River, regularly and often even ahead of schedule.[83] This, however, is a fundamental concern for all humanity, which, like the forest expansion against deserts, requires incredibly complex cooperation and coordination, including interdisciplinary analyses, scientific guidance, and the actions of numerous public agencies and private actors over decades. Citizens are encouraged, within the framework of these programs, to plant several trees each year.[84]

The *Kubuqi Desert*, for example, is the seventh largest desert in China and the closest to Beijing. It has long been partly responsible for the large sandstorms that have plagued Beijing and Hebei province since time immemorial. Its expansion, also caused by centuries of overgrazing, has been scaled back since 1988. Through decades of afforestation, control and mitigation of the situation were achieved. In this area alone, 3200 square kilometers of forest were created, restoring approximately one-third of the desert to greenery. This project was also highlighted by UNEP as a model example.[85]

Today, most of these forest areas no longer require irrigation and have become self-stabilizing systems. Desertification has been largely reversed, with 200 million tons less sand now being transported by storms into the cities. Even Japan and Korea, which were previously affected, benefit from these efforts. Residential areas that were once at risk remain habitable.

Worldwide, about 10 million hectares of forest are lost annually due to deforestation, resource extraction, and forest fires, which are worsening continually due to climate change.[86] Meanwhile, China afforests four million hectares of forest each year,[87] contributing to a significant reduction in the CO_2 content of the earth's atmosphere. NASA (see above) confirmed that China, as seen from space, has become significantly greener and leads the greening of the earth by a wide margin.

For this reason, humanity has a strong interest in ensuring that China can continue its successful path. In most countries, this is increasingly recognized and appreciated. Even Western green and left-wing political circles should, in fact, rejoice, but it is often easier to howl with the wolves.[88]

People as Carriers of the Eco-Revolution: Environmental Awareness, Popular Control, and Penalties for Companies' Pollutions

The required ecological revolution can only be achieved through a drastic change in the prevailing lifestyle and our concrete behaviors, and how people are mobilized for such a mega-project can be clearly seen in China. Here, all key players—including authorities, political leaders, the party and its top officials, companies and their executives, and of course private households—are involved. We will return to the different models of incentive systems for all these actors to promote future-oriented and ecologically sustainable behaviors.

As far as corporate action and managerial behavior are concerned, it is increasingly the residents near industrial areas who have become the driving forces in uncovering environmental offenses. Chinese newspapers[89] are full of cases not only involving political misconduct (corruption is publicly denounced but has been increasingly contained in recent years; more on that below)[90] but also cases in which residents report companies' ecological violations. The population is explicitly called upon to remain vigilant and report environmental pollution. The *China Daily* quotes a leading Chinese state representative as saying: "The protective umbrellas for polluting companies must be removed".[91]

Most of the time, action is taken immediately after such reports. Commissions from environmental ministries and agencies at the central, provincial, and municipal levels are quickly on site, meticulously verify the information, impose penalties if necessary, and announce a follow-up review to ensure that the issues have been resolved six months or a year later.

A report from the Ministry of Environmental Protection's investigation commission for 2016 and 2017 mentions 38,000 tips from the population, 5700 investigated companies, and 4300 punished managers, senior officials, and party officials. The penalties typically include travel and flight restrictions or credit limitations—not just fines, which, as in the West, can be paid out of the company's petty cash, but truly impact the managers. The report also cited 460 imprisoned managers and penalties totaling 77 million US dollars.[92] In addition to the possible blocking of private loans (for the individual, not the company), managers who have violated environmental regulations are primarily punished in the following ways:

- Ban on riding in the first class of the bullet trains for one year
- Ban on flying with business class for one year

- General ban on flying for one year

Penalties that personally "hurt"—and depending on the severity of the environmental offense, imprisonment can, of course, also be threatened.[93]

It should also be noted that since 2015, state actors and public officials, from the municipal to the central government level, can be held accountable for environmental offenses, and that their prospects for advancement are linked to their environmental records.[94] By contrast, environmental enforcement in Germany is comparatively lax, where one would hardly notice the existence of environmental criminal law: the automotive industry's exhaust manipulations speak for themselves.

"Circular Economy" and the "Blue Map"

With all these remarkable measures and projects, China is on the verge of becoming an "ecological circular economy", and it has enshrined this concept in law since 2009 with its "Circular Economy Promotion Law". As a result, the country is more advanced in developing closed-loop material cycles than even most developed industrial nations, according to the World Bank.[95]

The "Blue Map" app sets an even larger framework: a sensational interactive map in which all Chinese public environmental statistics have been localized since 2006. This includes 20,000 stations providing local environmental measurement and monitoring protocols— data from 338 cities in 22 provinces[96]—as well as real-time pollution data from 40,000 factories and other sources,[97] local information on air and water quality, weather, and much more, all of which can be used to guide the local behavior of users.[98]

The app has become a "hit" for environmental movements worldwide. Implementation is difficult, however: neither in the USA nor in the EU do environmental data exist in this quantity and quality, and they are far from being made publicly available.

Learning Ecological Behavior and Awareness in Play: The Tree-Planting App "Ant Forest"

As shown, China is the world leader in forestation and reforestation, and thus also a global frontrunner within the framework of the Paris Climate Accords (from which the USA withdrew under Trump) and the UN Millennium Goals (the so-called SDG—Sustainable Development Goals).

The previously mentioned payment app Alipay from Alibaba has become the "financial ant", Ant Financial, which handles the payments of over 500 million users. So far, so unspectacular. But how even the largest IT and internet companies in China are—or must be—involved in the national CO_2 strategy is illustrated by Ant Financial's sister app, *Ant Forest.* It specifically encourages environmentally conscious consumers and everyday behavior.[99]

The app was launched at the end of 2016 and already had over 600 million registered users by 2021.[100] Users can collect "tree points" for climate-friendly behavior. Points are awarded for, for example:

- Commuting to work on foot, by bicycle, or by train, leaving the car behind.
- Paying bills without paper.
- Refraining from using plastic bags when shopping.
- Buying products with a smaller ecological footprint. Information about the CO_2 balance and the ecological footprint of individual products can be accessed in the supermarket via the app.

After collecting points for some time, users receive a virtual tree sapling, which they must continue to "water" through climate-friendly behavior. At a certain point, the sapling becomes a real tree, and Alibaba, together with its NGO and UN partners, plants it in designated areas of China (usually in the fight against deserts, see above). By 2022, support for marine conservation projects, such as seagrass planting and mangrove restoration, was also added to the donations users can make with their earned green energy points.[101] By late 2019—after only three years of operation—122 million trees had already been planted through the app, resulting in a reduction of carbon emissions by 7.9 million tons.[102]

The game concept is reminiscent of the former Japanese Tamagotchis or today's Pokémon Go from Nintendo, but China demonstrates how the playful principle of caring can not only turn otherwise senseless, time-consuming "gaming" into something meaningful, but also actually improve the world. As of August 2023, more than 475 million trees had been planted, and 31 nature reserves established. These projects have furthermore created over 3.7 million income opportunities in planting, maintenance, and patrolling.[103]

Accordingly, this app has once again engaged the UN Development Programme (UNDP), which describes the Ant Forest platform as *exemplary*. In 2019, it was awarded the "UN Champions of the Earth Award", the United Nations' top environmental honor, by the UN Environment Programme (UNEP), which has become an official partner of Ant Forest.[104]

Of course, one can also anticipate the criticism from relevant Western media: all just to collect data, to perfect surveillance and dictatorship! Such a claim, of course, would be completely absurd in the case of Pokémon Go.

Every Day "For Future"

Should Chinese youth perhaps join the worldwide "Fridays-for-Future" student movement? After everything we have seen so far regarding "environmental and climate protection", such a thought might seem somewhat absurd. China is shaping its ecological future as a societal project: people are engaged in planting trees and exposing environmental violations, and they do not think about polluting their surroundings. And this happens every day of the week. China's young people do not need to skip school hours to gain attention for environmental and climate protection; this attention is part of a national state program. They can simply walk through the wide-open doors and participate.

In China, consumers do not need to laboriously educate themselves about eco-alternatives or fight for ecological products to appear on supermarket shelves. Here, innovative companies, embedded in the national eco- and climate strategy, provide ecological products and are at least as advanced as the eco-awareness of consumers. Companies act as pioneers. For example, one can already reach for a biodegradable item on the shelf instead of a plastic product. Straw instead of plastic is a reality, and the app guides consumers there. China is also one of the largest importers of bio-based products and materials.[105] These developments were already underway even before China's Ministry of Ecology and Environment announced in early 2020 that the country will phase out all single-use and non-biodegradable plastics—including plastic straws and bags—by 2025.[106]

In addition, government agencies and NGOs regularly place large advertisements in print and online media to raise public awareness of ecology, resource conservation, and health, thereby providing additional *nudges*:

- "Put your phone away sometimes!"
- "Watch out for your gambling addiction!"
- "Don't eat too much, and don't get fat on fast food!"[107]
- "Don't eat turtle soup! Even if it's offered to you in the restaurant. The killing stops only when the demand stops."
- "Protect sharks and say no to shark fin soup! The killing stops only when the demand stops."
- "Don't buy rhino powder! It's illegal. And the killing stops only when the demand stops."
- "Don't buy ivory. It's illegal. But the killing stops only when the demand stops."[108]
- "Say no to pangolin products. Humans are the only threat to these endangered animals. And only humans can save them."[109]

It is often young "influencers" who demonstrate how "uncool" environmentally damaging consumer behavior is.

For example, China has formed an alliance for Antarctica with Norway, Chile, and South Korea, which voluntarily imposes strict restrictions on krill fishing.[110] Elsewhere, it is reported that China operates joint eco-parks with other technologically advanced countries, where new natural materials for zero-energy houses and cities are researched and developed.[111] 3D-printed houses from recycled and natural materials can now be mass-produced at low cost, with excellent quality, equipment, and environmental properties.[112]

The list could go on, and every week new, surprising reports are added.

China the Only Country to Meet the Goals of the Paris Agreement 2016 Three Years Early (UN): "Ecological Civilization" Again Ahead of Climate Goals 2030/2040

According to the UN, China had already achieved its goals under the Paris Climate Agreement for the year 2020 by 2017.[113] The above-quoted myth of the "world's biggest polluter" should therefore be classified as "denial".

China's ecological revolution has now become constitutional, and the level of mobilization of the government, public administrations, companies, and citizens in terms of "ecology" is considerable.

This ecological revolution is explained by the well-known American Methodist theologian and philosopher John B. Cobb in his book *China and Ecological Civilization* as follows:

> Then, one of the oldest cultures of earth, China, stood up and said 'No! There are different ways to go forward. We could all benefit from the progress, without cannibalizing, and fully destroying our Planet.'[114]

Arthur Hanson, founding president of the *Canadian International Institute for Sustainable Development* and former chief advisor to the *China Council for International Cooperation on Environment and Development* (CCICED), defines China's conceptual framework of "Ecological Civilization", which was enshrined in its constitution in 2018, in contrast to mere "sustainable development", as follows: "in the emphasis placed on political and cultural factors, as well as on defining new relationships between people and nature that would permit living well, and within the eco-environmental bounds of planet Earth."[115]

Other international experts, such as the above-mentioned anthropologist, historian, ecologist, and Pulitzer Prize–winner Jared Diamond, confirm the "drastic and rapidly implemented measures of environmental protection that China has already adopted".[116] And that was back in 2005.

Even the *New York Times*, which is not suspected of having great sympathies for China, wrote in 2018: "Four years after declaring war on pollution, China is winning."[117]

Joyce Msuya, former Deputy Executive Director of the *United Nations Environment Programme* (UNEP), also praised China's successes in combating air pollution in 2019: "This improvement in air quality didn't happen by accident. It was the result of an enormous investment of time, resources and political will. [...] Understanding Beijing's air pollution story is crucial for any nation, district or municipality that wishes to follow a similar path."[118] Similarly, on plastic pollution, she urges that the "[w]orld should look to China for lessons".[119]

As the host country of the *UN World Environment Day* 2019, China was able to report on the successes of its "Blue Sky" initiative, which was only introduced in 2012. In just six years, the pollution load of Chinese cities was reduced by over 50 percent on average, as documented in the *China Air Quality Improvement Report*.[120]

Notes

1. See for example: Lauri Myllyvirta, "Analysis: Clean energy just put China's CO2 emissions into reverse for first time", *Carbon Brief*, May 15, 2025: https://www.carbonbrief.org/analysis-clean-energy-just-put-chinas-co2-emissions-into-reverse-for-first-time/ visited July 11, 2025.
2. As stated by the historian Richard Smith, for example in his article "China's drivers and planetary ecological collapse", *real-world economics review* 82, 2017.
3. Ibid., p. 23 ff., p. 27 f.
4. See also above Part I.
5. See for example: "Per capita CO_2 emissions", *Our World in Data,* June 20, 2024: https://ourworldindata.org/grapher/co-emissions-per-capita, visited August 14, 2024. See also: Kunzmann 2018, 87 ff.
6. For example: Kunzmann 2018, p. 88.
7. Kunzmann 2018, p. 95.
8. In detail: Larry Romanoff, "History of Chinese Inventions. The Present and the Future", *Transcend Media Service*, December 23, 2019: https://www.transcend.org/tms/2019/12/history-of-chinese-inventions-the-present-and-the-future-recent-chinese-state-of-the-art-innovations/ visited May 17, 2024.
9. Ibid.
10. Ibid.
11. Ibid.
12. Ibid.
13. Amanda Heidt, "'This is exclusion': Florida law restricts hiring of researchers from seven countries", *Nature*, March 6, 2024: https://www.nature.com/articles/d41586-024-00554-2 visited August 15, 2024.
14. Nature Editorial, "Why it would be a dangerous folly to end US–China science pact", *Nature*, February 26, 2024: https://www.nature.com/articles/d41586-024-00577-9 visited August 15, 2024. As of March 2024, the US-PRC Science and Technology Agreement (STA), which is

generally renewed every five years, was extended for another six months, its future however remaining uncertain. See: Nike Ching, "US-China Science, Tech Pact Is Renewed for Another Six Months", *Voice of America*, March 07, 2024: https://www.voanews.com /a/us-china-science-tech-pact-is-renewed-for-another-six-months/7518409.html, visited August 15, 2024.

15. "American and Chinese scientists are decoupling, too", *The Economist*, October 11, 2023: https://www.economist.com/science-and-technology/2023/10/11/american-and-chinese-scientists-are-decoupling-too visited August 15, 2024.
16. For example: Niu Honglei, Lekse, William, "Carbon emission effect of urbanization at regional level: empirical evidence from China", *economics* e-journal, 2018–44, July 12, 2018.
17. Yang FEI et al., "Can reducing carbon emissions improve economic performance? Evidence from China", *economics* e-journal 2019–13, February 12, 2019.
18. Ibid.
19. For example: ZHUANG Miao, Tomas Balezentis et al., "Environmental Performance and China's Atmospheric Pollutant Emissions: Evidence from 'Three Regions and Ten Urban Agglomerations'", *Environmental and Resource Economics* 74 (2019), pp. 211–242.
20. For example: "China's road to net zero: reshape the country and the world", *Economist Intelligence Unit*, February 23, 2023: https://www.eiu.com/n/china-road-to-net-zero-reshape-the-country-and-the-world/, visited August 16, 2024.
21. For example: WANG Mingjie, "Report claims China can fully develop and also cut its emissions to zero", *China Daily,* November 29, 2019: https://www.chinadaily.com.cn/a/201911/29/WS5de07a01a310cf3e3557 ad7f.html, visited January 11, 2025.
22. See Myllyvirta, ibid. (see above).
23. See for example: Isabel Hilton, "How China Became the World's Leader on Renewable Energy", *Yale Environment 360*, March 13, 2024: https://e360.yale.edu/features/china-renewable-energy visited August 16, 2024. Hilton notes, for example, that "[i]n 2022, China installed roughly as much solar capacity as the rest of the world combined, then doubled additional solar in 2023."
24. Brand, Ulrich, Wissen, Markus, 2021. *The Imperial Mode of Living. Everyday Life and the Ecological Crisis of Capitalism*. London: Verso.
25. Ruth Michaelson, "'Waste colonialism': world grapples with west's unwanted plastic", *The Guardian*, December 31, 2021: https://www.theguardian.com/environment/2021/dec/31/waste-colonialism-countries-grapple-with-wests-unwanted-plastic visited August 16, 2024.

26. Carly Cassella, "There's a Trash Crisis in The US Happening Right Now", *ScienceAlert*, December 6, 2018: https://www.sciencealert.com/the-us-has-nowhere-to-put-its-recycling visited August 16, 2024.
27. For example: Thomas Johnson, "Environmental protest in urban China", in: *Handbook on Urban Development in China*, 2019, pp. 329–342.
28. For example: Simon Göß, "Erneuerbare Energien in China 2019 [Renewable Energies in China 2019]", *Energy BrainBlog*, September 9, 2019: https://blog.energybrainpool.com/erneuerbare-energien-in-china-2019-erzeugung-und-foerderung-im-ersten-halbjahr/ visited August 17, 2024.
29. Andy Tay, "By the numbers: China's net-zero ambitions", *Nature*, April 5, 2022: https://www.nature.com/articles/d41586-022-00802-3 visited August 17, 2024.
30. Hilton, ibid. (see above).
31. Zheng Xin, "Nation biggest contributor to global renewables capacity amid green transition", *China Daily*, July 7, 2024: https://www.chinadaily.com.cn/a/202407/02/WS66835931a31095c51c50bd77.html visited August 17, 2024.
32. Yujie Xue, "China to remain renewable energy leader with strong capacity growth in 2022, despite subsidies phase-out", *South China Morning Post*, January 2, 2022: https://www.scmp.com/business/china-business/article/3161732/china-remain-renewable-energy-leader-strong-capacity-growth visited August 17, 2024.
33. Lauri Myllyvirta, "Analysis: China's clean energy pushes coal to record-low 53% share of power in May 2024", *CarbonBrief*, July 11, 2024: https://www.carbonbrief.org/analysis-chinas-clean-energy-pushes-coal-to-record-low-53-share-of-power-in-may-2024/ visited August 17, 2024.
34. For example: Jared Diamond, Liu Jianguo, "China's environment in a globalizing world", *Nature* 435, 2005, pp. 1179–1186.
35. Kavipriya, "China leads the EV revolution with 1.8 million public charging stations", *Telematics Wire*, June 23, 2023: https://telematicswire.net/china-leads-the-ev-revolution-with-1-8-million-public-charging-stations/ visited August 17, 2024.
36. Helen Davidson, "'High quality, low price and dizzying variety': how the Chinese switched to electric cars", *The Guardian*, July 24, 2024: https://www.theguardian.com/environment/article/2024/jul/24/high-quality-low-price-and-dizzying-variety-how-the-chinese-switched-to-electric-cars visited August 17, 2024.
37. Keith Bradsher, "China's Electric Cars Keep Improving, a Worry for Rivals Elsewhere", *The New York Times*, May 1, 2024: https://www.nytimes.com/2024/05/01/business/china-electric-vehicles.html visited August 17, 2024.

38. Madeleine Genzsch, "Suizid deutscher Autohersteller [Suicide of German car manufacturers]", *Ecological China*, October 29, 2018. See also: Simon Book et al., "Electric Shock: An Existential Crisis in the German Auto Industry", *Der Spiegel*, March, 27, 2023: https://www.spiegel.de/international/business/electric-shock-an-existential-crisis-in-the-german-auto-industry-a-266bd037-b63a-4c9b-97b5-423866d7080f, visited August 17, 2024.
39. For example: *Steingarts Morning Briefing* December 16, 2019.
40. Ly Yutong, Denise Jia, "China Could Have a Million Hydrogen-Powered Vehicles on Its Roads by 2035", *Caixin Global*, June 6, 2024: https://www.caixinglobal.com/2024-06-06/china-could-have-a-million-hydrogen-powered-vehicles-on-its-roads-by-2035-102203629.html visited August 17, 2024.
41. *Steingarts Morning Briefing*, December 16, 2019.
42. Frank Schumann, "China produziert hochwertigere E-Autos [China produces higher quality E-cars]", *junge Welt*, December 23, 2019, p. 3.
43. João da Silva, "EU hits Chinese electric cars with new tariffs", *BBC*, July 4, 2024: https://www.bbc.com/news/articles/cy99z53qypko, visited August 17, 2024.
44. "China's operating high-speed railway hits 45,000 km", *Xinhua*, January 9, 2024: https://english.news.cn/20240109/28b8075c73384fa894e90afd1b8d0dbc/c.html, visited August 17, 2024.
45. Micah McCartney, "China's High-Speed Rail Miracle", *Newsweek*, July 13, 2024: https://www.newsweek.com/china-high-speed-rail-miracle-1924185, visited August 17, 2024.
46. Frank Chen, "China sets railway building spree in high-speed motion", *Asia Times*, August 24, 2020: https://asiatimes.com/2020/08/china-sets-railway-building-spree-in-high-speed-motion/, visited August 17, 2024.
47. Xinhua, "China's bullet trains make five billion trips", *China Daily*, August 1, 2016: https://www.chinadaily.com.cn/business/2016-08/01/content_26292785.htm, visited August 17, 2024.
48. See for example: Irene Li, "Beijing-Shanghai Rail Trips Are Outpacing Flights, Here's Why", *The Beijinger*, September 5, 2023: https://www.thebeijinger.com/blog/2023/09/05/why-high-speed-rail-outpacing-air-travel-china, visited August 17, 2024.
49. See for example: "China-Europe freight train runs setting new monthly record in May", *Global Times*, June 16, 2024: https://www.globaltimes.cn/page/202406/1314206.shtml, visited August 20, 2024. And: Łukasz Kuś, "Large increase in container transport by rail from China to Europe in 1Q 2024", *IntermodalNews EU*, April 12, 2024: https://intermodalnews.eu/2024/04/12/large-increase-in-container-transport-by-rail-from-china-to-europe-in-1q-2024/, visited August 20,

2024. Kuś records a year-on-year increase of 44 percent in container transport from China to Europe via Russia for the first quarter of 2024. In 2023 alone, "1.9 million containers were moved from China westwards on the New Silk Road railway." By May 2024, the cumulative number of cargo containers transported via the China-Europe Railway Express reached 8.7 million, valued at over 380 billion USD, the *Global Times* reports.

50. For example: "Strengere Regeln: China geht den Lastwagen an den Kragen [Stricter rules: China is cracking down on trucks]", *FAZ* January 6, 2019. And: "China to crack down on diesel trucks, raise fuel standards", *Reuters*, January 5, 2019: https://www.reuters.com/article/business/environment/china-to-crack-down-on-diesel-trucks-raise-fuel-standards-idUSKCN1OZ066/, visited August 20, 2024.
51. tagesschau.de on January 5, 2019.
52. Ibid.
53. "U-Bahn fahren kostet 20 Plastikflaschen [Riding the subway costs 20 plastic bottles]", November 20, 2018; online at: genzsch.wordpress.com; visited June 6, 2019. See also: Ben Schiller, "In Beijing, You Can Pay For Train Rides With Plastic Bottles", *Fast Company*, August 26, 2014: https://www.fastcompany.com/3034 720/in-beijing-you-can-pay-for-train-rides-with-plastic-bottles, visited August 21, 2024.
54. Loz Blain, "China unveils new 600 km/h ultra-fast maglev train", *New Atlas*, July 21, 2021: https://newatlas.com/transport/china-fastest-maglev-train/?itm_source=newatlas&itm_medium=article-body, visited August 21, 2024.
55. Michael Li, Toby Mann, "China successfully tests maglev trains in vacuum tube, eyeing future speeds of 4,000 kph", *Australian Broadcasting Corporation (ABC)*, April 11, 2024: https://www.abc.net.au/news/2024-04-12/china-ultra-high-speed-trains-maglev-how-fast/103644930, visited August 21, 2024.
56. Joe Salas, "621-mph maglev vacuum train "T-Flight" test successful", *New Atlas*, August 09, 2024: https://newatlas.com/transport/tflight-chinese-maglev-train-test-successful/, visited August 21, 2024.
57. Diamond Liu (2005).
58. The term "moderately prosperous society" (小康社会 - Xiǎokāng Shèhuì) has become a well-known political slogan in China and was first used by Deng Xiaoping in 1979 in the context of Zhou Enlai's envisioned "Four Modernizations" (strengthening agriculture, industry, defense, science and technology) and the Reform and Opening-up period. It has subsequently been reused especially by former president Hu Jintao and more recently by Xi Jinping in connection with his "Chinese Dream" slogan. The term Xiǎokāng (meaning moderately or basically well-off) itself however originates in ancient texts such as the *Classic of Poetry* (11th to sev-

enth century BC) and the *Book of Rites* (5th to first century BC), which have become classics of Confucianism. See for example: Smith, Craig A., 2019. "Datong and Xiaokang". In: Sorace, Christian, Franceschini, Ivan, Loubere, Nicholas (eds.). *Afterlives of Chinese Communism: Political Concepts from Mao to Xi*. Acton, Australia: Australian National University Press, pp. 63–66.

59. Graham Hope, "Autonomous Street Sweepers Take to China's Streets", *IOT World Today*, January 20, 2023: https://www.iotworldtoday.com/smart-cities/autonomous-street-sweepers-take-to-china-s-streets#close-modal visited August 22, 2024.
60. Karla Lant, "China Has Officially Started Construction on the World's First "Forest City"", *Futurism*, June 27, 2017: https://futurism.com/china-has-officially-started-construction-on-the-worlds-first-forest-city visited August 24, 2024.
61. Lisha Liao, Chunkai Zhao, Xing Li, Jiahong Qin, "Towards low carbon development: The role of forest city constructions in China", *Ecological Indicators* Volume 131, 2021, 108,199.
62. Jun Yang, Wanli Yang, Yandi Zhao, "China to have 300 forest cities by 2025", *China Daily*, July 9, 2018: https://www.chinadaily.com.cn/a/201807/09/WS5b429dcba3103349141e169e.html visited August 24, 2024.
63. Ibid.
64. Liao et al., ibid.
65. Cheng Wang, Jiali Jin, Clive Davies, Wendy Y. Chen, "Urban Forests as Nature-Based Solutions: a Comprehensive Overview of the National Forest City Action in China", *Current Forestry Reports* Volume 10, 2024, 119–132, p. 122.
66. Diamond, Liu 2005.
67. "China trägt am meisten zur globalen Grünflächenausdehnung bei [China contributes the most to global green space expansion]", *german.china.org.cn*, February 28, 2019: http://german.china.org.cn/txt/2019-02/28/content_74515793.htm visited August 25, 2024.
68. Xinyue Fan, Weihua Xu, Zhenhua Zang, and Zhiyun Ouyang, "Representativeness of China's Protected Areas in Conserving Its Diverse Terrestrial Ecosystems", *Ecosystem Health and Sustainability* Vol 9, April 2023. For updated and extensive lists of all general and specialized protection and development zones, see for example also the Wikipedia page: "List of protected areas of China": https://en.wikipedia.org/wiki/List_of_ protected_areas_of_China, visited August 25, 2024.
69. "Estimated forest coverage in China from 1990 to 2022", *Statista*, July 18, 2024: https://www.statista.com/statistics/300977/china-forest-coverage/, visited August 25, 2024.

70. See: "Global Forest Resources Assessment 2020: Main report", *Food and Agriculture Organization of the United Nations*, Rome, 2020, pp. 15–18. In terms of total forest area, China is ranked fifth worldwide, comprising about five percent of global forest area (Russia at number one with 20 percent).
71. Diamond, Liu 2005.
72. Greg Beach, "China is fighting desertification with a Great Green Wall of trees", *Inhabitat*, August 31, 2017: https://inhabitat.com/china-is-fighting-desertification-with-the-great-green-wall-of-trees/ visited August 31, 2024.
73. "China's Great Green Wall", *Royal Geographical Society*, January 2015: https://www.rgs.org/schools/resources-for-schools/chinas-great-green-wall, visited August 31, 2024.
74. Bloomberg News, "China's 40-Year, Billion-Tree Project Is a Lesson for the World", *Bloomberg*, September 14, 2020: https://www.bloomberg.com/news/articles/2020-09-14/china-s-40-year-billion-tree-project-is-a-lesson-for-the-world, visited August 31, 2024.
75. Royal Geographical Society, ibid.
76. *Süddeutsche Zeitung* December 22, 2016 (quote translated by the authors).
77. According to the UN Environment Program UNEP: "China's desert greening efforts inspire world: UNEP chief", 10.7.2017; Video online at: youtube.com, visited August 31, 2024, and UN Environment, "List of Projects under Implementation as of 30 September 2018"; online at: wedocs.unep.org, visited June 7, 2019.
78. For a detailed example: Uwe Kerkow, "Chinas Grüne Große Mauer [China's Green Great Wall]", *Telepolis*, January 16, 2020: https://www.telepolis.de/features/Chinas-Gruene-Grosse-Mauer-4638653.html, visited August 31, 2024.
79. "China will aim to plant and conserve 70 billion trees by 2030 as part of the global tree movement", *World Economic Forum*, May 25, 2022: https://www.weforum.org/press/2022/05/china-will-aim-to-plant-and-conserve-70-billion-trees-by-2030-as-part-of-the-global-tree-movement/, visited August 31, 2024.
80. Abby Tabor, "Human Activity in China and India Dominates the Greening of Earth, NASA Study Shows", *nasa.gov*, February 11, 2019: https://www.nasa.gov/centers-and-facilities/ames/human-activity-in-china-and-india-dominates-the-greening-of-earth-nasa-study-shows/, visited August 31, 2024.
81. Kerkow, ibid.
82. World Economic Forum, ibid.
83. As an older example from the first Paris Round: "China erfüllt die Ziele für 2018 [China meets the goals for 2018]", *german.china.org.cn*,

January 21, 2019: http://german.china.org.cn/txt/2019-01/21/content_74393836.htm, visited August 31, 2024.

84. For example: Kunzmann 2018, p. 94.
85. "Grünes Wunder in der Kubuqi-Wüste [Green Miracle in the Kubuqi Desert]", May 20, 2019: http://german.china.org.cn/txt/2019-05/20/content_74803631_0.htm, visited August 31, 2024. See also: United Nations Environment Programme, "Review of the Kubuqi Ecological Restoration Project: A Desert Green Economy Pilot Initiative", *UNEP*, 2015: http://www.dl.edi-info.ir/Review%20of%20the%20Kubuqi% 20Ecological%20Restoration%20Project.pdf, visited August 31, 2024. And: Charlie Campbell, "China's Greening of the Vast Kubuqi Desert is a Model for Land Restoration Projects Everywhere", *Time*, July 27, 2017: https://time.com/4851013/china-greening-kubuqi-desert-land-restoration/, visited August 31, 2024.
86. James MacCarthy et al., "The Latest Data Confirms: Forest Fires Are Getting Worse", *World Resources Institute*, August 13, 2024: https://www.wri.org/insights/global-trends-forest-fires, visited August 31, 2024.
87. "How China brought its forests back to life in a decade", *Rapid Transition Alliance*, December 2, 2018: https://rapidtransition.org/stories/how-china-brought-its-forests-back-to-life-in-a-decade/, visited August 31, 2024.
88. With such metaphors, one should actually regularly apologize to nature. Wolves, for example, are smart, social, and cooperative creatures, and even contribute to mitigating the effects of climate change. See for example: Alison Stine, "How Wolves Mitigate the Effects of Climate Change", *Nonprofit Quarterly*, November 9, 2023: https://nonprofitquarterly.org/how-wolves-mitigate-the-effects-of-climate-change/, visited August 31, 2024.
89. We usually refer to the newspaper *China Daily*, which, similar to *USA Today* in the USA, reports in English for an international audience about recent developments in China. Among the most read domestic, national Chinese-language newspapers are, for example, *The Beijing News (Xinjing Bao)*, *People's Daily (Renmin Ribao)*, or *Workers' Daily (Gongren Ribao)*. Next to national newspapers there are many widely read regional newspapers for cities and provinces, such as the *Jiefang Daily (Jiefang Ribao)* in Shanghai, *Beijing Daily (Beijing Ribao)* in Beijing, and so on.
90. For example: *China Daily* July 6, 2018, p. 5; July 13, 2018, p. 4.
91. *China Daily* July 6, 2018, p. 8.
92. *China Daily* July 10, 2018, p. 5.
93. In China, "prison" does not result in lifelong stigmatization or a definitive descent into criminality; rehabilitation is the primary focus. If deficiencies are remedied within one year, the manager is fully rehabili-

tated, which can then also be reported in the newspaper. China has a lower incarceration rate than the US, which has a vast private prison system that creates incentives to maintain a large prison population. The US counts 531 incarcerations per 100,000 people, while China counts 119. Even in total numbers, the US exceeds China, with 1,767,200 prisoners compared to China's 1,690,000, despite China's population being over four times the size of the US. The numbers are from *World Prison Brief* in 2023: "Highest to Lowest - Prison Population Total". See: https://www.prisonstudies.org/highest-to-lowest/prison-population-total?field_region_taxonomy_tid=All, visited September 1, 2024.

94. For example: Kunzmann 2018, p. 91.
95. "China Circular Economy Promotion Law", *The World Bank*, August 25, 2020: https://ppp.worldbank.org/public-private-partnership/library/china-circular-economy-promotion-law, visited September 6, 2024.
96. Jonathan Landreth, "A rare environmental success story: The Blue Map app and its 3.8 million Chinese users — Q&A with Ma Jun", *The China Project*, May 2, 2023: https://thechinaproject.com/2023/05/02/a-rare-environmental-success-story-the-blue-map-app-and-its-3-8-million-chinese-users-qa-with-ma-jun/, visited September 6, 2024.
97. Jeff McMahon, "How An App Is Stopping Pollution In China", *Forbes*, November 17, 2017: https://www.forbes.com/sites/jeffmcmahon/2017/11/17/how-an-app-is-stopping-pollution-in-china/, visited September 6, 2024.
98. See for example: Ma Jun, Changhua Wu, "Blue Map: Here's how emissions reporting data is supporting the global green transition", *World Economic Forum*, June 18, 2024: https://www.weforum.org/agenda/2024/06/china-blue-map-green-transition/, visited September 6, 2024. The maps can be accessed via: https://wwwen.ipe.org.cn/, visited September 6, 2024.
99. Harry Kretchmer, "This app plants trees when people make lower-carbon choices", *World Economic Forum*, July 21, 2020: https://www.weforum.org/agenda/2020/07/china-ant-forest-app-carbon-emissions-trees/, visited September 6, 2024.
100. "Over 600 Million People Planted More Than 326 Million Trees via Alipay Ant Forest in Five Years", *Business Wire*, August 25, 2021: https://www.businesswire.com/news/home/20210825005340/en/Over-600-Million-People-Planted-More-Than-326-Million-Trees-via-Alipay-Ant-Forest-in-Five-Years, visited September 6, 2024.

101. "Leveraging digital platform to amplify green participation by the public: An Ant Group case study presented at COP28", *Asia Tech Daily*, December 1, 2023: https://asiatechdaily.com/leveraging-digital-platform-to-amplify-green-participation-by-the-public-an-ant-group-case-study-presented-at-cop28/, visited September 6, 2024.
102. For example: Muhammad Ashfaq et al., "You plant a virtual tree, we'll plant a real tree: Understanding users' adoption of the Ant Forest mobile gaming application from a behavioral reasoning theory perspective", *Journal of Cleaner Production*, Volume 310, August 10, 2021, 127,394.
103. "支持22个省份生态建设:蚂蚁集团通过"蚂蚁森林"累计协议捐资超34亿元 [Supporting ecological construction in 22 provinces: Ant Group has donated more than 3.4 billion yuan through the "Ant Forest" agreement]", *Ant Group*, August 28, 2023: https://www.antgroup.com/news-media/press-releases/1693215256000, visited September 6, 2024.
104. "Chinese initiative Ant Forest wins UN Champions of the Earth award", *UN Environment Programme*, September 19, 2019: https://www.unep.org/news-and-stories/press-release/chinese-initiative-ant-forest-wins-un-champions-earth-award, visited September 6, 2024.
105. For example: *prognos newsletter* May 2019, p. 14 f.
106. Sophie Yu, Huizhong Wu, "China moves to phase out single-use plastics", *Reuters*, January 19, 2020: https://www.reuters.com/article/world/china-moves-to-phase-out-single-use-plastics-idUSKBN1ZI0MQ/, visited September 7, 2024.
107. *China Daily* July 11, 2018, p. 17.
108. *China Daily* July 6, 2018, p. 16; July 14/15, 2019, p.7.
109. *China Daily* July 7/8, 2018, p. 7.
110. Zhang Chun, Tang Damin, "Krill fishers agree to partial ban in Antarctic", *Dialogue Earth*, July 16, 2018: https://dialogue.earth/en/ocean/3891-krill-fishers-agree-to-partial-ban-in-antarctic/, visited Sept. 7, 2024.
111. For example, in the huge eco-parks of the port city Qingdao: Frank Schumann, "Vorreiterrolle in Ökologie angestrebt [Aiming for a leading role in ecology]", *junge Welt*, December 23, 2019, p. 3.
112. For example: Victor Anusci, "3D printed house takes shape in rural China", *VoxelMatters*, November 27, 2021: https://www.voxelmatters.com/3d-printed-house-takes-shape-in-rural-china/, visited September 7, 2024. And: "China: Firm 3D prints 10 full-sized houses in a day", *BBC*, April 25, 2014: https://www.bbc.com/news/blogs-news-from-elsewhere-27156775, visited September 7, 2024.
113. "China Meets 2020 Carbon Target Three Years Ahead of Schedule", *United Nations Climate Change*, March 29, 2018: https://unfccc.int/

news/china-meets-2020-carbon-target-three-years-ahead-of-schedule, visited September 8, 2024.

114. John B. Cobb, Jr., *China and Ecological Civilization*, in conversation with Andre Vltchek, Jakarta, Indonesia: Badak Merah Semesta, 2019, p. 2.
115. Arthur Hanson, "Ecological Civilization in the People's Republic of China: Values, Action, and Future Needs", *ADB East Asia Working Paper Series*, No. 21, December 2019: https://www.adb.org/sites/default/files/publication/545291/eawp-021-ecological-civilization-prc.pdf, visited September 8, 2024.
116. Jared Diamond, *Collapse: How Societies Choose to Fail or Survive*, London, New York: Penguin Books, 2005, p. 377.
117. Michael Greenstone, "Four Years After Declaring War on Pollution, China Is Winning", *The New York Times*, March 12, 2018: https://www.nytimes.com/2018/03/12/upshot/china-pollution-environment-longer-lives.html, visited September 8, 2024.
118. CCAC secretariat, "Beijing's air quality improvements are a model for other cities", *Climate & Clean Air Coalition (CCAC)*, March 9, 2019: https://www.ccacoalition.org/news/beijings-air-quality-improvements-are-model-other-cities, visited September 8, 2024.
119. Dominic Faulder, "UN environment head: World should look to China for lessons", *Nikkei Asia*, May 8, 2019: https://asia.nikkei.com/Spotlight/The-Big-Story/UN-environment-head-World-should-look-to-China-for-lessons, visited September 8, 2024.
120. Hou Liqiang, "Major cities experience drop in air pollutants, greenhouse gases", *China Daily*, June 6, 2019: https://www.chinadaily.com.cn/a/201906/06/WS5cf867d8a31017657722fc98.html, visited September 8, 2024.

Selected and Recommended Literature

Diamond, Jared, and Jianguo Liu. 2005. China's environment in a globalizing world. *Nature* 435:1179–1186.

Further Cited Literature

Kunzmann, Marcel, 2018. *Theorie, System und Praxis des Sozialismus in China* [Theory, System and Practice of Socialism in China]. 2nd ed. Berlin: Verlag Mirco Kolarczik

CHAPTER 12

"Democracy? Dictatorship!"

Anti-Corruption, Rule of Law, Privacy Protection, and "Credible China": Internet and Everyday Behavior

Everyday Philosophy: Confucian Social Values, Respect for Difference, and a Focus on Learning and Cooperation

In China today, unsurprisingly, a revival of awareness of its own cultural history can be observed. In contrast to most Western countries, China does not have a comparable history of global aggression and subjugation through crusades, imperialism, or colonialism. In this context, the millennia-old Confucian philosophy and value system are being recalled and further developed. This reference to its own history often serves as a practical guide for ethical, socially responsible, and ecological everyday behavior.[1]

At its core, Confucianism is based on a holistic worldview: society as a system, rationality and emotion, body and mind, tradition and innovation, history and future—all belong together, form a whole, and are connected with the ideals of a just and harmonious social order.

Among Chinese everyday institutions (behaviors) and values is the search for opportunities for cooperation: Where are win-win situations? Where and how can we cooperate for mutual benefit? This is also associated with striving for constant exchange and learning from others: What can we do better? What can you recommend to us?

W. Elsner, E. Najmehchi, *The Rise of China*,
https://doi.org/10.1007/978-3-032-20260-4_12

The Chinese concept of harmony emphasizes peaceful coexistence and the acceptance of existing differences—and it also contains an idea of cooperation as "mutual doing good".[2]

An example of contemporary Chinese philosophy in the field of international politics was provided by then-Premier Li Keqiang in his speech at the World Economic Forum in Davos in 2015:

> In a world of diverse civilizations, we should all seek to live in harmony. Cultural diversity, like biodiversity, is a most precious treasure endowed to us on this planet. And human society is like a garden where all human civilizations blossom. Different cultures and religions need to respect and live in harmony with each other. While maintaining the natural close ties among those with whom we see eye to eye, we also need to respect those with whom we disagree. Like the vast ocean admitting all rivers that run into it, members of the international community need to work together to expand common ground while accepting differences, and seek win-win progress through inclusive cooperation and mutual learning.[3]

Skeptics may argue that this sounds like a soapbox speech—beautiful words cost nothing, after all, just "cheap talk". We in the West are all too accustomed to hearing window-dressing speeches. Nevertheless, we would be glad if our politicians, in front of international audiences, would at least *talk* about international harmony, cultural and religious diversity, respect for those who think differently, cooperation, and mutual learning, instead of constantly lecturing "the others", making rules for them, or threatening them—in short, wanting to impose our "worldview" on everyone else, forcing "them" to adapt to us. Since such ideas and words, if sincerely meant, could move and change us, they certainly have the potential to make the world a better place.

Optimism and Openness, Multi-Religions and Religious Tolerance

We have highlighted the generally relaxed nature of the Chinese in daily interactions, as well as the speed and ease with which they embrace change and innovation. This is grounded in a widespread optimism for the future. We have already noted several times the social embeddedness and long-term secured stability of the framework conditions for individual life, investment planning, and professional (including entrepreneurial) perspectives.

And indeed, according to an international comparative survey conducted by the market research company *Ipsos* at the end of 2023, 87 percent of Chinese were optimistic that the following year would be better than the previous one—a tied second place worldwide, only after Indonesia with 91 percent (USA at 65, Germany 57, and Japan at 39 percent; the global average being 70 percent).[4] It is also interesting to note a 2020 survey by the *European Investment Bank* (EIB) on climate change, which found that 80 percent of Chinese believe climate change is reversible, compared to only 59 percent of Europeans and 54 percent of US citizens.[5]

Practically all major religions of the world exist in China, often with many of their factions. They coexist largely pluralistically, tolerantly, and peacefully. This also applies to Islam, which significantly shapes the cityscape of central cities such as the old imperial city of Xi'an (formerly Chang'an), a major hub of Hui Muslim[6] society and culture, with its famous Muslim Quarter and the Great Mosque of Xi'an—one of the largest in China—whose history dates back to the Tang Dynasty (618–907 AD).

There is no "state religion" and no dominant church, and any religious movements, sects, or cults that aspire for state power and legislation guided by religion are generally met with restriction if they are perceived as a serious threat to the secular status quo. If asked, most Chinese people today would generally consider themselves not particularly religious, but they maintain a relaxed, pragmatic, real-world relationship with religions. They possess historical and, at the same time, modern ethical orientations and value systems, and many certainly have a form of spirituality—but for the most part without aggressive superstition, a sense of mission, or any inclination to harm others over religious conflicts.

This is also why the bloody attacks by Islamist terrorists since the 1990s surprised and shocked many in China so deeply. China was culturally somewhat unprepared for this new level and type of violence and brutality, even though the Chinese were already familiar with this kind of fundamentalist militias abroad in the form of the Mujahideen and later the Taliban from the Afghanistan war of the 1980s. Moreover, the western borders of Xinjiang were apparently still largely uncontrolled and permeable to terrorist intruders in the 1990s.

In the Chinese core regions, the old and generally humane and tolerant Buddhism has historically dominated much of the time, but almost always in coexistence—and sometimes even in syncretism—with Daoism,

Confucianism (which is generally considered a system of thought and philosophy rather than a religion), and various local folk beliefs and traditions. These have also coexisted with numerous other religions, many of which, like Buddhism, arrived in China via the Silk Road in the early centuries CE, such as Christianity, Islam, Manichaeism, Zoroastrianism, and even Judaism.

However, alongside periods of more harmonious coexistence, there were naturally also periods of increased strife and conflict, including religious intolerance of various forms, with Daoist, Buddhist, or Confucian dominance or even supremacy at different times. Nevertheless, many periods in ancient Chinese history demonstrate a surprising—and, by global standards, exceptional—degree of religious tolerance and peaceful coexistence. One famous example is the Tang Emperor Taizong (ruled 626–649 CE), whose reign is considered a golden age of Chinese history until this day. As a Buddhist himself, he believed in religious tolerance, allowing followers of Zoroastrianism, Manichaeism, Christianity, and Islam to practice their religions freely alongside Buddhists and Daoists. His tolerance also extended to diverse ethnic groups, many of which had representatives in high positions at the imperial court.[7]

Therefore, due to the historical dominance of Buddhism in China, most of the temples that can be visited today in cities of the historical Han Chinese settlement areas are Buddhist. These temples are, of course, open, unguarded, and unprotected, yet still somehow "in use".

Conversations about religion and faith with some Chinese people occurred during a brief visit to a temple in the port city of Tianjin. For example, I [W.E.] carefully observed an older Chinese woman in a temple. Friendly question, again in front of the temple: "Who is the figure to whom you just lit an incense stick?" She replied, "It is a local Buddha, a Buddha of the seafarers." I asked, "Do you have anything to do with seafaring?" She answered, "Yes, I come from a seafaring family. I visit our local Buddha from time to time and light the stick to protect the seafarers." The lady smiled, as if she knew that I couldn't really understand. Then she added, with overwhelming charm, "I think you respect my spiritual need and action." How could I do otherwise?

A relaxed spirituality, then, without a sense of mission or mania for conviction—no wonder that most Buddhist temples in China today do not play the role of aloof, distant, elitist sanctuaries owned by a caste of high priests but are integrated places of everyday life, offering daily small spiritual refueling and the consolidation of humane values of peaceful coexistence. Such a humane approach to religiosity and spirituality is desirable between religions all over the world.

But of course, China, the "fattest roast" in the eyes of colonialists, imperialists, and religious fanatics, is not immune to the global wave of religious extremism and fundamentalism. This is not limited to so-called "Islamist fundamentalism" or "Islamism", and certainly not a unique or inherent characteristic of "Islam" itself, as there have also been instances of Buddhist fundamentalism and extremism, such as the riots by Tibetan Buddhists targeting Hui Muslims in 2008,[8] a series of terrorist bombings in Tibet in 1996,[9] and the 2002 Chengdu bombing.[10]

However, these phenomena are much more closely connected to global geopolitical developments than to the inherent characteristics of the religions themselves. Meanwhile, to the south of China, a rising tide of Hindu fundamentalism and extremism—paired with and influenced by an increasingly belligerent ultranationalism and territorial expansionism—has been observable in India in recent years,[11] fueling an already tense situation at the India-China border, which has seen numerous minor clashes between armed forces.[12]

Anti-Lobbying, Anti-Corruption, and the "Rule of Law": Politicians, Managers, and Bureaucrats

After the painful historical experiences with colonial terror during the "Century of Humiliation", as well as with lawlessness and arbitrariness during the "Cultural Revolution", the desire for the rule of law and stability is deeply rooted in the Chinese population. It is therefore unsurprising that the rule of law plays a dominant role in public perception and discussion.[13]

In recent years, the Chinese judiciary has undergone a massive cultural change. This was also associated with the first measures addressing the negative social and behavioral consequences of the period of deregulation ("Reform and Opening-up") from 1978 onwards, which targeted massive individual enrichment, widespread corruption, and environmental crime. By the end of the 2000s, an increasingly serious and comprehensive fight against corruption began. The then-general secretary issued a dramatic appeal to the world in 2007, stating that the party and China would be lost if the problem of corruption were not brought under control. This was likely an extremely realistic assessment and functioned as a political emergency brake.

However, only from 2012 onward, under the leadership of the Xi-Li administration, did this policy seem to take hold seriously. Several times since 2014, we have heard the following sentence: "For 30 years we have been told about fighting corruption; rarely has anything happened, but now, for the first time, we notice that really something is happening."

The focus of the fight against corruption has always been local and regional state units, as well as corresponding party units, especially at the provincial and municipal levels. Given the relative independence of lower levels, corrupt alliances of party officials, senior civil servants, and regional companies had established themselves. Hundreds of politicians and businesspeople were sent to prison in the 2010s for passive and active bribery, including prominent figures in the highest positions of the administration.[14]

Colleagues confirm in conversations, by the way, that this had little to do with the "elimination of internal party competitors", as is often reported in the West. Rather, for the most part, these were already generally known cases that were finally being acted upon. An exception is probably the well-known case of Bo Xilai, former mayor, provincial governor, minister, and last party secretary of the directly administered municipality of Chongqing, who was dismissed in 2012 for "serious disciplinary violations" and "corruption", and subsequently indicted.[15] The background may have been connected to the fact that Bo opposed the expansion of market economy elements in China's development strategy, advocated a return to Mao, and had begun campaigns reminiscent of the Cultural Revolution.

Proceedings for bribery and corruption, particularly concerning the untraceable and inexplicable wealth of party officials, are now discussed publicly. Accusations from the population are followed up, and convictions usually result in prison sentences. In the specialist literature, there is a broad consensus that this cultural shift and the continuous fight against corruption are crucial for the sense of justice and the strong aversion to inequality among the Chinese population—and thus for China's political culture and stability.[16] Since the 2010s, the Chinese leadership has apparently managed to establish an integrated strategy for inequality reduction and anti-corruption, as the critical author Zhang Fan also explains.[17] Since then, a genuine anti-corruption movement has emerged.[18]

This is now being standardized, made transparent, and, above all, transferred into legal proceedings, so that reports from the population do not turn into revenge campaigns against unpopular local politicians, competing companies, or similar targets.

Thus, the Chinese government has declared that the three strands of distribution policy, justice policy, and anti-corruption policy—which have been in their usual experimental phases in recent years—will now be made transparent, standardized, and permanent elements of politics, society, and the judiciary.[19]

Studies such as Transparency International's *Corruption Perceptions Index* attest to the successes of the anti-corruption campaign, with China reaching a level of perceived corruption below the global average for the first time in 2021.[20] In a review of recent scholarship for the 2025 *Routledge Handbook of Anti-Corruption Research and Practice*, Jingyuan Qian and Feng Tang furthermore confirm that "[m]ost scholars agree that Xi's crackdown on corruption, to some extent, has been effective in curbing rent-seeking and graft in the bureaucracy", with the campaign having "yielded better results than most anticorruption efforts in other countries" and having "led to a visible decline in the illegal exchange of favors between politicians and entrepreneurs".[21]

As a result of the campaign, studies attest to "improved firm performance, [...] more efficient allocation of corporate resources, and reduced operational costs for private enterprises", as well as an increase in investment into research and development (R&D) activities due to decreased spending on political connections. Among potential negative factors, Qian and Tang note a possible impact on growth and GDP, as the new strict rules make local officials more cautious and reluctant to make public investments and disincentivize them from informal practices that might promote economic growth. They emphasize, however, that it is still too early to assess the long-term socioeconomic impacts of the campaign.[22] This may also indicate that initial caution under the new rules and regulations could settle over time, contributing to a more reliable, sustainable, and credible culture of public investment.

"Credible China" and Local "Social Credit"-Experiments

Since the period of "reform and opening-up" that began in 1978, the Chinese population, as already described, has been confronted with comprehensive and massive structural changes, general deregulation, enormous migration movements, and the associated social and spatial uprooting. As a result of these societal turbulences, the level of trust within the Chinese population has also declined since the mid-1980s.[23] The socially negative moral and behavioral effects of an almost 25-year period of deregulation had to be rebalanced in order not to endanger the national development path.

Redistribution and social compensation policies, reform of the Hukou system, the introduction of social insurance, as well as the rule of law and anti-corruption policies, were then massively developed in an integrated manner starting in the mid-2000s—and finally, from 2012 onwards, on an even larger scale. In recent years, these various initiatives have been summarized under the national development goal of "Credible China".

The level of trust in China was once again severely shaken by the well-known baby milk (melamine) scandal of 2008, in which six infants died from contaminated baby formula and hundreds suffered serious health damage. The scandal had a lasting impact on the Chinese people's sense of mistrust and continued to resonate in the collective consciousness and public discourse even ten years after the event.[24] At the end of 2018, a death following a rabies vaccination again caused public outrage.[25] Since then, the pharmaceutical industry has come under particularly close public scrutiny and has been politically committed to a "Credible China" in its production, with several severe crackdowns on corruption in the sector in recent years.[26]

In all these cases of consumer harm, the public investigations were immediate, effective, and transparent. The penalties imposed on leading managers—some of whom had even deliberately put inferior products into circulation (as in the melamine case)—were severe, exceeding even the public's expectations. This was also perceived as a success of "online democracy", that is, the intensive participation of citizens in discussions on online forums and social networks.[27]

"Credere": "Believe", "Trust", and "Trustworthiness"

The measures around "Credible China" consciously encompass the various dimensions and conceptual relationships of trust and trustworthiness. The Latin word *credere* simply means "to believe" but also carries an interpersonal dimension—in this sense, it means trust. *Credibilis* means "believable" and "trustworthy", or, in other words, credible. Following this semantic line, we eventually arrive at the more mundane notion of financial credit, often singled out in the West as the specter of "credit denial".[28]

Importantly, in Chinese, the word used for "credit", also in the financial sense, is 信用 (xìn yòng), which directly translates as "trust". Further below, we will return to this topic in the context of the broader behavioral incentives of the new experimental "social credit" point systems.

In terms of creditworthiness in the narrower sense, capitalist countries such as Germany have the so-called "credit rating", colloquially known as *Schufa*, named after the well-known German credit bureau. If one fails to obtain an apartment or a job, this may, in fact, be due to one's rating at the German "Schufa". At least now, rating data held by banks and insurance companies have become accessible.

In the West, individuals are not only "rated" in their Schufa file but also through police-issued certificates of conduct or criminal records, at their banks, and on platforms such as eBay, Amazon, or PayPal—as buyers or sellers—and even ranked in exam results and work certificates. Evaluations and rankings are ubiquitous, and some have existential importance. Everyone and everything is also "rated" for creditworthiness by the US "Big Three" or "three sisters", the rating agencies Standard & Poor's (S&P), Moody's, and Fitch—affecting companies and public bodies, sometimes with worldwide consequences.

Those who fall through certain private grids may also find themselves excluded by Facebook, Google, X (formerly Twitter), YouTube & Co., or even by email providers—recently through privately administered "upload filters"—without knowing what rule was violated or which communication was deemed "politically incorrect". Rankings and social point systems are therefore "depoliticized" and privatized in the West, outsourced to private internet oligopolies. Thus, IT corporations already shape behavioral and communicative norms today, often without our awareness.

After all, income and wealth inequalities represent the all-dominating—albeit underground, that is, untransparent and "privatized"—social credit systems of capitalism.[29] To what extent differences from China can already be identified in this regard would, however, require closer examination.

The fact that large IT corporations can easily block internet accounts for tens of thousands of people is becoming an increasingly visible reality of this global, privatized censorship regime. This is especially true when expressions of opinion fail to conform to the respective Washington geostrategy and its appendages such as Facebook, Google, X (Twitter), or YouTube. Such instances have, for example, been observed again recently in Cuba, Venezuela, or Hong Kong.[30] Likewise, Twitter (now X) has in the past collaborated with military propaganda units.[31]

Even in the West, a growing body of research in economics and the social sciences now recognizes that individual behavior must be brought into greater harmony with social and ecological goals if we do not wish to watch the world around us collapse. We have already mentioned examples of behavioral economists who call this process "learning new preferences". The approaches of the somewhat euphemistically termed "nudging"—psychological behavior control systems—were even awarded a Nobel Prize in economics a few years ago.[32] The concept of behavior control systems is now regarded as an "internationally established policy concept"[33] and is anything but a Chinese invention.

China, of course, approaches these issues in its own way, which, as we have already seen several times, fundamentally means multiple, localized, parallel processes, all initially experimental, time-limited, and accompanied by intensive public discussion on social networks, as we will report in more detail on the social credit systems below.

Two differences between the "Western" and "Eastern" systems of behavioral control are immediately noticeable. First, the Western concept of nudging is a technocratic instrument of government or agencies, often outsourced to private IT corporations, that is, privatized, while ideally the user should not notice it. This has the "advantage" of minimal public discussion but the obvious disadvantage of potential manipulative misuse.

The Chinese "social credit" point system, by contrast, consists of numerous, sometimes very different, local experimental approaches operating in parallel. A recent experimental system in Shanghai, for example, called "Honest Shanghai", focused on highly differentiated waste separation systems. Other systems concentrate, for example, on participation in local tree planting actions.

There was always scientific and public discussion about the different criteria, and, of course, some fundamental disputes:

- Which behaviors are socially and ecologically relevant and should be considered?
- What point values should be assigned to each behavior?
- Should only positive aspects (point gains) be rated, or should negative aspects (point losses) also be included?
- Where should thresholds for qualitative assessments, such as "high", "medium", or "low" creditworthiness, be set?
- Should sanctions be imposed? If so, when and of what type?

The comprehensive yet experimental nature of the Chinese approach can sometimes lead to overshooting the mark in individual cases. Controls within specific municipal or regional programs may go too far, as may the sanctions applied. Western media often focus exclusively on this aspect. However, we will address the overall picture of the so-called "social credit systems" and their potential for full implementation, if at all, further below.

How Much Censored Is the Chinese Internet?

Yes, the Chinese internet is regulated and censored, as are practically all networks worldwide, whether publicly or secretly controlled by IT corporations (see above).[34] The regulation and censorship of the Chinese internet are based on its *Cybersecurity Law*, which commenced in 2017, and the *Data Security Law*, which commenced in 2021. Article 12 of the Cybersecurity Law outlines the categories by which online content can be subject to regulation or censorship:

> Any person and organization using networks shall abide by the Constitution and laws, observe public order, and respect social morality; they must not endanger cybersecurity, and must not use the Internet to engage in activities endangering national security, national honor, and national interests; they must not incite subversion of national sovereignty, overturn the socialist system, incite separatism, break national unity, advocate terrorism or extremism, advocate ethnic hatred and ethnic discrimination, disseminate violent, obscene, or sexual information, create or disseminate false information to disrupt the economic or social order, or information that infringes on the reputation, privacy, intellectual property or other lawful rights and interests of others, and other such acts.[35]

Google, Facebook (now Meta), and other companies that do not wish to implement these restrictions in China—and probably could not—and that do not want to distance themselves from political interventions by Washington—or could not—are therefore blocked by the Chinese "Great Firewall" or "Great Cyber Wall". Western media outlets quickly interpret this as proof of censorship and dictatorship, which, according to the ideological warfare narrative, exists only in China.[36] The fact that Chinese people are, on average, better informed about "us" than "our" average citizen is about China has never prompted any of our opinion and "value" journalists to reflect.

The debate about degrees of freedom, regulations, and their criteria is probably nowhere as broad, qualified, and differentiated as in China itself. Opinions, discussions, and trends on social media are closely monitored: "evaluated", according to the literature,[37] and "censored", according to Western media. For example, in debates about Chinese live-streaming and internet ethics,[38] questions arise such as: Should teenage girls be allowed to pursue the maximization of their follower count as live-streamers and influencers, potentially posting sexist content? The risk of moral and proportional derailments, particularly after the experiences of the Cultural Revolution and the relatively unrestrained deregulation of the "reform and opening-up" period, seemed especially high in China.[39] In response to growing concerns about excessive social media use and online gaming addiction among children, China has thus recently strengthened regulations, including plans to limit daily usage for minors.[40]

Nationwide in China, so-called upload filters are also being implemented to identify unwanted content. Within the framework of a clear and serious moral and behavioral "re-cultivation" in China, there is indeed room for playful interactions between internet regulators and users. In the Chinese syllabary, for example, some regulations and deletions of linguistic transgressions—such as sexism, foul language, hate speech, or "shitstorms", which we in the West have already become accustomed to[41]—can be circumvented. It is often sufficient to replace certain forbidden words with similar-sounding syllables to bypass the filter. For instance, the forbidden phrase "Cào Nǐ Mā" (肏你妈), in English "F*** Your Mother", can become the "Grass-Mud-Horse" (草泥马 – Cǎo Ní Mǎ) when alternative but similar sounding Chinese characters are used. Circumventions of this kind have now become a kind of sport for young internet users and are tolerated within certain limits. However, severe penalties have been imposed when similar "jokes" were made in connection with rape or pornography.

Pornography, violence, harassment, and hate of all kinds are unlikely to be removed from a "free" internet in the West for the foreseeable future. On the contrary, it appears that the cultivation of a culture of hate, war, and violence online is gradually seeping into Western everyday culture and politics, potentially undermining what we have understood as liberalism and democracy. Let us set aside, for now, the question of whether our plutocratic and crisis-ridden neoliberal social system requires and promotes such excesses as a means of consolidating power, and whether parts of the elite, in light of the perceived decline of the West, are turning toward a more violence-oriented and ultra-right-wing system variant both domestically and internationally, as some observers claim.[42]

China, for its part, is treading uncharted territory on its national path of independence, including in "internet governance". It addresses these challenges, unlike the West—which apparently struggles to manage the growing culture of online hate and the worrying trends of social media addiction—with demonstrably positive results in everyday culture and behavior. As in all policy areas, China approaches this inductively, experimentally, pragmatically, result-oriented, and always provisionally. Some Western observers have therefore noted:

> Social values and consumerism are being negotiated and contested online. [...] Confluence of Big Data and online discourse is moving China's negotiation of social values, and hence also of CnSR [consumer social responsibility] and corporations' management of their social responsibilities (CSR), into an evolving online society.[43]

In Chinese society and politics, internet regulations and censorship are also constantly "up for review" in terms of further development. This review includes, above all, the risks of abuse, opportunism, and the restriction of political freedom of speech. The discussion process surrounding these issues is, by the way, unparalleled in both quality and intensity. Participation rates on social media, the involvement of users in the development of digital products, and the critical comments and suggestions from the public on draft laws speak for themselves.[44]

Cyber Space: Western Political Censorship to Be Executed By Big Tech … Versus a Future Mature Democracy

As we have shown above, China already provides an enormous infrastructure of data, analysis, and control, enabling a leap toward a developed and conscious online society of the future. It boasts extraordinary social and technical scientific analysis capabilities, supported by hundreds of thousands of scientists across national, regional, and local institutes and universities. In this way, the country not only manages to hold together a fifth of humanity within a highly complex, multicultural society, but it also organizes forward-looking structural change of unparalleled breadth, depth, and speed.

The fact that the latest technologies for data collection and analysis—including devices of all kinds (the IoT)—can also be used to observe, control, manipulate, or suppress individuals is obvious, and this applies globally, as all leading countries possess these technologies. Technologically, China can initially do no more than what all developed industrial countries are already capable of and are currently implementing. However, in China, public financial resources and organizational capabilities are also available to apply and test these technologies *comprehensively*. These capacities are no longer financially or organizationally available in neoliberal, financialized capitalism at the state and public level and are therefore transferred to private high-tech corporations and IT oligopolists. The perception that cybertechnology is used less intensively in the West seems primarily due to lower public investment capacity, and by no means to higher democratic insight or restraint.

The Chinese big data/AI/cyber/IoT complex, like its Western counterpart, will certainly continue to grow in political and practical management importance. The transitions to abuse, censorship, and suppression will always be fluid and visible—both in the West and in China. Such transitions can never be decided purely on technical grounds, either here or there. China develops and implements technological innovations quickly and comprehensively, often faster and more extensively than the West, but always with the possibility of correction, accompanied by intensive political discourse conducted in politics, science, and social media.

This leads to the principle by which humanity can succeed in controlling the dangers of the new big data/AI/cyber/IoT world while simultaneously exploiting its practical technical possibilities: a future democracy must decide and measure the extent to which society can distinguish the useful from the harmful effects of technology. Above all, it must decide democratically when and to what extent, for ethical reasons, we refrain from implementing something that is technically possible.

Contrary to common portrayals or perceptions, China does not necessarily offer worse conditions than the West for navigating this path into the future—a path all developed industrial countries must traverse—in terms of transparency, discussion, experimental character, control, and adaptability.

Once Again: Social "Nudging" and Social Credit Points: West Good, China Bad?

This brings us again to the small number of local experiments with the Chinese "Social Credit System(s)", or shèhuì xìnyòng tǐxì (社会信用体系) in Chinese, composed of the characters for *society*, *trust/credit* (as mentioned above), and *system*. In the West, social credit systems are often reflexively condemned as instruments of dictatorship, rather than being examined in terms of the associated challenges and opportunities for managing social and ecological behavior—issues that all countries face but which are largely taboo in Western discourse.

In China, various approaches to addressing corruption and low trust in society, the business sector, and government have been under discussion since the negative side effects of deregulation following the "reform and opening-up" period became increasingly visible in the late 1980s and early 1990s. It was partly out of these discussions that the first concepts of a "social credit system"—designed to address corruption and low trust across these three domains—emerged in the early 2000s.

Even several Western media outlets have, in recent years, recognized that their coverage of the Chinese social credit system has been distorted.[45] This distortion is often based on superficial observation, if any, and a lack of contextualization. One observer has even called it "one of the most misunderstood things about China".[46] Here are some of the most important and surprising facts about the envisioned Chinese credit point system:

- There is not a *single* credit point system in China, but rather a multitude of local experimental systems. The central government approved only a framework document in 2014, calling on decentralized state levels to develop and test behavior control systems aimed at combating corruption and financial crime, increasing financial trustworthiness, and promoting socially compatible and ecologically responsible behaviors. There are no central regulations. A standard was originally planned for introduction in 2020; however, this had still not been implemented, in part due to ongoing discussions within China and the challenges posed by the Covid-19 pandemic. The Chinese experimental political philosophy of "one country, 1000 systems" also applies in this context, although, for now, only a few local and regional systems exist.

- China's 13th Five-Year Plan (2016–2020) operationalized criteria for socially responsible behavior on the internet. However, in implementing these criteria within local and regional credit point systems, the plan increasingly relied on small networks to prioritize mechanisms of self-regulation among internet producers and consumers. The 14th FYP (2021–2025) mentions the social credit system only briefly, describing it as a "sound system of credit-related laws, regulations, and standards",[47] which may signal a potential reevaluation, a gradual phasing out, or at least a reduction in the relevance of the project.
- The systems have not been primarily aimed at private individuals, but rather at politics, authorities and governments, companies (the "Corporate Social Credit System" or CSCS, which accounts for the majority of all credit scores), banks, and the judicial and scientific sectors, with natural persons addressed only subsequently. They are therefore clearly associated with anti-corruption policy (politics, authorities, companies), legal policy (judiciary), policies aimed at improving working and environmental conditions (companies), and the banking and financial system (ratings and creditworthiness, including the behavior of lenders). Overall, they support the broader policy of a "Credible China".[48]
- The systems have generally been designed transparently and discussed publicly regarding their various goals and quality features, particularly concerning the reliability of the databases, the validity of the indicators used, the criteria incorporated into the systems, the weights assigned to these criteria, the threshold values for specific ratings, and the sanctions associated with certain thresholds (see above).[49]

  One could also put it this way:

> The Chinese – in contrast [...] to the commercial-intelligence spying and exploitation proliferation at CIA or Facebook – know about the data collection and can view their rating.[50]

- There has never been, and simply is not, a single score for every person that is used to monitor individual behavior, dictate one's place in society, or punish individuals (for example, through blacklisting) if the score is low. Only a few localized experiments with individualized rating systems have existed, and these were used solely for positive,

incentive-driven, encouragement-only "loyalty rewards programs" with voluntary participation. Behavior outside violations of laws and regulations cannot serve as grounds for punishment and is not continuously monitored—for example, excessive video game playing.[51]
- The social credit system was and remains largely human-driven rather than AI-driven, relying primarily on analog input. In fact, the Chinese government pledged to ban the use of AI for social scoring by endorsing the 2021 UNESCO plan on principles for the ethical use of AI.[52]

Indeed, even in Western media, socially compatible point criteria are occasionally mentioned. For example, besides the so-called "penalties for the wealthy" (depending on the details), criteria such as "helping to plant trees" or "regular visits by adult children to their parents"[53] are sometimes cited. Occasionally, Western media reports even state:

> Villager and farmer Mu Linming [...] the 62-year-old with the inviting smile invites us into his house, offering his visitors apples and peanuts. 'Our village has always been good,' says the former construction worker. 'But after the introduction of the system, it has become even better.'[54]

Or a 32-year-old entrepreneur:

> [...] I have the feeling that people's behavior has improved in the last half year.[55]

To conclude, the Social Credit System, although under development for nearly two decades, is far from complete and may not be fully established for another decade, if at all,[56] as recent developments suggest a possible downgrade of its general priority or even a gradual phasing out. Above all, it has been one of several attempts to systematically address the negative societal, governmental, and economic side effects of the deregulation period—such as low societal trust, corruption, and lack of compliance with market regulations—rather than a tool for mass surveillance or punishment. Throughout its development, it has been continually reevaluated, sometimes harshly criticized, and subsequently adjusted, with certain elements abolished when necessary, reflecting the Chinese experimental approach of "letting go" and "reining in", as described in numerous other instances. In fact, a 2018 opinion study from the Free University of Berlin revealed that, at the time of the survey, the social credit system enjoyed "very high levels of approval" among broad sections of society, particularly among higher-income and highly educated respondents.[57]

In many ways, the initial Western response to the Chinese "social credit system" reflects a broader contemporary attitude toward China as a whole. As a coping mechanism for their own failures and shortcomings, China is often treated as a psychological projection screen, constructing China, the Chinese, and anything originating from China as an "Other" that is inherently "bad". This positioning allows the observer to present themselves as "good", while projecting their own traits, failures, or concepts—such as credit scores and mass digital or AI surveillance—that originated in the West onto this "Other". In many ways, as in so many other cases, "every accusation is another confession".

Nothing is more telling than Western internet users' misinformed responses to the social credit system, which sometimes take the form of harmless but occasionally also borderline racist "memes". For example, a common meme shows "+15 social credit" alongside a caricatured, racially charged image of a Chinese person, mocking a version of the social credit system that the creators themselves have simply made up.[58] This narrative and widespread Western misunderstanding of the system have, in turn, been mocked by Chinese internet users, as Sinologist Manya Koetse translated from Weibo on Twitter (X):

> Weibo post that's nearing 70,000 likes: "There's this online rumor which some foreigners believe, that China operates this system of "credit points" similar to Sesame Credit and that everyone's closely monitored. If you behave badly, points will be deducted, and if your score's too low, you'll be locked up, and that these "credit points" can be transferred to each other […]." And quoting another user who mockingly imagines this made-up credit score: "-278 points: "to be executed immediately"[59]

This provides further evidence for the point made above: the average person in China is better informed about the West than the average person in the West is about China.

Notes

1. See for example: Xian Li, Fuming Wei, "What Confucian Eco-Ethics Can Teach Us about Solving the Dilemma of Interpreting the Concept of Sustainability", *Religions*, 2023, Vol. 14, No. 9, 1216.

2. Detailed for example: ZHANG Fan, *The Institutional Evolution of China*, 2018, p. 243 ff.
3. Li Keqiang, "Chinese Premier Li Keqiang's speech at Davos 2015", *World Economic Forum*, January 23, 2015: https://www.weforum.org/agenda/2015/01/chinese-premier-li-keqiangs-speech-at-davos-2015/, visited September 10, 2024.
4. Xiaohan Yi, Nick Chiarelli, "Global predictions for 2024: Optimism is on the rise as more think next year will be better", *Ipsos*, December 18, 2023: https://www.ipsos.com/en-ch/ipsos-global-predictions-2024, visited September 13, 2024.
5. "Chinese most optimistic climate change is reversible", *European Investment Bank*, June 26, 2020: https://www.eib.org/en/infographics/2nd-climate-survey-chinese-climate-change-reversible, visited September 13, 2024. The study also finds that, regarding the impact of individual actions on climate change, 72 percent of Chinese believe they make a difference, compared to 69 percent of Europeans and 65 percent in the US. Furthermore, in its 2023 climate study, the EIB found that 94 percent of Chinese were in favor of "eliminating subsidies and tax breaks for the aviation sector and industries that rely heavily on fossil fuels", compared to 74 percent in the EU and 78 percent in the US. Most notably, 74 percent of Chinese agreed that their country should compensate developing nations for the impact of climate change, compared to only 63 percent in the US and 60 percent in the EU. Additionally, 90 percent of surveyed Chinese "would be willing to pay higher income taxes to help lower-income households cope with the costs of the green transition", compared to 67 percent in the US and 59 percent in the EU. See: "People in major industrialised nations support compensating low-income countries affected by climate change", *European Investment Bank*, September 2023: https://www.eib.org/en/surveys/climate-survey/6th-climate-survey/world, visited September 13, 2024.
6. Of the ten predominantly Sunni Muslim ethnic minority groups in China, the Hui constitute the largest one at approximately 11 million, alongside the Uyghurs, who also stand at over 11 million. See for example: "List of ethnic groups in China", *Wikipedia*: https://en.wikipedia.org/wiki/List_of_ethnic_groups_in_China, visited September 13, 2024.
7. For an introduction, see for example: Emily Mark, "Emperor Taizong of Tang", *World History Encyclopedia*, March 9, 2016: https://www.worldhistory.org/Emperor_Taizong_of_Tang/, visited September 13, 2024.
8. Barbara Demick, "Tibetan-Muslim tensions roil China", *Los Angeles Times*, June 23, 2008: https://www. latimes.com/archives/la-xpm-2008-jun-23-fg-muslims23-story.html, visited September 13, 2024.

9. Associated Press, "Bomb at Government Offices Wounds 5 in Tibetan Capital", *The New York Times,* December 30, 1996: https://www.nytimes.com/1996/12/30/world/bomb-at-government-offices-wounds-5-in-tibetan-capital.html, visited September 13, 2024.
10. "China Sentences 2 Tibetans in April Bombings - 2002-12-05", *Voice of America*, October 29, 2009: https://www.voanews.com/a/a-13-a-2002-12-05-28-china-67258092/379318.html, visited September 13, 2024.
11. On the rising popularity of the irredentist Hindu nationalist vision of *Akhand Bharat*, or "Greater India", which lays claim to all of Afghanistan, Bangladesh, Bhutan, India, Maldives, Myanmar, Nepal, Pakistan, Sri Lanka and Tibet, not only among fringe extremist but increasingly also mainstream nationalist politicians, see for example: Rhea Mogul, "Why a map in India's new Parliament is making its neighbors nervous", *CNN*, June 13, 2023: https://edition.cnn.com/2023/06/13/india/india-akhand-bharat-map-parliament-intl-hnk/index.html, visited September 15, 2024.
12. See for example: "China says Indian troops fired 'provocative' shots in border dispute", *BBC*, September 8, 2020: https://www.bbc.com/news/world-asia-china-54067400, visited September 15, 2024.
13. For example: Zhang, *The Institutional Evolution of China: Government Vs Market,* 2018, p. 221 ff., p. 242 f.
14. Ibid., p. 171 f.; numbers are given by *Merics China Update* 6/2018: In five years (2013–2017), 1.5 million party cadres were punished, of which 440 were in high provincial and ministerial offices.
15. Zhang 2018, p. 213.
16. Ibid., p. 172.
17. Zhang 2018, p.212 f.
18. For example, also: Ruegemer 2018, p. 281 f.
19. Ibid., p. 218–221.
20. "Corruption Perceptions Index 2021", *Transparency International*: https://www.transparency.org/en/cpi/2021, visited September 15, 2024.
21. Jingyuan Qian, Feng Tang, "Tackling Corruption through Top-Down Political Campaigns: Assessing China's Anti-Corruption Crackdown under Xi Jinping", in: *The Routledge Handbook of Anti-Corruption Research and Practice*, edited by Joseph Pozsgai-Alvarez and Roxana Brutu, 2025, pp. 613–628. Also accessible via: https://juan-qian.github.io/Qian_Tang_Chapter.pdf, visited September 15, 2024, quotations from pages 15–16.
22. Ibid.
23. "General trust" in worldwide social and value research, including in China, is understood as, for example, the average number of "yes" responses to

the question "Do you believe you can trust the next person you meet?". The so-called "World Values Survey", supported by the World Bank, collects data on general trust in a standardized and representative way in most countries of the world, particularly because it correlates strongly with a country's economic and social success within the deep structure of socio-economics (for example: S. Dai, W. Elsner, *Declining Trust in Growing China*, 2015). Other institutions, such as the University of Michigan (Ann Arbor, USA), are also building corresponding datasets and analyses on the general level of trust in society.

24. Bloomberg, "China's parents still mistrust country's brands 10 years after lethal milk powder scandal", *South China Morning Post*, January 22, 2019: https://www.scmp.com/news/china/politics/article/2183116/ chinas-parents-still-mistrust-countrys-brands-10-years-after, visited September 21, 2024. It is also known that baby milk powder is a popular import from Germany to China. Chinese tourists in Germany still clear the shelves of baby milk powder and fill their suitcases for the journey home.
25. *China Daily*, October 17, 2018.
26. *China Daily*, July 14/15, 2018, p. 6. And most recently: Amy Hawkins, "China renews crackdown on corruption in healthcare", *The Guardian*, August 17, 2023: https://www.theguardian.com/world/2023/aug/17/china-renews-crackdown-on-corruption-in-healthcare, visited September 21, 2024.
27. Email communication with Prof. Dr. S. Dai on November 13, 2018.
28. Julia Buschmann, "China verwehrt Bürgern mehr als 11 Millionen Flüge – wegen schlechten Benehmens [China denies citizens more than 11 million flights – due to bad behavior]", *Handelsblatt*, May 25, 2018: https://www.handelsblatt.com/politik/international/chinas-sozialpunktesystem-china-verwehrt-buergern-mehr-als-11-millionen-fluege-wegen-schlechten-benehmens-/22602814.html, visited September 22, 2024.
29. For example: Florian Rötzer, "Sozialkreditsysteme im Kapitalismus [Social credit systems in capitalism]", *Telepolis*, August 29, 2019: https://www.telepolis.de/features/Sozialkreditsysteme-im-Kapitalismus-4509017.html, visited September 22, 2024.
30. For example: Sebastian Carlens, "Völkerentzweier des Tages: ›Soziale Netzwerke‹ [Divider of the Day: 'Social Networks']", *junge Welt*, August 24, 2019: https://www.jungewelt.de/loginFailed.php?ref=/ artikel/361429.v%C3%B6lkerentzweier-des-tages-soziale-netzwerke.html, visited September 22, 2024.
31. Archie Hall, Helen Warrell, "Twitter executive is British Army information warfare unit reservist", *Financial Times*, October 1, 2019: https://www.ft.com/content/53017272-e37f-11e9-b112-9624ec9edc59, visited September 22, 2024.

32. The award winners were Richard H. Thaler and Cass R. Sunstein; for example: The same, *Nudge: Improving Decisions About Health, Wealth and Happiness*, London, New Haven, CT: Yale University Press, 2008.
33. Deutsches Institut für Wirtschaftsforschung [German Institute for Economic Research], "Stupsen und Schubsen (Nudging): Ein neues verhaltensbasiertes Regulierungskonzept [Nudging: A New Behavior-Based Regulation Concept]", *Vierteljahrshefte zur Wirtschaftsforschung* [Quarterly Journal of Economic Research], 87(1), 2018.
34. Also for example: Monika Ermert, "China: Viele Regierungen filtern das Netz [China: Many Governments Filter the Net]", *Heise Online*, May 14, 2009: https://www.heise.de/news/China-Viele-Regierungen-filtern-das-Netz-219087.html, visited September 29, 2024. See also: Williamson 2017. Next to censorship by private companies, government censorship is also commonly practiced in the West. Just to name two recent examples: The blocking of online access to Russian state media (such as Russia Today and Sputnik) in the EU since the beginning of the war in Ukraine, which was strongly criticized by the European Federation of Journalists (EFJ), among others. See for example: Dirk Voorhoof, "EU silences Russian state media: a step in the wrong direction", *Columbia University Global Freedom of Expression*, May 9, 2022: https://globalfreedomofexpression.columbia.edu/publications/eu-silences-russian-state-media-a-step-in-the-wrong-direction/, visited October 1, 2024. Second, the "systemic online censorship" of pro-Palestinian voices by Meta (Instagram and Facebook) since October 7, 2023, as uncovered in a report by Human Rights Watch: "Meta's Broken Promises: Systemic Censorship of Palestine Content on Instagram and Facebook", *Human Rights Watch*, December 21, 2023: https://www.hrw.org/report/2023/12/21/metas-broken-promises/systemic-censorship-palestine-content-instagram-and, visited October 1, 2024. Also, pro-Palestinian voices and activism have been actively censored and criminalized by governments in Western countries such as in Germany, online and offline. See for example: Kumars Salehi, "Germany's unprecedented crackdown on pro-Palestinian speech", *The Hill*, December 17, 2023: https://thehill.com/opinion/internation al/4362806-germanys-unprecedented-crackdown-on-pro-palestinian-speech/, visited October 1, 2024. Here, as in many other instances of the West's attitudes towards China, "every accusation is a confession".
35. The full text in English translation is available at: Rogier Creemers, Graham Webster, Paul Triolo, "Translation: Cybersecurity Law of the People's Republic of China (Effective June 1, 2017)", *Digichina*, June 29, 2018: https://digichina.stanford.edu/work/translation-cybersecurity-law-of-the-peoples-republic-of-china-effective-june-1-2017/, visited September 29, 2024.

36. In fact, with its 2017 German Network Enforcement Act (NetzDG), Germany—not China—set a precedent and became an inspiration and model in censorship law for other countries around the world, due to its wide-ranging powers to compel platforms to remove "illegal online speech" under the threat of huge fines. This law and its various drafts, described as a "censorship infrastructure", have been criticized by organizations such as *Reporters Without Borders* and the UN Special Rapporteur on freedom of opinion and expression, who stated that it "violates human rights". See: Alexandra Zerkalo, "UN-Sonderberichterstatter: Netzwerkdurchsetzungsgesetz verstößt gegen Menschenrechte [UN Special Rapporteur: Network Enforcement Act violates human rights]", *Netzpolitik.org*, June 9, 2017: https://netzpolitik.org/2017/un-sonderberichterstatter-netzwerkdurchsetzungsgesetz-verstoesst-gegen-menschenrechte/, visited October 1, 2024. Free-speech expert Jacob Mchangama has thus aptly termed the law "The Digital Berlin Wall" in a detailed report on its global impact. See: Jacob Mchangama, "The Digital Berlin Wall: How Germany (Accidentally) Created a Prototype for Global Online Censorship – Act Two", *Columbia University Global Freedom of Expression*, October 10, 2020: https://globalfreedomofexpression.columbia.edu/publications/the-digital-berlin-wall-how-germany-accidentally-created-a-prototype-for-global-online-censorship-act-two/, visited October 1, 2024.
37. For example: Feng YANG et al., "Internet Governance in China: A Content Analysis", *The Palgrave Handbook of Local Governance in Contemporary China*, Singapore: Palgrave Macmillan Springer Nature, 2019, pp. 441–463.
38. M. Ermert, op. cit., ibid.
39. As also for example: Williamson 2017.
40. See for example: Zen Soo, "China keeping 1 hour daily limit on kids' online games", *Associated Press*, January 20, 2023: https://apnews.com/article/gaming-business-children-00db669defcc8e0ca1fc2dc54120 a0b8, visited September 29, 2024. And: "China proposes to limit children's smartphone time to a maximum of 2 hours a day", *Associated Press*, August 3, 2023: https://apnews.com/article/china-internet-restrictions-children-smartphone-limits-8435b530b117b70357856ddf6a5968d1, visited September 29, 2024.
41. In a most recent example the alarming increase of racist and sexist language as well as misinformation on X (formerly Twitter), since it was acquired by Elon Musk: Zoe Williams, "Racism, misogyny, lies: how did X become so full of hatred? And is it ethical to keep using it?", *The Guardian*, September 5, 2024: https://www.theguardian.com/technology/article/2024/

sep/05/racism-misogyny-lies-how-did-x-become-so-full-of-hatred-and-is-it-ethical-to-keep-using-it, visited September 29, 2024.

42. For example: "Der beginnende Abstieg des Westens [The Beginning Decline of the West]", *German Foreign Policy*, February 11, 2020, about the "Munich Security Report for the Munich Security Conference 2020; online at: https://www.german-foreign-policy.com/news/detail/8183, visited September 29, 2024. On the underlying economic causes of the "decline of the west", see for example: Owen Jones, "Politicians are right about the 'decline of the west' – but so wrong about the causes", *The Guardian*, April 5, 2023: https://www.theguardian.com/commentisfree/2023/apr/05/decline-of-the-west-causes-moral-decay-living-standards, visited September 29, 2024.
43. Williamson 2017.
44. For example: *Merics China Update* 6/2018.
45. For example: Louise Matsakis, "How the West Got China's Social Credit System Wrong", *Wired*, July 29, 2019: https://www.wired.com/story/china-social-credit-score-system/, visited October 4, 2024. And: Vincent Brussee, "China's Social Credit System Is Actually Quite Boring", *Foreign Policy*, September 15, 2021: https://foreignpolicy.com/2021/09/15/china-social-credit-system-authoritarian/, visited October 4, 2024. And: Cindy Yu, "Mythbusting the social credit system", *The Spectator*, June 13, 2022: https://www.spectator. co.uk/podcast/social-credit-system/, visited October 4, 2024. And: Bing Song, "The West May Be Wrong About China's Social Credit System", *Noema*, November 29, 2018: https://www.noemamag.com/the-west-may-be-wrong-about-chinas-social-credit-system/, visited October 4, 2024.
46. Viola Zhou, "People Don't Understand China's Social Credit, and These Memes Are Proof", *Vice*, October 25, 2021: https://www.vice.com/en/article/china-social-credit-meme/, visited October 4, 2024.
47. For example: "Outline of the 14th Five-Year Plan (2021-2025) for National Economic and Social Development and Vision 2035 of the People's Republic of China", *The People's Government of Fujian Province*, March 13, 2021: https://www.fujian.gov.cn/english/news/202108/t20210809_5665713.htm, visited January 11, 2025. See: "IV. Social credit system".
48. On the so-called "Corporate Social Credit System" (CSCS), which has been the largest part of the Social Credit System project, aimed to condition and shape the Chinese market to improve compliancy with regulations, see for example the detailed 2019 report by *Sinolytics* and the European Union Chamber of Commerce in China: "The Digital Hand: How China's Corporate Social Credit System Conditions Market Actors", *Sinolytics* and the *European Union Chamber of Commerce in*

China, 2019: https://www.sinolytics.de/cscs-in-china/, visited October 4, 2024.

49. For example, Williamson 2017.
50. Rügemer 2018, p. 285 (quote translated by the authors).
51. Mercator Institute for China Studies (MERICS), "China's social credit score – untangling myth from reality", *merics.org*, February 11, 2022: https://merics.org/en/comment/chinas-social-credit-score-untangling-myth-reality, visited October 4, 2024.
52. Melissa Heikkilä, "China backs UN pledge to ban (its own) social scoring", *Politico*, November 23, 2021: https://www.politico.eu/article/china-artificial-intelligence-ai-ban-social-scoring-united-nations-unesco-ethical-ai/, visited October 4, 2024, as also cited in Merics, ibid.
53. H. Steltzner, "Chinas Weg zur Weltherrschaft [China's Path to World Domination]", *FAZ*, January 7, 2018; H. H. Ankenbrand, "Ehrgeiz vernetzt Berge [Ambition connects Mountains]", *FAZ*, February 4, 2018; Andreas Landwehr, "China schafft digitales Punktesystem für den ›besseren‹ Menschen [China Creates Digital Point system for the 'better' human]", *Heise Online*, March 1, 2018: https://www.heise.de/news/China-schafft-digitales-Punktesystem-fuer-den-besseren-Menschen-3983746.html, visited October 4, 2024.
54. A. Landwehr, ibid. (quote translated by the authors).
55. Ibid. (quote translated by the authors).
56. Merics, ibid.
57. Genia Kostka, "China's Social Credit Systems and Public Opinion: Explaining High Levels of Approval", *SSRN*, July 23, 2018, p. 23: https://ssrn.com/abstract=3215138, visited Nov. 5, 2025.
58. Viola Zhou, "People Don't Understand China's Social Credit, and These Memes Are Proof", *Vice*, October 25, 2021: https://www.vice.com/en/article/china-social-credit-meme/ visited October 4, 2024.
59. Manya Koetse on Twitter (now X), November 13, 2020: https://x.com/manyapan/status/1327208138660077569?s=20&t=ouhprNpUl6vMhPWtQ0johw visited October 4, 2024. As found in: Cindy Yu, "Mythbusting the social credit system", *The Spectator*, June 13, 2022: https://www.spectator.co.uk/podcast/social-credit-system/ visited October 4, 2024.

Selected and Recommended Literature

Zhang, Fan. 2018. *The Institutional Evolution of China, Government vs Market*. Cheltenham and Northampton, MA, USA: Edward Elgar.

Further Cited Literature

Rügemer, Werner, 2018. *Die Kapitalisten des 21. Jahrhunderts. Gemeinverständlicher Abriss zum Aufstieg der neuen Finanzakteure* [The capitalists of the 21st century. A general outline of the rise of the new financial players]. Cologne: PapyRossa.

Williamson, Dermot, 2017. China's Online Consumerism: Managing Business, Moral Panic and Regulation. *SSRN*, July 29, 2017, https://papers.ssrn.com/sol3/papers.cfm?abstract_id=3181287. Accessed September 29, 2024.

CHAPTER 13

"A Multiethnic Country? Concentration Camps, Police State, Genocide!"

China's Nationalities and Minorities, Self-Governed, Multicultural, and Multi-Religious: Free Traveling Through Tibet or Xinjiang—and the Political Struggles Within and Around Taiwan and Hong Kong

56 Ethnic Groups, of Which 55 Are Minorities: Autonomous Peoples' Self-Governance and Chinese Population Policy

Much of the territory that is today known as the People's Republic of China has, at various times, been part of a unified political entity (empire or kingdom) of continental size during the last two to three thousand years. It has established and maintained a high level of cultivation, population subsistence, and infrastructure, including thousands of kilometers of canals and a continental water management system, and it has created a unified and centralized state under leading philosophies and traditions of governance and statecraft, such as Confucianism. Naturally, the country also harbors a high degree of ethnic diversity—more than Europe, for example. Without a long history as a unified political entity and, today, a clear and strategic national development policy, including a prudent active

W. Elsner, E. Najmehchi, *The Rise of China*,
https://doi.org/10.1007/978-3-032-20260-4_13

ethnic and minority policy, it would probably have long since disintegrated into dozens of small states and perhaps hundreds of warring "warlordships", as are common in peripheral, resource-supplying dominions of the West.

Thus, today China understands itself as a multiethnic and multicultural country, in which members of all ethnicities are considered *Chinese citizens*. The equation and conflation of the majority Han population with the term "Chinese" (often reproduced by people in the West) reflects a practice of "othering" of the non-Han population that stems from Han chauvinism and an ideology of ethnic supremacy, which the CPC officially opposes in the PRC constitution.[1] This ethnically *inclusive* understanding of the nation-state—uniting all the different ethnicities equally under the umbrella of the Chinese nation—has been described as the "Plurality and Unity in the Configuration of the Chinese People" by China's most famous anthropologist, Fei Xiaotong (1910–2005).[2]

China today consists of a total of 56 *officially recognized* ethnic groups, of which the so-called Han Chinese are by far the largest, not only in China but also globally, making up more than 90 percent of the population (over 1.2 billion). It is important to note, however, that among the Han there are numerous sub-groups, such as the Hakka, who alone have a population of about 80 million. All of the other 55 ethnic groups are correspondingly much smaller; some are among the smallest peoples or local communities, often living on the edges of Chinese territory. They are recognized as minorities and thus have an international legal status, which is associated with the guarantee of certain rights and privileges, such as education and language promotion. In China, many of the largest of these groups live in autonomous provinces or, if locally limited, in autonomous prefectures with special rights of self-administration (for example, the *Yanbian Korean Autonomous Prefecture* of the Korean minority in northeastern China).

Among the larger and internationally better-known minorities are, for example, the Manchu (满族 Mǎnzú in Chinese) in the northeast, numbering around ten million people, who from 1644 to the bourgeois revolution in 1911/12 (founding of the Republic) even ruled all of China under the Qing Dynasty. In Europe, the Uyghurs are also recently known—about 11 million inhabitants—who are a Turkic ethnic group mostly inhabiting Central Asia in western China, having in the past extended into Siberia and also made significant advances toward the West and East. In China, they are today predominantly Muslim and live, unlike the Manchu, in a so-called autonomous region: the *Xinjiang Uygur Autonomous*

Region. Xīnjiāng (新疆) literally means "new frontier" in Chinese and became the official designation for the region when it was incorporated as a single entity during the Qing dynasty. However, the region itself was already, in parts, an official protectorate of China as early as the Han dynasty (202 BC–220 AD) to secure safe travel over the Silk Road.

Furthermore, about six million Tibetans live in China today, many of whom, but not all, in the autonomous province of Tibet, officially known as the *Xizang Autonomous Region* or *Tibet Autonomous Region* (although other smaller ethnicities also live in Tibet). Xīzàng (西藏) is the Chinese name for Tibet, literally meaning "Western Zang", with Zang being a loanword from Tibetan that designates a part of the Tibetan plateau. In Tibetan, Tibet is known as Bod (བོད་), simply the name of the region, which has historically been pronounced as Tubo (吐蕃) in Chinese. The English word "Tibet" may also derive from this, though the etymology is not yet fully clarified and might alternatively stem from Old Turkic. The region of Tibet has historically been part of different political entities, including a Tibetan empire in the 7th to 9th centuries CE, and it has intermittently fallen under Chinese rule throughout the centuries, until it finally became a protectorate of Qing China in the eighteenth century. The main religion is Tibetan Buddhism (since the eighth century CE), although a considerable number of practitioners of the ancient indigenous Tibetan animist and shamanic religion Bon (or Bön) also exist, as well as syncretic traditions in which Buddhist and Bon practices have partly merged over the centuries.

About six million Mongolians live today in the *Inner Mongolia Autonomous Region*, which is in fact more than in the country of Mongolia itself (3.5 million). Mongolians also have a long and entangled history with China, with either the area of today's Mongolia having been part of the Chinese empire or Mongolians themselves ruling China for nearly one hundred years during the Yuan dynasty (1271–1368 AD), which was established by Kublai Khan. Mongol rule was, in fact, one of considerable development and even religious tolerance, with the Mongols adapting to Chinese styles of governance, reinstating Confucian traditions, and some Mongol emperors even mastering the Chinese language.

In addition, due to the enormous historical migration processes in Central and Northeast Asia, the extensive presence of early nomadic peoples, and the occasionally arbitrary border demarcations known from history, Koreans (1.8 million), Kazakhs (1.5 million), Kyrgyz (190,000), Russians (15,000), Uzbeks (11,000), and Tatars (3500) live in ethnic communities, as do Vietnamese and many other groups, some of which are so small that they can no longer be referred to as recognized minorities. In Taiwan, there are still some small communities of indigenous peoples, as Taiwan was the northwesternmost island once reached by Austronesian seafarers.

Among the lesser-known in the West, but numerically major, ethnic minorities in China are, for example, the Zhuang (19.6 million), Miao (11 million), and Yi (9.8 million), as well as the previously mentioned Muslim Hui (11 million). The reasons for their being less known in the West are multiple; what is observable, however, is that, alongside historical factors, there seems to be at least a correlation between a general lack of interest in the cultures and traditions of peoples and their (perceived) lack of political relevance for international politics from a Western (liberal) perspective.

Many of the recognized ethnic minorities are granted not only relative autonomy of self-administration *officially*, but they have also been favored in terms of population policy; for example, they were all exempt from the one-child policy, so that their population shares would not continue to decline. Furthermore, policies of affirmative action ensure that a certain share of ethnic minorities is present in university admissions, and language policies provide education, promotion, and protection of indigenous languages and scripts. These policies are in part also an acknowledgment that ethnic discrimination is a destabilizing threat, especially given the size of the majority Han ethnicity.

Taiwan: History, Cross-Strait Relations, and the Current Political Divide Within Taiwan

From the Origins of the Taiwan Question to the Current Status Quo

When telling the history of Taiwan, one must not leave out the perspective of its indigenous population, who were the first to settle the island and are little represented in Western discourse about the island today.

The island today known as Taiwan (originally called "Formosa" by Portuguese colonizers) and its surrounding smaller islets were first settled by the indigenous Austronesian population, whose descendants still live there today, around 6500 years ago, with some of them probably also arriving via what is today mainland China. (Taiwan itself was also settled some 25,000 years ago by ethnic groups that no longer exist there today.) There are thus many different smaller indigenous ethnic groups on Taiwan today, many of which have their own languages and cultures (not Sinitic languages, but Austronesian). Today, there are still about 600,000–800,000 indigenous inhabitants, between 2 and 3 percent of the total population. However, many of these groups, especially their languages and culture, are threatened with extinction (10 of around 26 known languages are already extinct, and six are endangered).

Taiwan was long known to mainland China as a trading partner, but major settlement movements of the Han Chinese to the island began in the thirteenth century CE, and then on a larger scale from the 16th to 17th centuries. Western colonial powers such as the Dutch and Spanish also attempted to claim, colonize, or "civilize" the island for themselves, in the face of constant resistance from the local population—Chinese and indigenous alike—many of whom were exploited or killed by the colonialists. Especially the Ming Chinese general Koxinga (Zheng Chenggong, 1624–1662) should be mentioned as a famous Taiwanese (Chinese) anti-colonial resistance figure who repelled the Dutch in 1661. However, the Dutch were later completely expelled from the island, also thanks to the indigenous resistance fighters. Taiwan was then systematically incorporated and settled, particularly under the Qing dynasty, becoming the Qing Empire's official prefecture from 1684. Here too, attempts were made to take the land rights of the Aborigines into consideration, albeit not always successfully.

It is important to note that the indigenous Austronesian peoples (formerly called "Aborigines") were not the only minorities on Taiwan, either historically or today. There are also settlers from different ethnic groups of mainland China, such as the Hakka from Fujian province, and there have often been conflicts between these different ethnic groups, or even uprisings against the Manchu-led Qing government, sometimes in cooperation.

However, today the proportion of the population has shifted, with the indigenous Austronesians making up only a small minority. The reasons for this are multiple. Of course, the "Sinicization" under the Qing is a factor (i.e., cultural assimilation as well as intermarriage), but the fifty-year Japanese colonial period from 1895 to 1945 deserves special mention, as Taiwan was taken by Japan as a colonial possession after the Qing lost the Sino-Japanese War of 1894–1895. The industrialization of the island under the Japanese brought Japonization, land seizure, and exploitation not only of the Han (or other Chinese mainland ethnic groups) but also of the indigenous Austronesians, against whom there was a racist mania for extermination, as they were regarded as a "lower (savage and brutal) race." There were several massacres of indigenous Austronesians, such as the Musha Massacre in 1930, and the forcing of indigenous women into sexual slavery ("comfort women") for Japanese soldiers.

Taiwan then became, after the capitulation of Japan in World War II and the founding of the People's Republic of China in 1949, the retreat for the military forces of the former bourgeois-conservative party, the Kuomintang. This party was founded in 1919 in the then Republic of China. Its right wing took power after the Communist Party gained influence in the 1920s, and from 1927 to 1949, under the well-known leader Chiang Kai-shek, it led the Chinese Civil War against the Communist Party of China, which had also built military forces, the Red Army (which was later reorganized into the People's Liberation Army, PLA). During the Japanese invasion, however, a united front was formed between the KMT and the CPC to fight back the invaders.

The Red Army, under the leadership of Mao Zedong, carried out the famous "Long March" in 1934–35, during which it was pursued by the state army under Generalissimo Chiang and repeatedly encircled. A major part of the Red Army had to cover more than 12,000 kilometers through difficult terrain in 370 days, losing 90 percent of its soldiers. The civil war weakened the Chinese front against the Japanese invasion, and Chiang's army increasingly terrorized its own population. After the victory of the People's Liberation Army in 1949, the forces of the Kuomintang fled to the island of Formosa and established themselves there as the Republic of China (Taiwan), militarily supported by the USA.

Back in Taiwan, the Kuomintang, under the nationalist Chiang Kai-shek, established themselves on the island with a military dictatorship and a reign of terror, known as the "White Terror", which lasted from 1949 to 1991 (the first democratic elections took place in 1996). Many Austronesian indigenous peoples, in addition to (supposed) political opponents, also fell victim, including through systematic discrimination. Since the 1980s, the situation of the indigenous peoples has gradually improved due to political struggles and the lifting of martial law in 1987, but discrimination still exists. Many indigenous activists remain active critics of the Taiwanese government, fighting for land rights and continuing to criticize the Japanese government's nationalist aspirations and Taiwan's collaboration with it. Paradoxically, many indigenous people in Taiwan today see themselves as more aligned with the KMT (Kuomintang) than with the currently ruling DPP (Democratic Progressive Party), from whom they feel—due to complex historical, ethnic, and current political reasons—not treated fairly, neglected, and, in some cases, discriminated against.[3]

Another division and influential factor on the political landscape in Taiwan has been the distinction between *Waishengren* 外省人 ("person of a foreign province"), which refers to those persons or descendants of persons who arrived in Taiwan from mainland China after 1945, following the Japanese surrender and the Kuomintang retreat, and *Benshengren* 本省人 ("person of this province"), which refers to those persons whose ancestral home is Taiwan and whose ancestors settled there before the Japanese colonial period of 1895–1945. These include members of Han subgroups such as Hoklo (the major ethnic group of Taiwan, making up 70–76 percent of the 23.8 million population today, most of whom can also speak their own language, Hokkien, to this day) and Hakka, but the terms do not refer to the Austronesian indigenous peoples of Taiwan. It is estimated that around 1–2 million Waishengren originally migrated to Taiwan from the mainland, but the exact number today is unclear, and the lines have become increasingly blurred after decades of intermarriage. Nevertheless, the distinction, along with the decades-long KMT military rule and the newcomers' dominance of the government, has also been a source of strife, discrimination, and economic inequality throughout Taiwan's modern history.

The People's Republic of China has never recognized Taiwan as a separate country and insists on the "One-China" position, according to which there can be no two "fatherlands". Taiwan is therefore considered part of the People's Republic of China and is to be formally reintegrated sooner or later. The method of national reunification is, for the time being, that of "functional" economic integration, which one day should facilitate political rapprochement.[4] Taiwanese are therefore treated by the People's Republic of China today as Chinese citizens. By receiving a so-called "Mainland Travel Permit", they enjoy significant advantages when entering and staying in mainland China, as it entitles them to stay indefinitely, for any purpose. The *Taipei Times* (Taiwan) wrote in July 2017:

> The government of mainland China cleverly addresses Taiwanese citizens directly, bypassing our government [...] and their strategy is catching on [...].[5]

Taiwanese citizens indeed rarely forego the offered benefits, whether for traveling, family visits, shopping, studying, or doing business.

On the other hand, officially, the Taiwanese government (Taiwan's official name being *Republic of China*, ROC) regarded itself as the sole legitimate government of all of China until 1991, with Taipei initially seen as a temporary capital until the mainland was "liberated" again. Until the *United Nations General Assembly Resolution 2758*, which was passed on October 25, 1971, and admitted the PRC government in Beijing as the only legitimate representative of China at the UN, this government technically represented all of China (although it controlled only Taiwan) at the United Nations. Following the US-China rapprochement initiated by Richard Nixon and Henry Kissinger in 1971–72, the USA formally recognized mainland China over Taiwan in 1979, and many other countries followed suit. As of 2024, only 12 UN member states (mostly smaller island nations) still recognize Taiwan, while 180 recognize mainland China. To become a full UN member state, Taiwan would, however, need to obtain a two-thirds majority vote of all members in the General Assembly.

The Taiwanese Political Split Over "One Country, Two Systems"? Guomindang and Parliamentary Majority in Favor of Peaceful Unification … Vs. US-Leaning DPP State President

Today's political landscape in Taiwan is interesting. The old, formerly right-nationalist and strictly anti-communist party, the Kuomintang (KMT), which had ruled Taiwan for most of the time since 1949, has seemed to increasingly accept the PRC's positions and align itself with the Beijing government. This is due in part to their lasting recognition of a shared Chinese identity, their overall stronger links to the mainland, and their party-political opposition to the Democratic Progressive party (DPP), the second of the two large political parties in parliament, which has increasingly developed a pro-independence stance in recent years (also known as the "One Country on Each Side" position).[6]

This party divide has at times reached almost absurd heights. For example, the then presidential candidate (and now president) of the "progressive" DPP, Lai Ching-te, accused the "conservative" KMT of being "pro-communist" in late 2023, a month before the election.[7] There are several smaller parties across the political spectrum, although most communist parties are routinely suppressed or banned, often due to alleged links to mainland China (even after the end of the "White Terror" in 1991).[8]

It was thus under then-Kuomintang-led Taiwan that the first rapprochement meeting between Taiwanese KMT and mainland CPC officials took place in 1992, resulting in the so-called "1992 Consensus": an agreement that there is "one China". This meeting and its exact contents have at times become points of contention in cross-strait relations (disagreements about what "China" means – Republic or People's Republic of China), as well as in the domestic party politics of Taiwan to this day, with the DPP outright rejecting the consensus, while the KMT, as of 2024, still at least nominally includes it in their platform.

In 2005, the KMT and the CPC agreed on a five-point plan for peaceful development toward a nation, with "full respect" from the CPC for the social system and lifestyle of the "Taiwanese compatriots".[9] Even the former chairman of the Kuomintang visited Chinese government representatives in Beijing for friendly talks in July 2018, as reported by *China Daily* and as corresponding photos clearly showed.[10] In March 2023, Ma Ying-jeou (KMT), whose presidency from 2008 to 2016 can be seen as a high point of friendly cross-strait relations, rapprochement, trade, and investment, became the first former Taiwanese president to visit the mainland since 1949, when he met with government representatives in Shanghai—a visit that was then criticized by members of the opposing, then-ruling DPP.[11]

The newer, neoliberal, and "social democratic", and thus strictly anti-communist Democratic Progressive Party (DPP), which became the ruling party in 2016 (majorities in Taiwan fluctuate strongly), has reacted with intensified anti-PRC politics, and cross-strait relations have largely deteriorated since then.

The Taiwanese population also seems increasingly divided into different conceptions and understandings of their own identity. On the one hand, there is a "Chinese" identity, referring to those who still mainly identify as part of a larger Chinese nation and cultural heritage, or *Huaxia* (华夏), and who might only reject mainland rule due to its current political system, while still believing in and potentially welcoming unification under favorable conditions. On the other hand, there is an increasingly growing number of people who promote a "Taiwanese" identity, which is distinct from the mainland and seeks to establish a new self-understanding and heritage, potentially culminating in a declaration of an independent Taiwan.

This bifurcation of national identity, however, merely demarcates two general overarching tendencies on a sliding scale, which themselves still contain numerous subgroups with different identity-political conceptions that might even contradict each other (which is why they should not be conflated with the Waishengren–Benshengren distinction, although certain correlations exist).[12]

For example, among those favoring independence, there is the more moderate position that still aims to retain a Chinese identity and the current legal status quo of semi-independence, referred to as *Huadu* (華獨—"Chinese independence") and commonly associated with the DPP, and the more radical position of *Taidu* (臺獨—"Taiwanese independence"), which aspires to a full formal declaration of independence from the mainland and the creation of an entirely new, purely "Taiwanese" country.

Everything, therefore, seems to be in motion, although a formal integration of Taiwan into the PRC—even after a longer coexistence period à la Hong Kong—would likely be met with the sharpest reactions from the USA. The USA sees Taiwan as an "unsinkable aircraft carrier"[13] in the so-called "first island chain"[14] of US-friendly territories (including South Korea, Japan, and the Philippines, with the US colony and military base of Guam being in the "second island chain"), which are intended to encircle and contain China to ensure US hegemony in the Asia-Pacific region.

Taiwan and the US-China Chip War: Taiwan Crashed by the DPP's "Big Brother"?

Today, Taiwan is one of the world's largest and most important computer chip (semiconductor) manufacturers, with the *Taiwan Semiconductor Manufacturing Company* (TSMC) accounting for over half of the world's market, which gives it additional geopolitical relevance to both Mainland China and the USA.[15] Therefore, the US and Mainland China are engaged in a competition to build up their own domestic semiconductor industries in order to reduce volatile dependencies and secure supply chains, in what some have called a "chip war".[16] Taiwan is thus in a precarious position, with some arguing that its semiconductor industry acts as a "silicon shield" that prevents US-China War from breaking out over Taiwan, as such a conflict would severely disrupt supply chains. Others argue, however, that this important position actually increases the risk of conflict.[17]

While Trump put the Chinese companies Huawei, ZTE, and the chip-maker SMIC (*Semiconductor Manufacturing International Corporation*) on trade blacklists during his first term, Biden has implemented export controls to cut China off from chips made in the USA.[18] The Biden administration also passed the CHIPS Act ("Creating Helpful Incentives to Produce Semiconductors") in 2022, which authorized around 280 billion USD to subsidize chip manufacturing in the USA. However, especially US deals with TSMC to establish semiconductor production inside the USA have been met with challenges. Plans to build TSMC semiconductor fabrication plants (so-called "fabs") in Arizona have encountered construction costs four to five times higher than in Taiwan and a lack of qualified personnel, which has increased overall manufacturing costs by around 50 percent compared to Taiwan. Furthermore, TSMC's disputes with labor unions and general cultural workplace differences have further impeded progress, with completion deadlines being pushed back repeatedly.[19]

In response, China, the world's largest semiconductor market in terms of consumption,[20] has increased the overseas expansion of its semiconductor business, especially to countries other than the USA, including the purchase of semiconductor equipment and the hiring of international professionals.[21] On the other hand, it has also introduced measures to boost domestic production and has, for example, established a state investment fund of an additional 47.5 billion USD into the industry in 2024 alone (it is already the global leader in "fabs" under construction). It has also introduced prohibitions on the use of US-made chips in government devices and state-owned company devices, as well as export controls on strategic raw materials.[22]

The large-scale, state-funded research and development for semiconductor production has already produced substantial results. A Japanese semiconductor research company revealed in August 2024 that China's current semiconductor technology, by companies such as Huawei and SMIC, is "just three years behind" industry leader TSMC, "showing the limitations of U.S. efforts to stem Beijing's development of cutting-edge chips." In fact, SMIC's 7-nm chip already rivals TSMC's 5-nm chip in terms of performance. Thus, TSMC "faces growing hurdles to stay ahead of Chinese rivals technologically as miniaturizing circuits become increasingly difficult."[23]

In another step toward self-sufficiency in semiconductor production, China has also reported "significant technological breakthroughs" by its state-owned companies, including especially the *Shanghai Micro Electronics*

Equipment Group (SMEE), in the production of its own chip-making deep ultraviolet (DUV) lithography machines. China has mostly depended on the Dutch manufacturer ASML (*Advanced Semiconductor Materials Lithography*), which has been under pressure from the USA to stop supplying China.[24] This development of China's domestic capabilities may therefore have been incentivized and accelerated by US containment measures.

This competition around "semiconductor geopolitics", in which Taiwan and its TSMC play a central role, is therefore likely to intensify under Trump's second term and beyond. Cross-strait tensions (and by extension the political future of Taiwan) are thus closely linked to the China-US competition and the dynamics of semiconductor production capabilities in the context of power relations in this New Cold War, and therefore seem far from over for the foreseeable future.

Hong Kong: From British Colonial Possession to "One Country, Two Systems"

Some who had already been in a fruitful learning process about China in recent years and had become open and interested quickly fell back into old Pavlovian reflexes and long-overcome devaluations, judgments, and condemnations during the Hong Kong events of 2019–2020. They seemed fascinated by the TV images and corresponding narratives of Western media, showing masked and helmeted, stone-, Bengal fire–, and Molotov cocktail–throwing, pepper spray–spraying, slingshot- and crossbow-using, pavement-into-projectiles–turning "freedom and democracy fighters" opposing mainland China. The fact that there were actual hunting scenes targeting mainland Chinese and supposed political opponents was usually reported on far less.[25]

What was going on there, and what has reached our emotions and minds? How does the sudden and by no means merely clandestine enthusiasm of Western media for orgies of violence and destruction carried out by small, well-organized, and well-equipped groups come about—groups whose actions would not be tolerated for a single day in Western countries such as Germany without the deployment of the army?

There is no way around addressing "Hong Kong 2019 onward" in a book about China. After the events have settled and some time has passed, one can at least clearly conclude: no, it was of course not "Tiananmen

2.0", despite the apparent hopes and efforts of certain Western governments and media institutions.

The 2019 protests were initially triggered by a proposed bill that aimed to enable the extradition of criminal fugitives in Hong Kong, including to Taiwan, Mainland China, and Macau, which has since been suspended. The proposal originally responded to the case of a Hong Kong resident who murdered his pregnant girlfriend in Taiwan and then fled back to Hong Kong, with no possibility of extradition due to the absence of a legal framework. However, many in Hong Kong criticized the bill—some claiming they feared it would be used to arrest political dissenters, and others arguing it would be "bad for business".[26] (The bill was also intended to curb financial, tax, and especially corruption offenses leading to capital flight.[27])

However, some observant and reflective contemporaries were unpleasantly struck by the fact that the young fighters for democracy and freedom in Hong Kong took to the streets carrying the old colonial flag of Hong Kong, as well as American flags and signs reading "Trump, free us!" The notion of marching for human rights and democracy under the banners of Boris "Brexit" Johnson and Donald "the Dealer" Trump seemed somewhat skewed even to many Western observers—as if there had ever been democracy and freedom for the ordinary working Chinese under British colonial dictatorship in Hong Kong.

For many ordinary Hong Kongers, a seven-day work week and twelve-hour workdays are still common practice. This also applies to the young bankers and junior managers who were demonstrating for "more freedom", without ever clearly articulating where the shoe really pinches in this city of almost 7.5 million inhabitants.

Not without reason has the American *Heritage Foundation*, a right-wing think tank backed by US corporations, been crowning Hong Kong as the "freest economy in the world" for 25 years.[28] Hong Kong's labor law is among the most employee-unfriendly in the world, leaving ordinary working people effectively in a colonial status reminiscent of the early twentieth century. In contrast, the International Labour Organization (ILO) of the United Nations praises Chinese labor law as one of the most progressive globally (as outlined in this Part, Chapter 9).

Many Hong Kong workers earn just enough to survive in tiny, few-square-meter apartments in a city that is at once one of the most densely populated and the most expensive property markets in the world.[29] The Employment Ordinance provides virtually no employee rights, and the

ILO has repeatedly urged Hong Kong to comply with the internationally binding conventions on collective bargaining—so far, without success.[30]

The city owes its high per capita income largely to the fact that it is also one of the most billionaire-dense cities worldwide. Yet the income share of the bottom 50 percent of the population has fallen over the last 40 years from 18.7 percent to just 11.6 percent, while that of the top 1 percent has risen from 10.7 percent to 16.3 percent. In terms of wealth, the richest 0.001 percent account for over half of the city's total income, making Hong Kong the most economically unequal city in the world by this metric.[31]

For example, the port tycoon and billionaire Li Ka-shing, one of the handful of oligarchs who effectively control Hong Kong's economy, led a campaign against the dockworkers in 2013 aimed at crushing their union. Wages in the sector had not been raised for 15 years. The crane and container bridge operators were prohibited from stopping the machines to go to the toilet during working hours.

Despite their good education and earning prospects, the protesting students and young bankers would probably never be able to afford an apartment under current conditions, nor to start a family. Like many others in Hong Kong, they are deeply frustrated with their financial and social circumstances, and with the overall economic and social outlook of the city.[32] Over the past 25 years, Hong Kong's contribution to China's GDP has fallen from 18 percent to less than three.[33] Meanwhile, increasingly affluent mainland tourists—including young bankers from the booming neighboring metropolis of Shenzhen or from the financial hub of Shanghai—now visit the city in large numbers, seeming somehow to embody a better future ...

Today, Hong Kong is steadily losing its appeal—even for its traditional clientele of Western oligarchs and tax evaders. It is therefore hardly surprising that critical observers of the situation have commented with biting sarcasm on the financial and material support behind the violent protests: "Washington and London are disabling Hong Kong of her West-serving money-laundering capacity."[34] A pragmatic banker remarked similarly: "Hong Kong: how much longer? [...] An end to the conflict is more likely to come with the continued decline of the local economy."[35]

As the so-called "freest economy in the world" located right next to China, Hong Kong has naturally long been a magnet for the mega-rich and for economic and financial criminals. For many years, this included individuals from mainland China, who typically amassed their fortunes through corruption between 1978 and roughly 2012, only to flee to Hong Kong once China began consistently pursuing and punishing corruption, financial crimes, and tax evasion in the 2010s.

These and other influential forces naturally supported the protest movement, as long as it served to maintain the status quo and secure their privileged elite positions. For example, China has accused the US government-funded *National Endowment for Democracy* (NED) of providing extensive funding for the demonstrations since 2014, including USD 310,000 in 2020 alone.[36] Meanwhile, platforms such as Facebook (now Meta), Twitter (now X), Instagram, Google, and others have blocked thousands of accounts of Hong Kong citizens whose expressions of opinion do not align with Western strategies of escalation and violence, as has occurred in Cuba, Venezuela, Bolivia, and occasionally in Western countries.

At the same time, Hong Kong media mogul Jimmy Lai, a British national and associate of former US national security advisor John Bolton, was able to use his tabloids to incite violence, promote destruction, and ostracize dissenters. The provisional climax came with the *Hong Kong Human Rights and Democracy Act*, passed by the US Congress in November 2019. Its economic and financial sanctions—previously requested in private meetings by Jimmy Lai with Mike Pompeo[37]—reflected the familiar pattern of the Trump era's assertion of global dominance, including sanctions, technology boycotts, and other measures.

For the first time, China responded in kind: US warships are no longer permitted to dock in Hong Kong's port, and foreign organizations involved in funding or organizing the demonstrations—including the NED, the party organizations of the Democrats and Republicans, the *National Democratic Institute for International Affairs*, the *International Republican Institute*, *Freedom House*, and *Human Rights Watch*—are now being monitored in their financial transfers.[38]

Eventually, the protesters achieved, in many ways, the exact opposite of their aims with the violent protests. In 2020, the Chinese government passed the *Hong Kong National Security Law* in response to the violence and unrest. This law established new provisions against "subversion, terrorism, separatism, and collusion with foreign forces" to prevent similar outbreaks in the future.[39]

How did we get here? Some background facts: The island of Hong Kong, which had been part of China's historical polities for over 2000 years, was stolen from China by the British Empire through so-called "unfair treaties", which forced the Qing government to cede it to the British after losing the First Opium War (1839–1842). This war was initiated by the British Empire to force the Qing to accept the import of their opium, which was sold to the addicted population, causing mass squalor, in order to rebalance their trade deficit with China, which had arisen from the purchase of luxury goods such as porcelain, silk, and tea (bought in part with silver that had itself been taken from America by European colonizers).

The colony was further expanded in 1898, when the British obtained a 99-year lease for the so-called "New Territories" around Hong Kong Island, which make up about 86 percent of its territory today. During British colonial rule, there were frequent anti-colonial protests by the disenfranchised Chinese population, such as the 1967 pro-CPC Hong Kong riots. Although based on an appropriation in a context of injustice and colonial subjugation, China honored its side of the "treaty" and waited until 1997, when the lease expired and the territory was officially handed back to the PRC. A similar history applies to the neighboring, smaller Macau, which was returned to China from Portuguese colonial rule in 1999 and today has the same legal status as Hong Kong.

The transition phase until full integration into the PRC is set for 50 years, extending until 2047. Until then, Hong Kong holds the status of an autonomous Special Administrative Region of China, with its own constitution, still influenced by its colonial past. China follows the deescalating principle of "One Country, Two Systems", which is practiced in relation to Taiwan, Hong Kong, and Macau, giving these regions time for adjustment and gradual national integration. China is therefore primarily responsible for Hong Kong's external border and territorial integrity and also supplies the region with food, energy, and other necessities. This became evident in August 2019, when China denied entry to two American warships into the port of Hong Kong. (Imagine two Chinese warships attempting to enter the port of New York while, in Washington, Congress is being pelted with Molotov cocktails and George Washington University is occupied and set on fire by students waving Chinese flags, demanding Xi Jinping to liberate the USA …)

It is clear that Hong Kong is apparently "an important battlefield for the declining West in the fight against the new main enemy, the economically successful People's Republic of China",[40] and that the script of the "color revolutions", with street violence and terror against dissenters—à la the "Right Sector" on the Maidan—was being used again.

Thus, ironically, the protests against integration with the mainland have, in many ways, only incentivized and even accelerated the process, with the government in Beijing probably slowly realizing that an abrupt system change in 2047 could become an even more dangerous and destabilizing undertaking. However, other factors work in Mainland China's favor in this process: over the remaining two decades, Shenzhen, Guangzhou, and Shanghai will likely have long since overtaken Hong Kong, while its status as an international financial metropolis continues to fade.[41] The protests and unrest have significantly contributed to capital flight from Hong Kong and to the city's economic decline. At the same time, China is building a financial center directly north of the provincial border, with Shenzhen already serving as an attractive "showcase" of twenty-first-century prosperity socialism compared to the socially and politically early capitalist financial center of Hong Kong. Shanghai and Shenzhen are financial hubs whose capital volume is already larger than that of Hong Kong.[42]

Furthermore, identity links and emotional attachment to mainland China are even stronger in Hong Kong than in Taiwan today. While the independence movement receives much more attention in the Western press, many Hong Kong residents still see themselves as Chinese and do not support independence. A Pew Research survey from 2023, for example, found that "[a]round three-quarters of adults in Hong Kong (74%) express an emotional attachment to China", with 53 percent identifying as "both a Hong Konger and Chinese", 36 percent as "primarily a Hong Konger", and 10 percent as "primarily Chinese".[43] A Reuters poll from December 2019—just a few months after the protests began—found that only 17 percent of Hong Kongers supported independence from China, and only 20 percent said that "China has abused the 'one country, two systems' model to favor Beijing", while the majority (57 percent) nonetheless wanted then-Chief Executive Carrie Lam to resign (she eventually retired in 2022).[44]

Tibet's Former Feudal Buddhism: Extreme Poverty, 95-Percent Illiteracy, and Mass Famine: The Liberation, Dalai Lama, and Mao Zedong ... and the Modern Development

The significance of the Tibet Autonomous Region in China is, of course, one of the perennial topics in Western reporting. The former religious ruler of Tibet's old Buddhist feudal system, the Dalai Lama, has often become a projection screen for widespread Western desires for feudal splendor. In the following section, we will present some facts that are crucial for a historical contextualization, which is often missing or inadequately addressed in certain superficial Western narratives about Tibet.

As already mentioned above, Tibet has been in a close relationship with, or part of, the Chinese empire on and off for many centuries, including during the Yuan dynasty (1271–1368 CE). It was during the Ming dynasty (1368–1644) that, in 1578, the title of *Dalai Lama* for the leader of the "Yellow Hat" or Gelug school of Tibetan Buddhism[45] was created by the Mongolian leader and high official (tributary) of Ming China, Altan Khan (1507–1582). "Dalai" is the Mongolic word for "ocean", while "Lama" is Tibetan for "master", making "Dalai Lama" roughly translate as "ocean of wisdom". With the bestowal of the title, Altan Khan, who was interested in bringing Buddhism to Mongolia, created ties with Tibet, to which the Emperor of China then gave his seal of authority. This Mongol endorsement ultimately established the Dalai Lama line, with its system of constant reincarnations and its theocratic claim of rule over Tibet under the supremacy of the Yellow Hat (Gelug) school.

As one might already suspect, the supremacy of the Gelug school also meant the suppression of other rival schools at various times in Tibetan history, including forced conversions of their monasteries. These inter-Tibetan conflicts and tensions caused by the Gelug claim to supremacy persist in part to this day. Some Tibetans, including those in exile who belong to other schools, view the current Dalai Lama's role as a global leader of Buddhism as highly problematic, as it implies a continuation and endorsement of the old Gelug claim to supremacy and rule over Tibet. According to some Buddhist observers, the Western Orientalized and distorted framing of the Dalai Lama as a global leader of Buddhism, and the resulting implicit conflation of all Tibetan Buddhism with the Gelug school, in fact contributes to the suppression of other Buddhist schools and may impede a genuinely progressive development of Tibetan society.[46]

With Gelug supremacy established, and although under nominal Ming rule, Tibet was then ruled de facto independently by the Dalai Lamas until coming under Chinese rule again during the Qing dynasty in 1720, when the Qing army drove out the forces of the Dzungar Khanate that were occupying Tibet. Since then, Tibet has been administered semi-autonomously under the Dalai Lamas, with oversight from the Qing government.

It was thus after the colonial subjugation of China in the nineteenth century that, through the influence of the British Empire, Tibet was once again fully separated from China. The British, who ruled India and were engaged in an imperial competition with Russia in the so-called "Great Game", were naturally interested in Tibet, north of India, from a geostrategic and imperial perspective. Despite Russian assurances that they were not interested in Tibet, the British saw a weak and disintegrated Qing government that was unable to maintain control over the region. Their imperial ambitions culminated in the *British expedition to Tibet* from 1903 to 1904. This expedition was effectively an invasion, incorporating parts of southern Tibet into the British Empire and massacring thousands of Tibetans in the process. After storming the capital, the British forced the *Convention of Lhasa* (1904) on Tibet without Chinese consent. This treaty followed the typical imperialist design of "unfair treaties", including land concessions, indemnity payments, full trade access, and denial of political sovereignty. However, the later 1906 *Anglo-Chinese Convention* with the weakened Qing government, although confirming the previous provisions, promised that Britain would not annex or interfere with Tibet, while China promised to prevent other countries from interfering. In reality, while Tibet was effectively isolated from other countries, the British maintained significant influence there through diplomats, trade representatives, and a permanent mission, continuing until 1950, when China finally regained full control over Tibet.

For Britain, the expedition was simply another step in the disassembly, fragmentation, and physical, economic, social, and moral devastation of China. After the Qing government fell in 1912, the fragmented China of the warlord era, Japanese invasion, and civil war was preoccupied with other matters and unable to exert any authority over Tibet, although it still maintained its de jure claim. Upon returning to Tibet, the 13th Dalai Lama declared Tibet independent from the weakened and fragmented China following the 1911 revolution, in 1913. Only a year later, in 1914, Tibet signed the *Simla Convention* with the British, which recognized China's *suzerainty* over Tibet but not full *sovereignty*, and effectively defined Tibet's borders as envisioned by the British—including the so-called "McMahon Line", which delineated the border between British India and Tibet. The Chinese government objected to the treaty and denounced it as illegal, prompting Britain to disregard China and sign a bilateral treaty with Tibet.[47] This position—that China did not have sovereignty over Tibet—was maintained by Britain until 2008.[48]

All the way until after the communists reclaimed it in 1951, Tibet was a class-based feudal society under the theocratic Buddhist rule of the Dalai Lamas. A small oligarchic caste of leading Lamas, together with a small caste of large landowners, dominated a system that made Tibet one of the poorest regions in the world, while enormous gold treasures were accumulated at the seat of the Dalai. This system included slavery and serfdom, widespread poverty and hunger, an illiteracy rate of 95 percent (and almost 100 percent outside the theocracy), the near-total absence of medical care—turning even minor diseases into deadly threats—as well as regular child abductions for the recruitment of new monks. While the 13th Dalai Lama (1876–1933) introduced several reforms and improvements in living standards, much of this social structure, including slavery, remained in place until the 1950s.

The current 14th Dalai Lama (as of 2025) was enthroned in 1940 at the age of four. His secular tutor was the German SA and SS member Heinrich Harrer. Dalai Lamas are raised in near-complete isolation from the outside world and especially from the common people, shaped into artificial products of their environment—and the 14th Dalai Lama was no exception. After the socialist revolution in China in 1949, the People's Liberation Army entered Tibet in 1950–51 and secured its outer borders as Chinese borders. The British governor was deposed. Instead, the Dalai Lama was prematurely recognized by China as the political leader of Tibet at the age of sixteen. In 1951, the *Seventeen-Point Agreement for the Peaceful Liberation of Tibet*[49] was signed between Beijing and Lhasa, Mao Zedong and the 14th Dalai Lama, which, among other provisions, included the following regulations:

- "[T]he Tibetan people shall have the right to exercise national regional autonomy under the unified leadership of the Central People's Government."
- "The central authorities will not alter the existing political system in Tibet. The central authorities will also not alter the established status, functions and powers of the Dalai Lama."
- "The policy of freedom of religious belief [...] shall be carried out. The religious beliefs, customs and practices of the Tibetan people shall be respected, and lama monasteries shall be protected."
- "The spoken and written language and education system of the Tibetan nationality shall be developed step by step in accordance with the actual conditions in Tibet."

- "Tibetan agriculture, livestock raising, industry, and commerce shall be developed step by step and the people's livelihood shall be improved step by step in accordance with the actual conditions in Tibet."
- "The local government of Tibet shall carry out reforms of its own accord, and, when the people raise demands for reform, they shall be settled through consultation with the leading personnel of Tibet."[50]

The 14th Dalai Lama was allowed to be elected to the National People's Congress of China, which also happened. As a young man, he was even elected Vice Chairperson of the Standing Committee there.

However, in the meantime, the large landowners, together with a significant part of the theocratic caste, rebelled against the gradual abolition of slavery and fiefdom, as social protests and demands for reform in Tibet had increased. From the mid-1950s, armed terrorist groups were secretly established in the Nepalese mountains with the help of the CIA of the USA,[51] which, as the 14th Dalai Lama noted in his autobiography, "were able to inflict considerable damage on the Chinese several times".[52] The cause of this CIA-backed "Tibetan resistance" was publicized in the West by government-funded organizations such as the *American Society for a Free Asia*—one of the forerunners of today's well-known, CIA-funded *Radio Free Asia*—and was part of the broader US-initiated anti-communist propaganda strategy during the Cold War. One of the organization's active members was, for example, Thubten Jigme Norbu, the brother of the 14th Dalai Lama. Another brother, Gyalo Thondup, organized guerrilla units for the CIA to fight against the PLA.[53] However, the People's Liberation Army was able to defeat these terrorist groups, and in return, a land reform in favor of the peasants was carried out. During the anti-Chinese Lhasa uprising of 1959, the feudal caste finally broke with the Seventeen-Point Agreement and fled to India with considerable wealth, where they have since been allowed to govern a smaller area as a mini-state, initially with only a few hundred Tibetans and a small local Indian population, from a former British garrison. As of 2025, around 70,000 Tibetans live in exile in India,[54] corresponding to about 1–2 percent of all Tibetans worldwide.

The 14th Dalai Lama, who was Mao's contractual partner in the Seventeen-Point Agreement and a vice chair of the National People's Congress of China, was originally "deeply impressed by Mao Zedong's extraordinary personality", as he himself noted,[55] and was seen in 1954, at the age of nineteen, shaking hands with Mao at the National People's Congress in Beijing. He was likely persuaded by his caste to join in breaking with Tibet's progressive development that had begun and to flee as well. The rest of the story of the 14th Dalai Lama is well known to the average Western media consumer as an esoteric, glorified, and romanticized tale of secret longings for spiritual leaders, princes, kings, and demigods.

However, a renewed "liberation" of Tibet under the aegis of feudal (Gelug-led) political Buddhism, as it is widely and prominently portrayed on the internet today, devoid of any reference to real history or the actual social conditions of ordinary people under that regime, within the framework of Western intellectual do-gooder longing for religion, a transfigured and misunderstood version of Buddhism, esotericism, and the glorification and admiration of feudal pomp, seems absurd at best and is unlikely to appear realistic to a neutral observer today.

Nevertheless, many people in Tibet also experienced hardships after 1951, especially during the excesses of the Cultural Revolution in the 1960s and 1970s, when, in violation of the PRC's own Seventeen-Point Agreement with Tibet, and as almost everywhere in China at the time, under the idea of abolishing the so-called "Four Olds": "old ideas," "old culture," "old customs," and "old habits," zealous young Red Guards vandalized and destroyed Buddhist temples and monasteries as well as other cultural sites, and monks and nuns were persecuted.[56] An improvement in the situation came with the beginning of the reform era in 1980, when, especially after a visit by General Secretary Hu Yaobang to Tibet, the atmosphere became more relaxed, and social controls were eased again.

Riots also flared up in 2008, which included, as documented above, attacks on Hui Muslim mosques and Han Chinese stores by Buddhist fundamentalists and Tibetan separatists, leaving several people dead or wounded.[57] The heavy handling and suppression of the riots by Chinese security forces afterward were criticized, especially in Western media.

But as with many other instances of Western media hysteria, the addressees of the Tibet campaigns of the US internet oligopoly hardly seem to be the general world public, which is scarcely reached anymore, or, in this case, the ordinary Tibetan population, which, even with a glorification of its own tragic feudal history, can hardly be influenced today. Rather, the target appears to be the Western public itself. A neutral and detached view from outside the real and mental state of the West—for example, today's Europe[58]—reveals much about the longings and irrationalities present there and holds up a mirror that seems to say: no impulses are to be expected from you in the foreseeable future. The mostly hysterical and aggressive political approach of the West toward Tibet and China, in any case, seems to have little to do with genuine cultural emancipation, modernization, or increasing prosperity in Tibet,[59] as it oscillates between distorted, romanticized, and Orientalized images of a harmonious indigenous Buddhist population, or simply instrumentalizes the Tibetans for its own geopolitical interests in destabilizing China (or Russia, during the "Great Game"). In both cases, a genuine interest in the real culture and traditions of the Tibetans, and in a real improvement of their living conditions free from ulterior motives, is rarely observable.

However, a forced modernization of Tibet, on the other hand, would be counterproductive for China itself, as would an alienation of the Tibetans from their own genuine history and culture. Through the Qinghai–Tibet Railway, the "world's highest train line" and a "miracle of engineering", which today connects Lhasa and Beijing, the other end of the Chinese continent is only about 40 hours away for Tibetans by regular direct train, and about 30 hours by bullet train when transferring via Xining.[60] Modernization and economic development, including a rise in living standards for all, must be possible without sacrificing culture and traditions, through development within the "Plurality and Unity Configuration" of a multiethnic country that upholds its promises of Tibetan autonomy in the Seventeen-Point Agreement. This would even align with the exiled Dalai Lama's "middle path" approach, which he adopted in the late 1980s, stating that "Tibet Wants Autonomy, Not Independence" in 2006. However, he has since seemingly deviated from that position, and in recent years has made headlines for controversial slip-ups and statements that some have deemed sexist and xenophobic.[61]

Nevertheless, the position he outlined in an interview with *Time Magazine* in 2006 should be quoted at length here:

> We Tibetans want modernization. Therefore, in order to develop Tibet materially as a modern nation, Tibet must remain within the People's Republic of China. Provided Chinese give us a full guarantee of preservation of Tibetan culture, Tibetan environment, Tibetan spirituality, then it is of mutual benefit. [Besides] foreign affairs [and] defense [are] all the things which Tibetans can manage by themselves. Tibetans should have the full autonomy.[62]

The Chinese government remains suspicious of the genuine nature of this position,[63] as the Dalai Lama and his government-in-exile have collaborated extensively with separatists and received funding and support from the US government and the CIA on numerous occasions in the past.[64] Nevertheless, the position has the potential to serve as a shared starting point for genuine rapprochement, especially if the complex geopolitical constellations and political entanglements surrounding it—partly fueled by Western public misconceptions and distortions—did not exist as major impediments. As the 14th Dalai Lama approaches advanced age (turning 90 in 2025), the question of his succession remains an additional potential obstacle to resolving the conflict. His death could potentially lead to a situation with two parallel Dalai Lamas: one appointed by the exiled leadership for the government-in-exile, and one by the government of China, acting as the official representative of the autonomous region, which would certainly complicate any further attempts at rapprochement and also strain relations with India. The USA has already threatened to sanction China should it "interfere in the selection process"[65] of the Dalai Lama—something in which the USA itself apparently believes it has the right to be involved.

Xinjiang: Old History, Terrorism and Counterterrorism from the 1990s Through 2010s, Current Geopolitical Significance, Its Socioeconomic Flourishing … and the Media War

Religion and ethnicity appear to be two areas in human history that can be radicalized to any degree and then used to create tensions and conflicts, divide nations, destroy states, or instigate wars. The trigger "You look different from us. So, you are a threat to us. So, we are afraid of you. So, we bash your heads in before you bash ours in" seems to reflect a deeply human instinct of tribal behavior. When ethnicity and religion combine as forms of "otherness", this tendency appears particularly likely.

The universalist ideals of peaceful coexistence, enlightenment, tolerance, diversity, and the resulting resilience of social systems emerged relatively recently in human history together with the rise of civilizations. Ideals of coexistence were developed in which we aim no longer to react in an exclusively reflexive and aggressive manner but instead recognize the benefits of cooperation—patterns that are accordingly controlled in our neocortex. At times, this has even been successfully put into practice, as in the ancient Achaemenid Persian Empire, with its peaceful ideals and religious tolerance.

In a world of explosive population growth, the struggle for ever-diminishing resources, systemic wars, and the resulting permanent stress, the attainment of such ideals seems once again to be a relatively hopeless endeavor.

We have already briefly touched upon the Xinjiang Uygur Autonomous Region (XUAR), the largest and westernmost region of China, bordering today's Afghanistan, India, Kazakhstan, Kyrgyzstan, Mongolia, Pakistan, Russia, and Tajikistan externally, and Tibet, Gansu, and Qinghai internally. What is today called Xinjiang has been part of Chinese empires on and off for more than 2000 years. As mentioned earlier, the so-called "Western Regions" became a protectorate of Han China in 59–60 BC, in order to secure trade routes along the Silk Road.

Throughout its history, Xinjiang was inhabited by numerous ethnic groups, such as the Indo-European Tocharians and the Sogdians, practicing a variety of religions, including Buddhism and Zoroastrianism. This high ethnic, cultural, and religious diversity was partly due to migration patterns, wars, the Silk Road, and resettlement policies.

The Turkic-speaking ethnic group today known as the Uyghurs settled in the region, specifically the Tarim Basin, beginning in the tenth century CE, following the collapse of the Uyghur Khaganate, which had been located in present-day Mongolia. When the Uyghurs settled in the region, they became the dominant and ruling ethnicity and only then adopted Islam as their religion, which had originally arrived via the Silk Road. The area was briefly conquered by the Mongolian Dzungars in the seventeenth century under the Dzungar Khanate (1634–1758). The Turkic Muslims, today collectively known as the Uyghurs, then asked the Qing dynasty for assistance in liberating them from Dzungar rule. With the help of Manchu armies, the Dzungars were defeated, and the area was reincorporated into the Qing Empire in 1759. The Uyghurs, who had been oppressed by the Dzungars and used for slave labor, held resentment toward their former rulers, which eventually contributed to what is today known as the Dzungar genocide, perpetrated from 1755 to 1757 by Uyghurs and other local ethnicities, such as Kazakhs, together with Manchu military divisions, and which wiped out much of the Dzungar population.

The resettlement policies of the Qing dynasty after the reincorporation of Xinjiang in the eighteenth century, and the official establishment of

Xinjiang as a province in 1884, also contributed significantly to the region's current ethnic composition. Large-scale Uyghur, Han, and Hui settlement throughout Xinjiang began. Today, of approximately 25.8 million inhabitants, about 11.6 million are Uyghurs, close to 10.9 million are Han, 1.5 million are Kazakh, 1.1 million are Hui, along with numerous other smaller ethnicities.

Although originally liberated from Dzungar rule by the Qing, the first seeds of separatism and Uyghur nationalism emerged in the 18th and 19th centuries, with growing resentment against the Manchu rulers. After the Revolution of 1911–1912, the new Republic of China formally treated all territories of the former Qing Empire, including Xinjiang, as part of the new China. As with many other regions at that time, the post-colonial instability of the warlord era led to country-wide destabilization and loss of central rule, which also affected Xinjiang. Parts of the region were claimed by local warlords, as during the *First East Turkestan Republic* (1933–1934) and the *Second East Turkestan Republic* (a Soviet satellite, 1944–1946), until Xinjiang was fully reintegrated into the People's Republic of China in 1949, after the Kuomintang, which had also ruled Xinjiang, was defeated. These republics were, however, unstable, extremely short-lived, and controlled only very limited areas. Nevertheless, they later served as inspirations for Uyghur separatists, Pan-Turkists, and Islamists advocating for an independent state of "East Turkestan", a term originally coined by Russian Turkologists in the nineteenth century.

After being reincorporated into China under communist rule, Xinjiang became an autonomous region on 1 October 1955, an official status it retains to this day. Since Xinjiang was not as severely affected by the famine of the Great Leap Forward in the late 1950s, many Han Chinese settled in the region at that time (especially in the north, while most Uyghurs today live in the south), fleeing the famine. During the Cultural Revolution in the 1960s and 1970s, Xinjiang suffered a fate similar to that described above for Tibet, with many mosques vandalized or destroyed and Muslim imams persecuted.

With the reform era of the 1980s, the number of mosques began to increase again, and restrictions on or persecution of religious expression were lifted. The loosening of border controls, following the overall relaxation of policies in the 1980s, also allowed an increasing number of Uyghurs to travel abroad, for example to undertake pilgrimage in Mecca or to visit Central Asia. This enabled a growing number of Uyghurs to attend fundamentalist Islamist schools in countries such as Pakistan, where some subsequently became radicalized. This side effect of the relaxation policies of the reform era eventually acted as a major facilitator for terrorism and separatism beginning in the 1990s.[66]

Simultaneously, however, living standards in Xinjiang have also increased drastically since then, with extensive economic development following Deng Xiaoping's visit in 1981. This included massive investments in public infrastructure and large-scale industry, as well as encouragement of small-scale businesses by Uyghurs. Furthermore, recent decades have revealed large gas, oil, and mineral reserves in Xinjiang, increasing its strategic importance for China in addition to its geographically volatile border position and major hub of the New Silk Roads.

Today, only slightly more than half of the Uyghurs are religious, most of whom are Muslims. While modernization has increased trends of secularism, the opening-up era also allowed a politicized, fundamentalist, and radicalized form of Islam to enter China, as described above. This form of Islamist fundamentalism developed toward using violence as a legitimate means, partly due to centuries of European and North American colonial and imperial oppression, and in parallel with tendencies in the Middle East and Arab world, as well as with similar tendencies in Christianity and other religions. That this is an expected reaction to, and in part a direct product of, centuries of colonial oppression and ongoing imperialist exploitation by the West remains a significant taboo in Western discourse to this day.

As a result of a long and only partially transparent process, which began in 1979 with the founding, radicalization, violent training, and organizational and financial support of the Mujahideen in Afghanistan and Pakistan (precursors of the Taliban) by the USA, news emerged a few years ago that thousands of Islamist Uyghurs, recruited by the *Turkistan Islamic Party*, were fighting on the side of ISIS and Al-Qaeda terrorists in Syria. Some observers estimate that around 5000 terrorists were involved in the conflict in Syria.[67]

After significant defeats and the partial dissolution of terror militias during the Syrian civil war, hundreds have died, some in suicide attacks. Among those who survived, some are reportedly still active within current Syrian forces but also participate in terror operations between the Near and Far East, such as the 2016 suicide bombing of the Chinese embassy in Bishkek. Others remain in exile in countries such as Turkey. A 2017 *Associated Press* report provided insights into the recruiting process, as well as the motivations and potential regrets of the terrorists. It states:

> Radical groups have aggressively recruited Uighurs. Al-Qaeda's leader promised in a video that Islamic militants would repay the Uighurs by striking at "atheist Chinese occupiers" after the Syrian war. The Islamic State has echoed similar pledges and the group in March released a Uighur-language propaganda video vowing to one day shed Chinese blood if Uighurs would join the Syrian struggle.[68]

One terrorist, interviewed in Istanbul and who spent two and a half years fighting in Syria, stated that while in Syria, in addition to being radicalized by ISIS or Al-Qaeda, they also studied Zionism as a model for building an independent homeland in China:

> We studied how the Jews built their country," [...] "Some of them fought, some of them provided money. We don't have a strong background of that.[69]

There was seemingly some regret about fighting and dying in a foreign land for a foreign cause:

> This is not our homeland," [...]. "We want our homeland, we don't need yours.[70]

The population in Xinjiang, and in China as a whole, which has been affected by repeated bloody attacks by terrorists since the 1990s, was clearly surprised and remained helpless for a long time in the face of these new forms of violence. There may even have been a certain social basis for religious extremism and terrorism in Xinjiang. After all, the attacks also demonstrated that the Chinese minority and autonomy policy of its multi-ethnic state had, in some ways, gotten out of hand and had long neglected the protection of its western border. The current situation might also be analyzed from the perspective of the dialectic of the Cultural Revolution, the reverberations, and negative consequences of which are still being felt in China today.

The numerous terrorist attacks starting in the 1990s were largely carried out by Uyghur separatists[71] and fundamentalist Islamists from organizations such as the East Turkestan Islamic Movement (ETIM)/Turkistan Islamic Party (TIP) (founded by an Al-Qaeda follower in Pakistan), the East Turkistan Liberation Organization (ETLO), the United Revolutionary Front of East Turkestan (URFET), or the Uyghur Liberation Organization (ULO), many of whom received funding from Pakistan and Afghanistan (especially from organizations such as Al-Qaeda) and trained their fighters there. Among the terrorist attacks are for example the 1992 Urumqi bombings (3 deaths), the 1997 Urumqi bus bombings (9 deaths), the 2008 Kashgar attack (16 deaths), the 2011 bomb and knife Hotan attack (4 deaths plus 14 attackers after a firefight with the police due to hostages taken), the 2011 Kashgar attacks (23 deaths including 8 attackers), the 2013 suicide attack on Tiananmen Square (5 dead and 38 injured), the 2014 Kunming knife attack on random railway passengers (35 deaths including 4 attackers, plus 143 injured), the 2014 Urumqi attack where two SUVs drove into a busy market (43 deaths including 4 attackers, plus 90+ injured), another 2014 Urumqi attack with bombs and knives (3 deaths and 79 injured), the 2015 Aksu colliery attack (16 dead and 18 wounded), and many more.

One of the most significant events, however, was the July 2009 Urumqi riots, which involved at least 1000 Uyghurs targeting mainly Han people. The riots resulted in the deaths of 197 individuals and 1721 injuries, mostly among Han or other non-Muslim ethnicities, along with the destruction of many buildings and vehicles.

It was this string of terrorist attacks and ethnic riots that led to the initiation of a harsh anti-terror campaign by the Chinese government in 2014, when the CPC launched a war against what it called the "Three Evil Forces" of separatism, terrorism, and extremism (the so-called "Strike Hard Campaign Against Violent Terrorism"). As of 2025, there have been no such terrorist attacks since 2017, due to strong crackdowns, increased surveillance, detention, and reeducation facilities, the existence of which China itself also acknowledged. The campaign was later criticized by human rights organizations such as Amnesty International, which allege that China has committed human rights violations in its repressive counter-terror policies.[72] These allegations have become a trigger for public criticism, primarily by Western countries, as well as a major reference point and justification for imposing sanctions. Since then, accusations have escalated, with the USA under the Trump administration (and, after it, several other Western countries) accusing China of cultural and ethnic genocide in January 2021.[73] This eventually led to collective sanctions by the USA and its Western allies against China in March 2021, including travel bans and asset freezes for senior officials in Xinjiang, to which Beijing responded with counter-sanctions.[74]

The USA based its accusations of genocide mostly on non-peer-reviewed reports by researchers who were either not independent or only partially independent, often with certain political agendas or funding from interest groups. These included Adrian Zenz from the US government-founded right-wing anti-communist think tank *Victims of Communism Memorial Foundation*, who is a fundamentalist Christian; the DC-based far-right think tanks *Heritage Foundation* and *Jamestown Foundation*; and the hawkish *Australian Strategic Policy Institute* (ASPI), which is largely funded by the Australian Department of Defence, the US State Department, weapons manufacturers such as Raytheon, Thales, and Lockheed Martin, and the governments of Taiwan and Japan.

These reports, especially those by Adrian Zenz (whose estimates of detained Muslims have ranged from 100,000 to 1.8 million, and which also allege forced sterilizations[75]) and ASPI, have been the subject of controversial discussion even among some Western China scholars and academics, with some voicing careful criticism of the validity and scientific integrity of the conclusions or of the employed methodology. The methodology is largely based on a mixture of analyses of allegedly leaked documents, satellite imagery (ASPI, for example, used satellite images of facilities they claimed were detention centers and approximated the number of inmates based on floor space), estimates from exiled Uyghurs who were interviewed, and government spending reports.

For example, in a critical response, political scientists Alain Brossat and Juan Alberto Ruiz Casado accused Zenz's reports of including "subjective and free interpretation" and containing "misleading" or "directly false" claims based on flawed methodologies and unclear source material. They problematized the fact that his conclusions "were presented as an irrefutable fact by Western media and, thereafter, Zenz became the preferred source and the ubiquitous expert supporting any claims about Xinjiang in Western media".[76]

On the charge on genocide, which according to the Rome Statute of 1998 requires evidence of "intent to destroy, in whole or in part, a national, ethnic, racial or religious group", they conclude that

> while it is possible to argue that the "re-education camps" resulted in significant physical and mental harm, along with harsh living conditions, it remains extremely difficult to justify with a high standard of evidence that this sought the physical destruction of those individuals and not, for instance, their indoctrination or acculturation—which we might condemn but do not entail genocide.[77]

Furthermore, they argue that

> […] the often exaggerated numbers, the way those numbers are presented—constantly repeating that millions of Uyghurs are being still and forever detained—and, principally, the unsubstantiated accusation of genocide, have to be criticized and presented as an attempt to accelerate the demonization of China to progressively bring it into submission through sanctions and international isolation. […] The label "genocide" waved by Pompeo on his last day at work perfectly illustrates the nature of the "post-truth" prevailing in US discourse since the arrival of Trump, which has continued after their replacement by Biden and Blinken.[78]

A 2022 report by the UN High Commissioner for Human Rights (OHCHR), following an official visit to Xinjiang, does not accuse China of genocide but does claim that "serious human rights violations" were committed. China has denied these accusations and responded that its so-called "Vocational Educational and Training Centres (VETCs)", which are part of its "counter-terrorism and de-radicalization efforts", are "learning facilities established in accordance with law intended for de-radicalization".[79]

On the whole, however, a certain reluctance to engage critically or in any challenging way with the conclusions of these non-academic reports, which have been readily instrumentalized by Western governments, or even with the topic of Xinjiang in general, can be observed among Western media as well as Sinologists and academia, with critical voices being comparatively rare. This is probably also due to the seriousness of the allegations on the one hand—nobody wants to be accused of denying a genocide—and fear of being branded as pro-China or "paid by the CCP" on the other hand, in a broader return of red-scare and "yellow peril" rhetoric of "us versus them" or "clash of civilizations" in Western public discourse. This lack of challenging criticism is thus probably exactly what is intended.

German Sinologist Mechthild Leutner has analyzed this tendency in the context of a long tradition of Sinophobia in the West, in which "fears caused by the large population and the associated potential of the people fed the assumption of an impending 'yellow peril'" reach back to colonial times. In this context of a negative perception of China, already firmly established in the Western public consciousness for decades, a general reluctance by Western media to consult actual Sinologists, who could provide objective and balanced analyses, now predominates, sometimes even leading to their vilification.

Today, one of the main drivers behind this strategy might be "the USA's claim to global hegemony, which also wants to draw its allies into the systemic conflict it has apostrophized. As early as the 1990s, US think tanks developed a foreign policy strategy that declared human rights to be a criterion", Leutner writes. "However, as these criteria are not applied in the same way to all countries, it may be suspected that the value-driven foreign policy relates in particular to China and is being instrumentalized to 'contain' China." She summarizes that Western perceptions of China thus "ultimately say more about the viewer's point of view than about the object of observation".[80]

One striking example is that of renowned German Sinologists Thomas Heberer and Helwig Schmidt-Glintzer, who, in 2023, after visiting Xinjiang, published an article in the major Swiss newspaper *Neue Zürcher Zeitung*. In it, they described how China's counterterrorism campaign has wound down, and circumstances have become less repressive, representing a "return to normalcy", with most camps already dissolved, a fact that Adrian Zenz himself has also noted in a recent publication and that was reported by the *Associated Press*.[81] They therefore argued for a discussion about a potential easing or lifting of EU sanctions.[82]

This, however, led to a media backlash in what might be called an attempted "cancellation" of the two experts. Not only did mainstream press outlets such as the German *Süddeutsche Zeitung* and *Frankfurter Allgemeine* accuse them of being "on the side of the CCP" and "too close to Beijing",[83] instead of constructively engaging with their arguments, but they also faced denunciations from other Sinologists.[84] A toxic and academically highly damaging atmosphere of paranoia thus haunts Western China studies today, where those reluctant to position themselves fully against China in an "us versus them" constellation may face serious defamation or "cancellation". This situation may incentivize many to follow the opportunist "party line", where only fully negative depictions of China are considered acceptable.

It is this complete negative portrayal of China in the media that has exacerbated the crisis in China studies. Who still wants to study Chinese studies in this toxic atmosphere of denunciation, when everything they hear about China is negative? There has, for example, been no growth in the number of Chinese studies students and graduates in the past 25 years in the United Kingdom, as a 2022 study by the *Higher Education Policy*

Institute shows. The study therefore diagnoses a "severe national deficit in China literacy and Mandarin speakers". Rana Mitter, Professor of Chinese History and Politics at the University of Oxford, notes in his foreword to the study:

> As in any democratic society, there will be varied views in the British public sphere on how to deal with China. Those views will often be robustly expressed, as is only right in a free society. But those conversations and debates can no longer afford to take in a swift and superficial view of China. The time to deepen the debate has surely arrived.[85]

Furthermore, a 2024 open letter signed by 63 China specialists in Australia warns that "research on Australia's giant northern neighbour has ground to a halt just when it is "most sorely" needed", as there is a "decline in funding for research with and about China".[86]

While the Chinese crackdown in Xinjiang must certainly be subject to objective scrutiny and criticism, the hypocrisy and double standards are not lost on many, especially observers from non-Western countries, when a US President such as Donald Trump, with his "Muslim ban" and migrant detention centers, from a country that itself initiated the brutal "war on terror" (while also being largely responsible for the emergence of Islamist terror in the first place), considers sanctioning China over its crackdown in Xinjiang.[87] The theory of Western projection against China, that "every accusation is a confession", is, however, most strikingly confirmed in the case of France. While condemning China's "unacceptable treatment of Uighurs",[88] including the use of "re-education camps", France itself first introduced re-education camps for "radicalized Islamists" after the 2015 Charlie Hebdo attacks. According to the plans presented by then-Prime Minister Manuel Valls, "suspects will be taught their 'patriotic duties' and forced to undergo psychological treatment across 13 centres".[89]

This hypocrisy and double standard applied by Western countries further accelerates the West–non-West divide, which is most strikingly seen at the United Nations Human Rights Council (UNHRC). At its 44th session in 2020, a group of 39 primarily Western countries condemned China's conduct in Xinjiang, while, in an immediate response, a group of 45 primarily non-Western countries defended China in a counter-letter, opposing the "politicization of human rights issues and double standards".[90]

That the issue of terrorism in Xinjiang does not interest most Western countries is hardly surprising. After all, terrorism in the West is not fundamentally condemned but is always pragmatically and tactically evaluated according to power and geopolitical usefulness. As US President Franklin D. Roosevelt once said about one of his Latin American executioners, the Nicaraguan dictator Somoza,

> He may be a son of a bitch, but he's our son of a bitch.[91]

Islamist terrorists, even if they were terrorist "sons of bitches", could still be utilized for one's own interests in the New Cold War against the new "challenger" of the empire. It is thus obvious that, to Western states, most prominently the USA, Uyghurs—many of whom were previously detained without charges at Guantanamo for alleged terrorist activities—have become nothing more than a means to an end in the power struggle with China. Their concerns are selectively championed only when they align with US interests.[92]

The experienced former US Secretary of State Henry Kissinger, who knew and had done much more than he publicly verbalized, already spoke in his 2011 book on China of the "possible effects" of Islamist terrorism on the province of Xinjiang.[93]

As outlined in the short historical overview above, the idea of a Uyghur Islamist "Khalifate" named East Turkestan, separated from China, already has a certain tradition. Uyghur exile organizations that have advocated the separation of Xinjiang from China have existed since the beginning of the People's Republic of China in 1949.

One of the most prominent organizations is the aforementioned Turkistan Islamic Party (TIP), which China regards as synonymous with the East Turkestan Islamic Movement (ETIM), an organization that has already carried out many attacks in China. Influenced by the Afghan Mujahideen and maintaining links with Al-Qaeda and the Taliban, they blend their Islamist ideals with a Pan-Turkist agenda, which seeks to establish an Islamic empire of all Turkic peoples stretching from Turkey to Xinjiang. The TIP has established an organization in Syria and reportedly commands at least several hundred professional fighters, with some sources claiming up to 5000.

It is officially recognized as a terrorist organization by 12 countries as well as the EU and the UN. The USA, however, *removed* ETIM from its terror list in 2020, citing "no credible evidence that ETIM continues to exist".[94] This is, of course, indicative of the US' strategic and selective use of terrorism for its own geopolitical aims, since after 9/11 China was still seen as a partner in the global "war on terror" until it became the US' major adversary. These "nonexistent" terrorists, however, "reappeared" after helping to topple the Assad government of Syria in late 2024, with a video message directed toward China: "Now here in Syria, in all the cities here, we fight for Allah, and we will continue to do this in our Urumqi, Aqsu and Kashgar in the future, [...] We will chase the Chinese infidels away", a member of the TIP proclaimed after conquering Damascus together with Hayat Tahrir al-Sham (HTS) forces, who themselves are an Al-Qaeda rebrand, on 8 December 2024. "Through God's support, the Chinese disbelievers will soon taste the same torment that the disbelievers in al-Sham have tasted, if God wills", TIP's emir Abd Haq al-Turkistani said in an official statement on 6 December 2024.[95]

In Germany, the headquarters of the *World Uyghur Congress* (WUC) is based in Munich and was formed in 2004, with numerous predecessor groups dating back to the 1980s. In its self-description, it presents itself as a more moderate group that officially rejects violent struggle and aims to separate Xinjiang as "East Turkestan" from China through largely peaceful means, although China has accused it of inciting unrest inside China, including the 2008 Tibetan uprising and the 2009 Urumqi riots. Its strategy, however, is largely one of public relations through mass media, with dissemination through outlets such as the US state broadcaster *Radio Free Europe/Radio Liberty*, based in Prague.[96] Its most prominent leader, Dolkun Isa, who temporarily stepped down as president in August 2024 due to sexual harassment allegations,[97] is designated as a terrorist by the Chinese government and was on Interpol's Red Notice list until being removed in 2017, a decision harshly criticized by China. China claims that he was vice-chairman of the *East Turkestan Liberation Organization* (ETLO), another secessionist group that does not reject violent means, having participated in terrorist attacks in the past and thus designated as a terrorist group by China in 2003.[98] He received the Democracy Award from the National Endowment for Democracy (NED) in 2019, which also funds the WUC.[99]

The USA, on the other hand, has hosted the *East Turkistan Government in Exile* (ETGE) in Washington, D.C., since 2004. Standing in opposition to the WUC, the ETGE is more radical in its approach and openly advocates violent means, including terrorism, for the establishment of an independent Uyghur state, with ties to the aforementioned Islamist groups such as the TIP and ETLO. However, a study by the US military concluded that these "exile government" projects are unlikely to succeed without external support.[100]

With the cartel of oil companies, it is known that, alternately, one company must take action to initiate the next gasoline price increase so that the others can follow suit. The situation is very similar to the media oligopoly. One must first put the story into the world and establish the language framework. Then a citation carousel begins, at the end of which no one knows where the "news" originated, but everyone "knows" that it *is* the truth.

In Germany, the *taz* once gave significant coverage to the topic of Xinjiang, benefiting from the presence of a correspondent of Chinese origin, Felix Lee. For him, Xinjiang was suddenly dead, or at least almost so: "Deathly silence", according to Lee, suddenly prevailed in what he described as the "large penal camp" of Xinjiang.[101]

And this, even though it is known that significant developments are now occurring there: the great New Silk Road route, with Urumqi as a main hub of goods transport and simultaneously the endpoint of a bullet train that takes passengers to Beijing in 30 hours. Surely, not all traditional Uyghurs will welcome such progress and change. But the depiction of this economically rising Central Asian region, including China's western neighbors, as completely silent because many of its inhabitants are supposedly all in camps (with circulating figures of up to three million, out of ten million) is a typical example of media framing.

A half-page photo in the *taz* reinforced the impression that life in Xinjiang is always gloomy or that thick yellow smog constantly fills the air. The photo was either taken in fog at dusk or edited with a yellow-gray filter. The science fiction classic Escape from New York, set in post-human Manhattan, came to mind. The sun never seemed to appear there either. And there it was: "The world's largest mass arrest of a minority population", one to three million in camps, and no one had noticed, probably because everyone was talking about the New Silk Road and how the western provinces are now gaining fast internet, modern infrastructure, e-mobility, and higher incomes. Yet suddenly, at least "one in ten" was supposedly in a "reeducation camp".

As a "source", an unverifiable "report of a US commission" was cited, in fact an unofficial group of experts. On his own journey through Xinjiang, Felix Lee had been unable to locate the mass camps to make more authentic statements. But such minor details do not matter when the story sounds plausible. Amnesty International admitted somewhat sheepishly that the camps were "invisible".[102]

China invited government representatives from around the world to inspection trips to Xinjiang, an invitation that was declined by Western governments and media representatives. However, numerous government representatives from countries that themselves have to deal with extremist Islamism, as well as UN representatives, accepted the invitations and conducted site inspections. Like Amnesty International, they found "no visible" internment camps—but also no invisible ones.

The waves of outrage in the Western media highlight a form of journalism prone to gross technical errors. The fact that these errors can be easily exposed afterward does not seem to bother anyone, because the insight of the ancient Greeks and Romans, going back to Plutarch, still applies: *Audacter calumniare, semper aliquid haeret*—"Slander boldly; something always sticks."

The discourse and attention around Xinjiang, and especially allegations of genocide, have, however, comparatively died down in Western media recently, particularly since 2022. On the one hand, this is because most "reeducation camps" (VETCs) have closed down and there is less to report on; on the other hand, the media has found new spectacles in the Russia-Ukraine war and, more recently, in Israel's wars in Gaza, Lebanon, and Iran. In this context, loudly continuing the accusations of genocide against China would especially expose its double standards, as many Western media outlets and governments seem reluctant to admit that Israel is committing genocide against Palestinians in Gaza, or will outright deny it,[103] despite it being, in this case, one of the most well-documented genocides in history, as it is being "live-streamed".[104]

The designation of genocide was also adopted by the Office of the United Nations High Commissioner for Human Rights (OHCHR) in a Special Committee report released on November 14, 2024,[105] while an International Court of Justice (ICJ) genocide case against Israel, brought forth by South Africa, is currently ongoing as of 2026, the court having already concluded the case as "plausible".[106]

Here, the narrative of an Islamist terrorist threat, employed by Israel as a justification for its conduct, is willingly and uncritically adopted, while in the case of China it was scrutinized to the extreme. One can, thankfully, only imagine the difference in reaction of the Western press if China were carpet bombing Urumqi, indiscriminately killing civilians in the process under the pretense of counterterrorism. Again, with Western charges of genocide or colonialism against China, "every accusation is a confession".

The issue of Xinjiang, together with the West's double standard exposed over Gaza, is just one more indication of a growing West–non-West divide in global politics, which opens up new areas of cooperation that circumvent the previous global hegemon. Some of these will be outlined in the following chapter.

Notes

1. A recent example of the official position on ethnic and population policy and philosophy of the Chinese government can be seen in a speech by Xi Jinping in 2021 at a central conference on ethnic affairs, as summarized here: Cao Desheng, "Xi outlines ethnic affairs for new era", *China Daily*, August 30, 2021: https://www.chinadaily.com.cn/a/202108/30/WS612c12b2a310efa1bd66bdf2.html, visited October 5, 2024. Here, Xi states that "Neither Han chauvinism nor local ethnic chauvinism is conducive to the development of a community for the Chinese nation". One can observe that here the rejection of any ethnic supremacy does not imply a rejection of nationalism: on the contrary, a strong nation might be seen as only achievable with an overcoming of interethnic strife.
2. Fei Xiatong, "Plurality and Unity in the Configuration of the Chinese People", *The Tanner Lectures on Human Values*, Delivered at The Chinese University of Hong Kong November 15 and 17, 1988: https://tannerlectures.utah.edu/_resources/documents/a-to-z/f/fei90.pdf, visited October 5, 2024.
3. For example: Alison Hsiao, "Tsai failing nation's Aborigines: KMT", *Taipei Times*, December 1, 2016: https://www.taipeitimes.com/News/taiwan/archives/2016/12/01/2003660344 visited October 6, 2024. And: Abraham Gerber, "Rights groups call on Tsai to return Aboriginal lands", *Taipei Times*, May 8, 2016: https://www.taipeitimes.com/News/taiwan/archives/2016/05/08/2003645783 visited October 6, 2024.
4. For example: Gang Lin, *Taiwan's Party Politics and Cross-Strait Relations in Evolution (2008–2018)*, Palgrave Macmillan Springer Nature, Singapore, 2019, pp. 137–180.
5. *Taipei Times* July 20, 2017.
6. Most recently with the 2024 election of DPP president Lai Ching-te, the successor of President Tsai Ing-wen (2016–2024), who in his inaugural speech proclaimed that "the Republic of China Taiwan is a sovereign, independent nation in which sovereignty lies in the hands of the people.",

earning a sharp response from mainland China. For the whole speech see: "Inaugural Address of ROC 16th-term President Lai Ching-te", *Office of the President Republic of China (Taiwan)*, May 20, 2024: https://english.president.gov.tw/News/6726, visited October 7, 2024.

7. "Taiwan presidential frontrunner accuses opposition party of being 'pro-communist'", *Reuters*, December 26, 2023: https://www.reuters.com/world/asia-pacific/taiwan-presidential-frontrunner-accuses-opposition-party-being-pro-communist-2023-12-26/, visited October 8, 2024.
8. For example: "Taiwan indicts 2 communist party members accused of colluding with China to influence elections", *Associated Press*, October 4, 2023: https://apnews.com/article/taiwan-china-communist-party-elections-b55ac61be9109aa54c8d8bf34bb99176, visited October 8, 2024.
9. *China Daily* July 14/15, 2018, p. 3.
10. *China Daily* July 14/15, 2018, p. 1.
11. "Ex-Taiwan leader visits China, first such trip since civil war", *Al Jazeera*, March 27, 2023: https://www.aljazeera.com/news/2023/3/27/former-taiwan-leader-arrives-in-china-first-such-trip-in-decades, visited October 7, 2024.
12. For example, a Pew Research survey conducted in 2023 found that 67% of respondents see themselves as "primarily Taiwanese", 28% as "both Taiwanese and Chinese" and 3% as "primarily Chinese". Among the former, support for the DPP is higher, and among the latter, support for the KMT is higher, although the numbers are not definite (most do not feel close to any party). See: Christine Huang, Kelsey Jo Starr, "Most people in Taiwan see themselves as primarily Taiwanese; few say they're primarily Chinese", *Pew Research Center*, January 16, 2024: https://www.pewresearch.org/short-reads/2024/01/16/most-people-in-taiwan-see-themselves-as-primarily-taiwanese-few-say-theyre-primarily-chinese/, visited October 7, 2024. These results should always be treated with caution, however, as opinions, especially toward the mainland can be highly fluctuating, based on current political events and the dynamics of party politics, among other things.
13. Taiwan was first likened to an "unsinkable aircraft carrier" by US General Douglas MacArthur in 1950. See: "National Affairs: An Unsinkable Aircraft Carrier", *Time*, September 4, 1950: https://web.archive.org/web/20 091125150338/http://www.time.com/time/magazine/article/0,9171,856644,00.html, visited Oct. 6, 2024.
14. The "island chain strategy" of containment against China and the Soviet Union was first formulated by former US secretary of state John Foster Dulles in 1951. While the third Island Chain includes Hawaii, American Samoa, Fiji, and New Zealand, recently, a fourth and fifth island chain

have been proposed that extend to the Indian Ocean (Sri Lanka, Maldives, etc.) and the East African coast, respectively, in order to stop any Chinese influence in the region and ensure a global US hegemony. See for example: Lt Col JS Sodhi (Retd), "Island chain strategy: Steps to checkmate China", *Financial Express*, June 18, 2022: https://www.financialexpress.com/business/defence-island-chain-strategy-steps-to-checkmate-china-2565232/, visited October 6, 2024.

15. For example: "China and Taiwan: A really simple guide", *BBC*, January 8, 2024: https://www.bbc.com/news/world-asia-china-59900139, visited October 6, 2024.
16. Most notably: Chris Miller, *Chip War: The Fight for the World's Most Critical Technology*, 2022, New York: Scribner.
17. See for example: Wu Jieh-min, "Silicon Shield 2.0: A Taiwan Perspective", *The Diplomat*, September 14, 2024: https://thediplomat.com/2024/09/silicon-shield-2-0-a-taiwan-perspective/, visited July 13, 2025.
18. Eduardo Baptista, Fanny Potkin, "Make new friends and boost hiring: How China's chip industry plans to deal with Trump", *Reuters*, November 11, 2024: https://www.reuters.com/technology/make-new-friends-boost-hiring-how-chinas-chip-industry-plans-deal-with-trump-2024-11-08/, visited November 12, 2024.
19. See for example: Viola Zhou, "TSMC's debacle in the American desert", *Rest of World*, April 23, 2024: https://restofworld.org/2024/tsmc-arizona-expansion/, visited November 12, 2024.
20. Mark Lapedus, "China Accelerates Foundry, Power Semi Efforts", *Semiconductor Engineering*, November 22, 2021: https://semiengineering.com/china-accelerates-foundry-power-semi-efforts/, visited November 12, 2024.
21. Eduardo Baptista, Fanny Potkin, ibid.
22. Laura He, "China is pumping another $47.5 billion into its chip industry", *CNN*, May 28, 2024: https://edition.cnn.com/2024/05/27/tech/china-semiconductor-investment-fund-intl-hnk/index.html, visited November 12, 2024.
23. Kotaro Hosokawa, "China's chip capabilities just 3 years behind TSMC, teardown shows", *Nikkei Asia*, August 31, 2024: https://asia.nikkei.com/Business/Tech/Semiconductors/China-s-chip-capabilities-just-3-years-behind-TSMC-teardown-shows, visited November 12, 2024.
24. Shinmei Shen, "China touts home-grown chip lithography machines amid semiconductor self-sufficiency drive", *South China Morning Post*, September 15, 2024: https://www.scmp.com/tech/tech-war/article/3278597/china-touts-home-grown-chip-lithography-machines-amid-semiconductor-self-sufficiency-drive, visited November 12, 2024.

25. "Black terror. Mainland Chinese are being attacked in Hong Kong", *The Economist*, November 7, 2019: https://www.economist.com/china/2019/11/07/mainland-chinese-are-being-attacked-in-hong-kong, visited October 8, 2024.
26. Eamon Barrett, "'We Fear Confidence Will Suffer:' Hong Kong's Extradition Law Is Denounced as Bad for Business", *Fortune*, June 10, 2019: https://fortune.com/2019/06/10/hong-kong-extradition-law-protest-business/, visited October 8, 2024.
27. Rolf Geffken, "Im Sinne der Konzernbosse [In the interests of the corporation bosses]", *Neues Deutschland*, September 6, 2019: https://www.nd-aktuell.de/artikel/1125429.china-und-hongkong-im-sinne-der-konzernbosse.html, visited October 8, 2024.
28. Werner Ruegemer, "Hongkong – der neue Systemkonflikt [Hong Kong - The new system conflict]", *NachDenkSeiten*, August 28, 2019: https://www.nachdenkseiten.de/?p=54420, visited October 8, 2024.
29. "Hong Kong Holds Spot As World's Priciest Residential Property Market", *CBRE*, June 8, 2020: https://www.cbre.com.hk/press-releases/hong-kong-holds-spot-as-worlds-priciest-residential-property-market, visited October 11, 2024.
30. Rolf Geffken, ibid.
31. "How Hong Kong Became One of the Most Unequal Places in the World", *Stanford Center on China's Economy and Institutions*, March 1, 2024: https://sccei.fsi.stanford.edu/china-briefs/how-hong-kong-became-one-most-unequal-places-world, visited October 11, 2024.
32. Detailed for example also: Andre Vltchek, "Some In Hong Kong Feel Frustrated, As Their City Is Losing To Mainland China", *Countercurrents.org*, October 10, 2019: https://countercurrents.org/2019/10/some-in-hong-kong-feel-frustrated-as-their-city-is-losing-to-mainland-china/, visited October 8, 2024.
33. "The transformation of Hong Kong in five charts", *Reuters*, June 28, 2022: https://www.reuters.com/ world/china/transformation-hong-kong-five-charts-2022-06-28/, visited October 8, 2024.
34. Peter Koenig, "Hong Kong - Pure Western Insanity", *Countercurrents.org*, December 3, 2019: https://countercurrents.org/2019/12/hong-kong-pure-western-insanity/, visited October 8, 2024.
35. *Solvecon Forex Report* 16.12.2019, p. 7 (quote translated by the authors).
36. Cyril Ip, "China accuses US group National Endowment for Democracy of 'ideological infiltration'", *South China Morning Post*, August 10, 2024: https://www.scmp.com/news/china/diplomacy/article/3274000/china-accuses-us-group-national-endowment-democracy-ideological-infiltration, visited October 8, 2024.

37. See for example: Brian Wong, "Jimmy Lai says he may have asked US official to sanction Beijing and Hong Kong", *South China Morning Post*, November 27, 2024: https://www.scmp.com/news/hong-kong/article/3288407/ex-media-boss-jimmy-lai-says-he-might-have-asked-us-official-impose-sanctions-beijing-and-hong-kong, visited July 13, 2025.
38. For example Stephen Lendman, "China Retaliates Against Hostile US Legislation", *Global Research*, December 3, 2019: https://www.globalresearch.ca/china-retaliates-against-hostile-us-legislation/5696675?pdf=5696675, visited October 8, 2024.
39. Clare Jim, Yew Lun Tian, "China passes national security law in turning point for Hong Kong", *Reuters*, June 30, 2020: https://www.reuters.com/article/us-china-hongkong-security/chinas-parliament-passes-national-security-law-for-hong-kong-cable-tv-says-idUSKBN241061/, visited October 8, 2024.
40. Ruegemer, ibid. (quote translated by the authors).
41. For example: Vltchek, ibid.
42. For example: Rügemer, ibid.
43. Manolo Corichi, Christine Huang, "How people in Hong Kong view mainland China and their own identity", *Pew Research*, December 5, 2023: https://www.pewresearch.org/short-reads/2023/12/05/how-people-in-hong-kong-view-mainland-china-and-their-own-identity/, visited October 8, 2024.
44. Kenneth Rapoza, "Interesting Poll Shows Hong Kongers Not Exactly Against China", *Forbes*, January 2, 2020: https://www.forbes.com/sites/kenrapoza/2020/01/02/interesting-poll-shows-hong-kongers-not-exactly-against-china/, visited October 8, 2024.
45. There are four major schools (and some minor ones) in Tibetan Buddhism: Nyingma, Kagyu, Sakya and Gelug. Gelug is in fact the newest of them, reaching back to the fifteenth century, while the Nyingma is the oldest, stemming from the eighth century CE.
46. See for example: Teahouse, "The Mongolian-Gelug shadow over Tibet: Six decades of failed US-Gelug policy", *Buddhistdoor Global*, August 28, 2024: https://teahouse.buddhistdoor.net/the-mongolian-gelug-shadow-over-tibet-six-decades-of-failed-us-gelug-policy/, visited October 13, 2024.
47. For an in-depth account of Tibet's modern history, see for example the authoritative *History of Modern Tibet* series by renowned Tibetologist Melvyn Goldstein, especially: *A History of Modern Tibet, Volume 1: 1913–1951: The Demise of the Lamaist State*, Berkeley: University of California Press, 1989.

48. As for example documented in: "Britain's suzerain remedy", *The Economist*, November 6, 2008: https://www.economist.com/asia/2008/11/06/britains-suzerain-remedy, visited October 11, 2024.
49. The full official name (in English translation) is: Agreement of the Central People's Government and the Local Government of Tibet on Measures for the Peaceful Liberation of Tibet.
50. The full list in English translation can, for example, be found here: "Seventeen Point Agreement", *Wikipedia*: https://en.wikipedia.org/wiki/Seventeen_Point_Agreement, visited October 12, 2024.
51. We again refer here for example to the authoritative work by Conboy and Morrison, 2002, *The CIA's Secret War in Tibet*, Lawrence, Kansas: University Press of Kansas, as already mentioned further above.
52. Sebastian Carlens: "Middle Ages ended. Sixty years ago the Dalai Lama fled from China. He could not stop the modernization of Tibet [Mittelalter beendet. Vor 60 Jahren floh der Dalai Lama aus China. Er konnte die Modernisierung Tibets nicht aufhalten]", *junge Welt*, March 16, 2019: https://www.jungewelt.de/loginFailed.php?ref=/artikel/351118.vr-china-mittelalter-beendet.html, visited October 12, 2024 (quote translated by the authors).
53. In detail, for example: "Tibet and the CIA's anti-China crusade: New Edition Articles from Workers World, including Sam Marcy's 1959 "Class War in Tibet." Updated to included reports from 2008.", *Workers World*, New York: Workers World Publishers: https://www.workers.org/ww_books/Workers_World_Tibet.pdf, visited October 12, 2024. See also: Associated Press, "Dalai Lama Group Says It Got Money From C.I.A.", *The New York Times*, October 2, 1998: https://www.nytimes.com/1998/10/02/world/world-news-briefs-dalai-lama-group-says-it-got-money-from-cia.html, visited October 13, 2024.
54. Reuters, "China says Dalai Lama succession issue a 'thorn' in relations with India", *Reuters*, July 13, 2025: https://www.reuters.com/world/china/china-says-dalai-lama-succession-issue-thorn-relations-with-india-2025-07-13/, visited July 13, 2025.
55. Carlens, Ibid.
56. An authoritative source on this topic is, for example: Melvyn C. Goldstein, Ben Jiao, Tanzen Lhundrup, 2009, *On the Cultural Revolution in Tibet: The Nyemo Incident of 1969*, Berkeley, University of California Press.
57. Barbara Demick, "Tibetan-Muslim tensions roil China", *Los Angeles Times*, June 23, 2008: https:// www.latimes.com/archives/la-xpm-2008-jun-23-fg-muslims23-story.html, visited September 13, 2024.
58. Andre Vltchek, "Europe in Irreversible Decay, EU Elections Are Proof of It!", *Countercurrents.org*, January 6, 2019: https://countercurrents.

org/2019/06/europe-in-irreversibly-decay-eu-elections-are-proof-of-it/, visited October 13, 2024.

59. We again also refer to the extensive documentation of R. Fitzthum 2018b, pp. 8–10.
60. Thomas Bird, "The Qinghai-Tibet railway: The world's highest train line", *BBC*, January 9, 2024: https://www.bbc.com/travel/article/20240108-the-qinghai-tibet-railway-the-worlds-highest-train-line, visited October 13, 2024.
61. Harmeet Kaur, "The Dalai Lama just said some (more) controversial things about women and migrants", *CNN*, June 27, 2019: https://edition.cnn.com/2019/06/27/world/dalai-lama-female-successor-europe-trump-bbc-trnd/index.html, visited October 13, 2024. And: Manveena Suri, "Dalai Lama apologizes after video asking child to 'suck' his tongue sparks outcry", *CNN*, April 11, 2023: https://edition.cnn.com/ 2023/04/10/india/dalai-lama-apology-kissing-boy-video-intl-hnk/index.html, visited October 13, 2024.
62. "Dalai Lama: Tibet Wants Autonomy, Not Independence", *Time*, April 15, 2006: https://time.com/archive/ 6939337/dalai-lama-tibet-wants-autonomy-not-independence/, visited October 13, 2024.
63. "China says Dalai Lama must 'thoroughly correct' his political views", *Reuters*, June 20, 2024: https://www.reuters.com/world/asia-pacific/china-says-dalai-lama-must-thoroughly-correct-his-political-views-2024-06-20/, visited October 13, 2024.
64. Again: Associated Press, "Dalai Lama Group Says It Got Money From C.I.A.", *The New York Times*, October 2, 1998: https://www.nytimes.com/1998/10/02/world/world-news-briefs-dalai-lama-group-says-it-got-money-from-cia.html, visited October 13, 2024.
65. Penelope Macrae, "Dalai Lama defies China to say successor will be chosen by Tibetan tradition", *The Guardian*, July 2, 2025: https://www.theguardian.com/world/2025/jul/02/dalai-lama-says-there-will-be-search-for-his-successor-ending-years-of-speculation, visited July 13, 2025.
66. See for example: Rémi Castets, "The Uyghurs in Xinjiang – The Malaise Grows", *China Perspectives*, No. 49, September–October 2003: https://journals.openedition.org/chinaperspectives/648, visited October 20, 2024.
67. Bassem Mroue, Gerry Shih, "Chinese jihadis' rise in Syria raises concerns at home", *Associated Press*, April 22, 2017: https://apnews.com/article/591f9b238c84477b87cfac68bfe169fc, visited October 20, 2024.
68. Gerry Shih, "AP Exclusive: Uighurs fighting in Syria take aim at China", *Associated Press*, December 23, 2017: https://apnews.com/article/79d6a427b26f4eeab226571956dd256e, visited October 20, 2024.

69. Ibid.
70. Ibid.
71. China uses the term "separatists", while the groups themselves will often describe themselves as "national liberation movements", etc.
72. For example: "Like We Were Enemies in a War: China's Mass Internment, Torture and Persecution of Muslims in Xinjiang", *Amnesty International*, 2021: https://xinjiang.amnesty.org/, visited October 25, 2024.
73. Edward Wong, Chris Buckley, "U.S. Says China's Repression of Uighurs Is 'Genocide'", *The New York Times*, January 19, 2021: https://www.nytimes.com/2021/01/19/us/politics/trump-china-xinjiang.html, visited October 25, 2024.
74. "Uighurs: Western countries sanction China over rights abuses", *BBC*, March 22, 2021: https://www.bbc.com/news/world-europe-56487162, visited October 25, 2024.
75. For example: Adrian Zenz, "China's Own Documents Show Potentially Genocidal Sterilization Plans in Xinjiang", *Foreign Policy*, July 1, 2020: https://foreignpolicy.com/2020/07/01/china-documents-uighur-genocidal-sterilization-xinjiang/, visited October 25, 2024.
76. Alain Brossat, Juan Alberto Ruiz Casado, 2023. "What Is Happening in Xinjiang?" In: *Culture of Enmity: The Discursive Struggle for Taiwan in the Making of the New Cold War*. Singapore: Springer. pp. 75–94., p. 78. The chapter offers a detailed analysis of all main conclusions of Zenz' reports.
77. Ibid, pp. 80–81.
78. Ibid, pp. 81–82.
79. "China responsible for 'serious human rights violations' in Xinjiang province: UN human rights report", *UN News*, August 31, 2022: https://news.un.org/en/story/2022/08/1125932, visited October 26, 2024.
80. Mechthild Leutner, "Kritik am Berliner Konfuzius-Institut: Falsches Feindbild China [Criticism of the Berlin Confucius Institute: False image of China as the enemy]", *Tagesspiegel*, February 19, 2020: https://www.tagesspiegel.de/wissen/falsches-feindbild-china-4683751.html, visited October 26, 2024. (Quotes translated by the author)
81. Dake Kang, "Terror & tourism: Xinjiang eases its grip, but fear remains", *Associated Press*, October 10, 2021: https://apnews.com/article/coronavirus-pandemic-lifestyle-china-health-travel-7a6967f335f97ca868cc618ea84b98b9, visited July 15, 2025.
82. Thomas Heberer, Helwig Schmidt-Glintzer, "Jenseits von Hass und Zorn – nach der erfolgreichen Kampagne gegen Terrorismus und Islamismus sollen sich nach dem Willen Pekings die Verhältnisse in Xinjiang wieder normalisieren [Beyond hatred and anger - after the successful campaign against terrorism and Islamism, Beijing wants condi-

tions in Xinjiang to return to normal]", *Neue Zürcher Zeitung*, September 11, 2023: https://www.nzz.ch/meinung/xinjiang-china-kampf-gegen-terrorismus-und-separatismus-ld.1753509, visited October 26, 2024.

83. For example: Kai Strittmatter, "Beschämend leichtgläubig [Shamefully gullible]", *Süddeutsche Zeitung*, September 24, 2023: https://www.sueddeutsche.de/kultur/deutsche-sinologie-pro-chinesisch-aufruhr-thomas-heberer-helwig-schmidt-glintzer-1.6252806?reduced=true, visited October 26, 2024. And: Hinnerk Feldwisch-Drentrup, "Ein Buch als Zerreißprobe für die Sinologie [A book that puts sinology to the test]", *Frankfurter Allgemeine*, October 8, 2024: https://www.faz.net/aktuell/wissen/forschung-politik/uiguren-region-xinjiang-ein-buch-als-zerreissprobe-fuer-die-sinologie-110031597.html, visited October 26, 2024.
84. Kai Vogelsang, "Die fatalen Fehleinschätzungen der chinesischen Diktatur zeugen nicht bloss vom Versagen einzelner Sinologen, sondern sind eine Bankrotterklärung jener Sinologie, für die sie stehen [The fatal misjudgements of the Chinese dictatorship are not just evidence of the failure of individual sinologists, but are a declaration of bankruptcy of the sinology they represent]", *Neue Zürcher Zeitung*, October 1, 2023: https://www.nzz.ch/meinung/die-fatalen-politischen-fehleinschaetzungen-von-teilen-der-sinologie-ld.1757905, visited October 26, 2024.
85. Michael Natzler, "No growth in Chinese Studies graduates during China's ascendancy", *Higher Education Policy Institute*, March 31, 2022: https://www.hepi.ac.uk/2022/03/31/no-growth-in-chinese-studies-graduates-during-chinas-ascendancy/, visited October 26, 2024.
86. John Ross, "China research at 'crisis point', Australian scholars warn", *Times Higher Education*, May 18, 2024: https://www.timeshighereducation.com/news/china-research-crisis-point-australian-scholars-warn, visited October 26, 2024.
87. Lily Kuo, "US considers sanctions on China over treatment of Uighurs", *The Gurdian*, September 12, 2018: https://www.theguardian.com/world/2018/sep/12/us-considers-sanctions-on-china-over-treatment-of-uighurs, visited October 20, 2024.
88. News Wires, "France denounces 'unacceptable' treatment of Uighurs in China", *France 24*, July 21, 2020: https://www.france24.com/en/20200721-france-denounces-unacceptable-treatment-of-uighurs-in-china, visited October 20, 2024.
89. Rachel Bishop, "Radicalised Islamists to be sent to re-education camps as France tackles 'biggest security threat since HITLER'", *Mirror*, May 10, 2016: https://www.mirror.co.uk/news/world-news/radicalised-islamists-sent-re-education-7939978, visited October 20, 2024. See also

for example: "French re-education camps" on *Wikipedia*: https://en.wikipedia.org/wiki/French_re-education_camps, visited October 20, 2024.

90. Catherine Putz, "2020 Edition: Which Countries Are For or Against China's Xinjiang Policies?", *The Diplomat*, October 09, 2020: https://thediplomat.com/2020/10/2020-edition-which-countries-are-for-or-against-chinas-xinjiang-policies/, visited October 20, 2024.
91. For example: Robert Funk, "He's Our Son of a Bitch", *Human Rights & Human Welfare*, Vol. 11, Issue 3, Article 4, February 1, 2011: https://digitalcommons.du.edu/cgi/viewcontent.cgi?article=1653&context=hrhw, visited October 20, 2024.
92. Colum Lynch, "U.S. Once Jailed Uighurs, Now Defends Them at U.N.", *Foreign Policy*, May 25, 2018: https://foreignpolicy.com/2018/05/25/u-s-once-jailed-uighurs-now-defends-them-at-u-n/, visited October 25, 2024.
93. Kissinger 2011, pp. 432–433.
94. Laura Zhou, "China could face greater terrorism threat as US 'delists' East Turkestan Islamic Movement, experts say", *South China Morning Post*, November 7, 2020: https://www.scmp.com/news/china/diplomacy /article/3108910/china-could-face-greater-terrorism-threat-us-delists-east, visited October 20, 2024.
95. Sophia Yan, "Uyghur fighters in Syria vow to come for China next", *The Telegraph*, December 13, 2024: https://www.telegraph.co.uk/world-news/2024/12/13/uyghur-fighters-in-syria-vow-to-come-for-china-next/, visited December 15, 2024.
96. "Ost-Turkestan im Visier (I) [East Turkestan in Focus (I)]", *German Foreign Policy*, November 15, 2018: https://www.german-foreign-policy.com/news/detail/7784 And "Ost-Turkestan im Visier (II) [East Turkestan in Focus (II)]", *German Foreign Policy*, November 26, 2018: https://www.german-foreign-policy.com/news/detail/7794, both visited October 25, 2024.
97. "Statement: Change in Leadership", *World Uyghur Congress*, August 5, 2024: https://www.uyghurcongress.org/en/statement-change-in-wuc-leadership/, visited October 25, 2024.
98. "China upset as Interpol removes wanted alert for exiled Uighur leader", *Reuters*, February 24, 2018: https://www.reuters.com/article/us-china-xinjiang/china-upset-as-interpol-removes-wanted-alert-for-exiled-uighur-leader-idUSKCN1G80FK/, visited October 25, 2024.
99. "Defenders of Human and Religious Rights in China to Receive 2019 Democracy Award on 30th Anniversary of Tiananmen Massacre", *National Endowment of Democracy*, May 21, 2019: https://www.ned.org/defenders-of-human-and-religious-rights-in-china-to-receive-2019-

democracy-award-on-30th-anniversary-of-tiananmen-massacre/, visited October 25, 2024. Another recipient was the evangelical Christian organization China Aid, which opposes abortion and aims to turn China into a Christian nation.

100. *German Foreign Policy*, ibid.
101. Felix Lee, "Grabesstille über Xinjiang [Grave Silence over Xinjiang]", *taz*, July 17, 2018, p. 1, 4–5.
102. Felix Lee, "Xinjiang: Im Land der unsichtbaren Lager [Xinjiang: In the Land of the Invisible Camps]", *Amnesty International*, August, 2019: https://www.amnesty.ch/de/ueber-amnesty/publikationen/magazin-amnesty/2019-3/china-uiguren-xinjiang-lager, visited October 26, 2024.
103. Jacob Magid, Jeremy Sharon, "Germany says will intervene at The Hague on Israel's behalf, blasts genocide charge", *The Times of Israel*, January 12, 2024: https://www.timesofisrael.com/germany-says-will-intervene-at-the-hague-on-israels-behalf-blasts-genocide-charge/, visited November 15, 2024. In response to the ICJ case, German government spokesman Steffen Hebestreit released a statement saying, "the German government decisively and expressly rejects the accusation of genocide brought against Israel before the International Court of Justice".
104. For example: Reuters, "World has failed Gaza in 'livestreamed genocide', South Africa's delegation says at ICJ – video", *The Guardian*, January 11, 2024: https://www.theguardian.com/world/video/2024/jan/11/world-has-failed-gaza-in-livestreamed-genocide-south-africas-delegation-says-at-icj-video, visited Oct. 26, 2024.
105. "UN Special Committee finds Israel's warfare methods in Gaza consistent with genocide, including use of starvation as weapon of war", *Office of the United Nations High Commissioner for Human Rights*, November 14, 2024: https://www.ohchr.org/en/press-releases/2024/11/un-special-committee-finds-israels-warfare-methods-gaza-consistent-genocide, visited November 15, 2024.
106. Scott Simon, Eyder Peralta, "ICJ finds genocide case against Israel 'plausible', orders it to stop violations", *NPR*, January 27, 2024: https://www.npr.org/2024/01/27/1227397107/icj-finds-genocide-case-against-israel-plausible-orders-it-to-stop-violations, visited November 15, 2024.

Selected and Recommended Literature

Conboy, Kenneth, and James Morrison. 2002. *The CIA's Secret War in Tibet.* Lawrence, KS: University Press of Kansas.
Kissinger, Henry A. 2011. *On China.* New York: Penguin.

Further Cited Literature

Fitzthum, Robert, 2018b. Der nächste Feind [The next enemy]. *Rubikon*, October 31, 2018, https://www.rubikon.news/artikel/der-nachste-feind. Accessed October 13, 2024.

CHAPTER 14

"Peaceful Coexistence, New Diplomacy, and the New Silk Roads? New Imperialism!"

The Other Globalization: South-South Cooperation in the UN, Shanghai Cooperation Organization+, BRICS+, BRI, Africa and Latin America, South China Sea and West-Pacific Military Buildup, Foreign Trade and Investment—And a New Immigration Wave

"All I have to say is: China, China, China."[1] With these words, in 1969, the then-German Chancellor Kurt Georg Kiesinger tried to stir up fear of the "communist threat" at a CDU (conservative) party conference. This is part of a long tradition: in the Kaiserreich (the German Empire), it was still the "Yellow Peril" that supposedly came from the "half-humans" of the Far East; then Germans were terrified of the "Red Menace" in 1919, 1933, and 1945, and this fear became deeply embedded in their political worldview ("better dead than red").

If the combined "Yellow-Red Peril" were to become economically successful, and a new Asian age were to establish long-term, historically normal international structures … unthinkable! And that is precisely where we are today. In what sense Kiesinger was somehow right at the time, he certainly had no idea. After all, it seemed clear then that China would return to the world stage and potentially disrupt the dominant structures of the last 150 years in a sustainable manner.

W. Elsner, E. Najmehchi, *The Rise of China*,
https://doi.org/10.1007/978-3-032-20260-4_14

China and the Global South: South-South Cooperation Since 1949

Historically, the People's Republic of China has considered itself a developing country from the first day of its existence, on October 1, 1949, a status to which it had been relegated due to colonial exploitation. It built its international relations with other developing countries, especially in Africa, under the framework of South-South cooperation. Initially, this had less to do with formal financial development aid, because as one of the poorest developing countries, still struggling with famines, China could not afford it. The focus was instead on political contacts, cooperation, and solidarity with anti-colonial and national-revolutionary liberation movements, the emerging independent African and Arab nation-states, and the liberation movements of Latin America.

Although those generations of national liberation movements are long history, this appears to be the tradition to which China, since its own stabilization in the 1990s and 2000s, could and still can connect. Today, it is gladly welcomed in Africa and Arabia, and partly also in Latin America. This is a tradition that apparently never completely broke off. The *Forum on China-Africa Cooperation* (FOCAC), for example, has existed for 25 years as of October 2025 and meets annually, always with concrete development policy and investment outcomes.

Only recently has China officially moved from being a recipient to a donor of financial development aid, and as such, it is of course also welcomed in Africa, Arabia, Central Asia, and South and Central America. Foreseeably, China is likely to overtake the USA as the most important donor to developing countries.[2]

However, this is not particularly difficult, as all neoliberal developed industrial countries are generally reducing their unpopular—and therefore always sparse—expenditures for development aid, which are multilaterally agreed, transparent, and UN-checked. As mentioned, these expenditures were never large amounts compared to military spending ("military aid") in these countries. The developed capitalist countries, with the exceptions of Sweden and Denmark, have never fulfilled their UN-pledged shares of GDP (0.7 percent) as development aid; for example, Germany contributed only 0.4 percent in 2014.

China's strategy, which it today calls *development cooperation*, is not primarily development aid in the conventional sense. The meager development aid of Western countries was always just drops in the bucket—"petty cash"—especially in view of the exploding economic, social, and ecological problems in these countries under neoliberal globalization, from which only the capitalist core countries benefited. Their "development aid" was objectively never designed to provide structural empowerment for ascent or catching up, but rather as a temporary patch for the worsening consequences of the global power distribution.

The worse this status quo under neoliberalism became for the developing countries, the more this "development aid"

- First, was reconfigured as a door opener for the businesses of Western companies.
- Second, was increasingly diverted into the hands of national, regional, and local elites, making a few powerful people rich, who then optionally invested in luxury goods, Wall Street speculation, or the consolidation of dictatorships. A positive, structural effect for the countries themselves, however, was mostly absent.

China thoroughly uproots these globally established structures and pursues a completely different approach to joint development, as we will see below. The well-known Chinese economist and former chief economist of the World Bank, Justin Yifu Lin, describes the Chinese approach to joint development—which we can also confidently call a *new globalization*[3]—using terms such as "openness to ideas", "experimental approach", and "joint learning". For this purpose, new special development banks and funds were created after developing countries rejected the neoliberal "Washington Consensus" and its instruments, the World Bank and IMF, which could no longer be trusted.[4]

Accordingly, "[t]he neglect of fundamental interests of emerging countries (Western geopolitics in practice) [...] was the catalyst that prompted China to take action".[5] Thus, "[i]n many developing countries, China is the only option" when it comes to development cooperation, as Matt Ferchen, the former research director of Global China at the *Mercator Institute for China Studies*, concludes.[6]

Indeed, one can say that the new alternative globalization through China's *New Silk Roads* also acts as a counterforce against the emerging deglobalization, the observable disintegration of the world economy, and the decline of world trade under the disruptions of Trumpism, thus representing a form of re-globalization.[7] Behind this, much unexpected and new lies ahead, as we will see.

The decades-long tradition of political solidarity, the shared understanding of developing countries in the same struggle for advancement, and increasingly, of course, financial aid are apparently all not forgotten in Africa, even among the grandchildren of the anti-colonial fighters. Therefore, it is not surprising that China in Africa in recent years encounters open doors and attentive ears, especially since it is not only interested in cheap resources, as is often alleged, but also in the industrialization of these countries. Even the elites influenced by the West apparently cannot resist the opportunity to have their infrastructure upgraded, to make a new departure from poverty, and finally to gain a new perspective on economic catching up.

China's Foreign Policy: No Wars, Peaceful Coexistence, and Diplomacy, Cooperation Agreements, and Infrastructure Investments

In contrast to the USA, with its over 750 military bases worldwide—many of them near Russia and China—its permanent global military maneuvers and operations, its leading role in armament, and its broad disregard for international arms limitation treaties,[8] China in its foreign policy primarily works through international legal state treaties, which focus almost exclusively on economic interests and exclude political interference in national development strategies. China offers infrastructure investments and industrial goods and services in exchange for raw materials in the course of further development of its partners. Increasingly, the reverse also occurs: with China's assistance in the industrialization of Africa, international trade becomes inter- and intra-industrial.

Thus, studies of 22 major developing countries show that their trade with China contributes to their industrial growth and that China is one of the key drivers of growth in the global South.[9] This has never been achieved by Western development aid.

Against this background, China has now abandoned its decades-long practice of extreme diplomatic restraint in international affairs and has adopted a more assertive foreign policy approach appropriate to its significance. China aims to pursue its development path peacefully[10] and therefore acts in accordance with the five long-standing principles of peaceful coexistence in international law:

- Mutual respect for national sovereignty and territorial integrity
- Mutual renunciation of violence
- Mutual non-interference in the internal affairs of a country
- Equality of all countries regardless of cultural, religious, or political-ideological orientation
- Cooperation for mutual benefit[11]

China in the UN and Its Organizations

As is well known, the PRC was admitted to the UN only in 1971. However, as we have seen from examples in environmental and climate policy, desert reclamation, and minority policy, China is now one of the most active countries in implementing resolutions across various development areas and policy fields. It is also active in the work of several UN sub-organizations (UNEP, UNDP, and others), making it an important partner for diplomats and UN representatives.

This includes, for example, UN climate resolutions, such as the Paris Climate Agreement of 2015, which China has fulfilled ahead of schedule, and the Sustainable Development Goals (SDGs) in general. Notable areas include poverty reduction, where China has accounted for the bulk of the global decline in poverty, desert containment programs, and the protection of ethnic minority rights. China has also achieved measurable successes in more specific areas, such as combating organ trafficking.[12]

UN representatives therefore come and go in China, see, learn, and often praise.[13]

The country has also participated militarily in UN peacekeeping missions since 1990, deploying approximately 2500 soldiers, primarily stationed in South Sudan, Liberia, Mali, and Lebanon. These forces can, in certain circumstances, even operate under US command.[14] China is also one of the largest financial contributors to these missions.

Thus, the country has established itself as an important voice for developing countries in the UN, and its draft resolutions regularly receive large majorities. Recently, for the first time, a Chinese candidate was elected—surprisingly quickly and decisively—against resistance from Western countries, to the head of a major UN organization, the Food and Agriculture

Organization (FAO). This outcome was widely seen as a reflection of China's strong relations with other developing countries.[15]

China's orientation in the UN today, like its domestic policies, increasingly focuses on the fundamental challenges facing humanity, a perspective reflected in the UN through the Chinese concept of a "community with a shared future for mankind".[16]

The Shanghai Cooperation Organisation (SCO) and BRICS

However, the UN has repeatedly proven itself highly incapable of effective peacekeeping. It can neither reliably secure peace nor prevent wars, and it has been unable to stop its military missions from occasionally being misused by "willing" parties for their own geostrategic interests. Today, imperialist intervention wars in resource-rich countries are usually conducted without a UN mandate. The UN is also vulnerable to paralysis, for example, through refusals to pay membership fees, whether generally or to specific sub-organizations it disfavors. As a result, it has long ceased to be an effective guarantor of classical international law, which arose from the experiences of the world wars and reflected a historical period of relatively restrained, liberal capitalism in international affairs for about four decades.

China's central negative experience in recent UN history came in this context with its abstention from the infamous UN Security Council Resolution No. 1973 of March 2011, which authorized an undefined form of intervention by "willing" parties in Libya. Following this resolution, Libya was bombed by NATO countries, transforming it from one of the last independent and secular Arab nation-states—albeit disobedient to the West and using its oil revenues to support the development of other African states—into a post-human state of total chaos and warlord despotism. Gaddafi's death was in part a consequence of his desire to exit the dollar system, develop and deepen cooperation with China, and, above all, use Libya's oil wealth for the strategic development of North Africa. China drew a clear conclusion: such a situation must never be allowed to occur again in the Security Council (Russia reached a similar conclusion).

However, China had already initiated the founding of the so-called Shanghai Five in 1996, essentially a UN-oriented group aimed at strengthening classical international law. This effort led to the establishment of the Shanghai Cooperation Organisation (SCO) in 2001, with six founding members: China, Russia, Kyrgyzstan, Kazakhstan, Uzbekistan, and Tajikistan. Since then, India, Pakistan, and most recently Iran in 2023 and Belarus in 2024[17] have also joined as full members. As of 2024, in addition to its ten member states, Mongolia participates as an observer, and fourteen mostly Asian countries participate as dialogue partners, with the UN serving as a strategic partner.

The objectives of the SCO include the restoration of international law, the promotion of a multipolar world system, a strict prohibition on the use or threat of military force among members and in international relations in general, non-support for separatism and extremism, and the pursuit of economic win-win cooperation, such as the establishment of free trade areas using local currencies, independent banking systems, and potentially the creation of a single SCO currency in the future.[18] The organization also emphasizes equality, respect for cultural differences, and cultural exchange programs (see above on China's contemporary political philosophy). The SCO does not consider itself a military alliance and therefore does not maintain any military bases. It has never participated in any military conflict, making its designation as a "counterpart to NATO" inaccurate.[19] Nevertheless, alongside its annual member state conferences, the member states engage in security cooperation and regular joint military exercises, primarily for counterterrorism purposes and the maintenance of regional stability.

With Pakistan and India, two additional nuclear powers joined the SCO in 2017, although both countries have long-standing tensions with each other, which have recently intensified again. India has at times also maintained a tense relationship with China. Under the nationalistic and Hindu-fundamentalist Prime Minister Narendra Modi (in office since 2014), India positions itself as a counterforce to China in the Indo-Pacific region and has regularly conducted naval exercises with the USA, Japan, and Australia in the Pacific and the Indian Ocean. In June 2017, Indian troops reportedly crossed Chinese territory in Sikkim, Tibet, triggering a tense border standoff that lasted over two months and left several injured.[20] The official Chinese response invoked BRICS and SCO principles: "India must end the troop confrontation in Chinese territory Donglang in its own interest and focus on the common interests."[21]

The Chinese-Indian border region remains highly contested and volatile, with both sides claiming parts of each other's territory and skirmishes continuing into 2020–2021. However, in October 2024, arrangements were made to de-escalate the situation, resulting in a bilateral meeting between Modi and Xi and a withdrawal of troops from the border stand-off. This development can be seen as a step toward Chinese-Indian rapprochement and as part of India's gradual reintegration into stable regional cooperation commitments. Even *The Economist* described it as the potential beginning of "a new era of closer ties"[22] and a possible shift away from India's previous role as a US instrument of economic and military containment against China. With India and Pakistan now in the SCO, the organization represents roughly half of humanity.

The better-known BRICS group—Brazil, Russia, India, China, and South Africa—also demonstrates clearly differing development policies and geostrategic orientations among its members. The development goals, strategies, and methods of today's Brazil (under left-wing President Lula, succeeding right-wing Bolsonaro), China, India (under Modi), and South Africa are noticeably different, raising the question of how relevant the BRICS group can be in global politics given this diversity.[23] Nevertheless, functional cooperation is advancing. The BRICS countries established their own development institutions in 2014: the New Development Bank and a currency fund, both of which serve as counterparts to the World Bank and IMF.[24] These institutions are already integrated into the financing system for projects along China's New Silk Road/BRI. To reduce dependence on the politically instrumentalized and therefore unpredictable US-dominated SWIFT system, the BRICS countries have implemented the Russian SPFS system for transactions among themselves. Additionally, BRICS Pay, an independent decentralized blockchain-based payment system for local currencies, is under development and received China's explicit backing at the BRICS summit in October 2024.[25]

In view of China's policy of non-interference in the internal affairs of sovereign states and its recognition of diversity among countries, the differing orientations and methods of the BRICS members do not preclude the realization of mutually beneficial opportunities. These win-win potentials are actively integrated into the projects of the New Silk Roads. In this regard, China's approach to foreign policy contrasts sharply with that of Western countries, which tend to rely on alliances built around strong political unity, as seen in NATO or the G7 (Canada, France, Germany, Italy, Japan, UK, USA). This fundamental difference, however, may ultimately disadvantage the West in the new age of globalization, as its rigid "us versus them" mentality could contribute to an increasing isolation from the broader global community.

In light of recent developments toward global multipolarity, the BRICS model has gained increased popularity, especially among non-Western countries, as a viable alternative for economic opportunities within the new globalization. Consequently, BRICS has expanded into "BRICS+", with Iran, Egypt, Ethiopia, and the United Arab Emirates joining on January 1, 2024, Indonesia on January 1, 2025, and Saudi Arabia potentially joining in the near future (as of 2025). As of 2025, the group also includes ten partner countries that may become full members in the future: Vietnam, Belarus, Bolivia, Kazakhstan, Cuba, Malaysia, Nigeria, Thailand, Uganda, and Uzbekistan.[26] In 2024, BRICS+ accounted for 35.4 percent of the world's economy, surpassing the previous leading Western G7 countries, which stood at 29.6 percent.[27] Representing over 45 percent of the world's population compared to the G7's 10 percent, BRICS+ has also overtaken the G7 in terms of economic growth and is projected to surpass the G7 in global trade by 2026, according to a report by *EY*.[28]

With these developments, together with the implementation of new payment systems that circumvent the US dollar, BRICS+ could potentially challenge the Dollar's status as the global currency hegemon in the near future. Such a shift would deal more than a symbolic blow to Western economies. In this context, a *political* unity like that of the G7 is not strictly necessary for BRICS+ or SCO members, as long as shared economic incentives—particularly the desire to reduce dependence on the USA—exist, as several observers have noted.[29]

A Cooperative Asian-Pacific System: ASEAN, RCEP, APEC, ACFTA, CPTPP ... and the US Military Buildup in the Asia-Pacific

The USA declared the Pacific its primary area of interest as early as 2012 with President Obama's "Pivot to Asia" strategy, which was later expanded into the broader "Indo-Pacific strategy" under President Trump.[30] Their military presence in East Asia is now greater than ever. However, this strategic shift has not altered their fundamental approach: it continues to prioritize building political and military alliances in the region with the primary goal of containing China.

Nevertheless, China is steadily increasing its influence among its neighbors, including countries bordering the South China Sea and throughout Southeast Asia. This includes the once US-dominated *Association of*

Southeast Asian Nations (ASEAN)[31]; the newly established *Regional Comprehensive Economic Partnership* (RCEP), a free trade agreement between 15 Asia-Pacific countries that emerged from ASEAN negotiations and received strong support from China, as examined by the US government-related Brookings Institution[32]; and the related new *ASEAN-China Free-Trade Area* (ACFTA), which has just been upgraded with further trade liberalizations at the *APEC* meeting in South Korea end of 2025. RCEP, which includes ASEAN members as well as Australia, Japan, China, and South Korea, came into effect on January 1, 2022, and has become the largest trade bloc in history, encompassing 30 percent of the world's population (2.2 billion people) and nearly 30 percent of global GDP (around 30 trillion USD).[33]

In contrast, although the USA formulated its "Pivot to Asia" strategy in the early 2010s, the results have been mixed. Its own Asia-Pacific free trade initiative, the *Trans-Pacific Partnership* (TPP), launched under Obama's strategy, was never ratified, as the USA withdrew from the agreement under President Trump in 2017.[34]

Paradoxically, the development—and subsequent failure—of the TPP, along with Washington's economic containment strategy toward China, which began with trade tariffs under the Trump administration and continued under Biden, may have inadvertently facilitated and encouraged China's deeper economic integration in the Asia-Pacific through agreements such as RCEP.

On the military front, the US strategy of containing China has also produced mixed, and at times even counterproductive, results. Earlier attempts to establish a US-led multilateral military alliance in East Asia—similar to NATO in Europe—have been less successful.[35] America's post-WWII anti-communist containment strategy, initiated under President Truman in 1947 with the "Truman Doctrine", primarily relied on bilateral security agreements in East Asia, known as the "Hub-and-Spokes" or "San Francisco" system. These arrangements were largely vassal-like, positioning US allies in the Asia-Pacific in a dependent relationship.[36] Today, many Southeast and East Asian states appear wary of such dependency and have increasingly turned toward more independent multilateral regional partnerships, such as ASEAN.

Among the more recent US-led attempts at regional military alliances is "AUKUS", which includes Australia, the UK, and the USA and was launched in 2021. This security partnership, ostensibly aimed at promoting "a free and open Indo-Pacific that is secure and stable"[37] (in practice arming Australia with nuclear-powered attack submarines to contain China), has been controversial from the start. Its creation led Australia to cancel a submarine deal with France, triggering a diplomatic fallout between the two countries and culminating in a settlement payment of 584 million USD. In addition to domestic criticism, several ASEAN members, including Malaysia and Indonesia, condemned AUKUS as a move likely to provoke an "arms race" with China in the Asia-Pacific and potentially lead to regional conflict.[38] In many ways, AUKUS may have drawn Australia closer to a confrontation with China that previously did not exist, effectively making it a tool of the US containment strategy to its own detriment. China, by contrast, is Australia's largest trading partner by far and has never posed a military threat—"Beijing is closer to Berlin than it is to Sydney", after all.[39]

Another military alliance, the "Quadrilateral Security Dialogue" ("the Quad"), which includes the USA, Australia, India, and Japan, was first initiated in 2007 under Vice President Dick Cheney and re-established in 2017 under President Donald Trump. As of late 2024, the alliance has achieved little beyond several diplomatic meetings and minor naval exercises. In many ways, its members still lack a shared strategic vision, particularly regarding their stance toward China.[40]

In general, US military engagement and power projection in the Asia-Pacific—including in the South China Sea, the Taiwan Strait, and the strategically important Malacca Strait—is viewed critically not only by China and Russia but also by regional states such as those in ASEAN. Many locals resist US military bases,[41] and US involvement is often seen as primarily serving its own (imperialist) interests, stoking tensions with a Cold War mentality and actually *increasing* the likelihood of a regional conflict, while potentially drawing non-aligned states into it. In many ways, US engagement in the region further *incentivizes* Chinese military buildup in response. These developments can also negatively affect regional trade and economic ties, given that China is a far more important trading partner than the USA for most countries in the region.[42]

In recent years, the USA and major regional allies, such as the Philippines and Japan—which have experienced a general trend of post-WWII remilitarization amid rising ultranationalism and historical revisionism—have renewed efforts to form an alliance akin to NATO in East Asia. While no major, coherent military alliance comparable to NATO has emerged as of 2025, ambitions to create one have grown, and more substantial developments may occur in the near future.[43]

Nevertheless, the USA has recently, at least to some extent, "repivoted" back to the Middle East and Eastern Europe, primarily through military involvement, including supplying weapons in the Russia-Ukraine war, Israel's war on Gaza and Lebanon, and its conflict with Iran and in the Red Sea. While the USA is increasingly engaged militarily in multiple conflicts, China is simultaneously expanding diplomatic and economic cooperation through organizations such as BRICS+, the SCO, and RCEP. Even in the Middle East, China has made diplomatic inroads, facilitating reconciliation and normalization talks between Saudi Arabia and Iran in March 2023[44] as well as between formerly opposed Palestinian factions in July 2024,[45] to name just two examples (more on the "New Silk Roads" below).

In light of recent developments since the Russia-Ukraine war, the relationship between China and Russia has grown in global significance and attracted increased attention. This relationship will therefore be examined in more detail in the following section.

China–Russia: From an Externally Enforced Collaboration to a Deliberate Strategic Partnership

While China and Russia (then as part of the Soviet Union) were not allied for much of the later part of the First Cold War following the Sino-Soviet split in 1961, a special strategic partnership emerged between the two countries after 1989, and a treaty of "friendship and cooperation" was signed in 2001. This partnership has intensified in recent years, partly as a consequence of the sanction regimes and economic warfare led by the USA and Western Europe since the onset of the Russo-Ukrainian conflict in 2014, during and after the so-called Ukraine Maidan uprising and the subsequent secession of Donbass and Crimea from Kyiv in 2015, and especially after the full-scale war began in 2022. China helped to mitigate the effects of Western sanctions on Russia quickly and effectively. As a result, Russia was able to recover economically and technologically after 2015 and avoided a prolonged crisis. Instead, it has advanced even further in the field of defensive technologies and has deepened its strategic partnership with China, which now represents some of the most advanced military defense capabilities in the world.

Russia can now easily sell its resources to China and is therefore no longer fully dependent on gas exports to Western Europe, making it less vulnerable to political pressure from Western European countries or the

USA (as with the now-defunct Nord Stream 2 project). The 3000-kilometer gas pipeline between Russia and China, called *Power of Siberia*—the world's largest energy supply project—was put into operation in December 2019. China's banks have also extended special credit lines to Russian banks,[46] and cooperation in this strategic partnership continues to expand. Through forums such as the annual SCO meetings, Xi and Putin meet regularly, with India's Modi also increasingly participating. By late 2024, China had become Russia's largest buyer of coal and crude oil, while the EU, despite sanctions and public condemnations, remained its largest buyer of pipeline gas, with China in second place. Considering overall fossil fuel exports, China is now Russia's largest buyer, followed by India, Turkey, the EU, and Brazil. The EU therefore accounts for only around 12–15 percent of Russia's top five fossil fuel buyers.[47]

The newly established strategic trade structures, value chains, research and development projects, and the military, economic, financial, and monetary cooperation into which the West has pushed both countries will not be easily reversed. Since the sharp escalation of sanctions on Russia in 2022, these ties have deepened significantly: trade reached a record volume of 240 billion USD in 2023,[48] up from 190 billion in 2022,[49] and Chinese cars now account for one-third of all sales in Russia.[50] This process of driving Russia into China's arms has therefore been described by some Western strategists as a major strategic mistake.[51] As of 2025, the sanctions appear to have had far less negative impact on the Russian economy than expected, while affecting the sanctioning countries—especially Germany—much more severely. For two consecutive years, Russia recorded higher GDP growth than both the EU and the USA, while the German economy in particular has continued to struggle.[52]

David Teurtrie notes in *Le Monde diplomatique* that Russia's economic growth is by no means limited to the military-industrial complex. Sanctions have led to the reinvestment of Russian capital within the country, spurring significant expansion in the construction sector and domestic tourism. The automobile industry alone grew by 19 percent in 2023, while the budget deficit remains at about 2 percent of GDP and the national debt at 17 percent—one of the lowest levels in the world.

He also writes that the failure of the sanctions is due not only to internal Russian factors but also to the refusal of most non-Western countries to support the measures against Moscow. Trade with China and Brazil has increased, and exports to India have even tripled within two years. Moreover, actions such as the freezing of Russian central bank assets have, in many ways, undermined the credibility of Western financial systems among non-Western states. The use of the US dollar for secondary sanctions against third parties trading with Russia has likewise led countries such as China and Saudi Arabia to reduce their holdings of US government bonds, while others are increasingly shifting toward trade in their national currencies.

Teurtrie thus concludes:

> By concentrating on the power struggle with Moscow, the Western elites have overlooked the collateral damage their policies are causing at a global level. All in all, the US and its European allies underestimated Russia's adaptability and industrial potential. This misjudgment is one of the reasons why the West is becoming increasingly isolated in the world.[53]

In the field of military technology, China and Russia now stand on nearly equal footing and have developed strong strategic complementarity under shared military pressure from the West—especially the USA, which maintains more than 750 military bases globally, many surrounding China and Russia, and conducts near-continuous maneuvers along their borders and coasts. On its 70th anniversary, the People's Republic of China showcased an intercontinental missile capable of reaching Washington with exceptional speed and precision, while Russia unveiled its most powerful supersonic bombers and continues to field the world's most advanced missile defense systems. China has also recently launched its second and most capable aircraft carrier. In addition, Russia, China, and Iran—three countries frequently targeted by Western hostility—have conducted joint naval maneuvers for the first time. These developments should serve as a credible warning to the USA to refrain from military "adventures" it can no longer win. Unlike the Soviet Union in the 1980s, Russia and China today cannot be outgunned. Rather, it is the USA that risks outgunning itself.

Indeed, it is gradually becoming known in the West that the combined Russian and Chinese defensive technology—missile defense, short- and medium-range missiles, missiles for the destruction of US aircraft carriers, early detection of US stealth bombers, and so on—has a technological quality that is in many ways not matched by the West and is unbeatable in the hypersonic range. US aircraft carriers, traditionally the golden calves of the imperial arms madness of the twentieth and twenty-first centuries, have thus become military dinosaurs. The trillion-dollar US stealth technology is now detectable early through Chinese quantum communication and has, with all its former military-imperial grandeur, become normal, vulnerable, and manageable. The Empire can no longer afford to attack the combined defense technologies of China and Russia. This is known today in the arms centers and among military experts of the West, and hopefully also in its political centers.[54] China's hypersonic missiles are almost all medium-range, with ranges of 1000 to 1500 kilometers, meaning they do not reach the USA and are therefore not offensive weapons—but they can fend off any attack from the hundreds of US military bases or aircraft carriers surrounding China.

And mind you, the starting signal for the development of new generations of weapons was given by the USA itself when it terminated the arms limitation treaties in 2002, long before Trump.[55] This triggered an arms race like we have not seen since the First Cold War, which the USA still hoped to win at the time, in order to remain the sole imperial world power.

The capacity to win an international arms race is no longer possessed by the USA and its NATO allies today. Russian-Chinese arms superiority now ensures that many wars can no longer be waged—or won. The Empire is increasingly resorting to economic, technological, and sanction-based warfare. Its failure to learn from the past is illustrated by the grand hegemonic gesture with which Trump established the *United States Space Force* as a new branch of the US military in December 2019.[56]

It will not help the USA. Puffed cheeks can no longer deceive anyone who has delved into the matter. All aggressive actions of the Empire, whether economic or military, including the once-celebrated "victories" in Afghanistan, Iraq, Libya, or Ukraine (see, for example, George W. Bush's 2003 speech "Mission Accomplished"), have so far only contributed to its own decline to the world's second position or are clearly designed to further that decline. Perhaps that is why US President Trump announced and carried out a series of, to put it mildly, surprising and partly confusing withdrawal maneuvers of the US military, culminating in Biden's Afghanistan withdrawal in 2021 and the takeover by the Taliban, the same group that rose to power partly as a consequence of US support for the Mujahideen in the first place.

The "balance of terror" has thus been restored due to the Russian-Chinese strategic partnership. It is now, as in the First Cold War, the second-worst situation; the worst would be an "imbalance of terror" in favor of the Empire.

How easy it would have been to accept the countless peace, cooperation, and negotiation offers from Russia or China. Talk and negotiate with the serious intention not to destroy the other but to reach a balance of interests. There was once such a culture in international relations, an attitude so simple yet apparently so difficult to achieve. Since 2022, however, this situation has become increasingly irreversible.

There are slight differences compared with the First Cold War. We are not faced with a bipolar situation of two opposing blocs and a non-aligned rest. Rather, China and Russia do not form a coherent bloc but maintain a strategic partnership that emerged in response to Western antagonization within an increasingly multipolar world, in which non-Western powers such as India and Brazil, as well as developing countries, are becoming increasingly integrated. Since 2022, multipolarization has *accelerated*, a development that in many ways favors China's diplomatic approach and will likely increasingly isolate the West, especially the EU and the USA in their seemingly unwavering partnership, from the rest of the world if it does not change course. Therefore, we will report on China's "new globalization" in detail in the section below.

BRI, A Novel Kind of Re-globalization: Re-coupling and Cooperation

Global Significance, Global Attention, and Accompanying Analyses

Not many things in the world today are as widely discussed or as constantly observed, documented, analyzed, and monitored[57] by numerous research institutes and observation centers worldwide as what has been described as "perhaps the most ambitious infrastructure project in human history".[58] We are, of course, talking about China's network of "New Silk Roads", also known as the "Belt and Road Initiative" (BRI) or "One Belt, One Road" (OBOR): "There is simply no other comprehensive, inclusive, far-reaching, and financially solid development program on the global market."[59]

The idea was only officially born, announced, and launched in 2014. In the first ten years of its existence, it has already transformed at breathtaking speed from a concept into the reality of a global awakening, especially for developing countries. Around the world, hundreds of projects are now being linked through a new global network of trade exchange, the infrastructural construction of trade routes, and the economic and infrastructural empowerment and development of BRI partner countries. This includes developing nations in the broadest sense—in Africa, Latin America, Central Asia, and also in Eastern and Southern Europe. Experts have assessed it as a "key element for global growth, poverty reduction, and greater economic stability".[60]

By the end of 2019, only five years after its announcement, the "project of the century"[61] already included 137 countries and 30 international organizations, connected through 197 international legal agreements.[62]

We do not need, and cannot, go into details here. Newspapers, journals, and blogs are full of project information and individual aspects every day, whether presented objectively or subjectively, accurately or distortedly. The overall picture that is emerging is too extensive and too dynamic. What is said about the BRI today is already outdated tomorrow, as is generally the case with China.

One of the most comprehensive, detailed, and comparatively objective sources is the Global Development Policy Center (GDP Center) at Boston University in Massachusetts, USA, which has documented the BRI from the beginning in its bi-weekly newsletter *Global China Roundup* and draws on worldwide media reports and academic studies.[63] Johns Hopkins University in Washington, D.C., also follows the BRI, particularly in Africa through its *China Africa Research Initiative*.[64] As the largest coherent investment program in the world, the BRI—or New Silk Roads—is necessarily and rightly the most researched and, therefore, the most transparent major project of our time. It is noteworthy that not only Chinese and American research institutes monitor the initiative but also the largest US consulting firms (McKinsey, KPMG, Ernst & Young, and others), as well as international consortia of Chinese, American, and other institutions and consulting firms. All of this is reflected in the ongoing adaptation, further development, and growing quality of its implementation.

The project could, of course, easily become a major financial and/or ecological disaster due to its sheer size and complexity, for example, if the increased trade volume that comes with it were to lead to an extensive and ruthless expansion of infrastructure corridors through many still untouched areas of the world. Indeed, new trade routes will pass through regions of Central Asia, Southeast Asia, and Africa that have never experienced such scale and intensity before. Therefore, it is crucial that the financing and productivity, as well as the ecological impacts of production, infrastructure, and transport systems, are analyzed early on and continuously monitored, managed, and improved.

Reform and Opening-Up 2.0: Cooperation with 140+ Countries Representing Five+ Billion People

The New Silk Roads have been compared to the "Long March" of the Chinese People's Liberation Army under Mao Zedong in 1934–35 and described as a "new development model".[65] It is indeed a new development model in the sense of being an alternative to imperial globalization based on the claim of global hegemony by a single country.[66] This "old" globalization has been driven against the wall—ecologically, socially, economically, and finally politically and morally—and, in the end, during the final years of the "Trumpist" Washington strategy of global disruption to stop China, it even (perhaps consistently) led to a new phase of de-globalization (see above).

The BRI has also been referred to as "Chinese Opening 2.0",[67] highlighting that it represents a performance and risk assumption by China comparable to the transformation and challenges associated with the "Reform and Opening-Up" initiated in 1978. However, the recent opening of China's industrial sectors to foreign corporations and capital may even constitute a more profound and riskier "Opening 2.0" than the BRI itself—especially in the automotive and financial sectors, now accessible even without joint-venture requirements, and through further reductions in import tariffs implemented since 2018 in response to Washington's economic war and the collapse of world trade. Yet it is also clear that both developments are not entirely independent of one another.

The BRI is essentially a project aimed at reconnecting the Eurasian continent. Historically, various routes of the old Silk Roads existed since the beginning of our era—trade routes that passed through Central and South Asia. Today's project, however, goes far beyond that: it includes Africa, Latin America, and Southeast Asia, consists of both land and maritime routes, and more recently even encompasses a northern maritime route that does not leave the 60,000 inhabitants of Greenland out.[68]

With its current projects and plans, the BRI already integrates more than 140 countries[69] and nearly 5 billion people,[70] *more than half of humanity*, and represents about 40 percent of world GDP,[71] with this share continuing to grow. Overall, according to a 2019 study by the Centre for Economics and Business Research, the BRI is expected to boost the world's GDP by 7.1 trillion USD per year by 2040.[72]

The significance of individual Silk Road routes has been compared to the historical importance of the Suez Canal and, in reference to Xi's formula of the "new socialism of our era", has been called the "Suez Canal of Our Era".[73] A "middle" route through Turkey has already been opened. A North Sea route is expected to revolutionize Eurasian trade, and the new fast freight train routes through Central Asia will connect Central China with Duisburg, Rotterdam, or Hamburg in a foreseeable eight days.[74] Newly opened train routes or sections, such as one over the German Baltic Sea island of Rügen or various Central Asian sections, have already been described in detail by many observers.[75] A Chinese-backed 3.5 billion US dollar megaport in Peru, inaugurated in November 2024 during Xi's visit to the Asia-Pacific Economic Cooperation (APEC) Forum, could potentially create trade routes that fully bypass North America. This is another indicator of waning US influence in the Western Hemisphere: Washington, which has historically viewed Latin America "primarily in terms of illegal migration and illegal drugs", "is now paying the price for years of indifference towards its neighbours and their needs", as even the *BBC* has observed.[76]

Transparent State Contracts and Infrastructure Investments, and Loans Without Political Interference

The main instrument of the international Silk Road initiative is public, transparent contracts based on international law. Within this framework, China's public banks and funds primarily finance public infrastructure in the partner countries, but they also support secondary private investments by Chinese companies (officially called "outbound Foreign Direct Investment", or oFDI in China) as well as private corporate investments within the partner countries. This stands in contrast to the often-corrupt structures that frequently turned the old globalization into a one-sided system of exploitation—raw materials exchanged for corruption payments to national or local elites—which produced very little real development or economic emancipation in these countries.

The funds are usually granted as long-term, flexibly repayable loans with interest rates below those of the market to the partner countries.[77] The US-based Brookings Institution has described China's credit policy as "friendly",[78] while others have called it "patient" in the sense of "Patient Local Capital".

Unlike Western countries and their institutions, such as the World Bank and IMF, China usually does not grant its loans bilaterally. Instead, loans are often provided on a different basis, for example, through consortium arrangements and secured within larger country communities, which can reduce risks and lower interest rates.

Above all, there are no economic policy prescriptions or political preconditions.[79] That is, except for inherent quality control of the projects, none of the usual neoliberal guidelines of the IMF and World Bank—such as austerity policies, privatizations, social cuts, and redistribution measures at the expense of the general population—are applied.[80] Cooperation without any political preconditions occurs, for example, with countries of Central and Eastern Europe (CEE), many of which are even EU members. In the BRI, the Confucian principle of "harmony in diversity" also appears to become reality.[81]

Global Effects

We have already mentioned some global economic assessments of the BRI above. Of course, the close scientific monitoring of the BRI also includes impact analyses. These cover the capacity effects of infrastructure and private corporate investments, the distribution of wealth gains, the ecological and social effects, and the net effects on global trade volume, including the balance between "trade creation" among participating countries and "trade diversion" at the expense of third countries.

Researchers from the World Bank have found that the trade volume among 71 examined BRI partner countries had already increased by over 4 percent by 2018,[82] which corresponds to an increase in total world trade volume of 2 to 3 percent. China's investments in BRI partner countries are thus, contrary to conventional economic wisdom, associated with greater rather than reduced trade volume, promoting trade rather than substituting it, as is usually assumed.[83]

Financial Overstretch?

China accumulated enormous currency reserves during its years as the world's extended workbench—at its peak, about four trillion US dollars. These reserves have already been reduced to around three trillion US dollars in the current decade as part of the new domestic economic development model, which includes planned lower export surpluses and increased financial foreign engagement (oFDI). They were usually invested passively—although relatively safely in earlier years—in US government debt securities, which financed US government deficits and represented, in principle, a purely speculative financial use on Wall Street.[84]

Today, they are being reduced on the one hand, but on the other hand also used differently and more proactively. The Chinese central bank can, in principle, provide the state-owned universal banks, various international and BRI-related Chinese special banks, and funds with resources for their tangible investments,[85] thereby leveraging the Chinese currency reserves, as with any normal bank-related money creation, to a multiple of credit volume. The figure of 15 trillion US dollars as potential BRI financing had already been publicly estimated early.[86] It is more toward 20 trillion today. China's EXIM Bank alone has recently exceeded the trillion-dollar mark in credit distributions.[87] This represents a financing potential that is rarely mentioned in current reporting, which is not yet fully mobilized but could be mobilized over the coming years. Chinese foreign exchange reserves are thus being subjected to a higher real interest rate than if they were only held in low-interest US government bonds.

We are thus talking about magnitudes that the world has not yet known, which also make the frequent "overextension" warnings, to which Western media often devote attention, appear somewhat less alarming. At present, there is no indication that the international BRI initiative could collapse or stall due to any form of financial mismanagement, particularly any overextension of China, as is often predicted in the West. As already mentioned (see above on China's financial system), a professionally managed and regulated financial system that prevents uncontrolled international speculation and excessive leverage—dangerous effects arising from investment and shadow banks using uncontrolled derivatives—remains within its own currency and retains sovereignty over national exchange rates, making it practically always stabilizable.[88]

Financial stability is therefore not primarily a question of the quantitative leverage of Chinese currency reserves into the multi-trillion range. Nor does it imply that China could now proclaim the world a land of milk and honey. The queue of countries seeking Chinese investments is already long enough. Rather, it is about a transparent and collectively rationally managed national, and in part also international, financial system.

The most important banks involved in the BRI are:

- The Asia Infrastructure Investment Bank (AIIB) (members now including Germany and the UK)
- The China Development Bank

- The New Development Bank (the BRICS Bank)
- The China EXIM Bank

In addition, a number of special funds have been established:

- A general Silk Road Fund
- A fund for global climate measures
- A fund for South-South cooperation
- A fund for projects in the Community of Latin American and Caribbean States (CELAC)
- Special funds for projects and regions in Africa, Arabia, a Eurasia Fund, and more
- The Kunming biodiversity fund for the poorest developing countries
- And more[89]

Overall, the capital endowments of these banks alone already surpass those of the World Bank and the development banks of the old globalization.[90]

The amounts that Western countries, particularly those of the EU, are now offering in response to Chinese international networking—for example, in their initiatives toward Southeast Asia or Africa, such as their new so-called connectivity strategy—are mostly in the lower billion range (four billion euros were pledged at the EU-Africa Summit in 2017) or are spread over the mid- to late 2020s (123 billion euros for Asia[91] and 150 billion for Africa until 2027[92]). As far as can be seen, these funds are not linked to a concrete real economic or infrastructural investment perspective. The EU, and especially former Chancellor Merkel and Prime Minister May on their Africa trips, were, like the USA in Latin America, primarily concerned with stopping refugees.[93]

Even the EU's "Global Gateway" initiative, which pledged the aforementioned 150 billion euros for African infrastructure by 2027, has been described as providing "misleading" figures, since "the investments are expected to come largely from the private sector, with the EU securing the money through its investment guarantees", according to Wilhelm Emmrich of the foreign trade agency Germany Trade and Invest (GTAI).[94] Beyond this private funding, almost no new public funding has been pledged until 2027. Furthermore, much of the investment focuses on infrastructure for raw material extraction, leading critics to argue that "the initiative could continue the extractivism of the colonial era. The fact that the old European colonizers now claim that they want to protect Africans from the Chinese is often seen as hypocritical on the continent", as one observer noted.[95]

The USA also responded to China's initiative in 2019 with an Indo-Pacific infrastructure program called the "Blue Dot Network" (BDN), with 60 billion USD pledged for initial funding. Essentially, it too appears to be a purely commercially oriented initiative, financed by private banks, which has also claimed to evaluate BRI projects in terms of quality and sustainability.[96] The Blue Dot Network later launched the so-called "Partnership for Global Infrastructure and Investment" (PGII) as a collaborative effort by the G7 countries to counter the BRI in 2022. It emerged from the now defunct and failed "Build Back Better World" initiative under the Biden administration, which never moved beyond the planning phase. While the figure of 600 billion USD has been cited as a pledge (compared to China's multi-trillion-dollar BRI), again largely through private investments,[97] few substantive details have been disclosed as of late 2024, aside from a commitment of "$2 million of seed money for the steering committee" by the USA.[98]

Thus, over ten years after the initiation of the BRI, Western countries have still failed to develop a substantial and effective response. The reasons for this go far beyond a mere lack of initiative: they are in part systemic, as will be outlined in detail in the third part of this book.

A "Debt Trap" for Africa?

One of the main criticisms in Western media and literature is the alleged danger of "debt bondage"—an irreversible credit dependency of partner countries on China, which would render them unable to service their loans. According to this view, China allows developing countries to take on such high levels of debt in their distress that they become overwhelmed by interest and repayment burdens and must either replace one loan with the next or eventually lose control over their own infrastructures.[99]

It seems that the actual reality of global debt traps under the old globalization and the regime of the World Bank and IMF is being projected onto a supposed future Chinese horror scenario. Some proponents of this narrative may be succumbing to a psychological projection ("every accusation is a confession"),[100] while others may simply lack the imaginative horizon for a "possible other world" and cannot conceive that development aid and cooperation could occur without exploitation.

China, as shown above, has a long tradition of solidarity with and financial development aid for developing countries, without any known cases of "debt servitude" so far. Moreover, China has repeatedly demonstrated that it can handle any "credit squeeze" through internal borrowing mechanisms within its flexibly regulated financial system.[101]

Moreover, the countries concerned are predominantly themselves involved, with voting rights, in the new financing instruments—the participating international banks and funds, such as the AIIB and the BRICS Bank—which should make it impossible to establish a system of Chinese debt servitude. As mentioned, Chinese loans are usually transparently based on multilateralism. Conversely, there seems to be considerable trust on the Chinese side in the validity of international law with regard to public and private foreign investments and state treaties, and in the contractual fidelity and willingness to cooperate of the partners, who are often, such as the EU and/or NATO member countries, strategically more tied to the US Empire. The repeated serious experiences with international arbitrary acts by Washington, London, and their allies in the EU, Australia, Canada, or Japan in cases of illegal confiscations of foreign bank balances, gold reserves, and other property (such as in the cases of ZTE, Huawei, or China Mobile) in numerous "insubordinate" countries, as well as against their companies and private individuals, should actually make China more cautious in its international capital investments. However, it can be assumed that, against this background, no US or EU bank is involved in the transfers of the BRI billions anymore.

The above-mentioned documentations of the GDP Center of Boston University on the BRI, as well as reports from several other research institutes, note numerous renegotiations of credit conditions, refinancing measures, deferrals, and even complete debt cancellations by China for individual developing countries.[102] China and its partners thus see themselves far removed from any debt trap.[103] To name one concrete example: in 2022, China forgave 23 loans for 17 African countries. Even a conservative estimate from a Johns Hopkins University study found that between 2000 and 2019, China canceled at least 3.4 billion USD in debt for African countries and restructured 15 billion, without any evidence of "asset seizures".[104] Even the US state-funded broadcaster *Voice of America* has therefore acknowledged that "the debt-trap narrative against China is unfounded", citing experts such as Deborah Brautigam of the above-mentioned Johns Hopkins University study, Shahar Hameiri of Queensland University, and Harry Verhoeven of Columbia University.[105]

And finally, the literature on the BRI is full of official documents, considerations, analyses, and proposals for improving "governance" in order to keep debts sustainable. For this purpose, there is now even an international "Debt Sustainability Framework".[106]

It is obvious that such a young, extensive, and complex project network, with diverse projects, financing forms, participating banks, funds, and partner countries that often have little experience in professional project management, requires permanent financial readjustments. This applies not only to individual distressed loans, but also to the level of a possibly distressed partner country with its numerous loans, and finally to the total credit volume that China can afford macroeconomically within a given period.

In financing matters, it should therefore be a reassuring sign that UN sub-organizations such as UNDP, UNEP, or FAO are increasingly becoming partners—for example, in the quality and impact control of projects[107]—or are also involved in necessary refinancing for individual recipient countries.

Ecologically Accompanied, Controlled, and Evaluated by International Research Institutes: The Green Silk Road[108]

All Silk Road projects are now also subject to strict ecological criteria and project oversight. In general, the New Silk Roads are shifting the focus of the global logistical "modal split" (the combination of different modes of transport along an international goods route) away from cumbersome and ecologically damaging ship transport toward rail. They are therefore replacing an increasing portion of cheap but slow, and above all ecologically harmful, overseas shipping, which accounts for the largest emissions in the global modal split. At present, only about 5–10 percent of ship traffic is being replaced by rail,[109] but the trend is rising. Rail also partially substitutes for fast but expensive, and still ecologically problematic, air transport.[110]

The "ecological BRI" also includes the concept of "Smart" or "Wise Cities", particularly along the rail routes.[111] We mentioned the Xinjiang capital, Urumqi, as an important hub.

The international accompanying project analyses and the increasingly intelligent control mechanisms demonstrate progressively stronger quality control. For example, in addition to avoiding debt traps, combating corruption, and improving general efficiency, a large cross-sectional focus is applied to ecological upgrading, such as combating deforestation, protecting rainforests, and similar measures.[112] The UNDP and the China Development Bank, for instance, have developed and published an international framework of financing standards for ecologically sustainable development, which includes the "Green Investment Principles" (GIP) for the BRI, released by China in 2018.[113] These were followed in 2021 by the "Green Development Guidelines for Overseas Investment and Cooperation" and the "Guidelines for Ecological and Environmental Protection of Foreign Investment Cooperation and Construction Projects". The green investment strategy pursues a dual goal: reducing coal-related investments on the one hand and increasing green energy investments on the other.[114]

This strategy has, in fact, been implemented. While "coal-related investments and construction projects dropped to around zero in 2021 and 2022", "investments in renewable energy and solar, wind, and hydropower in the Belt and Road region increased by 50 percent year-on-year in 2022".[115]

Such information must not only be sought with a magnifying glass in Western media, but the question also arises as to where the West—through its constant sharp criticisms of China on these issues of global importance, or more specifically within UN processes—actually stands. No comparable initiatives are visible. Instead, widespread obstruction is evident, as the annual UN Climate Change Conferences (COP) often dramatically demonstrate.

Again: "China in Africa"

China's close cooperation with most African countries is also a major point of criticism—or rather, fearmongering—by Western media. "Debt bondage", "new imperialism", "power politics", "environmental destruction", "resource theft", "land grabbing", and similar accusations form the familiar repertoire of projections drawn from past and present colonial and imperial globalization.

As already described, China has a long tradition of friendly solidarity and non-colonial relations with most African countries.[116] Today, it apparently pays off that China stood on the "right side of history".

Between 2015 and 2018 alone, Chinese companies made about 300 billion US dollars in direct foreign investments ("Foreign Direct Investments"—FDI) in Africa. Today, China accounts for more than a third of all infrastructure investments on the continent, and it has been calculated that Chinese public infrastructure investments predominantly target development bottlenecks.[117]

Studies from US sources have also produced notable findings regarding China's engagement in Africa. For example, the aforementioned China-Africa project consortium at Johns Hopkins University concludes, "Chinese engagement in Africa emphasizes infrastructure needs".[118]

The American Carnegie Foundation also concludes that China's Africa engagement contributes to the sustainable fight against poverty.[119]

The American consulting firm McKinsey, completely unsuspected of any sympathy for China's system or politics, had already examined and interviewed 1000 Chinese companies in Africa (out of a total of about 10,000 Chinese companies active on the continent) in 2017 and revealed surprising findings[120]:

- Already nearly 90 percent of employees in Chinese companies in Africa were local employees, i.e., Africans.
- Chinese companies already employ several million Africans (extrapolated to the 10,000 companies: up to ten million).
- Two-thirds of the companies provide training and further education for their African employees.
- One-third of the companies have already brought new technologies into the country.
- Already 44 percent of managers in Chinese companies are Africans (up to 80 percent in individual companies).
- Chinese companies in Africa are "primarily focused on serving the needs of Africa's fast-growing markets rather than on exports".
- "An overwhelming 74 percent said they feel optimistic about the future. Reflecting this, most Chinese firms have made investments that represent a long-term commitment to Africa rather than trading or contracting activities."

McKinsey summarizing:

> On balance, we believe that China's growing involvement is strongly positive for Africa's economies, governments, and workers.[121]

Similar findings are also present in other studies:

- A Ministry of Education report from 2018 showed that 80,000 Africans were already studying in China then, with 6385 pursuing a PhD, which was 20 percent of all foreign PhD students.[122]
- Chinese agricultural companies and agricultural experts secure and renew African agriculture.
- China competes with African countries primarily in the field of textile production, but otherwise mainly produces complementary goods, such as electronics for the local market, at prices lower than American or European offers, thereby increasing local purchasing power.[123]
- Chinese development aid (ODA) has increased fiscal autonomy in the African recipient countries and thus enabled increased spending of these countries in their health and education sectors.[124]
- The label "Made in China" is to be gradually replaced by the label "Made in Africa" for production from Africa.[125]

US studies on alleged Chinese land grabbing come to the following conclusion, among others[126]:

- Chinese land grabbing is not verifiable. China ranks only 19th among non-African countries with land ownership in Africa, far behind the main "land grabbers" USA, UK, Saudi Arabia, Singapore, Netherlands, India, Malaysia, etc.
- Instead of the six million hectares claimed in the West, only 240,000 hectares were verifiably owned by Chinese companies.

On the alleged resource theft:

- Africa is by far not China's most important partner to meet its resource needs; trade with Africa (including raw materials) accounts for less than 10 percent of China's foreign trade.[127]
- The majority of China's public investments in Africa therefore do not flow into resource extraction (only just under 30 percent flow into resource extraction in the broadest sense) but into infrastructure, information technology, and education.[128]
- Most of China's public investments flow into resource-poor countries like Zambia or Tanzania.[129]

All of this ultimately explains why the Chinese are welcome in Africa:

- A representative study by *Afrobarometer*[130] in 36 African states in 2015 already found that 63 percent of the Africans surveyed welcome China's economic and political role in Africa and see a positive influence of China on Africa. In addition to investments in infrastructure and development, the reason given is "the different way of dealing with each other" (as well as "negotiations on an equal footing").[131]
- The representation of the Konrad Adenauer Foundation of the German Christian Democratic Union (CDU) in Senegal reported back home accordingly:

> China enjoys a good reputation in Senegal and is praised for its efficiency and commitment [...] the media report very positively about the Chinese presence [...] [In contrast, overall] anti-western sentiments are increasing.[132]

This stands in stark contrast to Western projections of their own colonial mentality onto Africa, which often depict Africans and their governments as people and countries without real agency, who can only be exploited. However, this contradicts empirical research on the topic. For example, a major study by Christina Seyfried of Yale University, based on hundreds of expert interviews with policymakers and investors in Nigeria, South Africa, Kenya, Ethiopia, and Tanzania, has shown that rather than African countries being simply "price-takers", governments in fact have significant influence on investment conditions with Chinese companies, making them the "price-setters" instead.[133] With new competitors for investments emerging in Africa, many governments nevertheless turn toward Chinese competitors to Western companies out of their own volition—not only because of colonial resentments but also because Chinese companies have often been more open and flexible in negotiating conditions.

"Africa on the rise" can be read everywhere today, and there is feverish speculation about the "awakening continent" and its resources and potential. But who helps Africa develop industrially after decades of waiting and falling behind, after the phase of national anti-colonial liberation in the 1950s and 1960s, under the dominance of neoliberal, imperial globalization since the 1980s? For many, the answer is increasingly: China.[134]

In doing so, it also helps the EU more effectively combat poverty-driven migration and keep future refugees "at bay" than the EU does itself,[135] which relies on interception camps and Libyan coast guard operations, while otherwise holding EU-Africa conferences with lofty words but few ideas, projects, and, above all, little funding. Of course, as an African minister, you attend such events. But even a Kenyan or Nigerian foreign minister understands "Fortress Europe" and knows that Merkel, Scholz, Merz, Macron, and the like travel to Africa mainly due to domestic pressure—and also knows where and with whom real progress can be made.

BRI "Governance": Accompanying Analyses and Forums, Ongoing Adaptations

China organizes its international relations not like the USA, which increasingly operates bilaterally (for example, TTIP and similar initiatives), bypassing the once self-created multilateralism of the WTO, but rather multilaterally—both in financing and through cooperation forums and annual conferences. Thus, annual coordination rounds take place not only with BRI partners in Africa, Europe, or Latin America but also for the entire BRI. In October 2023, on its 10th anniversary, the third BRI Forum was held in Beijing.[136] And with the Central and Eastern European (CEE) countries, for example, there is the 14+1 format (more on this below).

In addition to the above-mentioned issue of the permanent, flexible adjustment of financing, it must also be noted critically that the Chinese and international law principle of non-interference in internal affairs, combined with existing old corrupt structures and cultures and overly lax controls, has sometimes led to labor and environmental standards not being fully observed, particularly in the early stages.

Chinese studies themselves have pointed out that 90 percent of the 10,000 Chinese companies are small- and medium-sized private enterprises, whose owners often lacked sufficient qualifications for their overseas activities and did not fully understand or comply with the required labor and social standards or local regulations.[137]

The development of mainly African countries into competitive industrial nations, and the long-term promotion of local production capacities rather than quickly displacing them through external superiority, is a development-policy balancing act that no Western industrial nation has ever seriously considered. In the short term, the African population is supplied with high-quality electronic products by Chinese companies, while at the same time high-quality domestic production is being established.[138]

Individual ecological problems related to oil, copper, cobalt, and gold extraction in countries such as Angola, Ghana, Chad, and the Democratic Republic of the Congo have been reported by Western media.[139] However, the conclusion that the BRI consists entirely of loss-making Chinese investments, that it is already overstraining the Chinese domestic economy, and that the "BRI bubble" would soon burst (as Western analysts predicted as early as 2018[140]), has largely proven to be wishful thinking.

China has continuously tightened its rules for overseas investments following these and other experiences,[141] and BRI investments in Africa, for example, have been accompanied and monitored by the China-Africa Institute for some time.[142]

China in Europe

"China in Africa", and, by the way, in Latin America[143] and Southeast Asia (already mentioned above),[144] seems bad enough for the European Union. However, "China in the EU" seems perfectly suited to trigger any register of panic. For example, the entire toolbox of the fear narrative "China is driving a wedge into the EU!"[145] is being pulled out of the closet. After all, in March 2019, China was classified by the EU as a "systemic rival".

But to continue the theme of Western "projection" onto China that runs through this book: as if the EU, through its botched neoliberal and monetarist brainchild of a currency union without an economic and social union—lacking even the most basic economic understanding, as if putting the ideology- and power-driven cart before the horse of economic integration—had not already caused enough division! The brainchild "monetary union" predictably became a monetary "rack" for the weaker (or "undisciplined", not sufficiently neoliberal-austerity wage-dumping) members, with an external value of the euro and a uniform discount rate both too high for most of the weak, and too low for Germany and the few other strong ones. Of course, Germany has always been happy to make compensation payments into the "structural funds". After all, that was the basic business of EU integration from the beginning, since the times of the customs union (from 1957): the counter-deal for the German export machine.

And as if this EU had not already sufficiently disintegrated itself through its bureaucratic-authoritarian fiscal and social policy directives to the weaker member states; through a dictatorial fiscal "European Semester"; through the imposed humanitarian catastrophe in Greece as a result of an arrogant "Troika" autocracy; through a "EU of two speeds", a "North EU" versus a "South EU"; the refusal of minimal compensation mechanisms by Germany; and so on.

And there they stand now—the left-behind countries of the EU in Central, Eastern, and Southern Europe—peripheral and without economic capacity to act, without headquarters or centrality functions, dominated by German corporations to whom, for example, Greek Telecom (Deutsche Telekom), Greek airports (Fraport), or the Eastern European automotive industries belong as a matter of course.

But this is also already the case within Germany: the "own" East cannot structurally catch up, no matter how many solidarity surcharges we pay for the next thirty years or how many financial patches we apply for village-core renovations, highways, and bypass roads. The Berlin puppet masters are facing the disaster of forty years of neoliberal narrow-mindedness—in Germany and in the EU.

And then comes China, with the offer of long-term cooperation on an equal footing: transparent contracts based on international law, attractive long-term loans, infrastructure investments, and job creation—real economic development instead of EU structural funds that have often disappeared into a corruption abyss. For the left-behind, this brings the prospect of an "upgrading", of a new "high road" for their development. And so, among other things, the following projects are being realized in European (not only EU) countries:

- An east-west corridor built through Macedonia.[146]
- A public transport system developed in Skopje.
- The Greek transmission system operator ADMIE (with a 24 percent share of Chinese companies) rehabilitated.
- A steel mill and thermal power plants constructed in Serbia.
- The high-speed line between Belgrade and Budapest built.
- The dilapidated Port of Piraeus rehabilitated (which the EU Troika had forced Greece to privatize, but for which no Western investor had been found). The port was then acquired by the Chinese company COSCO (51 percent), modernized through massive investments (at least four billion US dollars), and has since been operated

very successfully. Today, Piraeus is the largest container-handling port in the Mediterranean, with a several-fold increase in cargo turnover, significant job creation, revitalization of the entire region, and soon the first high-speed rail connection between Piraeus and Athens.[147]

Next to these developments that can be summed up under the designation of the "Balkan Silk Road", the list can easily be continued in the EU core countries:

- Italy's ports of Trieste and Genoa have been developed as additional endpoints of the New Silk Road.[148]
- The inner harbor of Duisburg in Germany has been developed into a hub of the New Silk Roads in Europe, with over 200 Chinese container trains per week,[149] rolling in over more than 11,000 kilometers of railway track[150] and now gradually returning fully loaded (and hopefully someday completely replacing the terrible container ships[151]).
- And even the German Railway (Deutsche Bahn—DB) was given a boost in freight traffic,[152] which DB and Berlin had run down under the neoliberal regime.[153]

Between 2015 and 2018 alone, China and Chinese companies invested approximately 380 billion US dollars, both privately and publicly, in Europe (including countries beyond the EU). Even the German Bertelsmann Foundation sought to temper the usual EU panic over Chinese foreign investments in a study, arguing that Western countries still invest more internationally than China—albeit differently, and perhaps less strategically and effectively.[154]

The EU Commission and Council bureaucracies reacted in their characteristic manner—defensively, authoritatively, and arrogantly. For example, the EU bureaucracy initiated a competition procedure against Hungary because of the "free-handed" awarding of the contract for the Budapest–Belgrade high-speed rail line to China.

Politically, the functionally incapable, "divergent", out-of-control, and politically–administratively failed integration project is backfiring on the EU. Greece suddenly blocked the EU's annual, uniform condemnation of China at the UN over human rights issues—a long-standing EU ritual and a true "taboo break".[155] Portugal and Hungary followed in the subsequent years. Hungary repeatedly refused to sign the EU's blatantly imperial human rights declarations against China.[156] And, as the first G7 country, Italy even joined the BRI in 2019—in open defiance. Naturally, pressure has been put on these countries, and "[f]irst Eastern European representatives have already complained that Brussels wants to alienate them from China".[157] In 2023, however, Italy formally withdrew from the BRI under its new EU- and NATO-aligned, neo-fascist prime minister, Giorgia Meloni.[158]

As mentioned, China and the Central, Eastern, and now also Southern European BRI participants have organized themselves in the "14+1" format (most of the 14 are EU members), which holds regular annual meetings and coordinates investments. Greece joined in 2019, while Estonia, Latvia, and Lithuania withdrew in 2022, citing the war in Ukraine and increased unofficial diplomatic engagement with Taiwan among other reasons. Due to its constant flux in membership, the format was previously also called the "16+1" or "17+1", which is why China today prefers the designation "China-CEEC".[159]

The seventh summit of the (then) 16+1 mechanism took place in Sofia in 2018, resulting in 20 newly signed projects[160]; the eighth was held in Dubrovnik in 2019, before the mechanism was temporarily put on hold due to the Covid-19 pandemic (a virtual summit took place in 2021).

The 14+1 format is multidimensional and "Asian-fluid" rather than rigid, formal, and "European-mechanical". It flexibly combines multilateralism and bilateralism,[161] something that the European partners apparently appreciate, not least in comparison with the formal integration structures of the EU.

And finally, even the prosperous, conservative, neutral Switzerland—not subject to Brussels' fiscal thumbscrew bureaucracy—Felix Helvetia, has expressed interest in becoming a partner country of the BRI.[162]

Possibly a reason for panic for those who celebrate "Europe" in soapbox speeches, yet trample on Europe's real Eurasian interests and understand "European integration" only in terms of their own partial power against the weaker states—their "backyard", the "lazy" in the south and east—opposing effective and balancing cooperation.

Who is truly fostering convergence in the EU periphery, promoting real integration, and thus enabling possible long-term stabilization of the EU? The then-Chinese Premier Li Keqiang put it succinctly at the EU–China Summit in 2019: China's cooperation with the CEE countries is "beneficial for a balanced development within the EU [and] also serves the unity of the EU […]"[163] before he traveled to the eighth 16+1 annual meeting in Dubrovnik.

In contrast, EU administrators in Brussels have frequently engaged in verbal warfare against China, often accompanied by sanctions that were met with countersanctions. This had the most noticeable effect on the "Comprehensive Agreement on Investment" (CAI), first proposed in 2013 and aimed at substantially improving investment conditions for EU companies in China—liberalizing the Chinese market through measures such as lifting joint venture requirements and technology transfer obligations, opening new investment sectors, and so on, essentially everything the EU has criticized China for not doing in the past. As of 2025, the CAI has still failed to materialize, with the EU announcing a freeze on its ratification in 2021, partly due to pressure from the USA.[164]

Chinese–EU relations, despite China's designation as a "systemic rival" and recent exchanges of blows, remain highly significant and substantial, particularly in trade. In 2020, China replaced the USA as the EU's largest trading partner for the first time, while the EU also became China's largest trading partner.[165] Recent announcements by the EU, such as the intent to impose tariffs on Chinese EVs of up to 45.3 percent,[166] are more indicative of a failed European industrial policy—resulting from decades of neoliberalism—than of Chinese practices. They reveal a European tendency to seek band-aid solutions for domestic failures by locating the problem externally, which will ultimately exacerbate these issues in a vicious cycle.

In opposition to Brussels' legislators, a rare case of European pragmatic thinking was occasionally offered by France's president, Emmanuel Macron (here in terms of foreign policy only), who, during his 2023 visit to China alongside French business leaders, called on Europe to develop a neutral position and reduce its dependence on the USA—including on the issue of Taiwan—while reconnecting with China in the post-Covid era in the fields of trade, energy, aviation (for example, the European company Airbus reached a deal to double sorely needed production in China after its 17-year-long trade dispute with its US competitor Boeing[167]), tourism, culture, and more.[168]

China in Germany

We have shown several examples of how the technological tables are now turning. In the future, German corporations, long at the global forefront of engineering, will increasingly benefit from China's technological knowledge. We highlighted the example of Bosch China. The official governmental and media panic over Chinese "Outbound Direct Investments" (ODI, or oFDI) in the EU and in Germany not only seems backward-looking, ideologically driven, or the product of helplessness and mistimed judgment but is also simply counterfactual.

What it has already achieved, however, is that Chinese FDI in Germany has significantly decreased since 2019, while England now receives more than twice as much Chinese FDI. Well-known cases of Chinese investment offers in companies such as Aixtron, Kuka, 50 Hertz, and Leifeld Metal Spinning were partly forbidden in a state-authoritarian manner, and thus anything but consistent with the principles of a "market economy".[169] The strong political faction of the "Transatlanticists", which has newly formed in recent years around figures such as German foreign ministers Sigmar Gabriel, Heiko Maas, and Annalena Baerbock; EU Commission presidents Jean-Claude Juncker and Ursula von der Leyen; and subsequent German ministers of Economic Affairs Peter Altmaier and Robert Habeck, has quickly developed new protectionist instruments to prevent Chinese investments. These instruments constitute modern capitalist-nationalist investment controls, now already applicable for sales of 10 percent or more of a company's value.[170]

From the spontaneous protectionist reflex, as already discussed above, a possible later rational, proactive, and structure-oriented industrial policy could certainly develop. Such a policy would again provide the state and collective capacity to act and to negotiate with China on broad, win-win cooperation on an equal footing. A prerequisite for this, however, would be an open, self-confident, future-oriented, problem-solving, and cooperative mindset.

The facts of Chinese investments in Germany at least speak their own language:

- In China in 2022, around 5200 German companies were represented with a record capital stock of about 122 billion euros,[171] while only about 2000 Chinese companies were represented in Germany. In 2021, Chinese investments in Germany amounted to only 4.6 billion euros and were on a declining trend.[172] By comparison, over 20 billion euros were invested in Eastern Europe in 2023.[173] Hungary alone received 44 percent of all Chinese FDI into Europe that year, more than France, Germany, and the UK combined.[174] The capital stock of Chinese companies in Germany still ranks among the lower tiers of foreign investments. For a long time, Germany and the EU as a whole invested multiples of what China invested in the EU.[175] This only began to balance out somewhat in 2018.

- In terms of the market value of listed German companies (DAX stock index), Chinese companies owned less than 3 percent as of 2024, while US investors held about 22.5 percent, roughly 10 times as much. All non-European and non-North American investors together hold only 3.9 percent of the DAX (only this number is reported).[176] As noted, "Chinese [...] investors, contrary to what media alarmism would suggest, [...] [in the DAX] play only a subordinate role."[177]
- The focus of German and EU intervention instruments against Chinese direct investments therefore demonstrably has no objective basis and is probably ideological, likely rooted in deeply ingrained perceptions of a "struggle for existence" against "the East". For dyed-in-the-wool transatlanticists such as the then-Minister of Economic Affairs Sigmar Gabriel (SPD—Social Democrats), "the (communist) East" naturally serves as an enemy image, because this enmity has been embedded in the SPD since 1918 and is more deeply ingrained in its political DNA than in that of many "bourgeois" parties.
- The real economic effects of mostly productive, real-investment Chinese company participations are generally greater than those of mostly speculative financial investments by American investment banks, hedge funds, or private equity companies, which often dismantle companies to sell the prime assets at a higher price, typically resulting in negative job development. Assessments from those familiar with the situation in German business associations are accordingly positive. For example, Hubert Lienhardt, former CEO of Voith and Chairman of the Asia-Pacific Committee of German Business, stated, "The German companies that have been taken over by Chinese companies are doing very well."[178]

Accordingly, the German Association for the Protection of Private Investors (DSW) criticized the then-Minister of Economic Affairs, Sigmar Gabriel, for acting as quickly as possible in the case of Aixtron at the request of the USA, without hesitation, calling him an "agent of US economic interests".[179] In this case, as is well known, the USA had asserted security interests.

Jürgen Heraeus, former board member of the Federation of German Industries (BDI) and head of the Heraeus Group, was quoted in the case of Kuka as saying: "If Kuka were so enormously important for Germany, then a few German or European corporations should have made an effort to secure larger shares. I know a number of companies in which the Chinese have invested. I have not observed the fears mentioned so far. On the contrary, look at the takeover of Putzmeister [concrete pumps]. The company is developing very well under Chinese leadership."[180]

And Hubert Lienhard again, similarly: "The fear that the Chinese were only interested in the know-how has not come true. On the contrary: Chinese investors have proven to be responsible and far-sighted in many cases."[181]

And from the perspective of employees, it is even said: "Worker councils in Germany are now happy when not a US 'locust', but an investor from China comes."[182]

- As a study by the Munich-based Ifo Institute already showed in 2019, "companies from the People's Republic [...] take over higher indebted companies than investors from other countries. [...] the debt ratio is 6.5 percentage points higher and the average profitability at the time of acquisition is close to zero, while other investors focus on companies with positive returns. [...] The preference for higher indebted and less profitable companies could [...] be explained by a longer-term investment horizon or better financing opportunities through state Chinese banks."[183] The study furthermore showed:

  Chinese companies often even purchase German companies with higher debt levels and lower productivity.

  They do not pay more for companies than buyers from other countries, indicating that they are not subsidized by the Chinese government for strategic purchases, as is often claimed.

  Companies acquired by Chinese investors often experience lower growth in capital productivity but stronger growth in wages.[184]

  Often, Chinese investors were therefore the only ones willing and able to buy, save, restructure, and invest in the long term, thereby maintaining German companies, as in the case of Piraeus. China's industrial investments almost always served to secure, stabilize, and upgrade the respective German company. Chinese companies generally do not hesitate to acquire undercapitalized German firms with significant long-term investment needs, for which there are otherwise no Western private buyers. This is precisely because Chinese companies, being systemically embedded, usually plan for the long term and often build their German subsidiaries as technological complements to their own capabilities. Nothing benefits the German industrial stock more than committed partners who are technologically engaged and capable of acting and investing competently over the long term.[185]

Chinese FDI: Western Scares, But Knowledge Transfers to the West and No Investment in "Cultural" and "Ideological" Industries

Thus, the tide of the old "technology theft" stories is shifting toward a more reciprocal dynamic, in which the West could potentially benefit more from China's leading R&D in emerging fields than vice versa.[186] We have presented numerous examples in which Western countries gain from China's technological lead. China has now moved away from the image of the "copycat". In fact, "copying" has never been a simple endeavor, either in China or in any other emerging country in history, because it always requires the learner's own effort and, as mentioned, sufficient "absorption capacity".

China has become an exporter of innovation and could, in cooperation with developed capitalist industrial countries, ideally contribute to *globally shared innovation*,[187] as it already does with the "developing countries" of the "Third World" and the partner countries of the New Silk Roads. Through its ODI, China not only supports their *industrialization* but, according to international studies, has also become a promoter of *institutional quality* on the path to sustainable modernization and development.[188] This includes, for example, the introduction of the rule of law and regulatory capacity in these countries, qualities that the West has apparently neither promoted nor been capable of fostering in decades of "development aid".

Chinese private oFDI (ODI) has generally undergone substantial correction since the 19th Party Congress of the CPC in October 2017, benefiting both the home country and the target countries and thus improving relations with the latter. Chinese FDI is intended to occur only for the purposes of mutual technology transfer, joint innovation, and learning, specifically in technology areas where China has identified its own deficits but can also contribute significant investments and know-how from other fields.

China's portfolio of foreign investments is currently being restructured, moving away from speculative, excessively risky, ideologically influenced, and "irrational" investments. The central government is now taking action against "unwise" and "risky" foreign investments by Chinese companies and investors. Examples include the mere purchase of real estate, hotels, football clubs, cinema chains, Hollywood studios, media companies, or other entertainment businesses,[189] as well as purely speculative financial instruments such as complex derivatives. For instance, the now-defunct Chinese investment company HNA sold its 26 percent stake in the Hilton hotel group and also reduced its stake in Deutsche Bank.[190] In these large-scale corrections of foreign investment, China even accepts price collapses and restructurings for companies such as HNA that are withdrawing from such commitments.[191]

This has already reduced Chinese foreign investments in certain "irrational", "unreasonable", speculative, and ideologically driven areas and is expected to increase investments in more rational, productive industrial sectors.[192] As a result, China's foreign portfolio is improving, and Chinese companies are withdrawing from symbolic, ideologically charged, and potentially conflict-prone investment areas in the West, particularly media companies. This trend could also contribute, and ideally should contribute, to reducing tensions with target countries over Chinese investments.[193]

Is China imperialistic?

In this popular accusation in the West, often repeated even by the left-liberal intelligentsia, it should be emphasized that the internationalization of Chinese investments—both in public infrastructure and private companies—occurs without any military dimension, accompaniment, or threat. This fact is highly significant, particularly in the context of the imperialism narrative.

After the above litmus test of "China in Africa", it should also be clear that China's foreign activities are economically different and driven by goals and mechanisms distinct from what we understand as "imperialism".[194] China's private foreign investments are apparently not simply the result of overproduction of capital seeking profitable outlets abroad to secure maximum returns. On the contrary, China's private returns can be adjusted at any time, as they are regulated and subject to the *primacy of politics*, as shown in several fields. China's private capital must therefore, when necessary, adapt to foreign principles, participate in common goods and infrastructure, invest, employ, and train locally, as illustrated by the example of Africa and by China's distancing from "irrational" non-productive investments.

China's private returns are the dependent variable, not the independent one. The independent variable is the political decision regarding the concrete design of international relations in the context of long-term, internationally cooperative national development. If an African country is to be promoted and economically developed under friendly or contractual conditions, the Chinese private company must subordinate itself and cannot pursue its own "foreign policy" to maximize private returns, which "politics" would then have to follow. The presence of the Chinese state abroad is therefore not intended to pave the way for its own "champions" or, if necessary, to force a path for them with violent means.

This view is shared by a number of critical analysts worldwide. Ali Kadri of the London School of Economics (LSE), for example, argues that China is not an empire and does not act imperialistically. According to Kadri, this notion is a construction of Western liberal intelligentsia, often pseudo-radical, which fails to perceive the breadth of debates about Chinese development, portrays actual imperialist actions as "democratic" and "humanitarian", and otherwise postulates "ideal socialism or nothing".[195]

Today, China's strength is once again promoting a global movement toward national independence. An expanded credit supply through China strengthens the purchasing power and choices of developing countries in relation to the established industrial nations.

Kadri goes even further, arguing that China represents a long-awaited civilizational shift in international relations. It acts without threats of war and without military operations in other countries. By contrast, the wars and interventions by the USA and EU in the Middle East, Ukraine, Afghanistan, and elsewhere serve, among other things, to disrupt the Silk Road project.

The aforementioned GDP Center at Boston University has also addressed the "imperialism" thesis regarding the Silk Roads and reached the interesting conclusion that the BRI is not primarily a geopolitical instrument. It is more economically than politically oriented and is "less geopolitical" than corresponding US programs.[196]

With China's BRI and foreign investments, we are likely witnessing a development that does not stem from a systemic compulsion to realize surplus capital through capital export. This also makes the option of "development without interference" possible.[197] In the words of a pragmatic banker, "China, unlike the USA, is not known for regime change but for implementing economic projects."[198]

International Immigration into China

In this context, we highlight another notable aspect that would have been surprising until recently but, in light of the developments discussed above, is no longer so. As already mentioned, thousands of young Africans are now studying in China, but they are not the only ones. As a German university professor [W.E.] who has sent students abroad to the USA for decades can attest, China has suddenly become an attractive destination for students seeking education abroad, even though it was not immediately clear when or how this "change of values" occurred.

Indeed, China has now become an immigration country. Many qualified ethnic Chinese, particularly from the USA, are returning to their homeland due to good job opportunities and, perhaps, a growing climate of mistrust in the USA. Hundreds of thousands of young people from developing countries across several continents are now studying in China. Beyond temporary study stays, entire African communities have formed in China, including many workers with longer-term or indefinite prospects of residence. Following the American model, China now also issues "Green Cards" for permanent residence and work permits. Its dynamic economic growth and demographic needs make this both possible and necessary. Finally, China now also accepts refugees from around the world.

Although the country has statistically only recently become a middle-income nation in global comparison—as we noted above—it is what the country makes of this status that matters. The unique approaches and practices we have sought to illuminate, analyze, explain, and understand—technologically, in employment, ecologically, and in terms of prosperity and welfare—have helped China become a global center of gravity, including for migrants.

An ancient and now renewed center of the world, potentially of a more multipolar one, is opening up for us to explore, observe, learn from, understand, negotiate with, and cooperate. If we could redevelop these best qualities and traditions of human coexistence internationally, we might have a chance to experience the end of this century in a more humane way.

Notes

1. Karen Andresen, "Ich sage nur China, China, China [All I have to say is China, China, China]", *Der Spiegel*, November 16, 2004; online at: www.spiegel.de, visited June 19, 2019.
2. *Merics China Update* 6/2018.
3. For example, Chen Xiangming, "Globalisation redux: can China's inside-out strategy catalyse economic development and integration across its Asian borderlands and beyond?", *Cambridge Journal of Regions, Economy and Society* 11(1), 2018, pp. 35–58.
4. Lin Justin Yifu, Wang Yan, "China's Contribution to Development Cooperation: Ideas, Opportunities and Finances", in: Shahid Yusuf (Ed.), *China and the Global Economy*, Cheltenham, UK, Northampton, MA, USA: E. Elgar, 2017, pp. 826–851.
5. *Solvecon Forex-Report*, March 19, 2019.
6. Johannes Heller-John, "Matt Ferchen: "In vielen Entwicklungsländern ist China die einzige Option" [Matt Ferchen: "In many developing countries, China is the only option"]", *Mercator Institute for China Studies*, March 24, 2020: https://merics.org/de/podcast/matt-ferchen-vielen-entwicklungslaendern-ist-china-die-einzige-option, visited October 27, 2024.
7. GAO Bai, "China's Belt & Road Initiative: A Counterforce to Globalisation Reversal", in: WANG Huiyao, LU Miao (Eds.), *Handbook on China and Globalization*, Cheltenham, UK, Northampton, MA, USA: E. Elgar, 2019; Vassilis Fouskas, Bulent Gokay, *The Disintegration of Euro-Atlanticism and New Authoritarianism: Global Power-Shift*, London, Cham (CH): Palgrave Macmillan, 2019.
8. These facts can be regularly read annually for decades in the reports of the *Stockholm International Peace Research Institute* SIPRI; most recently for example under: "SIPRI Yearbook 2024: Armaments, Disarmament and International Security", *SIPRI*, 2024: https://www.sipri.org/sites/default/files/2024-06/yb24_summary_en_2_1.pdf, visited October 29, 2024. On the number of US military bases in particular, for example: Hope O'Dell, "The US is sending more troops to the Middle East. Where in the world are US military deployed?", *Chicago Council on Global Affairs*, October 25, 2023: https://globalaffairs.org/bluemarble/us-sending-more-troops-middle-east-where-world-are-us-military-deployed, visited October 29, 2024.

9. For example: Tam Nguyen Huua, Deniz Dilan Karaman Örsal, "A new benign hegemon on the horizon? The Chinese century and growth in the Global South", *economics e-journal* 2019–60, November 13, 2019.
10. In detail for example Kunzmann 2018, pp. 95 ff.
11. Ibid., p. 98.
12. As an older example: *Merics China Update* 6/2018.
13. For example: "UN deputy chief praises China's investment in tackling climate change, forging 'new development pathway'", *The United Nations Office at Geneva*, June 30, 2023: https://www.ungeneva.org/en/news-media/news/2023/06/82547/un-deputy-chief-praises-chinas-investment-tackling-climate-change, visited October 29, 2023.
14. For example: *China Daily*, July 7/8, 2018, p. 17.
15. Jörg Kronauer, "Beijings Einfluss wächst [Beijing's Influence Grows]", *junge Welt*, June 26, 2019, p. 6.
16. For example: Kunzmann 2018, p. 99.
17. Elena Teslova, "Belarus joins Shanghai Cooperation Organization as 10th member state", *Anadolu Agency*, July 4, 2024: https://www.aa.com.tr/en/asia-pacific/belarus-joins-shanghai-cooperation-organization-as-10th-member-state/3265708, visited November 2, 2024.
18. For example: Zongyuan Zoe Liu, "China Is Quietly Trying to Dethrone the Dollar", *Foreign Policy*, September 21, 2022: https://foreignpolicy.com/2022/09/21/china-yuan-us-dollar-sco-currency/, visited November 2, 2024.
19. Vali Kaleji, "The Shanghai Cooperation Organization Is No 'New Warsaw' or 'Eastern NATO'", *The National Interest*, November 13, 2021: https://nationalinterest.org/feature/shanghai-cooperation-organization-no-new-warsaw-or-eastern-nato-196138, visited November 2, 2024.
20. For example: "What's behind the India-China border stand-off?", *BBC*, July 5, 2017: https://www.bbc.com/news/world-asia-40478813, visited November 2, 2024.
21. *China Daily*, July 14, 2017.
22. "Narendra Modi and Xi Jinping meet and resolve a border row", *The Economist*, October 24, 2024: https://www.economist.com/asia/2024/10/24/narendra-modi-and-xi-jinping-meet-and-resolve-a-border-row, visited November 2, 2024.
23. For example: Zhao Huanyu, "China and Global Economic Governance: Does BRICS Matter?", in: Wang Huiyao, Lu Miao, (Eds.), *Handbook on China and Globalization*, Cheltenham, UK, Northampton, MA, USA: E. Elgar, 2019, Chap. 20.

24. For example Erhard Crome, "Chinas Aufstieg und die geopolitischen Folgen" [China's rise and the geopolitical consequences], *WeltTrends*, December 2, 2017, https://welttrends.de/res/uploads/Crome-Chinas-Aufstieg-2017.pdf, visited May 20, 2024., p. 10.
25. Wolfgang Muenchau, "The West will pay a steep price if it ignores Brics countries", *New Statesman*, October 30, 2024: https://www.newstatesman.com/international-politics/geopolitics/2024/10/west-will-pay-steep-price-ignores-brics-countries, visited November 5, 2024.
26. "Vietnam joins BRICS as a Partner Country", *BRICS Brazil*, June 13, 2025: https://brics.br/en/news/vietnam-joins-brics-as-a-partner-country, visited July 17, 2025.
27. Ibid. Also: MG Chandrakanth, "How BRICS countries have overtaken the G7 in GDP based on PPPs", *The Times of India*, April 9, 2023: https://timesofindia.indiatimes.com/blogs/economic-policy/how-brics-countries-have-overtaken-the-g7-in-gdp-based-on-ppps/, visited November 5, 2024.
28. "BRICS+ Set to Overtake G7 in Global Trade by 2026, EY Report Reveals", *Outlook Business*, October 31, 2024: https://www.outlook-business.com/news/brics-set-to-overtake-g7-in-global-trade-by-2026-ey-report-reveals, visited November 5, 2024.
29. Wolfgang Muenchau, ibid.
30. Felix Heiduk, Gudrun Wacker, "From Asia-Pacific to Indo-Pacific", *Stiftung Wissenschaft und Politik*, July 1, 2020: https://www.swp-berlin.org/publikation/from-asia-pacific-to-indo-pacific, visited November 5, 2024.
31. These include Brunei, Cambodia, Indonesia, Laos, Malaysia, Myanmar, the Philippines, Singapore, Thailand, and Vietnam.
32. Jonathan Stromseth, "The testing ground: China's rising influence in Southeast Asia and regional responses", *Brookings Institution*, November 2019: https://www.brookings.edu/articles/the-testing-ground-chinas-rising-influence-in-southeast-asia-and-regional-responses/, visited November 5, 2024.
33. Laura Zhou, "What is RCEP and what does an Indo-Pacific free-trade deal offer China?", *South China Morning Post*, November 12, 2020: https://www.scmp.com/news/china/diplomacy/article/3109436/what-rcep-and-what-does-indo-pacific-free-trade-deal-offer, visited November 5, 2024.
34. The remaining countries have since established a new agreement without the USA, the *Comprehensive and Progressive Agreement for Trans-Pacific Partnership* (CPTPP).
35. One illustrative example is the now-defunct *Southeast Asia Treaty Organization* (SEATO), which existed from 1954 to 1977. This military

alliance primarily included Western members such as the USA, the UK, and France, with only Thailand and the Philippines representing Southeast Asia—both under US-backed regimes, including the dictatorship of Ferdinand Marcos in the Philippines. SEATO achieved little in practice, and as interest among its members waned, the alliance ultimately dissolved.

36. For example: Yasuhiro Izumikawa, "Network Connections and the Emergence of the Hub-and-Spokes Alliance System in East Asia", *International Security,* No. 45, Vol. 2, 2020: pp. 7–50.
37. "Joint Leaders Statement On AUKUS", *Prime Minister of Australia*, March 14, 2023: https://www.pm.gov.au/media/joint-leaders-statement-aukus, visited November 8, 2024.
38. See for example: Dian Septiari, "Indonesia chides Australia as Indo-Pacific tensions rise", *The Jakarta Post*, September 18, 2021: https://www.thejakartapost.com/seasia/2021/09/17/indonesia-chides-australia-as-indo-pacific-tensions-rise.html, visited November 8, 2024. And: Stephen Dziedzic, "Malaysia warns Australia nuclear submarine project could 'provoke other powers' in Asia", *ABC News*, September 18, 2021: https://www.abc.net.au/news/2021-09-19/malaysia-indonesia-criticise-australian-submarine-about-face/100474056, visited November 8, 2024.
39. As noted by Sam Roggeveen in an interview with *Foreign Policy*: Maddison Connaughton, "AUKUS Gets Awkward Down Under", *Foreign Policy*, March 24, 2023: https://foreignpolicy.com/2023/03/24/aukus-australia-submarine-deal-paul-keating/, visited November 8, 2024.
40. For example: "Has the Quad lost its way?", *The Economist*, September 26, 2024: https://www.economist.com/asia/2024/09/26/has-the-quad-lost-its-way, visited November 8, 2024.
41. Resistance to military bases countries such as the Philippines, Japan (Okinawa), and South Korea has been expressed by locals for many reasons, including abuses (such as rape) by US military personnel against the local population, environmental concerns, or negative economic impacts (land grabbing, etc.). Resistance, although substantial, has however in most cases been rather unsuccessful. See for example: Yuko Kawato, *Protests Against U.S. Military Base Policy in Asia: Persuasion and Its Limits*, Redwood City, CA: Stanford University Press.
42. On this topic, in detail, see for example: Lucas Myers, "The Problem of US Military Access in a Non-Aligned Indo-Pacific", *The Diplomat*, August 03, 2024: https://thediplomat.com/2024/08/the-problem-of-us-military-access-in-a-non-aligned-indo-pacific/, visited November 8, 2024.

43. A trilateral meeting between the USA, Japan and the Philippines (now under dictator Marcos' son "Bongbong" Marcos) took place in April 2024, for example. See: Ariel Cohen, Wesley Alexander Hill, "An 'East Asian NATO' is forming", *The Hill*, May 1, 2024: https://thehill.com/opinion/national-security/4636136-an-east-asian-nato-is-forming/, visited November 8, 2024.
44. "China-brokered Saudi-Iran deal driving 'wave of reconciliation', says Wang", *Al Jazeera*, August 21, 2023: https://www.aljazeera.com/news/2023/8/21/china-brokered-saudi-iran-deal-driving-wave-of-reconciliation-says-wang, visited November 5, 2024.
45. "Hamas and Fatah sign unity deal in Beijing aimed at Gaza governance", *Al Jazeera*, July 23, 2024: https://www.aljazeera.com/news/2024/7/23/palestinian-rivals-hamas-and-fatah-sign-unity-deal-brokered-by-china, visited November 5, 2024.
46. For example Küsters 2018, p. 30 f.
47. Vaibhav Raghunandan, "October 2024 — Monthly analysis of Russian fossil fuel exports and sanctions", *Centre for Research on Energy and Clean Air*, November 8, 2024: https://energyandcleanair.org/october-2024-monthly-analysis-of-russian-fossil-fuel-exports-and-sanctions/, visited November 9, 2024.
48. "China-Russia 2023 trade value hits record high of $240 bln - Chinese customs", *Reuters*, January 12, 2024: https://www.reuters.com/markets/china-russia-2023-trade-value-hits-record-high-240-bln-chinese-customs-2024-01-12/, visited November 9, 2024.
49. "China's 2022 trade with Russia hit record $190 bln – customs", *Reuters*, January 13, 2023: https://www.reuters.com/world/china-customs-says-trade-with-russia-hit-new-high-2022-2023-01-13/, visited November 9, 2024.
50. "China Drives Russia Car Sales After Global Brands Quit Over War", *Bloomberg News*, July 6, 2023: https://www.bloomberg.com/news/articles/2023-07-06/china-drives-russia-car-sales-after-global-brands-quit-over-war, visited November 9, 2024.
51. For example: Liam Garman, "Sanctions backfire, quite often", *Defence Connect*, June 28, 2022: https://www.defenceconnect.com.au/geopolitics-and-policy/10248-sanctions-backfire-quite-often, visited November 9, 2024.
52. "Deutsche Wirtschaft in der Krise, Industrie verzeichnet Auftragsminus [German economy in crisis, industry records drop in orders]", *Der Standard*, October 7, 2024: https://www.derstandard.at/story/3000000239713/deutsche-wirtschaft-in-der-krise-industrie-mit-auftragsminus, visited November 9, 2024.

53. David Teurtrie, "Warum die Sanktionen gegen Russland scheitern [Why the sanctions against Russia are failing]", *Le Monde diplomatique*, June 13, 2024: https://monde-diplomatique.de/artikel/!6006242, visited November 9, 2024 (quote translated by the authors).
54. Thomas Stölzel, "Chinas und Russlands Hyperschall-Raketen alarmieren Militärstrategen [China's and Russia's hypersonic missiles alarm military strategists]", *WirtschaftsWoche*, December 28, 2019: https://www.wiwo.de/my/unternehmen/industrie/moderne-kanonenkugeln-chinas-und-russlands-hyperschall-raketen-alarmieren-militaerstrategen/25277032.html, visited November 9, 2024.
55. Ibid.
56. For example: "United States Space Force: History", *United States Space Force*: https://www.spaceforce.mil/About-Us/About-Space-Force/History/, visited November 9, 2024.
57. Generally, for example: Peter Frankopan, *The new Silk Roads. The Present and Future of the World*, 2019; Jörg Kronauer, *Der Rivale. Chinas Aufstieg zur Weltmacht und die Gegenwehr des Westens* [The Rival. China's rise to world power and the resistance of the West], 2019.
58. Jörg Lichter, "Chinas Neue Seidenstraße: Das Versagen des Westens [China's New Silk Road: The Failure of the West]", *Handelsblatt Research Institute*, March 1, 2019: https://www.handelsblatt.com/downloads/2405 2840/2/01-03-19-analyse-chinas-neue-seidenstrasse.pdf, visited Nov. 10, 2024 (quote translated by the authors).
59. Pepe Escobar, "Xi's road map to the Chinese Dream", *Asia Times*, October 21, 2017: https://asiatimes.com/2017/10/xis-road-map-chinese-dream/, visited November 10, 2024.
60. *Solvecon Forex Report*, Annual Outlook, February 16, 2019, pp. 1, 12 (quote translated by the authors).
61. Stephanie Olinga-Shannon, Mads Barbesgaard, Pietje Vervest, "The Belt and Road Initiative (BRI). An AEPF Framing Paper", *Transnational Institute*, October 29, 2019: https://www.tni.org/en/publication/the-belt-and-road-initiative-bri, visited November 10, 2024.
62. Pepe Escobar, "A blue dot barely visible from New Silk Roads", *Asia Times*, November 7, 2019: https://asiatimes.com/2019/11/a-blue-dot-barely-visible-from-new-silk-roads/, visited November 10, 2024.
63. "Global China Round Up Newsletter", *Global Development Policy Center*: https://www.bu.edu/gdp/global-china-round-up-newsletter/, visited November 10, 2024.
64. "China Africa Research Initiative", *Johns Hopkins University*: https://www.sais-cari.org/, visited Nov. 10, 2024.

65. For example: Uwe Höring, *Der Lange Marsch 2.0. Chinas Neue Seidenstraßen als Entwicklungsmodell* [The Long March 2.0. China's New Silk Roads as a Development Model], Hamburg 2018.
66. For example CHEN Xiangming, "Globalisation redux: can China's inside-out strategy catalyse economic development and integration across its Asian borderlands and beyond?", *Cambridge Journal of Regions, Economy and Society* 11(1), 2018.
67. David Gosset, *Keynote*, Tianjin Forum 2017, mimeo.
68. For example: Werner Ruegemer, "Grönland: US-Militär gegen chinesischen Ausbau der Infrastruktur [Greenland: US-Military against Chinese infrastructure expansion]", *NachdenkSeiten*, October 16, 2018: https://www.nachdenkseiten.de/?p=46547&pdf=46547, visited November 15, 2024.
69. See for example: James McBride, Noah Berman, Andrew Chatzky, "China's Massive Belt and Road Initiative", *Council on Foreign Relations*, February 2, 2023: https://www.cfr.org/backgrounder/chinas-massive-belt-and-road-initiative, visited November 15, 2024. 100 countries had already participated in the first BRI summit in Beijing in May 2017. See: Jörg Lichter, ibid.
70. Pepe Escobar, "Xi's road map to the Chinese Dream", *Asia Times*, October 21, 2017: https://asiatimes.com/2017/10/xis-road-map-chinese-dream/, visited November 10, 2024.
71. For example: Michael Dunford, *Whither globalization?* Tianjin Forum, July 2017, mimeo.
72. "Belt and Road Initiative to boost world GDP by over $7 trillion per annum by 2040", *Centre for Economics and Business Research*, May 27, 2019: https://cebr.com/blogs/belt-and-road-initiative-to-boost-world-gdp-by-over-7-trillion-per-annum-by-2040/, visited November 15, 2024.
73. Geoffrey Aronson, "China Just Opened the Suez Canal of Our Era and No One Blinked", *The American Conservative*, December 6, 2019: https://www.theamericanconservative.com/china-revolutionizes-world-trade-while-washington-dozes/, visited November 15, 2024.
74. Britta Kuhn, "Chinas Neue Seidenstraße [China's New Silk Road]", *Wirtschaftsdienst*, 12–2019, pp. 880 ff.
75. For example Jörg Kronauer, "Fernost, ganz nah [Far East, very close]", *junge Welt*, November 20, 2019: https://www.jungewelt.de/loginFailed.php?ref=/artikel/367143.handel-mit-china-fernost-ganz-nah.html, visited November 15, 2024; Pepe Escobar, "New Silk Roads in Action at China-Kazakh Border", *Asia Times*, December 4, 2019: https://asiatimes.com/2019/12/at-china-kazakh-border-new-silk-roads-in-action/, visited November 15, 2024.

76. Robert Plummer, "China megaport opens up Latin America as wary US looks on", *BBC*, November 16, 2024: https://www.bbc.com/news/articles/ckg79y3rz1eo, visited November 16, 2024.
77. Details for example in Kunzmann 2018, pp. 100 ff.
78. Ibid., p. 100.
79. For example Mick Dunford, *Whither globalisation?* Tianjin Forum, July 2017, mimeo.
80. For example: Kunzmann 2018, p. 101; Jörg Kronauer, "Von wegen Kolonialmacht [Far from being a colonial power]", *junge Welt*, May 2, 2019.
81. For example: ZHENG Chongwei, XIAO Ziniu, ZHOU Wen, CHEN Xiaobin, CHEN Xuan, *21st Century Maritime Silk Road: A Peaceful Way Forward*, Singapore: Springer Nature Singapore, 2018.
82. Suprabha Baniya, Rocha Gaffum, Nadia Patrizia, Michele Ruta, "Trade Effects of the New Silk Road: A Gravity Analysis", World Bank, *Policy Research Working Paper* WPS 8694, January 10, 2019.
83. For example: Philipp Harms, Konstantin M. Wacker, "The special issue on FDI and multinational corporations: an introduction", *Economics* e-journal, Discussion Paper 2019–15, February 12, 2019.
84. For example: Rasmus 2017, pp. 252ff.
85. Ibid.
86. Thus David Gosset, *Keynote*, Tianjin Forum 2017, mimeo.
87. For example: *China Global Round Up* April 25, 2019.
88. For example: Rasmus 2017; Kadri 2017, pp. 40 f.
89. For example: M. Dunford, *Whither globalisation?* Tianjin Forum July 2017, mimeo.
90. Ibid.
91. Jörg Lichter, "Chinas Neue Seidenstraße: Das Versagen des Westens [China's New Silk Road: The Failure of the West]", *Handelsblatt Research Institute*, March 1, 2019: https://www.handelsblatt.com/downloads/2405 2840/2/01-03-19-analyse-chinas-neue-seidenstrasse.pdf, visited November 10, 2024.
92. Arne Schütte, "EU's Global Gateway keeps focus on investments in Africa", *Science Business*, February 1, 2024: https://sciencebusiness.net/news/eus-global-gateway-keeps-focus-investments-africa, visited Nov. 17, 2024.
93. Jörg Kronauer, "Von wegen Kolonialmacht [Far from being a colonial power]", *junge Welt*, May 2, 2019.
94. Arne Schütte, ibid.
95. Ibid.

96. Pepe Escobar, "A blue dot barely visible from New Silk Roads", *Asia Times*,November7,2024:https://asiatimes.com/2019/11/a-blue-dot-barely-visible-from-new-silk-roads/, visited November 10, 2024.
97. "G7 summit: Leaders detail $600bn plan to rival China's Belt and Road initiative", *BBC*, June 27, 2024: https://www.bbc.com/news/world-asia-61947325, visited November 17, 2024.
98. Steve Herman, "US-Led Initiative Aims to Make Mark on Global Infrastructure Development", *Voice of America*, January 31, 2020: https://www.voanews.com/a/economy-business_us-led-initiative-aims-make-mark-global-infrastructure-development/6183503.html, visited November 17, 2024.
99. For example: Uwe Hoering, *Der Lange Marsch 2.0. Chinas Neue Seidenstraßen als Entwicklungsmodell* [The Long March 2.0. China's New Silk Roads as a Development Model], Hamburg 2018.
100. "So far, the West has done exactly what it is accusing China of." (*Solvecon Forex Report* March 19, 2019, p.3. (quote translated by the authors).
101. Also, for example, Jörg Kronauer, "Von wegen Kolonialmacht [Far from being a colonial power]", *junge Welt*, May 2, 2019; see also Kronauer 2019; Willy Sabautzki, "Respekt vor staatlicher Souveränität oder: die Mär der chinesischen Schuldenfalle [Respect for state sovereignty or: the myth of the Chinese debt trap]", *isw* Munich, May 22, 2019.
102. An overview of 40 such cases since 2015 is provided by: Agatha Kratz, Allen Feng, Logan Wright, "New Data on the 'Debt Trap' Question", *Rhodium Group*, April 29, 2019: https://rhg.com/research/new-data-on-the-debt-trap-question/, visited November 19, 2024.
103. For example, *China Global Round Up*, August 1, 2018, p. 2.
104. Kate Bartlett, "China Cancels 23 Loans to Africa Amid 'Debt Trap' Debate", *Voice of America*, August 25, 2022: https://www.voanews.com/a/china-cancels-23-loans-to-africa-amid-debt-trap-debate-/6716397.html, visited November 19, 2024.
105. Ibid. See also for example: Robin Fall, "The Myth of the Chinese 'Debt Trap' in Africa", *Bloomberg*, March 17, 2022: https://www.bloomberg.com/news/articles/2022-03-17/the-myth-of-chinese-debt-trap-diplomacy-in-africa, visited October 23, 2025.
106. For example, *Global China Round Up*, July 18, 2019, p. 2; July 31, 2019, p. 2.
107. For example, *China Global Round Up*, November 15, 2018.
108. Detailed for example Zhou Lihuan, Sean Gilbert, Wang Ye, Miquel Munoz Cabre, Kevin P. Gallagher, "Moving the Green Belt and Road Initiative from Words to Actions", *BU-GDP Working Paper*, October 2018: https://www.bu.edu/gdp/files/2018/11/GDP-and-WRI-BRI-MovingtheGreenbelt.pdf, visited November 22, 2024.

109. An example from the early days: Valentin Raskatov, "›Neue Seidenstraße‹: Erster Warenzug aus China in Mecklenburg-Vorpommern angekommen ['New Silk Road': First goods train from China arrived in Mecklenburg-Western Pomerania]", *sputniknews*, November 13, 2019.
110. For example: Kunzmann 2018, p. 100.
111. For example: David Gosset, *Keynote*, Tianjin Forum 2017, mimeo.
112. For example: *Global China Round Up*, July 31, 2019, August 14, 2019, August 28, 2019.
113. UNDP China and China Development Bank (CDB), "Harmonizing Investment and Financing Standards towards Sustainable Development along the Belt and Road", *undp.org*, November 6, 2019: https://www.undp. org/china/publications/harmonizing-investment-and-financing-standards, visited November 22, 2024.
114. Anthony Xiao, Yifei Ding, "Evolution of China's Belt and Road Initiative: Green Silk Road", *Invesco*, April 4, 2023: https://www.invesco.com/apac/en/institutional/insights/fixed-income/evolution-of-chinas-belt-and-road-initiative-green-silk-road.html, visited November 22, 2024.
115. Ibid.
116. In addition to the sources already cited, for example Eom, Janet, Hwang Jyhjong, Atkins, Lucas, Chen Yunnan, Zhou Siqi, "The United States and China in Africa: What does the data say?", *China-Africa Research Initiative*, Johns Hopkins University, Washington D.C., *Policy Brief* 18–2017.
117. For example: Lin Wang, "China's Contribution to Development Cooperation …", 2017, pp. 10ff.
118. Janet Eom et al., op. cit.; also: Mthuli Ncube, Charles L. Lufumpa, George Kararach, "Infrastructure, political economy and Africa's transformational agenda", in: M. Ncube, C.L. Lufumpa (Eds.), *Infrastructure in Africa*, Bristol, UK, Chicago IL, USA: Policy Press, 2017, pp. 662–664.
119. According to Kunzmann 2018, pp. 104 f.
120. Kartik Jayaram, Omid Kassiri, Irene Yuan Sun, "The closest look yet at Chinese economic engagement in Africa", McKinsey, June 28, 2017: https://www.mckinsey.com/featured-insights/middle-east-and-africa/the-closest-look-yet-at-chinese-economic-engagement-in-africa, visited November 23, 2024.
121. Ibid.
122. Rachel Nuwer, "Why China has been a growing study destination for African students", *Nature*, June 5, 2024: https://www.nature.com/articles/d41586-024-01599-z, visited November 23, 2024.
123. Marianna Schauzu, "Land Grabbing: China als neuer Kolonialherr in Afrika? [Land Grabbing: China as new colonial master in Africa?]", *Marxistische Blätter* 2–2018, pp. 114–121.

124. For example: Matilda Dunfjäll, "Sino-African Relations and ODA in the Twenty-First Century: Chinese Aid and Public Expenditure in Education and Health Sectors of Sub-Saharan African Nations", *Chinese Political Science Review* 4(3) 2019, pp. 375–402.
125. Kristin Palitza, Jörn Petring, "Drache zu Gast bei Löwen – Warum Chinas Einfluss in Afrika expandiert [Dragon visiting lions -- Why China's influence in Africa is expanding]", *Allgemeine Zeitung*, August 31, 2018: https://www.az.com.na/nachrichten/der-drache-im-land-des-lwen-chinas-rasante-expansion-in-afrika-2018-08-31, visited November 23, 2024.
126. Cited from Schauzu, ibid.; see also Jörg Kronauer, "Von wegen Kolonialmacht [Far from being a colonial power]", *junge Welt* May 2, 2019; Kunzmann 2018, p. 104, referring to the source "Landmatrix. Web of Transnational Deals"; online at: https://landmatrix.org/charts/web-of-transnational-deals/, visited November 23, 2024.
127. For example: Kunzmann 2018, p. 103 f. See also: Zainab Usman, Tang Xiaoyang, "How Is China's Economic Transition Affecting Its Relations With Africa?", *Carnegie Endowment for International Peace*, May 30, 2024: https://carnegieendowment.org/research/2024/05/how-is-chinas-economic-transition-affecting-its-relations-with-africa?lang=en, visited November 23, 2024. In fact, Usman and Tang report that as of 2024, Africa constitutes only 4.7 percent of China's global trade, much of that being unprocessed commodities or semi-processed agricultural products, with crude oil imports from Africa actually even *declining* in recent years. Nevertheless, mineral and metal exports such as lithium have however increased at the same time, with China also building refining and processing plants in countries such as Zimbabwe and Nigeria, rather than simply importing the raw materials. Usman and Tang however conclude: "These trends in the fossil fuel and metals trade are crucial for a continent with more than ten major oil producers and twenty mineral producers."
128. Kunzmann, ibid.
129. Ibid.
130. An institution unsuspected of any China sympathies, embedded in and financed by "Western" state and private centers (Bertelsmann, US-State Department), similar to the "Eurobarometer" of the EU.
131. Schauzu 2018, ibid.
132. Quoted from Jörg Kronauer, "Von wegen Kolonialmacht [Far from being a colonial power]", *junge* Welt, May 2, 2019 (quote translated by the authors).
133. Christina Seyfried, *African Bargaining Power with China: Foreign Investment and Rising Influence*, 2023, London: Routledge.

134. A shift of Chinese investments from an emphasis on infrastructure to industrialization of African countries can especially be observed since the 2023 BRICS summit, as Tang and Usman report (see above, ibid.). The intention is to create a synergy with the previously still underutilized infrastructure: "In China's experience, the synergy between industrialization and infrastructure has proven to be essential in driving sustainable economic growth and social transformation", Usman and Tang write.
135. For example also: *Solvecon Forex-Report*, April 26, 2019, p. 3.
136. Extensive coverage was for example provided by the *South China Morning Post*: "Belt and Road: 2023 Summit": https://www.scmp.com/topics/belt-and-road-2023-summit, and on the forum's official website: http://www.beltandroadforum.org/english/, both visited November 24, 2024.
137. For example: DING Xiaoqin, "Development without Interference", 2018.
138. Ibid.
139. For example: ibid.; or: David G. Landry, "The Belt and Road Bubble Is Starting to Burst", *Foreign Policy*, June 27, 2018: https://foreignpolicy.com/2018/06/27/the-belt-and-road-bubble-is-starting-to-burst/, visited November 24, 2024.
140. Ibid.
141. For example: Kunzmann 2018, pp. 103 f.
142. *Global China Round Up*, April 25, 2019.
143. We have not addressed Latin America and the Caribbean (LAC) within the framework of the BRI, although Chinese investments from the China Development Bank and the EXIM Bank already exceed loans from the World Bank, the IMF, and the Inter-American Development Bank (all under US influence). For a detailed discussion of LAC in the BRI, see for example "GDP Center Dialogue - China-Latin America Finance" February 21, 2019.
144. Additionally, and as an impression, for example Thomas Berger, "Bahn frei für Schnellzüge. Laos, Thailand und China unterzeichnen beim BRI-Forum in Beijing Abkommen über Hochgeschwindigkeitsstrecke [Clear the tracks for high-speed trains. Laos, Thailand, and China sign agreement on high-speed line at the BRI Forum in Beijing]", *junge Welt*, April 29, 2019, p. 9. In English, for example: Geoff de Freitas, "BRI Success Stories: The Laos-China Railway Remains Clearly Well on Track", *HKTDC Research*, December 22, 2023: https://research.hktdc.com/en/article/MTU1NTUzNTAwOQ, visited November 30, 2024.
145. For example: Philip Pfleger, "Chinas Geld treibt einen Keil in die EU [China's money drives a wedge into the EU]", *ORF*, January 7, 2019: https://orf.at/stories/3102598/, visited November 30, 2024.
146. In the early days, e.g., *Süddeutsche Zeitung*, October 17, 2017.

147. For a detailed discussion, see for example Fred Schmid, "EU – China: Künftig mehr Rivalen als Partner [EU – China: More rivals than partners in the future]", *isw* Munich, April 14, 2019, p. 3 f.; *Solvecon Forex-Report*, March 26, 2019, p. 3.
148. For example: "Kampf um die Seidenstraße [Battle for the Silk Road]", *German Foreign Policy*, March 11, 2019: https://www.german-foreign-policy.com/news/detail/7884, visited November 30, 2024. In English, for example: Francesca Ghiretti, "Demystifying China's Role in Italy's Port of Trieste", *The Diplomat*, October 15, 2020: https://thediplomat.com/2020/10/demystifying-chinas-role-in-italys-port-of-trieste/, visited November 30, 2024.
149. German Foreign Policy, ibid.
150. For example: Michael Verfürden, "Chinatown Duisburg – Wie das Ruhrgebiet von der Seidenstraße 2.0 profitieren will [Chinatown Duisburg – How the Ruhr area wants to benefit from Silk Road 2.0", *Handelsblatt*, September 24, 2018.
151. The pollution of the world is then, of course, gladly taken over by the booming cruise industry, which brings European and American retirees to the penguins and to the remotest corners of the Arctic and Antarctic—infecting the penguins with food waste and leftovers, while ensuring the closest possible observation of the polar bear's death and a proactive acceleration of polar melting.
152. For example: Jens Kastner, "German rail group bets on Belt and Road with more trains to China", *Nikkei Asia*, June 29, 2019: https://asia.nikkei.com/Spotlight/Belt-and-Road/German-rail-group-bets-on-Belt-and-Road-with-more-trains-to-China, visited November 30, 2024.
153. For example: Luik, *Schaden in der Oberleitung. Das geplante Desaster der Deutschen Bahn* [Damage in the overhead line. The planned disaster of Deutsche Bahn], Frankfurt 2019.
154. For example: Thorsten Mumme, "Mehr westliche als chinesische Investitionen: Die Angst vor Chinas Neuer Seidenstraße ist unbegründet [More Western than Chinese investments: The fear of China's New Silk Road is unfounded]", *Tagesspiegel*, September 2, 2019: https://www.tagesspiegel.de/wirtschaft/die-angst-vor-chinas-neuer-seidenstrasse-ist-unbegrundet-6644620.html, visited December 1, 2024.
155. For example: Jens Bastian, „Chinas Einfallstor [China's gateway]", *Süddeutsche Zeitung*, October 17, 2017.
156. Philip Pfleger, ibid.
157. *Mercator Institute for China Studies*, Berlin, *merics China Update* 6/2018, p. 9.
158. Ilaria Mazzocco, Andrea Leonard Palazzi, "Italy Withdraws from China's Belt and Road Initiative", *Center for Strategic & International Studies*,

December 14, 2023: https://www.csis.org/analysis/italy-withdraws-chinas-belt-and-road-initiative, visited December 1, 2024.

159. The member list as of December 2024 is: Albania, Bosnia and Herzegovina, Bulgaria, Croatia, the Czech Republic, Greece, Hungary, Montenegro, North Macedonia, Poland, Romania, Serbia, Slovakia, and Slovenia.
160. For example: HU Yongqi, "China to boost economic links with CEE nations", *China Daily*, July 9, 2018, p. 3.
161. SONG Lilei, Dragan Pavlicevic, "China's Multilayered Multilateralism: A Case Study of China and Central and Eastern Europe Cooperation Framework", *Chinese Political Science Review* 4(3) 2019, pp. 277–302.
162. For example: *Global China Round Up* 25.4.2019.
163. Cited from "Volksrepublik fördert europäische Integration [People's Republic promotes European Integration]", *junge Welt*, April 9, 2019, p. 9 (quote translated by the authors).
164. Paul Taylor, "In defense of the EU-China investment deal", *Politico*, January 8, 2021: https://www.politico.eu/article/europe-at-large-eu-china-investment-deal/, visited December 1, 2024.
165. For example: Tom O'Connor, "China Celebrates Surpassing US in Trade with EU for the First Time", *Newsweek*, December 4, 2020: https://www.newsweek.com/china-good-news-passes-us-trade-europe-1552454, visited December 1, 2024.
166. Tina Teng, "EU and China advance towards alternative solution for EV tariffs", *Euronews*, November 29, 2024: https://www.euronews.com/business/2024/11/29/eu-and-china-advance-towards-alternative-solution-for-ev-tariffs, visited December 1, 2024.
167. See for example: Jens Flottau, "Airbus verdoppelt Produktion in China [Airbus doubles production in China]", *Süddeutsche Zeitung*, April 7, 2023: https://www.sueddeutsche.de/wirtschaft/airbus-endmontage-tianjin-a320neo-1.5785898, visited December 4, 2024. See also: "Boeing-Airbus trade row set to end after 17 years", *BBC*, June 15, 2021: https://www.bbc.com/news/business-57484209, visited December 4, 2024.
168. For example: Jamil Anderlini, Clea Caulcutt, "Europe must resist pressure to become 'America's followers,' says Macron", *Politico*, April 9, 2023: https://www.politico.eu/article/emmanuel-macron-china-america-pressure-interview/, visited December 4, 2024.
169. For example: *Handelsblatt* August 2, 2018; in detail also Schmid 2017, p. 50 f.; or: "Neue Industriestrategie: Staat fordert mehr Kontrolle bei Firmenverkäufen [New industrial strategy: State demands more control over company sales]", *Deutsche Wirtschaftsnachrichten*, December 8, 2019.

170. For example: Jens Bastian, "Chinas Einfallstor [China's gateway]", *Süddeutsche Zeitung*, October 17, 2017.
171. Sebastian Huld, Clara Pfeffer, "Rückzug, nein danke! Deutsche Firmen bleiben in China [Withdrawal, no thanks! German companies remain in China]", *Capital*, June 29, 2024: https://www.capital.de/wirtschaft-politik/rueckzug%2D%2Dnein-danke%2D%2Ddeutsche-firmen-bleiben-in-china-34838082.html, visited December 4, 2024.
172. "Deutsch-chinesische Wirtschaftsbeziehungen", *Deutsche Vertretungen in China*, 2022: https://china.diplo. de/cn-de/willkommen-in-china/wirtschaft/wirtschaft-bilateral-1,218,264, visited December 4, 2024.
173. Jakob Pflügl, "China investiert verstärkt in Osteuropa – und hängt Deutschland und Österreich ab [China is investing more in Eastern Europe - and leaving Germany and Austria behind]", *Der Standard*, July 3, 2024: https://www.derstandard.at/story/3000000226673/china-investiert-verstaerkt-in-osteuropa-und-haengt-deutschland-und-oesterreich-ab, visited December 4, 2024.
174. Agatha Kratz, Max J. Zenglein, Alexander Brown, Gregor Sebastian, Armand Meyer, "Dwindling investments become more concentrated - Chinese FDI in Europe: 2023 Update", *Mercator Institute for China Studies*, June 6, 2024: https://merics.org/en/report/dwindling-investments-become-more-concentrated-chinese-fdi-europe-2023-update, visited December 4, 2024.
175. For example: H. Steltzner, "Chinas Weg zur Weltherrschaft [China's Path to World Domination]", *Frankfurter Allgemeine Zeitung*, January 7, 2018.
176. Birte Penshorn, "So hat sich der Auslandsanteil bei den Dax-Unternehmen verändert [How the foreign share of DAX companies has changed]", *Das Investment*, August 8, 2024: https://www.dasinvestment.com/ dax-aktionaere-struktur-aktionaersstruktur-ausland-investoren/, visited December 8, 2024.
177. *Steingarts Morning Briefing* June 3, 2019 (quote translated by the authors).
178. *Handelsblatt*, June 10, 2016, all quotes from Schmid 2017, pp. 50 f. (translated by the authors).
179. Schmid 2017, ibid. (quote translated by the authors).
180. Ibid. (quote translated by the authors).
181. Ibid. (quote translated by the authors).
182. W. Ruegemer, "Die Volksrepublik China und ihre globale Bedeutung [The People's Republic of China and its global significance]", Part 2, *World Economy*, May 20, 2019.

183. Quoted from "Volksrepublik fördert europäische Integration [People's Republic promotes European Integration]", *junge Welt* April 9, 2019, p. 9 (quote translated by the authors).
184. Clemens Fuest, Felix Hugger, Samina Sultan, Jing Xing, "What Drives Chinese Overseas M&A Investment? Evidence from Micro Data", *EconPol Working Paper* 33, November 2019.
185. For example: Christian Rusche, "Chinesische Beteiligungen und Übernahmen in Deutschland [Chinese investments and acquisitions in Germany]", *Wirtschaftsdienst* 2–2020, pp. 144–146.
186. The major international publishers have all launched large series of Chinese engineering and natural sciences, and specialized Chinese books are now the best-selling titles. As of 2024, Springer and Palgrave alone "publish over 900 scholarly books by Chinese authors each year". See for example: Leana Li, "Celebrating China's Impact on Global Sustainable Development Research", *Springer Nature*, September 4, 2024: https://www.springernature.com/de/researchers/the-source/blog/blogposts-communicating-research/china-new-development-awards-2024-sdg/27504230, visited December 9, 2024.
187. For example, KE Dickie Liang-Hong, Enrique de Diego, "Chinese Innovation and Entrepreneurship Going Abroad: From Counterfeits and Copycats to Innovation Exporters"; ZHAO Weilin, "China's Innovation-Driven Growth and Its Emerging Impact on Global Innovation", both in: WANG Huiyao, LU Miao, (Eds.), *Handbook on China and Globalization*, Cheltenham, UK, Northampton, MA, USA: E. Elgar, 2019, Chpts. 3, 10.
188. For example: PAN Chunyang, WEI William, Etayankara Muralidharan, LIAO Jia, Bernadette Andreosso-O'Callaghan, "Does China's Outward Direct Investment Improve the Institutional Quality of the Belt and Road Countries?", *Sustainability*, 12(1), 2020, pp. 415 ff.
189. For early details, for example: *Reuters Business News*, July 19, 2017.
190. For example: *Handelsblatt* July 5, 2018. Regarding the commitment to Deutsche Bank, it had previously already been speculated that the HNA Group apparently had a credit crunch.
191. Ibid. As a result, HNA in fact eventually had to file bankruptcy after failed debt restructuring efforts in 2021. The Hainan High Court has since approved a civil case that aims to restructure, split assets, and transfer shares to creditors. See for example: "Debt-ridden Chinese conglomerate HNA Group resolves risks after 2 years", *Global Times*, April 24, 2022: https://www.globaltimes.cn/page/202204/1260207.shtml, visited December 9, 2024.

192. For example, "China curbs 'irrational' outbound investment", *Deutsche Welle*, September 14, 2017: https://www.dw.com/en/china-curbs-irrational-outbound-investment/a-40500798, visited December 9, 2024.
193. For example: *China Daily*, July 14, 2017, p. 1.
194. For example: Crome 2017, passim; also: Ncube, Lufumpa, Kararach, "Infrastructure, political economy and Africa's transformational agenda", in: Mthuli Ncube, Charles Leyeka Lufumpa (Eds.), *Infrastructure in Africa* (2017), pp. 662–664.
195. Ali Kadri, "The Saudi palace coup, the oil market, China and the US", *real-world economics review* 82, 2017, 29–46, especially pp. 34 ff.
196. Global Development Policy Center of Boston University, *Working Paper*, March 27, 2018.
197. Ding Xiaoqin, "Development without Interference", 2018.
198. *Solvecon Forex Report* March 26, 2019 (quote translated by the authors).

Selected and Recommended Literature

Kadri, Ali. 2017. The Saudi palace coup, the oil market, China and the US. *Real-World Economics Review* 82. http://www.paecon.net/PAEReview/issue82/Kadri82.pdf.

Further Cited Literature

Crome, Erhard, 2017. Chinas Aufstieg und die geopolitischen Folgen [China's rise and the geopolitical consequences]; *WeltTrends*, December 2, 2017. http://welttrends.de/res/uploads/Crome-Chinas-Aufstieg-2017.pdf. Accessed May 20, 2024.

Kronauer, Jörg, 2019. *Der Rivale. Chinas Aufstieg zur Weltmacht und die Gegenwehr des Westens* [The Rival: China's Rise to World Power and the West's Resistance]. Hamburg: Konkret.

Kunzmann, Marcel, 2018. *Theorie, System und Praxis des Sozialismus in China* [Theory, System and Practice of Socialism in China]. 2nd ed. Berlin: Verlag Mirco Kolarczik

Küsters, Günter, 2018. *Das Verhältnis von EU und China im Kontext globaler Machtverschiebungen und der aktuellen Kontroverse um Chinas Großprojekt der 'Neuen Seidenstraße'* [The relationship between the EU and China in the context of global power shifts and the current controversy surrounding China's major 'New Silk Road' project], presentation, *Attac*: https://www.attac.de/fileadmin/user_upload/Kampagnen/Europa/workshops/Guenter_Kuesters_Verhaeltnis_von_EU_und_China.pdf. Accessed January 14, 2025.

Rasmus, Jack. 2017. *Central Bankers at the End of Their Rope? Monetary Policy and the Coming Depression.* Atlanta, GA: Clarity Press.

Schmid, Fred, 2017. China im globalen Kapitalismus [China in global capitalism]. In *Krise des Globalen Kapitalismus. Und jetzt Wohin?* [Crisis of global capitalism. And now where to?]. Munich: Institut für sozial-ökologische Wirtschaftsforschung (ISW), Report Nr. 109.

PART III

"It's the System, Stupid!" Many Construction Sites, Many Building Blocks, Toward Another Future: The "Mosaic" and "System"

Former US President Clinton is said to have won his 1992 campaign with the slogan "It's the economy, stupid!", which effectively countered his opponent, the initially favored President George H.W. Bush, a "hero" of the Kuwait/Iraq war. We do not aim to counter anyone here, but instead argue, simply and hopefully just as effectively: "It's the system, stupid!"

So, let us "complete the picture" (the mosaic) or, expressed psychologically, understand the "gestalt" of the many individual phenomena, recognizing their meaning, inner connections, and future prospects.

This may seem simple at first—reality brought to a point—but it also points to something very complex. A "system" is more than the sum of its parts, elements, components, or dimensions. It contains non-linearities of all kinds and threshold values in its emergence and development, at which it may suddenly shift, creating or collapsing something entirely new. Even if we think mechanically, as with assembled Lego blocks: only when enough of them are correctly arranged do we recognize what the construction is meant to represent. We could then remove one block after another and still see the overall construction. But removing just one more block could cause the entire structure to collapse, leaving no mosaic, picture, gestalt, or "system" recognizable—only chaos.

So, let us ask: what could the system called "China" be, after ten chapters full of sometimes surprising facts? Is there something tangible? A connection, a goal, a purpose, something understandable despite much foreignness?

CHAPTER 15

What Kind of System? "Communism"? "Turbo Capitalism"? "State Capitalism"? "Socialist Market Economy"? "Autocracy"? Or What?—Sorting Out the Conceptual and Analytical Confusion

What kind of "system" is China today? This China, which had one of the geographically largest, longest-lasting, and most stable civilizations and generated a substantial share of humanity's knowledge? This China, which, after an extremely volatile recent history including near-destruction by foreign powers, mass poverty, and famines up until the 1950s, international boycott and obstruction by a dominant empire, civil war-like internal turbulences, regime-change revolts such as Tiananmen, and global proxy wars on its borders in Vietnam and Korea, somehow still found the strength and clarity to reinvent itself around 1978? This China, which would take existential risks and opportunities, expose itself to extreme change and tensions, pull itself out of poverty and underdevelopment by its own bootstraps, and since the 2000s has reinvented itself again, taking steps into an unknown future along paths no country has yet traveled?

What an individual cannot do, except perhaps Baron Munchausen pulling oneself out of a swamp by one's own hair, a system with cumulative circularities can accomplish.

Yet this country, this system, has quite obviously been "riding on a razor's edge" for decades, as has become clear.

What is this millennia-old and now renewed and emerging "number one", which seems to constantly reinvent itself, can restructure itself

W. Elsner, E. Najmehchi, *The Rise of China*,
https://doi.org/10.1007/978-3-032-20260-4_15

extremely quickly, awakens and shakes up itself and a large part of the world, while remaining surprisingly modest yet determined on its own path?

To this end, we have gathered extensive factual material, literature, our own reflections, and evaluations above. We have examined the "deep structures" of the system in the most important development areas and policy fields. We can therefore conclude with shorter and more concise considerations.

Hundreds of authors have tried to bring this system "to the point", to a concept, and each of a thousand authors has offered a thousand and one answers.

So, is China's system

- Capitalism? Even a "turbo-capitalism"? Or a "state capitalism" (whatever that might be)? Even a "state monopoly capitalism" ("sta-mocap"), as Marxists had characterized capitalism in the 1980s? Has China perhaps become "a new capitalist center"?[1]
- A "communist" or "communist-led" capitalism (which then, however, fares better than Western capitalism in practically all questions)?[2]
- Or something specifically Chinese: a "Sino-capitalism"?[3]
- Or simply a "dictatorship" (also often in combination with the usual qualifications "totalitarian", "autocratic", "party", and so on)?
- Even a very own "Chinism"?[4]
- Or perhaps a "socialist market economy"?
- Or rather a "market economy socialism"?
- Or a socialism at all, albeit in an early stage, and "with Chinese characteristics"?
- Or something completely different, something "third"? A "mixed system", composed equally of socialist and capitalist elements?[5]

"Capitalism"?

If capitalism is a system aimed at achieving and securing maximum profit through capital investment, labor exploitation, and accumulation of capital in competition with other individual capital, and if its institutions, parties, politics, and state bureaucracies follow the logic of securing this maximum profit both internally and externally, then China, based on everything we have seen above, would not qualify as a typical capitalist system.

Chinese capitalists, as we have observed in various areas, are clearly regulated and subject to the dictates of dominant politics. They must subordinate themselves to national development goals, contribute to common goods, accept in part high wage increases, social security benefits, and improvements in working conditions that are politically desired. They share their technologies with others, participate in a progressive and disruptive ecological strategy, allocate parts of their profits to infrastructure, forego maximum profit abroad in "irrational" or "unscrupulous" investment fields, and instead serve development policy cooperation goals. Rather than optimally exploiting other countries, they invest internationally where it best fits China's international cooperation strategy and refrain from ideologically charged investments in Western media and the entertainment sector, even if this reduces their returns.

And the richest entrepreneurs must now also submit to an income redistribution strategy aimed at making income distribution more equal.

Under these circumstances, however, they are well embedded and networked, participate in the rapid innovation and development of the nation's science and research, receive secured loans for their projects on favorable terms, gain access to new investment and expansion opportunities, and can still become very wealthy. An ideal form of capitalism, one might say.

Real capitalism, however, has always looked different. Even classical capitalism could never implement a long-term systemic preservation and development rationality with sufficient social balance, stable accumulation, robust economic and social infrastructure, and, if necessary, the rejection of individual interests of large capital owners and their organizations (cartels, associations). In practice, the state was anything but rational, neutral, or long-term oriented. Long-term preservation rationality repeatedly failed due to power structures that allowed short-term individual interests to dominate.

For the declining neoliberal capitalism of the last four decades, which has established de facto plutocratic rule by the top percentile, this is even more evident. Long-term rational politics overriding the profit rate, or a coherent national development concept, are impossible given the size of individual industrial-financial capital groups, which have become states within states and are internationally larger than most countries. The minimum collective state rationality required to regulate corporations or industries in the interest of the overall system has largely evaporated, replaced by the profit interests and financing capabilities of the 0.1

percent. As in almost all declining empires in history, private financing of politicians and the privatization of large parts of the state have emerged, undermining the ideal of a neutral state. In other countries, such practices would often be labeled systemic corruption.

Capitalism, as the system we know it as, is therefore probably not fully applicable to China. It is not the dominant feature of the Chinese system, even though private capital, capitalists, private profit, capital realization, capital accumulation, and surplus value creation through labor exist. All of these serve as instruments for the development of productive forces in the interest of long-term social and national development. To characterize China as "capitalist" would therefore be entirely misleading.

And if "state monopoly capitalism" means the close coordination between the government and the largest oligopoly corporations for the purpose of securing maximum returns for these companies—or even the complete instrumentalization of the state by such an oligarchy—then China does not fit this category at all. In China, most of the largest and strategically most important companies are state-owned. The focus is on maintaining their competition with the private sector so that they do not become sluggish, bureaucratic, or turn into oligarchies and political power centers. If they fail to achieve this, they are sometimes coldly allowed to go bankrupt. In China, nothing and no one is "too big to fail", and no one can rely on a taxpayer-funded bailout.

The pressure to compete and innovate, even for large state-owned companies, comes from the promotion of SMEs, millions of entrepreneurs, start-ups, spin-offs, and a society-wide, open innovation process supported by almost ten million science and engineering students. Exclusive state protection for large corporations or "too-big-to-fails" is far from the truth. Private large corporations that fail or engage in corruption can go bankrupt and are sometimes nationalized. Even wealthy and powerful oligopolists can end up behind bars, while oligarchic crime in neoliberal systems rarely faces prosecution. "Closed shops" for oligopolies? diesel cartels? steel cartels? cement cartels? government-protected auto industries? No, in China the wind of structural change, innovation, national development, or also income increase for broad masses blows through all the cracks of the corporations. "State monopoly capitalism" obviously works differently.

A market economy can be a long-term instrument for the development of productive forces, as we have shown repeatedly. But under capitalist rule, it quickly degenerates into an oligopolistic and then oligarchic power system. In China, this is not allowed. The market remains a subordinate *instrument*, not an end in itself. It is required to adjust, or it can quickly be replaced by other systemically available mechanisms. The state and society do not adapt to the market; the market adapts to them.

Is China a "turbo-capitalist" system? In terms of the speed of structural change and the pace set by politics, "turbo" might apply. This is likely what proponents of the Chinese turbo-capitalism thesis intend, which makes Western observers nervous. Systemically, China can achieve speed, adaptability, and development of the commons in ways that capitalism, if left unchecked, can no longer accomplish. Capitalism tends to degenerate, lose performance, and transform from a historically progressive system into a restrictive power structure.

So "turbo" may be accurate in one sense, but since there is no capitalism in China, there is no "turbo-capitalism" either. China has sublated and further developed the former turbo potentials of the capitalist market economy. Overall, China is not ridden by the capitalist tiger; it rides the tiger as a strictly regulated and instrumentalized market, made useful to the nation. This is unlikely to ever be reversed into capitalism as we know it. While China cannot be fully characterized as a market economy either, the following statement contains considerable truth: "The West will have to learn to accept this form of market economy."[6]

China HAS private capital, which strives to accumulate for profit as it does in capitalism, and it may in China, within defined limits and regulations. And China HAS capitalists, striving for the (political) power in a country, as they do in capitalism.

And China HAS markets that in large parts steer and allocate the economy through prices and incomes, but in the essences of the system, China is no ("liberal", neoliberal) "market economy", and even the term "socialist market economy", often used officially in China, seems to be very misleading.

And as shown, "capital" does not necessarily imply "capitalism" as the essence of a system, and the capitalists in China may earn money, and within defined limits, they may get rich. But they have no chance to organize as a class to grab the state power and transform China into a neoliberal financialized redistribution and private-enrichment machine. They are appreciated in some sense by the government and asked to meet with and advise both the prime minister and the state president two times a year.

But if they appear on the annual *Hurun* list of the rich and cannot prove having earned their wealth seriously, they get into trouble. *They* have to pay the taxes and contribute to the national infrastructures, while the average Chinese employee virtually does not have to pay taxes anymore.

If the capitalists would only try to buy the politicians, the political parties, the parliament, laws, politics, and the state bureaucracies—the core of the core in neoliberal financialized capitalism—they would fall into the abyss of the anti-corruption prosecutors and end in jail … Those who have tried it, some of them until the 2010s, ended there, or have left the country long ago, first to Hong Kong, later ending up in the City of London or at the Wall Street, where they fit better.

"Autocracy"? A Governance Through Networks, Rather

Those who consider China capitalist, yet *support* capitalism, are often the same people who also regard China as a dictatorship. From the classics of old liberalism, and even from the proponents of neoliberalism and capitalism, we hear that a market economy would guarantee political democracy. Experts, however, differentiate: the ideal market economy described by the eighteenth-century classical theorists—consisting of SMEs and a strong middle class, without oligopolies, cartels, and their economic, media, or political power—could indeed support political democracy. Capitalism, on the other hand, was, especially after the experience of capitalist terror regimes such as the Nazi dictatorship, fully compatible with political dictatorship, as later liberals recognized. This insight was also formulated by the so-called ordoliberals in the CDU's (German conservatives) first post-war program, the Ahlener Program of 1947.

Now we have seen how and why China mobilizes markets, keeps them on their toes, makes them flexible and innovative, and promotes and uses them for national development. This stands in stark contrast to developed capitalist countries that call themselves market economies, where markets are increasingly dominated by a shrinking number of oligopolies whose income, wealth, and power are protected under all circumstances. Expropriations, nationalizations, bankruptcy, prison, or even credit denial in cases of corruption or environmental crimes are rare. Political guidelines for the markets are what make markets in China flexible, innovative, functional, and useful—something not seen in real capitalism since the American New Deal or the short phase of German Keynesianism at the end of the 1960s and beginning of the 1970s.

So, China as a novel market economy of the twenty-first century—and still a dictatorship? This does not fit, especially from the perspective of China critics. The middle class and entrepreneurship in China are booming, and this is politically encouraged: a "middle-class society" in the sense of good incomes for millions of self-employed individuals and SMEs. A system collapse due to its market economy, middle class, or millions of new entrepreneurs is not imminent.

Political dictatorship and freedom of speech? Chinese society is based on extensive network structures, from the family to the clan, village community, personal professional networks (Guanxi), older workplace-related networks (Danwei), modern neighborhood networks (Shequ), and digital social networks. These structures have enabled and systematically promoted extraordinary social mobilization and political participation in resident-related, workplace-related, social policy, and even general political issues.[7]

It has even been said that the Chinese system, with its comprehensive social and physical connectivity, is a system of "governance through networks".[8] Not a bad characterization.

Regarding the core characteristics of the Chinese system, some have suggested that its microeconomic basis is a "Guanxi Economy", which some even present as a separate mode of production, akin to capitalism or socialism.[9] It is emphasized that party groups within companies are often the decisive driving forces behind increased R&D investment, broad participatory innovation, social mobilization, and improved company performance.[10] This is certainly another core characteristic of the system, but due to its microeconomic focus, it is not sufficient on its own to comprehensively characterize and define the Chinese "system".

In any case, what a China expert of the German trade union IG Metall once wrote should apply here: "The Western description of the current leadership [...] of China as a dictatorship from above does not do justice to these complex negotiation processes for controlling China [...]."[11]

The Chinese have demonstrated in countless cases—from labor disputes and urban development conflicts to social policy initiatives, from the melamine scandal to environmental controversies amplified on social networks, from public campaigns against companies that commit environmental violations to tens of thousands of submissions to draft laws, and even to the "tree app"—that they want to participate and refuse to be taken advantage of.[12] Often, the party supports this participation. The willingness to engage is enormous, and so is what it can accomplish.

This clearly has potential, and it remains to be seen which system can ultimately develop a more effective substantive democracy in the future: declining capitalism or the Chinese system. Much of this has already been illustrated above, including in discussions of the widely debated social credit systems.

Dictatorship? If we consult the Chinese constitution or the CPC party program, the answer is clear: yes, of course, it is a dictatorship. It is called a "people's democratic dictatorship". Over whom? Over the capitalists? Jack Ma would likely say: yes, the government dictates a lot to me, but I still respect the party, just as I respect my mother (see his famous statement quoted above). He means that he acknowledges the authority of the party. In America, he might be even richer, but he keeps all his capital in China because, overall, he can achieve much more here—from Taobao and Ant Financial to the massive tree plantings enabled by his "Ant Forest" app.

Even super-rich entrepreneurs can have ideals and want to make a difference toward a better world, and they can apparently do this more effectively within the Chinese system. That is why the multi-billionaire Ma, along with other capitalists, is also a member of a CPC advisory circle. However, he certainly has no opportunity to organize with other capitalists as a political party for capitalism.[13]

In cases of corruption, ongoing "irrational" foreign investments, or other misuses of capital and power, the classic dictatorship measures of expropriation or nationalization are also applied in China. Sometimes this takes the form of a forced sale, and sometimes control is even transferred to the workforce—actual instruments available in the Chinese system. In 2018 alone, more than ten private corporate groups were compelled to sell their companies to state enterprises.[14] Since the initial waves of the anti-corruption campaign, launched in 2007 and intensified in 2012, the government appears increasingly willing and capable of curbing the rent-seeking behavior of large companies and limiting excessive corporate power.[15]

How does this relate to individual freedom of speech? One of my [W.E.] Chinese colleagues, who teaches in Beijing and Shanghai, can criticize his government, receive applause in the lecture hall, and meet with government officials as a consultant the next morning. We have reported this. His ability to do so, however, may be linked to his relative prominence.

A keen observer of the systems of the GDR (former East Germany) and the FRG (West Germany, today Germany) once aptly illustrated the systemic difference in freedom of speech for the "common person" with the following metaphor: in the socialism of the GDR, you could say to your boss or company leader, "You are an a**hole", but if you said, "Honecker[16] is an a**hole", you might end up in jail. In the capitalism of the FRG, you could say, "Merkel is an a**hole", but if you said that to your boss, you would likely be out on the street the next day.

This metaphor reveals much about the respective social evaluations and mechanisms of rule in the two opposing systems. Democracy versus dictatorship? For whom—and by whom?

Terms such as "freedom", "freedom of speech", "democracy", and "dictatorship" remain highly relative and abstract without concrete reference to reality. Used in this way, they often become all-purpose weapons in ideological debates. Which rights and freedoms are better, and for whom? Those at the workplace, in the marketplace, the newspaper owner, the capitalist who can hire or fire employees, the freedom to post on the internet, or to play football? Are we discussing abstract "freedom" or concrete, tangible freedoms? Only private freedom of speech, or the full catalog of UN human rights? What actually constitutes the deep structures of these freedoms—the rights and duties, the rights of some as restrictions on the rights of others? Questions like these, and not abstract definitions, determine the nature of a system.

From another perspective, we perceive the Chinese in everyday life—similar to findings in comparative studies of international everyday cultures—as relatively fearless, self-confident, optimistic, well-informed, and highly engaged in discussion. They observe corruption being curtailed, greater equality being introduced, and the rule of law taking hold, while in other countries these qualities are declining. Today, they trust it when a president says, "Power must be confined in the cage of institutions" (Xi Jinping).[17] But what does all this tell us about "the system", and about the systems that exist in the world today?

Democracy: "In Asia, Results Count"

International polls on what people consider the main goal of democracy

The Western *Alliance of Democracies* carries out annual *Democracy Perception Indexes* with representative polls in the majority of countries in the world. The *Index 2025*[18] showed that in 52 percent of all countries the understanding of people about the main purpose of democracy is the *improvement of physical wellbeing and of social appreciation and welfare.* Only in 16 percent of countries, the Western understanding of democracy as liberal rights and freedoms to speak out and to periodically choose among several political parties prevails.

An East-Asian cultural and political heritage

This should mainly reflect the Global South as well as the billions of people in Asia. It also resonates with the thousands-of-years-old *Daoist* and *Confucian* conceptions of society and state governance.

Uncertainty about our own democracy and values is spreading in the West. What was, what is, and what will become of "our democracy"? On this question, the major German business magazine *Wirtschaftswoche* published a widely discussed interview with the political scientist Parag Khanna from Singapore back in 2020.[19] In it, he presented the cultural and political values of "Asian cultures" for the consideration of Westerners.

Democracy versus technocracy? Khanna argues, "It's not that simple" in Asia. People engage intensively and continuously with governance, and they expect *tangible results* from their government. Party democracy and elections according to the Western model are not necessarily the best methods to capture these needs and desires of the population. In Khanna's view, Asia's heads of state are often more popular than rulers in Europe, America, or Africa. Pragmatic governments are seen as guarantors of prosperity. "They rely on data, not political dogmas; they proceed systematically, strategically, wisely."

The journey is the destination. This old saying, which seems to originate from Asia, applies widely. The Western political party consortia and periodic election campaigns no longer convince many in the West, nor, for that matter, do they in most countries around the world. The saying applies again: "In the West, the government coalitions change all the time, but politics remains the same, in Asia, the government remains the same, but the policies further develop all the time."

The modern Chinese conception of the "Whole-process people's democracy", a "democracy that works"

And China? First of all, what does China want?

> China wants foreign resources, not colonies, does not want to expand, but to strengthen its interior. It acts neo-mercantilistically, not aggressively. And it pursues primarily defensive goals with the new Silk Road (...) China wants to diversify its supply chains.[20]

How relative Eurocentric, Western-capitalist perspectives and values suddenly become, when we look around, rub our eyes, and realize how much the world has changed—and apparently not *only* for the worse. China, for its part, is pragmatic and "communist" in ways unfamiliar to Europeans, Khanna says.[21]

Second, on democracy in particular.

The current reference source is the *White Book of the Chinese Government* of 2021 on a "democracy that works".[22] It includes elections, consultations, participative decision-making, and participation in policy realization and control.

It includes the basic organization of people in their neighborhoods, i.e., around 110,000 *Shequ*, where the candidates for the parliaments have to repeatedly appear and present and discuss their programs.

The political system is based on the value of *meritocracy*. The candidate has to prove that he/she has had a professional real-world life, where he/she has demonstrably worked for the common good, for national development, for people.

The system includes the *(National) People's Congresses* at more than 40,000 communities, 2700 counties, 330 districts, 23 provinces and the national level (the NPC proper), as well as the *Chinese People's Political Consultative Conferences* (CPPCC), which represents all regions, ethnicities, gender, industries, professions, mass organizations etc., all at the same 5 governance levels.

It also includes around 540,000 self-governed village committees for around 1 million villages.

China has, in this way, around 2.6 million political delegates.

There are labor committees in around three million enterprises, and employee conferences are to be held annually.

There are 690,000 self-governed *People's Mediation Committees* that care for conflicts of interests at village or county levels, which may substitute large parts of the bureaucratic state, namely the legal and court system (which may be appealed subsidiarily after a proposal of the committee has been made and rejected by one of the conflict parties).[23]

The substantial participative democracy "with Chinese characteristics" also includes some 10,000 walk-in one-stop citizen centers all over the place, where law drafts are displayed, legal advisors are available and may be consulted to explain the texts and political process, and people may deposit their proposals on the laws in the making.

For instance, the 15th FYP that started in 2026 saw 3.1 million legislative proposals by individual citizens and several thousand from organizations in the general public and organizations' consultative processes.

Another large part of the consultation and discussion processes takes place on social media … another story of its own that we have discussed already.

"Communist-Led"?

Absolutely. The CPC has stood at existential turning points countless times, for itself and the nation as a whole. From the Long March to the founding of the People's Republic, from the Great Leap Forward and the subsequent famine, from the Cultural Revolution to the great risk of "Reform and Opening-up", from Tiananmen to WTO accession, from the Western technology boycott to technological leadership, from large-scale anti-corruption campaigns to the entrepreneurial and founder revolution, and from the ecological revolution to the New Silk Road initiative. As one of the West's major pressure points, China had to open up immediately and extensively to foreign (US) investments at its WTO accession, unlike Japan, South Korea, or Taiwan, which all received more lenient transition periods.

The latest challenges include navigating the desperate global economic disruptions caused by the USA and its Western allies, confronting existential military threats, addressing fundamentalist Islamist terrorism, and managing the coronavirus pandemic. China must ride the capitalist tiger to avoid being ridden by it, and as noted, has always walked a razor's edge.

This party, with its 100 million members, is one of the oldest and most historically experienced in the world. It has consistently demonstrated internal intellectual capacity to process historical experiences and realign its actions. The CPC has reinvented itself multiple times without abandoning its overarching goal: socialism with prosperity at a high cultural and ecological level. Today, it appears capable of holding this vast country together—spatially, ethnically, and across municipal, provincial, national, and international levels. From what one hears in China, from professors to taxi drivers, the party's credible fight against corruption has significantly strengthened its authority and legitimacy compared with twenty years ago.

But what does "communist-led" mean for a system that so effectively demonstrates how markets can function, that promotes entrepreneurship, a middle class, SMEs, and top-level technologies? It suggests something very different from what we have understood through Eurocentric thinking. And it is precisely this conceptual exploration that this book has undertaken.

If more evidence of its communist-led character is needed, consider the perspective of Dieter Kempf, former president of the Federation of German Industries (BDI). While he also recognizes the aforementioned "Guanxi Economy", he evaluates it differently: in China, political leadership continuously expands its influence. The Communist Party "installs its followers" in companies and shapes business decisions—an approach that has alarmed him and his member companies.[24]

There is no reason for "schadenfreude", but every reason to continue engaging with each other, to reduce panic and hostility in conflicts of interest, and to seek compromises rather than allowing trust to collapse entirely. Europe can only benefit from China's new knowledge. Companies have largely understood this. The task of politics is to avoid destroying these opportunities for cooperation by escalating ideological or military hostility. Observers suggest that China could probably manage without us, alongside Russia and other Silk Road countries, but we likely cannot manage without China anymore.

"With Chinese Characteristics" or "Chinistic"?

Fortunately, no one has ever claimed that the Chinese way—the Chinese system—is a *universally* valid model or an export product for other countries. Certainly not the Chinese party or government itself, as shown above. This fact is sometimes even acknowledged positively in Western publications.[25]

Imperialistic attempts to "convert" other countries were typical Eurocentric thinking, both among past and present imperialists and among so-called progressive do-gooder (neo-)liberals or leftists. China has ended such disguised value universalism, behind which European master-race mentality and imperialism all too easily lurked.

China—its party, government, and people—has understood and internalized this: the system applies *only* to China. It is their own way, rooted in their history and experiences. China does not export models. Its system works only "with Chinese characteristics", like everything attempted in China today.

Among those specific features and historical experiences unique to China are:

- The two-thousand-year history of a rationally planning civil service state
- The specifically Chinese network structures, which, when modernized, have a great potential for cooperation and innovation
- The idea of protection against invasions of all kinds, thus on the importance of the "Great Walls"
- But also, the realization to never isolate oneself from the world again, as happened for example through the restriction of maritime trade during the Ming era sea ban

However, all of this is not "Chinistic", at least not in the sense of being so foreign that we cannot understand a word. On the contrary, we can understand China and its system. It has Chinese characteristics, but it is by no means "Chinistic" in the sense of being egocentric, introverted, or incomprehensible from the outside.

A "Mixed System"?

A communist party on the one hand, entrepreneurship, waves of founders, and highly flexible markets on the other—if that is not a "mixed" system, what is?

Since Deng Xiaoping (and later officially by Jiang Zemin), the term "socialist market economy" has been widely used, including in Western media. Whether Deng was correctly translated here is unclear. One could imagine he meant something closer to a "market economy socialism". However, the term "socialist market economy" (SME) had become firmly established in English and German since Tito's "Yugoslavian model", which many European intellectuals had admired after the Second World War, and people were quick to apply it to China.

As post-war Yugoslavia's experience with "worker self-management" has shown, a "mixed economy"—ideally combining socialist central planning and capitalist market elements on an equal footing—would be an inconsistent and therefore unstable conglomerate, likely to tip in one direction sooner or later.

China, however, has proven surprisingly stable, achieving technological innovation, income and welfare growth, radical environmental and climate protection, and growing international networking—alongside considerable market dynamism under strong state planning, diverse property rights, a growing sharing economy, and social mobilization. At first glance, this may seem like a wild mix. That this systemic diversity and complexity work does not need to be proven here.

So yes, "mixed"—but as a whole, it is not a "market economy" and thus not a "socialist market economy". At best, it is a "market economic socialism", a *socialism with markets*, as described. None of the standard system characterizations, even simplified "mixed" labels, can fully explain how China has caught up and risen in such a sustainable and stable manner despite significant external adversities.[26]

Notes

1. As for example Felix Wemheuer, *Chinas große Umwälzung. Soziale Konflikte und Aufstieg im Weltsystem* [China's Great Transformation. Social Conflicts and Rise in the World System], Cologne, 2019.
2. Werner Ruegemer, "Varianten des Kapitalismus. Ein Vergleich des westlichen mit dem chinesischen Kapitalismus [Variants of Capitalism. A Comparison of Western with Chinese Capitalism]", *isw* Munich, October 25, 2017.
3. Uwe Hoering, *Der Lange Marsch 2.0. Chinas Neue Seidenstraßen als Entwicklungsmodell* [The Long March 2.0. China's New Silk Roads as a Development Model], Hamburg: VSA, 2018.
4. Grzegorz Kolodko, "Socialism, capitalism, or Chinism?", *Communist and Post-Communist Studies* 51(4), 2018, pp. 285–298.
5. Similarly, for example, Schmid 2018, pp. 37ff.
6. David D. LI, "70 Jahre Volksrepublik China: Spektakuläres Laboratorium für Entwicklungspolitik [70 Years People's Republic of China: Spectacular Laboratory for Development Policy]", *Weltwirtschaft und Entwicklung*, 9–2019, p. 3 (quote translated by the authors).

7. In addition to the literature already mentioned above, for example: HE Shenjing, "Two waves of gentrification and emerging rights issues in Guangzhou, China", *Environment and Planning A*, 44, 2012, pp. 2817–2833.
8. Stephan Krüger, "Epochenwechsel auf dem Weltmarkt und in der Weltwirtschaft? [Change of Epochs in the World Market and in the World Economy?]", *Marx-Engels-Zentrum Berlin*, March 29, 2019, p. 60; online at: https://mez-berlin.de/veranstaltung/epochenwechsel-auf-dem-weltmarkt-und-in-der-weltwirtschaft.html, visited December 14, 2024.
9. For example: Manfred Nitsch, "Von China lernen [Learning from China]", *FU Berlin, Latin America Institute*, April 14, 2019: https://www.lai.fu-berlin.de/homepages/nitsch/2019-Von-China-lernen-DeltaFaktor.pdf, visited December 14, 2024; The same, Frank Diebel, "Guanxi Economics: Confucius Meets Lenin, Keynes, and Schumpeter in Contemporary China", *Intervention. European Journal of Economics and Economic Policy* 5(1), 2008, pp. 77–104.
10. On staff activities and controls in China for example also Kunzmann 2018, pp. 65 f.
11. Wolfgang Müller, quoted from Schmid 2018, p. 37 (quote translated by the authors).
12. For example: Kuang Wenbo, "New-Media Public Opinion Becomes Mainstream Social Opinion", in: idem, *Social Media in China*, Singapore: Palgrave Macmillan/Springer Nature, 2018, pp. 25–38.
13. For example: Kunzmann 2018, p. 65 f.
14. Ibid., p. 65.
15. For example: Zhang Lanying et al. (2018).
16. The General Secretary of the Socialist Unity Party (SED) of East Germany, from 1971 to 1989.
17. Quoted from: David D. LI, "70 Jahre Volksrepublik China: Spektakuläres Laboratorium für Entwicklungspolitik [70 Years People's Republic China: Spectacular Laboratory for Development Policy]", *Weltwirtschaft und Entwicklung*, 9–2019, p. 3 (quote translated by the authors).
18. Alliance of Democracies 2025: https://allianceofdemocracies.org/democracy-perception-index, visited November 6, 2025.
19. Dieter Schnaas, "In Asien zählen Ergebnisse [In Asia, results count]", *WirtschaftsWoche*, January 12, 2020: https://www.wiwo.de/politik/ausland/parag-khanna-in-asien-zaehlen-ergebnisse/25405972.html, visited October 24, 2025.
20. Schnaas, ibid. (quote translated by the authors).

21. See for example also: Parag Khanna, 2019. *The Future Is Asian: Commerce, Conflict, and Culture in the twenty-first Century*, New York: Simon & Schuster.
22. *China: Democracy That Works*, China State Council, Beijing 2021, https://us.china-embassy.gov.cn/eng/zgyw/202112/t20211204_10462468.htm, visited November 6, 2025. For a further in-depth analysis, see for example also: Paweł Wargan and Jason Hickel, "Building Whole-Process People's Democracy in China", *Progessive International*, November 10, 2025: https://progressive.international/blueprint/cb7dbaf4-b106-4105-8bde-fdab4bfc2fe8-building-whole-process-peoples-democracy-in-china/en, visited November 14, 2025.
23. E.g., Sonja Eiseman, "Mediation as a vehicle of restorative justice in China", *Peking University Law Journal* 12(2), 2024, 185–208; Mediation as a vehicle of restorative justice in China: Peking University Law Journal: Vol 12 , No 2 - Get Access, visited November 6, 2025.
24. "BDI-Präsident schlägt Alarm [BDI President sounds the alarm]", *Handelsblatt*, November 16, 2017.
25. Accordingly, the Director of Merics, as quoted by Schmid 2018, pp. 35 f.
26. As for example also: Schmid 2018, p. 35 ff.

Selected and Recommended Literature

Khanna, Parag. 2019. *The Future Is Asian: Commerce, Conflict, and Culture in the 21st Century*. New York: Simon & Schuster.

Zhang, Lanying, Guanqi Li, and Huili He. 2018. Controlling corporate power in China: Case studies of seed companies and water distribution. *American Journal of Economics and Sociology* 77 (2): 511–540.

Further Cited Literature

Kunzmann, Marcel, 2018. *Theorie, System und Praxis des Sozialismus in China* [Theory, System and Practice of Socialism in China]. 2nd ed. Berlin: Verlag Mirco Kolarczik

Schmid, Fred, 2018. Trumps Wirtschaftskrieg gegen China [Trump's economic war against China]. *Globaler Wirtschaftskrieg. Der Aufstieg Chinas. Zerbricht der Westen?* [Global economic war. The rise of China. Is the West falling apart?]. ISW Report Nr. 115, Munich, 22–39.

CHAPTER 16

"I Don't Know It; I Don't Need It!"

A New and Significant Kind of Socialism for the Twenty-First Century: Different from What We Believe, Different from Anything We Knew Before, Different from What We Are Told …

"Building Blocks" Again

Let's review some of the striking phenomena that make up the Chinese system and can give us final clues to the "system question":

- The companies are diversely institutionally embedded.[1] Their returns are subject to the primacy of politics and are more dependent than independent variables in the system. Parts of the profits are to be used for higher R&D expenditures, the construction of infrastructures, the safeguarding of natural commons, the increase of wages, and rising social security benefits.[2]
- China's development is associated with a continuous reorganization of the relationship between the state and the private economy, with the state acting with an ever-larger role in important industrial sectors and in the financial sector.[3]
- There is a clear "coordination and socialization of investment" alongside the emergence of "new and higher forms of economic planning".[4]

W. Elsner, E. Najmehchi, *The Rise of China*,
https://doi.org/10.1007/978-3-032-20260-4_16

- Strategic parts of the industrial and service sectors are under state ownership, and credit allocation is state-controlled.
- The forms of ownership (not property forms, but only lease forms) are diverse and flexible, sometimes even "fuzzy", as some say.[5] The various bundles of rights and obligations that can constitute "land ownership" range, as already described, from individual ownership, urban developer ownership, corporate ownership, cooperatives, and village community property to the rural HRS of individual farming families.[6] Public and private forms of ownership mix flexibly, though each is clearly defined by contract.
- Likewise, the types of companies are diverse and variable, as already described. The following forms coexist within the "system": state-owned enterprises, collectively owned enterprises, cooperatives, joint-ownership companies, equivalents of LLCs and corporations, sole proprietorships, self-employed individuals, and foreign-invested firms.[7] Since 2013, private investments in state-owned enterprises have also been permitted.[8]
- We have also reported on the various forms of China's expanding *sharing economy*, including private P2P and C2C sectors, which serve as indicators of socialization processes developing from below.
- Redistribution strategies play a major role, for example, through substantial tax relief for lower- and middle-income groups and stronger fiscal participation of the super-rich.
- We have also highlighted the high degree of social mobilization, participation, and engagement in different spheres of work and life.
- A new society also appears to be emerging in everyday philosophy and behavior, characterized by systemic thinking, an emphasis on social harmony and the balancing of interests, cooperation, acceptance of diversity, a keen interest in learning and communication, openness toward foreign cultures, greater relaxation in gender relations, and a generally more composed attitude. This increasing sense of serenity results from improved social security, rising income prospects, and above-average optimism about the future. Most Chinese also show a clear aversion to inequality; conspicuous consumption and displays of excessive wealth are largely rejected.
- In public life, there are few visible signs of poverty, deprivation, or social exclusion.
- Excess capital does not need to be exported merely to maximize returns. Chinese investments abroad therefore serve different

purposes in developing countries and are not secured through military means.

- For China, a military first-strike doctrine does not apply.[9] Rather, the country presents itself as a largely "self-sufficient" leading system.[10]
- Let us conclude the above exemplary list of already described phenomena with the previously quoted statement from Xi Jinping's party congress speech: "For China, development and working-class security are key to national security"—a formulation we have interpreted as an indicator of the system's social core.

Explaining the Particular Dynamics and Effectiveness of Markets in China: The "Productive Forces" and the "Relations of Production"

This also explains the distinctive *systemic* relationship between market and state in the Chinese model. China has traversed the essential phase of capitalist development—from a poor developing country to a leading industrial power—between 1978 and 2012, thus in less than thirty-five years. The advanced Western capitalist nations, by contrast, required roughly two centuries to achieve comparable progress, and under far less external pressure. Today, China is advancing toward the position of the new global "number one".

Nowhere else has the market been mobilized so comprehensively and dynamically—and with all its familiar, and partly still lingering, negative side effects. The market served as the central instrument for developing the productive forces, just as it once did in the capitalist countries. Yet without this massive expansion of the productive forces, the relations of production in an already formally and politically socialist framework could not have evolved toward a *substantive socialism* marked by rising prosperity for all and a successful national catch-up process.

What China has been able to extract *permanently* from the market—in terms of innovation, entrepreneurship, and social mobilization under socialist conditions—was achieved by the advanced capitalist nations only temporarily, during brief phases of their ascent, most recently in the two decades of post–World War II reconstruction.

What China is already achieving—despite its still relatively low per capita income—in terms of *multidimensional prosperity* and technological, ecological, social, educational, and cultural performance is, in many respects, without historical precedent. According to the former vice president of Peking University,[11] the evidence "that a market economy can function efficiently under the guiding hand of the state" now seems convincingly demonstrated. It illustrates what becomes possible in the development of the productive forces under corresponding relations of production—once the overall national development no longer has to pass through the narrow bottleneck of maximizing private capital returns.

Such a development of the productive forces can no longer be described as "capitalism" in any conventional sense—but neither as a "communist dictatorship", a "socialist market economy", a "mixed system", nor as some form of "Chinism". To single out any of these supposed core characteristics obscures rather than clarifies the reality of China's evolving system.

Economist Eike Kopf therefore considers China's self-description as an "initial stage of socialism" to be accurate. He even argues that China's consciously designed and, thus far, successfully managed "initial stage of socialism", projected through 2049, constitutes a world-historical transformation comparable to the bourgeois-Protestant Reformation of the sixteenth century—nothing less than a "transitional stage toward a new type of civilization".[12]

The Chinese Capitalists

The Marxist philosopher Domenico Losurdo further clarifies that the characterization of China's system as "socialism" is primarily grounded in political power, and that the internal class struggle has, at least temporarily, been decided—though the external, international struggle has by no means ended. Politically, Chinese capitalists have been effectively expropriated, though only partially economically. They can no longer convert economic power into political power, must subordinate themselves to the socialist national development goals, comply with regulations and guidelines, and can realize monopoly rents only to a limited degree. For example, the working class can demand that company owners allocate a fixed portion of profits to technological development.[13]

Socialism in China?: A Litmus Test

After all other test categories above have been discarded, the following points make the characterization of China as being in an "early stage of socialism" appear most plausible:

- No private ownership of land, natural resources, or key strategic assets.
- A large, modern, and strategically oriented state production sector, which drives and partly competes with the private sector.
- A likewise large, modern, and strategically oriented state finance and credit sector, independent and protected from international speculation.
- Chinese capitalists lack organized access to political power.
- The working class is politically promoted, with operational demands and co-determination activities supported and organized by the state.
- Social mobilization and participation at work and local community levels.
- Significant political influence of decision-making processes in social media.
- Redistribution policies and progressive taxation.
- Socialization and "sharing" of IT infrastructures and services, with open information flows.
- Extensive and expanding physical sharing economy.
- Massive ecologization of national and international development activities.
- Control over the real economic utility of investments, avoiding "irrational", purely speculative, or ideologically driven projects.
- Public discussions promoting socially and ecologically responsible ethics and behaviors.

An "Early Stage of Socialism": A Novel Way of Socialism That We Have Not Known Yet ... But Which Is Not the Old Eurocentric One

And so we arrive at China's own characterization: an "early stage of socialism with Chinese characteristics". In this sense, one could still describe it as a "mixed" system, featuring diverse forms of property and enterprise, multiple organizational solutions for production, and markets embedded within state planning.

What has emerged in China is a more effective model than both the declining neoliberal financial capitalism and the old Eurocentric model of socialism. The European-style socialism of the twentieth century was largely state-controlled and top-down, leaving little room for evolution. Under unfavorable external conditions, it became bureaucratic and rigid, unable to mobilize its population and ultimately discredited after military and financial defeats by the West. Unlike that model, China today has learned from history and does not aim to export its system, focusing instead on domestic development and stability.

Some observers in the West therefore perceive China's rise not only as a systemic challenge in the developing world but also within the core Western countries.[14] Its growing importance for global peace and security, as well as for technological, social, and ecological progress, is increasingly recognized.

China today has the capacity to overturn decades of discrediting and stigmatization of socialism. It demonstrates that twenty-first-century socialism is no longer a static, bureaucratic system of poverty but a dynamic model that can surpass existing capitalism in many respects and broaden human possibilities.

Notes

1. For example: Hardy et al. 2017.
2. In detail for example Kadri 2017, pp. 36 f.
3. Ibid., pp. 36 f.
4. Elias Jabbour, Alexis Dantas, "The political economy of reforms and the present Chinese transition", *Brazilian Journal of Political Economy* 37(4), 2017, pp. 789–807.
5. For example: Ireland, Meng, "Post-Capitalist Property", 2017, op. cit.
6. Ibid.
7. For example, ibid.; similarly: Zhang Fan, 2018, pp. 110 ff.
8. "Mixed Economy", *Wikipedia*: https://en.wikipedia.org/wiki/Mixed_economy, visited December 20, 2024. In depth, see also: Tessa Wong, "Investing in China's State Owned Enterprises: A Deep Dive", *Allianz Global Investors*, October 4, 2024: https://www.allianzgi.com/en/insights/outlook-and-commentary/investing-in-china-state-owned-enterprises, visited December 20, 2024.
9. For example: Kadri 2017, pp. 36 f., 41.

10. Ibid.
11. Quoted from Schmid 2018, p. 36 (quote translated by the authors).
12. Eike Kopf, *Eine chinesische Reformation. Zum Werden eines neuen Zivilisationstyps* [A Chinese Reformation. On the Becoming of a New Type of Civilization], Cologne, 2019.
13. Losurdo (2017).
14. See a series of quotes from studies and media articles in Schmid 2018, for example p. 37.

Selected and Recommended Literature

Hardy, Jane, Yassamin Imani, and Beini Zhuang. 2017. Regional resilience and global production networks in China: An open political economy perspective. *Competition & Change* 22 (1): 63–80.

Kadri, Ali. 2017. The Saudi palace coup, the oil market, China and the US. *Real-World Economics Review* 82. http://www.paecon.net/PAEReview/issue82/Kadri82.pdf.

Losurdo, Domenico. 2017. Has China turned to capitalism?—Reflections on the transition from capitalism to socialism. *International Critical Thought* 7 (2017): 15–31.

Zhang, Fan. 2018. *The Institutional Evolution of China, Government vs Market*. Cheltenham and Northampton, MA, USA: Edward Elgar.

Further Cited Literature

Schmid, Fred, 2018. Trumps Wirtschaftskrieg gegen China [Trump's economic war against China]. *Globaler Wirtschaftskrieg. Der Aufstieg Chinas. Zerbricht der Westen?* [Global economic war. The rise of China. Is the West falling apart?]. ISW Report Nr. 115, Munich, 22–39.

CHAPTER 17

Structural Problem Areas and Prospects of the Chinese Development

The Punitive System, The Death Penalty, and The Legal Culture

Death penalty: In the end, let's assume the innocent attitude of a naive, unknowing external observer, in a stark and deliberate contrast to a typical Western media or political representative, who a priori knows all the answers on China before any question has been put—and without ever having been in China. They know for sure that China's system is dictatorial, inefficient, "wrong", and collapsing soon anyway, as US think tanks have been repeating even in the year 2025.

And they also know for sure that China is helplessly uncivilized, as it still formally has the death penalty in its constitution. While another standard would apply to the USA anyway.

But we will try to sincerely ask and inquire: Why does China still have the death penalty? Can't they leave that to the Empire? The times of bloody and existentially destructive occupations by European and US colonial and imperial powers and Japanese racist mass-murderer troops, the times of the bloody civil war against the (in the end marauding) Kuomintang troops, are long over. The country is more stable than ever. The excesses of the Cultural Revolution are also gone. There appears to be no longer any need for a death penalty in times of high and increasing average education, high-quality factors of production, a friendly and

W. Elsner, E. Najmehchi, *The Rise of China*,
https://doi.org/10.1007/978-3-032-20260-4_17

relaxed public atmosphere, and societal developments toward a high-quality culture and civilization.

Even the mass stabbings and terrorist acts with cars driven into street markets, etc., by fundamentalist Islamists, which occurred throughout the 1990s up until 2016 in Xinjiang and beyond, have long been a thing of the past. The structural basis of fundamentalist violence has been eliminated over more than the past decade not primarily by punishment—although it *did* include death penalties for some known committed international terrorists—but mainly through comprehensive modernization, including societal reintegration and professional training. This has stressed better multicultural and multilingual schooling, a broad general and vocational education campaign (supported and accompanied by the World Bank), large-scale infrastructural and private investment, massive job creation for young people (both male and female), increasing economic growth, and the strengthening of Xinjiang's and namely Urumqi's role as a central hub within Central Asia and the Eurasian BRI-corridors.

Notably, the death penalty is still widely applied across East Asia, including in Japan, Singapore, Vietnam, Thailand, and also Taiwan.

Reforms of the death penalty: In China, the death penalty has undergone considerable reforms in recent decades. These include a sharp reduction in the number of death sentences and executions, a narrowing of the range of crimes eligible for capital punishment, and the requirement that the Supreme People's Court now has the final authority to review and approve all executions.[1] And its full abolition further down the line has been under discussion in China for some years now.[2]

Confucian ethics: Nevertheless, the death penalty still exists, is carried out, and apparently retains support among many people in China today. If you ask a Chinese person *"Why is there still a death penalty?"*, you might be told something about ancient Confucian or Legalist ethics, according to which a murderer—or someone who acts gravely against the community—must pay with his or her life, as has been the case for over two or three thousand years. Even internationally renowned Chinese professors may give you this answer.

But on this issue, one can certainly evolve and adapt, which would not seem to be contradictory to Confucius: While Confucius may not have explicitly rejected the death penalty, he also appeared somewhat lenient and seemed to prefer rehabilitation over capital punishment: "Morality is primary, punishment is secondary", a famous Confucian saying goes, together with the general respect for human life. Benevolence (仁) is indeed a core tenet of Confucian ethics.[3] A Confucian reading, therefore, might allow for a "sublation" of the death penalty in a harmonious society, where capital punishment is simply no longer necessary to maintain and reproduce society and allow it to flourish.

Thus, in a word, if we were asked for advice in China, we would recommend: "Get rid of it". Leave it to the split and decaying society of the Empire. As an uninvolved and, in that respect, deliberately naïve "impartial spectator", the role we assume here, we might provide a more innovative impulse than those more closely involved.

Judicial punitive and mediation system, Rule of Law, and Credible China: Judicial punishment in China appears in the mirror of our media as a-priori harsh and unjust and/or unlawful. However, they apparently know almost nothing about the laws, the criminal law and jurisprudence, or the legal culture in China.

This especially applies to the new strategic orientation since the 2010s of the judiciary sector, and the public sector and state in general, toward a strict *rule of law* and a "Credible China" under the new, highly modern and progressive *Civil Code* of 2021, the *data protection law*, modeled after Germany, and the new civil rights—for instance, the individual right to effectively prohibit private data collection with just one click in the internet, to have a look, in any of the thousands of new civic centers, into one's data set, or to have one's conflict issues immediately addressed in one of the 690,000 *People's Mediation Committees*—just to name a few examples of a dynamically elaborating substantial people's democratic culture "of the whole process" (see above).

Novel forms of punishment and a rehabilitation focus: As reported above, judicial sanctions and punishments in China today—meant especially for managers, officials, and politicians involved in corruption, financial, or environmental offenses—are original, flexible, adequate, and effective. They include credit bans, flight bans, first-class bans on bullet trains, and similar novel kinds of non-pecuniary sanctions, which always leave a patch open, too, for rehabilitation and resocialization. No manager, politician, or state bureaucrat can just simply buy their way out with petty cash.

Rehabilitation can thus be achieved relatively quickly. In China, the stigma of prison does not cling to the ex-convict as it does in many other, mostly Western countries, particularly in the "incarceration society" of the USA, where lifelong punishment and the enduring stigma of imprisonment, rather than reintegration, are often the (intended) outcomes for the lower social strata. In contrast, in China, an ex-convict is unlikely to drift back into crime, simply due to his/her imprisonment, and therefore is not permanently stigmatized by a judicial sanction.

Anti-corruption campaigns and trust of people in the CPC, in the system, in the government, and the state: Even here, a naïve outsider may note that the excesses of the late "Wild-East" phase stemming from the first Reform & Opening-up period (1978–2007), marked by rampant corruption, crime, internet and credit/financial fraud, and environmentally harmful practices, have largely been brought under control. This was achieved through major anti-corruption campaigns targeting CPC, state, and political ranks as well as entrepreneurs and corporate managers after 2007, and particularly in the 2010s. During this period, thousands of officials, mostly regional and local party and state cadres, as well as business people, who had caused moral, social, and economic damage to the country, were imprisoned. Both the party and the state have noticeably renewed themselves through these efforts. Internationally comparative trust surveys therefore show that public confidence in the CPC, the government, and the state has risen to levels that continuously have been among the highest levels globally. In this respect, one can take reassurance.

Positive incentives: Finally, could any future local, regional, or even national "social-credit" system, if they will not have fulfilled their purpose and become entirely redundant one day, be designed primarily around positive rather than punitive incentives, e.g., for safeguarding the environment and culture? The already mentioned playful *Ant-Forest* app, with its positive reinforcement for ecological and social behaviors, might serve as a role model in this regard.

The Long-Term Reinvestment Cycle

A country with a young physical infrastructure: No country in the world has ever invested as much as China in such a short period in recent decades. Infrastructure, buildings, machinery, and technological and research systems are mostly still at the beginning of their long-term life cycles—even the oldest, from the 1990s, are only halfway through. This is a highly modern nation, with infrastructure and building stock ranging from brand new to rarely more than 35 years old, considered against typical physical infrastructure life cycles of around 60 years.[4] Just note: 90 percent of the residential buildings that Chinese people live in today were built since 1990.[5]

We have reported above on related city appearances, and the internet is full of Western millennials' and GenZ's enthusiastic posts about spectacular modern Chinese multi-million cities and their natural surroundings, hundreds of posts reflecting the surge in international tourism to China in recent years (with largely no visa requirements anymore).

The neoliberal financial-oligarchic West hugely failed against the long-run reinvestment requirement: The USA was once like that, home to the world's cutting-edge cities of the 1950s to 1970s. But then neoliberalism was installed as a new paradigm of rule for the rich and powerful oligarchies, bringing with it aggravated austerity and public poverty, in the end along with public and private disinvestment and general deterioration. Since then, the country has largely lived off its existing public-infrastructural substance.[6] Much of the still standing infrastructure was built during the New Deal of the 1930s. US cities, like many Western cities, have developed their particular morbid charm, with often downgraded downtowns and large poverty-stricken areas in suburbs and ghettos, alongside small clusters of modern corporate and hotel skyscrapers that many tourists still appreciate. But overall, tourism to the US cities, touristic Mekkas up to the 2000s, has declined considerably recently.

Hardly any country has so far ever managed to systematically replace the long-term, decades-long life cycle of the building stock, infrastructures, or central basic technologies in a forward-looking manner, or to manage this in such a way that the cycle could be dissolved, stabilized, and transformed into a continuous, even, and "linear" development, one that does not fall into the straitjacket of a long wave of reinvestment, always echoing the first investment period. Should a downturn phase of a long wave then combine with a slack phase of a short-run business cycle, a massive crisis may even result.

Chinese planning options: The Chinese decentralized and flexibly planned system, as described, can definitely absorb or prevent a long wave, as it already has succeeded in smoothing out business cycles and critical macro aggregates' time series since the early 2010s. Major crises might, of course, be imposed from outside through geopolitical hybrid wars. But in that respect, too, China has increasingly become resilient, as we have seen. However, preventing a long-term modernization and reinvestment cycle in order to avoid becoming an "old industrial" entity sooner or later is something no country has achieved so far, least of all the beacon of the Western bloc and "only superpower" USA, which, on the contrary, is grappling with the consequences of decades of disinvestment and the aging of its capital stock.

China will (have to) address this reinvestment cycle issue early on: A gigantic renewal cycle is foreseeable over the next 25 to 60 years. Can the time structure of infrastructure and construction investments be dissolved and smoothed out in time? We can already see many efforts in Chinese cities, where older residential areas are modernized and upgraded, one possible step toward breaking up the time structure of reinvestment. After all, we have discussed in this book, if there is any country that can reverse long-term aging and decline, and even out the time structure of its capital stock, it is China.

Climate-Change Mitigation and Nuclear Power

Renewable and "new" energies: The energy transition in China, rushing before our eyes, is also historically unique, and every week we receive new data from international news sites on the expansion of renewable energies and renewable electrical power supply. Sun, wind, and water are replacing coal, oil, and gas at unprecedented speeds, as described above in different contexts.

Besides sun, wind, and water, nuclear power is considered one of the "new energies" in China. Nuclear power has contributed about 5 percent of China's electricity (planned to decline to 4 percent in 2035). There are mini nuclear-power plants, in container size, intended for villages in China's West, for accelerated rural development.

Revival of nuclear power in the West: In the West, and namely Germany/EU, nuclear power was considered strictly too risky a technology during the decades-long "green" wave and quickly was reduced to zero in Germany after the Japanese Fukushima accident. This caused industrial issues related to sufficient and sufficiently stable energy supply in Germany, namely against the backdrop of Germany simultaneously being cut off from its traditional Eurasian (Russian) energy lifelines (e.g., the Nord Stream 2 pipeline "shutdown", as previously pledged by then-US President Biden[7]), and cutting itself off through its years-long waves of "sanctions" against Russia. Now the political pendulum swings back in the West in the face of its self-imposed disconnection from the half-century-long Eurasian energy cooperation on gas and oil, and nuclear power is now politically set for a rescue and revival; old shut-down nuclear power stations in Germany are to be reactivated.

New generations of conventional nuclear-power technology: Conventional nuclear power may never completely lose its technical peculiarity, with the range of effects in the event of any technological failure quickly becoming unmanageable and uncontrollable, as Harrisburg (1979), Chernobyl (1986), and Fukushima (2011) demonstrated. The temporal range of conventional nuclear energy technology (the half-lives of radiation) is typically longer than the collective human memory and planning horizons.

China in particular has made significant advances in reactor technology in recent years, with conventional nuclear technology now being two generations ahead of the Fukushima-era systems, featuring now three independent cooling circuits and passive cooling, virtually prohibiting core meltdown.

Thorium and nuclear-fusion technologies: Much more important, however, and much praised in power engineering worldwide, seems to be the so-called *thorium technology*, based on molten-salt nuclear reaction, running without pressure and without uranium, and thus without long-term fissile material. Originally developed in the USA but abandoned there in the 1990s due to a number of unsolvable technical issues, China adopted and further developed the technology at the Chinese Academy of Sciences, succeeded in overcoming those issues over time, and now has its thorium reactor operating under real-world conditions in the Gobi Desert. This will then pave the way for further commercial/applied modular thorium-based reactors. This has made China the first country in the world to operate this novel kind of fuel reactor with fuel breeding and molten salt. Thorium-232 is used as an alternative to uranium-235 and is much more abundant on earth, thus allowing for a significant reduction in dependence on uranium. In China's case, thorium does not even need to be mined separately, as it is sourced as a waste product of its rare-earth mining operations, making the environmental impacts even smaller compared to conventional nuclear technology.

This would make it "a practically inexhaustible supply of fuel", as the *Institute of Electrical and Electronics Engineers* (IEEE) has described,[8] another evaluation stating that "China has enough thorium reserves to meet its energy needs for 20,000 years".[9]

Thorium-based reactors also produce less waste: more than 80 percent of the fuel material can reportedly be recycled, while the remaining radioactive residue is solidified into glass and transported "to a national nuclear waste disposal site deep underground in the Gobi Desert".[10] Moreover, the waste material itself has a significantly shorter half-life, remaining hazardous for only a few hundred years rather than tens of thousands. The risk of nuclear meltdown is also greatly reduced compared to uranium reactors, since in the event of overheating, the molten salt would drain into a container below the reactor, thereby posing "no threat to the surrounding environment".[11]

China will combine thorium power plants with new gas-cooled reactors, advanced pressurized water reactors, fast neutron reactors, and small modular reactors. In addition, it is advancing nuclear fusion technology and is already approaching a workable prototype fusion reactor.

China plans to build 150 advanced nuclear reactors by 2035, replacing conventional ones, placing it ahead of France and the United States, whose plants still largely rely on Cold-War era technologies.[12]

But can China get along without any nuclear power?

Overall reduction of energy consumption: While these advances can contribute to China's transition toward renewable and sustainable energy supplies, another challenge that remains is an ever more efficient energy use or one day even the reduction of overall energy consumption. This includes ongoing efforts to improve productivity and ensure sustainable population development (see below).

And it might include abandoning nuclear power in any form entirely.

During the 13th FYP (2016–2020), China had achieved an average annual GDP growth of 5.7 percent, while energy consumption grew at an average annual rate of 2.8 percent. Under the 14th FYP (2021–2025), it realized a reduction in energy consumption of 13.5 percent per unit of GDP. This, however, represents only a relative reduction in energy consumption. In the long-run, another world may emerge, in which China and the most developed countries, in a collective action, may afford zero or even negative growth rates. With increasing energy efficiency, this could translate into even stronger reductions in energy consumption, enabling a full-fledged green economy and a qualitative improvement in people's well-being rather than through mere GDP growth. We have discussed the broader context of a future Chinese ecological civilization and the transition to HDI- and happiness-based indicators above (see above, Part II, Chapter 6).

After all that we have reported and discussed about China in this book, one may assume that more of these developments will appear in the 15th FYP (2026–2030), and that China will take the lead in the long-term transitions toward less physical consumption and the increasing irrelevance of the GDP, the contours of which may become visible toward the end of the century as China's next major century goal after 2049.

Demographic Challenges: Population Development and Comprehensive Social Policies After the One- and Two-Child Periods

Was the one-child policy a failure? We have described the earlier one-child phase above and discussed its different effects. It was the only significant attempt in modern history by a country to address the challenge of rapid global population growth before natural limits and demographic pressures would have led to more severe socio-demographic crises. Those which namely the "Western liberal-democratic" India has run into, including intensified natural disasters, regional overpopulation stresses, increase of poverty-stricken areas, and fundamental social problems.

In contrast, humanity in total appears to be approaching these natural limits in ways that still reveal a collective incapacity to anticipate, react to, and prevent large-scale demographic and ecological crises. To date, still no other country except China has developed an adequate action capacity for a forward-looking population policy.

So again, was the one-child policy a mistake? In contrast to the (unsurprisingly) usual scandalization of it in the Western media, a less ideological-superficial look at it suggests a more complex picture:

- First, the policy decisively altered China's demographic trajectory, slowing down what was set to be a rapid population expansion, eventually contributing to a plateau and gradual decline. At the same time, most Western media reports on India, a country perceived as "friendly to the West", becoming the world's most populous country, remain blind to the challenges associated with India's rapid—and partly uncontrolled—population growth. While a large population can certainly provide potential demographic dividends, it may also intensify challenges of poverty, employment, social provision, and ecologically sustainable development if such population growth is not ensured within sustainable parameters. So, what a naïve, childish view on population numbers is such a "The more, the better". While India may well have 1.5 billion people by the mid of the century, there will just be a couple of hundred million more in poverty, more a burden for the country's development than an asset given the country's parameters.

- Second, the one-child policy has led to significant structural changes in China's population, most notably an aging population—a predictable, foreseen, and accepted outcome. And again, Western media often present aging in a distorted, sometimes alarmist way. As can be observed in China nowadays, and as we have discussed above, an older population can become a societal and economic asset. Accumulated knowledge and experience of the elderly may continue to contribute to goods and services production, provided that work and retirement systems are shaped and managed properly, flexibly rather than rigidly. China has addressed this by slightly adjusting retirement ages over the coming decades, which still remain very low, namely given the country's considerably extended life expectancy. And the elderly are always also productive consumers, or, in the terminology of the IT economy: "prosumers", contributing users, if they are properly integrated and connected and not marginalized. This has already contributed to the emergence of a "grayhair economy", encompassing commodities, services, and infrastructure tailored to older adults. Additionally, initiatives support self-organization and networking among older individuals, for example, with the "younger old" assisting the "older old". Of course, old-age insurance and healthcare systems must also be adapted. Overall, this represents a substantial structural change with however significant potential benefits for both the economy and society.

National "grayhair-economy" plans: In 2022, China's State Council introduced its "silver economy" or "grayhair economy" plans, aiming to promote public and private innovation and investment in services and products targeted at the elderly. By 2024, these plans were expanded to include social-support systems and infrastructure for elderly care, including, for example, ten so-called "silver economy industrial parks",[13] or canteens, advisory services, sports facilities, and leisure parks in feasible walking distances.

International median-age ranking: Against this background, the population issue in China after the one-child policy has presumably become smaller than it would have been under an unhampered population explosion, and it is different from how it is usually portrayed in the West. Even quantitatively, it appears smaller than often suggested, at least on average still: Mainland China's median age was 39.8 years in 2023, ranking China only 62nd in the world by age, well behind the EU (32nd), South Korea (18th), Taiwan (30th), or Japan (3rd), which has a median age of 49.5.[14]

But of course, the dynamics at the more recent margins count more than the means, and China's dropping fertility rate has recently been very dynamic.[15] The central government as well as provinces, cities, and companies have begun to support families with second and third children, with financial subsidies, generous maternity-leave regulations, and local child-related infrastructures (baby-change spaces, nurseries, and kindergartens, later reliefs for families with school children, etc.).

A shortage of workers? There is also always the specter of a worker shortage. In this respect, China's considerable increases in productivity (always cared to be above GDP growth!) are reflected in a relatively high level and dynamic of automation and robotization in goods and services production.

From one-child to three-child policy: The new cultural problem behind: The one-child policy as such had quickly become history. It had already been weakened early on, as we have reported. It had been stepwise transformed into a two-child policy, which, in recent years, was again replaced by an official three-child policy.

The background here is a new phenomenon, already well-known from the mature developed countries of the West, linked to increasing wealth, rising female labor-force participation, higher female education, and changing cultural patterns in female career-paths, in work, consumption, leisure, and consequently, family planning. The apparently "natural" weakening of population growth in this way is culturally conditioned.

China has been experiencing this much earlier, i.e., at a much lower GDP per capita level than the West, in fact already as a (still) developing and new middle-income country, coming from below. China's particular cultural traits, a large middle-income population of several hundred million, a still very competitive educational, labor, and work culture, and an extensive female emancipation, have contributed to a considerable decline in fertility and childbirth rates, now clearly below the reproduction rate.

The implications appear quantitatively more severe than those of the one-child policy.

Maternity and family policies and other policy challenges: Thus, China will need to adjust more profoundly today than in the aftermath of the one-child policy. Beyond the old-age policy measures mentioned, a substantial system of incentives and support for maternity and young families is already being implemented, and family reliefs in education include a less competitive schooling culture. Thus, it appears to be recognized that schooling, labor, and work cultures will need to become less harsh and competitive, while still balancing this against a high overall productivity growth.

Finally, China has already become an immigration destination, with many people from both the West and the Global South settling there to work and live. This appears to be a particular asset with a potential for China and should be further developed. As we have shown, China has been further opening to Western manufacturing and financial capital and their employees and is also pursuing some proactive tourism and settlement strategies through its new liberal visa policies.

Considering all of the above, it is comprehensible that China is widely considered an international population-policy model in the international community, from which the UN, international agencies, and many countries of the Global South do learn and seek guidance.

The Middle-Income Trap

Balancing supply and demand sides in a dynamic circuit and in a proper time structure: Productivity growth above GDP growth is a necessity in order to avoid falling into the middle-income trap, where production, investment, technology, productivity, and supply are neglected in favor of consumption, leisure, income, and a general drive for redistribution of the given (or then perhaps even shrinking) cake, as was experienced in the young industrializing and emerging economies of Latin America in the 1950s, 1960s, and thereafter.

On the household-income, disposable-income, and consumption-demand side, China continues to show considerable wage increases, significant tax relief for lower-income groups, and recent measures to strengthen domestic consumption, as discussed above (Part II, Ch. 6). Altogether, this supports domestic orientation, inclusive prosperity, and a more equal distribution.

Maintaining a balance in the economic circuit, as well as in the timing of investment and consumption, while ensuring dynamic development and avoiding pronounced business cycles and long infrastructure reinvestment waves (above), is not a trivial task. The balance must be maintained between advancing technologies, productivity growth, and production structures on the supply side, and household income, private and public investment, and state expenditures on the demand side, while accounting for exports and imports as well.

Countries stuck in the middle-income trap: Above all, productivity growth must be kept higher than income growth (national income, GDP). If this is not guaranteed in the longer term, a rising country risks falling into the infamous "middle-income trap". Many neoliberal and oligarchically structured countries, such as Argentina, Brazil, South Africa, Indonesia, the Philippines, and, to some extent, Turkey, were stuck in this trap for some decades.[16] Only a few climber countries, such as Japan, South Korea, Singapore, and above all China, have consistently avoided the trap and managed a continuous catch-up.

Social middle-income strata: The middle-income trap tends to occur at "middle" GDP levels, namely GDP per capita ("middle-income") levels, when consumption pressures, redistribution struggles, and rent-seeking behavior begin to dominate. The question is whether China can avoid such a "trap of a middle-class society": namely, avoiding the risk that productivity growth and innovation capacity lag behind income growth, especially of the social "middle-income" strata, leading to a gradual loss of the advantages achieved so far and resulting in a culture of redistribution struggles rather than efforts of production growth, at medium-income levels.

From manufacturing to a "service society"? China has, for a long time, planned for a general stabilization and careful slowdown of GDP growth in its FYPs since the 2010s. The secular structural change from more growth-intensive manufacturing to a less growth-intensive "service society" (less prone to productivity growth) has, of course, also been actively promoted. Many experts, therefore, have observed that

China avoids the middle-income trap. [...] To the extent that this change is the intended result of China's strategic realignment, a slowdown in growth is significantly less worrying.[17]

A key to this will remain the promotion of "intensive growth", namely productivity growth in manufacturing, and in service industries as far as possible. We may be optimistic for China in view of its huge skilled human capital, research, innovation, and technology, as well as its modernizing and highly invested capital stock, particularly in automatization and robotization, which now includes automatization of the service industries as well.

Others, however, have not seen the battle is already won:

How China overcomes the middle-income trap is arguably one of the greatest problems for policymakers and development economists alike.[18]

The middle-income trap into which Latin American countries once fell has also been analyzed as a problem of economic dependency following forced "neoliberalization", with excessive interest rates, overvalued currencies, debt traps, deindustrialization, and authoritarian oligarchic rule and their excessive enrichment, imposed through the policies of Washington's IMF/WB.[19] From this perspective, China again appears to have a good chance of avoiding such a mess.

Consumerism, Middle-Class Ideology, Elitism, and Nationalism

Social upward mobility—middle-class ideology sneaking in: This complex is not only a matter of making sure that productivity growth outpaces income growth but also has a social, cultural, and socio-psychological dimension concerning people's attitudes toward the growth of their own income and consumption and their relative status in society. It involves their cultural stance toward a predatory redistribution of a given "cake" rather than contributing to its enlargement, as mentioned above in the context of the middle-income trap. It is a question of consumerism and aspirations for individualistic advancement into an ideal of a "middle class", which appears to many people to be more than just being at a middle-income level. From there, they would aspire to some ideal "upper class", perhaps feeling supported by some political ideas of upward mobility, meant inclusively but interpreted exclusively by some. Such a culture can of course not be left to develop unchecked. Not the least because, as noted, a Western-style consumer society, the "imperial mode of living", would not be sustainable with 1.3 to 1.4 billion people.

While public political education and narratives, as well as the positive social role models that CPC members are personally expected to provide, do counter such tendencies, such aspirations, cultural patterns, and middle-class dreams often creep in slowly, tacitly, and hidden. They are frequently accompanied by emerging elitist attitudes regarding one's personal income, wealth, companies and entrepreneurship, and the education and academic status of one's children. Such elitist attitudes may easily extend to school and university rankings.

An elitist higher education? However, there is a clear, dominant political tendency in China toward more even development, downward distribution, and inclusive socio-economic progress, supported by a broad social basis both inside and outside the CPC, the government, and the state. In higher education, a field particularly susceptible to elitist ideology, recent scrutiny and discussion have addressed excessive gating and restricted physical access for the general public to the campuses of top universities.[20]

On the other hand, some leading universities have decided to withdraw from international university ranking systems, which still operate largely according to elitist US academic traditions imposed on China in the 1980s and 1990s. They are arguing that such rankings no longer fit their own new and politically supported educational ideals "with Chinese characteristics" and also threaten their educational autonomy.[21] Domestically, the criteria for individual academic promotion in China have in fact been broadened in recent years to include efforts at knowledge transfer and the "translation" of research to the general public, including publication in general-interest outlets.

Nationalism on social media? Social media platforms provide a space where people often (although mistakenly) feel more anonymous than in the analog world of in-person interaction. They therefore have proven to be a particularly difficult sphere of interaction worldwide. In the West, we have witnessed all kinds of excesses on the internet over recent decades. Today, it is subject (namely in the EU) to strict regulation and censorship, carried out not directly by the state but indirectly through corporate regulatory policies imposed by large private tech providers, often on behalf of state authorities (as in the EU and Germany).

In China, the digital communication sphere was regulated and placed under strict legal rules early on. As reported, public agencies engage with people on social media on an equal footing, and there is no way to fully conceal one's identity. The correct name and at least the name of the residential community must be visible. The state regulates directly (not through silent mass cancelations by the big-tech corporations, as practiced in the EU) and has established legal criteria for non-acceptable online behavior, as we have noted. Among others, incitement to war/violence, racism, personal degradation, sexism and pornography, as well as nationalism are prohibited, and such contributions will generally be deleted, usually after some warning from, and online communication with, the internet governance agency.

Since the turn of the millennium, new generations have grown up in China with an often-strong national consciousness and a more open, at times more aggressive, language. One factor behind this has been the ongoing excessive criticism of China by Western media and politics, while young Chinese, in turn, feel many reasons for some national pride. And as internet and social-media regulators have apparently become more permissive in recent years, often engaging, as said, in dialogue with rule violators rather than flatly cancelling them, some unprecedentedly offensive language has occurred, including, as a recent example, insults directed at entertainment or sports celebrities for allegedly insufficiently "patriotic" behavior. International sports contests, which serve as battlegrounds for nationalist emotions in the West, have also triggered some nationalist sentiments in China that were traditionally unknown.

But here as well, there are countermovements and many serious voices warning against nationalist overreactions. They suggest that the high degree of leniency on the part of regulators and policymakers may have become problematic.[22] Thus, a "battle" between a tendency toward greater liberalism in the social media and the maintenance of Confucian and socialist values and ethics is ongoing. Defining the border between sound national consciousness and nationalist excess will thus become another field for Chinese experimentalism.

Downward redistribution and inclusive development as the mainstream: More generally, China seeks to address people's mental models, dreams, and aspirations. This has included, for example, the transition from combustion-engine vehicles to NEVs and from individual to collective forms of public transport. It has also encompassed, as reported, public discussion of consumption patterns (e.g., meat consumption, treatment of animals, reduction of food waste), a redefinition of macroeconomic success criteria (GDP vs. HDI), ethics (Confucian traditions), and values of life (the conception of "spiritual civilization"). It has emphasized the environment ("ecological civilization"), justice (rule of law and the concept of "credible China"), equality, and the broader vision of a "moderately prosperous society" grounded in ecological and social commons.

On Paths We Have Not Known Yet ...

Experimenting, learning, changing ... the "green factory of the world": China, as we could see in many areas, is developing pathways that often look surprising and sometimes strange to us, simply as they have never been taken before. It has organized "the one large" and infinitely many smaller experiments, it evaluates its experiences, learns, and changes things—and often very quickly.

It is making enormous contributions to the global ecological commons, both domestically and in the Global South, and has made renewable energy cheaper than coal, oil, and gas. As the international consulting company *Roland Berger* says, China now is no longer just the factory of the world; it is the "green and sustainable factory of the world".[23]

But even China's massive "green" production capacities are still insufficient to meet global climate goals. As if "Chinese overcapacities"! Even China's huge renewable-energy expansion rates would have to be tripled to save the world's climate.[24] The *International Energy Agency* (IEA) has estimated that sales of NEVs would need to increase to 4.5 times the 2022 level, and PV-panel production and sales would have to rise to 10 times the 2022 level in order to reach the 2030 climate goals.[25]

That China (still insufficiently) enables Africa, Latin America, and Central and Southeast Asia in approaching their climate goals is well known and recognized in the Global South, but still widely ignored in Western official media and politics, which still speak of "overcapacities" and "price dumping", in order to further protect their own oligopolistic industries and keep price levels high. A regular young family in the West will never have the chance to get a cutting-edge family EV for below 10,000 USD as is the case in China.

China's sovereignty, integrity, and stability ... imagining our own future: China's national sovereignty, territorial integrity, economic stability, long-term planning, social inclusion, internal mobilization of human resources, and broad external cooperations are therefore to be considered, if anything, on the positive side of world development.

2025: The China-EU summit flopped: We would therefore do well to observe, understand, and learn for ourselves what the future "with China" might look like, and to make clearer to ourselves what *our* future should look like. Obviously, traditional Eurocentric arrogance and hubris are out of place; instead, some humility, willingness to cooperation, and mutual learning from and with China would be appropriate. But the EU missed a major chance to move in that direction with the latest China-EU summit in mid-2025, upon the occasion of the 50th anniversary of the establishment of diplomatic relations between the two parties (China–Germany). Belligerent remarks by EU officials in the run-up to the summit inevitably caused it to flop. No substantial results were agreed on. The EU will very soon realize how much of a disadvantage it is in in this relationship. The EU manufacturing sector will increasingly have to migrate to China in order to make sales, profit, and technological advances and gain access to badly needed rare earths. On top of this failure in EU-China relations came a complete defeat for EU officials in the US-EU trade talks, which was considered the beginning of an EU "century of humiliation" by Washington. In the end, even more EU companies and private investments will migrate to the USA (and China). After all, the EU appears to be on a reinforced path to global marginalization.

Squaring multiple circles: Domestic dynamic stability and a future multipolar global structure: If a country can manage the squaring of different circles—between domestic stability, a dynamic development, and a world structure changing toward multipolarity—trade-offs that most countries face today: stability, prosperity with inclusion, more equality, and saving the earth's ecology—then, as it looks today, China holds good cards.

But China's 19 percent of world population cannot—economically, ecologically—pull along 80 percent. And keeping itself isolated, even a large country like China would have failed. The country recognized that early on and cared for maximum global integration, be it into the UN-South-South cooperation, the BRICS+, SCO+, ASEAN, RCEP, and BRI networks, as we have reported, with more than five billion people in BRI partnership countries alone. And BRICS+, with its 4.5 billion people, now represents more than 55 percent of the world population. Just to remind ourselves of the global dimensions of the current multipolarity move...

A global lead for China? No matter which path the West takes, no matter how great the hostilities and disruptions in the international system become, the new "number one" will have both an economic and ecological lead in the foreseeable future—and nolens volens will have to assert this lead in international diplomacy. A chief economist of the *New Development Bank* ("BRICS Bank") and professor at the renowned Tsinghua University in Beijing described it as a major challenge for China:

> Beijing must learn to lead at a time when the USA is confused and paranoid. This may include tolerating attacks from some US politicians while carrying out domestic reforms and advancing climate protection [...] Ignore the noise and just do it![26]

And we remain cogitating and silent … no comment …

Some Critical Solidarity for Those Efforts Seems Fair

While researching literature, we accidentally found the following inspiring phrase on the website of a small German leftist group, in a long article about China:

> [..] socialist China truly deserves more in this struggle than unwillingly grumbling spectators who mutter something about a 'next attempt'. This is happening right before our eyes and deserves sympathy and support in our own interest […].[27]

Well, obviously an appeal from leftists who are not the usual China bashers, as many Eurocentric leftists are nowadays. Surprisingly, an appeal of ours would, in fact, be quite similar—perhaps a bit more down-to-earth, in a more traditional-pragmatist style. It would be an appeal to the Western pragmatic professional, skilled worker, technician, engineer, programmer, corporate manager, average student, simple tourist even, and academic colleague—representatives of whom we have met on flights to and from China, in the elevators and lobbies of hotels in China, on trains in Germany (see Introduction), and in considerable E-Mail communication about the original German edition of this book over years. But it would also be an appeal to high-school students and their teachers, to our neighbors, and just to the average reader.

Note China's mid-term and long-term overarching socio-economic, societal, and systemic goals:

- First, China's *15th Five-Year Plan* (2026–2030) is aiming to achieve a *socialist modernization by 2035*. For that goal, the plan emphasizes a high-quality development, comprehensive reform, cultural progress, improving the quality of life, and high-quality productive forces, among others. Particularly the latter conception is fundamentally socio-economic, as it implies people not only with high skills but high cultural and social standards. We therefore should expect China to focus on the human being in an ever more multidimensional and comprehensive way. A future socialism should have this at its core indeed.

- Second, after the 2021 centenary goal (100 years CPC) of eliminating absolute poverty and building a "moderately prosperous society", China has embarked on a journey toward its second centenary goal for 2049 (100 years PRC) of building a *modern socialist country that is prosperous, strong, democratic, culturally advanced, harmonious, and beautiful.* We have no clear idea yet how China's socialism will look like in 23 years. Many readers will be able to observe that development. Twenty-three years will have passed quickly. It will certainly be no pure ideal Eurocentric state socialism, and they will have "capital", "capitalists", and "markets". But it still appears to be a true adventure to envision a form of a socialist country in that short period of time, given the world might be rather more turbulent by that time, and the old empire and its trabants perhaps even more hostile to that project than less. So, here is perhaps *the* grand process on earth to be observed and analyzed.

So, China indeed deserves more than disregard, scorn, and hostility. It deserves to be perceived and comprehended, in our own interest, for trying out ways that no one has ever gone before, for taking risks on this path, making mistakes, and correcting them. And with that, yes, why not, it also deserves an honest, informed, and critical interest, if not solidarity. Why we advocate this, everyone may find out when traveling to China oneself at the next occasion. We hope this book will have well prepared the reader for his or her own travel and exploration.

Notes

1. E.g., Death Penalty Information Center, "China Moves to Sharply Restrict Use of Death Penalty", March 14, 2025: https://deathpenaltyinfo.org/international-china-moves-to-sharply-restrict-use-of-death-penalty, visited July 26, 2025.
2. E.g., Gui Huang, *On the Alternative Punishment to the Death Penalty in China*, Singapore: Springer, 2024.
3. E.g., Lan Chi LE, "Death Penalty in Confucian Legal Culture in China and Vietnam", in: *'Death Penalty in Asia: Law and Practice' Online Conference*, University of Melbourne, February 18–19, 2021: https://law.unimelb.edu.au/__data/assets/pdf_file/0004/3604972/Le-Lan-Chi.pdf, visited December 21, 2024.
4. This is very sensitive of the specific infrastructure, and the exact lifetime varies a lot, usually between 20 and 100 years.

5. E.g., Adam Tooze, "Global Green Transition and China's Role: A Historical Perspective", *The East is Red*, July 21, 2025, Center for China and Globalization, Beijing. Tooze's keynote at the CCG details the amounts of investments made in very short time, and the resulting huge structural challenges coming up to China.
6. Wildfires and natural catastrophes, not the least due to the climate crisis, are particularly disastrous in the USA, notably because of the collapse of power-supply systems, emergency services, and other infrastructure and maintenance services. Widespread power shutdowns affecting tens of thousands of households testify to the decline of the capital stock, result in enormous economic and social losses, and even signal of an impending system collapse. Similar patterns of non-provision and long-term neoliberal austerity and disinvestment in physical, human, and ecological capital have become visible in Australia's mega-fires, which have also revealed a frightening public inability to respond.
7. Andrea Shalal, Andreas Rinke, Jeff Mason, "Biden pledges end to Nord Stream 2 if Russia invades Ukraine", *Reuters*, February 8, 2022: https://www.reuters.com/world/biden-germanys-scholz-stress-unified-front-against-any-russian-aggression-toward-2022-02-07/, visited August 22, 2025.
8. Emily Waltz, Yu-Tzu Chiu, "Why China Is Building a Thorium Molten-Salt Reactor", *IEEE Spectrum*, December 30, 2024, https://spectrum.ieee.org/chinas-thorium-molten-salt-reactor, visited January 3, 2025.
9. Stephen Chen, "China sets launch date for world's first thorium molten salt nuclear power station", *South China Morning Post*, July 26, 2024, https://www.scmp.com/news/china/science/article/3271978/china-sets-launch-date-worlds-first-thorium-molten-salt-nuclear-power-station, visited January 3, 2025.
10. Ibid.
11. Ibid.
12. Ibid.
13. E.g., Arendse Huld, "Developing the Silver Economy – New Proposals to Cultivate China's Elder Care Industry", *China Briefing*, January 23, 2024, https://www.china-briefing.com/news/developing-the-silver-economy-in-china-new-proposals-released/, visited January 4, 2025; Chad de Guzman, Koh Ewe, "China Unveils Extensive 'Silver Economy' Plan to Adapt to Aging Population", *Time*, January 16, 2024, https://time.com/6555949/china-silver-economy-aging-population-plan/, visited January 4, 2025.
14. E.g., "List of countries by median age", *Wikipedia*: https://en.wikipedia.org/wiki/List_of_countries_by_ median_age, visited January 4, 2025. Data based on CIA World Factbook estimates.

15. E.g., World Bank, "Fertility rate, total (births per woman) - China, United States, Germany, Japan, European Union": https://data.worldbank.org/indicator/SP.DYN.TFRT.IN?end=2023&locations=CN-US-DE-JP-EU&start=1986, visited September 13, 2025.
16. E.g., "Middle income trap", *Wikipedia*: https://en.wikipedia.org/wiki/Middle_income_trap, visited January 4, 2025.
17. Stephen S. Roach, "China vermeidet die Falle des mittleren Einkommens [China avoids the middle income trap]", *Finanz und Wirtschaft*, April 18, 2019, https://www.fuw.ch/article/china-vermeidet-die-falle-des-mittleren-einkommens, visited January 4, 2025 (translated by the authors).
18. CAI Peter, "How China can avoid the middle income trap", *The Australian Business Review*, April 28, 2015, https://www.theaustralian.com.au/business/business-spectator/news-story/how-china-can-avoid-the-middle-income-trap/6ccc1e2695b4d48250a2c9aa9eea532d, visited January 4, 2025.
19. E.g., Luiz C. Bresser-Pereira et al., "An alternative to the middle-income trap", *Structural Change and Economic Dynamics* 52 (2020), 294–312.
20. E.g., Zichen WANG, "China's Ivory Tower in Lockdown: Top Universities Hide Behind Gates", *Pekingnology*, July 4, 2025: https://www.pekingnology.com/p/chinas-ivory-tower-in-lockdown-top, visited July 28, 2025.
21. E.g., Yojana Sharma, "Three major universities quit international rankings", *University World News*, May 11, 2022: https://www.universityworldnews.com/post.php?story=20220511170923665, visited July 28, 2025.
22. E.g., Zichen WANG, "Don't Fear Tesla's Lead: HU Xijin Warns Against Online Nationalist Overreaction", Center for China and Globalization (CCG), *The East is Read*, July 26, 2025.
23. Ma J., "China's standing as 'world's factory' difficult to replace: Roland Berger Global Managing Director", *Global Times*, March 7, 2024, https://www.globaltimes.cn/page/202403/1308410.shtml, visited May 20, 2024.
24. E.g., W. Pomrehn, "Von wegen ‚Überkapazitäten' [As if ‚overcpacities']", *junge Welt*, May 18–20, 2024, p.9.
25. E.g., *Newsletter Chinah*, Chinese embassy in Germany, special edition, 4–2024, p.11.
26. David D. LI, "70 Jahre Volksrepublik China: Spektakuläres Laboratorium für Entwicklungspolitik [70 years People's Republic of China: Spectacular laboratory for development policy]", *Weltwirtschaft und Entwicklung*, 9–2019, p.3 (translated by the authors).
27. "Chinas Kampf um den Sozialismus. Klassen und Klassenkampf in der VR China (Teil 2) [China's struggle for socialism. Classes and class struggle in the People's Republic of China (Part 2)]", *Kommunistische Arbeiterzeitung*, No. 364, 2018, https://www.kaz-online.de/artikel/klassen-und-klassenkampf-in-der-vr-china-teil-2, visited January 5, 2025 (Translated by this author).

Selected and Recommended Literature

Allison, Graham. 2017. *Destined for War. Can America and China Escape Thucydides's Trap?* Boston: Houghton Mifflin Harcourt.

Ang, Yuen Yuen. 2016. *How China Escaped the Poverty Trap*. Ithaca, NY: Cornell University Press.

Boer, Roland. 2021. *Socialism with Chinese Characteristics: A Guide for Foreigners*. Singapore: Springer.

Brand, Ulrich, and Markus Wissen. 2021. *The Imperial Mode of Living. Everyday Life and the Ecological Crisis of Capitalism*. London: Verso.

Brossat, Alain, Ruiz Casado, and Juan Alberto. 2023. *Culture of Enmity: The Discursive Struggle for Taiwan in the Making of the New Cold War*. Singapore: Springer.

Chang, Ha-Joon. 2002. *Kicking Away the Ladder: Development Strategy in Historical Perspective*. London: Anthem Press.

Chang, Ha-Joon. 2007. *Bad Samaritans: The Myth of Free Trade and the Secret History of Capitalism*. London: Random House.

Cobb, John B., Jr. 2019. *China and Ecological Civilization, in conversation with Andre Vltchek*. Jakarta: Badak Merah Semesta.

Conboy, Kenneth, and James Morrison. 2002. *The CIA's Secret War in Tibet*. Lawrence, KS: University Press of Kansas.

Dai, Shuanping, and G. Liu. 2017. Emergence of new products and agile innovation in a catching-up economy: Evidence from the low-speed electric vehicle industry in the Shandong Province, China. In *EAEPE Annual Conference, Budapest, mimeo*.

W. Elsner, E. Najmehchi, *The Rise of China*,
https://doi.org/10.1007/978-3-032-20260-4

Diamond, Jared, and Jianguo Liu. 2005. China's environment in a globalizing world. *Nature* 435:1179–1186.

Elsner, Wolfram. 2015. Speculative financial capitalism wacking out over an "impossible" profit rate. The infeasibility of a "usual" real average profit rate, considering fictitious capital, and its implications. In *Marx, Veblen, and the Foundations of Heterodox Economics. Essays in Honor of John F. Henry*, ed. T.-H. Jo and F. S. Lee, 199–227. London, New York: Routledge.

Elsner, Wolfram, and Henning Schwardt. 2014. Trust and arena size. Expectations, institutions, general trust, and critical population and group sizes. *Journal of Institutional Economics* 10 (1): 107–134.

Elsner, Wolfram, and Henning Schwardt. 2015. From emergent cooperation to contextual trust, and to general trust: overlapping meso-sized interaction arenas and cooperation platforms as a foundation of pro-social behavior. *Forum for Social Economics* 44 (1): 69–86.

Felipe, Jesus, Utsav Kumar, Norio Usui, and Arnelyn Abdon. 2013. Why has China succeeded? And why it will continue to do so. *Cambridge Journal of Economics* 37 (4): 791–818.

Frank, Andre Gunder. 1998. *ReOrient. Global Economy in the Asian Age*. Oakland, CA: University of California Press.

Funk, Andrea S. 2019. *Crowdfunding in China. A New Institutional Economics Approach*. Cham: Springer.

Guo, Wenbo, Jing Feng, Brad McKenna, and Pengzhu Zhang. 2017. Inter-Organizational Governance and trilateral trust building: A case study of crowdsourcing-based open innovation in China. *Asian Business & Management* 16 (3): 187–207.

Hardy, Jane, Yassamin Imani, and Beini Zhuang. 2017. Regional resilience and global production networks in China: An open political economy perspective. *Competition & Change* 22 (1): 63–80.

Hasnat, Baban. 2018. Big Data: An institutional perspective on opportunities and challenges. *Journal of Economic Issues* 52 (2): 580–588.

Herrmann-Pillath, Carsten. 2017. *China's Economic Culture. The Ritual Order of State and Markets*. London, New York: Routledge.

Hudson, Michael. 1972. *Super Imperialism: The Origin and Fundamentals of U.S. World Dominance*. London, Sterling, VA: Pluto.

Hudson, Michael. 2015. *Finance as Warfare*. Bristol: World Economics Association.

Ireland, Paddy, and Gaofeng Meng. 2017. Post-capitalist property. *Economy and Society* 46 (3–4): 369–397.

Jin, Keyu. 2023. *The New China Playbook: Beyond Socialism and Capitalism*. New York: Viking Press.

Kadri, Ali. 2017. The Saudi palace coup, the oil market, China and the US. *Real-World Economics Review* 82. http://www.paecon.net/PAEReview/issue82/Kadri82.pdf.

Khanna, Parag. 2019. *The Future Is Asian: Commerce, Conflict, and Culture in the 21st Century.* New York: Simon & Schuster.

Kissinger, Henry A. 2011. *On China.* New York: Penguin.

Knight, Jack. 2014. China as a developmental state. *World Economy* 37 (10): 1335–1347.

Lamperti, Francesco, and Clara Elisabetta Mattei. 2018. Going up and down: rethinking the empirics of growth in the developing and newly industrialized world. *Journal of Evolutionary Economics* 28 (4): 749–784.

Li, Minqi. 2008. *The Rise of China and the Demise of the Capitalist World Economy.* London: Pluto Press.

Lin, Justin Yifu. 2017. Lessons from China and East Asia's catch up: the new structural economics perspective. In *Mapping a New World Order*, ed. V. Popov and P. Dutkiewicz, 53–70. Cheltenham and Northampton, MA: Edward Elgar.

Liu, Qunyi. 2018. Rethinking Land Reform in East Asia: Egalitarian or Inegalitarian? *Journal of Economic Issues* 52 (3): 694–716.

Losurdo, Domenico. 2017a. Has China turned to capitalism?—Reflections on the transition from capitalism to socialism. *International Critical Thought* 7 (2017): 15–31.

Mazzucato, Mariana. 2013. *The Entrepreneurial State. Debunking Public vs. Private Sector Myths.* London, New York: Anthem Press.

Miller, Chris. 2022. *Chip War: The Fight for the World's Most Critical Technology.* New York: Scribner.

Needham, Joseph. 1954. *Science and Civilisation in China.* Cambridge: Cambridge University Press.

Rasmus, Jack. 2018. Trump's Déjà Vu China Trade War. *World Review of Political Economy* 9 (3): 346–363.

Roberts, J. M., and Odd Arne Westad. 2013. *The History of the World.* 6th ed. Oxford: Oxford University Press.

Ruegemer, Werner. 2019. *The Capitalists of the 21st Century: An Outline of the Rise of the New Financial Players.* Ahrensburg, Germany: Tredition.

Seyfried, Christina. 2023. *African Bargaining Power with China: Foreign Investment and Rising Influence.* London: Routledge.

Shen, Zhenjiang, and Miaoyi Li, eds. 2018. *Big Data Support of Urban Planning and Management, Advances in Geographic Information Science.* Cham: Springer.

Sieren, Frank. 2023. *Future? China! How The New Superpower Is Changing The West.* Singapore: WSPC.

Thuy, Tran Truong, John B. Welfield, and Le Thuy Trang, eds. 2019. *Building a Normative Order in the South China Sea. Evolving Disputes, Expanding Options.* Cheltenham and Northampton, MA: Edward Elgar.

van Bavel, Bas. 2016. *How Market Economies Have Emerged and Declined since AD 500.* Oxford: Oxford University Press.
Vogel, Hans Ulrich. 2012. *Marco Polo "Was" in China: New Evidence from Currencies, Salts and Revenues.* Leiden: Brill.
von Glahn, Richard. 2018. The Institutionalization of paper money in Song-Yuan China. In *Money, Currency and Crisis. In Search of Trust 2000 BC to AD 2000,* ed. R. J. van der Spek and B. van Leeuwen, 248–267. London, New York: Routledge.
Weber, Isabella M. 2021. *How China Escaped Shock Therapy: The Market Reform Debate.* London, New York: Routledge.
White, Colin. 2018. *A History of the Global Economy. The Inevitable Accident.* Cheltenham and Northampton, MA: Edward Elgar.
Woo-Cumings, Meredith, ed. 1999. *The Developmental State.* Ithaca, NY: Cornell University Press.
Wu, Shanlin. 2018. The Mercantilist Root of the United States, Europe and Japan's Refusal to Accept China's Market Economy Status. *World Review of Political Economy* 9 (3): 315–329.
Yep, Ray, June Wang, and Thomas Johnson, eds. 2019. *Handbook on Urban Development in China.* Cheltenham and Northampton, MA: Edward Elgar.
Yusuf, Shahid, ed. 2017. *China and the Global Economy.* Cheltenham and Northampton, MA: Elgar.
Zhang, Angela Huyue. 2024. *High Wire: How China Regulates Big Tech and Governs Its Economy.* New York, NY: Oxford University Press.
Zhang, Fan. 2018. *The Institutional Evolution of China, Government vs Market.* Cheltenham and Northampton, MA, USA: Edward Elgar.
Zhang, Lanying, Guanqi Li, and Huili He. 2018. Controlling corporate power in China: Case studies of seed companies and water distribution. *American Journal of Economics and Sociology* 77 (2): 511–540.
Zhao, Hongjun. 2018. *China's Long-Term Economic Development. How Have Economy and Governance Evolved Since 500 BC?* Cheltenham and Northampton, MA: Edward Elgar.

Further Cited Literature

Baron, Stefan, and Guangyan Yin-Baron, 2018. *Die Chinesen. Psychogramm einer Weltmacht* [The Chinese. Psychogram of a World Power]. Berlin: Econ.
Berthold, Rolf, 2009. *Chinas Weg. 60 Jahre Volksrepublik.* [China's Path. 60 years of the People's Republic.]. Berlin: Wiljo Heinen.
Brzeziński, Zbigniew. 1997. *The Grand Chessboard: American Primacy and Its Geostrategic Imperatives.* New York: Basic Books.
Chai, Shijun, et al. 2018. Social networks and informal financial inclusion in the People's Republic of China. In *ADBI Working Paper 802.*

Chang, Ha-Joon. 1999. The economic theory of the developmental state. In *The Developmental State*, ed. Meredith Woo-Cumings, 182–199. Ithaca, NY: Cornell University Press.

Chang, Ha-Joon. 2010. How to 'do' a developmental state: political, organisational and human resource requirements for the developmental state. In *Constructing a Democratic Developmental State in South Africa: Potentials and Challenges*, ed. O. Edigheji, 82–96. Cape Town: HSRC.

Chen, Ping. 2010. *Economic Complexity and Equilibrium Illusion: Essays on Market Instability and Macro Vitality.* London, New York: Routledge.

Crome, Erhard, 2017. Chinas Aufstieg und die geopolitischen Folgen [China's rise and the geopolitical consequences]; *WeltTrends*, December 2, 2017. http://welttrends.de/res/uploads/Crome-Chinas-Aufstieg-2017.pdf. Accessed May 20, 2024.

Dai, Shuanping, and Wolfram Elsner. 2015. Declining Trust in Growing China. In *Working Papers in East-Asian Studies No. 101/2015.* University of Duisburg-Essen. https://www.econstor.eu/handle/10419/109976. Accessed September 21, 2024.

Dai, Shuanping, and Guanzhong Yang. 2017. Does social inducement lead to higher open innovation investment? An experimental study. In *Working Papers on East Asian Studies 112.* University of Duisburg-Essen. https://www.uni-due.de/imperia/md/cont ent/in-east/about/publications_green_series/paper112-2017.pdf. Accessed May 30, 2024.

Diamond, Jared. 2005. *Collapse: How Societies Choose to Fail or Survive.* London, New York: Penguin Books, esp. chapter 12: "China, Lurching Giant".

Ding, Xiaoqin, 2018. Entwicklung ohne Einmischung [Development without interference]. *junge Welt.* February 7, 2018.

Elsner, Wolfram. 2010. The process and a simple logic of 'meso'. On the co-evolution of institutional emergence and group size. *Journal of Evolutionary Economics* 20 (3): 445–477.

Elsner, Wolfram. 2013. Financial capitalism trapped in an 'impossible' profit rate. *International Journal of Pluralism and Economics Education* 4 (3): 243–261.

Elsner, Wolfram. 2021. Collapse. Institutional decline and breakdown, its endogeneity and its asymmetry vis-á-vis emergence: A theoretical frame. *Journal of Economic Issues* 55 (1): 79–102.

Elsner, Wolfram, Torsten Heinrich, and Henning Schwardt. 2015. *The Microeconomics of Complex Economies, Evolutionary, Institutional and Complexity Perspectives.* San Diego, Oxford, Amsterdam: Elsevier/ Academic Press.

Fitzthum, Robert, 2018a. *China verstehen. Vom Aufstieg zur Wirtschaftsmacht und der Eindämmungspolitik der USA* [Understanding China. On the rise to economic power and the containment policy of the USA], Vienna: Promedia.

Fitzthum, Robert, 2018b. Der nächste Feind [The next enemy]. *Rubikon*, October 31, 2018, https://www.rubikon.news/artikel/der-nachste-feind. Accessed October 13, 2024.

Frankopan, Peter. 2019. *The New Silk Roads: The Present and Future of the World.* London: Bloomsbury.

Fu, Tong. 2017. What determines firms' access to credit in the absence of effective economic institutions: evidence from China. *Economics. The Open-Access, Open-Assessment E-Journal* 11 (31): 1–27.

Graebner, Claudius, Wolfram Elsner, and Alex Lascaux. 2021. Trust and social control: Sources of cooperation, performance, and stability in informal value transfer systems. *Computational Economics* 58 (4): 1077–1102.

Han, Byung-Chul. 2015. *The Burnout Society.* Redwood City, CA: Stanford University Press.

Hardt, Michael, and Antonio Negri. 2000. *Empire.* Cambridge, MA: Harvard University Press.

Höring, Uwe 2018. *Der Lange Marsch 2.0. Chinas Neue Seidenstraßen als Entwicklungsmodell* [The Long March 2.0. China's New Silk Roads as a Development Model]. Hamburg: VSA.

Kirner, Florian Ernst, 2018. Es geht um Asien, verdammt! [It's about Asia, stupid!]. *Free21.* May 29, 2018. http://www.free21.org/es-geht-um-asien-verdammt/. Accessed January 6, 2025.

Kronauer, Jörg, 2019. *Der Rivale. Chinas Aufstieg zur Weltmacht und die Gegenwehr des Westens* [The Rival: China's Rise to World Power and the West's Resistance]. Hamburg: Konkret.

Kunzmann, Marcel, 2018. *Theorie, System und Praxis des Sozialismus in China* [Theory, System and Practice of Socialism in China]. 2nd ed. Berlin: Verlag Mirco Kolarczik

Küsters, Günter, 2018. *Das Verhältnis von EU und China im Kontext globaler Machtverschiebungen und der aktuellen Kontroverse um Chinas Großprojekt der 'Neuen Seidenstraße'* [The relationship between the EU and China in the context of global power shifts and the current controversy surrounding China's major 'New Silk Road' project], presentation, *Attac*: https://www.attac.de/fileadmin/user_upload/Kampagnen/Europa/workshops/Guenter_Kuesters_Verhaeltnis_von_EU_und_China.pdf. Accessed January 14, 2025.

Li, Kai, Cheryl Long, and Wei Wan. 2019. Public interest or regulatory capture: Theory and evidence from China's airfare deregulation. *Journal of Economic Behavior & Organization* 161:343–365.

Lin, Justin Yifu, and Yan Wang. 2017. China's contribution to development cooperation: Ideas, opportunities and finances. In *China and the Global Economy*, ed. Shahid Yusuf, 826–851. Cheltenham and Northampton, MA: Elgar.

Losurdo, Domenico. 2017b. China und das Ende der 'kolumbianischen Epoche' [China and the end of the 'Columbian Epoch']. *Marxistische Blätter* 3 (2017): 52–62.

Luik, Arno, 2019, *Schaden in der Oberleitung. Das geplante Desaster der Deutschen Bahn* [Damage in the overhead line. The planned disaster of Deutsche Bahn]. Frankfurt: Westend.

Mackinder, Halford J., 2019. *Der Schlüssel zur Weltherrschaft. Die Heartland-Theorie* [The Key to World Domination. The Heartland Theory]. Frankfurt/Main: Westend. (A German translation of Mackinder's original article "The Geographical Pivot of History" from 1904.)

Rasmus, Jack. 2015. *Systemic Fragility in the Global Economy.* Atlanta, GA: Clarity Press.

Rasmus, Jack. 2017. *Central Bankers at the End of Their Rope? Monetary Policy and the Coming Depression.* Atlanta, GA: Clarity Press.

Rügemer, Werner, 2018. *Die Kapitalisten des 21. Jahrhunderts. Gemeinverständlicher Abriss zum Aufstieg der neuen Finanzakteure* [The capitalists of the 21st century. A general outline of the rise of the new financial players]. Cologne: PapyRossa.

Scheuer, Stephan, 2018. *Der Masterplan: Chinas Weg zur Weltherrschaft* [The Masterplan: China's Path to World Domination]. Freiburg: Herder.

Schmid, Fred, 2017. China im globalen Kapitalismus [China in global capitalism]. In *Krise des Globalen Kapitalismus. Und jetzt Wohin?* [Crisis of global capitalism. And now where to?]. Munich: Institut für sozial-ökologische Wirtschaftsforschung (ISW), Report Nr. 109.

Schmid, Fred, 2018. Trumps Wirtschaftskrieg gegen China [Trump's economic war against China]. *Globaler Wirtschaftskrieg. Der Aufstieg Chinas. Zerbricht der Westen?* [Global economic war. The rise of China. Is the West falling apart?]. ISW Report Nr. 115, Munich, 22–39.

Schmidt, Christian Y., 2009. *Allein unter 1,3 Milliarden. Eine chinesische Reise von Shanghai bis Kathmandu* [Alone among 1.3 billion, A Chinese journey from Shanghai to Kathmandu]. Reinbek: Rowohlt.

Schmidt, Christian Y., 2010. *Bliefe von dlüben. Der China-Crashkurs* [Letters flom ovel thele. The China Crash-Course]. Reinbek: Rowohlt.

Schmidt, Christian Y., 2011. *Im Jahr des Tigerochsen* [In the Year of the Tigerox]. Berlin: Verbrecher.

Schmidt, Christian Y., 2013. *Im Jahr des Hasendrachen* [In the Year of the Hare Dragon]. Berlin: Verbrecher Verlag.

Veblen, Thorstein Bunde. 1918. *The Instinct of Workmanship and the State of the Industrial Arts.* New York: B.W. Huebsch.

von Schomberg, René, and Jonathan Hankins, eds. 2019. *International Handbook on Responsible Innovation.* Cheltenham and Northampton, MA: E. Elgar.

Williamson, Dermot, 2017. China's Online Consumerism: Managing Business, Moral Panic and Regulation. *SSRN*, July 29, 2017, https://papers.ssrn.com/sol3/papers.cfm?abstract_id=3181287. Accessed September 29, 2024.

INDEX[1]

[1] Note: Page numbers followed by 'n' refer to notes.

W. Elsner, E. Najmehchi, *The Rise of China*,
https://doi.org/10.1007/978-3-032-20260-4

L

M

O

P

Q